THE RISE OF

WARREN GAMALIEL HARDING

1865–1920

&

THE RISE OF

WARREN GAMALIEL

HARDING

1865–1920

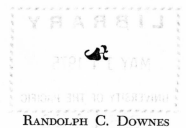

RANDOLPH C. DOWNES

OHIO STATE UNIVERSITY PRESS

Copyright © 1970 by the Ohio State University Press
All Rights Reserved.
Manufactured in the United States of America

STANDARD BOOK NUMBER 8142–0140–7

LIBRARY OF CONGRESS CATALOGUE CARD NUMBER 68–31421

TO MARIE McKITRICK DOWNES

CONTENTS

*The Frontispiece is reproduced from a printed
impression, on deposit as a part of the Harding
Papers, of an original drawing by K. Abelmann,
and is used here through the courtesy of the
Ohio State Historical Society Library.*

Preface

The opening to the public by the Ohio Historical Society in April, 1964, of the papers of Warren G. Harding made it possible at long last for scholars to attempt the preparation of an adequate biography of the twenty-ninth President of the United States. Much other material necessary to this effort had long been available. This included the Ohio newspapers of the period of Harding's life, especially Harding's own newspaper, the *Marion Daily Star*. The resources of the National Archives and such collections as the papers of Will H. Hays, Charles D. Hilles, Theodore E. Burton, and Ray Baker Harris invited study. New collections of the papers of Malcolm Jennings, Charles E. Hard, Fred E. Scobey, and Newton H. Fairbanks were also of considerable value.

This biography traces Harding's career from his Blooming Grove, Ohio childhood to his election to the Presidency. The account of his years as newspaper publisher has been taken largely from a study of the *Marion Daily Star* and the *Marion Weekly Star*. For his years of service in the state senate and in pursuit of the governorship of Ohio, this research relied mainly upon the Ohio newspapers of the period. However, the Harding Papers gradually became vital to understanding, as the future President became a power in state politics. Finally, during his United States senatorial years and the presidential campaign, the Harding Papers became the main basis for the narrative, though other sources were essential.

Readers may now try to understand more of the political nature of Warren G. Harding. Certain simple things are apparent. He was a loyal Marion booster, an ardent "Ohio Man," and a skilled politician of the Republican persuasion. Republican loyalty, discipline, and unity made up his central political faith. So thoroughly acquainted with the personalities and agencies of Ohio and national politics did he become, so eloquent and personable was he in his public appearances, that by 1920 he was considered to be of presidential timber.

There are certain qualities of Harding that we must be prepared to test. His understanding of the principles for which the Republican party stood may have lacked depth and breadth. His emphasis on politicking may have been greater than his abilities as a statesman. If so, these qualities illustrate something very basic in his character, namely a desire to subordinate his own mind to those of his ablest and most sympathetic counsellors.

Warren Harding lived through changing times. His politics did not keep pace with the change. It was easy enough for him to identify with progressive changes when it came to boosting the growth of Marion, Ohio, and in the gearing of Ohio political mechanics to national politics. But, when it came to such mighty problems as the guidance of the national economy, the interdependence of many nations in a world fearful of war, the gropings of laboring men for a more meaningful participation in their productiveness and an increased standard of living, he was ever the conservative man, searching for solutions. How near to, or far from, finding those solutions he came will begin to appear from the following pages.

THE RISE OF
WARREN GAMALIEL HARDING
1865–1920

CHAPTER ONE

The Ambitious Hardings
Come to Town

"As an awkward youth I witnessed the dreaming of a village which found itself at a railway intersection." : : : *Warren G. Harding in "Marion Daily Star," May 27, 1915*

Ancestor worship is not a characteristic American trait. But people with ambitions and a desire for status sometimes find it useful to do a little ancestral tinkering. The Hardings were that way when they came to Marion, Ohio in 1882.

The first Marion Harding was Warren Harding's father, Dr. George Tryon Harding, a former Morrow County, Ohio, farm boy who had taken a short course in medicine at the Homeopathic Medical College of Cleveland. Starting in 1873, he had acquired a practice in the boom town of Caledonia, and, in 1882, sought to do better in the nearby boom town of Marion because it seemed to have a greater future. As his practice grew, so did his ideas of family ancestry.[1]

The Hardings became very proud of their background. They had no ancestral priggishness, for they knew that the earth belonged to the living, but they also knew that it was good to have a worthy family background. Thus, in a society that did not always distinguish between the amateur and the professional genealogist, they constructed an ancestry occasionally based on fantasy instead of fact.

One of the amateur genealogists was Dr. George himself. The amiable doctor liked to trace the Tryon name back to the distinguished William Tryon, Tory governor of North Carolina at the time of the outbreak of the American Revolution. In 1920, shortly after his son had received the Republican nomination for the Presidency, Dr. George told a *Chicago Tribune* correspondent that the governor was the father of Dr. George's great-great-grandmother, who was promised a horse, saddle, and bridle if her first child was a boy.[2] Unfortunately it seems that the Tryon connection came from more humble sources. At least, so says the official family genealogist, Wilbur J. Harding, who

traced the Tryon connection to Huldah Tryon of Waterford, Connecticut. The humble Huldah seems to have priority over the Tory governor because it is reasonably established that her husband, Abraham
Harding, was living in Waterford at the time.[3]

Another Harding amateur genealogist was President Harding himself. In the happy hours following his election to the Presidency of the
United States, he told newspaperman Edwin C. Hill of an ancestry of
great heroism and achievement. He claimed that one of his pioneer
forefathers was Joshua Dickerson, "second child born in Monmouth
county, New Jersey, and the first white man to scale the Alleghenies."
The President also claimed descent from one Stephen Harding, who
was almost scalped by Indians in the famous Wyoming Massacre of
1778.[4] Actually the Joshua Dickerson, who was allegedly the second
child born in Monmouth county, New Jersey, could not have been the
same Joshua Dickerson first to cross the Alleghenies. The former
event, if it was an event, took place in 1634[5] and the latter in 1771 or
1772.[6] The first permanent English settlement in New Jersey took
place in Monmouth county in 1664, and no Dickersons are known to
have been in it. As for the almost-scalped Stephen, the President was
descended from his brother Amos who was not in the Wyoming fight,
and who was only fourteen years old at the time.

2

As the "official" family genealogists tell it, the Harding ancestral
story is somewhat less glamorous. Tracing back to John Harding of
Northampton, England (1587–1657), there is the account of an Atlantic crossing in 1623 of three sons to Massachusetts and the gradual
participation of descendants in the American westward movement.

This migration was of the typical short-step nature of the advancing
frontier. Sons did not usually strike westward to break far away from
parental ties. Matured sons accompanied parents, or else followed
close after one another, to benefit by co-operative soil-breaking and
farm-building. It was conservative, family-sponsored pioneering, and
it produced the skills and standards of property-minded, hard-working
folk. As Colonel George B. Christian, Sr., Marion friend and neighbor
of the Hardings, said with obvious exaggeration, "They weren't a
peasant race. They were men of strong character, of great independence and of considerable education, and they made Ohio pivotal."[7]

The short-step migration can be briefly summarized from the "official" family record. There was Stephen Harding (1623–1698), a blacksmith of Providence, Rhode Island, and his grandson, Captain Stephen (1681–1750) who migrated to Waterford, Connecticut, where he engaged in farming, business, and a bit of sea-going. The captain had a son and a grandson, both named Abraham (1720–1806, and 1744–1815), who together migrated to Orange County, New York, near Port Jervis. Old Abraham stayed in New York, but in 1774 young Abraham took his family to the not-so-distant Wyoming Valley country of eastern Pennsylvania. Here it was that one of Abraham's sons, named Amos (1764–1830), began farming part of his father's land, and then, after his marriage to Phoebe Tripp (August 21, 1784), moved a short distance to a new farm near Clifford in Susquehanna county. This Amos was destined to become known as the patriarch of the Ohio Hardings.

It was the patriarchal Amos who made the biggest hop in the Harding westward movement. It was indeed a family affair. It took place in the period from about 1818 to 1820. Amos was well along in years by this time, and the move was pioneered by his son Mordecai Rice Harding, who, in 1818 or 1819, settled in what is now Richland county near what later became the Morrow county line. Amos followed shortly after, as did three other sons, George Tryon [8] (Warren G.'s great-grandfather), Salmon E., and Ebenezar Slocum. They all purchased land in the same neighborhood, part of which was in what became North Bloomfield township in Morrow county. Thus appeared another "Harding Settlement" like the one back in the Wyoming Valley. Its center was the village of Blooming Grove, laid out by Salmon E. Harding at a crossing of the road to Mansfield in Richland County.

Amos Harding's third son was George Tryon (1790–1860) whose farm was on the Mansfield-to-Marion road about a half mile southeast of Blooming Grove. When he died the farm passed on to his son, Charles Alexander (1820–1878), who had built a log cabin on the parental acres at the time of his marriage. The cabin did not last long, being replaced by a small frame house built by Charles' father at the time Charles took over management of the farm, and occupied the large two-story home built many years before. It was in this small frame house that Charles' son, George Tryon Harding (Warren's father) and his wife, Phoebe Dickerson Harding, began their home life together, after the young husband's return from the Civil War. It was in this house that Warren Gamaliel Harding was born, November 2, 1865.[9]

3

Warren's father and mother had no intention of remaining in a rural environment. They were the last of the farming Hardings, so far as their line of the family was concerned. They saw villages and cities growing up in this new dynamic West, and correctly judged that more prosperity and distinction could be acquired therein. That is why, in the summer of 1873, George Tryon Harding began a full-time medical practice in the near-by town of Caledonia in Marion county. For a few years, while he worked on his father's farm and did a little school-teaching, he had been an apprentice to the family physician, Dr. Joseph McFarland. In the early 1870s he took courses at Dr. McFarland's medical alma mater, then known as the Homeopathic Medical College of Cleveland. By 1878 he was a full-fledged homeopathic M.D. (Many years later, after her child-bearing days were over, Phoebe Harding joined her husband in the medical profession, after taking the usual courses at the same school her husband had attended.) [10]

The Hardings were climbers, and quickly became part of the "elite" of Caledonia. The town may have been "just a plug tobacco village," [11] to use the phrase of Jack Warwick, one of Warren's friends, but it had expectations of being a great railroad junction, and the Hardings expected to rise with it. In 1876 Dr. Harding was an officer of the newly organized Caledonia Lyceum.[12] A year or so later, he and his son Warren were charter members of Caledonia Division No. 4 of the Sons of Temperance.[13] In 1879 Dr. Harding was sworn in as a member of a lodge known as the Caledonia Knights of Honor.[14]

Dr. Harding also had business aspirations. He was soon investing in banks and real estate. When the Caledonia Building and Loan Association was incorporated in 1874, Dr. Harding was one of the incorporators.[15] During Caledonia's short-lived boom he bought land, and in 1876 laid out an "addition" that was called "Harding's Addition to the Town of Caledonia," a 3.59-acre residential district, complete with lot divisions and projected streets.[16] However, it must be admitted that the doctor's financial speculations were less successful than his medical ministrations. As his son said good-naturedly in later years, "My father has always been a benefactor to his fellow man, and successful, too, as long as you could keep him to doctoring. But he did love to trade a bit on the side." [17]

4

The years at Caledonia were important ones for young Warren. There he grew from an over-sized seven-year-old into a teen-age collegian. He absorbed the ambitions of his father and mother, and acquired the virtues resulting from the disciplines of good family standards and hard work. His growing maturity was accentuated by his role as an older brother, resulting from the fact that his brother Charles died in 1878, leaving him the only son among three sisters and the newly born George, who was thirteen years younger. Relatives have commented on the impatience sometimes shown by the boyish Warren toward the childish traits of his brothers and sisters. A story comes down from Caledonia neighbors of the six-year-old Warren driving the cows daily to and from the town pasture for a stipulated sum from every cow owner. Jack Warwick tells of Warren's sense of responsibility in regard to family chores. "Chores is an important word in the lexicon of the son of a country doctor. It means horses to curry and feed, a stable to be kept clean, and a cow to milk morning and evenings. . . . I was often with Dr. Harding's son to see that the work was done right. A team that comes in after a hard drive over mud roads needs considerable attention. Dr. Harding's horses were not neglected." [18]

It may be that young Warren was too hard-working for his own good health. That was the opinion of his younger sister, Charity, who wrote after her brother's death, "He was large and strong and we thought him able to carry out anything he would undertake. He was taught to work at a very early age. The chores of a family home fell upon him as he was eldest and a boy. . . . During vacation days he helped neighbors thrash their grain and worked with all the men, and did as much as anyone, but he was only fourteen years old. He plowed and looked after much of the orchard work at this time on our farm. He helped with the construction work of the Ohio Central Railroad . . . they wanted those who could furnish a team. He worked hard every day, in fact too hard for one so young. I have often thought, *and so did he,* after he was older, that such heavy work (when so young and developing so rapidly) was not conducive to a strong physical foundation for after life. He was too tired to rest and sleep at night. He would drive those horses all night long, for we could hear him in his slumber." [19]

The heroes of Harding's boyhood were the men of skill and industry, the hard-driving men who did things, rather than the merchants who sold things, or the teachers who thought things. They were William Boughton, the wagonmaker; Ed Dodge, the band leader; and "an Englishman named Buck who taught me to swing the paint brush." Buck taught him to grain. "I could do a bully good job of graining," said Harding in 1920. "The greatest of them all," he added, "was Chandler Smith, who had a smithy and a water sawmill, a hard handed, resolute man with unbounded confidence that you could do anything you wanted to if you did it hard enough. He was an inspiration." To Harding, the blacksmith was "the captain of industry of the village." There was a completeness and thoroughness to village industry that satisfied the young man. The "shops and smithies were real wood and metal work establishments and not mere places for assembling parts already fabricated. A buggy cost $250, and it was all made there—painting and all." [20]

This sense of thoroughness in and appreciation for the practical things of life was not apparent in Warren's attitude toward the gentle arts. There was no such hard-driving industry and self-discipline in the Caledonia one-room schoolhouse as there was on the farm or the railroad right of way. Said Dr. Harding, "He studied his lessons, I don't know when. I never caught him at it and it used to worry me, so I asked his teacher what Warren was doing to bring in such decent reports when he didn't seem to work. 'Oh, he's just naturally smart, I guess,' his teacher said. 'I never saw him working yet.'" [21] This is confirmed by his boyhood pal, Jack Warwick, who said, "Nobody ever saw him at hard study, but he shone at recitations." [22]

In 1880 Warren went to college. However, his collegiate years were of as short and abbreviated a nature as were his father's and mother's short medical training at Cleveland's Homeopathic Medical College. It was a two-year institution known as Ohio Central College, located at Iberia about six miles east of Caledonia on the road to Galion. In its pre–Civil War days it acquired a bit of fame by being a militant Abolitionist center, but it seems never to have recovered from the adversity of its war years. Shortly after Harding's graduation in 1882 it was converted into a school for the blind, and a few years later it burned to the ground. It seems that the education that penetrated deepest was his editing with Frank H. Harris of the student paper, *The Spectator*.[23] Otherwise, he never praised his alma mater. Indeed, he was highly critical of it. He wrote in the *Marion Star*, October, 1894, "In the 1860's it was quite a notable institution of learning, the course of study comparing favorably with any western institution. Later on, though the classical course was still taught, the institution became more like an academy and normal school." [24] Warren certainly had no abiding respect for the basic sciences, as is shown by his liking for the pseudo-explorer, Dr. Frederic A. Cook, false discoverer of the North Pole. "Maybe we like him," wrote Warren in the *Star*, September 10, 1909, "especially because he isn't a full fledged scientist, though we have no antipathy to scientists beyond college recollections." He confessed that Cook "loomed up big to us when we read that he treated the Eskimos and dogs kindly."

Something of Harding's way of life at college was gleaned by Herbert Corey from Frank Harris and others and published in a Cincinnati *Times-Star* series from August 17 to September 2, 1920. The work seems to have been strenuous, but more on the breadwinning and extracurricular side than in affairs of study. He worked his way through college, as did his two roommates, John Deuly and John Gerber, each of whom provided his share of firewood, food, and bedding. Warren's share of food came from Mother Harding's larder in the form of pies, cakes, chickens, hams, bacon, bread, and so on, which he brought in every three weeks from Blooming Grove. Being the college's best paint-grainer, he was in great demand for embellishing houses, barns, and church steeples. When grading the railroad, he pastured his horse on the college campus, much to the annoyance of "old man" Busch, who had monopoly rights thereon and for whom, therefore, Warren had to do odd jobs. According to Harris, he knew every girl within a five-mile radius of Iberia, and they "frolicked together as innocently as young pups." With the aid of Mother Harding's cakes, he was received by them unchaperoned, and, when raided, was concealed beneath the kitchen table by the ample skirts of his hostesses. He was a "bear" in debate, "mental science," history, philosophy, and literature—"he read more than he has ever had time to read since of the masters of English prose." Other subjects, like geometry, he would put off until the last minute, and then shock the professor by doing all the problems in one grand flourish. When he did this last-minute, make-up work, he would "sit down with his face to the wall, head in hands and soak it up. Then when he was through, he would jump up with a yell and shout, 'Now, darn it, I've got you,' and slam the book against the wall." [25]

Following graduation Warren had one term, and one only, of school-teaching in a schoolhouse near Marion. His profound aversion for this occupation and his desire for something "better" were formally expressed in a letter to his aunt, February 12, 1883, as he neared the end of the term:

> Next Friday, one week, *i.e.*, the 23rd inst., forever my career as a pedagogue will close and oh, the joy! I believe my calling to be in some other sphere and will follow out the belief. . . . I will never teach again without better (a good deal better too) wages, and an advanced school. [26]

Warren's discomfort with some serious book reading was shown by his brief exposure to the study of law. "After graduation," he once said, "my father wanted me to study law." He entered the law office of a family friend, S. A. Court, prosecuting attorney of Marion County. "I entered the law office with misgivings," he continued. "Lashing my feet to the top of a desk and tilting back in a chair, I glued my eyes on Blackstone four or five hours a day. It was slow work and money ran out. Compelled to ask my father for some cash to keep the law mill grinding was humiliating for I realized that I was not earning a living." [27]

Light reading was much more appealing. This was true even with respect to the Bible. There were family prayers and parental Bible readings, but for his own reading he said, "I don't mean that the boys were Great Bible readers but we had books made up of stories rewritten from the Bible." Even more to his liking were the dime novels, "the Dare-Devil Dick kind of thing, but, of course, we had to read them on the sly." He also confessed to an enjoyment of the works of the humorist Artemus Ward (Charles F. Browne) and of Mark Twain. Nor was his great admiration for Alexander Hamilton arrived at by serious study. This had been, he said, an "early passion" in his boyhood. "What reawakened it was a novel—Gertrude Atherton's 'The Conqueror.' . . . It riveted me." He read other works on Hamilton and wound up by making his political bible Frederick Scott Oliver's *Alexander Hamilton*.[28] According to Herbert Corey's report, Harding "prefers Maurice Hewlett to Bernard Shaw and does not care a nail paring for O. Henry. . . . Hammock fiction would bore him." [29]

The Harding years at Caledonia were numbered because Caledonia's years were numbered. This became apparent in 1880 when the
New York, Pennsylvania, and Ohio Railroad (the Nypano) decided to
make Marion the junction of its Chicago branch rather than Caledonia, ten miles northeast. This decision made Marion a "three railroad town" and ended the dreams of Caledonia.[30] Young Dr. Harding
had no intention of confining his practice to a dead town.

In later years, when Warren Harding had become a United States
Senator, he had occasion to refer in an uncomplimentary manner to
the backwardness of the Caledonia of his childhood. It was upon the
occasion of an address to the National Association of Manufacturers in
the sumptuous Waldorf Astoria Hotel in New York City. He classed
his boyhood hometown as a sleepy village of folks who let progress
pass them by. It had had two railroads, but did not know what to do
with them. "Dreamers were abundant," he told his listeners, "but the
creative forces and constructive leadership were lacking. . . . It remains today a railway crossing town, whose territorial lines would be
lost in the expanse of agricultural glory except for the signs—'Speed
limit—8 miles per hour.'" Then, with a glance at the alleged utopian
and radical nature of Progressive and Democratic reforms of the
twentieth century, he added that Caledonia was a good example of
how backward places encouraged poorly thought-out reforms. "It still
has, as it had then," he said, "the ablest and most untiring exponents
of panaceas for all ailments, social, economic and political." He referred to one of his impecunious Caledonia kinsmen "who can reel off
advice by the hour as to how a big enterprise ought to be conducted,
and can settle any big governmental problem with a wave of the
hand, but his talent soars to such lofty heights that his threshing
machine, on which he employs three men, reverted to its maker under
the mortgage which guaranteed the payment of the purchase notes." [31]

5

Whatever it was that consigned Caledonia to a hick-town status,
this did not happen to Marion with its three railroads. The opening of
the Chicago branch of the Nypano in 1880 was the beginning of a new
era, and great was the local rejoicing. Headlined the *Daily Star*,
March 26, 1880—not yet, of course owned by Warren Harding:

HURRAH FOR MARION

MARION AND CHICAGO TO BE UNITED

BY THE NEW RAILROAD LINE

THE CHICAGO AND ATLANTIC

AWAKE! FOR THE BOOM IS ABOUT TO STRIKE US

Thus Marion had become a three-railroad city: the Bee Line (a road to Indianpolis), the Nypano, and the Columbus and Toledo (later the Hocking Valley).

Marion was, indeed, a boom-town when the Hardings came in January, 1882. A few days after they arrived the *Star*, on February 2, contained the following effusion:

> Marion! Marion! Change cars for Cleveland, Columbus, Cincinnati, Indianapolis, St. Louis, Chicago, New York, Pittsburgh, Toledo and all points east, west, north and south!

Central to Marion's dreams of greatness was the Huber Manufacturing Company, product of the genius of Edward Huber, former blacksmith and wagon-maker of Indiana. He had come to Marion in 1865 with his newly patented Huber hay rake. He had chosen Marion because of the prevalence nearby of abundant ash timber needed for mass production of his article. Gradually "the Works" grew to gigantic proportions, supplying to farms of the Middle West not only hay rakes, but harvesters, road scrapers, and corn planters.[32]

Also prophetic of the future was the appearance of a new specialty industry for Marion. On April 17, 1884 the Huber Company announced that the "Barnhart Steam Shovel" was about to be put into production. This led to the organization of the Marion Steam Shovel Company in August, 1884, by Huber and the inventor, H. M. Barnhart. The "Shovel Works" soon became famous the country over, not only for its steam shovels, but for its wrecking cars and ballast unloaders, so necessary for the upkeep of the rapidly improving railroad systems of the nation.[33]

As business boomed during the 1880s the old country town began to take on the appearance of a city. Out in the "west end" sprawled the "Huber Works" and its cousin, the "Shovel Works." Over in the east end new suburban residence districts were platted and built, such as

College Hill and Mt. Vernon Avenue, where Warren Harding was to build his well-known home early in the 1890s. Additions fanned out in all directions. At the city center, in place of the old wooden "rat-trap" courthouse of Jacksonian days, rose a dome-topped, marble "temple of justice" designed by the Toledo architect D. W. Gibbs. It was "Water Works Yes" in the special election of January 3, 1882, bringing a facility so necessary to the growth of the Huber and the shovel industries. Marion residents in general breathed easier with the drastic reduction in fire hazards and insurance rates. Business structures rapidly filled whole blocks of the city. The "palatial" Marion Hotel, owned by three of Marions's leading businessmen, Amos H. Kling, his brother George, and H. J. Hane, had its "Grand Opening" August 15, 1883. Public sewage and paving were "in the works." There was talk of an opera house, a union depot, and a new city hall.

Thus it was that Dr. Harding moved his family into a new and overflowing Marion, taking up residence in the center of the town in the "fine house" which he bought on East Street near the courthouse. His practice flourished too; as Warren wrote in a letter to his aunt on February 12, 1883, "Pa is very busy—making over $500 per month." [34] The real-estate dabbling was resumed and a "Harding Addition" in Marion was added to the county records.[35] Again Dr. Harding identified himself with the respectable folks in town as evidenced by his becoming, in 1884, the medical examiner of a lodge called the Prudential Order of America.[36] Politically, the Doctor had also established contact, as shown by the newspaper announcement five days before the election of 1884:

> First ward polls will be at
> Dr. Harding's office on East Street.[37]

In the meantime, son Warren came to town in search of something "better than school teaching," and was soon identifying himself with the boomer aspect of his adopted city. One necessity for a booming city was a brass band. Warren was ready for this because he had tinkered with horn blowing in his Caledonia days. What kind of a horn Warren blew in Caledonia is not clear. That did not matter. There was a horn to blow for Marion and Warren was a horn-blower. According to biographer W. F. Johnson the ambitious young man was so anxious to help that he professed a mastery which he did not have over the B-flat cornet, his talents being confined to the tenor horn. He was eventually drafted for the "helicon bass." [38] Whatever instrument it was, there was no doubt about his enthusiasm. For this was 1883, the year when the city of Marion was to attain its greatest achievement, the opening of direct railroad connections with Chicago.

May 1, 1883 was a great day for Marion. It was the day scheduled for the first train out of Marion on the Chicago division of the "Nypano." All was hustle and bustle in preparation for this great event. Just before the first west-bound passenger train pulled out of the "Nypano" depot at 11:25 A.M., thirty privileged Marionites boarded the cars with much pomp. Among them was the Citizens Band with W. G. Harding and his "helicon bass." They rode as far as Kenton, paraded smartly through this village, received the plaudits of its citizenry, and returned to Marion the same evening as from a triumphal tour. The *Star*, May 5, 1883 reported with bursting pride, "We learn that the citizens of Kenton are wonderfully praising the merits of our band. John Robison's circus band played there last Wednesday, but they say it couldn't be compared with the Citizens Band of Marion. We often wonder if our citizens appreciate what a splendid band we have."

Thus did Warren Harding make his debut as a booster for Greater Marion. Thus did the booming city sound forth its prophecies of future greatness. There was naturally a campaign for new uniforms. It began with Saturday evening concerts in the courthouse yard. The bright-colored outfits were rushed from Philadelphia by S. G. Kleinman, Marion's "enterprising clothier," in time for Decoration Day exercises. "Quite nobby," opined the *Star*, May 31. On June 8 there was a tournament at Findlay at which the Marion Citizens Band won third place and $100. On the way home, according to the *Star*, June 9, 1883, "W. G. Harding, 'Kid' Shute and Charley Mader stopped off and played with the Little Six at Upper Sandusky." According to Warwick, there was a peculiar detail to the Findlay trip that Harding had to handle. One of the rules of the tournament was that the band must demonstrate its marching ability. The band members evidently did not know this. Hence, as soon as they had played the required numbers, they got on the train and left for Marion—all but Harding. It was he who had to stay behind and fulfill the marching requirement. Thus "Warren G." alone paraded before the judges stand, playing a quickstep. He was determined not to be denied the trophies of the day. His daring carried him through and he brought home the big money prize of the occasion.[39]

Next was the grand round-trip excursion of August 1, 1883 over the newly opened Chicago line—for the benefit of the band. This was managed entirely by young Harding. On July 11, 1883 the *Star* reported, "W. G. Harding left on Monday evening for Chicago to make arrangements for an excursion from here to Chicago over the C. & A. to be run by the Citizens Band of this city." On July 19, 1883 the *Mirror* commented, "Mr. Harding was very fortunate in securing such admirable arrangements for the excursion, when it is known that the new C. & A. is pressed with business." A week later, the *Star* noted, "Warren Harding, returned home this morning from towns along the C. & A. where he had been arranging for the excursion to Chicago next week."

By 1884 the nineteen-year-old Harding had made something of a name for himself in the town of his adoption. For a teenage youth he had done well. As Jack Warwick, who had been in Kansas for a while and returned to Marion in 1884, said, "When I returned I found Harding one of the best known young men in Marion." [40] Warren Harding could be considered as Marion's young man of the year for 1884.

CHAPTER TWO

Boosting and Feuding for Marion

"Talk about Marion—Write about Marion—Be friendly to everybody
—Sell all you can—Buy all you can at home—Support your town
newspaper—Advertise." : : : "Marion Daily Star," May 16, 1887

It is clear that young Harding's talents were of an ambitious, outgoing, exhibitionist nature. It was not enough to be part of a fast-growing town; he must be at the forefront of the advance, exhorting, advising, cheering, and being cheered. His role at first was not in public-speaking, but it was very close to it—running a newspaper.

That is why it was not long before the teenage, firstborn son of Dr. George Harding had a more effective instrument for boosting Marion, and himself, than the tenor horn or the helicon bass. This was a daily newspaper, the hallmark of a city. As long as Marion was a small town, a weekly paper was sufficient; a weekly was designed for village folks and for country folks who came to town once in a while. There was nothing fresh about the advertisements, which were mostly the same, week after week. A successful daily was proof that a community had reached city proportions, with lots of people who had lots of money to buy what competing advertisers had to sell. The ambitious Harding would help ambitious Marion put on city clothes.

In 1884 Marion had a daily newspaper—of sorts—along with two much more successful weeklies. The daily, the *Marion Star*, existent since 1877, had not been successful because its editor was incapable of adjusting it to urban requirements. This was Sam Hume, a quixotic fellow, whose chief success, up to the time he took over the *Star*, was as a camp follower of county fairs and soldiers' reunions, where he sold cheap jewelry and roasted peanuts. His conception of a daily newspaper was to make it a vehicle for the amusement of his fellow townsmen with allegedly humorous news items and editorials written in a Josh Billings style, and characterized by a deliberately bucolic vocabulary and ungrammatical construction. The hard work of news-gathering, typesetting, printing, and circulating was done by his two teen-age sons and his ever-faithful wife. He had no dynamic advertising program. By 1884 his few subscribers had tired of their funny man, and his declining subscription list caused him to pine again for the open road. In other words, the *Star* was for sale—cheap.[1]

The declining fortunes of the *Star* in 1884 were described by Jack Warwick, one of Harding's Caledonia pals, who was also a partner with Harding in rescuing the *Star* from oblivion. After Harding had become President of the United States, Warwick wrote, "The history of the paper up to this time could be written in four letters—J-O-K-E. It had been kicked at and kicked. At the time we took hold, it amused everybody and inspired faith in nobody. The people of the town laughed at us." [2]

The paternal hand of the genial and ambitious Dr. Harding was observable in the purchase of this dying newspaper. In 1921 Dr. Harding was quoted in *McClures* magazine as saying, "Jack Warwick and Warren bought the Marion *Star* when they were both youngsters. I made most of the arrangements about buying the paper and went on their notes and helped them at the start." [3] By this help—it was only a few hundred dollars—Dr. Harding was doing for Marion and for his son what he had tried to do in Caledonia in the 1870s when he set up the *Weekly Argus,* and got Warren the job of "devil." It was with the *Argus* that Warren first learned how to "stick" type, feed the press, make up forms, and wash rollers.[4] Incidentally, this modest investment in the *Star* was by far the most successful business venture, outside of doctoring, in Dr. Harding's career.

The nineteen-year-old editor and publisher of the *Marion Daily Star* had supreme confidence in himself when he took over the paper in 1884. Such facts are usually left unsaid, but not in the case of Warren Harding. Four days after assuming his new responsibility, he announced in the editorial column, "Our egotism tells us that if we can't make the STAR a success no one can. That the STAR successfully managed is popular we are fully assured." [5]

There was more than bravado in young Harding's administration of the *Star*. He took hold with a firm and determined leadership. He knew that there could be no success for the paper under the management of boys and jokesters. Sam Hume had proved that. The public had to be shown that the new *Star* was serviceable and therefore stable. That was why Harding, at the very outset, gave his organization the name of the Star Publishing Company. "It was thought," he said in later years, "that under such a head the changes of ownership could go on forever without the weekly announcements of the changes." He had started out with two boyhood friends as his partners, Jack Warwick and John O. Sickle, but they were unable to continue in the partnership. Sickle was the first to go. As Harding said, "Mr. Sickle tired of it within two months and luckily withdrew." [6] Jack Warwick was more frank: "Sickle started in to learn to set type, but gave up in a week or two, not in despair but for fresh air." [7] According to Sickle, he got out because he wanted some of his invested money for Chistmas presents. "This is a dickens of a business to be associated with," he told Warren, "All you do is work and put up money. Let me out." [8] Soon Warwick himself withdrew from managerial responsibilities, "discouraged most completely," as Harding put it.[9] In later years, Warwick confessed his inadequacy. He was still merely a boy from Caledonia. "It was only nine miles from Saturday night and Mother at the gate," he said.[10] More specifically, Warwick objected to the installation of a telephone. "Wild extravagance," he told Warren, "You're ruining us." [11] And so, with the boys out of it, Warren was left to go it alone. "The *Star* was his baby now," said Jack, who stayed on as city editor and rewrite man.[12]

Under Warren's skillful and diligent guidance the *Star* quickly acquired "city clothes," as its new editor liked to say. New presses were installed, telegraphic news acquired, a greater variety of "side plate" included. Reporters with a nose for news were hired, enabling "W. G." to remain in the office writing editorials or to go about soliciting the all-important advertising. In this latter department, the young editor and publisher became highly adept. As Warwick said, "W. G." had the ability to "get on the right side of the cow. He convinced her that she ought to 'give down.'" This was achieved, added Warwick, without stressing the financial advantage to the *Star*, "but because it meant health and happiness to the cow." [13] Another friend, Sherman A. Cuneo, quoted the Harding pitch: "You can't afford not to. If you do not advertise, your competition will use advertising as a club to beat off your business head." How it worked was frankly described by one of the Marion advertisers, "His convincing argument won us all, one after the other. And once we began we couldn't stop." [14] Needless to say this "pitch" included display advertising.

By 1890 the *Star* had arrived. It was a six-page daily with an eight-page Saturday edition. It should be added that, after the marriage of Warren and Florence Kling in 1891, she was not the guiding spirit of the *Star*, keeping the editor and publisher in line. As Warwick said, "She did not at any time edit the paper, or dictate its policy; she did no reporting, neither did she write editorials." All that she did was to manage, for a while, circulation and the newboys. "She controlled those lads," said Warwick, "kept their accounts and spanked them when necessary." [15]

2

Warren Harding's progress as a newspaperman was inseparable from his progress as a Marion booster. One of the most profitable qualities of Harding's journalism was its enthusiastic promotion of the fortunes of the burgeoning city. Harding came to Marion in the full flush of its boom, and became one of its most effective promoters. "We started the *Star* off," wrote Warwick, "with a policy that has never been changed. It was to boom Marion and Marion men against all outsiders. Every enterprise was given all the attention the traffic would bear. . . . We exploited railroads that never got beyond the blue print and we saw smoke rolling out of the chimneys of factories before the excavations were made for the foundations." [16] As Harding himself said in a 1914 address to the American Railway Business Association concerning Marion's sponsorship of new railroads, "The newspaper workers were a part of the system of promotion, fostering friendly public sentiment, and shaming the tightwads who did not shell out in their donations in accordance with their proclamations of local pride." [17]

It is important to emphasize that Harding's interest in booming Marion was conditioned by his ardent admiration for men of skill and industry. As in his Caledonia days, when he found his greatest inspiration in the blacksmiths and wagonmakers, so in Marion, he felt the deepest regard for the town's leading industrialist, former blacksmith and wagonmaker, Edward Huber. According to Warwick, Harding found himself solidly backed by Huber's encouragement. "He was a man of great faith—faith in his own big factory, faith in the town, and faith in its citizens." [18] The *Star* early had his good wishes, backed by practical help in the way of printing orders. When Huber died in August, 1904, Harding wrote of the industrialist's kindness to him back in 1885: "'We can't advertise threshers with you,' he said that day, 'but any time you need twenty-five or fifty dollars, come and get it.' His generous offer was never accepted but the encouragement of that tender gave new determination in more than one hour of discouragement." [19]

Until about 1891 publisher Harding's activities were noisier and more contentious than constructive. They were the reactions of a youthful enthusiast rather than those of a mature civic builder. As he said in the *Star*, September 13, 1890, "Marion may be moving along with the industrial procession, but there is no brass band or noisy drum corps to give evidence of it. Somehow we like the music with the marching. It adds to the enthusiasm and leaves no doubt."

One of the blueprint railroads Harding boosted was the so-called Black Diamond, promoted by the aggressive Colonel Albert E. Boone, "as strong in the faith as he was short in financial resources," to use Harding's phrase of later years.[20] This was a line designed to supply Marion with coal from the mines in Coshocton county in eastern Ohio. "Marion will be the Central Ohio city of the future when the Black Diamond is completed," promised the *Star*, April 1, 1887. Harding no doubt realized that railroad promotion had helped newspaper rivals build up their good will in earlier years. Such promotion had been made since 1850 for every railroad that had planned to include Marion on its route, including many that had never made it. Hence the Black Diamond conducted the usual public meetings where the usual subscription lists were drawn up and circulated while the *Star* office, Harding recalled in 1914, became "a sort of civic center" for this project. The Colonel was the "Blackie Daw" in his combination "who furnished us with the ammunition and our office did the firing." He also recalled that the people were wary enough to subscribe on C.O.D. terms, *i.e.*, payment "on the arrival of the first train." But the enterprise soon faded, and Harding was eventually calling the Black Diamond a "flivver," and Boone a "blow-viator." [21]

More often than not the *Star's* pronouncements about Marion's future prospects were characterized merely by brag and bluster. "No Horse Cars for Marion," warned the *Star*, January 10, 1888. "Marion doesn't want any one-horse-or-mule-car street railway. If the step is to be taken it should be modern." When Findlay struck gas, Marion was green with envy. Said the *Star*, March 14, 1887, "If Marion had her natural advantages we would rival any city in central Ohio in three years." Thereupon ensued a great promotion of drillings in the Marion area, but, when no gas could be tapped, the *Star* went back to coal. It turned up its editorial nose on oil, remarking, March 7, 1888, that "there will be no flies on us. . . . Marion is doing pretty well just now. . . . There was never an instance where new industries have leaped into successful existence so quickly as here." As for Marion residents who helped boom other towns, that was downright disloyalty. "Whenever an alleged Marionite begins singing the praises of other towns and their booms," wrote Harding April 20, 1887, "walk away from him and leave an unfeeling lamp post stand the racket."

The time would come when Harding and the *Star* would dig into the technicalities of local problems and provide constructive and informational leadership, but not in these youthful years. All was enthusiasm of the "hurrah boys" quality. "Whoops for Marion's electric lights and whoops for the boys that worked up the company," shouted the *Star*, December 10, 1888 after the first street lights were turned on by the Marion Electric Light Company. "There isn't a city anywhere, great or small, that is better lighted than the arc district of Marion." Actually there were just 15 arc lamps that "blazed forth this marvelous transformation." "And yet," said the incredulous *Star*, December 6, "there were fellows who carried lanterns and the lanterns were lighted." As if the lanterns would not be needed on most of the way home.

Marion was really big-time, at least it was the biggest city in the Ninth Ohio Congressional district. "Newspapers," he said, August 18, 1888, "seem seriously concerned because we insist that Marion is the only real city in the Ninth [Congressional] District. Well, there is wicked Kenton—we're always ahead of her; sleepy Marysville is not to be compared; classical Deleware [sic] will do for a college, but we distance her every other way; [Mt.] Gilead did well and deserves much credit as Edison's [a nearby small town] suburb, but compared to Marion she is as copper to gold; Mt. Vernon is a fair country town, but we knock her silly, as the boys say, except in getting there politically." No, Marion did not want a "fragile boom" like Findlay, said the *Star*, January 27, 1890. That was a "little isolated gas city" whose businessmen were in constant fear of the gas giving out.

What other towns had, Marion should have also. "Oh, for an Orchestra," pined Harding in the *Star*, September 5, 1889. A band of "cornstalk fiddlers," sneered the *Star*, September 16, 1889, was superior to the outfit that produced those "nerve shocking strains that are so often heard at Music Hall." As for the ramshackle "Music Hall," let's have a real opera house. Of course, it probably would not pay, but he felt the town should have one anyway—even at public cost. "Some cheerful and half reckless person some day," said the *Star*, January 25, 1890, "will set a movement going to bond the city, and many conservative people who do not believe in putting these burdens on the tax duplicate will not oppose the plan." A year later, Harding himself became that "half reckless person" when he seriously proposed a publicly built opera house. "It is the only way," he said, May 28, 1891. And when churchmen prophesied "more work for the Devil if an Opera House was built," Harding, on February 8, 1891, declared himself on the side of the Devil. "There is no objection at this office to crediting the opera house to his Satanic Majesty, for we follow the rule of giving the Devil his dues." Also, a Summer Driving Association was as essential to a thriving town as summer stock theaters are now. "A good guarantee fund is the important thing, and good races will bring the necessary money. The flyers are as popular before a Marion crowd as anywhere."

Another civic difficulty in which Harding did his editorially vociferous best was the streetcar wrangle in 1890. This turned into a row between the haves and the have nots, that is, those neighborhoods which were on the projected line of the Marion Street Railway Company and those which were not. Members of the city council declined to grant a franchise for fear that a "real estate deal" was behind it. "What of it?" asked Harding, January 31, 1890, "If Marion is to be given what she needs, why object to it because a side line is to make a large addition of town lots of easy access to the business center. Selfishness has been a damper to Marion's prosperity already and it ought to be rooted out." As for the "sour grapes crowd" that would not invest in the company, one was supposed to ignore these smallminded folk and get the money from outside Marion. "A few fellows with old-time jealousy," he wrote, February 15, 1890, "are against it, and a very large number are chasing around wanting to know what to do about it. What to do, indeed! Why, do nothing, if you haven't something to do to push it along. We could cry for it for a half century to come if we waited for local capital to build it. That is why there is so much confounded foolishness in any set of fellows trying to head the thing off. Let them get out of the way. Such things deserve encouragement."

The seemingly unavoidable mixture of boom and discord in the Greater Marion movement, and Harding's inability to extricate himself from it, was remarkably illustrated by the arrival of Marion in 1890 at official city status. All hopes were fixed on Marion's becoming a city of 10,000 in this all-important census-taking year. This would not only bring the prestige of numbers but, according to Ohio law, it would bring the civic incorporation that would facilitate the construction of several projects useful to the city's expansion. The most important of these were street paving, sewers, and water supply.

A civic spirit of enthusiastic unity was abroad in the opening months of 1890. Everybody was counting on the Census Bureau's reporting the magic figure of 10,000. However, when that hope went glimmering, the enthusiasm continued because the law still permitted Marion to graduate from village status to that of city of the fourth grade, second class. This was carefully described in the *Star*, June 7, 1890. Preparations were, therefore, made for a referendum vote on the question.

In the meantime the *Star* went to great pains to show how the new form of municipal government would enable Marion to achieve what it had long desired—to get out of the mud by acquiring paved streets. Marion's primary need, wrote Harding, February 22, 1890, was street paving, "the kind that really improves." It was practically impossible for Marion to rid itself of mudholes under the village form of government. Ohio law required that all street improvement must be paid for from the general tax fund. This old-fashioned method led to a promiscuous dumping of crushed stone here and there, much to the dismay of wagon and buggy traffic, but much to the joy of the stone contractors who knew how to get the awards from the village council. This situation was locally characterized as "crushed-stone politics." Under city government it would be possible for the new city council to set up a formula by which the expenses of street improvement, *i.e.*, paving, could be assessed in large measure on the property owners who benefitted thereby.

At first the result was a happy one. On April 7, 1890, Marion voted overwhelmingly for advancement to city status. The election, according to Harding, April 8, was a "political cyclone." Not only did the voters endorse city status by the overwhelming count of 1,024 to 438, but they elected John Dudley, the first Republican mayor since 1872. Three of the four councilmen elected were Republicans, including the city's leading businessman, Amos H. Kling. "Probably the most plausible reason for this," wrote Harding, "is that crushed stone played an important part." The city was now ready for Council to adopt "the equitable plan of assessing street improvement on the adjacent property holders." When that is done, said the optimistic young editor, "we shall offer some carefully collected information on the matter of paving that improves and we entertain no doubt about the result."

But editor Harding never got a chance to offer his street improvement plan. Instead, on April 9, 1890, he offered some cutting remarks against the wealthy opponents of paving, which paved the way for no paving at all for several years. Evidently the political cyclone had gone to Harding's head.

This seemingly unprovoked April 9 editorial was, in effect, a declaration of war. It assumed that certain rich, but unnamed, Marionites would continue to block the city's progress as they had in the past. He practically invited them to leave town. These reactionary opponents of progress were Marion's "chronic kickers"—and he left no doubt as to whom he meant. They were certain big-property owners who "are not now, never have been and never will be of any earthly use to Marion. If they fear the city is to be killed by the new order let them get out. Their property is salable. They have roasted their shins and growled and grunted for ten years while the wide-awake, hustling classes were doubling Marion's wealth and extent, and have cast impeding rocks in the way while the hustlers were adding fifty to 100 percent to the value of their possessions, yet the same old miserable croak is heard. . . . Let the drones get out. . . . Property is up and in demand. Marion wants to move onward."

The asperity with which Harding denounced these property owners is surprising. When "some frightened individuals" wrote him asking if he was "not afraid of offending capital by your too plain remarks on the opposition to advancement to a city," he replied, April 12, emphatically in the negative. "It wouldn't hurt Marion particularly if what is termed her capital was considerably offended. The city would probably live and prosper just the same without the most of the able moneyed men, so if they want to pout because of a sinful lack of revenue let them pout. A few of them have dealt out somewhat in aiding enterprises, but it had been the exception rather than the rule. All the distinctly [sic] 'capital' here is of a mortgage-at-eight-per-cent order. . . . If the bulk of Marion's capital has been of any special use to Marion it has been fully rewarded, but those who know the inside facts pay no special reference to moneyed men for the impetus they have given Marion."

What encouraged Harding in this attack on Marion's property owners was his great admiration for Marion's industrialists, particularly Edward Huber. It has been pointed out that young Harding had the good wishes of Huber from the beginning of the revival of the *Star*. Huber had given Harding many printing orders. Harding liked the self-made Huber and said so. He bluntly declared that it was people like Huber, and not the real-estate men, who were the true builders of Marion. "The factories have made Marion," he said. Huber, he wrote, January 11, 1890, "was the pioneer and struggled along almost alone for many years before capital came to his aid."

Bitterly did Harding berate the real-estate men and their rent gouging. In *Star* editorials on February 4 and 11, 1890, he deplored the atrociously high rates of return on Marion real estate. "We are opposed to having a growing and highly successful future threatened by blind greed. . . . Property owners must be satisfied with a fair return on a good investment or they will commit a grave error." On May 26, 1890 he again deplored the speculation in real-estate additions and the alleged shying away from industrial development.

Chief property owner and butt of Harding's diatribes was Amos H. Kling, his future father-in-law. (He was courting Kling's daughter Florence at the time.) This hard-driving businessman was of Pennsylvania Dutch background, as was Huber. He was Marion's richest citizen. By the taxpayer's list, published in the *Star*, June 15, 1887 and June 21, 1888, Amos Kling's name was at the top: properties valued at $119,350 in 1887 and $117,138 in 1888. (The Huber Manufacturing Company's properties in these years were listed at $58,912 and $66,800; The Steam Shovel Company's at $14,300 and $14,330.)

It was with this mighty man of Marion that editor Harding found himself contending in 1890 over the future of the city. The coolness between Harding and Kling increased as a new crisis arose. This was the purchase of the Chicago and Atlantic Railroad by the Erie, and the possibility of transferring the division terminal facilities from Marion to Galion. Out of this Erie Railroad crisis arose the creation of the Citizens Board of Trade, headed by Kling. After much delay the Board was eventually created, with Harding a member and Kling as chairman of its executive committee. Harding's attitude was most provocative. He repeatedly reminded the Board, via the *Star*, that it was he who got it started in the first place, and that it was failing to live up to public expectations. On October 20, he commented rather superciliously, "The board of trade is to look after our industrial progress. The inquiry may arise, who is to look after the board of trade?" On November 19, he asked, "The new board of trade was inspired by the newspapers, but how many give them credit for it?"

As the new year opened and nothing had been done, Harding, on January 3, 1891, delivered another of his blasts at the moneyed men. "Last summer," he wrote, "a public meeting was hurriedly called to consider means to secure the Erie division and shops for Marion. Fifty or more men of moderate means, but much enthusiasm and interest, responded to the call and did considerable talking. The next day our moneyed men elevated their noses in a sneering way and ridiculed the idea as the windwork of fellows without means. But this meeting started the Citizens Board of Trade, from which we now hope for great things. It doesn't always do to sneer at the fellows who are not yet wealthy. They haven't been financial barbers long enough to attain fortunes, but they get there just the same."

And so Kling's Board of Trade fizzled out to the accompaniment of ridicule from the *Star*. According to Harding, the Board would have been pleased if the publicity-mad editor would only go out of business. "About all that has been accomplished so far," he wrote, March 26, 1891, "is the belly-aching whines of a few members because the *Star* doesn't stop publication." On March 31 Harding gave the Board a full treatment of sarcasm. The Board met yesterday, he said, "but a new resolution provides that none of the board's transactions shall be made public, so we announce the state of affairs in a half apologetic way and leave the public in suspense as to what is being done. Marion probably has the first board of trade ever known to pursue such a course, a new bit of wisdom that the world has never known before, but we shall not complain. Indeed, why should we? We can go along unconscious of having such an organization and wake up someday to find new factories, new institutions and a substantial boom, all done on the quiet, a still hunt, as it were."

Time and time again the needle was applied. The Board was a "quiet fizzle," said the *Star*, May 26, 1891. When someone suggested a "swell banquet," Harding, on June 13, proposed a "wake" instead. When a ladies' group conducted a successful cooking school, he commented, January 17, "We expect we shall yet have to depend on the ladies for a public fountain and the longed for opera house. . . . without their progressiveness Marion would alas! be a Delaware or a Galion."

Harding's courtship and marriage with Amos Kling's daughter, Florence, was part of the feuding. It was no secret that, among the things that Warren and Florence had in common, was the hostility of Amos Kling. In the late 1880s Florence Kling had offended her distinguished father by her marriage to Henry DeWolfe. This had turned out unhappily, and a divorce had ensued. Then Florence, perhaps as a result of seeing Warren when she gave his sister piano lessons at their home on Center Street, became enamored of the promising young editor. Amos Kling made known his bitter opposition, but she was as strong-willed as her father. She had set her cap for Warren, and she would have him.[22] They were married by the Reverend Richard Wallace of Epworth Methodist Episcopal Church at Warren's new Mt. Vernon Avenue home at 8:30 Wednesday evening, July 8, 1891.[23] The invitations were sent out, not by Kling, but by Warren himself.[24]

Jack Warwick told the story of Harding's courtship in a rather cloak-and-dagger way, but his meaning was quite clear. He spoke of "a dark complexioned man" who "entered the life of the young editor and sought to circumvent him." This villain, of course, failed utterly, and the editor triumphed "after the manner of the hero in the melodrama." "The dark man who entered the life of Warren Harding," wrote Warwick, "was Amos H. Kling . . . . reputed to be the wealthiest man in Marion and as such was accustomed to have pretty much his own way, because most people let him have it." But Amos did not have his way with Warren Harding and Florence. His opposition to the match was as well known as were the reasons for it. Said Warwick, "My sympathies were with the lovers and the time came when the sympathies of most of the town were with them. The exceptions could be traced to persons who feared the enmity or poor opinion of the Dark Man." The boys in the office were all with Harding in this affair of the heart. "While they couldn't help in the one they could dig into their work and assist him in making a success of the paper. They liked Florence Kling, as they liked her after she became the wife of their employer."

The fact of the general awareness of this Capulet-and-Montague love affair by the Marion community was well described by Warwick. "The town of Marion," he wrote, "was deeply interested in this affair between Warren Harding and Amos Kling's daughter. Many of the things I passed in my masculine way were vitalized in the minds of the women of the town and put in circulation on the wings of the morning. There were clandestine meetings—there always are when there are Capulets—and at times the counter in the Star office, with its two towering ends, furnished protection during a short whispered conversation. But I'll be doggoned if I'm going to tell anything I don't know, like a romancer."

"Then," wrote Warwick, "came a period of excitement." This was when the "Dark Man and some of his sattelites had circulated a damnable and impossible lie about W. G." Warwick was referring to the story that still lingers among Marion folk that Kling gave circulation to the claim that the Hardings were of Negro ancestry, and that was why he opposed the marriage. Warwick continued, "This is the one time in his life that Harding came to me in a two-fisted state of anger. He told me about it all, as near as I can recall, and then said: 'I am going to this man with a fair warning and I shall tell him that he must go no further with this lie—that if he does I will clean up the street with him the next time I meet him.' The Dark Man was pretty nervous about it, but managed to say: 'I shall be prepared for you, sir.' But the damnable lie went out of circulation so far as the Dark Man was concerned. And the love-making went forward. . . . "

Warwick carried his well-told story to its inevitable climax.

> Early in the year 1890 Warren Harding's love making had advanced so far that the subject of matrimony was obsessing his mind. Don't misunderstand me. He didn't tell me his thoughts on the subject, but I knew he was head over heels in contemplation. How did I know? Simple enough. He advised me to get married, and it would not have been like him to advise me to take the precipitous plunge had he not been expecting to follow. That would have been contrary to the old swimmin' hole rules. The Dark Man no longer worried W. G. In fact, the young editor said to me something like this, in substance: "I have about decided that I would rather have Amos Kling's enmity than his friendship. As it is, he now lets me alone. If he were friendly, he would want to tell me how to run my business." Verily, I believe the Dark Man's campaign against W. G. was an asset. They say "all the world loves a lover." However true that may be, an overwhelming majority of the people of Marion were in favor of the young editor of the *Star*, as against the prospective father-in-law.[25]

3

One of Harding's best editorial performances was his boosting of the campaign to get Marion out of the mud, *i.e.*, to adopt city paving. Everything centered around the special election of May 11, 1894. This was the day set aside for the local voters to decide on a new paving era. The Ohio Legislature's House Bill No. 696, passed May 1, authorized "any city of the fourth grade of the second class, which at the last federal census had a population of 8,327," to issue up to $30,000 a year of 6 percent bonds to a total of not over $100,000 for the purpose of paying one-fiftieth of the costs "in addition to intersections" for "paving and macadamizing the city's streets and alleys." [26] Since 8,327 happened to be Marion's population, as determined by the census taken in 1890, the city council immediately designated May 11 for the vote.

Harding proceeded to do an excellently constructive job in promoting this bond issue. Each day, starting May 2, the *Star* published promotional material, explaining the bond issue, showing its moderation, exhorting the people not to be influenced by the "certain element arrayed against it," and which would be against it ten years from now. Costs were discussed in detail with the appropriate figures and diagrams showing the brick, stone, and sand necessary, with a total of $1.25 per square yard suggested as the maximum figure. Testimonials from various Ohio cities, obtained by Harding himself were printed. Assurance was given for the use of home labor and material. Reference was made to the need for getting the pavement down before the street-railway tracks were laid.

On May 5 Harding presented one of his Sunday-best editorials on the subject:

> If one of the glories of the new Jerusalem lies in its streets of gold and onyx stone, Christian men and women should favor its nearest approach here below—cleanliness will come, like a balm and blessing to us all. The disease-breeding quagmires will go, and pestilential visitations cease. The cesspools of filth that pollute busy Marion streets after each Saturday of trade and horrify strangers who note them, will go, happily forever. The present condition is unendurable. Let us then be fair-minded citizens and with some show of public spirit endorse the proposition that is a favorable step toward improvement, and place Marion up with the times in this respect as she is in most others.

"Not a Marion paper except the star," he wrote May 8, "is lending its influence for a favorable ballot." And a favorable ballot they got—1,442 to 137. "Only 137 opponents of progress," wrote Harding May 12, " . . . As old Galileo said, 'it does move.'"

Carrying out the pavement program was certainly no perfunctory affair. Marionites went into it with gusto—and so did Harding. In fact, before the dust had settled on the new streets, the spirited young editor found himself in another feud—with the opponents of progress, of course.

If we may believe the *Star*, the awarding of the first paving contracts by city council for Center and Main Streets was the occasion of a great public controversy amongst Marionites. "It was the one subject discussed in the city today," wrote Harding on August 14, 1894, "and never before in Marion were those unpleasant things that break into the peace and happiness of the lives of councilmen so conspicuously apparent." The trouble was that the award had not gone to the lowest bidder. As the *Star* headlined it:

TALK OF THE TOWN

Is the City Council's Street Paving Contract

COLEMAN & HALLWOOD'S BID ACCEPTED

The Bid Was Not the Lowest by a D. S.

The *Star*, however, vowed to set the minds of people at ease. "The STAR will publish a tabulated statement of aggregate amounts of brick paving bids received on Center and Main Streets. We will give every bid received, and on different kinds of material so comparisons can be made, and the public may know the situation. Rumors of wide discrepancies between bids are not very reliable."

The *Star*'s publication of facts and figures did not prevent a first-class civic controversy. The disappointed lowest bidder, the Canton Shale Brick Manufacturing Company, sought a court injunction against the carrying out of the award. Moreover, it obtained the technical assistance of Edward Huber and J. J. Hane of the Marion County Bank. These men claimed that the bricks of the Canton company were superior to the Coleman and Hallwood bricks. They relied on Huber's testing the bricks of the two companies in his "rattler." Coleman and Hallwood bricks, weighing 3 pounds 11 ounces each, came out weighing 3 pounds 4½ ounces, whereas the Canton bricks, weighing 3 pounds 12½ ounces, came out weighing 3 pounds 10 ounces.

Harding, of course, was disturbed. He asked the "Canton kickers," on August 21, 1894, why they did not submit their tests to council at the proper time, and why similar tests made by Councilman B. P. Sweney showed "diametrically opposite results." Moreover, Harding cited what Council had cited, the testimony of dozens of other cities. "It is preposterous to assume that the widespread Hallwood sentiment throughout so many cities is corrupt." Not only that, but why, he asked, had not such experienced businessmen as Huber and Hane accepted public urging to seek election to the city council? "Now and heretofore they refused to accept. For just this reason the STAR believes their attitude of opposition indefensible."

Harding took special offense at the claims that he was being bribed by Council to suppress the facts about corruption. "In ten years experience, the STAR was never but once even offered a cash considera- tion for the suppression of news." This was when "a big hearted citizen generously proferred a quarter, after he had been pityingly promised freedom from publicity in a matter that could not have interested the people save as an ugly bit of gossip." For shame, this talk of corruption by councilmen known so well! "In big cities where councilmen are less well known, and less likely to be detected corrup- tion exists." But not in places like Marion. This sort of thing was not attempted in "interior cities, where councilmen are citizens instead of ward politicians and boodlers." He challenged the readers to "go over the list of councilmen and ask himself if he truly believes this member or that member is purchasable."

As the hearings on the injunction were put off day after day, Harding's impatience at the alleged small-mindedness of the "Canton obstructionists" increased. This claim of wasting taxes was nonsense. With winter coming, he said September 8, the delay and loss of work "will far exceed the difference in bills, which is alleged to be the moving cause of the offended taxpayers. Bosh! there is no tax paying grief in a single step of proceedings. A gauzier pretext never shielded an outrageous proceeding." It was a case between the masses of the people and a "disgruntled paving firm, to whom Marion owes not a farthing of consideration." Finally, after a month's delay, the Court of Common Pleas denied the injunction. "KNOCKED CLEAR OUT," rejoiced the *Star*, September 22, "The People Win the First Victory. Case of the Canton Kickers Kicked Out of Court."

But the impatient young editor was wrong. A new obstruction occurred which was to trigger him into injudicious tactics and pro- duce still another feud. A man named Lewis Gunn brought a taxpay- er's suit for an injunction against the city's using tax money to pay the allegedly illegal contract with the Coleman & Hallwood Brick Com- pany. According to the *Star*, October 4, 1894, the litigation was begun after a conference between J. J. Hane and an official of the Canton Shale Brick Manufacturing Company.

Harding was disgusted. "Public sentiment is utterly disregarded and a small coterie seeks to run great and modern Marion in the selfish interest of a brick concern a hundred miles away." This was trifling with public sentiment. It was downright petty. Messrs. Hane and Gunn were insincere. "How do the 1500 people of Marion who voted for the paving like it? Who runs Marion anyway?" "Pshaw," wrote Harding on October 5, "Mr. Gunn is not the petitioner. It is the Canton Brick Manufacturers that want Marion buried in the mud to further their selfish interest."

Harding's anger soon got the better of his judgment. He permitted himself to become personally insulting to Lewis Gunn by calling him a pensioner. Harding's point about a poor man acting like a taxpayer was illogical and rude. "What a spectacle," he wrote on October 4, "to have a pensioner under the Dependent Pensioners Act, bringing an injunction suit as an injured tax-payer, when he is interested in only his mite of the 2 per cent of the paving to be paid by the city in general! The STAR makes no fling at any old soldier—all honor to every one of them—but we can not help noting the incongruity of a dependent pensioner, who must swear he is unable to support himself, bringing suit as a suffering taxpayer."

The angry young editor became even more personally insulting. He offered to pay Gunn's tax of $16.30. He wrote a sarcastic letter in the Star of October 5 reflecting on Gunn's civic spirit, his poverty, and his being a puppet of the "Canton kickers." An altercation resulted when Gunn and his younger and more muscular brother called at the Star office, demanding an apology. The casualties consisted of a black eye for Dr. Harding, and numerous abrasions for young Gunn and Charles Kramer, Harding's chief job printer, who acted on behalf of his employer. Harding himself refrained from fisticuffs on the ground that he had "spent the greater part of the past eight months in a studious effort to avoid undue excitement." The melee ended with the Gunns leaving "under the escort of a city officer." They were bound over to court under $500 bond for committing an assault.

The paving did go on. Gunn's injunction petition was dismissed. On October 12, the first brick was laid by city solicitor, D. R. Crissinger. This was followed by a flood of petitions from side-street property owners. Harding took great credit for this, and on October 15 he wrote, "Just as we have all along insisted, without adopting I-told-you-so habits, the paving fever is spreading before a single block of work contracted is done. One paved street begets another, so to speak, and already there are positive signs of an epidemic, as it were." He felt added pride in the fact that several petitions were for asphalt. He liked the forward look of these "asphalt boomers." "Brick or block is not rich enough. . . . It has always been a hobby with the STAR to see Marion have a couple [*sic*] new asphalt streets."

4

Thus did editor Harding boom, build, and "bloviate" for Marion. The time would come when the city would fall flat upon its financial face in trying to finance its improvements, but the time would never come when the people of Marion would lose confidence in the *Star* and its ardent publisher. The *Star* was Marion's spokesman and the people were proud of it and its owner.

CHAPTER THREE

A Young Political Opportunist

"Most newspapers are run for money, 'tis true, and this is one of them."   : : :   *"Marion Daily Star," June 14, 1888*

◢ Warren Harding took his political principles very lightly in the early years of his newspaper career. They were subordinated completely to his desire to be a successful and profit-making publisher. If partisanship endangered his circulation, as it would in the *Daily Star*, he must suppress his Republican preferences. If, on the other hand, political partisanship would win him the recognition of the Republican county organization and the Republican share of the public printing, he would wave his editorial hat aloft in ardent enthusiasm in another newspaper, the *Weekly Star*. Moreover, if the time should come, as it did, when he was so successful as a daily newspaper publisher that he did not need the public printing, and ran no risk of losing circulation from revealing his Republican preference, his normal Republicanism would appear in both newspapers. Finally, if there should be a rival Republican paper to challenge his leadership, as there was in the Marion *Independent*, he would turn the full force of his wrath upon it, reveal its political as well as business ineptitude, and drive it to the wall, leaving the field almost entirely to himself. Harding's early politics were clearly dominated by a desire for revenue and a feeling of personal vengeance.

Harding's first political decision as a newspaperman was that it was more profitable to keep his daily newspaper out of politics. In the Ohio gubernatorial campaigns of 1885 and 1887 the *Star* was completely silent editorially about issues and candidates. Not until the reelection of Governor Joseph B. Foraker in 1887 did the young editor explain his reticence. "To be brief and very candid," he wrote on November 7, "the editor of this paper endeavors to conduct it so as to get the necessary support, regardless of politics, to sustain a daily here. With this view we have kept mum during this campaign, offering scarcely an hundred lines of editorial matter in the entire campaign. . . . It has been a clear case of shutting one's mouth to save offense, a thorough example of saying nothing political whatever."

Harding followed the same line in presidential politics. Personally, he had been an ardent supporter of Blaine against Cleveland in 1884, even to the extent of being fired from his job as reporter with the *Democratic Mirror* for his public conduct in Republican parades. After Cleveland's election, in which Marion county and city voted their usual Democratic majorities, he wrote, "Inasmuch as the election is settled, how would it be to cease talking about the 'solid south'? We do not suggest this from any political standpoint, but for the ordinary newspaper reader." As the day of Cleveland's inauguration approached in 1885, he wrote, "Only one month until we live and breathe under a Democratic administration. The sun will shine just the same and the great political change will be scarcely noted except by office-holders." After almost two years of Cleveland's administration, he commented, "Why criticize every little thing the man did? Party organs lay too much stress upon every act the Chief Executive of the land does. It has a tendency to make the country feel unsafe, while, if they would pursue a more lenient course, more confidence would pervade the masses."[1]

Elimination of the "bloody shirt" from the *Star*'s columns was also a good circulation booster. "Bloody shirt waving" was the exasperating practice of blaming the Democrats for the Civil War and for all its misery. The *Star*'s rival Republican paper, the *Marion Independent*, still engaged in the practice for political reasons. The Democratic paper, the *Marion Mirror*, fired back volley for volley. On the occasion of Jefferson Davis' death in 1889, Harding made much of the need to let bygones be bygones. "Mr. Davis is now in his grave," he wrote on December 12, "That is, the ceremonies are over, and they have been all that he could have wished. The sorrow of the Southern people has been as wonderful as it has been sincere, and Northern people have said very little that was harsh or unkind. It was proper for the late confederates to show their sorrow, and it is proper to have sectionalism buried with its late chief."[2]

Political-religious bigotry also came in for Harding's criticism. He strongly regretted Reverend S. D. Burchard's famous "Rum, Romanism and Rebellion" castigation of the Democrats in the 1884 campaign. In 1887 he told his *Star* readers that he hoped that Burchard's voice would not be heard in the coming campaign. "If he will remain Reticent, Retired and Regretful next campaign the friends of Blaine will take it as a favor." When Burchard finally passed away in 1891, Harding wrote graciously, "None were grieved over the effect of his unfortunate remarks more than he was." [3]

2

It was at this time that the young editor extended his horizons in hope of gaining a wider influence for his views among the general public. In 1885 the spectacle was suddenly presented of Harding furling the "bloody shirt" in the *Daily Star* and waving it vigorously in a new sheet called the *Weekly Star*. The publishing of the *Weekly Star* grew out of Harding's desire for income from the public printing. The *Independent*, now a semi-weekly, had had the Republican share of it ever since Civil War days. The impecunious young Harding wanted it. He believed that he had a better paper than his "bloody-shirt-waving" Republican rival.

However, the *Daily Star* did not qualify for the public printing. The law required that such printing should be awarded to a paper having a general circulation throughout the county. The *Daily Star* could not have that kind of circulation. To obtain this, it was necessary to have a weekly edition of the *Star*, and, again with the helping hand, financially, of Dr. Harding, such an edition was launched and published with the usual Harding hustle.

The objective of a county-wide printing for the *Weekly Star* was, of course, not openly declared by Harding. But it was frankly admitted in later years by Harding's partner, Jack Warwick. "W. G.," wrote Warwick, "incubated the idea that it was possible to make a field for a *Weekly Star*, to circulate in the farming district and gather in some of the county printing that must be published under the law in two newspapers. He was after the semi-weekly Independent's dry bone." [4]

Harding quickly put his new weekly to work grinding out a vigorous brand of Republicanism. Choice flourishes of the "bloody shirt" were offered in his editorials. One of them, dated June 20, 1885, and borrowed from the Cleveland *Leader*, castigated the new Democratic administration for appointing to office former Confederates guilty of denouncing Abraham Lincoln as a tyrant, and calling Union soldiers "Lincoln's dogs and hirelings." At the same time, taking a Republican out of office was "in a majority of cases punishing a man for having proved true to his country in the darkest hours of peril, and risked his life in its defense when attacked [by] powerful hordes of armed traitors." A week later the *Weekly Star* lamented, "When rebels and rebel sympathizers have preference to crippled soldiers, it seems as if it ought to raise the patriotism of every Union man in the entire party." This sort of thing went on week after week. The Republican ticket of J. B. Foraker and R. P. Kennedy for governor and lieutenant governor was called "the soldiers' ticket." Secretary of Interior L. Q. C. Lamar of Mississippi was blasted, August 8, 1885, for allegedly saying that southern officeholders were more reliable than northern ones. Ohio Democratic Governor George Hoadly was accused, September 19, of having thanked God for the Solid South, but of having omitted the name of God from his Thanksgiving Proclamation. Defamers of President Grant were given a vigorous treatment of invective.

But it took more than the "bloody shirt" to convince Republicans that the *Weekly Star* was orthodox. The Democrats had to be assailed at many points. On June 13, 1885 they were roundly denounced for their alleged inconsistency in posing as civil-service reformers and then removing Republicans for partisan reasons. In the same issue the Democratic Secretary of State, Thomas F. Bayard, was accused of political naïveté and ignorance. The June 20 issue contained a choice variety of anti-Democratic remarks. Cleveland's Indian policy of moderation was called unrealistic. Young Harding's advice was, "As there is no room for Indians and no food, let them be killed off." Cleveland was also said to be playing politics with Indian-agent appointments. The Republican-supported Scott law of Ohio, taxing retail liquor dealers and prohibiting Sunday saloon openings, was praised. On June 27 the Democratic party was denounced for causing a lack of business confidence and, hence, for producing panics. On August 1 Foraker was enthusiastically supported for governor, and the talk that he was anti-Negro was ridiculed. On July 18 the campaign of 1876 was rehashed, and the Democratic claim that the Republicans stole the contested votes was counteracted by recent "revelations" of the stealing of votes and of the intimidation of voters by Democrats. On July 11 and September 26 the election by the Ohio Democrats of Henry B. Payne to the United States Senate in 1884 was said to have been accomplished by bribery from the Standard Oil Company of the "coal-oil" Democratic legislators. On September 26 the wealthy Cincinnati Democrat and publisher of the *Enquirer*, John McLean, was said to have similar intentions and to have plenty of "boodle" with which to back them. In another issue, the Democrats were blamed for promoting the contracting-out of prison labor. On several occasions Adna B. Leonard, the Prohibition candidate for governor, was called a "pulpit pounding demagogue," and said to be in alliance with the Democrats. Democrats were charged, on September 19, with lowering wage levels by allowing prison-made brooms and harnesses to be sold in competition with the products of private enterprise. On the day following Grant's death, A. R. Bell of Bucyrus was quoted as calling Grant "a G-d d----d thief." Bell was thereupon referred to by the *Weekly* of August 1 as a "vile blow fly. . . . a loathsome maggot." [5]

3

As the two papers became financially self-sustaining, the fierceness of Harding's political journalism gradually declined, but not the fierceness with which he did battle with his rival Republican editor, George Crawford, and eventually drove him out of business. Crawford continued to live in the post–Civil War "age of hate," and added to his "bloody shirt waving" against the South a torrent of abuse, and sometimes filth, against his more clever rival. No stripling like Harding could rob Crawford of leadership in defending the Republican party, and receiving its public-printing largesse.

The bitter exchanges between Harding and Crawford became part of Marion's diversions for over ten years, that is, until 1896, when the aging Crawford threw in the towel. Harding spoke for the young Republicans, Crawford for the declining "old guard." Crawford called Harding a skunk and the *Star* a "slop bucket," a "smut machine." He accused Harding of being "a Republican for revenue only." Harding called Crawford "Old Nancy," a "driveling old idiot," "a sneaking whelp," "a lying dog," "a lickspittle," a "disgrace to the Republican Party," and a "sour, disgruntled and disappointed old ass." Eventually Harding caught Crawford in the act of overcharging the city for printing. He proved it beyond any doubt, and that was the end of Crawford and the *Independent.*[6]

4

By the turn of the century Warren Harding had become a pretty good political opportunist. Many things help account for this. One

was his success as a newspaperman in learning how to please all kinds
of people. Another was his belief that the natural leaders of society
were the businessmen. This derived not only from his relation to
businessmen as advertisers, but from the "blacksmith admiration"
concept of his boyhood. On popular politics, Harding was peculiarly
ambivalent: he professed a distrust of the direct primary because it
promoted demagoguery, but few could turn a demogogic phrase—in
print or on the stump—better than he, *viz.*, his indulgence in the
all-American support of high tariffs and overseas expansion. Finally,
there was an inability within him to rise to moralistic fervor in
opposing the possibilities of the evil influence of money in politics. All
these factors left the talented and politically ambitious Harding unable to move into the growing Progressive movement.

Harding thus floated to the top of that element in his section of
Ohio that may come under the label of conservative. This element was
held together by the belief that businessmen were the "true" progressives, the talented few who built the new factories, produced the new
inventions, and made the nation's industry and commerce hum with
increasing efficiency. Harding naively believed that these men should
enter into politics, and keep it from being contaminated either by
Democratic demagogues and place-hunters or by Republican bosses.

In the late 1890s, when the business element and the "asphalt
boomers" had succeeded in getting Marion to "wear city clothes," the
local Democrats introduced a new political gadget, the direct primary
for the nomination of city officials. The ensuing Democratic victory
led Harding into a mood of despondency as he saw local Democratic
demagoguery displacing the levelheadedness and nonpartisanship
that had, so far, characterized Marion's modernization. For the local
Republicans to adopt such rabble-rousing tactics in city politics was
unthinkable. In Harding's estimation the direct primary substituted
popular clamor for the calm and deliberate selection of candidates by
conventions and the "better minds" of those who attended conventions. The direct primary, he said, introduces "excessive partisanship
into the municipal elections and has a tendency to place city affairs
under partisan control, when the best judgment of the times and the
advanced movements of the day favor the divorce of municipal affairs
from partisan politics." (Harding's voice in behalf on nonpartisanship
was always loudest when the Democrats were in power.) "In Marion
county the excessive interest in Democratic primary nominations
brings out the full party vote and the partisan spirit is so aroused that

many voters make a party day of it, and give less attention to the merits of candidates than they do to party success. The few hangers-on at the public crib take advantage of easy party victory." Men with high ideals of public service, said Harding, will not expose themselves to such clamor. Marion needed this type of man, according to Harding, to protect it from "pap seekers and job hunters . . . but we can't expect this if our city elections are held in the midst of such partisan hurrah as the primary system promises to make permanent." [7]

Harding put some of his best journalistic devices to work against this "primary political lottery," this Democratic "free-for-all." On February 11, 1897, his new cartoonist, A. P. Porter, presented a front-page cartoon satire on the alleged vulgarity of the approaching April 5 local primary. There were portrayed the trappings of a circus: tents, performers, acrobats, each labeled with some references to local personalities and situations. The main title read:

WILL POSITIVELY APPEAR APRIL 5

NO POSTPONEMENT ON ACCOUNT OF RAIN

Some of the signs read:

A FEW OF THE ALMOST EXTINCT

HONEST POLITICIANS ON EXHIBITION

THRILLING LEAPS FOR NOMINATIONS

AMBULANCE ACCOMODATIONS PROVIDED

FRESH ROASTED PEANUT POLITICIANS INSIDE

A RARE COLLECTION OF MARBLE HEARTS

BARNUM IS DEAD BUT—THERE ARE OTHERS

The effect of this on Republican politics was very real. Democrats won elections without even trying. The Democratic victory of April 5, 1898 was headlined:

JUST LIKE FINDING IT

So Easy Was the Victory Won by Democratic

Hustlers Monday

The Republican caucuses in June for the county nominating convention were ridiculed in the *Star* of June 10:

DIDN'T TURN OUT

In Large Numbers. Delegates Chosen, Allee Samee

It was noted that at one precinct a total of four Republicans voted, at
another six and another eleven. "No voter seems to 'cara cuss' what
happens," he lamented October 8, 1898. "The local Republicans have
little or nothing to say, but, like the maiden of uncertain years, they
are in a receptive mind and are open to propositions."

The direct primary was but one of the new political nostrums that
Harding despised. The winds of reform were blowing rather fitfully in
the late nineteenth-century America, but they did not gain Harding's
enthusiasm. Reform, if we may use Harding's approach, was the
crochety side of the Progressive movement. Anything that was "really"
progressive he subscribed to or purchased, like asphalt paving, the
waterworks, or a linotype machine. As for the reform fads, such as
prohibition, women's rights, "Coxeyism," he treated them as curiosities
or, at best, tolerated them. In the case of free silver, he, of course,
fought it.

No, the *Star* was not a reform paper. As Jack Warwick said, "We did
not let the paper dabble in reform. It tried simply to be decent,
respectable and reliable, minding what little business it had to mind.
. . . We did not take ourselves too seriously and never thought about
bringing about a revolution of the world, morally or politically."
Reform apparently gave young Harding nightmares. Warwick recalled how "W. G." once woke him up at a weird hour in the morning
to listen to a speech. "As I recall the incident," Warwick wrote, "we
had followed him to the point where he struck a dramatic attitude
and, pointing toward the ceiling, insisted that there stood out in bold
cotton batting relief this legend: 'R-e-f-o-r-m!'" [8]

There was a certain rationale to Harding's skepticism about reform.
Society could not rise above its own level of morality. It could not lift
itself by its own bootstraps. As he observed the reform leaders trying
to get society to adopt their cure-alls, he came to the judgment that
they were trying to inject moral principles into people who did not
take their morals from strangers. Morals were things that people got
from family training or from religious indoctrination. (Schools and

colleges were not mentioned.) To seek to promote moral uplift by political action was impossible. "The force of moral law," he wrote in the *Star* December 19, 1911, "has been ignored in seeking cure-alls in statutory laws enacted by men. There has been more concentration on civic correction than moral redemption. . . . The latter must come first and must have its beginning in the individual heart." He blamed church leadership for the failure. "The American people are not drifting from the influence of the church, but the pulpit has too often failed to convince and carry the needed conviction. The great truth has never failed, the failure is in its utterance. Not enough preaching has stirred the individual conscience."

5

These assumptions were at the basis of Harding's middle-of-the-road attitude toward the temperance movement. When he became editor of the *Star*, the issue on this subject was state taxation versus prohibition, with Harding strongly on the side of the former method of control. "Restraint," he wrote August 28, 1885, "people will submit to. They do so in every relation, and there are very few who will not make every reasonable concession for the public good. But absolute interdiction—that is felt to be destructive of personal liberty, when the object sought is believed to be practically attainable without it." Nearly half of the American people, he said upon another occasion, June 1, 1887, did not think it a crime to drink a little beer, and they would break the law "because they think they are doing what they have a perfect right to do." Experience with prohibition in such places as Maine, Iowa, and Georgia, he said, demonstrated this fact. Therefore, he concluded, prohibition was a theory that violated the facts of life. "Theories that contravene all facts will not solve the question. It must be dealt with in the practical way which experience unmistakably points out." Experience had also shown, he claimed September 9, 1885, that high restrictive taxation closed the "doggeries" and materially lessened the sale of intoxicants. That was achieving more in the interests of temperance than prohibition could achieve. "If it is found impossible to enforce the law," he said on December 21, 1885 of Iowa's experience with prohibition, "it would be vastly better to have it repealed and some other means resorted to for the control of the traffic." Hence, in 1886 when, at Governor Foraker's suggestion, the so-called Dow Law was passed, taxing liquor sellers $200 a year and beer-and-wine sellers $100 a year,[9] Harding was satisfied.

Harding much preferred the moderation of the Anti-Saloon League approach to the temperance problem. He contrasted it with the Women's Christian Temperance Union's "prohibition or bust" attitude which made it a "side show" of the Prohibition party. The League's "plan of putting the question of temperance outside of politics," he wrote June 9, 1894, "is the only rational one." He drew on his own legislative experience as he described the League's work in a *Star* editorial on March 27 of that year. First it got a friendly legislator to introduce a local-option bill into the General Assembly. The bill was perfunctorily referred to a committee. Meanwhile the League was quietly promoting propaganda and collecting peititions in support of the measure from all over the state. The effect was quite startling. The committee had expected only a few "cranks" at its hearings. But the members were surprised to find a large representation of Anti-Saloon Leaguers present "who backed their requests and arguments by 150,000 petitioners over 60,000 of whom were voters." The effect of this was that "every legislator knows positively that if he votes for this bill he will have the combined liquor strength against him in the future campaigns he may make. If he could positively know the contra from the temperance people, the outcome of this fight could be easily predicted. The anti-saloon league is doing much for the cause."

Harding was no enthusiast for local option. Even though it made possible prohibition in a limited area, the same objection applied to a small group as to a large group of people: temperance was a personal matter subject to control mainly by personal, family, and religious influences. When Xenia, Ohio voted dry in 1901, Harding had his doubts about the prospects of success. Xenia was the largest city to try the experiment and it would be surprising, Harding thought, if there were not many speak-easies and well-stocked cellars to provide the basis for much law violation. "Local option," he wrote November 27, 1901, "is a splendid thing where everybody thinks alike and when appetites are in harmony. That place has not been found in Ohio up to date. If Xenia proves to be such a town it will have the distinction it deserves."

What local option really did, thought Harding, was to produce a certain inter-community arrangment concerning saloons. The cities voted wet and the villages and small towns voted dry by a sort of unexpressed agreement. The drinkers in the small towns were willing to depend on nearby cities for their satisfaction and the city merchants were glad to have their business. These ideas may be gleaned from several *Star* observations in 1902. On June 29, after Bellefontaine had voted wet by a big majority, Harding commented on the significance of such a decision "in the most pronounced temperance town and county in Ohio." The nearby towns of De Graffe, Belle Center, Rushsylvania, Quincy, and West Mansfield, as well as the countryside in general, were dry by "decided majorities." "This is partially explained, perhaps," he wrote, "by the well-proven statement that most people want to do their drinking away from home." He was much more sweeping in this idea on July 10, when he wrote, "The tendency of the small town to go dry will help the larger towns which remain wet. It may shock a great many good people to contemplate a commercial advantage growing out of the temperance question, but the business history of local option justifies the belief that there is a large class of people who prefer trading in the places where there is no limit to gratifying a possible appetite for something on the side."

Harding was also convinced that if the local saloonkeepers would be more careful in regard to such laws as related to Sunday closing, the hours of closing on weekdays, and the non-sale of liquor to minors, there would be no uprising of the temperance element in favor of prohibition. On February 13, 1894 Harding attributed the growth of the local-option movement to the organized lawbreaking of the saloonists in many localities. Several years later the popularity of local option seemed to decline as the result of a new law-abiding attitude. Thus on January 27, 1903 Harding commented on the action of the saloonkeepers of Shelby, Ohio in asking the mayor to fine heavily all violators of the liquor laws. "It is well known," he wrote, "that saloonists are responsible for many of the temperance wars made against them by taking advantage of the leniency and laxity of officials, when a strict adherence to existing laws would forestall agitation and bring about their complete overthrow. The Shelby liquor dealers have taken a sensible course." A few weeks later, a narrow victory for the wets in Ashtabula had the effect of frightening the saloonkeepers into more careful law enforcement. "While the saloons have won a temporary victory," he wrote, March 19, 1903, "the strength the opposition has shown has been sufficient to bring them to their senses, and they have entered into an agreement to strictly observe the law and assist in the prosecution of violators. When saloonists unite for the purpose of teaching their own members respect for law they will have succeeded in disarming much of the opposition directed against them."

6

What about reform in Marion? There were spasms of uplift by the ministry, by citizens' committees, by the mayor, by the police. Yes, there were even spasms promoted by Harding and the *Star*. But these movements never geared together to provide the much hoped-for, but never realized, general "clean up." Thus, Harding said, Marion exemplified the general rule that society cannot rise above its own level of morality. In this respect Harding provided more than editorial observations about the rule. He had his spasms and then cooled off.

Marion's vice district was known as the Bowery. According to the *Star* of March 20, 1897, which contained a drawing of the Bowery by Porter, its center was on Mill Street and Railroad Street between Main and State Streets. Effective exhibits of Marion's vice offerings were displayed from the windows and porches of the houses facing the railroad tracks for the benefit of incoming passenger trains. There were scattered "houses" in other parts of town. The operating units were the saloons, gambling rooms, and houses of prostitution. They bore such names as the Red House and the Blue Goose. Their habitués were alleged gangs, card sharks, "soiled doves," "yellow canaries," and a motley assortment of "bums," "bar flies," and rowdies. The existence of these dens of iniquity and their denizens was almost daily testified to by reports and stories in the *Star*. The organized prostitutes came to be referred to as the "Bag of Tricks." [10] Every once in a while there was a movement to "clean up the Bowery," a slogan which became a standing joke and served to advertise the institution more than to threaten its existence.

The most spectacular spasm of the "reform Marion" movement came in 1895. It was a sort of echo of New York City's great reform movement of 1892–94. The Reverend Charles H. Parkhurst of that city's Madison Square Presbyterian Church sparked a "good citizens" movement which revealed such rotten vice conditions that the voters upset the Democratic city government and replaced it with a Republican one that gave Theodore Roosevelt his famous term as reform police commissioner of New York. An investigation of conditions by a committee headed by State Senator Clarence Lexow revealed a vicious system of police protection of criminals and mobsters that shocked the nation.

The Parkhurst-Lexow revelations produced a Marion reform movement in 1894–95. The sensational facts were newsworthy, and Harding gave them much front-page coverage and frequent editorial comment. His editorials were encouraging to the reformers but never thoroughly insistent or persistent. As early as April 8, 1892 he had noted Parkhurst's New York technique of collecting evidence by visiting houses of ill fame and swearing to the observation of nude girls dancing before their customers. "This reverend gentlemen," he wrote, "has hit upon a plan to see things as the 'boys' do, to raise a big muss and possibly do good all at the same time." But, he added, "all men can not be Parkhursts." On January 1, 1895 he commented favorably on the Lexow revelations and declared that more Lexow committees were needed.

Harding's announcement that Marion was due for a Parkhurst movement came in December, 1894. On December 13 the *Star* announced, under the headline, "The Tiger Riders," that "the Parkhurst reformation has struck Marion." It was reported that Mayor Dudley had ordered the Bowery closed, and that the city marshal had visited the joints and ordered the residents to move and "do it quick." Editorials expressed the feeling of general public approval. "Marion," he said, "does not want to be winter quarters for the 'sure thing gamblers,'" Indeed, Harding could claim credit for needling the city officials into this action. On December 3 he had written, "If Mayor Dudley and the police department want to win the regard of every good citizen in Marion they will proceed to clean up or out the Bowery. This tough section of Marion has become a disgrace to the city, and its toleration is inexcusable. . . . Come, gentlemen, you who have Marion's reputation to guard, rid us of the thugs, thieves, burglars, highwaymen, gamblers and scarlet women that are making a small hades of the middle block of Mill Street. The people have been patient long enough."

The removal did not take place. A new mayor came into office in April, 1895, and by June another removal campaign was reported. How effective it and its predecessor were may be judged by the *Star* remark of July 24, "It must be nearly a week now since anybody declared that 'the Bowery gang must go.' Are we to infer from this that the gang has gone?" A week later it was remarked, "So 'the Bowery gang must go.' Can it be possible that we have heard that before?"

Suddenly something began to happen. On August 5, 1895 committees from the Marion churches met at the Y.M.C.A. and organized a Good Citizenship League. Weekly meetings were held throughout August, and a constitution and by-laws drawn up.[11] By September 2 the League had engaged the services of private detective James McEldowney of Bucyrus to accumulate evidence against the lawbreakers. By September 25, according to the *Star* of that day, he procured thirty-six indictments against local saloonkeepers and sporting-house proprietors.

The campaign was not a success. The persistence and ingenuity by which the Bowery lawyers brought delaying and discrediting tactics against McEldowney were amazing. The *Star* reported these events in great detail, and, it must be asserted, with amusement rather than with any sense of resentment. Witnesses showed a surprising propensity to be ill or out of town. When they did appear, attorneys befuddled them with rapid-fire cross-examination. Postponements protracted trials interminably. McEldowney himself was badgered almost to desperation. His boarding house was reported to have been threatened with a dynamiting. When he moved into another house, firecrackers were thrown down the chimney. He was arrested and tried for allegedly seeking to beat a board bill. Bond posted for his court appearances was alleged to be based on inadequate security. He was openly insulted in court, with the judge assessing a dollar on him for contempt. He was charged with seeking to intimidate potential witnesses. Talk of fear of assassination was bandied about. The few convictions that he got of law violators resulted in light fines. For over a month the daily stories of McEldowney's misadventures were news. Then they died out, as did the crusade itself.

In the process, Harding and the *Star* showed a strange lack of confidence in the movement. From the very first, the *Star* referred to the fees that McEldowney was promised in case of the conviction of a violator as a "rake-off."[12] On September 17 the *Star* predicted the failure of the campaign. "There is a lingering suspicion getting abroad about the town," wrote the editor, "that after the first eighteen or nineteen weeks of the private detective's method of reform have come and gone, somebody is apt to be afflicted with an ailment closely resembling 'that tired feeling.'" On September 28, there was a peculiar editorial remark that "it really seems almost like asking too much of an inoffensive public to choose between a 'private detective' and the detected."

And so Marion returned to normal. Raids on the Bowery took place periodically. "Hell in East Marion" continued to flourish.[13] The Reverend S. C. Wright was reported, on January 4, 1898, as having his spotters out observing saloons open on Sunday—for their Monday-morning complaints to the mayor. "No arrests are planned," observed the *Star*. "The slot machines must go," droned the editor on December 3, 1898. About all the citizens could expect, he said June 1, 1897, commenting on the gambling dens, was that "the officials can at least suppress the open games. It is too much to expect all clubs to be ferreted out. They can be reduced to a minimum by the influence of home and companionship."

As for any reform that would get at the basis of social problems, Harding had no solution and he frankly said so. Charity was "all right," and he praised the Women's Relief Association for its benevolent enterprise in behalf of the "worthy poor."[14] He supported these and other fund-raising campaigns with sincere enthusiasm. But he could not avoid expressing his contempt for "loafers on relief." On November 13, 1886, while congratulating the Relief Association for "gladdening the hearts of the suffering and of those unavoidably in distress," he wrote that "it is revolting to think that there are those who impose upon the sympathetic heart of the institution." He roundly denounced the "great lazy hulks" who "either will not work to support their families, or if they do, spend their earnings foolishly, leaving their homes barren of real necessities, and compel the wife or children to seek subsistence for themselves at the bin of public charity."

Harding's bewilderment as to what to do about the problem of charity was well expressed in the *Star* of February 6, 1894 in mid-winter of the severe depression following the Panic of 1893. He told of the general relief system in Cleveland, which reminded him of the maxim that the "indiscriminate charity of yesterday has brought forth a harvest of tramps of today." "Indiscriminate giving to chance beggars is not charity, it is almost wanton wickedness, working an injury both on the recipient and the country." And yet he was puzzled. "Who," he asked, "can turn from his door a starving man? The country is full of poor fellows who are out of a job and are persistently seeking work, tramping from town to town in search of employment. Where is the genius who will solve the problem?" When a congressional committee began a study looking into the possible causes of the depression, Harding, on May 16, 1894, offered the "rough guess" that it would find that "a certain portion of the community will be poor despite all blessings, all legislation and the most promising opportunity." He then went on to describe the necessity of a high protective tariff as a basis for general prosperity.

Tramps and bums annoyed him. They were "worthless characters," he said on July 29, 1885, who "bode no good and a sharp look out for them will not be out of place." When found, it was to the city stone pile with them, lest free lodgings at the jail make Marion a mecca for more of them. "Why not try them at stone breaking, Mayor Dudley?" he asked April 13, 1891. "It has been a good hit in the past."

Harding had a most interesting theory about tramps and how they worsened the effects of a depression. He described it in the *Star* of June 6, 1894. It seems that a depression created a paradise for them. By swarming upon the authorities they swelled the costs of relief to such a degree as to decrease the amount available to deserving cases. At least that was the conclusion Harding drew from the policy of the city of Baltimore during the winter of 1893–94. By requiring all tramps to work for their lodging Baltimore was almost entirely relieved of their presence. The result, Harding wrote, was that the city was able to confine its aid to the deserving unemployed on a work-relief basis. This "came so near to paying for itself that only an insignificant sum of money was required to prevent actual suffering." He therefore concluded that "this interesting sociological result has, therefore, again demonstrated that it is the tramp—the idler who does not want work—that causes the demoralization in a time of distress and prevents the involuntary idle from finding proper aid."

As for drunkards, harmless though they were, Harding believed that they should be dealt with very harshly. It was his judgment, expressed in the *Star* on March 18, 1887, that "every man knows what condition drinks puts him in, and the action in becoming drunk is perfectly voluntary." He even looked with favor upon a proposed law to make drunkenness a criminal offense with severe punishment for repeated offenses. "Some such treatment of habitual drunkards," he said, January 30, 1892, "would doubtless bring many of them to a halt."

Harding, of course, had no use for the drastic relief proposals of Edward Bellamy and Jacob S. Coxey. In 1893 a "Model City" was projected by some of Bellamy's followers, to be located near Niagara

Falls. It was inspired by the novel *Looking Backward,* and proposed a utopian community where everything was to be owned in common. "These dreamers," wrote Harding, June 24, 1893, "will have to create a new race, upon a revised model, before they can succeed." The Bellamy theory was charming reading, but in practice it had to fail. As for Coxey and his plan for a large-scale, public-works construction program for the unemployed, Harding treated it with ridicule. The march of Coxey's army of unemployed men on Washington was given much boisterous front-page publicity. But the program was never analyzed or evaluated in the *Star.* It was simply laughed at and called "tomfoolery." Its supporters were mostly hoboes with "wheels in their heads." [15]

In the field of high crime and its punishment, Harding repeatedly expressed his firm belief in the necessity of holding criminals to rigid personal accountability by the strictest enforcement of the law. The reform movement for the abolition of capital punishment found him entirely unsympathetic. "The good thing about hanging," he remarked January 7, 1893, "is the certainty of finishing the job, while imprisonment for life is never absolutely certain until the burial." As for substituting electrocution for hanging, he wrote August 9, 1890, "It never struck us as important how a murderer was disposed of, so his miserable career is ended. If electrocution has more terrors than hanging, let the current be turned on." When the Ohio Senate passed the electrocution bill in 1896 he cracked, "The death penalty should be more shocking to the criminal and less shocking to society in general." He had no use for paroling murderers "to prey upon society again." [16]

Harding's stern sense of rigid law enforcement led him to frequent expressions of doubt as to the efficiency of the jury system. Too often, he wrote on July 9, 1886, juries are made up of "eleven damphools and one wise man." Upon another occasion, December 17, 1889, when a verdict displeased him, he reversed the ratio and blamed the result on the persistence of one fool against eleven wise men. He therefore strongly supported proposals to abolish the unanimous-verdict rule, as well as the rule of complete impartiality. It was foolish, he said on February 26, 1894, to waste hours looking for twelve men too ignorant or disinterested in public events to have read the newspapers. When the Ohio legislature in 1898 passed a law requiring judges to sentence murderers to life imprisonment if the jury recommended mercy, he felt that that was the end of the death penalty. "It is a safe guess," he wrote April 25, 1898, "that it will be difficult to find a jury unanimously disposed to inflict the death penalty when there is a clear way to avoid it, except in extraordinary cases." He was, of course, opposed to putting women on juries because of the danger of getting jurors "of the sickly sentiment class, who sometimes carry bouquets to the worst prisoners who break into jail." [17]

Harding took an equivocal position with regard to the subject of lynching. He frequently condoned this resort to mob action. When "the good people" of Eaton, Ohio, followed the acquittal of four alleged murderers with the lynching of a fifth, Harding commented on December 22, 1886, "Lynching scrapes are to be deplored but cases like this one can be looked upon without any fear." Similarly on June 23, 1887, the elimination of the "Tolliver gang" in Kentucky "by an army of determined men who were armed with Winchester rifles for that purpose" was emphatically approved.

Harding was even specific in his approval of some lynchings. On August 26, 1891, he wrote, "There are occasional lynchings of murderers now and then that do not worry the law-abiding people. In cases where there is no doubt of identity or guilt a little hasty justice doesn't shock law abiding people and has a wholesome effect upon the tougher element. Mob law isn't to be commended, is indeed deplorable, but there are acceptable exceptions, so to speak." When an especially vicious Negro rapist was lynched in Urbana, Ohio, in 1897, he emphatically condoned the action of the mob. On June 4 he wrote, "Ohio will please defer any contemptuous remarks about Kentucky and Texas mobs until that unfortunate Urbana affair is forgotten." Three days later Harding described the affair in detail, declaring that, in spite of all the criticism by outsiders of the Urbana action, "there is no regret for the hanging of the wretch who was responsible for the trouble." Philosophers might moralize and suggest remedies, but "there seems to be but one. It is evident beyond question that public sentiment demands more severe punishment than that which is provided by law. . . . Until this is done the Urbana affair may be duplicated at any time and at any place to the disgrace of the whole state."

Harding, of course, had to face up to the fact that sometimes lynchers got the wrong man. His reaction to this was that, if the victim "really" was a bad character, it did not make much difference. But if the victim was "really," or "possibly" innocent, then the lynchers were the bad ones. Thus, on December 2, 1891, when it was reported that there was reasonable proof that a confessed robber named Blinkey

Morgan was not guilty of the murder for which he was hanged, the *Star* commented, "Doubtless, but a good robber got his just dues." On May 30, 1898, upon reading the reports of the possible innocence of two victims in Tennessee and Maryland, the *Star* was very bitter. "Spaniards or Turks do not commit worse crimes against civilization than these," wrote the editor. "How long must such continue to disgrace a nation which claims to being in the front rank in respect of law?"

7

Harding also showed considerable ambivalence about such things as political "boodle" and gerrymandering. He regretted their existence but felt they were necessary evils.

Boodle was the money spent by and for political campaigners. Harding blamed former Ohio Governor Charles Foster for boodleizing local politics. "Foster," he wrote in the *Star*, January 7, 1890, "did more toward introducing money in Republican campaigns in this country than any other living man. Campaigns have been a source of heavy expense ever since."

However, all boodle was not bad. Boodle was good if it was spent in Marion county. For example, there was the proposal to deepen the channel of the Scioto River. Harding's comment, March 19, 1892, was, "We should be pleased to see over $100,000 of good government boodle spent in Marion county, rather than some place else, but we have never had a moment's faith in the Scioto scheme." And yet, on January 21, 1887, he had expressed undying contempt for the "pap-suckers, ward bummers, and boodle politicians."

Another example of Harding's cynical acceptance of boodle was shown by his attitude toward the election of millionaire railroad promoter Calvin S. Brice of Lima, as United States Senator from Ohio in 1890. As in the Scioto scheme, if the boodle was spent in the right place, that made it all right. "Harping about Brice's purchase of the senatorship ought to begin to cease," wrote Harding, January 20, 1890. "The election is over and there is no evidence that the Lima statesman purchased any votes. Sure, he may have spent a few dollars in subscribing for various papers, but in that event the few dollars have gone where they are most needed." Besides, all the other candidates had boodle. Brice's rival, a gentleman named Thomas from Spring-field, boodled. "The trouble is," said Harding, January 30, 1890, "Thomas was beaten at his own game. He boodled just as obnoxiously as the Lima man, though not so successfully." As for the proposals to investigate Brice's use of money in the campaign, Harding warned that that would be fatal because Republican boodling would be revealed in the process. "This question of boodle is not monopolized by any one party, even under the McKinley tariff." "It is no secret in this section of Ohio," said the *Star* editor on November 20, 1891, "that Fostoria dollars have made campaigning with scant funds very hard sledding."

Harding believed that it was good to have rich United States Senators because the country needed the use of the qualities that made them rich. "Brice's opponents should shift their point of attack," he wrote on December 19, 1889. "Boodle don't [*sic*] disqualify from the position of the U.S. Senator. Besides, it makes an invulnerable fortification." Again, he wrote, on December 21, 1889, "The talk of an office seeking the man has been principally confined to the past, and is not a part of the present method of campaigning. However praisewor-thy the former method, we have outgrown it to a great degree, and the man does about all the seeking, and does it too, aggressively and thoroughly. In such cases it becomes natural to use the influence at command. If the influence is wealth it will be used to advance the interest of the candidates. It is powerful, and unless objections are strong and reasonable, it is not difficult to predict the result. Unless the opponents of Mr. Brice can find objections other than his wealth they will have made a fruitless fight." Moreover, reasoned Harding, rich men deserved to be rich. "It is undoubtedly true that nine out of ten statesmen who possess great fortunes have earned their money themselves by the exercise of those qualities of energy, industry, and enterprise which have likewise made them prominent in politics."

The time would come when Harding would resist boodle a little. He did not like its stultifying effects on the consideration of political principles. "It would be a diversion and a comfort," he wrote September 23, 1893, "to have a campaign without it." But in the meantime Harding assumed a resigned attitude. For example, as the campaign of 1894 opened, Harding offered the following in the *Star* of September 15, reflecting on the fact that Brice was more a resident of New York than of Ohio:

To Brice, senator from York, Ohio: Loosen thy purse strings as you have of yore and harmony, happiness, hope and Henchmen are thine. We suspect Calvin, old boy, knows this already. The scoring that the Democratic state convention will give Brice is all imaginery. It will never be heard of in convention. Denouncing Brice is like reading the Democratic Cincinnati Enquirer out of the party—it never comes to pass. The man with a barrel is a potent factor and powerful manager in politics, among Democrats, Republicans, Prohibs and Pops.

Gerrymandering was bad too. But, for the same bipartisan reason, there was nothing that could be done about it. In 1889 the Democrats won control over the Ohio legislature, and set about revising the boundaries of the twenty-one congressional districts in the state so as to create a majority of Democratic districts. Harding commented resignedly on February 12, 1890, "This is said to be very unjust, but is the way of politics." When the congressional election of 1890 resulted in the selection of fourteen Democratic congressmen and seven Republicans, Harding, on December 1, analyzed the vote to show how unfair it was to the Republicans. But what right had the Republicans to complain, he asked, when they themselves had been doing it all along? "The infamy of political scheming is apparent in the recent congressional election in Ohio. The republicans cast 362,625 votes and elected but seven Congressmen, an average of 51,804 votes to each member, while the democrats cast 351,528 votes to elect fourteen members, an average of 25,109 votes each. It is but a little of their own medicine in stronger doses for the republicans, however, so the kicking could not be excessive. It is a shameful disfranchisement of voters."

An interesting example of Harding's sense of resignation at the iniquities of politics was shown in the Star of February 3, 1890 when he commented on minority rights. It seems that in Congress the southern Democrats were complaining about the arbitrary Republican interference with the southern minority, if the Force Bill were passed to ensure Negroes the vote. At the same time, in the Ohio Senate, a Democratic majority was seemingly abusing the Republican minority by declaring the Democratic candidate for lieutenant-governor elected in spite of a small popular majority for his Republican opponent. According to the Secretary of State's report, Republican Elbert L. Lampson received 375,090 votes and Democrat William V. Marquis 375,068. In Harding's mind the two evils canceled out. "Of course minorities have rights in this country. So have the majority, and the latter ought naturally to have the best of it. The Republican majority

in Congress is taking good care of itself and the Democratic majority
in the Ohio Senate has taken good care of Mr. Marquis and ousted
Mr. Lampson. It is a horse apiece in the way of politics. Naturally the
national house attracts the more attention and is the more amusing,
for Southern gentlemen kick hardest when things aren't all their own
way."

Harding's refusal to get excited about what he himself called "infamy" and "shameful disfranchisement" was remarkable. When the
Findlay *Courier* said that the Republicans, by gerrymandering the
state's common pleas judicial districts so that there were ninety-three
Republican judges and only nineteen Democratic ones, had thus
created a situation "dangerous to the cause of justice and civil liberty,"
Harding observed on January 19, 1895, "We don't believe justice and
civil liberty are in any danger whatever from the cause you indicate,
but we know that some good Republicans down this way would just
throw up their hats if somebody would gerrymander them into a
district where Republican ambition would not be frosted to death."

8

Although Warren Harding's political opportunism was a dominant
quality in his character, it does not follow that he was lacking in a
certain fixity of outlook. On occasion in times of conflict of opinion, he
could show himself capable of independent decisions. He could be
loyal to friends who were unpopular, he could insist on party responsibility in the face of radical, though popular, attacks. He could be a
stabilizing force when such was needed. But this does not rule out the
fact that his ambitious nature made him more of an opportunist on his
way to fame than a man of profound thought and conviction. As will
be seen, Republican bosses and businessmen with power could always
count on the co-operation of Warren G. Harding.

CHAPTER FOUR

United States Militancy Abroad

"What Turkey seems to need is a good licking by some progressive nation like the United States."   : : :   *"Marion Daily Star," April 21, 1900*

⊄ Clear-cut evidence of Harding's political opportunism is provided by his concept of aggressive overseas Americanism. The zeal that he could not muster for Progressivism, reform, and even political morality found enthusiastic expression in his proclaiming the superiority of the United States over foreign countries. Although he no longer waved the bloody shirt, Harding was still adept at waving the American flag. It was easy for Harding to make sweeping comparisons between the United States and other nations of the world, always to the latter's disadvantage.

There can be no doubt that, right from the start, young Harding's views on foreign policy were chauvinistic and that the *Star* was his sounding board. He was an America-firster throughout his life. He thought as the man in the street thought. He thought of the power and glory of his own country, and he believed that the United States was superior to all other countries. According to Harding, its standard of living was the highest, its government was the best, its people were the most highly educated. In controversies the United States was always right. This was the Republican viewpoint, generally the most popular in the United States. It was also Harding's viewpoint, and in Marion there were few who dared to challenge him, unless politics was at stake.

There was often a show of smug condescension or even insolence in the *Star*'s comments on foreign countries. When the perennially brittle relations between Russia and Turkey approached another breaking point in 1886, the young editor suggested that the Czar and the Sultan fight it out in a duel or prizefight, preferably the latter, and under the "Marquis of Queensbury rules." When affairs grew ominous on the island of Crete in 1897, the *Star* remarked that "the European situation still looks Greecy. The conditions remain favorable for sliding into war." When the rabble-rousing opponent of the Third French Republic, General Georges Boulanger, was reported planning to visit the United States, the *Star* called him "a freak" and added that "a dime museum would have afforded us a cheaper means of seeing him." [1] An outbreak in Rio de Janeiro in 1893 led the *Star* to comment that the report that "Rio has fallen" did not refer to "coffee" which still "holds its own like Mother and Java."

Foreigners were treated with a certain amount of disdain. Czar Alexander II of Russia was a "drunken helpless sot"; Canadians were "Canucks"; the bewhiskered Boer leader, Oom Paul Kruger, a "lulu." The outbreak of the Sino-Japanese War in 1894 was dismissed with thoughtless remarks such as "The man who undertakes to read the Chino-Japan war names to his family is running the risk of losing the respect of the whole household, aside from endangering his nether jaw." [2]

Any problems the United States might have with territorial neighbors could always be solved, according to Harding, by annexation. Hawaii would be "a fat take," said the *Star* on February 11, 1893. Those who objected were un-American. "Probably a good many of the opponents of the annexation of Hawaii have never enjoyed the inspiring sight of the stars and stripes afloat across boundary lines," wrote Harding on February 27, 1893. As for Cuba in its struggle with Spain, the impatient Harding was of the opinion on November 22, 1897 that "the whole business may be quickly settled if President McKinley and Congress would only say the word. We could use Cuba as a United States annexation." This sort of policy was a characteristic of American history. "One needs only to recall the story that history teaches that annexation has always been our national policy."

Of course, the process of annexation was not yet over. Whenever the United States ran out of land at home, all it had to do, Harding said, was to annex more. That is what happened in 1889, as Oklahoma was opened up. The *Star* wrote on April 25, "The scramble for Oklahoma land is indicative of the scarcity of public land in the United States and points to the necessity of annexing Canada and settling her vast unoccupied area." It occurred to the *Star* again on January 7, 1896, when it wrote, "Up in Canada the other night the Canucks roundly hissed the American flag. . . . But never mind. When we have to annex Canada we will gently spank the ill-behaved child and teach her better."

Naturally the justification for this right of annexation was that the United States was a self-governing democracy. The "proof" was very easy to come by. When Ohio's Senator John Sherman returned from Europe, the *Star* reported on September 1, 1889, Sherman's opinion that "all the old governments over there are gradually remodelling on the plan of the American government." Thus, said the editor, "we have another evidence of this being the foremost nation on earth."

Important among the evidence of United States superiority was the lack of a standing army. The United States was no "soldier ridden nation," cursed with a half million idle soldiers sapping its vitality. So said the *Star* on January 6, 1887. "Even more than to the virgin soil, free institutions and industrious genius is America indebted for her prosperity to her freedom from the burden of a great standing army." As European countries lived uneasily in the shadow of international jealousy and hatred, said the editor a few months later on May 18, "America is going serenely on her way to the front rank of civilized nations. No enormous standing armies are kept to suck the life blood out of the purses of the tax payers, nor does the country go into hysterics over the trivial demonstrations against her." Somewhat illogically, the *Star* editor, on March 7, 1887, boasted that the United States pension roll exceeded the cost of Europe's armies.

2

Russian autocracy was a favorite butt of the *Star's* ridicule. Czar Alexander III, "poor fellow," drank because he was a nervous wreck in the midst of assassination plots and counterplots. He ought to have had sense enough, wrote the editor on March 21, 1887, to have given his country a constitution and thus have become "the greatest benefactor of his people." With constitutional government "he would sacrifice no power really worth possessing." As the czar lay on his death bed, the *Star*, on November 1, 1894, printed the macabre rejoicing of the horrible Nihilists, who issued bloody circulars decorated with sketches of bombs, revolvers, and daggers, and warned the czarevich of the terrible fate that awaited him. When finally the new czar, Nicholas II, had ascended the throne, the *Star* observed, on May 27, 1896, "At least there is an end to the tomfoolery connected with the coronation exercises in Russia, and the blessing of the Almighty have been invoked. The surprise may be that the autocrat of all the Russians thought of the Almighty at all."

There was power to support the virtue of this American democratic superiority. The United States did not need a great standing army, but it did need a mighty navy to show these foreign nations that it was ready for anything. As the navy grew larger, Harding's boasts and threats grew louder, until, on November 27, 1897, he bluntly announced that Secretary of the Navy John D. Long had just ordered "the largest lot of guns and ammunition ever purchased at one time." He then warned, "Uncle Sam is not going about looking for trouble, but foreigners must be given to understand that he will not be to blame if anything happens." Back of the navy, of course, was a booming commerce, which was also showing the businessmen of the world a thing or two.

3

Another example of foreign depravity was Turkey. The *Star* editor's first reflection on "the unspeakable Turk" was a sly remark about the Sultan Abdul Hamid and his harem. On September 1, 1885 the first audience of the new United States minister to Turkey, S. S. (Sunset) Cox, with the Sultan was noted: "If Sunset's overmastering love of fun does not lead him to investigate the inside life of His Majesty's domestic establishment the relations will undoubtedly continue pleasant."

Wise cracks gave way to horror as a new image of the "terrible Turk" emerged in 1894 out of the Armenian massacres. These were played up in the American press without reference to the roots of the difficulties. Beginning in 1894 certain family or clan feuds among the Armenian Christians and non-Christians of northeastern Asia Minor were looked upon by Anglo-Turkish politicos as threats to Turkish sovereignty and to English interests in Persia. Turkish troops, therefore, moved in to clean up the situation. Armenian retaliation, in the form of a movement for independence, led to counter-retaliation, and the hideous mob-slaughter of thousands of Armenians throughout Turkey. American missionaries in Armenia reported the terrible doings. Resentment in America reached fever heat.

This resentment colored all the reports and editorial comments in the *Star*. Armenian horror stories got page-one headlines from November, 1894 well into 1896. The Turkish magistrate of Armenia was headlined as "A Modern Nero" responsible for the butchering of thousands of defenseless people and the destruction of scores of villages. It was "A Story of Fiendishness Probably Not Equalled at Any Time in the World's History." Brutal Kurdish soldiers were reported rushing to the struggle with the cry of "Islam or Death." A "Horde of Hyenas" was said to be feasting on "Corpses by the Wagon Load" tossed upon the ground in Armenian cemeteries. Massacre followed upon massacre, Christian monasteries were burned, prisoners were tortured, women were outraged. The eloquent Reverend Dr. F. DeWitt Talmadge was quoted as calling upon the "Throne of Grace" to grant a mandate "to hurl back upon their haunches the horses of Kurdish calvary. . . . With the earthquake of thy wrath shake the foundations of the palaces of the Sultan. . . . Let the crescent go down before the cross, and the Mighty One, who hath on his vesture and on his thigh a name written King of Kings and Lord of Lords go forth, conquering and to conquer." When diplomatic efforts to solve the Armenian question bogged down, the *Star* dismissed the whole thing as a farcical poker game. "The allied powers of Europe are apparently not certain whether the Sultan has a full hand or a bobtailed flush. Abdul possesses a great phiz for working a bluff." [3]

4

Harding's attitude toward China was equally disdainful. When the first railroad line from Tientsin to the interior was opened, the *Star*, January 9, 1889, made a jibe at Chinese ancestor worship with the remark, "The government has authorized for the first time the right of way through graveyards—a tremendous innovation." When Anglican and American Methodist missionaries were murdered in the summer of 1895, the editor spat out, August 9, "It is a reasonable inference that China is not deserving of Christian missions. It would not harm Mongolian murderers to go to perdition. They seem to deserve such a fate."

The *Star*'s attitude toward the Sino-Japanese War of 1894 for the control of Korea was conditioned by the same considerations of contempt for reaction and praise for progress. Japan was the favored one.

As early as February 15, 1889 the *Star* had praised Japan for its prospects of becoming "at no distant day a member of the great family of civilized nations, with a place inside the limit of Christendom." The recent industrial progress was noted with favor and the new constitution commended. Harding was a bit worried when the Japanese won the first victories. He likened Japan to the "hilarious fellow who had his fun before he got on the side of the fence with the bull. When China is aroused in her might Japan will be crushed." But it did not happen that way, and Harding was glad. "If there is anybody grieving over China getting the worst of it in the peace negotiations," said the *Star*, March 14, 1895, "they have not held up their hands. We have never gotten in the habit of sympathizing with China and the Chinese." The "walls of conservatism" were now broken down, the editor added April 19, 1895. "The world is ready to applaud little Japan as the victor of progress over civilization."

5

With backward Samoa, the problem was different. Here Harding's sympathies, like those of most Americans, were with the backward people and against the chief intervening power of Germany. The United States had been committed to an interest in Samoa since 1878, when a treaty gave us the right to use Pago Pago on the island of Tutuila as a naval station. American commerce was involved because of the location of the islands on the trade route to Australia. After 1878, German influence increased until, according to the *Star*, May 15, 1889, the Germans inflated the ego of a Samoan royal pretender named Tamasese by supporting his claims to the throne. The *Star* of May 31 was convinced that the Samoan natives, "when untroubled by German greed . . . are a quite orderly race, competent to settle their own affairs." (Compare this with Harding on Cubans and Filipinos, pp. 63–73.) That was why the United States, at the Anglo-American-German-Samoan conference at Berlin, stood for Samoan integrity. If Harding was to be believed in the *Star* of June 17, 1889, the settlement favorable to the natives choosing their own authorities according to their own customs was "due to the firmness of the decision of our government." Thus "the great Republic, with its exhaustless and practically unlimited resources of offense and defense, is arrayed in behalf of a feeble and distant people who have been the victims of the outrages of the German understrappers." Our attitude, Harding concluded, "convinced Bismarck that graceful concessions are in order."

6

England, of course, came in for some of Harding's gibes when occasion offered. In 1896, he said, "Bryan and McKinley are both agreed on twisting the lion's tail, but they differ as to methods. Perhaps it is well they do not agree, else the poor lion would lose his tail entirely." [4] An excellent series of opportunities was offered in the 1880s and 1890s by the Bering Sea seals controversy. The Americans claimed that the homes of these interesting animals were at their breeding grounds on the Pribilof Islands off the coast of Alaska. Conservation regulations were, therefore, made by the United States, limiting the number to be killed. However, the seals were nomadic in nature and loved to take long summer trips into the high seas and along the Canadian coast. In these waters they were indiscriminately hunted by foreign companies whose weapons included dynamite. Offending British vessels were, therefore, seized by United States revenue cutters beyond the three-mile limit. The ingredients of a first-class international row were thus provided, with the United States clad in the righteous armor of ethics, and the English supported by international law. Chief defender of the United States position was the eloquent Secretary of State James G. Blaine, a great favorite of Harding's. Blaine's main opponent was the learned British Minister of Foreign Affairs Lord Salisbury. A treaty of arbitration was eventually drawn up with Great Britain in 1892. Protracted hearings were conducted in which American diplomats argued with more fervor than factuality in behalf of their right to seize British ships on the high seas. Agreement was not reached until 1898 when the decision was against the United States, which was obliged to pay British vessel owners about half a million dollars damages.

Throughout these years the *Star* vigorously supported the cause of the United States. Harding never discussed the legal aspects of this affair. He denounced the Canadian and British seal hunters as "poachers and pirates." He completely Americanized the issue. He engaged in personalities in praise of his great hero, Secretary Blaine, at the expense of the seemingly insufferable Lord Salisbury. For example, on January 7, 1891, he wrote, "Secretary Blaine is all right. He is not twisting the British lion's tail for effect, but he is maintaining the right of his country and he is doing it in a statesmanlike way. Mr. Blaine is a much bigger man than Salisbury and knows what he is doing." As the arbitration got under way, Harding belligerently declared, March 11, 1892. "If English poachers insist on destroying Uncle Sam's seals there ought to be no question what to do about it. The navy wants a good opportunity to distinguish itself." When at last the arbitration commission decided, in effect, that the United States was doing its share of bulldozing, and required damages to be paid to British traders as well as the refraining from seizing vessels beyond the three-mile limit, Harding ruefully observed, August 16, 1893, "If the British lion is wagging his tail in delight, let him wag." He found considerable consolation in the fact that the internationally arranged conservation measures destroyed the industry of the "seal pirates." [5]

The biggest tail twists of all came in the years 1895–97 in the Venezuela boundary dispute, with the United States cast in the role of Sir Galahad defending little Venezuela against mighty Britain. As in the seals controversy, the United States was partially right in principle, wrong in law, and defeated in the showdown. The dispute concerned the Venezuela–British Guiana boundary line, which had never been run. Venezuela had never made any effort to use or claim the area until the British discovered gold therein. The British asserted that her fifty-year, unchallenged possession of the land constituted in international law a claim superior to that asserted for Venezuela by the United States via the Monroe Doctrine. President Cleveland declared that the Monroe Doctrine gave the United States the right to determine the proper line by means of an "arbitration" commission appointed by him. Lord Salisbury asserted that international law required arbitration by an international commission. The latter was agreed to and the award was favorable to British claims.

The Star's news and editorial coverage was patriotic, as usual. When President Cleveland, on December 17, 1895, bluntly announced to Congress that Venezuela was right and Britain was wrong, and that the United States commission should be authorized to go there and determine the line, the Star the next day shouted its approval and joined the war cry:

A PATRIOTIC RING

President Cleveland's Special Message to the Point

JINGOISM ENOUGH IS IN IT

The Attitude of the United States Very Clearly Defined

MONROE DOCTRINE SUSTAINED

England Is Given A Chance to Show Her Hand in the Matter

United States Stands Firm

. . . . Wild Scenes of Enthusiasm. . . . Old Veterans Sing

Rally Round The Flag, Boys.

Editorially, Harding made it quite clear that the United States had possession of all the necessary facts, and that that was all there was to it: "All needed information relative to the boundary question is in the possession of the state department, or the American-English controversy would not have gone this far. . . . the commission can only confirm what is already known—that the English have sought to take desirable territory from Venezuela because the little republic is physically too weak to offer serious resistance. England must back down and accede to arbitration or there will be war. That's the whole story."

7

American relations with Hawaii illustrated, for Harding, another facet of expansion. To Harding, as to most business-minded Americans, the introduction into the islands of American capital and landowners resulted in the Americans paying most of the taxes and the Hawaiians doing most of the governing. This was not right, said the *Star* editor on July 13, 1887, in commenting on an American outbreak. "The leading cause for the dissatisfaction is that in the Sandwich Islands the foreigners pay the taxes, and have no votes in the government while the natives who attend to the law part spend all the money they raise and more too."

Hence it was that the Hawaiian Republic, maintained under the influence of American investors from 1893 to 1898, had no more ardent supporter than Warren Harding of the *Marion Daily Star*. To Harding, the revolution on January 16, 1893, by which the American element deposed Queen Liliuokalani, and set up a provisional republic, was like the American Revolution of 1776. It was a substitution of self-government for a reactionary monarchy. President Harrison was praised for supporting the new regime and converting it into an American protectorate with marines, recognition, and the preparation of a treaty of annexation. But when President Cleveland, immediately following his inauguration on March 4, 1893, repudiated everything, great was the disgust of the *Star* editor.

For four years Harding agonized over the "disgrace" of American Hawaiian policy and praised the Hawaiian Republic which endured despite the refusal of our "monarchists in Washington" to protect it from a return to the "cannibalism of a few decades ago." When Cleveland, on December 19, requested the new government to restore "the rotten monarchy," Harding, December 23, called the act "a formal declaration of war against the provisional government of Hawaii." "Who can tell," he exploded, "the end that will reverberate over our own country for the firing of a single gun upon the men who have done in Hawaii what our fathers did in '76'?" President Cleveland "must restore Texas, yes, he must restore the colonies to England. . . . The liberty loving heart of this country will not stand by and see the wrong rule applied to Hawaii and no one can forsee the end." Hawaii's president, Sanford B. Dole, was praised as a masterful statesman who desired only the establishment in the islands of the American way of life. (*Star*, January 15, 1894.)

Harding gloried in the perseverance of the Hawaiian Republic. "The Hawaiian monarchy," he wrote May 5, 1894, "can never be restored." Was America to permit the return of Queen Liliuokalani, so that she could "chop off the heads of President Dole and others who have destroyed her peace and happiness?" Financially the Dole government was, in Harding's view, "all right." In 1896 it wound up with a surplus of $93,627, after paying $236,459 in interest and taking up $100,000 in bonds. "This is a pretty good showing for a little government like Hawaii," said the editor on April 27, 1897. When, at last, McKinley came to power and raised over Honolulu the flag that Cleveland had hauled down, Harding was relieved. "This," he wrote, "is in full accord with the eternal fitness of things."

8

As tiny Cuba, in 1895, resumed its war against Spain's anachronistic colonial policy, it was natural that the American people should sympathize with its fight for independence. Cubans could hardly avoid a desire to be free from Spain's haughty intransigeance and to join the company of Spanish-American republics which had long since thrown off Spain's shackles. Considerations of proximity to the United States and its economic interest were also involved in determining American attitudes.

Harding was ready when revolt broke out in the spring of 1895, and he approached the problem with characteristic light-heartedness. The leaders of the Cuban revolutionary party, José Martí and Calixto García, were immediately hailed as heroes. Annexation was his first thought for a solution. "If we can let things drift with Spain," he remarked on March 20, "until we can take Cuba as a peace offering, why a little international disturbance will not be in vain." He was sure that most Cubans "will agree to any proceeding that will accomplish that result." When the American mail steamer *Allianca* was fired on by a Spanish gunboat in search of filibusters, the *Star* supported, belligerently, the demand for an apology. When Spain expressed a willingness to do so, the *Star,* March 30, affected disappointment and remarked, "Thus Uncle Sam will be deprived of the opportunity of turning the little government over his knee." When the apology was made, the editor, on June 6, asked, "By the way, for what was Spain apologizing?"

As the revolt progressed and the atrocity stories began coming in, Harding became more serious. Sympathy was not enough. We could at least make it a fair fight by recognizing Cuba's belligerency so that arms and ammunition could be delivered to the desperate rebels. "Spain," he said on September 25, 1895, "recognized the rights of the Southern Confederacy within forty days after the outbreak of the late Civil War. Why need liberty loving Americans longer delay in recognizing the patriots of Cuba who are fighting for independence and liberty? The fires of liberty are ablaze in Cuba." He scoffed at President Cleveland's caution as expressed by Attorney-General Judson Harmon, "The statesmen of this liberty loving country must get in out of the wet. The mighty wave of American sentiment will soon sweep everything before it. Cuba must be free." He repeated these sentiments in almost daily editorials. When, at last in February, 1896, Congress, by overwhelming majorities, passed a joint resolution recognizing a state of war in Cuba, the *Star* editor, March 3, asked, "Why worry over the attitude of Spain toward the United States? If she wants to expose the point of her jaw to a pivot blow from Uncle Sam, why that's her own funeral." The Cuban fighters, he added, April 6, can now "take a tighter grip upon their machetes."

Atrocity stories added fuel to inflamed American passions. The *Star* carried lurid headlines throughout 1896. Thus on March 6:

WEYLER THE BUTCHER

Further Reports of His Almost Incredible Brutality

MAKING MASSACRE OUT OF WAR

Again, on April 11:

POOLS OF BLOOD

Wounded Soldiers Assassinated by Spaniards

Stories of strangulation by slow degrees were reported April 1. These were said to be so horrifying that the executioner fled in nausea from his own handiwork. Yellow fever was reported racking the island. "Yellow Jack has assumed command," was the *Star's* lugubrious comment on July 13. Again the spirit of 1776 was invoked as headlines ran, November 26:

CUBA'S STRUGGLE FOR FREEDOM

COMPARES WITH OUR OWN

Forces Arrayed Against the Island Patriots

Five Times More Numerous Than Our Revolutionary Foes

Surely, Harding prayed, on November 17, America would help these heroes in remembrance of the help it had in its own independence fight.

As actual war became more imminent in 1897 and early in 1898, Harding's belligerency seemed to cool. This temporary change of mind seems in some measure to be related to his discovery that much of the news reporting from Cuba was extremely bad. He developed considerable skepticism about the reliability of certain reporters whose "Havana dispatches, Key West specials and Jacksonville scoops" were constantly being punctured by contradictions. This feeling was apparently strengthened by his own winter visit to Florida in March, 1898. He read pacifistic articles and commented darkly on the local jingoes.[6]

Nevertheless, the war came. Harding returned to Marion, installed the Scripps-McRae wire service, and accelerated the warmongering to a higher pitch than ever. In the process the *Star* reached the pinnacle of its success in scooping every rival in sight with its red-hot, Spanish-American war news.

Thus did Harding change his tune on Cuba and commit himself again to the "large" policy of American expansion. And the largest part of it was the paternal necessity to take all the unfortunate victims of Spain, "the rotten monarchy," and put them under the benevolent protection of the enlightened United States. "Cuba, Porto Rico, the Philippines and the Ladrones, freed from the hand of oppression, blossoming and blooming under the protection of the rippling folds of Old Glory—what excellent souvenirs by which Uncle Sam will be enabled to remember the Maine." In these words the *Star*, on July 13, 1898, summed up its concept of the "true" purpose of the Spanish-American war.

It should be emphasized that it was protection of Cuba, not independence, that dominated Harding's thinking. That meant, to his pragmatic understanding, annexation. Annexation talk resumed when Americans discovered that the Cuba revolutionists expected to set up a republic immediately upon the surrender of Spain to the United States. The Cuban insurrectionists showed this in their dealings with the American occupying forces. In the expectations of the Cuban fighters, the American army had simply come to their assistance. In the estimation of the American commander, General William R. Shafter, this was ridiculous. The Cuban rebels were heroes, but they could not be considered representatives of any responsible government. Harding was quick to sense this situation. On June 20 he expressed his editorial opinion that the Cubans were good guerrilla fighters and were useful as scouts, but they were not in the same class with the United States Regulars. And so far as government was concerned, "the greatest surprise will be when anything is found which can be identified as the Cuban republic."

After the occupation of Santiago, Harding was quite convinced that the Cubans would have to be put in their place. When General

Calixto García, in the name of the "Republic of Cuba," protested against leaving the government of Santiago in the hands of the Spanish instead of turning it over to him, the *Star*, July 21, carried a page-one dispatch with the following headlines:

GEN. GARCIA IS DISGUSTED

AND WILL NOT COOPERATE

With the American Forces in the Future,

So He Tells General Shafter by Letter—

Says He Was Not Treated Right at the

Surrender of Santiago and Will Act

Independently Hereafter.

This led Harding to announce that the United States might have to subdue the Cubans and annex their territory. "The Cubans are evidently bound to furnish all the excuse necessary for Uncle Sam to take the island and keep it. General Shafter's disgust at their actions will be shared by every American. It is shocking to thus have the fine sentiment rudely knocked out of the work of rescuing the island, but the consciousness of being engaged in the performance of a duty still remains. If it becomes necessary to whip the Cubans before peace can be permanently established that work ought to be entered into with the same vigor that is manifest in driving Spanish soldiers out." Harding was quick to approve of the stoppage of arming the Cubans after the Spanish were dispersed. "The Cubans are lucky," said the *Star*, July 23. "Hereafter no arms will be given them, but food supplies will be furnished, and eating three meals a day will be all that is expected of them." When, on January 1, 1899, Spanish Evacuation Day was celebrated, Harding fully approved of General John R. Brooke's refusal to permit the Cuban military leaders to participate in the Havana ceremonies. On December 31, 1898, the *Star* sternly declared, "Some influential Americans down in Havana should not neglect tomorrow to impress upon the Cubans the idea that the reasonable thing to do is to resolve to go to work."

Harding simply could not reconcile himself to permanent Cuban independence. Only American statesmen and businessmen could bring stability. Uncle Sam, he wrote on August 13, 1898, will have to teach the Cuban people "what twentieth century progress means." When that happens, Cubans will themselves admit, he wrote on August 17, "that they never knew what business was until American energy and enterprise began to exert an influence among them." Thus it was that American military occupation was really a blessing, first under the leadership of General Brooke, and then under General Leonard Wood. "Cuba may not want complete independence after she has had General Leonard Wood as military governor for a while," said the *Star*, December 18, 1899. The United States was bound by the Teller Amendment to let Cuba go, but, according to Harding, surely the Cubans would let the United States out of that promise when they discovered its benevolent intentions. "Let Cuba ask to be annexed to the United States" he wrote January 12, 1901, "and see what a rush there would be to accomodate her. Why can't the Gem of the Antilles see that we are dead in love with her anyhow, and only restrained by the resolution from popping the question." On February 2, 1901, he wrote, "Of course Cuba should be free and independent, but why can't she see how thankfully Uncle Sam would consider an annexation proposal from her, the blackeyed beauty!" Or, as he put it on February 4, 1902, "What better can Uncle Sam do than marry the girl?"

It was much easier to take the Philippines. There was not any "tomfool" Teller Amendment to block the way. The chief reason for this was that most Americans did not know where the Philippines were when the war began. Everybody was thinking about Cuba. Then, when Commodore George Dewey suddenly routed the Spanish Pacific fleet in Manila harbor on May 31, 1898, the United States practically had the islands as an unexpected, but very welcome, gift. All the United States had to do was to keep them. At least that is how Harding and most of his countrymen reasoned.

In Harding's estimation the chief reason for annexing the Philippines was Dewey's recommendation. The "logic" was very simple. Dewey ought to know because he won the battle of Manila Bay. Editor Harding wrote in the *Star*, on August 31, 1898, "Dewey's opinion of the Philippines will be enthusiastically accepted as a pretty safe guide to follow in settling the question. He won that empire of the East and afterwards conducted affairs so capably that his knowledge now is an essential factor in fixing the destiny of the islands. Dewey wants the stars and stripes to fly there forever. Gauged by his attainments, Dewey's judgment is worth more than that of all the hopelessly fanatic old mugwumps and learned college professors in the whole country." To let the Philippines go would be to repudiate Dewey—and, Harding said, one could not do that to the nation's heroes. "It was Dewey," wrote Harding on November 30, 1898, "who made us expand. Instead of weighing anchor on the memorable May morning and sailing away he laid his hands on a new land for the stars and stripes, and expansion was on. It would never have done to go back on Dewey."

While others said the question of annexation was one for diplomats and government officials back home to decide, Harding gloried in the fact that the army plunged ahead and occupied the islands, and thus gave the policy makers no choice. Dewey and General Wesley Merritt, he said on August 17, "have gone out and succeeded in bringing about the surrender of the whole Philippine group of islands. They now hold possession of everything in sight. To those who have been opposing the acquisition of the islands this is a terrible blow. The American flag covers them all." Americans do not do things half way. "Dewey and Merritt didn't skim off the cream, take the best and leave the rest for Spain and the insurgents and possibly other nations to fight over. . . . Nothing is left to Spain." "Dewey and Merritt," he said on August 20, "practically settled the Philippine question when they received the surrender of the islands."

Other reasons for annexation of the Philippines were added as they occurred to the *Star* editor. One, as described on August 12, was that the Japanese would take the islands if the United States did not. Another was the trade argument. The American home market was no longer sufficient for our industry, Harding said on September 21. "Our manufacturers will have all kinds of trouble in European markets because of competition. Therefore the Eastern Asian market is the one where competition is less." Still another argument was the duty of the churches to exert their benign influence on the natives. The *Star*, October 7, quoted with warm approval the *Chicago Tribune* endorsement of the Methodist Church Epworth League's resolve to expand its work in the Philippines: "The Epworth League marches under the American flag." It gave Harding much comfort that we had a President who had his ear to the ground to catch public sentiment. "No man," he wrote on August 20, "is quicker to recognize the drift of public sentiment than President McKinley and none place greater value upon public opinion."

Then there was Emilio Aguinaldo who, on June 18, 1898, proclaimed a provisional dictatorship to pave the way for a Philippine republic. Harding viewed this Filipino patriot as a vain pretender. The *Star*, on July 23, contemptuously announced that Aguinaldo would look like an "Indian Snake Charmer" in his new insignia of office. "If General Aguinaldo is so fond of wearing a big badge perhaps he would be satisfied with a job on the Manila police force." To give the Philippines back to Spain, opined the *Star* on July 30, "would present Aguinaldo a splendid opportunity to use his new whistle." As for the claim that the General was the George Washington of the Philippines, the *Star* sneered on November 22, 1899, "The few Americans who look upon Aguinaldo as a second George Washington will have some difficulty in identifying Mrs. Aguinaldo. There is no record to show that Martha Washington ever kept her wardrobe in a barrel."

The American mission to the Philippines received its supreme indignity when Aguinaldo and his followers turned their guns on American troops because the Spanish sovereignty was succeeded officially by that of the United States. This turned him into one "who arranged for a massacre of American soldiers whose only offense had been to rescue him and his people from the oppression of the Spanish government." It turned his insurgent followers into a "lawless mob," a "blood-thirsty riff-raff." [7] Moreover, it turned those Americans who opposed the war against the Filipino insurgents into traitors who helped kill American soldiers. The *Star*, January 12, 1900, quoted with warm approval Senator Albert J. Beveridge's remarks to this effect: "I have seen our mangled boys in the hospital and field. I have stood on the firing lines and beheld our dead soldiers, their faces turned to the pitiless southern sky; and in sorrow rather than anger I say to those whose voices in America have cheered those misguided natives on to shoot our soldiers down, that the blood of those dead and wounded boys of ours is on their hands; and the floods of all the years can never wash the stain away." On October 2, 1900, Harding had his own special curse for the "Tajal hero [*sic*] who fired the bullet that killed the beloved General H. W. Lawton," one of the American officers in the war against the insurgents.

9

Thus it was that the United States had to proceed on its unappreciated task of "accepting a God-given mission in spreading civilization," as the *Star* put it September 13, 1900. The editor praised McKinley on December 5, 1899, as one who was "the guiding hand of providence" in accepting the opportunity to help the Philippine people learn the hard lessons of freedom. In the presidential campaign of 1900 McKinley ran for reelection with that mandate as the key issue. When the Democrats cried "Imperialism," Harding laughed and wrote, September 6, "Uncle Sam is engaging teachers to be sent to the Philippines. What a tyrant is Uncle Sam becoming anyhow?" It was plain "tommy-rot" to criticize the American republic for "holding out the torch of liberty and enlightenment to the Orient."

CHAPTER FIVE

Tariff Americanism and the
Right to Work

*"If all consumers would boycott everything that's imported the de-
mand created would open many factories and help many idle men to
employment."* : : : *"Marion Daily Star," January 3, 1894*

⟐ Further evidence of Harding's belief in a vigorous Americanism is
found in his views on tariffs and organized labor. According to Harding, low tariffs made for the flooding of the American market with
cheap foreign goods, thus causing American unemployment. Militant
labor union action and its accompanying strikes were the result of
foreign agitators, in Harding's view.

Harding's main device for supporting the high-tariff position was
exaggeration. Repeatedly he identified a low tariff with free trade.
This enabled him to point with scorn at "free-trade Europe." In the
summer of 1885, when there was a falling-off of business, Harding
wrote, "advocates of free trade as a remedy for the prevailing business
depression are confronted by the fact that business in England is even
worse than in the United States and quite as bad in Germany and
France and the outcome for free trade countries is no more favorable
than for protective countries." [1] Lowering the tariff on wool would be
death to American farmers, and life to "the free-trade Britishers," he
wrote on October 23, 1886. Duty-free sugar from Hawaii was condemned by Harding on November 2, 1886, as the cause of the failure
of a St. Louis refinery. On December 19, 1887, free traders were
compared to the farmers of a piece of lowland digging a drainage
ditch when the river was low. "They may expect to be overflowed and
drowned out with the cheap labor production of the old world." In the
Weekly Star, April 21, 1888, a cartoon in *Judge* magazine was praised
for showing Uncle Sam as Moses, John Bull as Pharaoh, and the
Atlantic Ocean as the Red Sea. The parted waters permitted great
streams of laborers to come to the "promised land," as Uncle Sam said,

"Why, O Pharaoh, are your hosts migrating to my protected land if the free trade which your country enjoys is such a blessing?" Harding added, "The question states the situation in a nutshell."

When Harding sought to argue the merits of tariff protection, the results were remarkable. It may have seemed logical to him to say that tariff duties helped American people by enabling them to manufacture their own goods, but, when challenged by arguments that tariffs caused higher costs of production, higher prices, a narrowed market, lower buying power, and monopolies, he was not able to apply skillfully the canons of logic to his rebuttal. An example of Harding's views is taken from a speech made in Carthage, Missouri, in support of Taft in 1912: "While it is true it costs more to live with a protective tariff," he told his listeners, "We can have more to live with. What difference does it make how cheap a thing is if we haven't anything to buy it with?" [2]

Another example is seen in Harding's attempt to prove that a protective tariff did not promote trusts or combines. "The greatest trust on record is the Standard Oil Company, and oil is 'free,'" he wrote in the *Daily Star*, August 6, 1888. "The next greatest is the anthracite coal trust, and William L. Scott, the President's [Cleveland] right hand adviser, and a rabid free trader, is the head and soul of this trust. The sugar trust is engineered by Havermeyer [*sic*] who has subscribed $20,000 to the Democratic campaign fund. There are railroad trusts, and whisky trusts. All these except sugar are admitted free and the sugar that is imported never has been raised in this country."

Harding's faulty logic is shown in one of his efforts to demonstrate the tariff's effect on wages. He compared the increase in United States production of wool and cotton cloth between the years 1860 and 1880, with the increase in wages during the same period. Cotton production increased 67 per cent, woolen production increased 286 per cent, and wages to woolen workers increased 330 per cent. This, said Harding, demonstrated the effect of the tariff on cotton and woolen manufactures imposed between 1860 and 1880. He made no effort to demonstrate how other factors might have contributed to this increase in wages and production.[3]

By this kind of argument Harding could "prove" anything he wanted —and he proceeded to do so. The next effort was to demonstrate the "fact" that a tariff increased the United States' ability to trade with foreign countries. This was true, said Harding, because a tariff enabled "the manufacturers to build up their business to such an extent that they could not only supply the home market, but sell their goods abroad to foreign markets." How the manufacturers could sell more in the European market at higher prices resulting from the tariff, Harding didn't even try to show.[4]

On October 16, 1888, editor Harding set out to prove that high tariffs on manufactured goods protected the farmers in general. In this he failed miserably. All he did was to assert that the home market, created by protected industries, was a blessing to farmers. "The manufacturing establishments which have been encouraged by the protective tariff have been of more pecuniary advantage to the farmers than the foreign market." He gave no consideration at all to the farmers' higher costs of production and consumption resulting from the higher prices of protected articles that the farmers were compelled to buy.

2

Harding was rescued from the inadequacy of his "lucubrations" on the tariff by the "logic" of events. The main event was the Panic of 1893. This enabled Harding and his fellow Republicans to say that the cause of the panic and its ensuing depression was the election of Cleveland to the Presidency in 1893, and of the resulting fear in the business community of the effects of the expected reduction of the high McKinley-tariff rates.

As usual, Harding did not prove that the fear of Democratic tariff tinkering caused the panic; he merely said so. Following the Republican party line, he rejected, with a partisan shrug, the claim that the panic resulted from the drain of the government gold reserve, caused by the inflationary effects of the Sherman Silver Purchase Act which the Republicans passed in 1890. "We have never thought the silver situation of such import as many have claimed for it," he wrote on October 31, 1893, "but the country was very much like the man who had dyspepsia but believed he had heart trouble and insisted that he would not be well until his heart was made good."

That the businessmen's fear of a low Democratic tariff was what caused dyspepsia, only the businessman could know. Therefore, only the businessmen could know the remedy. The "wonderful" McKinley tariff of 1890, said Harding, had led investors to make basic commitments looking toward industrial expansion. "The larger part of our people has studied business conditions," he wrote, "and basing their risks upon them, have [*sic*] gone into debt." The decline in the value of the dollar was bad enough, but its harmful effects were minor and could be easily offset by the business preparations made possible by the McKinley tariff. Such preparations, if allowed to proceed, would soon increase the volume of business and thus end the inflation.[5] The essential thing was to restore prosperity by leaving the McKinley tariff alone. As he wrote on May 16, 1894, "For prosperity like we enjoyed two years ago the main essential is a declaration to quit tariff tinkering."

The 1893 panic situation was made to order for another outburst of the Harding brand of all-Americanism. He actually allowed himself to say that the best way for America to recover from the panic was to stop all importations from Europe and make everything in America. Said he, on January 3, 1894, " 'American manufactured goods for America' is coming to be a popular cry. There's more in it, too, than first thought would tell. If all consumers would boycott everything that's imported the demand created would open many factories and help many idle men to employment." On February 6, 1894, he declared:

> The market which is a profitable one to American farmers is the home market. The home market is kept up by having a home consumption. Home consumption is kept up by keeping our mechanics and other laboring people employed. Our mechanics and other laboring people are kept employed by our manufacturers. Our manufacturers can give employment by making goods at home instead of importing them. If goods are imported instead of made at home, foreign manufacturers receive the pay, to pay it to foreign labor, to buy foreign agricultural products or our own reduced in price by the cost of transportation to a foreign country. The importing business is arrayed against home business.

Again, on March 22, 1894 he commented on the falling-off of imports during the latter part of 1893 by $113,000,000. "If Americans would do their duty to Americans," he said, "they would fall off many millions more." He referred to the practice of labelling prison-made goods as such. "If the word 'imported' should suddenly work the same result there would be such a revival of factory and other business enterprises as America has never seen. Every time an American buys an imported article in competition with home manufactured goods he builds up the foreign factory and labor against America."

Harding's all-American tariff enthusiasm convinced him that even

Democrats had learned the folly of their free-trade faddism. The panic had taught them a well-deserved lesson. They would never again dare tinker too freely with the McKinley tariff. He became convinced that the "free trade" bill introduced into the House by William L. Wilson was "pretty near a goner." And it was. On April 2, 1894, Harding rejoiced when the Senate Democrats discarded the measure by amending it into a protective tariff. The Wilson bill, he rejoiced, has become "a thing of shreds and patches." As Democratic Senators rushed to restore high rates, Harding declared that the McKinley bill might as well have been left alone.[6]

Events seemed to justify Harding's faith in tariff Americanism. The Democrats passed the Wilson-Gorman bill, which, at least, saved the country from free trade. Then in the fall election the country voted the Democrats out of power in Congress. Harding's joy was supreme. "EVERYTHING IN SIGHT," headlined the *Star* on page one of the post-election issue of November 7, 1894, in describing the Republican "avalanche." "OVERWHELMING!" screamed the page one headline the next day. "MAJORITY THE REPUBLICANS WILL HAVE IN THE HOUSE MAY BE ALMOST A HUNDRED." Among the prominent victims of the Republican landslide was William L. Wilson. "History has simply been outdone. . . . the most astounding upheaval we have ever known," editor Harding rejoiced on November 7. The victory was the more remarkable because the Republicans won nineteen of Ohio's twenty-one congressional seats in spite of the Democratic gerrymander of the congressional districts. Business had triumphed over "tariff monkeying," farmers had registered their protest at the promotion of trusts while they were denied protection, Congress had been punished for trifling with the country. The crisis was past. America was saved.

Harding's supreme faith in the tariff was not disturbed by the free-silver crisis of 1895–96. To be sure, a revolution swept the control of the Democratic party from gold-standard Cleveland to free-silver Bryan. The Chicago convention that did this was a thing of madness so far as Harding was concerned. It put the Populists in control of the Democratic party, with their inflationary platform of the unlimited coinage of cheap silver. But Harding was not worried. The "matchless McKinley" was sure to win and bring about currency and tariff sanity. The very radicalism of the "Popocrats," their "roorbacks" and "jim-jams" would defeat them. He rightfully predicted that Cleveland and his conservative Democrats would drag their heels in the campaign. "The silver will-o-wisp will not be chased by the business Democrats of the East and Middle West, and while party fealty prevents an open revolt, there isn't a shadow of doubt but they will quietly oppose the ticket." He cast some choice ridicule on the hysterical free-silverites, the "faddists from the way back townships." [7] He waved the American flag furiously in fifteen editorials, claiming that the silver crackpots were trying to "Mexicanize" the currency.[8]

It all came to a happy conclusion on election day as the nation went for McKinley, and even Marion itself cast a majority of thirty-four for the great promoter of the tariff and the "full dinner pail." [9] The spring of 1897 came, and, with it, the inauguration of McKinley and the calling of a special session of Congress whose primary purpose was to re-enact the McKinley measure under the name of the Dingley tariff. This meant that the prosperity that had set in during the campaign of 1896, and had assured Bryan's defeat, would now become permanent. "With plenty of cash in the treasury," wrote Harding on July 3, 1897, "and with the prospect of an early settlement of the tariff question for a long time to come, there is no reason why the recuperative business tendency should not be permanent." The golden age of McKinley had begun. Harding summed up the mood of the time: "Let's be happy."

3

Harding's views on labor were essentially conservative and paternalistic. According to Harding, management usually knew what was best for the workingmen, each of whom had the right to work for whatever hours and wages he was willing to accept. Strikes which interfered with this right to work were wrong. Unions were too often led by demagogues who relied on threats and violence. There were, in Harding's opinion, too many foreigners in the labor-union movement.

Harding's viewpoint on labor had its beginnings in Marion. The city's comparatively small working force served mainly the Huber Works and the steam-shovel factory. Wages were satisfactory in view of the relative scarcity of labor and the low cost of living. There was a home-town loyalty and a neighborliness that made the workingmen more or less contented home owners and civic-minded city boosters. In an essay-editorial in the *Star* of June 3, 1887, entitled "Marion As It Is," Harding noted that "the workingmen, on whose thrift mercantile business largely depends, are intelligent and enterprising citizens.

Instead of spending their time and money in studying how to control their employers, they are paying for homes and for their families, and just now are enthusiastically engaged in perfecting a Mechanics Library and Reading Room Association that will be a credit to any city. Their homes give them an interest in the city's improvement and their actions are governed accordingly." The workingmen had not yet lost that somewhat personal relationship with management which came from mass production. Harding revealed a bit of this quality in a *Star* editorial on August 24, 1892 when he wrote, "We cannot speak advisedly concerning the great workshops of the larger cities nor of the men who labor for gigantic corporations, but in the employment field in Marion the workman who is devoted to his duties and to his employer's interests is always well cared for: he is indispensable."

The fact of the scarcity of labor in Marion was attested by an occurrence in the summer of 1887 when many day laborers were needed to help build the new water works. Outside workers were brought in, and the *Star* expressed the hope that they would not stay after they had completed their work—especially since they were Italians. The *Star* commented on the situation on August 8, 1887: "A great deal of comment is being made by our people upon the bringing into the city of a gang of Italian laborers to work for the Water Works Company. The company would not have brought foreign labor among us had it not been compelled to, but laborers are very scarce in Marion, so much so that it is impossible to secure even a small number of them."

It is important to emphasize that a strong feeling of unneighborliness was felt by Marionites toward these dark-skinned outsiders. Harding, in his editorial just quoted, went on to say, "We hope that the city will not be afflicted with this class of people a great while, but until there is a large number of white laborers it will be necessary to bear with these garlic eaters." Two days later, August 10, he enlarged on the subject, "We like to see Marion grow but not with cancers, or carbuncles on the body politic. . . . About one Italian in a thousand makes good, and the STAR, if it could have its own way, would devote its free passes for a whole year toward packing every mother's son of them and shipping them back where they came from. With all due respect for what few law-abiding Italians we have as residents, we have no use for the imported class of Italian labor, for it is one of the monster abuses that is completely rending the American social fabric." On September 23, 1887, the *Star* revealed the local snobbishness in another respect. It became necessary for the Italians to sue for their wages in the local court. Whereupon Harding made editorial comment, "For the enlightenment of our readers who cannot go abroad we give them a little of Italy in the copied names of the plaintiffs." Twenty-six such names were then listed, from Tomaso Fortinati [sic] to Angelo Duputro [sic]. The editor then added, "It is needless to say they go on the justice's docket by number." Four years later the Star, August 3, 1891, was still harping on the Italians. "The dago is a long way from being a promising or desirable citizen, as a rule."

Hence, it may be concluded that Marion and Marion labor were very self-satisfied. On May 1, 1886, the day set by the national organization known as the Knights of Labor for launching the country-wide crusade for the eight-hour day, the Star sarcastically commented that the effect of the movement was "not noticeable with Marion laborers and manufacturers." At Huber's, where the men were paid by the hour or by the piece, "to lessen their time of labor would be foolish for them." It was the same at the steam-shovel works and at the other shops in town. There were, of course, local units of such labor organizations as the machinists, the typographical union (in Harding's own shop), the Knights of Labor, and the American Railway Union. But the one which appealed to Harding was the Huber Beneficial Association. This was a company organization set up in 1884 on an insurance basis to provide sickness and death benefits to the workers. According to the Star, January 21, 1887, it cost the members $2.50 a year and paid a maximum of $4 a week for sickness and $45 for death benefits. "It will be seen," he wrote, "that the H.B.A. is the best and cheapest organization of the kind in the state, and the Huber boys are justly proud of it."

What Harding, while still a teenager, thought of the Typographical Union was frankly expressed in the Star on September 1, 1886: "The STAR has some knowledge of printers, both union and non-union, and while we consider them as a class a bright and intellectual body of men, we are intimately aware that a number of them are a drunken, worthless set, the majority of whom are supported by and sail under the prestige of typographical unions."

4

With these local standards Harding approached the general labor problem. On the question of hours, he was against the eight-hour-day and for piece-and-hour payments. As for wages, he had a homemade "philosophy" which combined: (1) self-adjustment of laborers to the local standard of living, (2) determination of rates by the craft involved, and (3) the right of the employer to a fair profit. As for unions, men were free to organize, but so were they free not to join the union. Union leaders were too often demagogues and anarchists who believed they had a right to interfere with management affairs which were none of their business. What constituted such interference was for the management to decide. That meant that an overly aggressive labor movement would cause costs of production to be so high that capital would withdraw from production. Without capital America was doomed. Strikes were usually futile, and they were to be crushed if the strikers used the boycott or direct violence. There were too many foreigners in America who provided the anarchistic elements that reduced an ordinary strike to a riot. Nevertheless "scabs" were to be protected because this was a free country. Most of this is summarized in two *Star* editorials: one on the eight-hour day, April 29, 1886; the other on "The Evil of Strikes," August 24, 1892.

Harding, in his eight-hour-day editorial, said that the eight-hour day disrupted society as a result of workers seeking more money for less work. This discouraged capital. He maintained that a man should be permitted to work as long as he wanted. How he reasoned is best seen by observing his own words:

> An eight-hour labor system has little to commend it. . . . Employment can be given to more people but [that]. . . . will bring inferior labor into competition with superior and the disadvantages arising therefrom are at once apparent. With the reduction of hours will come that struggle between capital and labor for the old wages under the new hours and a field is open for continued strife which will further unsettle the business interests of the country. The proposed system will also revolutionize piece and hour work and few workingmen whose labor is paid for in that way will choose to work eight instead of ten. In a general way the more a man works the more he will earn and save, and few men working for themselves stop at eight hours a day, but choose to give twelve, thirteen and even more hours to labor. Upon the kind of labor depends to a great extent the amount of time that should be devoted to it. In many employments eight hours a day is as much as should be required, while in others twelve would be no hardship.

The 1892 editorial on "The Evils of Strikes" was the most concise example of his "demagoguery" theory of labor unrest. The basic point was that the United States could solve its labor problem if the demagogues would only leave the workers alone. To be sure, the nation had problems. Both labor and capital were selfish. "Man never acquires riches or honors enough. . . . we see wealthy men, with means ample for absolute luxury and ease, still chasing the almighty dollar, the greed for gain being absolutely insatiable so long as there is the necessary vitality to acquire it. . . . Labor acquires power in organizing and with increased power it seeks to conquer." However, as between the two, labor and capital, the people should put their trust in the capitalists for the simple reason that upon them depended the nation's prosperity. And such trust was justified because, although there were "heartless and unappreciative employers . . . the great body of employing men find it to their interest to pay good wages." Such people had an economic stake in society and their survival required them to be more responsible.

But the demagogues spoiled it all. These were the "less responsible and the professional agitators" who "conceive the grievances of the unions." They then proceeded to instill a false loyalty in the men. "With a fidelity deserving of a higher cause and worthier reward than the many failures that are recorded, the many deserving union men march bravely into the industrial conflicts that seem to threaten the social fabric, and invariably do the greatest damage to the great masses of the laboring world." In so doing they committed "the greatest evil of all." This is "the denial of any right to the non-union workingman, [to] whom all fair-minded men must concede the right of an honest living wherever he chooses to toil it out."

5

Harding was a sincere believer in the fundamental importance of "the right to work." There was no objection to "an honorable control of the labor market, so long as no monopoly is claimed to exclude workingmen who do not happen to be union members." To Harding, a strike, under the leadership of demagogues, interfered violently with this right to work. "It is more tyrannical than has yet been charged against capital to deny any man the right to earn an honest living. Nothing is more brutal or horrible than the assault upon any man who seeks to earn bread for himself and family in a place voluntarily vacated by another. The hounding persecution and effort to starve a fellow man who seeks honest toil can not be tolerated, and the union that does it establishes a precedent far worse than the tyranny that it professes to be battling against."

Harding's interpretation of the labor-capital conflict was fed in considerable measure by the violence of the "era of strikes" which took place from 1885 to 1895. Out of his observation of the bloodshed that began with the Haymarket strike of 1886 and culminated in the Pullman strike of 1894, he found himself explaining the difficulties by blaming the allegedly anarchist-led foreign element.

Harding was given to a foreigner-anarchist interpretation of labor disturbances before the anarchist threw the bomb in the Haymarket riot of May 4, 1886. He did so on July 17, 1885 when he commented on "the riotous foreigners" who were on strike at the Cleveland Rolling Mills. This affair, he wrote, "seems to have been brought about by a Chicago Anarchist who had just got out of jail." He added, "Experience is every day teaching that the sooner this country is rid of blatant and inciting anarchists the better it will be off. The manner of removing them cannot be too severe. The oppressed laboring classes of this country can not acquire the desired state of affairs by resorting to deeds of violence and acts of lawlessness." Over and over again Harding associated foreigners with violence. On December 19, 1885 there was the story of "foreign cut-throats" who organized an "association of Socialists" in San Francisco for the "secret assassination of certain public men and police officials." On January 25, 1886 it was a strike in the Pennsylvania coke regions characterized by "the violent conduct of the belligerent strikers, nearly all of whom are foreigners." On April 24, 1886 labor disturbances in certain Long Island, New York, sugar factories were attributed to foreign communists. "The bloody rioters at Williamsburg and Greenpoint [near Brooklyn] wore the red ribbon of the communist, which in a measure accounts for their lawlessness." Two days later it was "the blood red colors of the Commune" which predominated an eight-hour-day demonstration in Chicago. "Only four small editions of the stars and stripes were counted in the procession. . . . Speeches of the usual Anarchist order were delivered by August Spies, Michael Schwab, and Parsons, the well-known agitator."

Then, early in May, 1886, hell broke loose on the front pages of the *Star*. The dispatches were from Chicago. On May 4 the headlines ran:

RIOT AND DEATH

Chicago the Scene of an Awful Carnage

Shot Down Like Hogs

The next day it was:

MORE RIOTING

Chicago the Scene of Several Bloody Demonstrations

The Anarchist Element

The Police are Mobbed, Stoned and Shot

Anarchist Blood Shed

Fifteen Men Reported Killed

What had happened? The Knights of Labor, a nationwide organization of workingmen, planned a great Chicago May Day demonstration in its campaign to promote the eight-hour day. Tension had been heightened by the fact that the employees of the McCormick Reaper Works had been on strike since February, 1886 in protest against the lockout of several hundred men for union activity. Apprehension was also felt because of the outspoken tactics of the anarchist clubs of Chicago and their paper, *Die Arbeiter Zeitung*, which urged the workers to arm themselves to fight the "hired murderers of the capitalists." The anarchists took part in all the demonstrations—the Knights of Labor parade and the mass meetings of the locked-out McCormick employees. The Knights had called for a general strike on May 1, but called it off at the last minute. On May 3 the McCormick men held a protest meeting near the works and, when the strike-breakers came out, a riot ensued in which the police killed several workers. Most of the police shooting, however, was purposely aimed over the heads of the struggling workmen. The anarchists thereupon called for a revenge meeting in Haymarket Square for the evening of May 4, the circulars calling the "Workingman to Arms." When the meeting was almost over, no violence having occurred, and most of the crowd having gone home, the police suddenly appeared and charged the remnants. Thereupon some person, never identified, threw a bomb into the police squad, and shooting from both sides followed. When the smoke cleared seven police were dead, sixty-seven wounded, and an even greater number of workmen either dead or wounded.[10]

This affair gave to Harding, as it did to most American editors, an opportunity to announce that what they had feared all along was true: the labor movement in America was a tool of the foreign anarchists.

Selecting his facts from the confusion of inadequate Chicago dispatches, Harding came to his own logically inescapable conclusions in editorial observations of May 5, 6, and 14. The McCormick strikers were said to be "composed principally of foreigners with communistic ideas, who hope to accomplish the betterment of their condition by violence." Their May 3 meeting was an attack on the McCormick works. The work stoppage was not a lockout induced by the firing of union workers but a strike against the McCormick company's retention of workers who refused to join the Knights of Labor. The May 4 riot was interpreted as follows: "Last night the anarchists exhibited their accursed desire for blood, and the murdering and wounding of fifteen or more policemen in the discharge of their duty was heinous, outrageous and a disgrace to civilization." Harding concluded, "It is at the mass meetings of these irrational strikers where the evil results are engendered, and it is the inflammatory speeches that excite the mob to bloodthirsty vengeance. To disperse these gatherings may be difficult, yet this should be done, and the tongue of the anarchist should be stilled quickly and effectively."

Harding's interpretation of the facts made heroes, not of the "poor duped strikers," but of the strike breakers, who opposed "these Czars of labor." "The laborer that dares to assert his rights and resist their authority—they crush him. Every avenue to a life of honest labor is closed against him, he is subject to increasing threats, annoyances, and humiliation, even violence, until he is a beggar in purse and hope."

Society must protect the free worker in his right to work. Riots begotten by immunity from punishment must be met with the rioters' own weapons. "They should be taught a lesson, one not to be forgotten, and the sooner the better. Circumstance will not admit of moral suasion even if it could be understood by the raving numbskulls." Referring to the efforts of the police in the May 3 demonstration to avoid shooting into the crowd, Harding wrote, "The Chicago police made a mistake when they shot over the heads of their fiendish socialistic assailants. Decisive action in the way of gatling guns would have been more effective."

Back in New York, according to Harding, was the sinister cause of it all: Johann Most, the much-publicized European exponent of the anarchistic ideas of Michael Bakunin. "What a pity," Harding remarked, referring to the firing into a mob by the Wisconsin militia in a Milwaukee riot, "that he [Most] was not at the head of the Milwaukee

Polacks Wednesday. The entire militia might have turned their rifles on him for one round and riddled his abominable carcass in a manner satisfactory to the law-loving American people. Some unmitigated nuisances can only be cured by allopathic doses of cold lead."

6

A less immediate but probably more effective measure for curbing labor unrest was the restriction of immigration. According to Harding, on May 27, 1886, that source of American growth which was once our glory had become a curse. "Foreign nations have piled in with their thrifty emigrants, their paupers, their outlaws, the offscourings of society and a disreputable mass that so contaminates the respectable element that the foreign importation has become a perfect dump of Oriental garbage. Immigration has become a sewer that empties onto American soil the pauper, the heathen, the contract laborer, the Mosts and Fieldings [one of the Chicago anarchists]. This daily arrival is numbered by the thousands and they are infesting the American social body with sores that no civilization and education, as a physician, can cure." Chicago was the worst example of this: according to Harding, it was no longer an American city. "We can not wonder," Harding said on November 17, 1886, "at it being a hot-bed of socialism and anarchism and all other devilish isms so detrimental to respectable government."

Few exceed Harding in the vindictiveness with which he hoped for the conviction and execution of the Chicago anarchists. Such vindictiveness was clearly shown by the trial judge, Joseph Gary, in helping the prosecutor place upon the jury men who had formed opinions against the anarchists from reading the newspapers. Harding was quite frank in praising the ruling of "this excellent judge." At one point, wrote Harding on August 7, 1886, "Judge Gary decided that, because a man had formed an impression as to the guilt or innocence of accused parties from reading the newspapers, this need not disqualify him from serving as a juror. He held also that it was impossible for an intelligent man to read about any occurrence without forming some sort of an impression with regard to that occurrence. But the impression received would not prevent a man from arriving at an honest and fair judgment concerning the matter from the evidence offered to him." This new principle of allowing newspaper-prejudiced jurors to serve was an easy one for journalist Harding to accept. It was one of the "good rulings" that "may be cited as authority to expedite future trials."

As for the basic fact that the anarchists on trial had not thrown the bomb, and that nobody knew who did, this did not bother Harding. One could not believe anarchists anyhow. "Just how much emphasis a jury can place in the testimony of those who seek to murder by whole-sale is hard to tell unless they have none at all," wrote the editor in the *Weekly Star* on August 7. "The red-mouthed bombthrowers would not hesitate to swear to a lie that would make the common perjurer blush with shame." It did not make any difference whether they threw the bomb or not. When, at last, the Illinois Supreme Court upheld the verdict that the "seven red devils" would have to hang, Harding wrote on September 16, 1887, "The fact is the anarchists have so conducted themselves in the eyes of law abiding people that popular sentiment would have them hanged whether the law would seem to prescribe that course or not."

When a strike was lacking in violence, such as was the case with the Chicago meat packers in 1886, Harding convinced himself that the sentencing of the Haymarket anarchists was the controlling factor. Said the *Star* on November 15, 1886, "The conviction and sentencing of the Haymarket rioters had a salutary effect in preventing the idle and the vicious from precipitating conflict by interference in a matter which was none of their business!" When appeals delayed the execution of the condemned men and gave rise to public meetings demanding mercy, Harding saw anarchy on the rise again. On January 17, 1887 he demanded that the meetings be suppressed "else a repetition of the events of last year may be expected." The same was true of the "silly talk and claims" for pardon. Only when "the monsters are strung up as high as the legal rope will pull them," he wrote on September 23, 1887, "will the millions of law abiding citizens give a joyful sigh of relief." When, on November 11, 1887, four of the seven were "strung up" (one committed suicide, and two had their sentences commuted to life imprisonment), "the universal anxiety" came to an end.

Imagine Harding's feelings when, almost six years later, Illinois Governor John P. Altgeld pardoned the anarchists who had been sentenced to life imprisonment. Altgeld claimed that the trial had been unfair. "Perhaps they were unjustly convicted," cried the *Star* editor June 27, 1893, "for a jury could not well be unbiased, but law and liberty demanded decisive action." "Lawless fanatics" would not become emboldened and a wave of anarchistic labor rioting might be expected. Harding could say no good word for Altgeld. The governor's decision could only be the result of an old grudge against Judge Gary, said the *Star* editor on July 1, 1893. He vented his rage on Altgeld with such epithets as "distinguished demagogue," the "fool governor," the "Illinois lulu," and "Anarchist Altgeld." [11] Riots were attributed to his influence. On May 28, 1895 Harding attributed a lynching in Danville to the effect of Altgeld's action. The mob was almost persuaded to disperse when it was reminded "that the 'Anarchist' had pardoned the last three rapists convicted in the State."

7

Harding's right-to-work convictions received another test in the famous Homestead strike of 1892.[12] This was a contest between the Iron and Steel Workers Union and the Carnegie Steel Company of Homestead, Pennsylvania, near Pittsburgh. In 1889 the union had negotiated a three-year wage contract with the company. At its expiration Andrew Carnegie insisted on a wage reduction. The union prepared to strike, but was suddenly confronted, on July 1, with a lockout. A back-to-work movement was begun by the company superintendent, Henry C. Frick, who engaged several hundred armed men, supplied by the Pinkerton Detective Agency, to come to the plant to protect those who desired to work in the mills. The "scabs" were opposed on July 5 and 6 by the armed strikers, who captured the "enemy," disarmed them, and ran them out of town. In the melee several men on both sides were killed. The Pennsylvania militia was called. On July 24 an anarchist named Alexander Berkman came to Homestead, forced his entry into Frick's office, and shot him point-blank, but without mortal results. The strike dragged out until November, during which period the back-to-work movement was successful and the strike a failure.

Harding made up his mind quickly about the merits of the strike. On July 27 he announced it as "about broken," with the men fast returning to work. He criticized the strike leaders, who had no hopes of returning to their jobs, for prolonging the strike and keeping hundreds of men from getting back to work to take advantage of the company's offer of amnesty. "The company asks no renouncement of the union, but will not recognize it as such, treating with the men as individuals."

However, Harding had announced his judgment of the affair nine days before in an editorial entitled "The Lesson of Homestead." He admitted that the strike was a lockout and that, at first, the union had the public sympathy. But, he claimed, the union made two fatal mistakes: one was to deny the rightful owners of the plant "either the use of it or access to it"; the second was to deprive "non-union workmen the inalienable personal right of accepting employment." The first mistake was bad enough. It was lawless, and "without law there is nothing but anarchy, followed by communism."

But the exclusion of the "scabs" was the most inexcusable mistake. Only the pressure of the Pennsylvania militia to protect these men in their inalienable right to work prevented a terrible conflict. "What atrocities might have been inflicted upon non-union men by the reckless and unreasoning class, were the militia not present, can only be judged by the experience of former conflicts." By seeking to interfere with the right of these men to work, the actions of the union leaders "approach nearer to despotism and absolutism than their capitalistic employers have ever been charged with." Said Harding, "The most essential of personal rights was violated. Every man had the right to seek employment as he chose. When that is denied, whether by capital or united labor, the social condition is threatened. Therein is the chief weakness of united labor. No matter how sneering the non-union workmen are, scabs or rats, they possess just as many rights as citizens as the organized men."

Harding believed in protecting strikebreakers for another reason, namely, that it was sound policy for big business to have reliable friends in the ranks. The leading *Star* editorial of November 22, 1886 contained this sentiment in the form of a quotation and endorsement of a *Cleveland Leader* statement on the subject. In a meat packers' strike, after the "scabs" had succeeded in achieving their employer's purposes, application was made for railroad fare back home. This payment was justified because the men "broke the back of the strike and helped the packers out of a bad fix. In case of another strike they would be needed again, and the packers ought to treat them well for policy if not for the sake of their honor. If they are deceiving or ill-using to the men who aided them in their hour of need, they are not only increasing the power and number of their enemies and weakening themselves, but they are playing into the hands of demagogues and tryannical labor organizations—and doing something to make trouble for employers everywhere." This duty to strikebreakers was expressed by Harding in connection with a strike on the Chicago, Burlington, and Quincy Railroad in 1888. "What just employer," he asked March 21, "could be expected to discharge those who helped in his great hour of need to make room for those who voluntarily go out to force submission?"

Harding's right-to-work interpretation of the Homestead strike led him to admit his belief in a certain fatalism—that labor must lose in most of its contests with capital. In a very significant passage of the July 18 editorial, just quoted, he wrote, "If there is a weakness, if there is a partiality, it must be charged to the more effectual influence of capital upon the execution of the law." In other words, one could not win, so why try? It was a one-way street. "Labor can't exist without capital," he declared on June 18, 1886 as a furniture workers' strike failed in Chicago. "It will be a happy day for all wage workers when they recognize the fact that strikes are profitless,"—this on November 18, 1886 during a lull in the conflict. On December 2, 1886 he quoted his favorite, Robert A. Ingersoll: "Making a living in this world is an individual affair, and each man must look out for himself." This, said Harding, "is a sensible idea of domestic economy." Of a longshoreman's strike, he wrote on February 4, 1887, "The practical workings of this, as well as most other strikes, render it more and more manifest that it is an unwise, unjust and unsuccessful method of attempting to right alleged wrongs." He was prone to refer to the financial losses to workers during a strike. "Strikes seldom pay," he declared January 9, 1889. After the failure of the protracted Chicago, Burlington, and Quincy strike in 1888, he commented, May 3, on its cost, saying, "When organized labor concedes the same right to the employer that they insist upon themselves, all strikes and boycotts will cease. No man has a right to force labor at a price for which the laborer is unwilling to hire, but neither has the laborer a right to insist on a man buying his help at a figure he does not see fit to pay."

Harding eased a bit as the 1890s wore on, but the price he demanded of labor was an agreement to arbitrate. "What a glorious thing," he said May 22, 1894, as a coal strike dragged out, "enforced arbitration would be." But he quickly turned against the miners at the first report of violence. "The coal strike will be a failure, mark that. No cause can win in this country through lawlessness and riot, no cause conducted on these lines can have public sympathy. The people did hope the miners might succeed, and wish them well today, when they are law abiding." Again, in 1897, an Ohio coal strike aroused his sympathy for the miners. "The situation is serious enough to give arbitration a trial," he wrote July 7. "The fact that the strikers have expressed a willingness to submit to arbitration will elicit no little public sympathy." But the next day he condemned them for "intimidating those who have remained at work."

8

The great Pullman strike of 1894 [13] found Harding supporting the strikers at first, and highly critical of the autocratic, intolerant George M. Pullman. The strike was largely a sympathetic one, when the American Railway Union, led by Eugene V. Debs, called out the railroad men in support of the workers of the Pullman Corporation, makers of the well-known sleeping cars. The Pullman people struck when Pullman reduced wages without reducing the house rents and store prices in the town which he owned, and in which his workers lived. The strikers offered to arbitrate, but Pullman refused, saying that there was nothing to arbitrate. Public opinion in general turned against the uncompromising Pullman, and Harding followed the trend of opinion upon the occasion of the refusal of arbitration. "Mr. Pullman's refusal to accept this proposition," he wrote July 22, 1894, "has led a great many to believe that he is wrong; that he would have nothing to lose by accepting the proposition if he was not. The sleeping car magnate may go a little too far in his stubborness for the satisfaction of the public." In November, when the United States Strike Commission made its "exhaustive report" on the affair, Harding accepted the findings, which were adverse to Pullman. The *Star* editor commented on November 14, "That part of the report that roasts the Pullman company and the Pullman system, however, is not likely to excite much sympathy in the public mind for Pullman and his company. By the report, what was once considered the model town of Pullman is not a model town at all. Independence is not a privilege among the residents of the town or Pullman employees. Life is a submission to the Pullman 'system' of exacting rents or other privileges, regardless of a sense of right or wrong." On January 4, 1895 Harding showed no sympathy for Pullman's report that he lost

$1,700,000 in 1894 and had to pay dividends out of the company surplus. "Still," said the *Star* editor, "there will be no sympathy wasted upon the Pullmans."

Nevertheless, the strike failed and Harding blamed Debs for the violence that developed and which President Cleveland suppressed, along with the strike itself, by calling out the United States Army. So far as Harding was concerned, all violence was the fault of Debs and the American Railway Union. He wrote on July 7, "President Debs in his proclamation to the striking employees says: We must triumph as lawabiding citizens or not at all. According to Debs' statements either the cause of the strikers is lost or they are to be considered responsible for the situation." Harding admitted on July 12 that "it is pretty generally believed that the strikers, the workingmen, were not directly responsible for the recent rioting." Yet the rioting ruined the strike, according to Harding, and Debs was bitterly criticized for refusing to order his fellow unionists back to work, so as to retain their jobs. The strike, said Harding on December 11, 1894, "was dictated by Debs and prolonged by his persistency when disaster confronted thousands of his followers. The sooner such selfishly inspired leaders as Debs are deserted the better it will be for the workingman." Harding had no sympathy for Debs when he was sentenced to prison for violating a federal injunction against doing anything that would prolong the strike. The *Star* editor saw no merit in Debs' side of the case. "Mr. Debs," he wrote on December 17, 1894, "furnishes the world a fair example of a man who may be said to have talked himself into jail." When Debs was reported to have said that he would rot in jail before accepting a pardon, the *Star*, on August 25, 1895, said that this was "right in line with his former ideas of raising a stink." Again, when Debs was reported to have advised the country "to read, study, think and vote," the *Star*, March 14, 1898, remarked, "This is probably a Debs scheme, to keep everybody quiet to give him a chance to do all the talking."

9

The Pullman strike gave Harding an occasion to renew his diatribes against foreigners, especially the Poles. Thus, on July 9, 1894, he commented, "A glance through the list of killed and wounded among the mobs which battled against the militia at Chicago tells the tale of who are engaged in the riots. It will hardly be believed that Szcepen-ski, Kocminski and Gazewaki were doing much for the cause of American labor."

The Poles and other foreigners in the coal-mining towns of eastern Pennsylvania were especially annoying to Harding. In an outbreak at Latimer, near Hazelton, in 1897, he blamed the violence on the excitable aliens. He wrote on September 11, "Cheka, Stanisk, Kulick, Keriovich, Krego, Shabolick, Wawensko, Sleshok and Erakuki are a few of the names that appear among the list of killed and wounded striking miners whom the sheriff's posse fired upon near Latimer on Friday. The other names given are equally as unfamiliar to Americans. They indicated the composition of the mob that has caused the first bloodshed as the result of the coal strike. It is the misfortune of the American laborers that their contests for better wages are so often brought into disrepute with law-abiding citizens through the influence of the foreign element."

It was the same story again in an eastern Pennsylvania hard-coal strike in 1900. When riots were reported, the *Star* again, on September 22, listed the "unpronouncable names" in the casualty list. "The Ska-maniczes, Sazelakus and Stalmocovickes, etc., always get hit when a sheriff's posse finds it necessary to defend itself against a mob of strikers. And these are the men whom the strike leaders find it easy to influence when a strike is desired. Once idle, grievances are magnified, bitterness is engendered and frenzy and rioting follow. The leaders who ordered the strike lost control of the men and appeals to the reason fell flat upon the ears of excitable Poles, Slavs and Huns."

Harding's anti-foreignism did not include the Jews. In the autumn of 1895 a German anti-Semitic lecturer named Herman Ahlwardt toured the United States. He received much publicity, mostly unfavorable. Harding shared the general antipathy and took editorial occasion to express his admiration for the Jews, and his dislike for Dr. Ahlwardt. "The doctor may as well return," he wrote on December 6, 1895. "America has found the Hebrews to be among her most patriotic and devoted adopted citizens. . . . We confess the Hebrews are getting their full share of the wealth of the world, but we should have to be dishonest not to admire them for their ability to get there." Harding contented himself by emphasizing the Jewish material success, giving no attention to their cultural and spiritual characteristics. He included Ahlwardt in his name-calling and jibes. The doctor was a "jew-baiter," a "bump on a log." [14] When the great Jewish philanthropist Baron Maurice Hersch died, Harding had words of praise for "one of the world's richest capitalists and indisputably one of the greatest philanthropists of the age." In the *Star*, April 23, 1896 he praised Hersch for his generosity in spending millions to improve the lot of the Jewish people. Special praise went for the Baron's benevolence for the Jews driven out of Russia, and his aid in bringing many of them to America.

10

In 1897 Harding showed signs of moderating his anti-union position. During the summer a strike of coal miners had broken out in southern Ohio. From the very outset Harding emphasized that public sympathy was with the miners. That was all right with him on the express condition, he said on July 7, that "there is no resort to lawless destruction of property." For a while, however, he was very apprehensive as he commented first on the serious injury to business, then on the "expected" intimidation of those who remained at work. It will be unusual, he wrote on July 8, "if lawlessness does not follow." But evidently it did not follow. At any rate, on August 12, Governor Asa S. Bushnell issued an appeal to the people of the state for aid to the suffering miners. Thereupon editor Harding denounced the mine owners for not paying a living wage. "For years," he wrote on August 13, "the condition of labor in the bituminous coal districts has been a blotch on the escutcheon of American industries, and so it will continue to be until some measure is adopted which shall solve the existing problem and do justice to the miner." What this could be, he confessed he did not know. He enthusiastically supported Bushnell's call for relief.

11

Harding's views concerning anarchy, unions, and foreigners reflected the feelings and opinions of the type of people found in Marion, as well as rural America as a whole, toward these issues, which were primarily big city problems. In years to come, Harding would moderate his anti-union and anti-foreign views as his constituents began to soften on such matters. The forthright leadership of President Theodore Roosevelt was to give Harding and the entire nation much confidence in this respect.

CHAPTER SIX

Of Ballyhoo and Bandwagons:
Election to the State Senate,
1890–1899

"Ohio has a little politics that is purely her own." : : : *"Marion Daily Star," February 10, 1897*

◢ Warren Harding entered Ohio politics in the 1890s with a display of the same qualities of boisterousness and promotionalism that accompanied his entry into journalism and civic boosting. He first conducted a campaign of anti-bossism that endeared him to his local political admirers. Then, in the name of Republican unity, he sought and gained the respect of Mark Hanna, one of the greatest bosses of them all. Finally he engaged in an exhibition of super-Americanism in the Spanish-American War that helped him sweep triumphantly into the office of state senator in the election of 1899.

In the early 1890s the young Marion editor felt obliged to challenge his Republican elders with the idea that the time had come for a youth movement in the leadership of the party. The Civil War heroes and founders of the party had had their day. Under the leadership of the superannuated United States Senator John Sherman,[1] who was completing his fifth term and wanted a sixth, there had been built up a patronage-based, Washington-centered organization of state, county, and local committeemen, judges, court officers, customs collectors, postmasters, and party-subsidized newspapers that seldom admitted new blood. So jealous were these party nabobs, so proud were they of their wartime rescue of the nation from the prewar Democratic "unholy" alliance of southern slavocrats and northern "doughfaces," that it was near-treason to question their continuation in party control.

One of the perennial satellites of the Sherman machine, whom Harding sincerely detested, was his fellow Republican George Crawford, editor of the *Marion Semi-Weekly Independent*. Ever since the

Civil War Crawford had abased himself before the local GOP hierarchy in order to gain from the public printing the income necessary to
keep his paper solvent. Although Crawford was not Marion's postmaster, his brand of "lick-spittle," "bloody-shirt" journalism had long
disgusted the *Star* editor, who likened Crawford's "bilge" to that of
scores of "post office editors" who prostrated themselves before the
"Washington throne" in order to keep their shabby journals alive.[2]
Such papers engaged in what Harding called "desperado methods,"
i.e., denouncing all Republican critics of Sherman as traitors because
they split the party and caused the election of Democrats.[3]

A basic difficulty in the Republican party was that the Old Guard
could not obtain for Senator Sherman his much-deserved and sought-
after elevation to the Presidency of the United States. His services as
Reconstruction leader, as President Hayes' hard-money secretary of
the treasury, as author of the famous Sherman Anti-Trust Act, and the
Sherman Silver Purchase Act surely warranted his promotion. But he
was a crusty, pompous personality and had little vote-getting appeal.
And so he hung on to his senatorship while office-hungry younger men
wished that he would gather up his well-won honors and retire.

Harding was historically sound and politically sure-footed in his
young-minded, locally-oriented concept of the Republican party. The
Republicans, like their Democratic rivals, had originated at the local
level to meet both local and national problems.[4] Actually the Ohio
Republicans had, in 1855, been the first to demonstrate to the nation
the ability of the Republican party to win state control in support of a
national antislavery-expansion program. That was when Salmon P.
Chase was elected the first Republican governor. Other states had
quickly followed suit so that, in 1856, a national convention of delegates from the states organized the national party and ran a presidential ticket. National Republican victory, of course, had come in 1860
with the election of Lincoln to the Presidency.

In the process, a state and local system of party representation and
responsibility had been created and maintained. To meet the Democratic opposition, a set of local party conventions, committees, and
officials had been created. In most cases Democratic models had been
followed. The main differences were party principles and the belief
that the southern-dominated national administration was too powerful
in controlling local and state machinery.

The elements of this local machinery were very simple. At the bottom were the county conventions, with delegates selected at precinct,

ward, and township caucuses. County central and executive committees controlled and managed county election campaigns. Associations
of county delegates formed similar conventions and committees to
handle election campaigns in districts made up of more than one
county. These involved state representatives, state senators and district
congressmen. At the state level there was the state convention made up
of delegates from the counties. There was a state central committee
and its agent, a state executive committee, to handle state election
campaigns. All along the way there were efforts to make declarations
of local, state, and national party principles that insured party unity.
In general, decisions concerning party principles and candidates were
made with reference to the membership of the party throughout the
state. Of course there was the national committee, made up of one
delegate from each state.

Harding was strongly in favor of the morale-building effect of
political participation at the local level. "In a republic," he wrote on
August 12, 1887, "politics is the people's business." His own involvement had been that way in the days when Dr. Harding's office had
been an official caucus center for party primaries. Such procedures,
with the bestowal of sundry patronage favors, brought about enthusiasm and loyalty among the party faithful. The future of the party, said
Harding, lay in the hands of a new generation of younger men, the
real party workers, "who toe the mark whenever a fight is on." Harding liked to think that the "Ohio Man" was a special political "species"
in the nation's history. "Get on whatever side of the political fence you
will," he said on April 30, 1895, "the Ohio man is a conspicuous figure
in politics." On April 12, 1895, he was moved to declare, "It does not
pay to fool with an Ohio man or a buzz saw." Again on February 19,
1897, as the nation looked forward to the inauguration of William
McKinley as the twenty-fifth President of the United States, he
bragged, "It is probable that 'the Ohio man' will always remain a
conspicuous entity at Washington. And still we have plenty more of
him at home. He is a smooth article politically and otherwise."

Harding's political hero and favorite Ohio Man was Joseph B.
Foraker, governor of Ohio from 1885 to 1889, the years of the young
editor's first serious thinking about things political. Harding liked
Foraker very much. Variously called "Little Breeches," "Fire-Alarm
Joe," and "Boom-ta-ra" for his spread-eagle Americanism, Foraker
appealed to those who thrilled to his "stand-up-and-fight" conduct on
the stump, to his stubborn refusal to return to the Confederates their

captured regimental flags of Civil War days. To Harding, Foraker was the "dashing leader," Ohio's "brilliant ex-governor." Foraker was the idol of Harding's opening and impressionable years of political commitment. He demonstrates, said the twenty-year-old editor of the *Star*, on April 24, 1886, "the practicability of electing young, wise and vivacious men to the governorship." He comes to us "whole souled from the people." "Little Breeches is a large man and still growing." It was a good thing to have keen-minded fighters like Foraker around to scalp old timers like Sherman, who did not know when to retire. "There is too much vim and vigor about Joe, old boy, to suit the Democracy." [5]

Harding had begun to eliminate from his editorial and forensic style the political appeal to the emotions which was characteristic of the showy Foraker. With Foraker, such ballyhoo was still useful to a large number of Foraker's adherents. As Senator James E. Watson said, "He is a wizard and a hypnotist who can make men forsake their families and their homes and their political principles and their bank accounts." [6]

Thus Foraker rose to power on the crest of a sea of words, promotionalism, and political deals. The states-rights appeal helped, but the cheering of the crowds was not so much for that as it was for the Foraker forensics. Sherman's popularity fell off, partly because of the dislike of his overweening desire for reelection and his use of "newspaper editor" patronage, and partly because he had no oratorical appeal, no personality capable of matching the magic of "Little Breeches." Time would come, and very soon, when the opponents of Foraker would have that personality, if not the oratory, in Mark Hanna. And Harding would then bow to it and its power, even while retaining his greater admiration for the more eloquent "Little Breeches."

Signs of concern in Harding's mind over Sherman's bossism appeared in the *Star*, November 9, 1891, when the editor commented favorably on the bold campaign of ex-Governor Foraker to unhorse the aging Sherman in the United States Senate. What riled Harding was the allegedly hypocritical claim of Sherman supporters that the Senator was "quietly awaiting the wish of the people, without soliciting support to retain the place." Actually, wrote Harding, "Mr. Sherman has been hustling all season, indeed he has been so persistent in some instances that he has injured his chances where they were first favorably inclined." Two days later, Harding was extremely caustic in declaring that the ambitions of the promising younger generation of

Ohio Republicans were being blocked by Sherman. William McKinley could have been nominated for the presidency in 1888, said he, if the unpopular Sherman had not prevented. And now he wanted to hang on to his senatorial toga at Foraker's expense. "Let the young Republicans of Ohio take notice," Harding warned, "that there is no use for them while Mr. Sherman enjoys his seat in the Senate. . . . of course Mr. Sherman is a great man. . . . but he ought to be in touch with the boys on the 'fitness of things.' "

Harding was also annoyed by the assumption that for a Republican to challenge Sherman was party treason. Sherman's stiff-necked, pompous, and monopolistic attitude was in striking contrast to the spirited but good-natured, unity-preserving campaigning of Foraker. "The notion," wrote Harding on November 20, 1891, "that the election of the brilliant Foraker to the senate means a disruption of the Republican party in Ohio is so silly as to be ludicrous. If honoring a dashing leader like Foraker is to burst the grand old party, why, let the explosion explode. The party that has but one man fit for the senate or but one deserving of such a place, can let the smash come, for it is needed. . . . Of course Mr. Sherman is a great statesman, no doubt about that, but if the Mansfield statesman and his suggestions are going to rule the roost or raise a racket, let the band play." Harding said, "Sherman's our choice, but we do not have any pick at Foraker." Moreover, he admitted, November 24, that a lot of the Sherman talk came from some of his "fool friends."

The Sherman mill moved on inexorably, and on January 3, 1892 ground out, from the servile Ohio legislators, the required sixth senatorial term for the venerable Mansfield statesman. Harding acquiesced, of course, but, in doing so, he made it quite plain that, in his opinion, the people's will had been thwarted, and Foraker unwarrantedly thrust aside. Harsh indeed were his comments in the *Star* of January 4: "The bankers and federal office holders have combined with Senator Sherman's national following and the prestige of his honorable career, and have downed the sentiments of the masses."

One more Shermanistic power play, and the people—yes, and Foraker too—would have their day. The presidential campaign of 1892 was not a very inspiring one for Ohio Republicans, or any Republicans for that matter, considering that Grover Cleveland led the Democrats to an impressive victory. But it was not Foraker's fault, said Harding. Indeed, Harding's hero was the one shining ray of hope in a campaign characterized by dullness and ineptitude. In Ohio, the bull-headed Sherman and his manager, the "ineffable" William H.

Hahn, tried to dominate the state convention at Columbus by engi-
neering a Sherman-committed delegation to the national nominating
convention at Minneapolis. They were stopped by Foraker's brilliant
maneuver which did not seek a Foraker-committed delegation, but an
uncommitted and united one in which Ohio might maneuver in behalf
of McKinley's nomination for the Presidency. The feature event was
Foraker's eloquent speech for party loyalty, with its broad hint and
hope of rescuing the Republicans from the unglamorous President
Harrison. As Foraker spellbound the Ohio convention into cheer upon
cheer, everybody knew that he was putting on a clever show to rebuke
the Sherman dictatorship. "The great crowd went wild," Harding
wrote. "It was the ovation of ovations." [7]

So far as Harding was concerned, and probably Foraker also, the
rest of the 1892 campaign was a dull one, dominated by dullards. At
Minneapolis, Hahn clumsily failed to support the "stop Harrison"
drive so as to create a dark-horse McKinley movement, whereupon
Harding snorted and suggested the muzzling of the stupid Hahn. The
Sherman-Hahn fizzle ended it for the Ohio Man enthusiasts. After the
long agony was over and Cleveland was elected, Harding salved some
of his misery by suggesting that the Republican party would be better
off for "its good sound drubbing." Maybe, after four years of dismal
Democracy under Cleveland, the day of the Ohio Man—McKinley in
the White House, and Foraker in the Senate—would yet return. [8]

3

By 1895, in Harding's estimation, the time had come for a Republican deliverance. Now was the opportunity for the Ohio Republican
party to enrobe itself in the habiliments of purity, and engage in a
long-delayed "back-to-the-masses" crusade, with the dashing Foraker
as its standard-bearer. There was plenty of ballyhoo ammunition at
hand. The Democrats deserved to be punished by a true man of the
people because of the depression brought upon the American economy through the Panic of 1893. The Marion editor therefore proceeded to join with others of the journalistic "young Turks" to make
their journals sounding boards for the elevation to the United States
Senate of "Little Breeches," the best Democrat-buster in Ohio. The
plan was to make the Ohio legislative and gubernatorial election of
1895 look like a grand demonstration of a righteous people rising in
their might to elect a "good" Republican to the Senate to replace the

"bad" incumbent, Calvin S. Brice, a "boodle" Democrat under the control of Wall Street and President Cleveland.

It is doubtful that the election of a Republican legislature, and, therefore, of Foraker, in the campaign of 1895, was the thing of states-rights, grass roots purity that Harding described. The Foraker victory was part of a deal between several promoters: Mark Hanna, who wanted William McKinley to run for President in 1896; boss George B. Cox ("Coxie, old boy," as Harding dubbed him), who was seeking to make his control of Cincinnati politics indispensable to the Ohio Republican party; and a group of Forakerites who wanted to make Springfield industrialist Asa S. Bushnell governor of the state. Behind the scenes was the direction of one of the most astute political managers in Ohio's history, Charles L. Kurtz. In other words, as worked out at the state Republican convention at Zanesville, the "Zanesville program" meant Foraker for United States senator, McKinley for President of the United States, and Bushnell for governor of Ohio, and "Coxie, old boy"—for Cox.[9]

Nevertheless, Harding found great pride in pointing to the campaign of 1895 as a grand example of Ohio Republicans solving their own problems in a democratic and Ohioan way, while the Democrats "boodled" with Brice, who was said to spend more time in his New York business office than on his job in the Senate or in his home in Lima, Ohio:

> The action of Ohio Republicans in uniting upon a candidate for United States Senator, so declaring themselves in convention and constant reiteration upon the stump, is a notable acknowledgment of the popular sentiment favoring the election of United States Senators by a direct vote of the people. Ex-Governor Foraker has contributed to this idea by coming out in a bold and unequivocal canvass. Had Senator Brice done as much, with the democracy declaring in his favor instead of momentary silence as a subterfuge by which to deceive voters, the senatorial question would have been presented in such a manner as to have been, practically, a submission to a direct vote of the people. Mr. Foraker has contented himself with the belief that the people should know who is to represent them in congress in case the next legislature is republican. Mr. Brice, on the other hand, has not even presented himself before the people of the state.[10]

When the Ohio legislature met in 1896 and Foraker was elected as planned, Harding rejoiced as he described the new unity and purity of Ohio politics. With an oblique glance at the "seizure" of the senatorship by Sherman in 1891–92, he said, "When the will of the people is followed in the election of United States senators there is no scandal in connection. Ohio had no senatorship for sale this year." [11] Thus was the principle of local control of Ohio politics given seemingly high justification and hopes for an enduring era of sweetness and light.

4

But Harding's joy at the apparent overthrow of "bossism" by popular Forakeristic action did not endure. A new threat to unity and localistic sensibilities suddenly appeared in the manipulations by Mark Hanna to make himself United States Senator. Harding instantly donned the armor of localistic righteousness and sallied forth—editorially, of course—to combat this new threat to party unity. As was the case in all his contests with Hanna, the Marion publisher was defeated, but he emerged from the contest with the respect of both sides.

At first, Harding was quite naïve about Hanna. He liked Hanna's management of McKinley in the 1896 fall campaign, and was glad to have such a good money raiser on the Republican side. If "Uncle Mark's" money was the dominant factor in the McKinley campaign, so much the better. "It was worth it," said the young editor. As for Hanna's continuing to be the power behind the throne when McKinley became President, that was as foolish an idea as to assume that Bryan's manager, Altgeld, would be the real President in the event of a Democratic victory. [12]

Harding soon had reason to change his mind about Hanna's intentions. It developed that McKinley planned to appoint Senator Sherman to be Secretary of State in order to enable Governor Bushnell to send Hanna to the Senate. [13] Harding was astounded. Ohio politics had not been cleansed after all. A new national political dictatorship had appeared to make a travesty of party home rule. New "hirelings" and "fawning sycophants" would now bow before the "mighty Marcus." Hanna should have done as Foraker did in 1895, appeal to the people of Ohio, instead of resorting to trickery via presidential maneuvering.

Never before, and never again, did Harding lambaste more vigorously what he considered to be the disuniting dictators of the Republican party. Also he left no doubt as to the identity of the head dictator. It was "the scheming, capable and ambitious Marcus." "Every other hungry Ohio aspirant for a pull at the government teat is whooping it up for Hanna. . . . With an obeisant smile to the President elect and an obsequious whoop for the great campaign manager, the clamor goes on, while the clamorers pay no attention to the considerations of politics, or to obligations that grow out thereof. They make believe that Mr. Hanna is the only grand mogul, the statesman of statesmen, and Santa Claus of patronage, and every Republican in Ohio ought therefore to hold his breath until the great and good Mark has satiated his political appetite." [14]

In opposing Hanna, Harding, of course, was blocked by a Hanna-Cox power play. While the Marionite was brazenly predicting the decline of the Hanna boom, the announcement was suddenly made that "Boss" Cox of Cincinnati had declared for Hanna. This appeared in the *Star* on February 18, 1897. Harding had always diluted his Forakerism with large doses of Coxism. Hence he now jumped on the Cox-Hanna bandwagon with an announcement on February 22, 1897, the day that Governor Bushnell announced that he intended to appoint Hanna to the United States Senate as soon as Senator Sherman resigned. "The governor trusts," wrote the *Star* editor, "that the action will meet with the approval of the people and there is little doubt that it will. There is no denying a strong public sentiment in favor of Mr. Hanna." Harding could not resist a jibe at the Shermanites who had blasted Cox for his corruption in 1892. As he said in the *Star*, February 16, 1897, "The gentlemen who have been industriously training with the so-called Sherman-Hanna faction will have to revise their opinion of Mr. Cox. Watch the Cincinnatian grow in the esteem of the beforementioned."

Thus did Harding change from an anti-Hanna to a pro-Hanna Republican, and, for a while, unity was restored. The *Star* chronicled the fact good-naturedly on March 6, 1897, when Hanna and Foraker walked arm in arm down the center aisle of the Senate to receive the oath of office together. A home-made cartoon accompanied the item, showing the crowned Hanna and Foraker sitting on thrones with local politicians seeking post-office jobs kneeling before their respective patrons. Before Hanna's throne was Old Guard Republican George Crawford, wearing his "Aunt Nancy" nightcap; before Foraker's throne knelt Harding's friend and leader of the young Marion Republicans, M. B. Dickerson. The title read:

Local Post Office and Other Candidates

Some Prefer to Worship at One Shrine

Some at Another

Harding's retreat before the superior strength of the Hanna maneuvers was fairly gracious, and was done, of course, in the name of party unity. Perhaps his own state senatorial ambitions were involved, because, as will be presently pointed out, the idea had already been broached to him by Governor Bushnell's private secretary, J. L. Hampton.

Nevertheless, Harding was still merely an editor-publisher, and, therefore, he could refuse to show admiration for Hanna when Hanna bossism seemingly went too far. This happened when Hanna asserted his power in the Republican state convention at Toledo in 1897, and caused the expulsion of Foraker's manager, Charles L. Kurtz, from the chairmanship of the state executive committee. Hanna wanted, and obtained, the selection of Charles Dick of Akron in Kurtz's place. Harding thereupon obstinately came out for Kurtz for governor in 1899.[15] When the election of legislators in the fall of 1897, conducted on the issue of Hanna's reelection, brought the choosing of 75 Republicans and 70 Democrats, Harding refused to recognize it as a Hanna victory because the dictatorial tactics used by the Senator resulted in some Republicans being anti-Hanna. The result, he said, "is not to be counted as a Republican victory. It is certainly not so emphatic as to be counted an endorsement and as Hanna may have wished." He hinted at high pressure, behind-the-scenes maneuvering in Marion county. "The Star is ready," he wrote, "to offer a chapter or two that can be made interesting reading." The "fool friends" of Hanna, he said, acted as if they owned the party and sought "to dictate to every private in the ranks." The opponents of Hanna were better sports. They were loyal Republicans who "take the bitter with the sweet without bellowing like calves or growling like disgruntled bosses."[16] When Governor Bushnell's disposition to treat the Hannaites and the anti-Hannaites equally caused the governor to be denounced as a traitor, Harding declared that "neither man is licensed to carry the liberty of Ohio Republicanism in his pocket."[17]

When, at last, on January 11, 1898, Hanna received a 73–70 legislative vote for reelection, Harding rather reluctantly climbed aboard the Hanna bandwagon, but deliberately chose a back seat on it. He showed that he really favored the grand fight of the local Kurtz-Foraker Republicans against the dictatorial Hanna. He rebuked the Hannaites for the bitterness of their tactics. "The contending element," he wrote in the Star, January 12, 1898, "that has proven its majority, assailed its opposition with a bitterness and a vehemence that ought to have been reserved. If they have caused wounds that will be slow in healing, the fault is theirs. However, the Star looks for no such unhappy results. The Kurtz Republicans of Ohio are of the true-blue kind. They take their medicine in defeat, and gird on their armor for the next fight for the party. How fortunate it is that they have not won, for their mightier opponent had almost threatened a desertion of the ranks if they did not have their own way."

5

Harding's technique of opposition to Hanna bossism did not long continue to partake of the nature of emphasis on the principle of self-determination. If it had, Harding might have become a Progressive. Instead, he revealed his opportunistic sense of values by choosing to pitch on Hanna with war talk. As the war fever mounted in the spring of 1898, Hanna advised caution. This was the signal for Harding to belittle Hanna by claiming that the latter was more interested in petty politics than in patriotic uplift. On April 6, 1898 the *Star* editorially reminded Hanna that here was something "in which the whole nation is interested, and postmasterships and political jobs are not involved." When Dewey's fleet sank the Spanish fleet in Manila Bay, the *Star* sneered, on May 4, "Mr. Hanna's method of getting the Spanish fleet from the harbor would have been to open a political campaign to vote it out." When the war ended and the peace treaty became an issue between Republicans and Democrats, the editor, on November 3, sneered at the idea that Hanna's reelection was an issue. "Mr. Hanna is too small a potato for an issue this year."

Harding's wartime needling of Hanna was symptomatic of what was happening to the Marionite as he approached his campaign of 1899 for state senator. Instead of stressing Hanna's bossism and the principle of local party control, Harding was rapidly, under the impact of events, becoming a war hawk and patrioteer. It has already been shown in a previous chapter how his militant patriotism had sensationalized the *Star* and enhanced its circulation and profit-making as he proudly added the Scripps-McRae wire service to his printing plant. He was now the patriotic editor, as well as the journalistic darling of the Foraker editors, and the Barkis-is-willing supporter of Hanna.

The time for a political entree was opportune. The year 1899 was

Marion county's year to name the Republican nominee for the state senatorship of the reliably Republican thirteenth Ohio senatorial district. Although Harding-for-senator was not part of the Zanesville program of 1895, which cast McKinley, Foraker, and Bushnell for political preferment, it is not without significance that the Harding state senatorial boom had some of its origin in the inner sanctum of Governor Bushnell's office. It was Bushnell's private secretary, J. L. Hampton, who had been urging the move. On July 18, 1899, the day following Harding's nomination for state senator, Hampton wrote, "This is the nomination I have worked and talked for for the last six years." [18] Many years later, in June, 1920, following Harding's nomination for the Presidency, Hampton recalled "how I labored with you to become a candidate for the State Senate the first time, and how you pleaded that you could not afford to neglect your business." [19]

There were few who played the politics of the Spanish War more ardently than the editor of the *Marion Star*. That the war was a part of Republican boosterism no one can deny. The *Star* made full use of the issue as the "matchless McKinley" toured the country in the campaign of 1898 to strengthen his position in Congress and his plans for reelection in 1900. Here is a *Star* report for October 14: "MC KINLEY AT OMAHA/ A magnificent Speech Heard by a Cheering Multitude/ THE STERN VOICE OF DUTY/ The Nation Must Unfalteringly Follow Wherever It Leads/ EVEN IF EVERY DESIRE OPPOSES/ The Temptation of Undue Aggression Must be Avoided/ WILL BE EQUAL TO EVERY TASK/ The Faith of a Christian Nation Recognizes the Hand/ of God in the Ordeal Which Has Just Passed, and/ Right Action Will Follow Right Purposes." At a "jubilee" two days later, McKinley was quoted: "My countrymen, the currents of destiny flow through the hearts of the people. Who will check them? Who will divert them? And the movements of men, planned by the Master of men, will never be interrupted by the American people." To this Harding added his blessing: "It is a keynote which is in perfect harmony with the advanced ideas of the country, an inspiration to those who have an abiding faith in the future greatness of the country."

A most fruitful part of this mixing of war and politics was Harding's emergence as a friend of all factions. With Mark Hanna so thoroughly possessed of the support of the United States Senate and the White House, the Republican preliminaries in the nominating convention in June, 1899 were a Hanna pushover. The states-rights people never even got started on a candidate of their own. The ardent Hannaite,

George K. Nash of Columbus, easily achieved the gubernatorial nomination, to which editor Harding bowed in a good-natured, but not abject, submission in a June 2 editorial:

> To Senator Hanna: The *Star* doffs its new straw hat. We haven't always admired you without reservation, but you're the real thing, all right. What you want among the Republicans goes. We say this in all conscience, and, honor bright, we have neither a post office, consulship or census job in mind. It is the *Star's* concession to a strong proposition.

A month later, on July 5, when Harding announced his bid for the Republican nomination for the state senatorship, he wrote as if he were no factionalist and had never uttered an anti-Hanna word in his life. Boldly, and blandly, he denounced all who were claiming that he was not a good Republican. He deplored "the system of organized misrepresentation that would make me wonder that I have not been drummed out of the Republican camp." He was confident that "the good, hard sense of the people," would reveal "the true inwardness of the matter." He offered himself as "one who has cared to be only a private in the ranks and has stayed through thick and thin."

The Marion Hannaites thereupon proceeded to try to make Harding eat his own words. In a county preference convention preceding the district nominating convention, they put forth Harding's friend, and well-known supporter of Hanna, Grant E. Mouser, for the senatorship. And they almost won. They were supported by a new Republican paper, the *Marion Transcript*, which had, throughout 1898, opposed Harding as a "straddlebug," an opportunist, who was using the war to carry water on both shoulders.[20] The factional line-up at the county preference convention of July 15, 1899 was so close that the outcome depended on six votes from a Marion precinct which sent in two sets of delegates. If the six votes had been counted, Harding would have lost to Mouser and the Hanna faction. By the chairman's disqualification of both delegations Harding was selected by a margin of two votes. The affair was punctuated by "thunderous yells" and by vigorous protests. After it was all over Mouser pledged his loyalty, Harding said the victory was not factional, and everybody shook hands and vowed to denounce only Democrats from then on.[21]

So it was on with the ballyhoo on July 18, 1899 as the Republican senatorial district convention met at the Marion county courthouse for the formal nomination. It was the first of many "Harding and Harmony" spectaculars that Marion was to stage for its favorite son. It was all boostership and hoopla as the Peoples' Band, resplendent in smart blue and gold attire, marched to the tune of "There'll Be a Hot Time in the Old Town Tonight." Harding badges were worn by nearly everybody. The convention made a grand demonstration of unity by endorsing President McKinley, Prosperity, Harmony, the Spanish-American War, American expansion, Governor Bushnell, Senators Foraker and Hanna, gubernatorial candidate George K. Nash, and everything else Republican that it could think of. Harding was nominated in a rousing speech denouncing factionalism —"we spell Harmony with a big H"—and Harding crowned it all by saying a few felicitous words to prove it. The whole affair occupied twenty-five minutes. There followed an inspection of the *Star* plant, a ride about Marion over the recently opened trolley line, and a final serenade by the Peoples' Band at the Harding and Mouser homes.[22]

The ballyhoo and the bandwagoning were on. In the campaign that followed Harding put on his first oratorical demonstration of how to smite Democrats. Prosperity and overseas expansion were the keynotes. The people were reminded how fortunate it was that Bryan and free silver had not been allowed to harm the marvelous good times in which they lived. The *Star* proudly dubbed its publisher-candidate as "the *Star's* prosperity editor." Patriotic fervor was aroused to the highest pitch by castigating Democratic criticism of the war and the peace terms. Democrats were accused of treachery in seeking to deprive Cubans and Filipinos of the protection of the Star Spangled Banner—in other words, of wanting to throw them to the mercies of the wolves of European and Asiatic imperialism. Much merriment was shown by Harding at the Democratic assaults on the Republicans for being ruled by Hanna and his fellow millionaires and all their "boodle." What gall, said Harding when the Democratic candidate, John R. McLean, was the millionaire publisher of the *Cincinnati Enquirer*, a "boodler from Boodlersville." Typical was the *Star* headline of November 2:

BOODLE

Being Used Freely to Debauch the State

of Ohio. Crisp New Bills Are Being

Lavishly Spent in Ohio Saloons.

McLean's Money Distributed from Residence

of the Boss.

Delighted indeed were Harding's fellow Republican editors with the discovery that the party had a new Demosthenes. The display of his oratorical talents came as a distinct surprise to them, and they made much point of it. The *Marysville Tribune* of November 1 observed that he was a remarkable exception to the rule that newspapermen were poor speakers. From the *Kenton News Republican* of September 9 came the report that Harding's first public appearance was a "smashing success." The most striking testimony came from the *Bellefontaine Republican,* October 17: "Mr. Harding was a stranger among us, but he soon won the admiration of the entire audience by his beautiful introductory remarks. . . . It is the universal expression that his picture of the signs of prosperity . . . in Logan county was one of the most beautiful combinations of word painting and effective oratory that was ever heard from the rostrum. It was beautiful, apposite, and, like the quality of mercy, was not strained."

More important was Harding's demonstration of cooperation with the Hannaites who controlled the state organization and its speakers' bureau. When Nash planned a caucus of Republican leaders for September 9 at Bellefontaine, F. O. Batch, chairman of the Logan County central and executive committees, summoned Harding, saying, "It would be well for you to be with us on this occasion and get acquainted with the boys." Harding was there, and the *Bellefontaine Republican* reported that "both gentlemen left a very good impression wherever they went." [23] A similar call for a Nash conference came from John H. Smick, chairman of the executive committee of Hardin county. Harding was there too, and the *Kenton News-Republican* reported that "the hustling young man" from Marion "made about the best short speech they ever listened to." [24] From each county, Hardin, Logan and Union, came requests for the usual campaign assessments of $50 and Harding promptly remitted. Before the campaign was over Harding was swamped with requests for speeches. [25]

Toward the end of the campaign Harding had the supreme pleasure of conspicuously producing Hanna as one of his supporters. John P. Bower, the Democratic candidate for the state senatorship, had been taunting Harding for not being "a regular worshipper at the Hanna shrine." [26] But so loyal had Harding been in answering the calls of party duty that he was finally able to elicit a specific telegram of support from Hanna, which the proud editor gleefully published in full in the *Star* of November 4: "Lima House, Lima O., Nov. 3, 1899. W. G. Harding, Marion, Ohio. 'I regret I cannot visit your district again to aid in your election, but you will have the support of a united party.' M. A. Hanna" [27] Harding commented briefly on the telegram, saying, "The Star is pleased to publish this because it refutes any intimation that factionalism has an excuse in Marion county."

And a great Republican victory it was. Harding received the usual Republican majority of the senatorial district. Nash and the entire Republican state ticket were elected by unusually large majorities. A Republican legislature was swept into office. Above all, in Marion county the Democratic majority was reduced to one of the lowest figures on record.[28]

Thus was Warren G. Harding, the anti-boss leader of crossroads Ohio, elected to the Ohio senate with the aid of both boss and anti-boss Republican votes. It was an early display of the success of the Harding way of building Republican unity. In the midst of war and prosperity hysteria, he matched ballyhoo with ballyhoo, showing talents and temperament that would soon make him indispensable in party affairs.

CHAPTER SEVEN

Lawmaking and Politicking, 1900–1902

"Party unity is more important than conscience." : : : *Harding, as quoted in the "Columbus Evening Dispatch," February 15, 1900*

When politics and conscience clashed, Harding chose politics. As a conscientious lawmaker, he was deficient. As a political fence-mender, he was the best. He emerged from his two terms as Ohio state senator without sponsoring any legislation of enduring importance. He missed a great opportunity to lead in bringing about a needed revision of Ohio's municipal code. But he did achieve the remarkable result of becoming a Hannaite, and of receiving the endorsement of the Hannaite governor, George K. Nash, for the succession to the governorship in 1904.

Harding was a Nash man, and there are Harding's own words to prove it. On September 6, 1920, in the midst of the campaign for the Presidency, he told a *Cincinnati Enquirer* reporter the story. Before he came to the legislature in 1900, he said, some of his friends told the governor that Harding was a Forakerite and would "bear watching." Thereupon Governor Nash sent for him and said, "Senator Harding, some of our friends have told me that you will be a hard man to get along with. I want to tell you that I think we can get along together. I wanted to have this little conference so that we could talk about the points we agree on and the points we don't agree on. And I want to have lots more conferences like it. Whenever you have anything on your mind to trouble you come to me and come out with it. I'll also come out with the things that are on my mind. In other words, I'll play square with you and you'll play square with me and we'll get along together."

Harding continued, "And the Governor and I did get along together, We did it so well in my first term that it was he who urged me to break a rule of 50 years standing in my Senatorial district and seek re-election when my first term was out. He gave me so much help in my contest that he was a considerable factor in my success. Furthermore when his term was drawing to a close he actually proposed me, the man he had been warned against, as his successor. It resulted, to be sure, only in the Lieutenant-Governorship."

Perhaps the most important influence that Nash had upon Harding was that he convinced the Marion editor to subordinate his own will to that of the party and to trust its leaders. As Harding put it, the political consequences of Nash's influence "were of less significance than the personal consequences to me." He "taught me that a certain faculty which I think is fundamental to my temperament can be and ought to be reconciled with effectiveness and success in politics and government. He taught me that the first thing to do with a man, no matter what side he may be on in a political controversy, is to trust him."

In other words, by his own admission Harding had few ideas of his own that he trusted; he depended on the ideas of others. Whether it is called self-effacement, subordination, puppetry, the desire for unity, or the search for good judgment—his approach to public problems was cautious and derivative, not bold and original. From 1900 to 1923 he was constantly trying to fit himself to the party's and the people's will. It was the newspaperman's way—trying to judge the nature of his constituency. It happened in respect to his decision not to wave the bloody shirt, in his ardent support of the war fever of 1898, in his legislative leadership of the Nash ideas, in his attitude toward World War I and the League of Nations, and in seeking nomination and election to the Presidency of the United States. He held up a political looking-glass to the people and tried to keep himself out of what he saw. He was decisive and bold only when he had a strong organization behind him.

2

The first example of State Senator Harding's sacrifice of legislative responsibility to the requirements of Republican political unity came during his legislative service in 1900. It was important to subordinate state legislation to the necessity of getting the Ohio electoral votes for President McKinley in the November election. This required concessions to boss George B. Cox of Cincinnati in order to secure a Republican majority in Hamilton county.

Governor Nash had a debt to pay to Boss Cox for Republican

support in Hamilton county in the gubernatorial election of 1899. This took the form of the so-called Cox Ripper Bill, introduced into the Ohio legislature by friends of the Governor.[1] It was a measure to change the form of government in Cincinnati so as to return to the Cox machine the control of city and county patronage appointments. Previous legislation—also of a "ripper" nature—had decentralized city administration and put the reformers or "fusionists" in power. The Cox machine had fought back in 1899, and elected local legislators pledged to introduce the "Cox Ripper." Cox had supported Nash in the election in the hope that the latter, if elected, would use his influence to get the bill through the legislature. If all went well, as it did, it would guarantee the loyalty of the Republicans of Cincinnati to the party, and to the reelection of McKinley in 1900.

The "Cox Ripper" was obviously part of a political job, and Harding knew it. He felt that he ought to vote against it. However, he knew, or at least he was told, that if it was defeated, the Cox machine would sabotage the Republicans in the election of 1900, probably cause the state to go Democratic, and might even bring about the defeat of McKinley. The Marion Senator, therefore, voted for the bill. And he openly admitted that he was voting against his personal convictions. On February 15, 1900 the *Columbus Evening Dispatch*, a Republican paper, quoted him as saying that "if he were to follow the dictates of his own conscience, he would vote against the bill. But party unity was more important than conscience. He felt it his duty as a Republican to vote for it." Or to quote the Democratic *Cleveland Plain Dealer*, "Mr. Harding's address was sensational. In substance, he said that he was opposed to the principle of the bill, that he could find no reason to give why the bill should be passed in the interest of the people and the city of Cincinnati, but that he proposed to support the bill because of the only argument that could possibly be made in favor of it—that it was for the party and was party politics." [2] The *Cincinnati Enquirer* was even more blunt. Harding was reported as calling the bill a "monstrosity," that he was "barely able to swallow it," but believed it to be a "party measure and would cast his vote accordingly." [3]

Harding was in full consultation with the top Ohio Republican leaders in subordinating his conscience to party unity on the Cox Ripper. There were conferences with Governor Nash. There was a letter from Senator Hanna dated February 9, 1900, urging the Ripper's passage because "it is the only way Republicans can get in a position to have a chance to carry Hamilton Co."[4] From Senator Foraker, in a letter of the same date, came the earnest hope that the bill become law. Assuming that certain "Fusionites" had factionalized the Cincinnati Republicans, Foraker said, "Let us now heal the factionalism in the important presidential year of 1900." The present Republican legislature should "make good to the Republicans of Cincinnati who have behaved so splendidly."[5]

3

An even greater danger to the Cox machine, and to an Ohio Republican majority for McKinley, was the Pugh-Kibler Municipal Code Bill. This was a progressive measure designed to wipe out the evils of ripperism. It was opposed not only by Cox but by all the city machines in the state, Republican and Democratic. It was a 260-page measure, prepared by a commission composed of Judge David F. Pugh of Columbus and Attorney Edward Kibler of Newark, Ohio, appointed by Governor Bushnell in 1898. The code would have set up a fairly flexible system of government for Ohio cities. Municipal control was placed in a city council, a mayor, and administrative boards elected by the people. This was called the "federal plan" because of a separation of powers in legislative, executive, and judicial functions similar to that in the framework of the government of the United States. The merit system of civil service was provided for as well as popular control of bond issues, awards of charters to public utilities, and the right to acquire municipal ownership of such utilities. There was a provision for non-partisan elections in all civic voting.[6]

The Pugh-Kibler proposal put Harding in the same embarrassing position that the Cox Ripper Bill had done. It came to him as chairman of the Senate Municipal Government Committee and became known as the "Harding Municipal Code Bill." He got it approved by his committee, introduced it into the Senate, spoke eloquently in favor of it, and almost got it passed on April 11.[7] That is to say, on the afternoon of that day it passed through its final reading and was scheduled for a vote when the Senate reassembled in the evening.

But Senator Harding was only going through the motions in his work for municipal reform. He knew that Nash was opposed to it, and that its passage would lose the support of Cox and others in getting an Ohio majority for McKinley in November. He actually let it be known to the public that he expected the bill to fail. According to the *Ohio State Journal* of April 12, "he frankly confessed that he did not believe that the bill would be enacted into law at the present session of the general assembly."

And yet, in the Senate discussion of April 11, Harding spoke eloquently in behalf of the adoption of the Pugh-Kibler code. The leading papers praised him for his "gallant fight," the *Ohio State Journal*, April 12, featuring his picture with the heading "Who Led the Fight for the Bill." According to the *Cleveland Leader* of April 12, "his speech bordered on the sensational at times."

If we may believe the *Journal*, Harding's defense of the bill was "simple, straightforward, masterful," and, "for the first time during the session, called forth enthusiastic applause from his colleagues of both sides of the house." According to the *Journal*, Harding urged Senate passage of the bill so as to remove municipal government in Ohio from the "pall of petty politics." He referred to "the high position which Ohio holds among the states of the Union," and earnestly appealed "to make her still more worthy of honor by the purification of the government of her cities and villages." "The opposition to the bill," he concluded, "is twofold—I speak deliberately—political and corporate. Now politics should have absolutely nothing to do with local elections. The problem of municipal government is merely a business proposition. The political system is incompatible with the wholesome conduct of municipal affairs." As for the provision that the people of a city could adopt municipal ownership, "I say, if the municipal code bill in any degree lessens the greed of corporations, godspeed its passage." This was rather progressive talk, coming from Harding.

But the bill was not adopted by the Senate. When Nash heard what Harding had done, the Governor made short shrift of the measure. According to the *Cincinnati Enquirer* of April 12, after its preliminary passage in the afternoon of April 11, Governor Nash sent his private secretary to the Senate with reasons why the senators, at least the Republican senators, should reverse themselves. The Governor's reasoning was very simple. Said the *Cleveland Plain Dealer*, "It . . . would prevent the Republicans from raising campaign funds from the corporations." [8]

Where was Harding when his bill was killed? He was on the night train bound for Washington, D.C. When he returned a few days later to find his bill dead, he did nothing. This is not surprising in view of the greater strength of his faith in the Republican party and its need for financial contributions than in municipal reform. Nevertheless, two years later, on June 28, 1902, he wrote in the *Star* that, after its passage, the code bill was "reconsidered a few hours later at the dictation of the politicians and the street railway magnates."

It is quite likely that neither Harding nor any other member of the legislature understood the Pugh-Kibler code proposal well enough to be able to handle it in conference and debate. At least that is what the *Columbus Dispatch* claimed over a year later in its issue of November 17, 1901. "The provisions of the measure," said the *Dispatch*, "as a matter of fact were not well understood even by the members themselves." On its face it seemed to be such a radical departure from the prevailing system that it was impossible to interest any politicians of importance to support it. It was too voluminous for legislators to read and master during a single session.

There was one man who saw in Harding's support of the Pugh-Kibler bill the sign of a prophet who might lead the forces of reform in Ohio politics. It was one Franklin Rubrecht, a Columbus attorney, who was so thrilled by Harding's speech of April 11, that he wrote to the Senator on the same day, calling upon him to assume the leadership of the forces of Progressivism. Harding's speech, wrote Rubrecht, showed a "spirit of honesty, frankness and championship of truly just legislation." It was "convincing, sensible, frank, able and logical and created much favorable comment." He said that "the people need such service as you are rendering, and they will not lose sight of any man, be his party faith what it may, who stands by their true needs and defends their just rights. . . . Your place is in Congress, and I hope you will go there before many years." [9]

But who was the unknown Rubrecht to encourage the ambitious Harding into uncharted Progressive paths? There was another path to fame—the path of Nash, Hanna, and the "organization"—and there was plenty of encouragement from those sources, and plenty of willingness to follow.

4

Senator Harding did other things in his first term in the legislature, but they were locally directed and even squeamishly carried on. In a *Dispatch* interview and in a *Star* editorial, both on April 15, 1900, he asserted that municipal reform was the "one real problem before the assembly." However, he confessed that it was snowed under by an "avalanche of local measures," lobbied for by "bloodsuckers who would indulge in legislative blackmail," and supported by legislators, many of whom were "utterly incapable of the work they are expected to perform."

Yet Harding himself was guilty of indulging the "bloodsuckers." For example, there was a bill, endorsed by Harding, for the encouragement of manufacturing in Marysville. Its promoter was George M. McPeck, president of the Marysville Light and Power Company, who agreed that the bill was probably unconstitutional, but said that "we will take care of that here." [10] Then there was House Bill No. 603, designed to protect small-town fire insurance companies against out of state competition.[11] Harding sponsored this bill when it came to the senate, along with a law enabling counties to get out of the mud by laying brick turnpikes,[12] another in behalf of greater newspaper publication of the county commissioners' annual reports.[13]

An example of Harding's lawmaking maneuverings was the Clark local-option bill. The Cincinnati Republican wets threatened to defect if the Clark bill passed; the Anti-Saloon League drys threatened to defect if it did not. Some device for escaping this dilemma seemed to be needed to keep both in line for the reelection of McKinley. Harding supplied it in the form of a last-minute amendment which would raise the number of county petitioners for a wet-dry referendum from 25 per cent to 33⅓ per cent of the electors.[14] This caused the Senate to defeat the bill by one vote with Harding voting for it. It was too late in the session for the two houses to get together on a single measure because both were swamped with local bills. There was talk of important people, including Harding, engaging in a game of buckpassing.[15]

Thus was the Ohio Republican party held together for 1900 presidential election purposes. The Cincinnatians were satisfied because no bill was passed, and the Anti-Saloon Leaguers were not yet strong enough to retaliate for the failure of local option by turning toward the Democrats. As the politically sophisticated W. Clay Huston of Bellefontaine wrote Harding, "I have no doubt but that your vote and influence concerning the Clark Bill will be to the best interest of the Republican party in this Presidential year. There are too many Methodist Anti-saloon people in Ohio who will always vote for McKinley to enable that organization to hurt us much however aggrieved its members may feel."[16] Individual drys privately criticized Harding for causing the bill to fail, but Huston was right—McKinley was too revered by Ohio Republicans.

5

There was an Ohio Man to keep in the White House in 1900, and a reputation for Harding to make. Harding was now in close cooperation with the man who held the reins in Ohio politics, Senator Marcus Alonzo Hanna.

Harding's new enthusiasm for Hanna was deliberate and conspicuous. The legislature had scarcely adjourned in April, 1900, when Harding made a move for Hanna's favor. He persuaded his fellow Thirteenth Republican Congressional district delegates to a Columbus convention to adopt a resolution proposing Hanna as an Ohio delegate-at-large to the national presidential nominating convention. It was an unnecessary thing to do because Hanna had been chairman of the Republican executive committee in putting McKinley over in 1896, and was in full control of the McKinley renomination movement in 1900. Nevertheless, the young Marionite took his delegation to Hanna's apartment in the Neil House in Columbus where, with reporters looking on, the proposal was made with Harding reading the resolution.[17] According to the *Ohio State Journal*, April 25, 1900, Hanna was "visibly touched," but made it clear that, though the gesture was appreciated, it was unnecessary. Thus Harding had to be content with being a member of the convention's resolution's committee, which drew up the usual Republican extravaganza.[18]

Back home, Harding made the *Star*, now being more widely quoted, a source of the most succulent praises of the "mighty Marcus" and his troupe of name performers. Modern political campaigns, according to the *Star*, had to produce power to be impressive, and this could be done only by headline personalities. "The public has become extremely exacting"—this from the September 15, 1900, issue. "Only the famous will draw. . . . The big guns are demanded. . . . The Hon. Jeremiah Skates, who has worked up a speech while waiting for clients, is not to fill an aching void in the rural audience. . . . But men who have faced the calcium light of fame will draw." And they *must* be able to spellbind. "We have always had the spellbinder," wrote editor Harding, October 8, 1900, "and if he does no more than stir up enthusiasm he will continue to come, with his hot air and his eloquence, and, after all, we could not well get along without him. We must be thrilled."

But Harding was doing more about spellbinding than writing about it. He could do a bit of it himself. The party leaders had found this out in his Columbus legislative outbursts. Hence, came the summons from state executive committee chairman and Hanna henchman Charles F. Dick to "hold yourself in readiness to meet any call that may be made on you." [19] And the calls came pouring in from every leader in his senatorial district. As one of them said, in making his request, "Experience has shown us that . . . a great deal of the campaign is made up of 'wind.'" Harding was billed "single and double," that is, with and without notables such as Governor Nash, Senator Foraker, and others. When it was all over, some of the large gains were ascribed to his credit. Friends wrote that he would be easily renominated for a second state senatorial term.[20] Best of all, came the report from Nash's secretary, Charles C. Lemert of Kenton, that "the Governor has the very highest opinion of your abilities and regards you as one of his most valued friends." [21]

So far over to Hanna did Harding go in 1900 that the resounding McKinley victory justified booming the President-maker for President himself in 1904. Two days after the election the *Star* headlined: "HANNA BOOM/ The Senator Is Seriously Discussed for/ The Presidency." The era of the Ohio Man seemed destined for a vigorous extension, and there was a place for Harding on the bandwagon.

The campaign of 1901 was even more important for Harding. This was the time when a Harding-Nash alliance bore fruits of mutual advantage. The Governor turned the full force of his office to the renomination of State Senator Harding, who, in turn, responded with a series of orations for the Governor's reelection. This was preliminary to Nash's use of Harding to act as floor leader for the new state tax-reform program that Nash proposed in order to demolish the drastic designs of Tom L. Johnson, mayor of Cleveland.

Evidently the entire gubernatorial staff worked to insure Harding's renomination in the Thirteenth State Congressional District. Lemert helped out, eventually reporting that he had "not the least fear" how the delegates would vote at the nominating convention. "Your friends there will see to it for you." Lemert's colleague in the governor's office,

Frederick N. Sinks, wrote, "Certainly all of us in this office hope to see you in the northwest corner of the State House next winter." [22]

The Nash push for Harding was matched at home by another district convention outburst, on June 17, of Marion county boosterism for its favorite son and for all things Republican, including Hanna, harmony, and prosperity. The resolutions in testimony thereof were, according to the *Star* of June 17, 1901, "a jingling poem" in praise of its great leaders. "Metaphorically they put the Republican party in the position of inserting a thumb in either armhole of its vest, throwing back its shoulders and inviting inspection." It was a new era for local Republican politics, the end of all factionalism. " 'Harmony' was written on the outer walls; 'harmony' was the shibboleth which admitted to the interior, where proceedings were set to consonant chords. Everything was in tune—a rythm [*sic*] of symphonic cadences. It was a day for letting bygones be bygones."

The chief gain for Nash in the Harding promotionalism was Senate leadership for the Nash tax-reform program. This had been announced at the June, 1901 Republican state convention which renominated the governor. This would abolish the state tax on real and personal property and make up the loss by moderate tax increases of income from the state excise taxes. Nash said that he hoped that the legislature would make his proposal a "must" in its 1902 session. It was offered as an allegedly saner program than the proposition by Democrat Tom Johnson of making possible the lowering of local taxes on farmers and city dwellers by requiring the assessment of railroad and public utility properties and franchises in the same proportion as farms and homes.[23]

Harding supported the Nash tax proposal with stump speeches and widely quoted *Star* editorials. They emphasized ridicule and name-calling instead of discussing the merits of, and making basic distinctions between, the Nash and Johnson programs. While characterizing the utterances of Johnson and the Democratic gubernatorial candidate, James Kilbourne, as "diversionary claptrap," the *Star* did its own diverting by playing up the free-silver past of the Democrats. They were a combination of "Simon-pure, Bryanistic, Silver-Billy-Smith, octopus-dreading Demmies." Johnson's tax ideas were invented to make people forget radical free-silverism. "In order to forget about the blunders of the past, think about something else," cracked the editor. Johnson and his seeming interest in the people were always good for a horse laugh. "Every time Tom Johnson gets his office full of applicants for positions he calls the janitor to open the windows." Besides, according to Harding, prosperity proved that Johnson was wrong.[24]

6

The sweeping state Republican victory on November 5, 1901, was but an incident in the pathway of Harding's march to local fame and party service. Before the winter of 1901–2 was over, the state was thrilled by the discovery of a new Buckeye Demosthenes. On three major, well-staged, and widely publicized occasions, and several minor ones, Harding stood before inspired audiences and aroused thousands of impressionable hearts with his spellbinding. These were: his nominating speech of January 14, 1902, in the Ohio Senate in behalf of the reelection of Senator Foraker; his memorial address of January 29 before the entire Ohio legislature in eulogy of the martyred McKinley; and his Lincoln Day oration at the annual meeting of the Ohio Republican League at Springfield. In the midst of this histrionic display came Governor Nash's announcement of his choice of Harding as his successor.

The speech for Foraker was triple-plated bombast—the kind that the "masses" were said to enjoy, and which "Fire-Alarm Joe" appreciated. Foraker himself had given his blessing to Harding. "I leave it all to your good taste and sense of propriety," [25] Foraker wrote on November 15, 1901. Whether Harding's performance was in good taste and proper, it was certainly super-laudation.[26] It ascribed the Republican victory of 1901 to Foraker's "all-conquering and unconquerable leadership." The whole nation was looking on because a Republican victory in Ohio meant "an unimpeded highway in the march of destiny." Ever since the world received the joyful tidings of Foraker's triumph "the great American hosts have been marching on, tramp, tramp, tramp, irresistible in the peaceful commercial conquest of the world, incomparable in rearing new standards of liberty, and spreading heaven-sent blessings of new-world freedom." In that election battle, "wherever the conflict was fiercest, wherever a line wavered, wherever courage and dash and leadership could turn the tide, there gleamed the defiant crest of the inspiring Foraker who charged on and on, until the day was grandly won." Describing the United State Senate as "the greatest political body in the whole world," and Ohio as most exacting in the requirements of her representation therein, Harding declared that Senator Foraker met every test. Greatest of his achievements had been to lead the party into overseas expansion. Referring to "Fire Alarm Joe's" spread-eagling on the Spanish-American War, he said, "The rescue of the union was heroic self preservation, but nothing less than the flaming torch of highest statesmanship could blaze the way of colonial expansion."

With the suggestion that Foraker had yet to reach the zenith of his career, that is, the Presidency of the United States, Harding closed with an exhortation to unite behind this "inspiring and always unfaltering Ohio leader, who lifts the head of a real statesman above the chorus of factional storm where, in the clear sunlight, he can look upon a million of Ohio voters who are proud to recommit him to the services of the nation."

Fifteen days later, on January 29, 1902, on the fifty-ninth anniversary of McKinley's birth, with memories of the Buffalo assassination still fresh in the public mind, Harding did it again.[27] This time he was the official spokesman for the entire state of Ohio. The occasion was a memorial joint session of the Ohio lawmakers in the hall of the House of Representatives in fulfillment of the joint resolution of the Seventy-fifth Ohio General Assembly. It was a solemn state ceremony with all government offices closed and all state officials and other dignitaries in attendance. The robed choir of St. Paul's Episcopal Church of Columbus sang some of McKinley's favorite hymns—"Nearer, My God to Thee," "Lead, Kindly Light," and "Jesus, Lover of My Soul."

Harding was at his soul-stirring best. He was "masterful," said the *Cincinnati Times Star*; the speech was a "masterpiece," said the *Ohio State Journal*. His words were extravagantly loving, tender, reverent. He spoke of the people's "enduring love" for the martyred President. "He was Ohio's offering of her most precious jewel to enrich a priceless tribute to New World progress. He grew because he was honest. If he had left no other heritage to a loving, worshipful republic his fame would still endure as the highest type of the honest politician." He pictured McKinley "as the inspired apostle of new world liberty and the emancipator of the oppressed far across the seas. . . . He was conservative: he ran not to rashness and unconcern." He stressed McKinley's humility; he was "a man of the people, believing in them and confiding in them." He emphasized the President's strong religious faith; "he walked unfalteringly on, in the light of conscience and faith in the omnipotent God." McKinley led the South back into the fellowship of the Union through participation in the war with Spain: "If in the crowning wreaths of immortality there is a separate bloom for every noble achievement, then the angel of the South will place on William McKinley's brow the richest garland that has blossomed there."

At Springfield, on February 12, with a host of Republican greats doing homage to the draped likenesses of the martyred Lincoln and McKinley, Harding was again at his best in shaping American history with a view toward the political. His theme being "The Newspaper in Politics," he declared that the press had made America "in one century the invincible conquerors of the commercial world."[28] The relation of the press to the Republican party was "closer than that of family ties." Alluding to the outbreak of the Spanish-American War, he told how "the American press echoed a nation's wrath when the cowardice of Spain led to the murder of American sailors who slept in the supposed security of guests in Havana harbor and spread the war cry for humanity and vengeance for so damnable a crime." And in the mighty conquests that followed, which the Democrats sought to relinquish, "the Republican press followed the flag whether the dear old constitution did or not, and had its reporters to herald every star of glory added there." When the war ended, "the Republican press preached American sovereignty, proclaimed the gospel of national expansion, glorified the purpose of the first of all republics, which has lighted the mission fires of progress and civilization in the benighted orient." And he closed, of course, by claiming approval of the Republican press by the "great spectral throng of heroes of the nation," including the "first of all patriots, George Washington. . . . The immortal emancipator, Abraham Lincoln. . . . And the noble and beloved William McKinley."

7

Suddenly, on January 28, 1902, the day before the McKinley eulogy, an event occurred which made Harding, for a while, the number one Ohio gubernatorial contender. In the evening of the same day, the Central Ohio Paper Company entertained the Associated Ohio Dailies with a dinner at the Columbus Club. Harding was toastmaster and Governor Nash was the main speaker. Harding introduced the Governor in very glowing terms: "No governor the state has ever had has been more honest, more faithful, more completely consecrated to his work than Governor George K. Nash." When the Governor rose, he replied by remarking, humorously, "If I had not been trained in cheek as a newspaper man in my early days, I should blush on account of this tribute from my friend, who is also regarded as a probable future governor of Ohio." At this point, the papers reported, the Governor was interrupted by the enthusiastic clapping of hands which was long and continued and accompanied by the waving of napkins by the ladies. The *Columbus Citizen* of January 29 could not refrain from the comment that such a testimonial for Forakerite Harding was most unusual coming for Hannaite Nash.

Remarks such as these have a way of being misquoted, with resulting public check-ups for accuracy. In the process Harding suffered no losses. Some papers reported Nash as saying that Harding would be his successor. Public "correction" of this came the next day when reporters confronted both Nash and Harding as they left the Governor's office after a conference. One reporter facetiously called Harding "Governor." The embarrassed Senator modestly replied that Governor Nash had been joking, whereupon the Governor replied, "Whether I was joking or not and whether or not I really said what they say I did, I am perfectly willing to stand for it." [29]

8

In the meantime, Harding "delivered" the Nash program. His first step was to make himself leader of the Ohio Senate. He did this quite openly in the name of party unity and the senate's integrity. He chose to spike, at the outset, the usual newspaper gossip accompanying the organization of the legislature that called the maneuvering a display of factionalism between Hannaites and Forakerites. "The legislature," Harding announced in the *Star*, on December 7, 1901, "ought to be and is something more than an assembly of 142 dummies in a Punch and Judy show." He rebuked his fellow journalists with the wry remark that "political writers have their salaries to earn in the dull season between elections and the holidays." If any petty, job-seeking Forakerite thought he could outmaneuver Hanna, he had an awakening coming. If any "fool friends" of Hanna thought they could do the same with Foraker, they were "due for a jolting when they learn the truth." He told the *Dispatch*, on December 11, 1901, that the members of the legislature "have the good sense and requisite party interest at heart to organize acceptably to themselves, and to the great, triumphant party of Ohio." He warned that "if anybody gets under the wheels as the procession moves on the fault will probably be his own."

The job was secretly and firmly done. With Harding presiding, a series of meetings of Republican senators-elect was held early in December. It was announced in the press that a majority of them had agreed on Harding to preside over their party caucus on January 4, 1902 for the naming of officers, committee chairmen, and committee assignments. The meeting was held as scheduled, Harding was made chairman of the Committee on Committees, and he immediately asked senators to show their preferences.[30]

Harding's show of openness concealed the fact that his control had been prearranged in December, and patronage assurances given. As Senator George H. Chamberlain of Elyria wrote to Harding on December 11, "I fully agree with you that there ought to be no difficulty in arranging the patronage between ourselves. I am pleased to know the view you take of the supposed factional war between Senators Foraker and Hanna. I am clearly of the opinion that the legislature ought not to be organized in the interest of any one or two men and if our senators cannot agree between themselves, it seems to me it would be a good plan to select officers who are friendly to both. A factional war at this time would be as disastrous as it would be idiotic." Other letters to similar effect were received from state senators F. B. Archer of Bellaire, and D. H. Moore of Athens. There was no sense, wrote Archer, for any of them being "let out in the cold and the prerequisites of office handled by outsiders." He listed nine senators who were "all right." Archer was sure they could "muster up 11 or 12 votes absolutely certain, not counting Hamilton County, which I understand is O. K." [31]

The details left little to be desired as to what patronage control meant. Senator Moore, who, as the senate's only banker, wanted the chairmanship of the finance committee—and got it—also told Harding that he wanted "one cloak room man or assistant doorkeeper and one of the 5 and 6 sergeants at arms." He added, "You can surely arrange to have enough to go around." At another time he suggested, "I hope we can arrange for enough of these positions to give each of us two. Some of the Senators would probably prefer one or two pages rather than the other positions." [32]

Mark Hanna left no doubt about what he wanted. On November 20, 1901, he wrote Harding that, since Cleveland had no Republican senators in the legislature, he would like to have W. B. Uhl reelected clerk of the senate; "I would personally appreciate it if you would see your way clear to support him." Since Uhl did not get this job and Harding's personal friend, F. E. Scobey of Piqua did, it is not clear what Hanna meant when he wrote Harding on November 23 that he appreciated very much "your willingness to oblige me in the matter." [33]

Upon these foundations Harding and his machine proceeded to do Governor Nash's will. In a message to the legislature on January 6, 1902, the Governor proceeded to lay down the details of his tax program.[34] In the days that followed Harding was very much in evidence in helping the Nash bills over the legislative hurdles. When Senator Nicholas Longworth of Cincinnati was having difficulty getting his committee to report the bills out, Nash sent a hurry-up message to the hesitating senate Republicans. Sensing Republican dissension, Democratic Senator William E. Decker of Paulding suddenly moved that Longworth's committee be relieved of further consideration of the bill. That was the signal for Republican floor leader Harding to move the tabling of the Decker proposal. The Harding motion carried by a strict party vote, and, before the day was over, Longworth had prodded his committee into reporting out the Nash measure.[35]

When the first of the Nash bills finally came up in the senate on April 10 for a showdown vote, Harding was at his best in not only outsmarting the Democrats in debate but in reminding the Republicans of the virtues of party loyalty. The Democratic substitute for the Nash bills was a Tom Johnson measure of the single-tax variety, taxing all public utilities franchises and requiring the assessing of their properties for tax purposes at 60 per cent of their true value. This was considered to be a radical measure, and Harding aimed to show that the Democrats were not really sincere in offering it. He therefore quoted the Democratic platform to the effect that acceptance of free railroad passes by a man in public office was just cause for his removal from office. He then asked Senator Decker if he had accepted such favors from the railroads. Decker admitted that he had. "Then I submit," said Harding, "that the gentleman from Paulding is not sincere." For the benefit of Republicans, Harding, who was himself a chronic railroad-pass receiver, then engaged in a bit of history to show

how, throughout history, Republicans could always be trusted to be true to their pledges, which, of course, did not include opposition to receiving free railroad passes. Moreover, he declared that "those who feared that a future legislature might increase the tax upon corporations to the point of gross injustice, have no faith in popular government." Not only that, but the measure would relieve the people of a tax burden of over $3 million. Thus was the Nash program saved.[36]

9

The greatest test of Harding's loyalty to Nash came in the summer and fall of 1902 when the Governor undertook to prepare a municipal code bill, forced by the Ohio Supreme Court's declaration that all Ohio "ripper" legislation was unconstitutional. On June 26 that august body had nullified the Cleveland city charter of 1891 and the Toledo Police Board Act of 1902 on the grounds that they were special legislation forbidden by the Ohio constitution.[37] In effect, this outlawed all Ohio city governments. The Governor therefore called a special session of the legislature to draw up a new code for the cities.

Governor Nash believed that it was his responsibility to draft a municipal code for the legislature to consider. The drafting was done by Senator Longworth and attorney Wade Ellis of Cincinnati, who framed a code modeled after the government of Cincinnati. As usual, it was necessary to remain true to Boss Cox. The measure was called the "board plan" because the executive departments were elected by the people instead of being appointed, as in Cleveland, under the "federal plan." Politicians favored the "board plan" because it fitted well into ward politics by enabling more wards to support more candidates.[38]

As senate floor leader and Nash-sponsored aspirant for governor, Harding favored the Nash code. It never for a moment occurred to him to revive the learned and progressive Pugh-Kibler bill that he had introduced in 1900. Harding wanted the Nash code, even before he saw it. It was another of those "party-line" measures. All rival plans and suggestions, including "home rule" for cities as provided by Progressives in the future amendment to the Ohio constitution, were sidetracked as politically inspired. A plan espoused by the State Board of Commerce he called "worthy of Democratic support." [39] On July 17 Harding wrote in the Star, "The governor is laboring conscientiously to give the legislature something tangible to work upon, while his critics are knocking, knocking, knocking without giving intelligible advice. Almost anybody can use a hammer and make a noise." Harding saw the code late in July when Longworth showed it to him and the Governor. "I should like very much to have you see what we have done," wrote Longworth, "and to have your advice and assistance in the matter." [40] Harding's support was then more vigorous than ever. "Governor Nash," he wrote in the *Star* on August 6, "is the man who is willing to assume responsibility for the code, and when he does it may be put down as a creditable piece of legislation, suitable for future monumental purposes." When at last the code was published, he wrote, "The Governor's code is not the frightful document a great many were led to believe a few weeks ago. Those who felt secure in the governor's well-known good sense were amply justified in their faith." In neither of these pronouncements did Harding analyze the merits of the code's provisions.[41]

During the senate debate on the Nash Code, floor leader Harding directed the repulse of Democratic attacks. At the very outset he announced that "the governor's code will be passed substantially as introduced." When the Democrats tried to introduce "irrelevant" bills, he and Longworth served notice on the "lobbying gang that nothing will be considered here save the subjects we were called to act upon." When the Democrats sought to have the code considered in joint committee sessions of both houses, Harding declared indignantly that the proposal was "the most impractical suggestion ever made on the floor of the chamber." [42]

Harding's contributions to the discussion of the merits of the Nash measure were limited. On September 16, according to the *State Journal*, the discussion degenerated into a squabble over who was the worse boss, Cox with the Cincinnati "board plan," or Tom L. Johnson with the Cleveland "federal plan." Harding took the side of Cox because the "board plan" made possible "a conference of ideas," *i.e.*, it was less dictatorial. Anyhow, he was for bosses because "I should rather have the advice of a political boss upon this subject than all of the theorists in the world." The only criticisms he had of the Nash plan were: (1) the terms should be made more flexible so that small cities could have one-member boards, and (2) the civil service provision should be made more meaningful than the mere provision that advancement should be by promotion.[43]

An unusual Harding contribution to the code debate was made with respect to municipal control of the franchises (charters) of public utilities. In this, Harding and Nash succumbed to the pressure of the utilities' lobby for less stringent control. The Nash proposal was to limit the terms of franchises to twenty-five years. This was called unfair to corporations who were said to be serving the big cities so well, and risking so much in modernizing streetcar and electric power service. Mark Hanna was said to be in favor of perpetual franchises, and Cincinnatians wanted a fifty-year one.[44]

Harding was at first opposed to perpetual franchises, and support from Nash made him bold. When Republican members began to quail under the Hanna-Cox influence, Harding spoke with vigorous condemnation of his colleagues' cowardice. Lobbyists suggested that, since the problem was so technical, its consideration be postponed to permit a more careful study of the merits of the question. Harding objected, saying, "The franchise question is fairly before us and it would be cowardly to dodge it." He admitted that there had appeared "some disposition to fight shy of it," but a good deal of "earnest discussion had developed an emphatic sentiment in favor of facing the question now." The legislature, he said could "do no better work than to incorporate franchise legislation in the code."[45]

Much applause came to Harding for his courageous stand. H. E. Owen of the Marion Y.M.C.A. wrote, "It pleased me very much to read the newspaper reports which credit you with taking such an outspoken stand in regard to the franchise matter. I believe the people are more interested in that question than any other one question covered by the proposed New Code."[46] On September 19 the *Columbus Dispatch* gave an entire editorial to Harding's efforts. "If the rebuke which the distinguished senator from Marion gave his weak-kneed brethren does not fall on ears too deaf and minds too small, the franchise section of the proposed municipal code will not be slighted nor omitted. . . . It was plain unvarnished language. . . . It means that one senator . . . if he means what he says, is willing to handle the franchise question without gloves, as an independent representative of the people, regardless of party affiliation or the dictates of party leaders with the private interests."

It did not mean any such thing. Harding quailed, as did Nash, and the utilities' lobbyists had their way. Harding changed his mind over the weekend of September 19–20, on the occasion of the Fall Festival in Cincinnati, which the Ohio senators attended en masse as guests of the Big Four Railroad and the Cincinnati Traction Company.

The affair reeked with the atmosphere of corporate hospitality to highly impressionable senators. The Big Four "Senatorial Special" was remarkable. It was a very heavy train, but, notwithstanding this, the run from Columbus to Dayton was "reeled off in the exceptional time of a mile a minute." A special joint session of the legislature was held on board, and Harding bespoke the members' gratitude, "thanking the Big Four company and its agent, Joe Moses, for the courtesy of the company in furnishing the special train." At the Cincinnati depot the party was met by Benson Foraker, son of the senator and vice-president of the Cincinnati Traction Company. The legislators were escorted to a special trolley and conducted on a two-hour tour of the city. As the *Columbus Citizen* remarked, "It was carefully pointed out to each member of the assembly that the company had spent fortunes the past two years in improving the tracks and in betterments." It should also be added, if we may believe the *Dispatch*, that on the trip several members got to discussing next year's gubernatorial campaign. Apparently, most of the talk favored Harding: "State Senator Harding, they say, possesses the qualities of leadership and statesmanship to make him the ideal compromise candidate." [47]

There was other pressure on Harding concerning the franchise question. It came from Senator Hanna, and was entirely political. It suggested dropping the whole discussion because the Democrats would make a political issue out of it. On September 3, Harding had written to the Ohio senator asking for his opinion. On September 8, Hanna replied, showing his support of perpetual franchises but advising dropping the discussion so as to foil the Democrats. As Hanna wrote, "The proposition then came to me to know if I would favor removing the limit of time on franchises with the ten year renewal of contract." (That was the technical way of defining a perpetual franchise—one with no time limit and subject to a council or popular vote every ten years on whether to continue it). "I thought," wrote Hanna, "that this might cover the situation and help our Cincinnati friends out of their dilemma, but, as the opposition party is disposed to make political capital out of it, saying that I am seeking perpetual franchises, I have decided to do nothing more about it." [48]

Harding thus had two problems on his mind in regard to franchises: (1) was it true that public utilities and their technical difficulties would be better understood by future study? (2) would it be best to protect the Republican party by keeping the question out of politics? Harding answered both these questions in the affirmative.

It was hardly a coincidence then that, back in Columbus on September 24, 1902, floor leader Harding arose to offer a joint resolution, providing for the governor to appoint a bipartisan commission to investigate the question of franchise grants to public utilities and to report to the next legislature. Senator Harding preceded his proposal with a humble confession that he had been wrong. His own convictions had been against postponement. "I have said and am still of the opinion that the general assembly ought to take a step forward in franchise legislation at this time." However, "if it is in order to make a confession, I will say that I have devoted no inconsiderable time to studying this matter, and I will admit that I find I am not big enough to meet it." Describing his views on taxation of public utilities and limited terms for their franchises, he described how variable were the practices in a few other states he had examined, and his own need for further information. Therefore, he concluded, "In view of the fact that there is a public clamor for an early adjournment, and a demand that we make no attempt to solve the franchise question, I will have to support the substitute." The *Dispatch* reported Harding's explanation a bit more bluntly: "Investigation of the subject proved it to be such a stupendous question, with vested interests here and there endangered, that a postponement of the matter seemed to be the proper course to pursue." [49] Thus it was that the franchise aspect of the Nash code was omitted and left to future study.

There was much scorn and ridicule of Harding for his alleged truckling to the utilities. The *Columbus Citizen* of September 24 headlined:

BOSS HANNA'S BANDWAGON

Boarded by Entire Aggregation of Republican Senators

The *Citizen* laughed at "the pirouting [*sic*] of Senators Harding, Godfrey and others who tramped on each others toes to tell the senate how they had changed their minds." Harding's speech was called mock heroics. After delivering it, "he sat down much relieved. He had gone on record." Rather cruelly the *Citizen* went on to say that Harding used the occasion to "grandstand" for the governorship. He was quoted as saying to a reporter, "I have been getting the worst of it all along, be as easy as you can with me." The *Dispatch*, too, was cruel: "What a spectacle is this? . . . Oh, there's politics in the code." [50]

Harding's greatest contribution to the victory of the Nash Code came in the conference committee after the senate had passed the Nash version, but the house had amended the "board plan" out of it. This so alarmed the Governor that he went to Harding, saying, "I am greatly worried by what I hear of the condition of affairs in the Conference Committee." The Code Bill, as passed by the senate "is much more satisfactory then the one which has been passed by the house." The boards, Harding said, had to be restored, and the strong civil-service provisions of the house bill "are a very grave mistake. . . . A fearful blunder is about to be made." Therefore, wrote Nash, "I wish you would show this letter to the Senate members of the Conference Committee. They should stand together because they are right and do everything they can to bring the House Members to them." [51]

And so it came to pass that, on October 21, the house surrendered, and the Nash Municipal Code Bill with its "board plan" was adopted. Again Boss Cox had been placated. Two weeks later, in the congressional election, the Republicans, with Harding stumping as usual, won another smashing victory. It was scored by the Republican leaders as a vindication of Nash, the legislature, and Warren Harding. In the light of increased Republican pluralities, Longworth wrote to Harding, "all of which is a compliment to those men who shaped the policy of the majority in the last legislature." [52] From Lewis C. Laylin, reelected secretary of state, came the following: "I heartily congratulate you as a member of the seventy-fifth General Assembly for the splendid endorsement given by the people of the excellent work of the general assembly at its regular and extraordinary sessions. Your wise counsel and leadership are well known and appreciated by the people of the state." [53]

Not so did the Democrats react. It was the triumph of bossism and Republican party hypocrites. On the day following the adoption of the Nash Municipal Code bill, the *Columbus Citizen* parodied,

> Praise Cox, from whom all blessings flow,
> Praise him, you people of Ohio,
> Praise Hanna, Nash and all the hosts,
> But praise George B. Cox the most.

Harding had come full circle. He who had once fought the bosses in the name of party unity was now in line to become the darling of the bosses in the name of party unity. He was showing his "reliability."

CHAPTER EIGHT

The Mirage of Ohio Republican Unity,

1903–1910

"There isn't any need to assassinate anybody." : : : Harding in *"Marion Daily Star," September 5, 1906*

ᏁᏔ Harding early established the reputation of being the Ohio Republican party's mirage-maker. While his party and its bosses floundered, quarreled, and factionalized, he was the one who said it was not so. While he himself was buffeted by bosses and denied the governorship he so much desired, he never, for an instant—publically, at least—lost his poise and eloquence. When, in campaign appearances, it was necessary for the Republican party to be seen in public, Harding could gloss over the inner, jangling discord with exhibitions of that personality and oratory which gave the appearance of harmony, efficiency, firmness, and dignity.

Harding had been in public relations for a long time. The *Marion Star* had contributed daily to the creating of over-all social and civic images. As the years went by, there emerged the images of a boosterized Marion, a militant and protective-tariff Americanism, and the ideal of harmony in the labor class founded on the right to work. The glorification of the Spanish-American War and its imperialistic sequel as a great humanitarian crusade was a newspaperman's masterpiece of image-making. His floor leadership of the state legislators in unified-party support of the Nash program was a consummate job of glossing over contradictions. He had concealed his own ideas on municipal home rule and public utility control for the good of party unity. And so it was "party unity forever," a mirage that was required to preserve the existence of the two-party system.

The Ohio Republican party was sick in 1903, and neither Harding nor any other earthly power could make it well. It was sick because its nominal leader, William McKinley, was dead, and two Ohio men and their followers were fighting for the crown—Senators Mark Hanna and Joseph B. Foraker. Harding was able to soothe this rivalry in the halls of Ohio's legislature, but he had no ability to touch with the slightest effect the desire of these two Ohio senators to be President of the United States. The desires of Foraker and Hanna were imperious and conflicting, and the Republican party split wide open as its members chose one or the other for their hero.

Conflict lurked behind any party problem. In 1903 the chief problem was whether or not Ohio Republicans should endorse President Roosevelt for reelection in 1904. Foraker said yes, because that would enable him to seek to be Roosevelt's successor in 1908. Hanna said no, because he had his own eyes on the White House. In the maneuvering, Foraker won out as the 1903 state convention endorsed Roosevelt for the Presidency and Hanna for reelection to the Senate. This meant no Presidency for Hanna, and, therefore, in the minds of vengeful Hannaites, no Presidency for Foraker and, after Hanna's unexpected death early in 1904, no senatorship either. And so a feud was deepened, and the future of the Republican party was prepared for the sacrifice.

How vengeful Hanna felt toward Foraker was revealed in one of the last letters the mighty Marcus wrote before his death. It was a letter to Governor Myron Herrick, written from Washington, January 30, 1904, outlining plans (1) to keep Foraker from "poisoning" Roosevelt concerning certain Ohio appointments, and (2) to win the President away from Foraker by controlling, in favor of Roosevelt's renomination, the Ohio Republican selection of delegates to the national Presidential nominating convention. This is how the angry Hanna wrote:

> On my return to W. I found that Foraker had got the Prest well poisoned and I have expected he would succeed in making a row by sending in those P. O. appointments over my head which would certainly call for a contest to know who controlled the situation in Ohio. I have had no opportunity to see the Prest so am letting things drift. Meanwhile we must organize our full strength and choose the Roosevelt delegates from among our friends.[1]

2

In the larger field of Ohio Republican politics Harding was not as prominent as he had been as senate floor leader for Nash's tax program. Nash could talk up Harding for governor, but he could not produce the goods. That result lay in the decrees of power higher than those wielded by a mere governor. For such a decision it took United States Senators with presidential prospects and patronage command.

This was the golden age of bossism in Ohio Republican politics, and the bosses' names were Hanna and Foraker. In unholy alliance with them was another dictator, George B. Cox, who had built up a regional overlordship of Hamilton county and its capital, Cincinnati. To be sure, this tyrannical trio was all but to destroy the Ohio Republican party in the first decade of the twentieth century, but this was not yet apparent to anyone in 1903, least of all to Warren Harding. All that the bosses cared for about Harding, in 1903, was to employ, for their own ends, his talent for spellbinding and his obsession for party unity. And all that Harding cared about was to oblige them.

Thus, in 1903, the Harding gubernatorial boom of 1902 became a boomlet in the hands of little people. It came from men who did not count, from brother Elks like Henry M. Stowe, from brother editors, from local enthusiasts who bragged, like W. Clay Huston of Belle-fontaine, about "that future which your friends have or think they have, mapped out for you." It was a "Hurrah-for-Harding" call from the backwoods. "Go in to win, old man," it said. "You are a cinch . . . a cracker jack." It liked his "ginger and git," his "heroic mold," his "nerve to beard the lion in his den." There were those who heard him match Lincoln Day metaphors at Springfield with his rivals, including the Hanna favorite, Myron T. Herrick, and wrote, "You skinned 'em a block." One, Frank E. Smiley, went so far as to make the familiar Ohio boast that Harding's election to the governorship would be his "second step toward the threshold of the White House." This was the kind of people who still believed in the David-and-Goliath myth.[2]

It was different when he consulted the top Republican bosses, Foraker and Hanna. Harding wrote to Foraker for encouragement on the governorship, and got the curt telegraphic reply, "Do not feel able to give advice." He visited Hanna in Washington and was given the ambiguous assurance that the field was "an open one." It was small consolation to hear from the once mighty Nash that "while I do not wish to mix up in the governorship matter, I have never hesitated to tell my friends how loyal you have been to me, and how implicitly I have relied upon you for important work in the General Assembly."[3]

All of this Harding knew, and he ventured forth his own candidacy in such a tentative way that he was ridiculed as a "quasi-candidate."

His announcement of January 16, 1903 accepted the "seemingly authoritative" statements of Hanna and Foraker that the field was still open. He mentioned these mighty ones by name, avowed their great eminence in national affairs, and vowed unfailing loyalty to their party leadership, closing with the pious assertion that the days of factionalism were over. "The time has come when we need be neither Greeks nor Trojans, but all Republicans." Yet just before the state nominating convention met, he publicly confessed, in the *Star*, April 20, "The dominance of Senator Hanna was recognized before any candidate entered the field, and it is fair to several of the men named in connection with the governorship to have it said that they made public their aspirations only after being assured that Senator Hanna had no preference and would ask for no particular nomination." And when, a few days later, Hanna did show his preferences, and did indeed put over Myron Herrick as the party nominee, James M. Faulkner, astute analyst of the *Cincinnati Enquirer*, good-naturedly jibed Harding, asking for a copy of the *Star's* comments on the outcome. "I want to hear," wrote Faulkner, "about the Greeks and Trojans which exist despite your declaration to the contrary some months ago." [4]

Hence it was that, well before the June, 1903 Republican gubernatorial nomination, it was decided that Myron T. Herrick, wealthy Cleveland banker, perennial underwriter of Republican debts, long a servant of the GOP in city council, state, and national conventions, and now Ohio's member of the Republican national committee, would be the party's standard-bearer against the expected Democratic nominee, Tom L. Johnson. The decision had really been made when Boss Cox of Cincinnati announced, on April 14, that he was casting his massive influence for Herrick. It was better for business and prosperity, Cox said, to have a solid businessman like Herrick for governor than a person like Harding who was not well enough known in business circles.[5]

In all of this power-politicking Harding meekly and publicly acquiesced. There might be some "mild opposition" as a matter of "political principle," he wrote in the *Star*, April 20, "but we are accustomed to it in practice, and complaint would come in ill grace." After all, he confessed, "any aspirant would rejoice to have the avowed support of Senator Hanna and George B. Cox. Now that Colonel Herrick is so fortunately possessed, it is in perfect order to doff hats to the coming leader from Cleveland." Power was the thing, not principles. If this sounds satirical, consider the rest of Harding's editorial. It was only fair to Hanna, wrote Harding, because the Senator was up for reelection by the next legislature, and Ohioans owed such a great national leader this act of confidence:

> This is Senator Hanna's year. There is not a Republican in all the state to dispute his title in the re-election, there are very few Republicans who are not really enthusiastic about it. He is more than a great Ohio leader. He is the head of the national Republican organization. This makes his re-election by the next general assembly of greater importance than the Governorship, and the unfortunate conditions attending his first election have put the party in power in Ohio in the humor to make Senator Hanna's wish little less than party law this year. Had he at any time declared Colonel Herrick's candidacy essential to his re-election, or the candidacy of any other aspirant, it would have assured a nomination this year. The alliance with Mr. Cox's powerful organization simply strengthens the situation and removes every possibility of doubt.

In 1920 Harding joked about it, telling a *Chicago Tribune* reporter that when "Hanna got Cox to support Herrick's friends, friends asked me what that meant. I said 'It means I'm through.'" [6]

As for the lieutenant-governorship nomination, which Harding got, this too was determined by the bosses, with Cox doing the dictating. Harding himself said so. As he related it in this same *Chicago Tribune* interview, "Then Hanna and George Cox talked me over for lieutenant-governor on the ticket with Herrick. Cox had told Hanna that I was a good companion, but Hanna wanted an old soldier on the ticket. He finally told Hanna as much when I went to see him and frankly asked him what his intentions were. Then, too, Hanna knew of the report that Roosevelt was supposed to want Herrick for vice president, and that would have opened up the governorship to me, which was something Hanna did not want to have happen." [7]

How much Harding was influenced to take the lieutenant-governorship nomination by the possibility of gaining the governorship via the back door cannot be said. There were rumors that Herrick would take the vice-presidency, if Roosevelt wanted him to. There was also the unmentionable possibility of Hanna's death—his health was not good—and the elevation of the ambitious Herrick to the vacant senatorship. If such thoughts occurred to Harding or anybody else, they could scarcely realize that the very fact of Hanna's death would steel the Hannaites against the Harding succession to the governorship because of their belief that he was a Forakerite at heart, which he was.

As good a reason as any for Harding being on the ticket with Herrick in 1903 was the sheer ballyhoo of it. This was the campaign of the four H's—Hanna, Herrick, Harding, and Harmony. One could always add "and Prosperity," or "and Progress," though the Democrats tried to spoil it with "and Cox," or such needling as "What about Foraker?"

But, if the truth be frankly said, it was the "Demosthenes factor" that did the most good in the campaigning. Harding simply stole the show. It was unprecedented for the second man on the ticket to do such a thing. "It has been a long time since the aspirant for second place has been so well equipped for the work. . . . He is one of the best stumpers in the state." So said the *Ohio State Journal*, June 6, 1903. After a blazing rally in Cincinnati's Music Hall on October 29, Mayor Julius Fleischman was so carried away that he called Harding's speech "the best ever heard on the subject of Republicanism." When the vote count showed one of the biggest Cincinnati majorities in history for the Republican ticket, the mayor telegraphed Harding, "My hearty congratulations—see what your speech did in Hamilton county." Even Hanna offered his plaudits, "I know that a large share of credit is due you, and am sure that the people recognize it." [8]

Everywhere he spoke, the magic of Harding's eloquence, so masterfully subordinated to the party he served and the leaders he praised, endeared him to Republican hearts. "A week on the Republican rostrum," said the *Columbus Dispatch*, October 7, "has given him the well earned reputation of being one of the most eloquent as well as one of the most pungent speakers in the State." From Sandusky came the *Register*'s report, September 30, that Senator Harding's address was a "marvel of eloquence." The *Toledo Blade*, October 14, was extravagant in its praise. "Senator Harding is convincing. . . . Cool, deliberate, suave in manner, and with a splendid vocabulary, he makes a delightful speech. His remarks stamp him as a thorough student of public affairs and a deep thinker. . . . His sincerity is at once evident. . . . His speech making in the present campaign has already placed him in the front rank in the state with a long array of notable public speakers and he suffers none by comparison." "Seems to us here," wrote S. A. McNeil of Richmond, "that you are shouldering the heavy part of the State campaign." [9] Invariably the Democrats taunted the Republicans with Harding's superiority over the rest of the stumpers. "Senator Harding's witty sallies and eloquence aroused the only real enthusiasm of the evening." So commented the Sandusky *Evening Star*, September 30, adding irreverently, "Senator Hanna's speech was nothing unusual."

When he came to an issue he could not understand, Harding slaughtered it with eloquent misinterpretation. Harding twisted entirely out of shape Johnson's program of making nominal the tax on farm land and residential property by shifting the burden to corporations and utilities via the equalization of property valuations and assessments. He did so by showing that Johnson believed in the Henry George theory of the single tax on land. The 1903 Johnson tax program was not that radical, but Harding's twist made it appear that it was. That is why farmers and homeowners blanched with fear when Harding mentioned Johnson and his "single tax on land." [10] They saw *all* the tax on *their* land, whereas, if the theory of the single tax on land were to prevail the tax would be vastly more on the land value, or rent value, of the big commercial and industrial holdings than on the tiny holdings of individuals.

But the greatest exaggeration of all was that the main issues were prosperity—and the United States supremacy based thereon—that only Republicans could produce. "The one real issue, encompassing all others," he blandly declared at the party opening at Chillicothe on September 19, "is the permanence of progress and prosperity. Amid such gratifying conditions in Ohio, amid incomparable advancement and achievement which have made us the first of industrial, commercial, financial and civilizing powers of the world; amid a manifest betterment of the commonwealth, and the entrenchment of all the essentials of American life, the people of Ohio will hesitate to be led astray by a threatening and destroying Democracy. Let us go ahead with the leadership of Herrick and Hanna." [11] Not even Hanna, who also spoke, could bait the Democrats more convincingly.

It was ridicule and counterridicule, with a belly laugh thrown in for good measure, that sent Republicans home from Harding rallies with stars in their eyes. When Democratic senatorial candidate John H. Clarke jibed at Hanna as a boss who wanted to look like the Biblical Joshua, Harding turned the taunt to his own advantage. "I remember," quipped Harding, "the Lord put Joshua at the head of the children of Israel and said, 'No man shall prevail against thee all the days of thy life.' The Lord delivered into Joshua's hands the Hittites, Jebusites,

Nibites, etc., and into Hanna's hands shall be delivered the Jonesites, Johnsonites, Bryanites, Monnettites, and, if that's not enough, I'll include the get-tights." [12]

Harding was especially effective in Cincinnati. He told his conservative, Cox-led listeners what proud Cincinnatians liked to hear. He recalled how the Nash code had first sought to cut the franchise limit from fifty to twenty-five years, but was revised when the legislators observed the "magnificent modernization" of the Queen City's transportation system, made possible by capital under the fifty-year franchise. "We Republicans voted that way, not through corruptive influence, not under the party lash, but because we know the people of Ohio, with whom common honesty is not a forgotten virtue, would approve our action." It was the old, old ruse of avoiding issues with the bunkum of seeming morality. As if that were not enough, he went on into "prosperity talk." In this election, he said, there were three issues, "the issue real, the issue paramount and the issue mountebank." The "issue real" was the "prosperity that is marked by the clink of the dollars in the counting room, by the rush of business everywhere and the rumbling of railroad trains that are laden with the commerce of the world." The "issue paramount" was that "to Senator Hanna, more than any man living, we owe the change from the wails of distress of 1896 to the prosperity of the present time." The "issue mountebank" was Johnsonism and the preposterous idea that anyone should want a change from prosperity to a single tax. To this the crowd shouted, "We don't. We don't." [13]

It was an easy victory for Ohio Republicans in 1903. The mirage of Hanna, Herrick, Harding, and Harmony won the day. Perhaps it was the figure of Hanna that did the most, with an assist from Cox, prosperity, and the feared radicalism of Tom Johnson. But, if the victory was mostly Hanna's, it would not endure. The mighty Marcus died on February 15, 1904, and the Ohio Republicans became more divided than ever.

3

Test was following upon test for Harding's loyalty to a stricken party. Always he survived as the great concealer of the terrible truth. Hanna's death produced the next such test.

If the Ohio Republican party had been united in 1904, Harding would have become governor of the Buckeye state. The man who wanted most to make way for Harding, in order to wear the fallen Hanna's senatorial toga, was Governor Herrick. If the legislature had chosen Herrick for the senatorship, Lieutenant-Governor Harding would have succeeded to the governorship. But it was not to be. The stunned Republican legislators, in a frenzy of grief and fear of Forakerism, refused to allow Herrick to create a vacancy for Harding. As C. C. Dewstoe, Cleveland postmaster and Hanna appointee, wrote Congressman Theodore E. Burton on February 17, 1904, "The legislature will not permit Herrick to leave the Governorship." [14]

Herrick, in his letterbooks, has left full testimony of this great factional and anti-Harding decision. To James R. Garfield, on February 24, he wrote, "I could not stand before the country in the light of having apparently disrupted and abandoned the organization which Senator Hanna had been so long building, and put it in the hands of his chief enemy." [15] To Cox, he wrote, "I think it is not an exaggeration to say that had we engaged in party strife, creating a new faction, it might have later on landed the State in the Democratic column." [16] "It was a great sacrifice," he told H. H. Kohlsaat, "I felt consolation at having at least served my party and our friends and especially my dead friend." [17]

Cox also had his fears of what the Harding succession to the governorship would do to his favorite scheme of getting the Ohio legislature to award the old canal lands to the interurban interests for a right of way. As Dewstoe wrote to Burton on February 17, concerning the succession to Hanna, "Cox is likely to be the master of it. He is going to hold all he can control to influence the passage of the canal bill, in which he is vitally interested." [18] Herrick confirmed this sentiment. "It would have raised havoc with pending legislation," he wrote R. B. Bokom of Chicago on March 3, 1904, "and created a new faction in the party." [19]

How touchy the leaderless Hannaites were about preserving their patronage rights against the hated Foraker was revealed when President Roosevelt started to appoint Forakerites to office without waiting for Hanna's successor in the Senate, Charles R. Dick, to get to Washington. On March 10 Governor Herrick wrote President Roosevelt in sharp rebuke for this. "You perhaps are not aware," said the Governor, "of the far reaching and unfortunate effect of this decision upon Senator Hanna's friends in this State." These friends have "been coming to my office in great numbers in the last few days [and] feel that it is your intention to wholly ignore the element which is dominant in this State." Herrick, therefore, included a copy of Hanna's last letter "which plainly indicates that it was his intention to have his friends give you their earnest support in Ohio." [20] This was Hanna's letter of January 30, previously quoted, in which he described his plans to deliver Ohio to Roosevelt's renomination, and in which he said that Foraker was "poisoning" the President's mind.

How Harding, as governor, would have upset the applecart of the Hanna organization patronage was alleged in a Columbus dispatch to the *Cleveland Leader* on February 18, "The new Governor might be seized with an uncontrollable desire to do something, and when he got through doing it, all that would be left of the Hanna organization could be put in one of the squirrel holes of the State House yard. Then, too, various measures pending in the Legislature have practically been settled by the organization, but if Mr. Harding got into the Governor's office they might be knocked out." Some of the political plums involved were listed: two oil inspectorships, decided on by Hanna for Frank Baird of Toledo and John R. Malloy of Columbus, both of whom had opposed Harding for lieutenant-governor. "In addition . . . there is a mine inspector, an insurance commissioner, a Lieutenant Governor, a board of penitentiary managers and no end of other appointments to be parceled out."

But the faithful Harding was undismayed. He quietly swallowed his pride, retained his $800 a year job as lieutenant-governor, and played his Harmony role as if he had not been hurt and as if the Ohio Republicans really were one big, happy family. He did this as keynoter to the Ohio Republican convention in Columbus on May 18, 1904, which carried out Hanna's dying wish to deliver Ohio to Theodore Roosevelt in the 1904 election. The way to do this was to name all the Republican prima donnas—Hannaite and Forakerite—as the so-called Big Four delegates-at-large to the Republican national convention, instructed to back Roosevelt's renomination. The Big Four were, of course, none other than that discordant quartet of Herrick, Dick, Cox, and Foraker. And who could perform such a noble task better than Warren G. Harding?

This produced Harding's famous "deference and devotion" speech which was long remembered in days to come when all four had become symbols of Republican discord. It was the "hit of the day"—a grandstand performance. It had the usual tone of sweetness, light, and harmony, and drove Harding's admirers into raptures. Harding spoke of four men "big enough to represent the grand old Buckeye state, big enough to be honored in state and nation, so big that, when they march down the aisle of the convention hall at Chicago, arm in arm as harbingers of harmony, you will hear the assembled Republicans exclaim: 'Hail to Ohio, prolific in her great sons. Her field marshals are in battle array reaching for victory in 1904.' " First was Governor Herrick, who "smote the allied hosts of Johnson Democracy to the tune of a hundred and fourteen thousand." Then there was George B. Cox, "a great big, manly, modest, but mighty grand marshal of an invincible division of the grand old Republican Party." Next was Dick, to whom the party turned "with unanimity and one accord" as the bearer of the "mighty mantle" of Hanna. Finally, there was Foraker, "a man so great that Ohio has given him to the nation." [21]

Thus Harmony spread its great wings of party unity with Lieutenant-Governor Harding again stealing the show. The 1904 campaign roared on to its expected conclusion with Roosevelt carrying the Buckeye state in a grand display of party loyalty and Prosperity promotion. Assorted Republican congressional and local aspirants coat-tailed with Roosevelt in the usual majority of districts and counties.[22]

Through it all Harding rose higher than ever on the list of speakers. "We will want all the time you can give us," wrote Julius W. Whiting, chairman of the party's state speakers' bureau. "Requests are coming in very rapidly for you." Similar requests came from the national committee followed by assignments in Indiana, Michigan, and New York. Always there were assurances of big crowds—"acres of people," "all the Big Guns will be there," "You are down on our big posters as 'it.' " There were reminders that the appearances "will do you personally lots of good," congratulations "on the part you took on the stump," hopes that "the day may not be far distant when we can all unite in something more expressive," and promises "to come to Ohio to campaign when you run for Governor which I hope will be next year." [23]

4

In 1905 Harding had the opportunity of a lifetime to try to unify the Ohio Republican party without the use of mirages. The issue of bossism came sharply into focus as Governor Herrick tactlessly alienated important segments of his party, and successfully railroaded the old Hanna organization into a boss-driven endorsement for reelection. Harding saw the so-called Herrick steal, and many of his followers saw it, predicting disaster to the party if Herrick were allowed to get away with it. They were right, too. By acquiescing in the continuation of bossism, Harding and the Ohio Republican party handed the anti-boss issue over to the Democrats and the Progressives. The result was the eclipse of the Republicans by the Democrats and the continuation of Harding in the role of mirage-maker and spellbinder for a sick and disunited party.

The Ohio Republican party was in the grips of a petty tyrant in 1905, and the tyrant was Myron T. Herrick, governor of the state. Like the venerated Mark Hanna, Governor Herrick was of the breed of businessmen-politicians who thought that they knew what was best for the party. Unlike the mighty Marcus, Herrick lacked the masterful personality and becoming tact to get what he wanted with a minimum of friction.

There was no doubt that Herrick, in his first administration, had become unpopular and was imperiling the future of the Ohio Republican party. Overly conscious of his sacrifice of the U.S. senatorship the year before in order to save the Hanna organization, he tried to dominate as Hanna had done. It was a pale and futile imitation of the original product. With a repeated revelation of self-righteousness, with the assertion of high-sounding principles, Herrick alienated one set of Republicans after another. He vetoed a bill legalizing race-track betting, thereby gaining the disfavor of sports lovers of the trotting fraternity, who resented his over-moralizing.[24] In the name of economy he vetoed appropriations for the promotion of Ohio State University's College of Agriculture and incurred the hostility of many usually Republican farmers.[25] And he accelerated the switch to the Democrats of many agricultural and small-town Republicans by resisting the Anti-Saloon League. Herrick believed that the League was unfair in trying to force counties into local-option prohibition via the so-called Brannock Bill. In the process he collided with the clever machinations of Wayne B. Wheeler, the League's brilliant Ohio superintendent, who was able, via the churches, to convince many Republicans that it was no sin to vote Democratic to save society from the evil influence of the saloons and the Ohio Brewer's Association. Wheeler, with his Anti-Saloon League weekly, the *American Issue*, launched a fierce campaign against the "Herrick saloons." In swift retaliation the Governor indiscreetly came to his own defense in his campaign speeches for

Roosevelt in 1904, much to the disgust of organization leaders who were trying to keep the wet-dry issue out of politics.[26]

But as the 1905 gubernatorial campaign approached, the Republican organization dared not challenge the imperious Herrick in his demand for renomination. The Governor insisted that any opposition to him was of a "bolting nature" and was inspired by Foraker's desire to get Harding in as governor and promote Foraker's desire to be the Republican nominee for President in 1908. Any gubernatorial candidacy besides his own, Herrick wrote A. D. Alderman of Marietta on January 10, 1905, "must be based upon a movement adverse to the administration and, therefore, must be adverse to the party and would be of a bolting nature." [27] To Vice-President Charles W. Fairbanks, Herrick wrote on January 20, 1905, claiming Foraker to be the instigator of the Anti-Saloon League campaign against him. "You know, my dear Senator," continued Herrick, "why he is doing this. He is a candidate for the Presidency the next time, and knows that he cannot succeed unless he succeeds in breaking down the old Hanna organization." Herrick closed by offering to support Fairbanks for the Presidency in 1908.[28]

The overbearing Governor proceeded to get the help of Cox to subdue Harding. Cox and his "wet" Cincinnati German supporters were naturally pleased with Herrick's opposition to the Anti-Saloon League. In a letter to Mark Hanna's former secretary, Elmer Dover, Herrick wrote on January 7, 1905, "Cox told me over the telephone about twe weeks ago that Harding would not be a candidate if I were a candidate." [29] In fact, Herrick had it arranged that Harding, an alleged Forakerite, would not be a candidate at all. The Governor informed Senator Dick, "Mr. C. insists that Harding will not be a candidate in case I am, and in the event that I am not, that Harding will not do." [30] Harding, himself, Herrick said, confirmed these sentiments. As he told Dover, "Harding told me that he would not be drawn into anything of this sort, as he would regard it as suicidal in the event that he should be nominated." In order to keep Harding firm in his committal, Herrick urged Dover to write Cox "a good strong letter on the situation." [31]

Herrick was implacable in his work against Harding. Rumors came to him that the Anti-Saloon League was putting money into the Harding boom. He, therefore, asked Dover to get the goods on this secret maneuver. "I would be glad if you could get it in definite form, so it could be used, the offer of $3,000 by the Anti-Saloon League towards conducting a campaign for Harding in Cuyahoga County. . . . This would, in my opinion, practically put these people out of business." [32] Of course, it did not work—Wayne Wheeler was too smart to be caught in that kind of a trap.

But the Governor bore down unmercifully to get his man. The plan was to start a movement to get the Republican organizations in easily controlled counties to hold mid-winter meetings to select Herrick delegates to the June, 1905, nominating convention. This had been arranged at a November 12, 1904, meeting in Cincinnati by the Herrick organization. Present were Cox, Dick, and Herrick's two right-hand men, State Attorney-General Wade H. Ellis and State Auditor Walter D. Guilbert. A "literary bureau" was set up in Columbus, managed by the organization's press secretary, T. C. Raynolds, who sent out to county committees and local Republican newspapers prepared editorials entitled "For Republican Fair Play" and "Stand By the Governor." [33] A few of these editorials were clipped and sent to Harding. Senator Dick, another Hannaite, as state executive chairman, followed up with a circular letter to local organization officials, warning against signing "anti-Herrick petitions," which were said to be sponsored by the Anti-Saloon League. Copies of Dick's letter also found their way to Marion, picked up here and there by Harding boomers. [34] The first county to fall in line with the early delegate plan was Hocking, where, in mid-January, 1905, local boss John F. White engineered a rump meeting of his county central committee, which selected Herrick delegates to the June convention. A local newspaper war revealed the inner workings of the so-called Hocking steal. [35] Herrick was delighted and wrote to J. C. Duncan of Killbuck in Hocking County on January 28, "The action of the Hocking convention was very pleasing to me." [36]

The last act of the Herrick steamroller, which left Harding completely subdued, was a maneuver at a Toledo Lincoln Day convention of the Ohio League of Republican Clubs, attended by both Herrick and Harding. The League was not a Republican organization agency. Indeed, it was a loose-jointed outfit with Forakerish backgrounds. The Harding boomers had planned a spontaneous demonstration for their man, but parliamentary maneuvers, managed by local Republican boss Walter F. Brown, caused a bolt by the Herrick faction on the grounds that the League's Harding delegates were not dues-paying members.[37] Then at the evening banquet Brown produced a spontaneous demonstration for Herrick instead of for Harding. At least that was the way Herrick described it. It seems that Brown had arranged for Herrick, the speaker of the evening, to be introduced by the distinguished Toledo jurist and Herrick follower John H. Doyle, the toastmaster. This is how Herrick described the affair, in a letter of February 14, 1905, to Senator Dick: "Harding was very much broken up after leaving the Toledo banquet. We came away on the train together. It was expected that a grand ovation would be given him and that he would be the hero of the evening. As it was, it turned out otherwise. Judge Doyle was toastmaster and carried everything with a strong hand. He had them all rise and stand in silence in respect to Senator Hanna's memory. Then, to my own surprise, I was able to make a better speech than usual. . . . The Toledo incident practically ended the opposition, so far as the nomination is concerned." [38] To Dover, on the same day, Herrick wrote, "Harding has practically given up, and is going off to Cuba." [39]

There were even more sinister forces supporting Herrick—forces of corruption looking for protection—and Harding was fully informed. They were in the sheriff's office in Cuyahoga County, and were headed by the sheriff himself, Edwin D. Barry. It was a little matter of the overdrawing of fees to the amount of $8,000, and Herrick's attorney-general, Ellis, knew about it. As Harding's friend F. E. Scobey reported, after a visit with Barry in mid-January, "You'll remember several of Co. officials overdrew their fees to an extent of several thousand dollars. Mr. Barry was one of these. It was not criminal, they merely followed precedent. He had been trying to avoid paying back into the treasury about $8,000. It has been referred to Atty. Gen'l Ellis. I suppose he is working Ellis through the Gov. . . . The reason he is afraid I think he has the promise that he won't have to pay back the over charge in fees." As Barry told it to Scobey, "If he [Herrick] were to go down in defeat there would be only one thing for us to do and that is to go down with him. . . . We all love Harding in this county, and we will always remember him with pleasure for the many kindnesses shown us at Columbus, but as long as Herrick stands for the second term we have got to stand with him." This assurance Barry made directly to Harding: "You may be assured that after we pay this obligation to Mr. Herrick that we will not forget your kindness to us." [40]

5

Against these devious and high-riding Herrick tactics, Harding had every reason to be resentful. And he was, for a little while. So were his friends and many other Republicans who were getting tired of Hanna bossism when not directed by a master hand like Hanna's. There thus developed an anti-boss movement in the Ohio Republican party that might have developed into a big thing if Harding had had the courage to fight for the principle of party self-government against the bosses.

There is no question about Harding's wanting the governorship in 1905 to save the party from a Herrick-and-Cox-imposed disaster. He said so rather mildly in his announcement of January 1, 1905, and he said so again most emphatically after Cox, on January 17, had declared for Herrick.[41] To Foraker, he wrote the next day, "Plans received a rather severe jolt yesterday when Mr. Cox of Hamilton made a clean cut declaration for renomination. It was an illogical statement, but it was a bomb well exploded. I am determined to stand pat." He had no intention to jump on the Herrick band wagon and promised that "we might have a bomb or two ourselves." "At any rate," he concluded, "I can't keep my self respect and recede from my position until I am dragged out and buried."[42]

Publicly Harding was just as emphatic in denouncing the Cox-Herrick dictatorship. In the *Star* of January 17, 1905, he exploded a few of those bombs he had mentioned. He bluntly reported that during the campaign of 1904, when Herrick was injecting the "wet-dry" issue into the discussion, "Mr. Cox was advising against Governor Herrick asking for the place again." Moreover, "Mr. Cox's statement, big as he is, does not settle nominations. If Mr. Cox's approval determines candidates, there is no need to hold conventions, no need to ask the Republicans of the state what their preferences are. If Mr. Cox can determine the governorship in 1905, he can name the U.S. senator and governor in 1908 and 1910, and the more than a half million Republican voters of the state can go about their private affairs reaping of the harvest of prosperity assured that the present party organization has things adjusted for all time to come."

The Harding boomers kept up their spirits. It looked as if their man had finally acquired the gumption to fight for a housecleaning of the Ohio Republican party. Letters poured into Marion. "The fight is on.

Let it be to a finish." "Come out with your colors flying. . . . This is
your hour to solidify the party now crumbling out of shape." "Push
hard and we will help you." "You are the natural leader for the
present emergency." "I glory in your spunk." "Strike while the iron is
hot." The "Hocking county steal" was denounced. "Take up the challenge of the Hocking Co. gang." "Are you going to let the Hocking Co.
delegation stand without a protest?" "The Herrick machine is working
overtime to make it appear that he has a certainty of nomination."
"Governor Herrick is taking advantage of the state organization to
thus further his interest." "For the love of God and the Republican
Party don't let the ghost of the honorable George B. Cox chill you." [43]

There were more indignant voices encouraging the fight—some with
a boss-busting ring which, if accepted, might have lined Harding up
with the nascent Progressive movement. Herrick, wrote W. L. Muller
of Winchester, is "the last of the Hanna bargain" which had made
Ohio Republican conventions "annual ratifications of the two or three
men's desires and suggestions." Silas E. Hurin of Findlay urged Harding to oppose Herrick so that the "splendid results of the last election
should be retained by the Republican party and not frittered away in
the vain attempt to satisfy one man's ambition." So, also, advised
Reverend E. Lee Howard of Columbus, who was now "ready even to
become politician for conscience sake." Then there was Toledo liberal
Frank L. Mulholland and Columbusite David F. Pugh of the well-re-
membered Pugh-Kibler home rule bill of 1900 that Harding had
weakly sponsored. Mulholland advised invoking the direct-primary
option of the state's Baber law to rally the local anti-boss people
againt Herrick and the Walter F. Brown machine. "I am positive that
you have the united support of all these men and they are vastly in the
majority in Lucas county at the present time." Pugh wanted primaries
and was confident Harding could win. It would take the "hardest
work and the expenditure of a large sum to hire workers," but it was
worth it to overcome "the combination of State, county and city officer
holders, employers, contractors and possibly some of Federal office
holders." [44]

Most tempting of the Harding boosters were the leaders of the
Anti-Saloon League. They really could deliver votes to Harding, at
least they said they could. For one thing, said Wayne Wheeler, in the
League's campaign against the "Herrick saloons," it had left Harding's
name entirely out of it in order not to "embarrass you." When the
"Hocking county steal" was revealed, Wheeler was convinced that

"the time is ripe to let things loose. . . . I find the people all over the State want to know definitely that you are going to be a candidate." Even the League's national superintendent, Reverend Purley A. Baker, was pushing Harding to come out against bossism. "You can win if you fight. If you fight and fail, you will have a tremendous following for the future. If you fail to fight, you are without a following, and your friends will be slower to take hold the next time." [45]

Finally, there was Foraker. Acting as if his candidacy might hurt Foraker for 1908, Harding wrote seeking the Senator's blessing. To this Foraker replied that he did not want to be an albatross for Harding. The big thing was that, since it was Harding's candidacy, it was up to Harding to do "some aggressive talking and some aggressive work. . . . I do not wish to prejudice your canvass by seemingly taking possession of it." From Reverend Baker came the assurance that he had talked with Foraker who "expressed a great desire that you become a candidate, but said he did not himself want to urge the matter to such an extent that in case of failure he would be compelled to bear all the blame. . . . if you are a candidate he will get behind your candidacy with all his power." [46]

But Harding was not of the mold to fight. He had behind him the anti-boss liberals, a widespread opposition to Herrick, the Anti-Saloon League, and Foraker. He could have exposed the defalcation in the sheriff's office in Cuyahoga County, and thus have kept the Democrats from stealing the corruption issue. To be sure, the League and Foraker might cost him votes. But to fight with gusto, with charm, and for the convictions that were in his heart might have gone far—if not far enough to win in 1905, perhaps to do so in 1908.

The moment of decision came on January 30, 1905 when Foraker permitted himself to be quoted in the *Cincinnati Times Star* as being in favor of Harding's nomination: "If there should be a contest between Herrick and Harding, my support and whatever help I can give will be on the Harding side." At once the *Times Star* telegraphed Harding for a reply. "This is construed," said editor Joseph Garretson, "to mean an invitation for you to make an open declaration of candidacy." The *Cincinnati Post* also asked for a statement. Harding declined to make one. [47]

Thus did Warren Harding decide to crusade for Ohio Republican unity, but not on an anti-boss program. It seemed more promising to continue with mirage-making and fence-mending. He took the advice of friends to wait his turn for the governorship of Ohio. As his Canton friend H. B. Webber wrote, on February 2, 1905,

> Do not at this time permit anyone to take you to the mountain top. Just now that machine is greased for someone else, but the people will see to it in good time that you are not forgotten. I am not a politician, have no axes to grind, plums to give out, or favors to ask, but I do wish to see the day when mortgages filed on future crops in Ohio by some men, shall expire and the people will see that there shall be no re-filing. Wait, just wait. Nothing will get away by so doing. In this you can't be mistaken and in doing something else, you may be mistaken. Within the next two years, with your acquaintance that you make in Ohio, you will have with you the young men of this State, and when you have them you have the power behind the throne.[18]

One of Harding's closest friends and associates on the *Star*, Malcolm Jennings, advised him to make up with the bosses, especially Cox. "Don't you think it would be a good plan for you to drop in on Geo. B. accidentally and have a 'heart to heart' talk with him—clear up all lies and liars. It wouldn't do any harm. Then if they want to throw the harpoon we will be in shape later to organize the 'boss busters' and go out in two years for 'blood.' " [49] Or, as another friend, B. F. Freshwater of Delaware, Ohio, advised, "Steady with your eyes 'sot' ahead—looking for the promised reward that awaits the 'faithful.' " [50]

6

Yes, it was back to mirage-making for Lieutenant-Governor Harding, as he mounted the stump for the doomed Herrick. From the day of the Cleveland opening, on October 7, 1905, to the end of the campaign, Harding was booked daily, with several speeches a day. And the usual reports came in of the magic of his words. From Urbana came the notice that "Lieutenant Governor Harding is getting to be a prime favorite with Urbana audiences." After his performance at Marietta on October 31, the editor of the local *Leader* wrote, "The brilliant and eloquent Warren G. Harding can be depended upon to deliver the goods in whatever he undertakes. . . . He carries to the listener an irresistible appeal by his convincing manner." At Pomeroy, in Meigs county, the editor of the local paper was convinced that Harding would be the next governor: "Lieutenant [*sic*] Harding is one of the brainest [*sic*] most loyal and most popular Republicans in

Ohio, and thousands of admiring friends in Ohio would like to see him the next chief executive of this great commonwealth." [51]

Of course, Harding had to eat his words of criticism of Boss Cox made earlier in the year. He did it most illogically and convincingly by calling Tom Johnson worse than Cox. At Cleveland, Harding admitted that the "Republican party sometimes skirts dangerously near to a ready-made ticket." But, oh, those Democrats, those Johnson hirelings and puppets! Johnson far outbossed Cox. He bossed legislatures, state and county conventions, city councils, obtaining for himself tax favors and perpetual franchises for utilities owned by him. Cox never went that far. Besides, what was wrong with accepting political help from Cox? "The Hamilton county delegation," said Harding, "yes, Cox, if you please, had one tenth of all the delegates to the last Republican state convention. Show me any man seeking a nomination who would say that he did not desire the support of this delegation and I will show you a man who does not tell the truth. If I should be a candidate before a Republican convention, I would want the support of Cox and would be proud to have it." [52]

Such talk was, of course, music to Democratic ears. They made the most of it, and probably won the election because of it. Especially helpful to Democrats was the partial defection of Secretary of War William Howard Taft over the Cox issue. At Akron, on October 21, Taft spoke in support of Herrick, but, in the process, scorched the Cox machine and advised Republicans to vote against Cox's puppet ticket in Cincinnati. [53]

How skillfully the Democrats outmaneuvered the Republicans on the Herrick-Cox boss issue was revealed by the Democratic gubernatorial candidate John W. Pattison's statement that, if it had not been for Cox, Harding would have been nominated and elected governor of Ohio. This convincing barb was delivered by Pattison on October 21, in Harding's own home town. "Had it not been for George B. Cox, W. G. Harding, your fellow townsman, would have been nominated governor of Ohio and with his high standing throughout the state he would have been elected by a grand majority." Harding could not openly admit the truth of this claim, but it was too close to the mark to be comfortable. [54]

Herrick lost in 1905, [55] and the Ohio Republican party was never the same again. A new era of Ohio politics opened with the Democrats having the advantage. To be sure, the Republicans got an undeserved and unexpected break when the Democratic victor, Governor Pattison, died in June, 1906 and the Republican Lieutenant-Governor Andrew L. Harris succeeded. But the Republican bossism and disunity had been exposed and could not match the Democratic seizure of the anti-boss issue and the revelation of Republican corruption. This unhorsed the innocent Harris in 1908, putting the Democrats in the saddle in Ohio politics for ten of the next twelve years.

So far as is known, only one of Harding's correspondents blamed the Marion leader for the disaster. This was a gentleman whose anonymous missive was found in the Harding papers attached to a newspaper clipping bearing an alleged Harding post-election statement, saying that Cox and Herrick bossism was responsible for the Republican defeat. "Why didn't you have the manhood," demanded this irate critic, "to come out and say this before the election? It would have done some good. As it is, you went around the state endorsing the gang, and pleading for votes for them. You have proved yourself a cheap gang politician and anything but a leader. You are a dead one like the rest of the bunch." [56] In other words, he was no Progressive.

7

But Harding was indomitable in his belief in mirage-making. The unexpected accession of the non-factional Harris to the governorship was looked upon as the restoration of Republican unity at the state level. If only Senator Foraker and President Roosevelt could be made compatible, perhaps all vestiges of Republican factionalism in Ohio could be made to disappear. Foraker could be President of the United States; Harris, the Governor of Ohio; Hannaite Dick, the senior United States Senator; and some other good Republican—Herrick perhaps?—the junior United States Senator. That would leave the governorship open for Harding in 1910. What a prospect for the deliverance of the GOP from its threatened decline!

This proposition of creating harmony between Roosevelt and Foraker was one of the most fantastic ventures in mirage-making in Harding's career. The complete enmity of these two political opposites gives cause for wonderment at Warren Harding's sanity. The best explanation is that Harding was a sheer opportunist, and that each campaign must be fought with the easiest weapon—or mirage—at hand. For purposes of the campaign of 1906, and the Ohio Republican congressmen who wanted to be reelected, it was well to have "good old" Warren Harding on the sawdust trail, saying that the Foraker-Roosevelt disagreement over various measures should not be allowed to break party unity and elect Democrats. Harding tried exactly that.

Harding's position in the 1906 feud between Roosevelt and Foraker was more than a straddle—it was a sprawl. The central issue was the Hepburn bill, giving the Interstate Commerce Commission rate-making powers over the railroads. Roosevelt was for it, and Foraker was against it. The discussion began in the House of Representatives with the President pushing hard for its passage. It was a popular measure and a majority of the Republican congressmen were in favor of it. So was Harding, until Foraker came out against it. In fact, said Harding from his editorial throne in Marion, anybody who was against the bill was a factionalist. "If the Republicans in congress expect to do any effective work," admonished the *Star*, January 25, 1906, "it's up to them to realize that it can be done only by working in harmony." Opponents of government fixing of railroad rates were "insurrectos." Such people "should remember that only one insurrection in a score pulls through, and the present doesn't appear to be the time for the overthrow of the big stick." As for the Senate, with its seeming majority of "railroad senators," it was a "do nothing" body, and it was "gunning" against Roosevelt. "It's to be expected," sneered the *Star* on January 19, "that a man who is a friend of the common people should be full of glaring faults in the eyes of the railroad senators. . . . The trusts and the great railroad interests have given the word to the senate to down Mr. Roosevelt, and the fact that many members of the upper house begrudge him the great hold he has attained upon the public doesn't in the least detract from the celerity with which they are endeavoring to execute the order." [57]

Then, in March of 1906, Foraker spoke with powerful logic in severe condemnation of the Hepburn bill, with particular respect to its denial of judicial review of the Interstate Commerce Commission's rate making.[58] Harding was at once overwhelmed with awe and admiration for Foraker's seeming wisdom and integrity. "He has argued the senators . . . to a standstill," wrote the editor on March 24. "Mr. Foraker's contentions that the bestowal of legislative power [on the I.C.C.] is in opposition to the constitution, and that denial of review by the courts is contrary to constitutional provisions, was so ably sustained in logical arguments, that none can make successful refutation." The *Star* likened Foraker to an unmovable rock on which a popular government could always rely with safety.

In spite of the differences between the President and the Senator, there was no incompatability—so said Harding. The Republicans needed big men like Roosevelt and Foraker even if they did disagree. In fact, the *Star* editor, with a few strokes of his agile pen, made the two complementary to each other—even as Roosevelt fumed and Foraker challenged. Said the *Star*, one was a courageous trust buster, the other a courageous trust defender. One must lead, the other must scrutinize. "President Roosevelt will long be remembered as leading to bring complete respect for the popular will, but the able senators who are contending for a law that will stand the cold scrutiny of the courts and command the approval of our soberest public opinion, will share with him the American regard that is written in the history of the republic." [59] People who clamored for the one as against the other were, of course, factionalists. Here was harmony with a big H, and Harding was the choirmaster who made it all sound so good, as he prepared for the party convention at Dayton in September of 1906.

The Dayton Republican convention was a "love feast," where the Ohio Republican party resolved to bless everybody and everything Republican and switched the discussion from controversial railroad matters to unassailable tariff Americanism. "The party," predicted the *Star* editor on July 21, "will declare its unwavering faith in President Roosevelt. It will express its approval of the senators and congressmen who brought credit to the state and participated nobly in the statesmanship of the nation. It will declare for a protective tariff and rejoice in the gratifying prosperity that we enjoy under a protective policy . . . and make such allusions to Republican contributions to Ohio advancement and progress as are seemly." It was all so simple, so reassuring, so harmonious.

And the Dayton convention seemed to produce this blessed Harmony—with Harding having much to do with it. Not only were Roosevelt, Foraker, and Dick all endorsed with equal enthusiasm, and Dick reelected as chairman of the state executive committee, but Harding, as platform committee chairman, engineered the platform with thorough harmony-making efficiency. It was framed after hearings from all who desired to be heard, and was the most progressive that the Republican party had ever adopted, which, of course, is not saying much. It contained such reform proposals as moderate tariff revision, primary elections for nominees and delegates to party conventions, and senatorial preference primaries. This was in line with the need to show the Ohio Republican party to be unbossed. What a glorious prospect was created in the promise of future Republican conventions being thoroughly representative of the people. Foraker was there, and made a unity-provoking speech featuring great self-denial in declining to accept the kingly crown of a presidential endorsement for 1908. This was a noble thing for Foraker to do, commented Harding. He was now a statesman who had "dropped all connection with party management and has given his thought and energies entirely to great public questions." [60]

Nor did the Harding-for-governor boom suffer. Newspaper references to his future were many. Said the *Dayton Daily News*, "Warren Harding of Marion, who would be governor today but for a row with Herrick, looks as handsome as ever. He's one of the very popular young men of the party." The *Columbus Citizen* headlined, "HARDING SLATED FOR GOVERNOR," reporting, "The Foraker-Dick men are saying that the victory of yesterday and today in the state convention presages that ex-Lieutenant Governor Warren G. Harding of Marion will be the slate of the senatorial combine for the nomination for governor in 1908. It is pointed out that Harding is the only one in the list of gubernatorial aspirants who came out of the contest either unblemished or not under suspicion." [61]

The campaign of 1906 was a tumult of tariff talk and railroad rate-control evasion. All the Republican congressmen desired Harding's oratorical talents, and the Marionite was not one to deny the calls. As usual he was booked daily, and the reports came in of rousing responses to his flaming Americanism and effective denunciation of Democrats. At Price Hill near Cincinnati, he was "greeted with a roar of applause and the audience went wild with enthusiasm." [62]

When it all culminated in another easy Republican victory in November, Harding was given his usual high credit for the outcome. Carmi Thompson of Cleveland, who achieved his heart's desire in election to be secretary of state, telegraphed, "No man in the state of Ohio contributed more to the success of the party than you. . . . I shall hope some day to be a soldier in the ranks when you are commanding the forces." From Bowling Green, B. F. James wrote, "Now get ready for 1908. You are still my one and only candidate for Governor." [63]

8

But all the platforming, spellbinding, glad-handing, *i.e.*, all the mirage-making, could not conceal the truth that the imperious Roosevelt was going to make William Howard Taft president of the United States in 1908. All who stood in the way—Foraker, Harding, or anybody else—were marked for extinction. Foraker, for reasons of his own, was willing to suffer that punishment, but not Harding. When Harding saw that party unity meant to drop Foraker, he dropped Foraker. But the man from Marion did it in the characteristically charming way that kept his Foraker friends—without Foraker—and won him Roosevelt and Taft friends even though he did not sincerely endorse their seeming Progressivism.

What was happening, although Harding possibly did not know it, was that, as the mirage of party unity glimmered, faded, then glimmered again, under the force of presidential and senatorial personalities, another mirage of unity, less bright but more persistent and growing slowly brighter, was beginning to form. That was the mirage of "Harding unity."

This was something far different from the concept of Harding as the politician representing only this or that special interest. It was the image of something constant in the midst of bickering and discord. To be sure, it was not founded on great idealogical principles or concepts. But for years it hovered in the Ohio political atmosphere above the smoke of battle and lingered after the battle. Harding was the one man who could at least talk and act unity, and appear unscathed as contests ended and the combatants nursed their wounds and marked their opponents for reprisals. In this role there was a certain strength, and no managers, be they Malcolm Jennings, Harry Daugherty, or another, created or maintained it. Harding created his own image and kept it alive even unto the days when he became important presidential timber.

Nevertheless, in 1907 and 1908, the let's-all-be-friends attitude of Harding's attempt to unite Ohio Republicans took cruel punishment. The attack on Foraker and Harding was commanded from the offices of four leading Republican newspapers, as they seized upon the new fad of Progressivism and built up the Taft boom. These were the *Ohio State Journal* and the *Columbus Evening Dispatch*, controlled by Robert F. Wolfe; the *Cleveland Leader*, controlled by Dan R. Hanna; and the *Cincinnati Times-Star*, controlled by the Taft family. These powerful journals headed up a neo-Progressive movement with the idea of liberalizing the Ohio Republican party. As the *Journal* said, November 8, 1906, "Great social, industrial and political changes . . . have taken place," and President Roosevelt was their great exponent. Whenever the President came out with something new like trust-busting, railroad-rate control, tariff revision, or conservation, the *Journal* and its allies applauded. Woe to those like Foraker who criticized these innovations. Such people were standpat reactionaries, constitutional finessers, picayunish, ill-tempered, disgruntled obstructionists.

As Foraker's fortunes declined, so did Harding's—for a while the Marion "professional unifier" with his "incongruous plaudits" was having his bluff called. Such people, said the *Journal*, November 7, 1906, "had no more principles than a dead snake." The *Cleveland Leader* said the same thing in more elegant language on November 9. The *Journal* had many very harsh words for Harding, and his part in building up Foraker for the Presidency and himself for governor. To be sure, said the editor on November 11, 1906, if the Republican convention were held right away, Harding would be the nominee. But that was all a put-up job by Foraker and Dick, who "starred Harding in the stumping campaign" for their own selfish purposes, boycotting the Progressive speakers when calls came in for them. Readers were reminded that Harding was a friend of Boss Cox. They were also reminded that a gubernatorial boom for Harding's fellow townsman, Congressman Grant E. Mouser, had been started "in hopes of staying the progress of the Harding boom."

Harding's decline in Republican favor did not last for long because he did not stay with Foraker beyond the danger point. When the Taft boom reached steamroller proportions, it was clear that the demands for party unity required the desertion of the senator even though it meant surrender to a new brand of bossism, this time emanating from President Roosevelt and Secretary of War Taft. Nevertheless, Harding maintained his Foraker preferences long enough to retain the respect of that wing of the Republican party. In fact, Harding was able to establish his role of Horatio at the bridge, who stood his ground when almost all others had fled, and retired only when Foraker himself failed to justify being supported by his followers. This happened early in 1908, when the Ohio Republican central committee, prodded by Taft and ably led by its chairman, Walter F. Brown, called a mid-winter party primary to choose either Taft or Foraker delegates to the state convention which, in turn, would pick Ohio's delegates to the Republican national nominating convention in June of 1908.[64] At this crucial primary Foraker failed to give Harding and his embattled pro-Foraker forces the necessary encouragement. Thus Harding was justified in declaring openly for Taft and putting the blame on Foraker.

The 1908 Harding switch from Foraker to Taft was really somewhat

of an agonizing process for Harding. It was the experience to which
Dr. Harding referred in 1920 when he said, "Warren was a Foraker
man until he found out Foraker himself was a Foraker man." [65] In a
political sense, Harding gave his all for Foraker in 1907 and early in
1908. When the Roosevelt-Taft juggernaut showed its intention not
only to blast Foraker's presidential prospects but to purge him from
the Senate, Harding wrote purple passages in Foraker's defense. This
was bossism at its worst, said he. He called Taft a "runner, but not a
competitor." For such a person, in alliance with Boss Cox, to be
Roosevelt's "divinely appointed legatee" was a travesty of political
decency. Harding branded Walter Brown, who had called the
"sneaky" mid-winter primary, "the Judas of Toledo . . . the odious
Toledo boss." Harding accepted the "unfair" primary and mounted
locally a crusade for Foraker. "It is a square-toed Republican contest
. . . and we are going to settle some vital questions. . . . We shall
decide whether the people of Ohio are sovereign in their political
liberties or whether the government at Washington dictates our actions. We like the man who is big enough to contribute to our
Republican statecraft, and at the same time is of the metal that makes
a fighter for Republican success. Foraker is both." But Foraker did not
fight this time. All he did was to claim that the Brown primary was
unfair and unconstitutional. And, while Brown plotted, Harding
fought back, expecting Foraker to produce petitions from all over the
state for Foraker candidates to contest with the Taft candidates in the
primary. Deadline day, January 20, 1908, came, and no Foraker petitions. Then, and then only, did Harding surrender. On January 22 he
published a *Star* editorial entitled, "Foraker Is Defeated and Ohio Is
For Taft." "The senator," Harding confessed, "was out-primaried. . . .
It was poor business to quit the game. . . . We think Senator Foraker
should have fought to a finish under the call. His Marion friends were
ready in eagerness to make the test of strength." And now, wrote
Harding, came the desertion of those "pretended friends," those "bargainers of politics," who encouraged Foraker "to make the decisive
battle and then scurried to the tall timber to await the commissary
wagons of the Taft armies." [66]

Publicly, Harding had preserved himself from the charge of disloyalty to Foraker; privately, he proceeded to write a letter, on January
24, 1908, telling the Senator a few things relating to the same subject:
"The best lot of Indians that ever banded together were pow-wowing
and skirmishing every hour in your behalf. The things we said, we

would not repudiate when you declined to contest the state and had to quit." "Mind you," he added, "I have joined no Taft movement. . . . I have simply followed the command of the political conscience which I expect to retain—which forbade the pursuit of a contest which seemed to me only obstruction." [67]

There was one who bespoke his profound disappointment in Foraker at the time of Foraker's failure to back his friends. This was Harding's friend Malcolm Jennings. Early in 1908, in a letter to Harding, Jennings was very outspoken in describing Foraker's delinquency. "Affairs on the Foraker side," wrote Jennings, "have been horribly mismanaged. He has led his forces into a cul-de-sac from which there is no escape except by death or surrender. . . . In every county there are local officers to be nominated and elected . . . congressmen, judges, state officers to be chosen. These are the people for whom I feel." Foraker "loftily told us that he had never had a machine and did not want one. . . . He pursued the dog-in-the-manger attitude until his friends in many counties were forced to either relinquish control or climb on the [Roosevelt-Taft] bandwagon." [68]

In his July 24, 1908 letter, Harding did not tell Foraker the whole truth, *viz.*, that he had trusted the Ohio Senator far beyond the call of the requirements of party loyalty, and expected defeat in the very hour of fighting for Foraker. But he did tell it six years later when he was running for the U.S. Senate. Harding wrote, "My admiration for you, ever growing for nearly thirty years, is no less today than when I enrolled for the contest in 1908, which I knew at the hour of enlistment would end in failure." [69] If Harding knew at the outset that Foraker was not going to fight, it was the one time in Harding's life when he subordinated individual friendship to the demands of party loyalty.

There is plenty of evidence that the prodigal, Foraker-worshipping Harding was welcomed back to the fold of the Republican majority. Chief rejoicer was the *Ohio State Journal*, which headlined January 23, 1908:

HARDING JOINS TAFT'S FORCES

FORAKER LEADER OUT FOR TAFT

"That is what harmony means," moralized the *Journal*, "getting with the main body of the army and marching along with it. . . . If a few more in the state would follow his footsteps, the G.O.P. of Ohio would be as serene as a May morning." E. M. Fullington, organization candidate for state auditor was very happy. "I have always admired your courage in politics as well as in public life," he wrote Harding. "Your statement . . . means much for the success of the Republican Party in Ohio this fall." [70] Then there was Harding's fellow townsman, Congressman Grant E. Mouser, always an organization man, who, as Harding stayed loyal to Foraker, had written, "I love to see this unselfish loyalty and devotion to Foraker's candidacy you give, and while under the circumstances I am not for him, yet have the greatest admiration for his courage and ability. . . . I have admiration for your talents and strong faith in your political future." When Harding's switch took place, Mouser was greatly touched and wrote that he talked it over with the other Ohio Republicans in Congress "who congratulate you on your stand." Mouser looked forward to the coming campaign when we "will get together for the sake of oratory." [71]

How highly the Taft men rated Harding in 1908 may be gauged by the latter's claim that he was offered the honor of nominating Taft at the Chicago national convention. He told this to Foraker in a letter of May 1, 1910. "Those who claim that I had sold out to Taft," he wrote, "do not know how I rejected overtures to ride on a high seat in the Taft wagon in 1908 when I could have had the honor of offering his name to the Chicago convention." [72]

Again it was back to the sawdust trail and stump talk in the campaigning of 1908, with mirages and music all the way. Harding spent four weeks in touring the state in behalf of Taft. In the final week he accompanied Governor Andrew L. Harris, candidate for reelection, in a cross-country "trolley trip." In all his appearances, Harding was billed as speaking on "national issues," *i.e.*, the tariff. This must have been embarrassing to the relatively inarticulate Harris who confined himself to state issues and the defense of the party against Democratic charges of corruption. The result was sad. Harris lost Ohio and Taft won it. [73] The difference may not have been due entirely to the contrast in oratorical aptitudes, but there is no question that Harding put on his usual display of personal charm and energetic oratory. Consider the *Journal's* report of Harding's appearance in Columbus on October 27. William Jennings Bryan was the Democratic opponent of Taft, and there was need for oratorical fireworks to combat those of the "silver-tongued" Nebraskan. Quoth Harding, "Mr. Bryan has raised the question of whether the people shall rule. Do you know what that is? That's punk, that's what it is. The Republican party, years ago, inaugurated the protective tariff system under which our manufacturing industries were conceived and prospered." He cited the reported fate of Welsh coal miners who were obliged to live on horse meat. "The American laborer had never reached the condition where he has to eat his friends." Harding continued in this vein in his soul-stirring rebuttal of Bryan's "punk." [74]

9

There was a great deal of the usual mirage-making in 1910 when Harding ran for governor, but it did not fool a majority of the Ohio voters. He presented a combination of anti-bossism, belated Progressivism, and general obfuscation, and sustained a devastating defeat by over 100,000 votes, the worst the Ohio Republican party had ever suffered. The reason was very simple: disunity had delayed too long the party's correction of corruption and the endorsement of sound Progressivism. Hence the Democrats, under the skillful leadership of Governor Judson Harmon, revealed the horrible truth that the Grand Old Party was no longer as grand as it ought to be. And yet, so far as Harding was concerned, he escaped the blame. It was becoming clear that, although Harding was not another Hanna, he was indeed bigger than his party.

Many were the Republicans who warned Harding that his cause in 1910 was hopeless. "The chances of success are against us," wrote former State Treasurer Robert P. Kennedy. "Republican prospects do not look rosy," warned W. E. Mallory. Another, W. S. Culp of Lakewood, wrote, "I personally regret that you are in the race. . . . You are too good a man to be defeated." "If you are not elected this Fall, do not be surprised, as the educated young men of this country propose, from now on, to vote for men that stand for the people and not the Bosses," said M. H. Frost of Cleveland. "You will be the worst defeated Republican candidate that ever ran for governor of Ohio," wrote R. L. Templin, also of Cleveland. Attorney Charles C. Pavey of Columbus felt sorry for Harding, writing, "I feel that you have been put up to make a 'sacrifice hit' and I do not think it fair to you to have been put on the ticket this year." [75]

The chief trouble in 1910 was that a new political hero had emerged in Ohio in the person of Governor Harmon, United States attorney-general under President Cleveland. A conservative Democrat, a Cincinnati corporation lawyer of great competence and prestige, he was not a Progressive. But he was enough of a reformer and tactician to confront Harding and the Ohio Republican party with well-founded revelations of scandal which the GOP could not deny. Harmon had followed up his 1908 campaign charges of Republican corruption with investigations that revealed the unmistakable truth of his attacks. It was shown that Republican officials had kept no records of the deposit of state funds; that Republican state treasurers had been stockholders in banks receiving state funds, interest on which was lower than it was for private depositors; that state funds were shifted back and forth between the state treasury and the banks, so that they were in the treasury at audit time and in the banks the rest of the time. The state treasurers thus pocketed the interest unbeknownst to the public. Prominent Republicans, such as Boss Cox, were officials in the favored banks. Other investigations revealed waste, incompetence and padded payrolls in state institutions.[76]

To put it bluntly, something serious had happened to the GOP. Its halo had dimmed; its old-time glory was tarnished. It would take far more than Harding's oratory and personality to capture the new political mood of the people. Progressives saw no virtue in loyalty to a corruption-ridden outfit. It was no longer a sin to be a Democrat.

One of Harding's Republican correspondents described this new reform feeling which was becoming respectable in politics. This was George P. Waldorf, old-guard, Brown Republican of Toledo. "I believe you realize," Waldorf wrote on July 28, 1910, "that the day of winning upon party pride and regularity is past. It is broad principle that will win the day. Roosevelt planted an idea in the public mind and, consequently, the demand for the 'square deal' is universal and will not down. The people are rising in their might to eliminate the control of the law making power and Executive function from 'political bosses,' and the 'interests.' It is a new deal and the leaders that do not read the times aright will go into political eclipse. The man that can correctly gauge the thinking of the masses and responds to same can win this fight. I believe you are in entire sympathy with the advanced idea." [77]

Harding was not the man for this new political idea of challenging old-time leadership. His stock in trade was adjustability to popular opinion; but when it came to granting concessions to progressivism, he could only go so far. They were involuntary and watered-down gestures.

The expediency of Harding's token Progressivism was partially illustrated by the advice he got from his friends. This was as hollow as it had been in 1905 when the Harding boom against Herrick was in the making, and the suggestions were made to follow the "Dineen-Folk racket" and some La Follette-like reforms for the benefit of "the dear common people," as Scobey had put it. In 1910 Scobey was at it again, writing to Harding, "Get in line and be as progressive as possible." [78] There came to him the cynical advice of his friend and old-guard stalwart, former State Attorney-General Henry E. Sheets: "If you don't agree with progressive ideas in all particulars, soften your views to theirs. Make it easier for them to remain in the party than to get out of it, for just as certain as death you will find the liveliest bunch of progressive republicans in the state of Ohio that were ever labeled 'dead' or 'dying.' You will find them everywhere, in all walks, in all businesses, and they are, generally speaking, the most outspoken and strenuous of any body of voters there are in the state today." [79]

And so Harding softened. He even softened on the tariff, mainly, of course, because of the outcry against the Payne-Aldrich tariff of 1909, which Taft had dared not to veto even though it was too favorable to the trusts to suit him. The measure came to be symbolic of a boss-ridden job, dictated by two autocrats, Speaker of the House Joseph G. "Uncle Joe" Cannon and Senate millionaire Nelson B. Aldrich.

The way to soften on the tariff was to emphasize the "scientific" part of the Payne-Aldrich Bill. That was the provision for a tariff commission which would study international comparative costs of production and recommend rate changes accordingly. "Harp on the tariff commission," wrote Scobey. Harding should show the people "that you stand pat when you know you are right, and that you have brains enough to progress as the times and business interest demand." [80]

Harding accordingly harped, changing his old tariff-Americanism line to one of tariff reform. For example, in Columbus on January 29, 1910, he emphasized the progressive idea that tariffs in the future would be made under scientific and unselfish auspices. "The details of the tariff law are settled until the next move is made in the light of an intelligent and unprejudiced tariff commission which is the first really progressive step in tariff unselfishness this nation has ever made. The footprint is that of William H. Taft." In Cleveland on April 21, he told his listeners, "The protective policy must yield to common sense devotion, like any other correct and valid principle. I like my tariff like the Methodist liberality in baptism—sprinkling at least, pouring if you believe that way, immersion if necessary, and redemption under one of these." Evidently some people liked this kind of tariff talk. T. H. McConica wrote, "It had the right ring, and ought to go a long way toward securing you the nomination." [81]

Another necessity in the Harding 1910 buildup for the gubernatorial nomination was for Harding to appear as the unbossed candidate. His adroitness in this regard was most conspicuous. The first announcement was staged as a response to a New Year's call at his home by the Marion county central and executive committees.[82] Circular letters began to appear, saying that he "truthfully" had not intended to be a candidate, and wondered if his friends were not "unintentionally" deceiving him. Another letter went out June 1 to all delegates to the nominating convention, admitting that he would like the nomination, but declaring, "I will conduct no campaign for the nomination nor organize any machine to promote my candidacy." He would seek no alliances, make no pledges, offer no declarations of views. He criticized President Taft for trying to dictate the appointment of his assistant, Attorney-General Wade H. Ellis, to the chairmanship of the Ohio executive committee.[83] He publicly declared that he did not "care a rap about the machine, wouldn't head one if I could. . . . I have no liking for political intriguing, and won't join in any such game." The party should name a candidate "in the good old-fashioned way." His manager, Malcolm Jennings, made similar statements, adding that Harding had made several public speeches "but has not referred to his candidacy." [84] All of which enabled the *Ohio State Journal* to headline on the eve of the convention:

HARDING OUTLINES CONVENTION HOPES

Says He's Here As No Man's Man, a Candidate Because

He Thinks He's Wanted, Knows When to Stand Pat and When

Progress is Demanded.[85]

It must be confessed, however, that Harding did considerable preconvention maneuvering in his own behalf. One move was the successful attempt to keep Foraker from even being present at the convention. Foraker was now an ex-senator and more hated than ever, having been denied reelection to the Senate for his past sins, especially for the so-called Archbold letters. These were published in 1908 by William Randolph Hearst, and revealed that, during his senatorial years, Foraker was in the employ of the Standard Oil Company and was importuned by his employer for certain favors in regard to national legislation and court action.[86] Foraker had written Harding that the practice usually followed by the Ohio Republican party of inviting notables to be present at state conventions had been omitted this year (1910). Harding replied that there was a general wish to see him at the convention, but that he (Harding) did not want to file a request with the committee "that will so greatly delay your summer vacation." [87]

Another not-so-coy maneuver by Harding was to assure the Taft presidential machine that he was no longer pro-Foraker or anti-Taft. Taft was using the 1910 Ohio election as a test of strength for his hoped-for 1912 reelection. The Taft managers were definitely against the Harding boom because, as Charles D. Hilles, one of Taft's backers, reported, "Harding's success would mean the return to power of Foraker's friends," and thus lose the President many Progressive votes. Taft had already suffered losses to the Progressives on his high Payne-Aldrich stand, his seeming anti-conservationism in the Ballinger-Pinchot dispute, and in his support of Speaker of the House Cannon. It was, therefore, incumbent on Harding, as the nomination maneuvering got under way, to disarm the Taft opposition. He did this quite frankly—verbally, to be sure—but one person, Joseph Garretson, editor of the Taft family's *Cincinnati Times-Star*, was present at the crucial conference and carefully described what happened. "Harding," wrote Garretson to the President on July 28, "reiterated and declared his loyalty to you in the most fervent terms. He insisted he had been at all times your most consistent supporter in the state, both in his speeches and in his newspaper. . . . He protested that he regarded the Payne bill as the best tariff measure that had thus far been secured, and that he was heartily in sympathy with the course you had pursued, that he owed no allegiance to Senator Foraker or the senator's old friends; that he felt that Foraker was politically dead, and could never be resuscitated; that if an attempt at resuscitation was ever made, he would oppose it with all his power and might." Garretson added that Harding assured everybody that he wanted only one term. To United States Senator Theodore E. Burton, who was present, he promised not to challenge him for reelection to the Senate in 1914, and to oppose Foraker, if he challenged. According to Arthur

I. Vorys, similar assurances had been made by Harding prior to the Garretson conference.[88]

Even though Harding, in his own estimation, got an unbossed nomination, at the 1910 convention, he was suffering from the "curse of Cox" anyhow. Cox was intent on humiliating Taft, and he used Harding as a tool to do so. The Cincinnati boss had never forgiven Taft for being against him in the Herrick campaign of 1905. Therefore, when the Taft managers failed to get their favorite, the progressive Judge Reynolds R. Kinkade of Toledo, to sacrifice himself by being nominated, Cox maneuvered to foil the Taft men in their second choice, Nicholas Longworth, Cincinnati son-in-law of former President Roosevelt. In the balloting, Cox kept his own candidate, Judge O. Britt Brown of Dayton, in the field long enough to encourage the Taft men to build up the Longworth vote to the point where Cox or Harding would have to switch to Longworth. Then, as the Longworth vote approached the bandwagon stage, Cox switched from Brown to Harding. The Taft men had suffered a Cox-inspired insult, and Cox had had his revenge. It was a nice piece of spite work.[89] "The old boy is well satisfied," commented J. W. Heintzman of Cincinnati.[90] Harding could hardly be proud of a nomination obtained under such circumstances. Actually, with the possible exception of Harding, none of the candidates—Kinkade, Brown, or Longworth—wanted the nomination because they knew that they would lose to Harmon in November.

Thus did Harding enter into a campaign that many important Republicans considered hopeless from the start. Cox sabotaged the ticket in an interview published in the *New York Sun* and headlined, "Few Unprejudiced Observers Believe That Harding Has Any Chance in the Large Cities of the State." Cox was quoted as saying that there was a strong anti-Taft and anti-Roosevelt feeling among businessmen, who deplored "that all party affairs must be managed to suit Taft's and Roosevelt's personal aims and wishes." It was felt, Cox presumably said, that the party "should not be run for the benefit of two men no matter how distinguished they may be."[91] Cox and Senator Burton engaged in a public and unedifying feud over who betrayed whom in nominating Harding, Cox calling Burton a "pinhead," and Burton saying Cox was "no gentleman."[92] Taft's man, Wade Ellis described the feeling of unenthusiastic resignation for Harding's nomination. This, Ellis reported, prevented "the maximum opportunity for success" that would have come with Kinkade's or Longworth's leading the ticket. "The only comfort we have," wrote Ellis, "is the consciousness that we did the best we could and that after all Harding was a natural choice and will make an able campaign." [93]

Other Taftites were more frank. Harding meant nothing to them, and they were glad it was he who would bear the brunt of the defeat. The members of the Republican party needed a shock which would cause a repudiation of the grafters and reunify the rank and file in support of Taft for reelection in 1912. Cincinnati distiller T. J. McNamara told Taft, "As at Balaklava 'Some one blundered.' . . . Harding is a nice gentleman but if you nominate him we lose Ohio this year as sure as God made little apples." But it was not really fatal: "A 'd——good licking this year' would help the party and wouldn't hurt the party nor you in 1912." Another believer in the cauterizing effect that Harding's defeat would bring to the party was D. K. Watson of Columbus, who wrote on October 27, 1910, "Many things have been done by Republican officers in this state which as an honest man I can not and will not apologize for. . . . the Republican party in Ohio deserves defeat; the people ought in reality to reprove us. . . . We are telling the people that the grafters belong to the past." [94]

McNamara and Watson were right. Harmon and the Democrats sallied forth clad in the armor of righteousness, damning Republicans with stinging revelations of corruption. He fed out his exposés one by one, a new scandal with each speech. The result, according to the *Ohio State Journal*, was "a fetching picture in the public mind of Harmon as a disinterested foe of graft." Mix this with a little "Harding-and-the-curse-of-Cox," and Foraker's insistence on attacking Roosevelt, and the Marionite looked little short of ridiculous. [95]

All that Harding could do was to engage in countersmears and pretended Progressivism. The Harding men dug up evidences of some Democratic-padded payrolls, but Harmon met this charge with revelations of new Republican treasury defalcations and with a lengthy list of Republican payroll padding. Then Harding tried the Wall Street argument, alleging Harmon to be the associate of J. P. Morgan in certain railroad receiverships in contrast with Harding's simple, honest, small-town background. This, too, Harmon threw back in Harding's face, not only with the skillful portrayal of the receiverships as judicially justified, but with Harding's defense of Cox, whose benefits from the treasury favoritism to Cox's bank were undeniable and hardly worthy of the label of pure-mindedness. [96]

Harding's efforts to represent himself as a Progressive were pathetic.

On October 10, he harked back to the days of 1900 and 1902 when he sought to get the Pugh-Kibler municipal government reform bill passed, and when he spoke for public utility franchise reform. "This is a progressive age," he declared, "and ours a progressive party. . . . I refer those interested to the legislative session of 1901[1900], when I introduced and championed the Pugh-Kibler code. Ohio spent $10,000 to have that code drafted and it was then the most advanced measure proposed in any state in the Union." [97] Harding did not tell his listeners that he had nothing to do with the originating or framing of the Pugh-Kibler bill, that he sponsored it because it came to him as chairman of the committee on municipal affairs, that he was abysmally uninformed about its content, that his support of it was casual, non-persistent, and anything but championing, and that he gave the conservative Nash Code bill his enthusiastic support as part of his partisan duty as floor leader of the Ohio senate. [98]

On the subject of franchise legislation, Harding described how he urged "extensive franchise changes," but was overruled by the party majority. [99] He did not tell about the famous senatorial trolley ride on the lines of the Cincinnati Traction Company, after which he returned to Columbus imbued with the great efficiency of the Cincinnati trolley system and voted to give such a "big question" further investigation. [100] Harding criticized Harmon's killing the Wood bill for the creation of a state public utilities commission for the regulation of public service corporations. But he did not say that in the *Marion Star* of April 9, 1910, when the Wood bill was being discussed, he too opposed its passage. "It is conceded," he had written, "that there is no general public demand for this legislation at this time. The system is being worked out in other states and when brought to perfection should be adopted in Ohio. But business should not be needlessly disturbed by experimental laws drawn by a visionary and pushed by aspiring politicians in search of winning votes." Such contradictions made ridiculous Harding's November 2 declaration to a Columbus audience, "I speak for a progressive Republican party. It wouldn't be a party worth while if it were not progressive." [101]

As the campaign closed, Harding became the victim of a ludicrous display of Republican mismanagement. Somehow or other, Foraker got himself into the campaign, and, on October 22, at Marysville, berated Theodore Roosevelt's "new nationalism" as "treasonable as secession." This so angered Roosevelt's friend, James R. Garfield, that, in a Ravenna speech on October 24, he roared back at Foraker as a reactionary, and, in the process, forgot all about mentioning Harding. Then, while Foraker kept on attacking Roosevelt, the former President himself was drafted into Ohio and supported Harding by practically using Harding's own words about Harmon as a Wall Street man. The lugging of Roosevelt into the campaign was so ineptly done that it was interpreted as outside interference. As the Republican *Ohio State Journal* ruefully admitted, "In every state where his personality became an issue, the Republican candidates whose election he urged were heavily cut." After the election Foraker reported to Harding that, when he got to Toledo just before election day, "I heard only one report, and that was of a sort of wholesale stampede to Harmon on account of Roosevelt's attack upon him there and at Cleveland." [102]

The campaign frittered out to an inglorious conclusion—for Harding. He tried to divert the issue from graft to the tariff. But it did not work. R. L. Miller of Kenton reported to Taft, "If, as I have done, you talk Tariff to them [the farmers] they begin to talk graft." James Boyle, Columbus Republican, reported that "Harding is making a splendid campaign, and, were it not for the Cox and the graft issues, I would be absolutely confident of his election but he is under tremendous disadvantage with these two loads." Taft worker Arthur Vorys wrote likewise, "The desirability of getting the campaign out of the petty larceny rut has been obvious all the time, but Harding and others have kept saying, and I believe they were right, that they could not get the people to listen to anything else but graft." And after it was all over D. K. Watson was quite blunt in telling Hilles, "Our defeat in Ohio is due more to the existence of graft in the state house and Governor Harmon's conduct in that connection than any one cause." [103]

Other factors that helped crush Harding were Taft's coolness on patronage issues and the failure to get "cabinet colossals" to speak for Harding. On the patronage matter, Taft worker Lewis C. Laylin informed the President, "We will be greatly embarrassed by announcements in the public press of proposed further extension of the civil service rules to a large number of offices, including assistant postmasters." [104] Or, as Republican chairman in Licking county, George H. Hamilton, reported, his workers complained, "What's the use? A Democrat is as good to appoint as a Republican, why should I work for the Republicans? My chances are just as good under Democratic administration as under Republican." Hamilton cited the Taft merit rulings in regard to census takers and the second and third class postmasters. These people asked, "What inducement is there for me to Be a Republican. . . . It takes away every incentive, inducement, ambition or anything else to be a Republican." Hamilton thought the President ought to know "just how the Proletariate [sic] feel in regards to this." [105] As for the "cabinet colossals," the failure of the national Taft leaders to get big names to come to Ohio in time to counter Harmon's use of the graft issue was maddening to some local loyalists. On November 4, S. J. Flickinger of the *Dayton Herald* complained, "Why on earth did not these cabinet officers come to Ohio sooner?" [106] This enabled a lot of loyal Hardingites to blame President Taft for the disaster. As James M. Walker of Dover, Ohio, Grand Chancellor of the Knights of Pythias, wrote to brother knight Harding in 1912, "Taft and his gang did not break their necks trying to elect you Governor, at least not in this part of the country." [107]

On the other hand, the Taft men blamed the Harding managers, Ohio executive committee chairman Laylin and his secretary, Malcolm Jennings, for the debacle. This was based on the premise that the real issue in Ohio was Taft's reelection in 1912. A Harmon victory in 1910 would make him presidential timber for 1912 and create a big weakness in Taft's plans for reelection. At least that was the way Taft's manager, Hilles, felt about it when he wrote his post-mortems to Vorys, "The President probably shares the views of most persons that Laylin was himself unequal to the task, and that Jennings was obsessed with the idea that there was only one interest in the campaign and that was the success of Harding." [108]

However, there may have been a deeper managerial problem than either side to this blame-throwing realized. This was the Bronson direct-primary law of 1908, requiring that all members of county central committees be chosen in direct primary elections. This upset the relatively even tenor of local political management by bringing into party affairs a lot of "new blood." At least that was what Malcolm Jennings offered as his post-mortem explanation. "Last year," he wrote Hilles on August 1, 1911, "was the first in which all central committees [county] were elected at direct primary, and it brought out a lot of inexperienced and in many cases disgruntled men. You know we had no means for a complete organization and could do little to make the county organizations effective. This should be carefully looked after before the next primaries." [109]

It was a stunning defeat for Harding—he lost by over 100,000—but there were consolations, especially self-made ones. After thinking things over he wrote to Taft that he was fully persuaded that no Republican could have won. There was "lack of harmony in national affairs," and "specific Ohio embarrassments" locally.[110] To his friends, he could write that "this was one of the times that all the people could be fooled. I was opposed by the drys as being too wet, by the wets as being too dry, by the bosses as being too independent, by the un-bossed as being too much subject to bossism, by the friends of Taft as a slap at Roosevelt, by the progressives as a slap at Taft, and generally by a lot of people as a rebuke to the party for passing of the tariff bill alleged to increase the prices of commodities with which the tariff had nothing to do."[111] In the *Star*, he admitted that Harmon and the corruption issue had had much to do with the outcome. He admitted that the "curse of Cox" was also a factor, alleging, of course, that he (Harding) was the only Republican gubernatorial candidate in twenty years that was not Cox's choice.[112]

There were greater consolations for Harding than those improvised by himself. They came from party leaders and predicted great things for him in spite of all. Foraker expressed the regret of many that the "heavy blow of such a cruel defeat should have fallen on you. . . . It was a Democratic year and we all knew it long before the end of the campaign. You will be victorious next time."[113] From Congressman Frank B. Willis came the advice, "Do not give up the game. You are the strongest man in the state. . . . Stay by it—your day will come, and that very soon."[114] From Charles S. Gongwer of Cleveland came equally consoling words: "You don't have to 'come back' to be what you are, what many thousands of people have come to recognize, the biggest man in the Republican party in the state."[115]

Things were worse for Harding and the GOP in 1910 than these consolations revealed. The mirages had disappeared. They were gone with the ghost of Hanna and the shadow of Foraker. No ballyhoo, no spellbinding could prevent the ultimate in Republican disunity—the great party split of 1912 and the election of the Democrats nationally. Taft, with his combination of clumsy politics and high statesmanship, could not hold back the high-flying Progressives and their prima donna leader, Theodore Roosevelt. Harding must go down with the wreck, hoping that the time might yet come when he could lead his party to safer harbors.

CHAPTER NINE

The War of 1912 in Ohio

"Roosevelt has convinced us that so-called progression is principally political fol-de-rol." : : : *"Marion Daily Star," February 22, 1912*

The years 1912 and 1913 were heroic but tragic ones for Harding and the Ohio Republican party. Political treason was abroad in the land, and Harding was battling against it. The result was Democratic triumph in state and nation, as the future darkened for the GOP and the man from Marion.

Harding played a dual role in the fight against the Progressives in the campaign of 1912. On the one hand, he said and did some very sound and sensible things about party unity and loyalty as the Bull Moosers staged their disastrous bolt. On the other hand, he participated in some political maneuvering which typified the kind of thing against which the Progressives were revolting. The manipulation of the Ohio Republican delegate-selecting convention of June 4–5, 1912, from a potential Roosevelt majority into a Taft majority was as expert a piece of bossism as had ever been perpetrated in Ohio politics. It was only by tricky methods that Harding was selected to be a Taft delegate-at-large, and, without such selection, he could not have made his well-known nominating speech for the President at Chicago.

In 1912 Harding no longer flirted with the Progressives as he had in 1910; this time he fought them. He was his conservative self again. The mirage of the compatibility of the incompatible disappeared to the accompaniment of mutual recriminations between the two factions. There had to be a disaster worse than that of 1910 to teach the Ohio Republicans the folly of their factionalism. That was the national victory of the Democrats, and Ohio's voting Democratic in a presidential election for the first time since the birth of the Republican party.

The open and shameless defiance with which the Progressives treated President Taft disgusted Harding. Taft's politicking may have been clumsy, but Harding liked his honest and competent statecraft.

In Harding's estimation, everything that the President did was states-manlike. There was, for example, Taft's support of the businesslike Ballinger against the troublemaking conservationist, Gifford Pinchot. There was Taft's high-minded scientific tariff reform as against the hit-and-run tariff tinkering of La Follette. Harding also admired Taft's refusal to debauch the civil service with promiscuous patronage politics in the 1910 census administration, as well as in the rapidly expanding post office department.

On many an occasion Harding, and his editorial alter ego, Malcolm Jennings,[1] worked with honest zeal in Taft's behalf, and against factious criticism. When Ohio's one-time glorious defender of the GOP, the *Ohio State Journal*, "defected" to the Progressives, Harding voiced the indignation of stalwart Republicans. He selected some rash remarks of the *Journal* which praised Pinchot, placed "more faith in the popular intuition than in a government report," and called the "vox populi the vox dei." "Balderdash," roared Harding in reply, "It was the voice of the people which sent Christ, bearing his cross, to His death on Calvary, martyrs to the stake, and clamored for the burning of witches. . . . The inconsidered, the intuitive judgment of the people is the verdict of the mob, and he who upholds the work of the mob is an anarchist."[2]

How ridiculous it was, said Harding, that normal Republicanism should be called reactionary. "A real reactionary in the United States," he told the Union League of Cleveland, February 11, 1911, "today would be trodden beyond all recognition by the irresistible onward pressure."[3] The Republican party had grown with the times. Taft, judicious and businesslike, was "the most progressive president ever elected. . . . A more progressive citizen of higher conscience, capacity or courage has never been named for that office. To progression he adds the poise of statesmanship and lofty patriotism that is making for needed conscience." What was so reactionary about Taft's vigorous enforcement of the anti-trust laws, the continuation and enlargement of the nation's conservation and reclamation program, scientific tariff-rate determination, the promotion of such things as the postal-savings bank service for rural depositors, campaign expenditure publicity, international arbitration, workmen's compensation insurance, the income tax, good roads, scientific farming and reduction of child and woman labor?[4] In short, said Harding, "We are for President Taft, not because he is a progressive, but because he is Old Man Progressive himself."[5]

According to Harding, and the *Star*, the trouble with the Progressive movement was that it was based on personalities, not principles; it was anti-Taft and pro-Roosevelt. "The whole progressive movement," said the *Star*, "is based on an unreasonable antipathy to Taft." Charges that Taft was a betrayer of Republican principles simply did not jibe with the facts. Therefore, Roosevelt's talk about fighting for the common man against special interests was "claptrap." Roosevelt's main goal was a personal "lust for power." He was a "limelighter," unhappy in the shadows. Along came the flatterers, "the money kings who had failed to win favor from Taft," the "malefactors of great wealth," who had been indicted by Taft's vigorous anti-trust-law enforcement. There came also "the rabble of place hunters, for whom Mr. Taft had not provided. . . . All the failures, the incompetents, the political tramps, the political soldiers of fortune, willing to fight under any banner which promised excitement and loot." Roosevelt was too vain to resist. He looked around for an issue, and "found it in an assault upon the integrity of the courts" through his doctrine of the recall of judges and judicial decisions. "He had always been inherently lawless." He accepted help from the very apostles of privilege he denounced, from George W. Perkins, the Morgans, the Rockefellers, the Hannas. The *Star* likened Roosevelt to Benedict Arnold "for he won his country's plaudits and turned traitor when he might have joined in a victory." He was a "master drunk with ambition . . . an insufferable boss . . . intolerant . . . an unheeding dictator . . . a traitor in the camp. . . . His prototype in history was Aaron Burr, the same towering ambitions; the same overbearing disposition and ungovernable temper; the same ruthlessness in disregarding the ties of friendship, gratitude and reverence; the same tendency to bully and browbeat . . . the same type of egotism and greed for power." In short, "if the party survives only in hero worship, its dissolution ought to be recorded." [6]

With such assumptions, Harding engaged in high praise of party loyalty. Party organization and discipline were great virtues, not symptoms of corruption. Only through political parties could effective choices be made in the conflicting views on public problems. As Harding later recounted the situation, in a *Star* editorial of 1912, popular government was "made operative through the party," and the success of the party was made possible only by "cohesion, discipline and leadership." By this means "great questions were forged in the hearts and consciences of the people, hammered into shape on the anvil of the party caucus and tested and tempered in the bath of the ballot. Each new party was born of some great issue so vital and pregnant that it occupied the minds of the people, subordinating for the time all other matters and bringing about new alignments, and, until that question was finally settled, that alignment was maintained, and, of necessity, carried with it adherence to the party formation on other and related policies." And so the people divided into two great armies. "Every office was an outpost or an entrenchment. Loyalty and vigilance were necessary at every point. A Republican postmaster or sheriff had nothing personally to do in the fixing of a tariff schedule, but the power and patronage of his office might elect a congressman who would have the deciding vote. And so we were ruled by parties, and in our ignorance we prospered and were content. A man, before he submitted his claims and his ambitions to the electors at a general election, had to pass through the winnowing process of a party caucus or convention. Back of him, when elected, was a party responsibility, and the party was jealous of its prestige and its standing." [7]

The *Star*'s preachments were particularly choice in defending party responsibility against the chief projects of the Progressives—the "ephemeral fads": the direct primary and other direct legislation such as the initiative and referendum. "The direct primary," wrote the editor, "is almost daily being demonstrated to be a huge political job." Candidates get their names printed on a ticket "merely by request, without the backing, selection or responsibility of any party, and without party designation." The direct primary made too easy the selection of nominees by cliques. People simply were not interested in turning out to vote. Not yet in Ohio, said Harding, had a majority of the voters of any party gotten out for the primaries. Through the initiative and referendum lawmaking became "subject to the momentary whims of the people. . . . Intuition takes the place of knowledge." Mass meetings take the place of legislatures. Judges could be unbenched as a result of "public clamor." Why not, asked the *Star*, instead of the recall, have the "remain" by which an office holder who was satisfactory could retain his office indefinitely? He scorned the new "petition collectors," a by-product of the initiative, referendum, and recall, who, at a certain rate per signature, would get the required number of petitioners for any cause or candidate paying the price.[8]

What was wrong, asked the *Star*, with representative government? To be sure, there were occasional abuses. But "abuse would be impossible if the people always exercised the interest that is incumbent on good citizenship." Representative government permitted "conference, comparison of notes and exchange of opinion." The experience of the GOP and its levelheaded stalwarts was still a sound reliance. "If representative government is endangered, the Republican party will furnish the veteran defenders, about whom the hope of the nation may be enlisted." [9]

2

The trouble with the *Star's* pious preachments was that its editor and publisher did not always practice them. Enough of Harding's record has already been described to show that he more than once succumbed to selfish or ill-advised interests: to the Cincinnati Railway Company, the Cox machine, Governor Nash's dictates about municipal home rule and taxation. There was a lack of conviction in his claims that Ohio already had workmen's compensation, adequate direct primary laws, and sufficient child-labor legislation.[10] Ohio's workmen's compensation law in 1912 was optional, and, therefore, actuarily inadequate. As for child-labor laws, Ohio Republicans in these years were always several steps behind the standards favored by Progressives. On the direct-primary issue, one could hardly credit Harding's citing of a system that he had so bitterly criticized. With respect to his admiration for Taft's trust-busting record, there is no indication that Harding ever understood the "rule of reason" included in the idea that the right to decide what was fair profit was essentially a judicial one.

Harding was a beneficiary of a clever deal made in the Ohio Republican state convention of June 4–5, 1912, which railroaded the selection of Taft delegates-at-large, including Harding himself, to the Chicago national nominating convention. The state convention was the culmination of much spring politicking between the Ohio Progressive Republican League and the Taft organization. The League was masterminded by Walter F. Brown, chairman of the Republican state central committee, who supported Roosevelt. The Taft organization was headed by Louis C. Laylin, chairman of the Republican state executive committee, which had run the Harding campaign in 1910. Secretary to this committee was Malcolm Jennings, associate editor of the *Marion Daily Star*. The executive committee was officially appointed by the central committee, but retained its Taft leanings because of the circumstances of the 1910 election. Neither Brown nor Laylin, of course, could officially declare their respective committees to be for their particular candidates, but they did use their official contacts with the county organizations in behalf of their favorites. Taft and Roosevelt toured the state during May, exchanging verbal blows while Brown and Laylin were using their offices for their opposing contenders.

There were two sets of primaries, both of which showed a popular preference for Roosevelt. One, held on May 21, was by congressional districts, and produced 34 delegates to the Chicago convention pledged to Roosevelt and 8 pledged to Taft. The other primaries, held by counties at various dates up to June 1, some by direct primary and some by convention, produced delegates to the June 4–5 state convention, which was to pick 6 delegates-at-large to the Chicago convention. Harding was a candidate for delegate-at-large. As the state convention met, these county delegates lined up 349 for Taft, 335 for Roosevelt, and 74 uninstructed, 53 of whom were from Cuyahoga County. According to George B. Harris of Cleveland, there was an agreement between Brown and Cleveland Republican leader, Maurice Maschke, that Cuyahoga's 53 delegates should be divided in proportion to the popular votes for Roosevelt and Taft in the county primary. Since Roosevelt received 71 per cent of the vote, 38 of the Cuyahogans could be counted for him. This put Roosevelt ahead of Taft by 373 to 364, with 21 uninstructed. Roosevelt needed only 7 of the uninstructed votes for a majority. As the final count on June 5 showed, most of the uninstructed votes outside of Cuyahoga were for Roosevelt. If Maschke had lived up to his promise, Roosevelt would have won the six delegates-at-large, thus preventing Harding from going to the convention.

Maschke did not live up to his promise to deliver the 53 Cuyahoga delegates at 38 for Roosevelt and 15 for Taft. He delivered them all to Taft. He did this, according to Harris, at the insistence of Senator Theodore E. Burton of Cleveland, who told Maschke that the 53 Cuyahoga delegates must go for Taft because Taft insisted upon it. Burton said that he could not face the President again if Cuyahoga was for Roosevelt. Burton also told Maschke that the latter owed it to Taft to deliver these votes because Taft had reluctantly made Maschke Collector of Customs in Cleveland at Burton's insistence.[11] Thus did Taft dictate a majority for himself and the selection of six Taft delegates-at-large, including Harding, to go to Chicago. But, even so, it was small consolation to the GOP because it made the total Ohio delegates for Taft 14 as against 34 for T. R. And it was much consolation to the Progressives who would claim, accurately, that Taft had stolen his state convention majority.

The Burton-Taft-Maschke maneuvers at the convention were further aided by the retention of a gag rule in regard to polling county delegation votes. The prevailing rule permitted a poll only by a challenge from the county delegation itself. Walter Brown wanted a poll upon the call of any delegate in the convention, and was able to get the rules so amended on June 4. This would have enabled the Roosevelt men to have challenged Maschke's delivery of the Cuyahoga delegation to Taft. But the Taft men outfoxed Brown by calling an early-morning meeting of the rules committee, presumably with enough Roosevelt men caught napping, so that the gag rule was restored before nominations were begun, when the convention opened at 9:30 A.M. on June 5. Incidentally, the *Star* described this incident as if it were a tricky move by Brown against Taft.[12]

Although the Taft men manipulated the delegates-at-large selection in their own favor, they did not get the June 4–5 convention to endorse Taft. The President's managers worked mightily to get this to come to pass, on the natural assumption that Taft would look very bad if not endorsed by his own state convention. Taft's Washington manager, Charles D. Hilles, pulled every string he could to bring about this result. He reported to the President that Laylin, Jennings, Daugherty, and others were in full control of the situation, and assured him that they would control the state convention. Harding's part in this was specifically arranged. "It is desired," Hilles informed Taft, "that Harding go to Washington for a conference with the secretary [Rudolph Forster] on the subject of the platform." Harding proceeded forthwith to Washington to be a member of the high-bracket conference which prepared a platform praising Taft.[13]

But the Roosevelt men were fully aware of the Taft machine maneuvers and used the knowledge to their own advantage. They made so much publicity of the Harding puppetry than they were able to eliminate the Taft endorsement from the platform as finally accepted. The pro-Roosevelt *Columbus Dispatch* made much ridicule of Harding as a tool of the bosses. "Warren G. Harding . . . is back from Washington," it was reported on June 2, "carefully carrying a very precious document in the shape of a platform for the Republicans of Ohio, as President Taft wants it. The president . . . has already decided who he wants for the Big Six, so if the president should by any chance control the convention, it will not be necessary for the delegates to do any work. It has all been done for them in advance, reminding them of the good old days when George B. Cox and the railroad and liquor lobbyists controlled all of the state's policies." Mr. Harding will guard this document "unassisted by the National Guard or Burns detectives, until the time comes to tell the delegates what they must do." [14]

Harding was no hero in the June 4–5 Ohio Republican convention. This time he was the spokesman of a most unpopular cause. He was denied membership on the convention's resolutions committee and had the thankless task of introducing and defending his Washington-prepared platform on the floor of the convention. For the first time, Harding was greeted by hisses and catcalls. He began with his old-time, florid eloquence: "It was just such a convention as this that nominated John C. Frémont. It was just such a convention as this that gave us the immortal Lincoln, Hayes and Garfield. It was just such a convention as introduced to the nation our illustrious William McKinley. It is such as gave its hearty endorsement to Theodore Roosevelt, but that was when Mr. Roosevelt was a leader of the Republican party." That broke the spell. There was a torrent of hisses. The magic was gone. Losing his poise, he retorted, "You can be for Roosevelt if you want to, but remember that you are sailing your Titanic at full speed. Be careful for there is ice ahead." This led to more hisses and cries of "Shame." Thoroughly angered, Harding rebuked his hecklers, "I have spoken more than 300 times to Republicans, Democrats and Socialists, but it is the first time that I ever was hissed." This brought some applause from the Taft side of the hall and shouts of "Go on." But when Harding likened the abuse of Taft to the crucifixion of Christ, the storm of hisses revived. "O, you'll be appealing to Calvary yet," was Harding's retort.[15] The behavior of the convention "would have disgraced a prize fight," wrote Roosevelt delegate Arthur L. Garford, in his "Recollections of a Rumpus." In spite of it, added Garford, "he did wonderfully well amid a storm of insults. No man in Ohio is so handy with words as Harding." [16]

Harding, of course, with his assumption that conventions were more reliable than primaries, assumed that there was nothing wrong with this affair of June 4–5, 1912—at least with his part in it. It is possible that he did not know about the Burton-Maschke-Taft deal. Assuming that the selection of the Taft delegates-at-large was unbossed, he wrote in the *Star*, June 8, that the delegates to it "had their commissions as directly from the people as the Roosevelt district delegates to the national convention." However, he did admit to some betrayal of constituents by delegates, when he wrote, "It is remarkable and pleasant to know that few of them betrayed the people who named them." Certainly "there was no effort on the Taft side to resort to coercion, intimidation or bribery. . . . There was no steam roller and no machine."

3

However much Harding may have been troubled by the questionable status and tactics of the GOP in Ohio, he could find solace in being chosen as the orator to put the President into nomination at the Chicago convention. He had been rumored for the assignment ever since the New York *Sun* on March 31, 1912 had mentioned it. For over two months Harding had been conspicuously coy in disavowing any responsibility for the rumors. Finally, on June 5, when the Ohio GOP managed to make Harding one of the "Big Six" delegates-at-large to Chicago, Taft made it official by a personal letter of invitation. Harding accepted with much gratitude, and proceeded to prepare a speech which the President approved without change.[17]

Harding was no hero at Chicago. He was one of a distinctly unpopular minority of fourteen in a total Ohio delegation of forty-eight. As the ardently pro-Roosevelt *Cleveland Leader* said, "The Taft instructed delegates-at-large from Ohio are a sham 'Big Six.' They will go to the national convention with less of prestige than any one of the forty-two delegates elected by the people. It's dollars to doughnuts that none of the six will be selected even as chairman of the delegation and when the roll is called Ohio's vote will be announced as thirty-four for Theodore Roosevelt to fourteen for William H. Taft."[18] The *Leader* was right. There were no appointments for Harding at the national convention even though the Taft men controlled it. That was simply because he was a minority member of his own state delegation. All that Harding got was a gentleman's agreement with Arthur L. Garford, majority leader of the Ohio delegates, to vote Ohio thirty-four to fourteen on all occasions.[19]

Harding's nominating speech for Taft was an anticlimax. The convention met on Monday, June 17, but it did not get around to

nominations until Saturday, June 23. The week was taken up mostly
with a dogged fight over contesting Roosevelt delegates. There were
more than two hundred of these. Most of them were technically
without merit because they had been chosen by one sort of primary
process or another that was not recognized by law and, therefore,
barred by the official rules of the party. Harding often vigorously
declared that the Roosevelt delegate contests were rigged to give
Roosevelt a chance to make publicity for his claim of Taft thievery.[20]
That the Roosevelt contesting delegates represented more popular
support than did their Taft rivals, in most cases, cannot be doubted.
There were over 400 uncontested Roosevelt delegates and most of
these were elected by direct primary processes. This contrasted with
the fact that the Taft delegates, which were safely in the majority, had
been elected by convention methods with a goodly proportion coming
from the non-Republican South. In other words, if there had been a
legal way of getting popular Republican sentiment, Roosevelt would
have been nominated in a landslide. That is why, by Saturday, June 23,
tempers broke down as contests were all settled in favor of the Taft
delegates. That is why hot charges of "burglars and pirates" and "naked
theft" were flung at Taft men, and fist fights broke out on the floor of
the convention. And that is why, when Saturday came, the beaten Progressives were simply waiting for the official nomination of Taft,
before marching in a body from the Chicago Coliseum to Orchestra
Hall to bolt the Republican party and set up a new one with Roosevelt
as the standard-bearer.[21]

Harding's nomination speech for Taft was another hissing-and-
cheering affair. The Progressives, having made up their minds to bolt,
were determined to make as much trouble for Harding as possible.
Before Harding was introduced, one leather-lunged Roosevelt delegate roamed up and down the aisles bellowing through a megaphone
that the next speaker on the program would be "Funeral orator
Warren G. Harding." At one juncture, when Harding referred to Taft
"as the greatest progressive of his time," another Rooseveltian became
so profane that fisticuffs resulted and were joined in so generally that
it took a score of policemen to restore order. How little attention was
paid to Harding by the Taft people was indicated by the fact that,
when he mentioned Taft's name about halfway through the address,
the cheerleaders engaged in a premature sixteen-minute demonstration of yelling and marching.[22]

Harding's speech bristled with barbs at the Progressives and re-

sounded with calls for sober and righteous leadership. There was
warning against demagogues, against "the party expediency," against
"ephemeral whims," against "disloyalty in our ranks inspired by pap
rather than patriotism." There was glorification of representative and
honest government, judicious leadership, moral stamina, poise, and
patience.[23]

The speech was variously received. The *Ohio State Journal*, though
defending Roosevelt, called it a "fine effort both in language and
sentiment. . . . Harding stood for his side of the case with courage
and good sense. . . . He declared some mighty sound doctrine, that
will stand the test of a real Progressive statesmenship." [24]

Another commentator on Harding's conduct was "Princess Alice,"
Roosevelt's daughter and wife of Nicholas Longworth. In her book
Crowded Hours, Mrs. Longworth stated that her dislike of President
Harding began at this convention. His Taft speech, she said, was
"run-of-the-mill. . . . We must have been obstacle struck not to leave
before then." She condemned Harding for coming to them in the
gallery and offering her husband the governorship of Ohio. Before
Longworth could answer, his wife told Harding "that we could not
accept favors from crooks." She wrote that she thought it was "a little
obtuse and raw of Harding to make that offer to Nick in my presence."
Longworth pleaded with Alice to apologize to Harding for calling him
a crook. She declined on the grounds that "that was what I had meant
to say." [25]

4

Harding's role in the rest of the campaign of 1912 was to help the
Ohio GOP run a good second instead of a poor third behind Roosevelt. This is what happened, and Ohio was one of the few states with
such a record. Nationally, in November, Taft received 3,484,980 votes
to Roosevelt's 4,119,538, whereas in Ohio Taft led Roosevelt by
278,168 to 229,807. Woodrow Wilson was, of course, the leader and
winner in both cases.[26]

The recovery of the GOP from the Progressive bolt may be said to
have begun in Ohio in the early summer of 1912. This is seen in the
fact that the Republican convention which, in June, was so evenly
divided, reassembled on July 2 and endorsed Taft by a majority of
125. Perhaps the very shock of Roosevelt's political treason accounted

for this, or, perhaps, it was the "Ohio, Mother of Presidents" feeling coming to the defense of its native son against an outsider. At any rate, Harding performed masterfully in the restoration of Taft prestige, as he did throughout the campaign.

The Progressive tactics at the reassembled state convention in Columbus were for the Republicans to be united on state issues but disunited nationally—in other words, to join with the Regulars in naming a governor but to refuse to support Taft for President. The issue was joined when the platform committee made a majority report endorsing Taft and a minority one without such an endorsement. Both platforms bristled equally with full-fledged Progressive commitments.

For the Ohio Republican party to be united on local issues and at the same time disunited on Taft was unthinkable to Harding. The Progressive proposal at the reassembled convention made him very angry. There were cries from the delegates of "Harding, Harding." With fire in his eye, he mounted the platform, thanked them for the courtesy, and reminded them that he had been hissed the last time he spoke to them. He said he was for Taft then, and was for Taft now. Someone shouted, "We know what kind of a Republican you are." To this, Harding fired back, "I am not used to courtesy in conventions." Then, referring to the doctrine of loyalty of the half-and-half variety, he said, with bitter sarcasm, "If the temper of this convention represents that better and cleaner party, I resign my connection with it beginning today. I wouldn't want to belong to any party which wouldn't endorse its standard bearer." "Let's be Republican," he shouted. If the "half-and-half" Republicans wanted to oppose their officially chosen national leader, let them go over to the Democrats who were assembling in Baltimore to nominate Woodrow Wilson. "If any one wants to go to the Baltimore convention, let him go and he will come back with repentance. If we refuse to stand by the standard of William Howard Taft we are no longer Republicans." He then moved the tabling of the "half-and-half" report. That stopped the debate, and, in the ensuing vote, the report was tabled 426½ to 301½. The majority report, *i.e.*, the endorsement of Taft, was thereupon adopted by the same vote.[27]

Harding had won a stirring victory. The convention majority of 28 for Taft in the June session had been increased to 125 in July. There could be no bolt of Ohio Progressives under these circumstances. No one could claim, as had been the case in the June 4–5 affair, that the convention had been stolen. Harding had put the issue squarely up to a group of over 700 delegates, and they had voted emphatically for party unity.

The convention could now proceed to the nominating of a gubernatorial candidate with the expectation of loyal support. The Progressives proposed Arthur L. Garford, Elyria businessman. There were four other names presented, including Bernard H. Kroger of Cincinnati. Harding was not one of them. He did not say so publicly, but he had no desire to be a candidate in a contest more hopeless than that of 1910. In the first two ballots no majority was given to any of the five. Garford led with the 300 or so Progressives supporting him, but he could not get a majority because he was unalterably committed to opposing Taft for President. A few scattered votes had been cast for Judge Edmund B. Dillon of Columbus.

According to the *State Journal* it was Harding who started the concentration on Dillon. At the end of the second ballot, Harding came to the platform and proposed to the chairman, Senator Burton, that all agree to name Dillon by acclamation. Harding then went to Walter Brown, the Progressive mastermind. Exactly what he proposed was not stated. The supporters of Kroger followed Harding to the conference with Brown to see what was going on. The central aisle was blocked by conferees. The result was that neither Kroger nor Garford budged. Nevertheless, on the third ballot, Dillon's vote increased and on the fourth, he went into the lead. On the fifth the Kroger and Cleveland delegation went to Dillon, who was thereupon nominated.[28]

The Ohio Republicans evidently thought they had survived the crisis. When the fifth balloting was completed, pandemonium prevailed. Dillon was "dragged" toward the platform. Had it not been for Harding, said the *Journal,* "he might have suffered some embarrassment." Harding stopped the shouting until the count was officially announced, and led Dillon to the platform where the judge received a great ovation. Dillon said a few words, the gist of which was: "You will not need to ask to what faction I belong. I belong to the people. Later on I will set forth the principles on which I expect to make my campaign."[29]

It was too good to last. On August 1 Dillon presented his resignation to the state committee. He said that he had accepted on the understanding that there was to be no third party in Ohio. This understanding had been shattered, he said, by the action of the Ohio

Progressives in circulating petitions for the preparation of a sample ballot containing presidential electors for Roosevelt. Dillon put the blame squarely on Roosevelt. "As everybody knows, or soon will know," he said, "his peremptory demand has from the beginning been that with respect to the regular nominee for governor, that the nominee must declare for him or he will nominate another candidate who will. This was true in my case and I refused." [30] There was nothing "half and half" about Dillon.

With the gubernatorial nomination going begging, it looked for a while as if Harding might have to take it. The *Ohio State Journal* started a belated boom which culminated on August 8, with headlines: "HARDING'S NAME UP AS A PARTY MOSES." The article told of a meeting of Taft leaders in Columbus, at Harry M. Daugherty's invitation. Harding "came to hear what Daugherty had to say, not to get into the race, but was greeted with the suggestion that he was the Moses to lead the harrassed Republicans out of the Egyptian darkness." The next day it was reported that "in the Taft camp yesterday, the strong impression, if not assured understanding, was that Harding could be drafted if the state committee so desired." Harding refused.[31]

Whether the gubernatorial nominee was to be a Moses or a goat, the Republicans finally found a man willing to run, but, in the process, gave the Progressives an excuse for nominating a candidate of their own. The Republican state central committee was the "little convention" to which was confided this last-minute selection. It met in Columbus on August 10 with Walter Brown presiding, and with a Progressive compromise candidate as a peace offering. He was Brown's fellow Toledoan, U. G. Denman, former state attorney-general. Denman, said the Brown peacemakers, "was for Taft, but if nominated, he would be endorsed by the Progressive party, which would accept the whole state ticket, the unsaid but understood fact being that he would not declare for Taft or Roosevelt, but make a campaign on state issues. They offered him as the one last hope of amalgamation of the disrupted party in support of the state and local tickets, leaving factions free to support Taft or Roosevelt as they pleased." This, of course, was the same old "half-and-half" proposal that Harding had so spiritedly opposed, that the July 2 session of the convention voted down, and that Dillon had rejected. Hence the committee, having a slim majority for Taft, turned the Denman offer down. According to the *Ohio State Journal*, they "feared being led into a trap and that they would wake up to find that Denman, absent in Michigan, with no one here to speak for him, would declare for Roosevelt." Therefore, they voted to nominate General R. B. Brown, editor of the *Zanesville Courier*. General Brown was an out-and-out Taft man, and his newspaper "had lambasted Colonel Roosevelt in strong words." "This simplifies matters for us," said Walter Brown. He thereupon resigned from the state central committee and set the wheels in motion for the nomination of Arthur L. Garford as Progressive Republican candidate for governor of Ohio. Harding countered the resignation of Walter Brown and some of his colleagues with the remark, "It's the only nice thing the Republican faction has done in the campaign. It was the only thing they could do in honor. Now the lines will be closely drawn and the battle will be between the straight Republicans and the bolters and hero-worshippers." [32]

5

Thus did Ohio Republican hopes for unity and victory in 1912 officially expire. The Taft men admitted it. So did the *Ohio State Journal:* "Freely Taft leaders admitted that the break-up presented the prospect of defeat, in November, of the national and state tickets at the Ohio polls. Rather that, they said, than covet attack. 'We know now what we have to face,' they said." [33] Even Harding allowed himself to talk publicly about possible defeat. He told a *Journal* reporter, August 14, 1912, "I would much rather it be defeat than to attain a temporary victory by hypocritical appeals to the masses of the American people."

The Republican nominee also expected to be defeated. He told Harding so two days after the nomination. In a sentimental letter to "big hearted, chivalrous 'Warren' G. Harding, the friend of my younger manhood," General Brown wrote, "You filled my soul with gratitude and inspired a courage which I mean to maintain to the end. Let's fight a straight-out, old time Republican campaign. There are glories in temporary defeat, defeats that end in holding the banner aloft, as you held it and still hold it. Of course, you are to help—and mightily—and we shall win the respect of mankind by manly courage. I am ready and un-a-fraid." [34]

Once more, Harding gave himself freely to that which he loved—

the free-for-all of political campaign. Again, as in 1910, he worked up a hopeful outward appearance to a hopeless cause. "Ohio Republicans," said the *Star*, "wear brighter and cheerier faces. The ranks have been cleared." It called General Brown "a stalwart, true blue, loyal fighting Republican . . . every inch a man . . . a square dealer . . . a valiant warrior." Brown was aided by vigorous disciplinary measures by the new state central committee chairman, Harry M. Daugherty, who became his own state executive committee chairman, and called on all county committeemen to declare for Taft or resign. This had the effect of bringing over to Taft the candidates for county office and also had the added effect of causing many of them to be defeated by Democrats. Similarly, Daugherty cracked down on the candidates for state office. Many of them came over to the Taft side when the Roosevelt men refused to let them run on both Republican and Progressive tickets. Such vigorous discipline helped the Ohio Taft candidates to run second instead of third, and forecast a collapse of the Roosevelt movement in Ohio after 1912.[35]

Of course, there was no Republican victory. Harding expected the defeat, and when it happened, he made no concealment of his satisfaction. He rejoiced at the rejection of Roosevelt, and the ruin of the Progressive hopes for the future. "Well," the *Star* chortled, "the mad Roosevelt has a new achievement to his credit. He succeeded in defeating the party that furnished him a job for nearly all his manhood days after leaving the ranch, and showed his gratitude for the presidency at this party's hands. The eminent fakir can now turn to raising hell, his specialty along other lines." The *Star* reminded the Bull Moosers how they had forced many minor Republicans out of office, "a fact which should not be forgotten when they seek to return to places of power in the Republican party." This was the fate of all bolters. "Stalwart Republicans are so incensed politically that years will not reconcile them to any party formed under the banner of bolters. . . . Thousands of Republicans, born, bred, and battle scarred as Republican Stalwarts, would go to Democracy under ordinary political conditions, before enrolling with the Roosevelt wreckers." The rank and file of commonsense Americans would support the regular parties while the radicals would not join the Progressives, but would "take their stand with the parties of agitation, like the Socialists, which do good by forcing some worthy ideas upon the attention of the large parties, but which can never be trusted with power."[36]

6

For Harding and many other stalwart Republican souls, there was a new hero in the Ohio Republican party. He was Harry M. Daugherty, who had taken over the chairmanship of the state central committee from the "traitorous" hands of Walter F. Brown. "Our hat is off to chairman Harry M. Daugherty," wrote the *Star* editor. "He never wavered in the fight, though his ammunition was short and the odds heavily against him. Men of the Daugherty type will eventually come to reward." [37]

Thus began the famous Harding-Daugherty political friendship. Though imperiled in 1918, it was based on the principle of party loyalty. Daugherty described it in a letter of January 13, 1913; he wanted to resign from party leadership, but could not do so in fairness to Harding and the party. With the true ring of sincerity, Daugherty wrote, "It was only on account of such support given me by you and others, but principally you, that made it possible for me to go through this terrific fight. . . . I should like very much to resign this chairmanship, but it is impossible and while I have it I propose to show my willingness at least to stand by the men as well as the Party they supported." He was thinking of appointments and offices he could salvage from the Democratic victory. He concluded with words prophetic of power and appointments to come: "I think it can be said now that you and I are two men who do not change colors, nor did we retreat. I am proud to be associated with men who would rather fall than falter in a contest such as we had." [38]

Let it be clearly understood that Daugherty's part in this 1912 disciplining, with its promise of a future to the Ohio Republican party, was patronage-based. He insisted upon full use of Taft's patronage power in the state. On March 6, 1912, Hilles prepared a memorandum which read, "If the Prest. will make a personal request of Daugherty to take hold of the fight in Ohio, he will do it; he can get more men to work than any man in the state." [39] Precisely what this meant to Daugherty in terms of patronage was specified in a letter which he wrote to one of Taft's secretaries, Carmi A. Thompson, on August 27, 1912. "My Dear Carmi," wrote Daugherty, "I am advised that the sundry civil appropriations bill provides for the employment of 300 clerks, not to exceed $1200 each, in connection with the new pension bill. When will these jobs be available? I understand the civil service registration has no control over them. I was in hopes that more than 300 would be created for Ohio men, but we will be content with the 300. I wish you would advise me where these positions are, the kind of service that is to be rendered, etc., in order that I may put in first claim for the full number." [40] How a couple of these appointments were arranged for was indicated on September 15, 1912, when Daugherty wrote Thompson, "I wish you would, upon receipt of this letter, hold two places, one for a very deserving woman and one for a colored man who is a lawyer and very capable, both of whom I will recommend doing the work." [41]

Daugherty was not entirely happy in this 1912 job-placement operation. It developed that Taft's postmaster-general, Frank Hitchcock, was not too careful in depriving Progressives of political appointments. "I'll be damned," Daugherty wrote Thompson on September 11, 1912, "if I don't propose to resign this job if Hitchcock's conduct in putting things over on us is not stopped. I spend half of my time listening to stories of the damage being done by employees of the Postoffice Department. I can't understand it and neither can anybody else here. I hope if the President does not do so before you get this letter that you will see that the appointment of J. M. Master at Pittsburgh is stopped. He is reported to be absolutely poisonous and vicious." [42]

Whatever President Taft did about Hitchcock's attempt to keep Progressives loyal by patronage, he appreciated what Daugherty was doing in keeping Progressives out of the patronage. "I congratulate you," wrote the President on September 16, 1912, "from the bottom of my heart on the success of the course you have taken in Ohio. We know our friends and we know our enemies, and we are in the fight to stay." [43] Hilles told Daugherty on September 13 that Taft would not make specific pledges, but, "if he is elected, no doubt he would have an opportunity to make many appointments agreeable to the Ohio crowd." Hilles added, "I must confess that I have slipped in and got a couple of places for good Ohio people . . . two of the boys who did good work for us in the preliminary campaign." [44]

7

However he might rationalize the Republican disaster of 1912, Harding was really a very gloomy and depressed man in the days that followed. His political future looked dim indeed. The Democrats were in control of the state and nation, and the one leading Ohio Republican officeholder, Senator Theodore E. Burton, was entitled to a renomination in 1914, if he wanted it. The governorship was no longer attractive—this was for the "small fry."

Harding was even denied a consolation prize, which he very much deserved—appointment by Taft to some foreign diplomatic post. On November 12, 1912 he wrote to Lewis Laylin about the vacancy caused by the resignation of the American ambassador to Japan. Laylin immediately conferred with President Taft, who told him that the Japanese post was going to Larz Anderson, minister to Belgium. There was no other suitable vacancy at the moment, but the President "commended your loyalty" and hoped that some other vacancy would occur before his term expired.[45] Laylin and Carmi Thompson took the problem to Daugherty, who gently rebuked Harding for not consulting him in the first place. Daugherty seemed most optimistic and promised to use his influence with Taft. "I want this to come to you," he wrote to Harding, "as a spontaneous and generous offer on behalf of the President, and be able to say that you never asked anything." [46] Nothing, however, ever came of these maneuverings.

Harding's political depression continued throughout the non-election year of 1913. Especially calamitous to him was the new Ohio constitution, which had been adopted by the people on September 3, 1912. This document, the *Star* believed, turned the state over to the Democrats and Socialists. What bothered the editor was not the social legislation involved, like workmen's compensation. Rather, it was the provisions for "home rule" for the cities where the ignorant rabble, the radical immigrants, the unscrupulous agitators, and the yellow press would vote into effect municipal ownership of public utilities. "The unrestricted powers of municipalities, the provisions for public ownership, the initiative and referendum in law making and constitutional changes—these are the avenues for socialistic advance." So lamented the *Star* the day after the vote on the constitution:

> The smaller cities and rural communities voted conservatively. But the cities with the great socialistic organizations and the propaganda of the syndicated press overwhelmed them. The experience of Tuesday will be easy to repeat. Ohio has broken her moorings. The revolution is on. . . . A crowd of selfish schemers and socialistic dreamers . . . have opened the floodgates for every form of government experiment and folly; they have swept away the legal safeguards of a century. In blind indifference, half the electorate remained away from the polls and

turned their affairs over to the domination of the Bigelows, Scripps, Debs, McNamaras and Gompers and their kind. The judiciary has been revolutionized and no man can henceforth be said to have a certain knowledge of the law. Property has been stripped of its rights, and provision made to plunder it in the interest of the idle and improvident.

Yes, Ohio industry and commerce were doomed. "Burdens have been placed upon enterprise which will drive capital into other and saner states." [47]

Harding's gloom deepened as President Wilson and a Democratic Congress took over the guidance of the nation. This meant tariff revision and, therefore, economic disaster. The low rates of the new Underwood tariff, for example, were sure to produce a depression. It was "a shame," the *Star* lamented, "to give to Europe access to our wonderful market and spoil years of prosperity. When we produce less at home we will employ less, and the present state of nation-wide employment will be rended. Then we cease to be able to consume, having less money to buy with." Moreover, said the *Star*, "if we are going to have a depression, we might as well have a big one. We wish the proposed bill were very much more radical. We have no hesitation in predicting that there will come a paralysis of many industries, and attending depression and the lowering of American wages. We need the experience and the lesson which will attend. There never was a better time to have it than now." In Ohio the editor predicted "the utter ruination of the wool industry." As the debate on the Underwood bill proceeded, the *Star* urged, "Quit fooling, Senate. If the Democrats are right the effects will not be half so harmful as waiting uncertainty. If they are wrong the quicker people find it out and correct the blunder registered in 1912 the better for all concerned." When the Bureau of Foreign and Domestic Commerce reported a favorable trade balance as of June 30, 1913, the *Star* predicted that it was the "last . . . that will be recorded of this country until the American people reverse the economic policy . . . in process of enactment." After the Underwood measure had been passed, the *Star* recorded the rejoicing of foreign manufacturers who at once were said to have increased imports to the United States and the prices thereof. Then came the usual forecast of disaster, "If he [the foreigner] ever dominates the market one of two things will happen—American producers will reduce wages or suspend production—and in either case there will be a depression that will send prices tumbling until we return to protection." These depression-predicting editorials became regular fare in the *Star*. "Prices will tumble, but not because of declining import prices, but on account of impaired American ability to buy. It will not take long for lagging and lessened production to have depressing effect on prices." [48]

Lamentations were also in order concerning the new income tax. "It is the socialistic drift of the day. One man has talent and industry, and saves and acquires; he must be penalized for these because the man who spends his all, or lacks talent and industry, demands the unnatural equalization. . . . An income tax, once levied, will never be repealed. . . . The only change will be to increase its burden." Upon another occasion the *Star* declared, "The blatherers will never be satisfied until the thrifty share all the burdens and are obliged to contribute of their accumulations for the comfort of the spendthrifts." Once again, "Most people who are wealthy are looked upon as favored by privilege or profiting in dishonesty and this majority of politicians from now on to doomsday will assail them, because the great mass out numbers them in votes." [49]

In state affairs, the *Star* commented, things were said to be in a deplorable condition under the "dictatorship" of Democratic Governor Cox. It did not take the editor long to come to this conclusion. On January 29, 1913 he wrote, "As the days go by, it is becoming very apparent to all students of Ohio affairs that the people's rule is Governor Cox's rule. But the coordinate branch of the government known as the general assembly will be kept going to maintain appearances." When businessmen sought to invoke the referendum in the workmen's compensation act, and Cox objected, the *Star* gave the Governor the editorial laugh: "It is childish for Cox to wail when he campaigned for it." Then there were the "Cox boards," those administratively appointed county boards of license commissioners which supervised the state liquor control system, and the appointive county assessors under the Warnes tax law. These new laws created over 10,000 appointive positions, which put the Governor at the head of "the most gigantic political machine in any state in the Union. . . . Many people shuddered at Boss Cox, the Cincinnati Republican, as a spoilsman and machine politician. When measure is taken, he isn't one, two, three to Boss Cox, the machine builder, who is today's chief executive." [50]

The "War of 1912" had been a searing experience for Harding. His idols had fallen, Democrats ruled, Socialism was "creeping" in, and the refuge of a lame-duck foreign post had been denied him. Was there a political future for Warren Harding?

CHAPTER TEN

A 100,000-Plurality Senator
via Politics and the
Protestant Crusade, 1914

"Let us forget 1912." : : : *Harding, as quoted in the "Cleveland Leader," July 19, 1914*

"The sectarian wave of that year [1914] would have made a Chinaman successful on the Republican ticket." : : : *James W. Faulkner, in the "Cincinnati Enquirer," March 21, 1920*

Recovery from the madness of 1912 came unusually soon for Harding and the Ohio Republican party. The GOP had run second in the voting, and Daugherty had kept the party morale high by his strict denial of patronage hopes to the Progressives. The conservative leaders had sense enough to realize that, with a little graciousness and some side-stepping of controversial issues, partial reunion with the Progressives might take place. And the genial Harding was the ideal man to head such a movement. Add to this the Protestant crusade of the Ohio Guardians of Liberty against Harding's opponent for the United States Senate, Timothy S. Hogan, a Roman Catholic, and Harding became one of those political rarities, a 100,000-vote plurality winner.

Reconciliation required much avoidance of controversial principles and people. The quarreling of 1912 had to be forgotten and the leading candidates and incumbents of that year by-passed. It meant soft-pedaling the Progressive issue in party platforms. It meant the conservative United States Senator Theodore E. Burton would do the Ohio Republican cause a service by not running for reelection. It meant letting the popular involvement in politics gradually subside while party managers gathered together semi-secretly to make arrangements for nominations without arousing much public interest.

Thus it was that early in January, 1914, the Ohio Republican Regulars inaugurated a reunion-by-avoidance movement by undertaking discreet maneuvers to coax the Progressive prodigals back into the fold. The initiative came from a caucus of the Republicans in the new legislature that assembled in Columbus. On January 7, the state central committee followed up with a call for a reunion banquet in Columbus for February 26. A friendly gesture in the Progressive direction was to schedule the liberal Idaho Senator William E. Borah as the main speaker. A reception committee was appointed containing prominent members from both sides: Harding and Daugherty for the Regulars, and Dan R. Hanna and David Mead Massie for the Progressives.

This "forget-together," as Daugherty called it, or "love feast," to use the *Ohio State Journal's* phrase, was a very pleasant affair. Controversial discussion was taboo, except to denounce Democrats. All shades of Republicanism were represented from Foraker and Senator Theodore E. Burton on the far right to a sprinkling of Progressives on the left. Telegrams of regret were read from distinguished absentees such as Harding—all "good old souls," as the toastmaster remarked. The Columbus Republican Glee Club sang "Hail, Hail, the Gang's All Here," and other well-chosen reminders of the "grand old days." Daugherty was introduced as "Horatius, who held the bridge." The Progressive *Ohio State Journal* called the meeting "historic," and its Cleveland Progressive counterpart, the *Leader*, remarked on the "atmosphere which made it easy for Progressives to feel at home among their Republican brethren." [1]

Essential to the Republican-Progressive reunion was the confession by the Progressive press of the error of its 1912 ways. Dan R. Hanna, son of the "mighty Marcus" and publisher of the *Cleveland Leader*, was quite frank about this. In the year of the great folly, Hanna had supported the Bull Moosers, partly out of pique at Taft because the President had included the M. A. Hanna Company of Cleveland in his trustbusting program. Early in 1912 Attorney General George W. Wickersham brought suit against Dan R. Hanna and his company, alleging illegal rebate arrangements with the Pennsylvania Railroad. But the election figures of 1912 did much to cool emotions, and Hanna said so to George W. Perkins, Roosevelt's financial angel, in March, 1914 when Perkins attempted to revive Progressivism in Ohio. It was Roosevelt, not Progressivism, said Hanna, who gave Ohio Progressives their 215,000 votes in 1912. Without T. R.'s coattails in 1914, Hanna claimed, the party could not get 50,000 votes in the state of Ohio—a remarkably close prediction. Therefore, wrote Hanna to Perkins, he had decided not to "send for Walter," as Perkins had urged. Walter, of course, was Walter F. Brown of Toledo, the Ohio manager for Roosevelt in 1912. "Regarding sending for Walter," wrote Hanna, March 8, 1914. "I have thought it over and don't believe I will do it. . . . I like Walter and enjoy seeing him, but I am absolutely set in my ideas this time—and conscientiously believe in the 'get-together' movement." Hanna criticized vigorously the Progressive plan of getting Democratic Governor James M. Cox to give the Progressives minority party rights in patronage appointments in bipartisan committees and boards.[2]

Harding took full advantage of Hanna's return to political sanity. Indeed, the Marion publisher insisted upon it if he was to be a candidate for the United States Senate. This is confirmed by the report on April 10, 1914 of J. S. Hampton, former secretary to Governor Nash and one of Harding's political aides, who had conferred in Columbus with William H. Miller, secretary of the state executive committee. "I told Bill," wrote Hampton," that you would not go into the fight unless D. R. agreed to support you with his newspaper. Bill was delighted; he said it solved the whole problem; that he would at once talk with Harry Daugherty who was almost sure to be able to get D. R. to agree. . . . The D. R. support would come to you naturally. I'll bet my hat on that." [3]

It was Harding's opinion that the great Bull Mooser himself, Theodore Roosevelt, was encouraging Republican-Progressive reunion because he wanted the party nomination in 1916. In June, 1914 Harding commented wrily on the sore throat suffered by T. R. "I am not much of a doctor," Harding told Scobey, "but I saw this throat trouble or some other disability developing several days ago. . . . He is setting his sails for the Republican nomination for president in 1916. There will be little doing, on that account, in the Progressive party for 1914." [4]

2

Before the non-controversial Harding could run for the United States Senate, the rules of reunion required that the controversial incumbent, Senator Burton, should not run. This eventuality was not only hoped for by Harding but by a large number of Republican leaders. For the Progressives it was an absolute requirement. The scholarly and conscientious Burton had become almost as much of an embarrassment to the Ohio GOP as Taft had been. He was a sort of Taft hangover. He had not only praised the much-hated Payne Aldrich tariff but had committed the unforgivable sin of supporting President Wilson in seeking the revision of the Panama Canal Act so as to abolish the exemption of United States vessels from canal tolls. Burton and a few other Republicans, such as Henry Cabot Lodge, felt that this was an obligation of honor to England resulting from the agreement in 1902 to let the United States go ahead with the building and fortifying of the canal.[5]

Progressive opposition was causing the senatorial toga to rest uneasily on the shoulders of the learned Burton. On November 23, 1913 the Progressive *Columbus Dispatch* headlined:

SENATOR BURTON FEELS THE GAFF

DOES NOT LIKE IT

The *Dispatch* nagged the Senator for his Payne-Aldrich ardor and his Panama Canal "treachery." Even the *Star* encouraged the injection of barbs into the tender hide of Ohio's senior Senator. A newspaperman with public-relations sensibilities like Harding's could hardly appreciate the high-mindedness of a Burton. On the occasion of the Senator's birthday in December, 1913 the *Star* admitted that Burton was "a scholarly, Christian man, and a great, big statesman." But he "does not appeal to popular acclaim." The *Star* said it would like to write him a birthday greeting urging his renomination and reelection, "but knowing readers would question our understanding of popular sentiment among Republicans who fight for victory." [6]

Senator Burton was a sensitive man. He was also loyal. Hence, as the direct primary of 1914 approached, he told Republican leaders that he would be glad to get out of the way if he was an embarrassment to them. He told them this frequently—altogether too much so. On January 7, he informed the state central committee that a trip through Ohio convinced him that the people wanted a change, that he did not want to be a "deadhead," and that if his withdrawal would help bring the Progressives and Regulars together "no one would go further than he to serve this end." He said it again to the Western Reserve Club on Lincoln's birthday, and still again at the February 26 "love feast." On the latter occasion, he said, "In case no reunion is possible. . . . I am perfectly willing to step aside if that seems best." [7]

Most top Ohio Republicans were delighted at Burton's squeamishness and hoped that the Senator would heed the call of duty and retire. That was why the Harding-for-Senator movement followed so closely upon the heels of the Burton retirement movement. In fact, the expediter of both movements was Burton's closest political friend, Maurice Maschke, GOP leader in Cleveland and engineer of the Cuyahoga delegation maneuver at the Columbus convention of 1912. The moment that Burton, on April 7, made known his intention to retire, Maschke unhesitatingly turned to Daugherty, who at once alerted Harding. Hence, a few days later, when Burton sought to recall his decision to withdraw, it was too late. [8]

The speed with which Harding acted on the Burton retirement notice was matched by his frankness in giving reasons. According to the *Star* of April 7, 1914, Burton was a "real statesman . . . a big man in the Senate," but he was not a "big man" in Ohio. Indeed, he was "one of the least popular men in public life." Of course, a Progressive would not do, either. [9] What the *Star* meant without saying so was that what the Ohio Republicans needed as a candidate for the United States Senate was a man who had a better public record and personality than Burton. Such a man, of course, was Warren G. Harding.

3

The reason that Burton changed his mind about retirement was that a man more conservatively controversial than he took advantage of the withdrawal to become a candidate. This was former Senator Joseph B. Foraker, who had been sacrificed for Burton in the senate race of 1908 and who ached for a chance to revenge the mistreatment he had received from the repudiated Progressives.

For Foraker to be the Republican senatorial candidate for 1914 made the cold shivers run up and down the spines of party managers. It violated all the rules of political avoidance necessary for forgetting and reuniting. For the Republicans to nominate a Roosevelt-hater (and a Standard Oil attorney) was a sure guarantee of a Democratic victory. The Republican press, Progressive as well as conservative, were in full agreement on this. Hanna's *Cleveland Leader* fumed with indignation. Foraker's candidacy would "throw away the Republican party's chance of holding the one Ohio Senatorship which it still possesses." (Democrat Atlee Pomerene had replaced Republican Charles F. Dick in 1911.) Foraker was "reactionary to a degree which mocks the hopes of these who have believed the Republican party pledges to progressive ideas and principles, men and methods." The Foraker movement was "a fatuous and menacing effort to turn back the hands on the dial and retreat to the days of other aims, different leaders, and ways which the state and nation have outgrown." The *Columbus Dispatch* was equally outspoken. The conservative *Cincinnati Times-Star*, from Foraker's home city, envisaged a renewal of "old charges and old acrimonies," and the inevitable victory of the Democrats.[10]

Harding also shared the sense of impending calamity if Foraker were to become the Republican standard-bearer for the United States Senate in 1914. Of course, Harding could not bring himself to tell this to his old friend until after the primary. Then, in a touching letter, he wrote Foraker the terrible truth, "Now that the primary contest is all over, I want you to know that I entered the race, hoping you would incline to retire. I could not and would not ask it, but I hoped for it. I know the drift of Republican sentiment." Harding emphasized the "widespread feeling of independency" against Foraker. "It was because of this that I entered and hoped for your voluntary retirement." [11] Incidentally, this revolt of Harding against Foraker indicates fuller realization by the Marionite of the truth of his father's remark to a reporter in 1920 about Foraker's selfishness.[12]

As the May 31 deadline for entry into the primaries approached, the vengeful Foraker refused to withdraw. Thereupon, the same GOP unifiers, who had engineered the elimination of Burton, now turned to fight for Harding, who had delayed casting his hat into the ring. The only declarant against Foraker was the relatively unknown Ralph D. Cole of Findlay, who simply could not stop the former Senator. If Harding did not declare, Foraker would surely be nominated and either the Progressives or the Democratic nominee would win in November. Thus the popular Marionite was the GOP's only hope. Harding was therefore summoned to Cleveland to confer with Burton, Hanna, Daugherty, and Maschke. Harding was told in no uncertain terms that the fate of the Republican party depended on his running for the Senate. He thereupon took the next train for Cincinnati, told Foraker to his face that he was going to run, and, on May 28, announced his candidacy in behalf of party unity.[13]

The result was purely Hardingesque. He put on a campaign of such sweetness and light as would have won the plaudits of the angels. It was calculated to offend nobody but Democrats. No Progressive felt any sting in Harding's calm and dignified platitudes. The effect was as of old. Harding emerged from the primaries with friends on all sides. So frustrated was Cole that the fiery Findlayite exclaimed, "If he is not going to fight some one, why did he enter the contest. . . . If a man's not against somebody or something he has no business in a fight." [14]

4

There was no doubt about it, Harding simply would not fight. "How can I," he asked his friend Scobey, "consistently go out and bat either Senator Foraker or Ralph Cole over the head and tell the dear people they will never do?" To fight was to violate the canons of party unity. Party primaries should no more be scenes of personal discord than, presumably, old party conventions had been. He said so quite frankly at a Cleveland party picnic: "The Senatorial campaign has been quiet, but that is natural and proper. The Senatorship is not to be decided by sensationalism. . . . So far as I am concerned I am trying to make a canvass under the new conditions that came with the primary in such a way that I will have nothing to repent after August 11." It was the old soporific magic, the soothing spellbinding for a patchwork unity. "Let us forget 1912. Those who were with us before will be with us again, because they believe as we do and know that this party, reconsecrated to a people's service, is the highest agency of a nation's good. With no apologies offered, and none demanded, we look above and beyond the mistaken differences of an unhappy year, and see before us the line forming and the way clearing for the triumphant Republican comeback and the great state and the rejoicing nation will be ready to acclaim it." [15]

The Republican press, especially the formerly Progressive organs, beamed in benign approval of Harding's peace overtures. The *Ohio State Journal* unctuously described Harding "waving white flags of peace to the candidate who will emit fire and brimstone and 'burn 'em up.'" Dan Hanna's *Leader* was even more unctuous and general. It stressed Harding's political experience, his propensity for hard work, his common sense, sound judgment, and clean living, his friendly and neighborly spirit, and his loyalty to friends. It liked his business success and the fact that he had a "moderate competence." Of course, there was his oratorical ability. "He is a man of the people. His life has known the struggles and trials of those who win a hard fight against heavy odds." He was certainly no reactionary—actually he was a "moderate Progressive." He was "far too big to be anyone's catspaw." When the war in Europe broke out, the *Leader* claimed that his "strength and breadth" were needed "whatever the business of the nation may be before the world can quiet down." At the close of the primary, the *Ohio State Journal* commented that Harding had barely made any campaign at all.[16]

Harding made much, in a quiet way, of his business and newspaper connections in the state. His campaign manager was Hoke Donithen, Marion attorney (Harry Daugherty was not involved). Postcards went out to his fellow editors, containing his picture and an "address to Republican Electors." This contained a mild statement of principles evincing a belief in "representative government" and in a tariff to promote "maximum employment." But the most noteworthy item was Harding's comment on his rival candidates—that all of them were good Republicans. He asked his fellow Republicans to "bear in mind the capacity, character, belief, habit of mind of the candidate and his availability for the nomination in the exigencies of the contest." Nothing specific was said about anyone.[17]

Harding's business contacts were well exploited. At the head were two of Marion's big industrialists, W. H. Houghton of the Houghton Sulky Company, and George W. King of the Marion Steam Shovel Company. Houghton sent out circular letters to his customers urging Harding's election, citing his "sane and progressive principles," his "statesmanship and business judgment." King wrote similarly suggesting that the lowering depression needed the influence of a business-minded man like Harding in the halls of Congress.[18]

Working for Harding were assorted traveling agents who cadged votes for their favorite in a systematic and rather inconspicuous way. One group was composed of railroad men under the leadership of E. M. Costin of Springfield, assistant general superintendent of the Big Four Railroad (the Cleveland, Cincinnati, Chicago, and St. Louis). Taking advantage of a business recession that idled thousands of railroad workers and factory employees, Costin headed a team of his office subordinates to whom he gave time off to carry Harding promotionalism among the Big Four workers and those of the Big Four's customers. How Costin operated was shown in a report to Harding on

August 3, a week before primary day. He told him he had arranged to have Stephen A. Stack and W. F. Hanrahan off duty on the last three days of the campaign working with the aid of two Negro men on a big colored picnic at Buckeye Lake. Then there was J. C. Carney, business agent of the Big Four, who knew personally the heads of firms using the Big Four's shipping facilities. "Carney," said Costin, "has done more for you, and can do more for you than any one man that I know of. He has been in politics for a long while, and has a host of friends, and understands the game from the ground up, and I never saw him quite so enthusiastic over anything as he has been over your campaign. Carney will take care of the distribution of any funds that are furnished him toward the other workers here in Springfield." Costin also requested 6,000 more Harding cards for distribution by Carney, and "a little expense money" for J. J. Fishbaugh, yardmaster at Middletown, to be used "where it will do good." Costin also put in a good word for Harding with Edward B. Myers, of the Robbins & Myers Company of Springfield, who employed about 900 people and was doing "everything that he could" for Harding. It was suggested that Harding write Myers a personal acknowledgement of his kind offices.[19]

How enthusiastically J. P. Carney worked for Harding was shown by his report to his colleague "Steve" Stack on July 30. Carney reported that Frank P. Johnson, vice-president of the American Seeding Machine Company, employing 700 men, had pledged to "do all he could" for Harding. So had George H. Brain of the Brain Lumber Company and the Brain-McGregor Real Estate Company in Columbus—"a very influential man." Carney mentioned others such as Hammond and Tejan, Dayton contractors, who were said to be influencing their men for Harding. All in all, said Carney, "it looks like Harding every place. The business men in general are for Harding," he added, "Now if the railroad men will only do as they say they will and what few colored men we can get, I think Mr. Harding should pull through with a large majority."[20]

Similarly indefatigable in Harding's behalf was railroader "Steve" Stack. His reports to Harding on August 2 and 10 showed tremendous coverage of the state "during the period that I have been in charge of your work." He listed twenty-two cities and towns, not to mention smaller places which he had personally visited. He told of "good work" done at Van Wert and on the Cincinnati Northern Railroad. There was F. J. Willige of Logan, locomotive engineer of the Hocking Valley Railroad, who was "working through Hocking, Vinton, Jackson and Meigs counties." George Wilson, ex-employee of the Ohio Traction lines, was at Columbus "meeting all employees." He named three men "working" the Toledo and Ohio Central Railroad. Others were canvassing the Detroit, Toledo, and Ironton Railroad. Stack himself had spent several days in the mining districts. Stack was most optimistic. "In all my territory," he wrote on the day of the election, "I found your standing first class with the people and with those who had decided to support other candidates, and from my point of view of the situation I think there will be a general landslide for the Republican Party and that Mr. Harding will be nominated for United States Senator." [21]

One who claimed to be highly effective in delivering the vote of work gangs on large construction jobs was C. C. Hamilton of Dayton. He named as one of his clients the Dayton contracting firm of Hammond and Tejan. Hamilton said that Tejan had done good work with his construction crews in the past, and now was pledging that "he will vote his men for you, but same must be quiet as he is now working on State & County Work." Hamilton admitted, "Mr. Harding, this may not look square." [22]

What worried Hamilton more than the ethics of this sort of vote-catching was that, without it, the light primary vote that was expected would defeat Harding and permit Cole or Foraker to be elected. (This was the first statewide primary in Ohio for United States Senator.) Therefore, reasoned Hamilton, "we will have to get a bunch lined up the 11th [election day] and go right after them." The way to do it was to get three other firms to vote their work gangs in the Tejan manner. Here are Hamilton's words: "I figure to get 400 Votes from Davis Sewing Machine Company. I have a good man taking care of them[.] The Barney & Smith Car Company will Come all O.K. I closed a Contract yesterday for the draying of all material for the new Hotel which is to cost one million and by the 11th the Contractor advised me He would have at least 100 Colored men employed. He advised me to come right on the job and he would help me vote the Bunch now that is not bad." He added that a leading Toledo contracting firm had three large jobs "and I have the same with them." [23]

A significant phase of the Harding senatorial build-up was a mailing campaign based in Marion and managed by Hoke Donithen. Of Donithen, W. H. Houghton said, "Some glory belongs to your efficient campaign manager, Hoke Donithen." [24] Thousands of names poured into Donithen's office, resulting in post cards being sent out and bundles of smaller cards mailed for widespread distribution. Mailing lists were prepared from reports sent in by three agents: Charles E. Hard, secretary of the Republican state executive committee in Columbus, and J. S. Hampton and E. Howard Gilkey, two roving emissaries. Hundreds of names of important Republicans were supplied. Voluminous reports contained details on local political conditions. One from Hampton in Akron, dated July 1, reported that a fellow Ohioan "regards you as a great big brainy, broadminded fellow who made a chump of yourself two years ago but he loves you and thinks you will carry Summit Co. by about 2 to 1." A report from Gilkey in Marietta, dated July 2, told of a peculiar situation resulting from the Progressives "keeping things stirred up until no old line Republican knows where any other old Republican stands on any question without hiring a detective to find out." Hampton wrote on July 9 from Celina that another Ohioan "is for you and can get every Republican in his Co. if you jolly him." Hampton added, "I am working until 8 and 10 o'clock every night and taking 6 o'clock trains every morning so that I hardly have time to make lists." [25]

5

When the ballots of the Republican primary election were counted, Harding had won a narrow victory in a very light vote. It is tabulated as follows:

	Vote	Number of Counties Carried
Harding	88,540	51
Foraker	76,817	21
Cole	53,237	16

Regionally the count showed a much wider support for Harding. Fifteen of Cole's sixteen counties were from his section of northwestern Ohio. Harding usually ran a strong second in the counties he lost. It was this good showing by Harding in all parts of the state that impressed observing politicians. It should be added that the vote in the Progressive party primary, where there were no contests, showed only 7,519 votes for its senatorial candidate, Arthur L. Garford.[26]

The reaction of the Republican press showed that party leaders felt that they had a strong candidate, and that Harding was the ideal man to overcome the two greatest weaknesses in the party: reactionary Forakerism and radical Progressivism. As the *Akron Beacon-Journal* said, "On the republican side the most significant feature of the vote was the failure of Joseph B. Foraker to 'come back.' Despite his old popularity and his ability as a speaker, Foraker had no chance. What he didn't realize apparently, and what the party did, was that the day of the Forakers has passed in Ohio." The formerly Progressive *Leader* was happy in the general spread of Harding's vote, "He showed great strength in all parts of Ohio. His support came from cities, villages, and farms. It was hearty and spontaneous in the most popular counties and in the rural districts of the state. This in spite of the fact—or because of it—that he carried on a quiet, moderate and altogether creditable campaign. He will be a great asset to draw back to the Republican ranks the few Progressives who have not yet decided to return, at the same time keeping the Republican party of this state always safely and soundly progressive." The *State Journal* was also pleased that in Harding the party had a "widely popular man and a campaign orator who has few equals in Ohio or elsewhere." The *Journal* was impressed with Harding's courtesy and consideration in his "desperately close rivalry with Foraker." [27]

6

Harding was in his element again. As the restored Republican spokesman for Ohio, he sparked a campaign of wooing Progressives and denouncing Democrats which set the pace for a restoration of his party's unity both nationally and statewide. In this role of prominence he became what had previously been only whispered about and hoped for, a Republican party Moses. He was leading his party back to unity and, in so doing, was directing his own steps toward the White House. No "Ohio Man" as successful as he was about to become could avoid being mentioned as a presidential candidate. The year of 1916 was to demonstrate that.

With Harding's ingenious and tireless campaigning for United States Senator as an inspiring example, the Ohio Republican party opened a dazzling campaign in 1914 that was supposed to demonstrate party unity, and be in striking contrast to the "War of 1912." Harding was quite frank about it, for he sought to make it easy for both kinds of Republicans to confess their sins and forgive the sins of others. He made it a matter of state pride. If Ohio Republicans were to return to their former high place in the councils of the nation, they must be united. If Ohio did that, it would again be in the lead as the chief factor in the restoration of national Republican unity. At Cleveland, on August 15, in his first political speech following nomination, he told the Cuyahoga county central committee: "We could triumph on state issues alone, but we shall add thousands of enlistments and magnify the victory, because Ohio Republicans mean to lead the way to the national restoration. The people of this great state have come to realization and regret over the surpassing blunder that grew out of our differences in 1912, and mean to unite to correct that blunder. Ohio, strong in agriculture, ranking high in industry, important in commerce and finance, and second to none in the attainments of modern progress, means to be the advance guard in battling for the restoration of the national policies which have made us what we are." [28]

In the campaigning of 1914 Harding was no dictator over his running mates. The lead was taken by his buoyant young partner, Frank B. Willis, candidate for governor. This was simply following custom, because never before in Ohio had there been a popularly elected United States Senator. In the party caucuses of August he deferred to Willis and the rest of the Republican state ticket in the selection of the new state central and executive committees. That meant the continuation of W. L. Parmenter as chairman of the central committee and the appointment of a new man, Edwin Jones, businessman of Jackson, as chairman of the executive committee and former state auditor E. M. Fullington of Delaware as campaign secretary. It meant enlarged membership of both committees with each district member bringing in new colleagues to please their vanity. It meant the ratification of all this in the state convention of August 25, presided over by a rising young politician, professor, and congressman, Simeon D. Fess of Ada. It meant a platform declaration filled with denunciations of Democrats, Wilsonian free trade, and the Governor Cox "dictatorship." [29]

Important also to the new Republican state policy was the avoidance of subjects said to be irrelevant to political campaigns. This meant the liquor question and woman suffrage. It happened that the issues were on a separate ballot in November, in the form of proposed amendments to the state constitution. It also happened that the Ohio Progressive party unwisely committed itself in favor of woman suffrage and state prohibition. When Progressive senatorial candidate

Arthur L. Garford challenged Harding for his evasiveness on the prohibition question, Harding replied, "Let the people of Ohio not be distracted by the feint of the Progressive allies who seek to expose our flanks to the real enemy. The simple uncontrovertible truth is that the citizenship of Ohio must decide the pending amendments without violating his partisan fidelity, and the wettest liberal in all the state may register his liberality without regard to the vital differences between political parties." [30] Willis was really a dry, but the political advice of Harding and other Republican veterans kept him fairly silent on the issue.

Thus the state referenda—they had one every year on the wet-dry question in those days—was a great aid to Harding's buck-passing propensities. "My attitude," he wrote in 1916, "is unavoidably fixed by the pledges which I made during the campaign in 1914. I told the people openly and above board, in response to persistent inquiries, that I would be guided by the expressed will of the people of Ohio, as expressed in the vote on the Constitutional Amendment, and I do not see how I can honorably or consistently change my attitude." [31]

Woman suffrage was also not a party matter, said Harding, and, besides, he was not much interested in the subject anyway. So he told Mrs. Harriet Taylor Upton, president of the Ohio Woman Suffrage Association, when she asked him. Party platforms, he informed her, contained the official statements of party principles, and the Ohio Republican document contained no committment on the subject. He, therefore, felt himself unauthorized to make a statement. Personally, he said, "I am not opposed to woman's suffrage. By this, I mean to say that while I have never been exceedingly interested in the question I am utterly without any opposition to the proposition and could very willingly support the proposal, unless our party platform should make a contrary declaration." He added for what it was worth that in 1912 when the woman suffrage amendment was up for ratification "our newspaper took a friendly attitude." When Mrs. Upton failed to be impressed with his political purity and continued to work for a committment, Harding became very impatient and curtly reminded her that the ladies could do no more good for their cause by not making enemies of the Republican voters through being overly persistent. He gave Reverend Purley A. Baker, of the Anti-Saloon League, a similar scolding.[32]

Having helped guide the state Republican campaigning into "proper" channels, Harding concentrated on national all-American subjects. Accordingly, he made his campaign slogan "Prosper America First." This was the title of his keynote address at the campaign opening at Akron on September 26.[33] It was a full-dress presentation of the need for a restoration of the protective tariff to rescue the United States from the calamity of a depression which Harding predicted as an "inevitable" result of the Democratic Underwood tariff. The speech was the usual eloquent and thrilling diatribe, without benefit of economic understanding. It was geared to appeal to patriotic emotions, not to the intellect.

Harding made much of his denunciation of the Democratic depression which, he said, was paralyzing American industry. "Not alone has our favorable balance of trade, which was enriching us as no other nation ever experienced, vastly diminished; not alone has a mounting treasury surplus been turned into a deficit, in spite of added income tax; but worse than that, it has spread discouragement and paralysis among American producers, it has thrown hundreds of thousands out of employment and put others on short time, and halted the distribution of American dividends—all of which have turned the joyous flood-tide of American good fortune into a most distressing ebb."

The war in Europe, which had just broken out, Harding assumed would not last very long. Our depression would then become a calamity. Disarmament and the disbanding of the armies would throw 5,000,000 European men who had been withheld so long from the industries of Europe, into production. With lowered American tariffs a flood of cheap imported goods would stifle American industry. "Five million more consumers turned to producers—turned to competitors, against whom the American producer 'must sharpen his wits' under existing tariff law. Five million more battering at the American standard of wage by which we maintain our boasted standard of living. It is unavoidable that we shall have increased competition in the markets of the world."

Still more calamity did Harding ascribe to the Democrats. There was the merchant marine which we did not have, and which the Democrats had kept us from having for fifty years. Think of the opportunity for American business growth we were missing by that lack! "When grim war halted the commerce of Europe and scurried its ocean carriers into friendly ports, when we found the world awaiting our cargoes and new markets beckoning, a Democratic Congress awoke to the error of its party policy of 50 years." Now, when it was too late, they were "learning that though it may repent a half century of mistaken obstinacy in one moment, it takes years to establish a great merchant marine."

Throughout the campaign Harding worked the hard times and unemployment theme over and over again. There is a pocket-sized campaign book, kept by Harding, now in the possession of Don L. Tobin of Columbus, who was press secretary to Harding. On one page is a rough draft of a speech in Harding's own handwriting in which he wrote, "I ask men in every section what they want discussed. Whether it is an audience of villagers and farmers or an audience of working-men in a city, the answer is invariably the same—'Talk Prosperity!' Men are out of work. Business affected. Farmers are apprehensive." [34] So he gave them what they wanted—calamity talk plus a rousing declaration of the need for a high tariff and a U.S. Merchant Marine to rescue us from disaster. At Wadsworth, he told of the talk in Cleveland of "possible bread riots this winter." At Columbus, he told his hearers that nearly 40 per cent of the employables in their city were "either out of work or working on reduced schedules with reduced pay." At Newark, he asked the workers, "Why is it you are working short time?" At Youngstown, he told of an informant who declared, "I state to you as a fact, in the Mahoning and Shenango Valley with 42 blast furnaces, 23 are out of blast." In Cincinnati, he quoted a Democratic congressman who said that there was no unemployment for men who really wanted a job. Harding did not deign to reply. He left the answer "to the thousands in Cincinnati and the millions in the nation who are out of employment. It is enough ill fortune to be idle, it is an affront to the American toiler to be told that he is idle of his own choosing." [35]

Since Harding's senatorial campaigning took place in the opening months of World War I, it is important to emphasize his isolationist and political use of it in behalf of his "Prosper American First" doctrine. It has already been pointed out how he used the European conflict to bolster his tariff talk and his advocacy of the United States Merchant Marine. The only kind of international involvement he thought of was that of American gains from European calamity. That was implicit, as well as explicit, in all his campaign utterances in 1914.

Taking advantage of the European War was made baldly explicit in one of the last *Star* editorials written before he took to the stump. The title of this editorial was "Our Golden Opportunity," and it told how one of the main effects of the World War should be to make us self-sufficient. The writer described how the making of potash was being undertaken in California because we could no longer get it from Germany. "And thus," he wrote, "we have another, and pleasing, result of the war in Europe which we hope and expect will prove but a forerunner to many more of like kind. We might have gone along for years, content to look to the Old World for this mineral, that drug, that dye or that manufacture had the war not cut us off, in whole or part, from their importation. The war has thrown us upon our own resources and we look to this land of ours to arise and meet the issue." But it was not only our home consumption that was involved. "Canada must be supplied. Mexico will buy, as will also the countries of Central America. The markets of South America—and two or three of them are really great—will want our goods. . . . It's a simply wonderful commercial vista which this misfortune of European lands had opened to us. It's a wonderful opportunity . . . and will bring wonderful results if we embrace it wisely and steer clear of the works of reckless or inferior production." [36]

Harding, of course, always denied any partisan use of President Wilson's foreign policies, especially in Mexico and in Europe. The Republicans were perfect patriots. Harding's speeches were studded with rousing references to Old Glory. At the Akron opening, he said, "As Republicans we will offer no dispute. When the safety and sanity of our foreign relations, in time of peril, are under consideration we cease to be partisan. When Old Glory goes to the border, or is unfurled beyond, we yield to none as patriotic Americans. Even though we sometimes doubt the wisdom of a proclaimed policy, but not always doubting, we are Americans first, all the time ready to support and sustain the honored head of this American republic." [37]

However, Harding's utterances were not always in keeping with his non-partisan claims. At Westerville, on October 12, he said that President Wilson had no more difficult a situation in Mexico than had Taft, and the latter had handled the problem without the loss of a single American life. As for neutrality toward the European conflict, he told his audience at Greenfield, on October 15, "that any man worthy to be president of the United States would naturally maintain American neutrality." He added, "I believe that Theodore Roosevelt, as much as he loves a scrap, would have maintained peace." Harding had a further word of praise for the peace-loving Roosevelt when he said, at Cincinnati on October 20, "Neutrality and peace advocacy are not novel with us. Ex-President Roosevelt maintained neutrality between Russia and Japan and finally delivered a master stroke that brought

the benediction of peace to the Orient." When the Democratic administration claimed that it was necessary to pass a deficiency revenue bill
to make up for the temporary losses caused by the war's curtailment of
imports, Harding declared at New Philadelphia, "President Wilson
and his cabinet are using the foreign war agitation as a curtain to hide
behind and are blaming the financial deficiency in government revenue on the war, when it was really due to the faulty tariff." "We are
pointed," he said at Springfield on October 22, "to the smoke of
foreign battle in order to take our minds from the disaster that has
come to American industry and trade." [38]

Tireless, hard-hitting, and enthusiastic as Harding was in the campaign of 1914, he was annoyed at the excessive burden placed upon
him by the party managers. County chairmen, he wrote to his friend
Malcolm Jennings, have the notion "that physical and nervous endurance are not to be considered and they expect a speaker to be
mentally alert through [sic] driven to the limit for twelve to fifteen
hours every day. It is really unfair to a man who seeks to leave an
impression that he is fit for the governorship or a seat in the senate."
He had no illusions about the motives of most of these party managers. "Of course, nearly every man at headquarters is a hundred times
more interested in the candidate who will deal out the loaves and
fishes." [39]

7

Harding's victory in the 1914 election was the basis for the illusion
of the great majority. The statistics showed a plurality of 102,373 votes
over his Democratic opponent, Attorney General Timothy S. Hogan,
as compared with only a 29,270 plurality for Willis over Governor
Cox. But the statistics also showed that over 70,000 Democrats who
did vote for Cox did not vote for Hogan. In fact, about 50,000 of them
did not vote at all. The reason for this was that several anti-Catholic
agencies, including the Guardians of Liberty, the Junior Order of
American Mechanics, and two newspapers called the *Accuser* and the
Menace, agitated vigorously against Hogan's election. Harding was,
therefore, not noticeably much more popular than Willis. Yet, as the
years went by, Harding's statistical plurality was exaggerated into a
tremendous popular mandate with special emphasis on wooing back
Progressives. Actually Harding got a majority of only 8,970 of the total

votes cast for senator, whereas Willis got a majority of 41,530 of the total votes cast for governor.[40] Harding was even the beneficiary of Socialist votes cast to prevent a Democratic victory.

Harding was fully aware of the anti-Catholic campaign in his behalf, and he encouraged it. According to Foraker, Harding told him before the campaign was over that his big majority would be due to the anti-Hogan Protestant crusade. In a letter to Charles L. Kurtz, on October 29, 1914, Foraker wrote, "Harding will have the largest majority of anybody on our ticket. I do not think he will claim that it is due to his personal popularity altogether. In truth, he said when here he thought his excess vote over other candidates on the ticket would be due to the opposition to Hogan on account of the religious question that had been injected into the campaign." Harding admitted this quite frankly to his friend Scobey early in the campaign. "I shall probably get a very large vote through the hostility to Hogan, and I learned yesterday that I am to have a very large percentage of the Socialist vote for the same reason. . . . In all my experience in Ohio, I have never known such a disaffection in the ranks of the Democratic party." [41]

Proof of Harding's encouragement of the anti-Catholic crusade also exists. This aid took the form of helping the *Accuser* get out a surplus of the anti-Hogan issues. Harding was invited by the editor of the *Accuser* "to help to make the next two issues very large so that we can cover Ohio thoroughly. . . . Sure you are the man who will gain the most from our fight." "We will agree," wrote William Long, the *Accuser*'s editor, "to distribute one half of the numbers you may order." To this Harding replied that "the matter of distributed publicity" would be "taken up with you doubtless by another party. . . . Naturally," Harding added, "I am interested in your campaign activities and I shall be very much interested in a personal interview." Long thereupon instructed his business manager, Charles Middleton, to inform Harding that they could meet him at specified hours on weekdays or Sundays or "any evening" to "talk matters over." "You will also probably be able to give us some materials for future articles. . . . Other matters can be discussed better personally, and I assure you we await an interview with interest." [42] Here the correspondence ended.

The Junior Order of American Mechanics, a nativistic organization, also had an agreement with Harding that savored of anti-Catholicism. This was a campaign pledge to work for immigration restriction when he got into the Senate. Harding himself referred to this in a 1917 letter to Malcolm Jennings apologizing for supporting such a mild restriction as a literacy test on immigrants. He voted for the bill, he said, with great reluctance "much as one takes a dose of castor oil. . . . I had allowed it to be inferred, to say the least, that I would support the Immigration Bill." If he had opposed it, he told Jennings, he would have been "unspeakably embarrassed." He added, "I do not care to put in writing the details of the inferential understanding, but it dates from the campaign of 1914." [43]

Particularly vituperative against Hogan was a newspaper called the *Menace*, published in Aurora, Missouri. Anti-Catholicism was soft-pedaled in the "respectable" press, but it found weekly airings in the *Menace*. For example, on August 15, it "exposed" a "plot" by the Knights of Columbus to "steam-roller" Hogan into the Senate by putting "the whole force of Rome in Ohio behind Attorney General Hogan." "What are you thinking about," it cried, "while these Nits of Columbus march by 350,000 strong, armed and equiped, shouting as they march: 'The pope is king,' 'On to Washington by the way of the Senate,' 'Hurrah for Hogan,' 'To hell with nations opposed to the pope.'" The September 12 *Menace* featured an article entitled "The Priests for Hogan," and a special rate of 50 cents for 100 copies was offered so that "the patriots of Ohio should see that every voter in the state received a copy." Finally when Harding was elected, the *Menace* took full credit. "For three years *The Menace* has shouted the alarm from the housetops, and promoted the way of escape. At last the people have heeded and the nation is saved. Can you blame us for feeling proud of the achievement?" A week later, Harding received his only specific reference in the *Menace* when one of its commentators scribbled: "Whew!/Hogan Hardingized." [44]

There was much more to this side of the campaign. The Guardians of Liberty got out a leaflet addressed to their "Fellow Citizens" calling upon them to "unite to protect and preserve the free institutions of our country." They appended a slate of men for whom to vote on November 3, all of them "guardians of liberty." This slate included the name of Warren G. Harding and excluded that of Hogan. [45] The night of October 27 was a big one in Columbus, when, under the auspices of the Guardians, the Reverend George P. Rutledge of the Broad Street Church of Christ, climaxed a year of anti-Catholic lectures with a mass meeting at Memorial Hall. Here he assailed Hogan with choice vituperation, "The Catholic church stands for an enthralled press, muzzled speech, the suppression of the public schools, the exemption of her clergy from prosecution in our courts, the nullification of all marriages not solemnized at their altars, the elimination of all Protestant children, the union of Church and State, the universal supremacy of the Pope, yet no matter what Mr. Hogan may say from the platform, in private conversation, or in print over his signature, his membership in the Roman Catholic Church endorses these un-American ideals that are as treasonable as anything advocated by the Tories of the Revolution." [46]

There are dozens of letters in the Harding Papers from anti-Catholics telling of the alleged progress of the movement to win Protestant Democrats over to the Harding cause. One of these was from S. P. Humphreys, secretary of the Ohio Farmer's Cooperative Fertilizer Association of Toledo. Humphreys wrote, "You can win if you can land the anti-Catholic Democrats who are largely Masons, I.O.O.F.'s, K. of P.'s, and the True Blue Democracy." He also advised Harding to go easy on President Wilson. "Praise Wilson," he wrote, "just enough not to offend Republicans, but to please Wilson Democrats. . . . Talk tariff, but slow down on the War tax a little." [47]

8

Thus was Warren Harding elected a senator of the United States. He was accompanied by the legend of his great Ohio plurality—a legend which grew and gradually gave him great political prestige.

On the night of November 10, 1914 he and Governor-elect Willis attended a "jollification" at Bucyrus. As they rode down the main street together in the back of a big open touring car, a man called out, "The next president of the United States is sitting in the back of that auto." [48] This, however, is more significant as an indication of the resurgence of the "Ohio, Mother of Presidents" obsession than as a proof of Harding's popularity. The *Cincinnati Enquirer* of November 9, 1914 reported that in New York four Ohioans were being mentioned for the Presidency: Harding, Willis, Myron T. Herrick, and former Senator Burton.

CHAPTER ELEVEN

"Prosper America First," 1915

"The Republican party reflects the best conscience of the best civilization the world has ever witnessed." : : : *Harding address to the Grant Memorial Dinner in Boston, April 27, 1915; quoted in Schortemeier, "Rededicating America," p. 149.*

The year was 1915, and Warren Harding, United States Senator-elect and Ohio's latest offering to national politics, already had whispers of the Presidency circulating about him. The world picture was in the process of tremendous change, and America itself was changing. But the views of Warren G. Harding remained firm—in fact, he became more of an isolationist than before. He still thought of world affairs only as an Ohioan and as an America-firster, while the world about him was on the verge of a new era.

Harding's guiding thought during these days was to "Prosper America First." He had little more conception of the significance of the grim struggle going on in Europe than that America should profit by it. It made no difference to him who caused or won the European war or what its sequel might be, except that the Republican party should return to power before the war ended and should put the United States ahead of Europe economically and commercially by a program of tariffs and ship subsidies. Then the postwar drive of the European victors for restored commercial supremacy would fail because America would be in command. "Above all else," the *Star* readers were warned July 27, 1915, "there will be the mighty struggle everywhere in Europe for commercial and industrial rehabilitation. There is keen competition ahead, and these United States, to maintain their eminence, must get back to the policy which made them eminent. Prosper America first!" It was isolationism to the very core.

It was a good political, crowd-pleasing theme—a normal part of the Harding way of thinking. It made full use of the two great alleged American failures of the day: (1) the depression which he said was

caused by the Wilsonian economic policy, especially the non-protec-
tive Underwood tariff, and (2) the collapse of the Progressives, which
Harding viewed as a righteous punishment for their "crime of 1912."
These failures could be remedied by the reunited Republicans winning the state and national campaigns of 1916, restoring the protective
tariff, and removing from the statutes such foolish Progressive legislation as the compulsory direct primary and other forms of "pure
democracy." American industrial and commercial dominance could be
further promoted by the ship-subsidy program which would keep
European nations from recapturing much of their trade lost by the
war, especially in Latin America.

2

Now that he was Ohio Senator-elect, a party sage, and in national
oratorical demand, Harding had a wonderful opportunity to present
to audiences, in Ohio and beyond, these ideas of how to prosper
America first. He did it with zest, grace, and confidence. He charmed
thousands of listeners and readers with his good nature as he blessed
Republicans, wooed Progressives, blasted Democrats, praised private
initiative, glorified businessmen and their ingenious leadership, and
predicted prosperity.

The Senator-elect's first chance to speak as a party sage in behalf of
the hoped-for Republican restoration came on December 10, 1914 in
an address at the Waldorf-Astoria Hotel in New York to the members
of the Railway Business Association.[1] The setting was made to order
for him. It happened that the railroads were in a state of approaching
bankruptcy as European war tension upset the even tenor of peacetime transportation ways. American markets were in a chaotic condition. As business commentator S. S. Fontaine showed in the New York
World, stock market values had slumped by almost three billion
dollars in 1913 and 1914. Hundreds of millions of dollars worth of
American stocks had been sold by apprehensive foreign holders.[2] The
Democratic House of Representatives was said to be largely to blame
because it had passed the so-called Rayburn Railroad Bill. This gave
to the Interstate Commerce Commission control over the issuance of
new railroad securities, in order to squeeze the "water" out and insure
proper valuation of properties.[3] Indeed, as Fontaine said, the midsum-

mer session of Congress in 1914 had frightened American business "far more than the farmers fear the cinch bug, the army worm, or the black rust." [4]

The Democrats were frightened also. In the closing days of 1914 and the opening days of 1915 the Wilson administration had recognized the economically depressed conditions by moderating its program. In the first week of 1915 the Interstate Commerce Commission had authorized a freight rate increase. Wilson had already dropped his desire for strict business supervision, and had let Congress water down trust control by the passage of the mild Clayton antitrust bill.[5] This presaged a dropping of the Rayburn bill by the Senate. As Fontaine said, in summing up the depression of 1913–14, the new Democratic policy "will probably mark the end of the trade pendulum's downward swing." [6]

The admission by the Democrats of the existence of a depression and their efforts to stop it were music to Harding's ears. He had been predicting one ever since the campaign of 1912. In his speech to the Railway Business Association he ripped into the Democrats bitterly, at the same time praising American business leaders. The United States should be done with the "excess of commissioning" by the Interstate Commerce Commission, he said. Let Americans have government by encouragement of "the unalterable honesty that is essential to right management." Then "we shall hail a new era, which shall mark a greater and swifter stride to our American astonishment of the world." The American railway giant was "vastly superior to any on earth, it was the best and cheapest rail transportation in the world." [7] This rousingly buoyant and optimistic vow in praise of American genius was easy to listen to by those who thought themselves exemplars thereof.

In the spring of 1915, after a winter's safari in Texas, the Pacific coast and Hawaii, Harding was back home, more convinced than ever that the country was in an industrial decline under the Democrats, and needed a rescue operation by the Republicans. In a series of eloquent speeches from March 20 to April 29, he spread the gloomy message of the "Democratic depression." On March 25, at a noonday luncheon of the Columbus Chamber of Commerce at the Hotel Southern, he said, "The West is languishing under an industrial depression. I passed through many states where the conditions were pitiful." "Business," he said, "is at a standstill." [8] He admitted that there were "spots" of prosperity, that farm prices were up, and that the munitions industry, the clothing trades, and food processing were beginning to boom because of the European war demand. Indeed, the balance of trade had turned sharply in our favor as exporters rushed to fill their war orders. But, he said, as he had in his campaign speeches in 1914, beware of the collapse that peace would bring. "Exports for purposes of destruction can not keep up forever," the *Star* told its readers. "Were such exports to be applied to upbuilding, profit would be realized from them and the barter and trade go on, but when constructive work is abandoned and the work of destruction increased, the time is bound to come when those engaged in it will no longer have the means with which to buy. There can be no doubt about it, the markets afforded by a world at peace are much to be preferred to those of a world at war." One saving grace of it all was that "we confidently look for marked improvement because the country already is confident of making a sweeping change in 1916. It is that very confidence which is helping the situation." [9]

Over and over again Harding warned that alleged Democratic folly and failure were ruining the country. He blamed the shortage of dyestuffs, formerly imported from Germany, on the failure of the Underwood tariff to protect that industry. The sugar supply was short for the same reason. "We should be independent of the world. We then would control our own market and make our own prices, dictating to the world instead of paying as it dictates. . . . The day of destruction has been delayed by the war prices now prevailing. But it is only disaster deferred." [10] The Democrats were also blamed for the inability of the United States to profit by Europe's loss of its shipping dominance in Latin America. What a great opportunity had been missed by the Democratic failure to subsidize the American shipping industry. "I want to tell you fellows," he said at the Columbus Young Men's Business Club on March 25, "that when I get to the senate, if I can have anything to do with it, I want to see brought about subsidies that will send American ships into all parts of the seas." [11] In the *Star*, it was written, "The war has given us exceptional opportunity for the development of South American trade. If we fail to take advantage of it now, no such golden opportunity may be offered for a century to come, if ever again." [12]

Harding's doctrine of the need for a Republican restoration reached a wider audience in a stirring address at the Ulysses S. Grant birthday dinner of the Middlesex Club in Boston on April 27, 1915.[13] Likening the 1915 Republican situation to that of General Grant's time, during the last years of the Civil War, he said, "We stand today, as in the party's beginning, committed to the fundamental principle of representative democracy and the American policy of tariff protection, and we mean to fight it out on these lines 'if it takes all summer,' this year and the next. Millions of volunteer enlistments are awaiting the call, and everywhere, north, south, east and west, is manifest eagerness to see the Republican reunion, confident that Republican victory means the country's restoration." And so he pitched the Republican future on the good, old-fashioned Republican political principles: representative democracy and tariff protection.

According to Harding, representative democracy was the Republican virtue that the Progressives, in 1912, failed to appreciate. It was the soundest basis for any enduring republic. "The Republican party endures because of its unalterable faith in our representative form of government, as conceived by the inspired fathers upon whose foundation we have builded to surpassing national glory. We believe in representative democracy as adopted in the Federal Constitution, and proclaim it to be the highest and best form and plan of people's rule ever fashioned by mankind for the commonwealth. We believe that upon this principle we have made orderly progress and unequaled advancement, until the record of that progress is the greatest heritage of American citizenship. We believe sincerely in the role of the people, not through unthinking broadened responsibilities, but through the conscience-driven, reasoning exercise of a citizenship made sovereign from the beginning."

To those Republicans of 1912 who, momentarily, had forgotten the virtues of representative democracy, he openheartedly offered the right hand of fellowship. "The country's restoration is not in recrimination, but reconsecration. . . . There need be neither foreswearing nor apology on the part of those who enlisted in the Progressive cause of 1912. I can utter a cordial and sincere welcome to the reenlistment of any or all. The country is calling, the cause is the people's need, and the glory of things to be will make trivial the bitterness that came over things which could not be. Let us turn from the unhappy wreck of 1912 and look to relieving the country of the misfortune which attended."

As for tariff protection, Harding gave it no new thinking. It was the old pragmatic test of alleged Democratic failure in the new 1914–15 depression. "It seems characteristic of our American life that we must have periodical Democratic paralysis to bring us to appreciation of the

healthful glow of Republican activity." He recalled the 1893 "visita-
tion of Democratic disaster and depression, wrought in the name of
cheapness and the freedom of buying in the markets of the world."
Again in 1913 "Democracy delivered," and again "a nation was distressed." And the "fullness of Democratic destruction, was averted by
the cataclysm of European war. . . . It is political history that Democratic revision invariably makes for depression and hold [*sic*] it uninterrupted until we apply Republican relief."

One of Democracy's greatest follies, said Harding, was its alleged
betrayal of the American industry of its failure to subsidize shipping,
and by its opening of the Panama Canal to equality in tolls for all
nations. Recalling the days when the founding fathers, by "subsidies
and subventions and discriminating tonnage taxes and preferential
tariffs . . . whitened the seas with American sails and acquainted the
world with the American flag," he cited the pledges of McKinley,
Roosevelt, and Taft to restore these glorious times. But alas, when, as a
result of war in 1914, the "unsupplied markets of the world turned to
us, and trade beckoned as never before, and opportunity awaited as
opportunity rarely does await, we found ourselves unable to respond,
and missed the opportunity for the miracle of expansion. Democracy
awoke to the error of its persistent opposition." He called Wilson's
Panama Canal tolls equality program the gift of $40,000,000 to non-
American fortunes.

Harding, in 1915, offered no more penetrating economic analysis of
why protection made for a higher living standard than he had in the
1890's. It was the same old negative doctrine that to buy abroad was
to penalize home labor and production. "It is not what the consumer
pays, it is the consumer's ability to buy that counts. Democracy's error
lies in thinking only of the consumer, but a Republican knows that it
is the producer that counts. One must produce before he can consume,
and American eminence is the reflex of a well-paid, fully employed
nation of producers. . . . We like 'made in the U.S.A.,' and mean to
protect the making and the maker. . . . 'Made in the U.S.A.' is the
making of the U.S.A., and the Republican party would make it a glad
reality, an assurance of accomplishment at home and a herald of
American superiority abroad."

This all seemed so simple to Harding because of what he claimed
were obvious results. To him, history proved that the Republican
party was the only party that actually did constructive things. "We are
political sponsors for things accomplished. We have not dreamed, we

have realized. We have not obstructed, we have constructed. We have not pretended, we have performed. We have not halted or faltered, we have attained and sustained. We have pride in things done—the highest reward of human endeavor."

A month later, on May 27, 1915, Harding gave another address promoting American business, this time before the annual banquet of the National Association of Manufacturers at the Waldorf-Astoria Hotel in New York City. Speaking in the presence of former President Taft, Harding made his theme the glorification of business and the excoriation of its critics.[14] In this, he ridiculed President Wilson's "new freedom," and its alleged efforts to protect the small manufacturer. He called the Democratic business-baiters "the greatest menace of American progress." Harding continued in this vein:

> I want less of ignorant hindering and more of helpful encouragement.
> . . . It is big capital and big enterprise and highly developed efficiency
> that makes a hopeful entry into the gigantic activities of nation-wide and
> world-wide competition. Reasonably left alone, business will adjust itself
> to the small competitor, because we can not abolish mediocrity nor elimi-
> nate failure. The survival of the fit will obtain so long as competition
> endures. . . . We can not escape the wail of the disappointed, but we
> can avoid the unreasoning influence thereof. Cheapened output means
> larger production attended by lowered percentage of profit, and the
> pinch of competition will ever remain until paternalism or socialism, or
> both, abolish the rewards of merit.

To Harding, the bloody struggle of the nations of Europe was both a warning and an inspiration to the United States to maintain the strength of business by policies of government encouragement. He especially admired Germany's might, which, he said, was made possible by her protective-tariff system. "We know," he said, "that Germany's phenomenal development in manufacturing and commerce is not due alone to thoroughness and efficiency but to government encouragement. Imperial Germany has done for manufacturing most of the very things we have legislated against, and Germany attained the commercial independence which has locked productive Europe in unspeakable carnage. Disagreeable as it is, the truth remains—commercial rivalry led to war, and the wealth of industrial development holds England and Germany able to fight on, wasting fifty million dollars a day. From the dawn of civilization commerce has been the inspiration of developing nations and it will continue so until the millenial day." Harding failed to mention England's low-tariff policy.

Liberty and culture in all the arts were dependent on business, said Harding. "Industry has transformed us from a struggle for subsistence to a contest for accomplishment. It has made our great states, for none makes its way to the front rank except over the manufacturing heights. Manufacturing and attending trade makes the nation. It is so in the case of our own country, because our eminence is in commerce and the encouragement of its reflexes. . . . Financial standing and educational advancement are in exact accord with manufacturing and commerical development. We have attained in art in accordance with the developed wealth which encourages it. I do not overlook the advantage of broadened liberty and higher political freedom, but I do know that these alone will not accomplish."

As for labor relations, Harding evinced a great distrust of unions and their allegedly irresponsible leaders, whom he called agitators. He felt great trust in the benevolence and wisdom of manufacturers, who are "necessarily leaders of men." Such doctrine could not be displeasing to the gentlemen of the National Association of Manufacturers. Every corporation, "in big manufacturing particularly," should have "an especially human agent acting for it in its department of labor." This man would be a "trained specialist, whose specific task would be to bring and hold employer and employee in closer touch and more candid relationship." There can be a profit, he said, in giving attention to conditions of production as well as in watching the conditions of marketing. This kind of "factory assistance to the cause of enhancing conditions of labor and adding to labor's rewards ought to enlist organized labor's cooperation in making for efficiency." But it was his opinion, resulting from experience as an employer, that organized labor "does not give a due proportion of attention to the increase of efficiency." The factory department of labor would "end the profession of agitator and make for the mutuality of interest which must be established to guarantee tranquility." He agreed that there would be "lack of appreciation and failure of so many efforts to establish the ideal." But let America not be discouraged. "We have had the crime of ingratitude since the world began. If men were halted by ingratitude, every effort to attain the ideal might as well be abandoned." Nevertheless, Americans must trust the "manufacturers, who are sponsors for the weal and woe of every community which their activities enlarge." These natural leaders must "take the advancing step themselves, rather than yield to advances promoted by those of less responsibility."

Harding's exhortations to businessmen that they ought to dominate labor relations, but were not doing so, were matched by similar advice that they should dominate politics but were not doing so. This was brought out by two addresses made in Columbus, Ohio on October 13, 1915: one to the Columbus Rotary Club and the other to the Retail Grocers and Meat Dealers Association of Ohio.[15] In these he did, in effect, blame the businessmen's aloofness from politics for causing the triumph of the demagogues and "blatherers" of the Progressive movement. The result was that these rabble rousers, through the direct primary, had established false and irresponsible leadership. "The primary has enlarged the obligations of the citizens to the state. It has introduced the alphabetical lottery in choosing men for office; it has added to the expense of the office seeker; it has taken away the honor of being chosen in a representative convention and opened the way to possibilities for the self-seeking and incompetent. . . . We are confronted with a struggle to maintain old-time standards, and I warn you it cannot be done unless the business men of Ohio are newly consecrated to the full exercise of their part in politics."

This failure of businessmen had permitted the false notion to get around that the "muddy pools of politics" were that way because of business. This was an utterly false assumption, said Harding. The muddiness was caused by businessmen not going into politics. "We have had 10,000 pools in politics as clear as the crystal spring, else we should have no republic today. And the dirty pools were what they were because business men who deplored conditions were not awakened to the call of duty, which demanded them to make correction. . . . It is thrice as important for the business man to perform the duty of citizenship, because of his leadership—sometimes unconscious—among his fellow men. . . . They ought to have been busy years ago. The business men of Ohio could have removed every semblance of odium from the caucus and could have made corruption too hazardous to undertake. We had the best system in the world and let it go to ill repute through neglect."

Throughout 1915 Harding stormed away at Progressive "uplift." His undisputed six-year tenure as Senator, and his confidence in the return of Republicans and business supremacy in 1916 enabled him to fill the editorial pages of the *Star* with anti-uplift diatribes. He delivered scores of public denunciations of the follies of Progressive legislation. He called the wave of referenda and "professional uplift legislation" a pestering of the public. "The great rank and file doesn't care a conti-

nental. . . . Great is reform, but the bunco game surpasses it." "Our
government is intended to be representative, and the people are
competent to choose representatives whom they will trust to act for
them. . . . We are reformed and repentant that we are reformed. Like
the measles and the mumps, we had to have them." As for the
primaries, he regretted the loss of the "old days" when, at party
conventions, "we touched elbows and felt the fraternity of citizenship." "Under the old convention system we had party sponsorship,
party counsel, and party concern, and the availability and desirability
of candidates were discussed before they were made nominees." We
could not draft good men as we used to because they preferred not to
chase after votes. "Who does not recall how convention after convention, recognizing the need of certain men in the public service, has
uttered a public call to serve, and rarely called in vain? We can't do it
now. We must choose among men seeking to enter the public
service." [16]

Significant of business-minded Harding's indifference to reform was
his position on woman suffrage. On June 24, 1915 he appeared before
a meeting of the Franklin County Equal Suffrage Association, each
member of which proudly wore the white, purple, and gold colors of
the Congressional Union for Woman Suffrage. The women were not
as bold as their colors might indicate because their spokesman sought
Harding's support for the national suffrage amendment without asking
him to commit himself at that time. The Senator-elect's answer was
frank. He said that he was quite indifferent to the subject and that he
feared it would lead to the destruction of popular government. "I am
frank to say," he told the ladies, "that I have never been committed to
the subject of suffrage for women. Up to this time I may say that I
have been wholly indifferent on the subject." This was not because he
believed that they lacked intelligence. "On the contrary, I even believe that women are better read and are better students of current
affairs than men for they have more time at their disposal to keep
informed upon the problems." However, he was concerned about the
fact "that it is a matter of history that the broadening of the franchise
has been the forerunner of the destruction of every popular government." He therefore enjoined the ladies to bring their influence to bear
on public affairs by influencing the votes of their men folk at home.[17]

Harding's belief in the superiority of the business mind, and in the
need to prosper America first, led him time and time again to the
utterance of highly isolationist remarks. Back in the 1890's, in the days

of the "Democratic depression" following the Panic of 1893, he had advised suspension of foreign trade as a recovery measure. Now, in 1915, with another "Democratic depression," he was at it again. In a *Star* editorial, on October 25, entitled "Beyond All Question," it was written, "One of the leading industrial nations of Europe once urged its citizens 'never to forget when you buy a foreign article, your country is the poorer.' This was sound advice, no one can deny. The truth of the proposition is too plain for even a schoolboy to question. And yet it is a truth that one of the great political parties of this country has persistently refused to recognize. The whole purpose of a protective tariff is to discourage the purchase of foreign goods and to induce citizens of our country to buy goods purchased at home. The whole purpose of a low tariff is to make it easier to buy in foreign markets. The Democratic party stands for low tariffs or free trade and expects lower tariffs to produce relatively more revenue because of larger importations. It refuses to recognize the important fact that 'when you buy a foreign article your country is poorer.' "

3

Harding sincerely believed in the economic independence of the United States with regard to Europe. As he observed American neutrality violated by both Germany and England, he soon found himself declaring that the best way to handle them was by a trade embargo. "We can live without Europe quite as well as Europe can live without us," the *Star* told its readers on August 15. He backed his claim by turning to one of his great American heroes, Thomas A. Edison, who, when asked if he could perfect a process of making aniline dyes, replied, "We Americans can make anything that anyone else can make, and I will show you that we can." Yes, echoed the editor, and all we needed to do so was to restore the protective tariff. "We can't make it and prosper while paying thrice or twice the wage which foreign competitors pay!" [18]

Particularly annoying to Harding's Republican and xenophobic sensibilities was the LaFollette Seaman's Act of March 4, 1915.[19] This was a measure to improve conditions of labor on United States ships, guaranteeing seamen a nine-hour day while in port, minimum standards of safety aboard, and a degree of protection against tyrannical captains. Another provision required that ship crews must have at least seventy-five men in each department able to understand any order given by the officers. This disgusted Harding even though it increased the number of Americans in the crews. As he wrote in the *Star*, June 17, 1915, "to get firemen and trimmers acquainted with the English language, to say nothing of other departments, at a wage which made competition with foreign shipping possible, has been found out of the question." The law was passed as a "sop" to organized labor, and should be called "A Measure to Drive American Shipping from the Seas and Make Its Rehabilitation Impossible." It drove the Pacific Mail Steamship Company to sell out to a Japanese company. Americans "must go, hat in hand, to the Japanese owners of the trans-Pacific ships to apply for the transportation which Mr. LaFollette's legislation makes it impossible for Americans to supply." [20] But Harding spoke quite otherwise in his address to the San Antonio Chamber of Commerce and Rotary Club on January 19, 1915. "If I had my way," he said, "I'd have ships made in America, manned by American sailors, bearing the American flag, loaded with American products and carrying the message of American peace, civilization and good will to all parts of the world." [21]

The xenophobia and isolationism of Harding's earlier newspaper days were on the rise again as he approached his senatorial responsibilities. This was sharply brought out in this widely publicized San Antonio address. He was quoted as favoring the "civilizing" of Mexico by the United States. "There is a destiny in the affairs of nations," he told the San Antonians. "That was demonstrated at your Alamo and again in the Civil War, but the magnificent resources of Mexico will never be given to mankind and that country never will come into its own until it is brought under the civilizing influence of the American flag. How that condition will be brought about is not for me to say." [22]

Harding had no faith in President Wilson's policy of encouraging the formation of a Mexican constitutional republic under Venustiano Carranza. The revolutionary armies in Mexico, said the *Star* on September 7, 1915, "are made up of the riffraff and criminal elements of the land, led by men equally vicious." Carranza "has preached intolerance, confiscation and hatred, even preaching the doctrine of anarchy in states which had already yielded to him without resistance. He has discoursed sonorously of ideals he does not entertain, perpetuated or sanctioned, and advocated every form of crime, and has forfeited every particle of respect of the better elements in Mexico. Under his supervision property has been seized on all sides without compensation, and he has continuously proclaimed the right of confiscation, so that farmers have been robbed of their crops." [23]

To Harding, the hero of Mexico was its longtime president, Porfirio Diaz. When the aged and expatriated dictator died in July, 1915, the *Star* mourned the passing of the man it believed to be Mexico's savior. Diaz's death, said Harding,

> removes the one great figure which had proven the strength to meet the difficulties of governing Mexico. . . . He ruled with an iron hand because it was necessary. No other course could have succeeded. The Mexican mass was unfitted for self-government, so Diaz dictated, but he did so with a lofty patriotism, and a high consideration for his country's good and its advancement. The revolution which led to his resignation and final retirement from the land he loved and fought for, was the forerunner of all the strife and bloodshed which has prostrated the republic during the last four years. A dozen ambitious Mexicans wish to do as Diaz had done, but none has the strength to succeed him and live to his measure. . . . He was constructive, he advanced civilization, he was just, he was lion-hearted, and he did more for his country in his long term of leadership than a thousand Maderos, Carranzas, Villas, Zapatas, and Huertas could accomplish in fifty years of harmonious endeavor.[24]

Wilson's Mexican policy, said the *Star*, was complete folly. He was a theorist "aglow with ideals and inexperienced in practical problems." He rejected the "bloody handed Huerta," Diaz's disciple and instigator of the assassination of Francisco Madero, "when only a bloody-handed rule was known and none other could deal with a people utterly unfit for self-government, as we know it. Huerta had the strength to have dominated the situation, had we strengthened him through recognition, and it was the normal, easy, proper thing to do." Instead, Wilson brought "chaos" by supplying arms and ammunition to the "ruffian armies" of Carranza and Pancho Villa.[25] Harding solemnly hoped that the United States would not repeat in Mexico in 1915 the blunder of 1898 in Cuba—that is, the failure to annex the country. Mexico would be as ungrateful for our altruistic help as was Cuba:

> Cuba owes quite everything in the way of independence and prosperity and tranquility to the United States. She owes to us her present state of health. The blunder on our part was in disavowing annexation when we unsheathed the sword. Cuba ought to have been made a part of the United States, and there would have been gratitude and respect, where we now encounter ingratitude and contempt. There is no undoing the

blunder of Cuba, not until strife calls us thither again, then we will stay
and govern. But we can avoid incurring like ingratitude in Mexico. . . .
We can let Mexico very much alone, until our guardianship is so
manifestly demanded there is no excuse for withholding it, then we can
and ought to go in, and go to stay.

So said the *Star* editor on September 13, 1915.[26] Harding repeated
this assertion on a visit to Frank Scobey at his San Antonio home in
January, 1915—a fact which he recalled with only mild embarrassment during the campaign of 1916. The press, he wrote, was digging
this up for campaign purposes, and he supposed candidate Hughes
would be annoyed. But, said the Senator, "I do not greatly care. I am
still of the opinion that I uttered at that time, and think the day will
come when we are bound to take possession. However, I am quite
agreed that the preaching of such a doctrine would not be helpful to
the Republican cause." It was only the publicity that gave Harding
qualms, not the principle. Shortly after he made the remark, he wrote
to Scobey, "I see the San Antonio speech was quoted all over the
country. It is all right, but had I dreamed of that I would have been a
little more careful." [27] It might be added that he would have been
even more careful if the large Mexican population in southern Texas
had had the right to vote at that time.

The *Star* conferred more of its criticism on what it called President
Wilson's creation of another Mexico out of the Philippines, *i.e.,* in
preparing to give the islands their freedom. In these remarks, the
editor had the support of the Taft policies and advice. "There is a
bunch of designing crooks in the islands," he told his readers, "who
have planted widely the promises of the Democratic party." The
simple fact was, said the writer, that "the Filipinos are not ready for
self-government. A generation must pass and a new generation, educated to western civilization, must come on the scene before the
Philippine people even approximate readiness for self-reliance. . . .
the professional politicians, the Aguinaldos, the adventurers and self-
seekers want self-government for the purpose of exploitation and will
halt the advance of civilization the moment they acquire it." [28]

The *Star* also allowed its apprehensions about foreigners to grow as
it viewed the need of an "Americanization" movement stemming from
the tensions resulting from the threats to our neutrality by Germany
and England. "The plain, startling, all-important truth," wrote the
editor, July 5, 1915, "is that all our citizens are not Americans, and
thus might come a crucial test which would prove it at incalculable

cost." He was concerned about the fifteen million foreign-born in the United States, three million of whom could not speak English. "We have looked with indifference on 'Little Italies' and 'Little Hungaries,' without a thought of their menace to our social solidarity." More effective assimilation was necessary to guard against "the dangers from invasion from without" and from "convulsions within."

The war-prevention activities of world-minded peace promoters left Harding cold. When, on May 13 and 14, the World Court Congress met in Cleveland to promote the establishment of an international court of justice, Harding, as Ohio's Senator-elect, was present, and presided over some of its sessions. Many distinguished jurists and scholars were present and spoke for progress along the lines of effective peace preservation. These included Taft, Elihu Root, John Hays Hammond, Bainbridge Colby, Alton B. Parker and others. On May 13, Harding made a few eloquent remarks on the "new baptism of peace supreme" which would result from bringing "nations into greater fraternity." But he was frank to say that he could speak only on the "desirability of the proposed court" rather than on its possibilities.[29]

Harding simply could not escape his own isolationist views when American neutrality was subjected to the test of German submarine attacks. To be sure, on "Peace Day," May 18, 1915 the *Star* made the usual lamentations about a "world gone mad," and about the need for sacrifice to preserve peace. But there should be no sacrifice at the price of "our honor as a nation." This was a wide-open exception when left to *Star* thinking. It came out in the aftermath of the German sinking of the British passenger liner *Lusitania*, when Wilson required of Germany "strict accountability" for the sinking of such craft in the future. The *Star* went farther than Wilson. It insisted on the immunity from submarine attack of all merchant vessels on which Americans were present—liners, tramp steamers, ammunition ships, or what not. This was good 100 per cent Americanism. The words were, "The life of the humblest American who ships as a stoker on a freighter and the life of the American farm boy who tends a dozen mules on a tramp steamer is just as dear to them as the life of Alfred Vanderbilt on the 'liner' Lusitania was dear to him. We promised the same protection to the American stoker on the ammunition ship which we promised to the American traveler on the liner. We told the Kaiser in impressive tones that we should expect 'strict accountability' for the death of the stoker and the death of the traveler alike."[30] That was not what Wilson promised. Harding himself would eventually have to back off from this kind of thinking, for the simple reason that it was too anti-German for his own political safety among the many Germans in his Ohio constituency.

4

Harding had a six-year senatorial mandate now to boost and "bloviate" for his country. He was at his America-first best as he approached the entry of the United States into the World War. There was no place in his mind at this time for idealistic hopes for world democracy, a kind of wishful thinking that he claimed was characteristic of demagogic Progressives and dreamy-eyed Democrats. There would be plenty of opportunity for Harding to say these things in the war-torn years to come.

CHAPTER TWELVE

Approaching the Summit, 1916

"It appears if a man talks he is a damn fool, and if he keeps his mouth shut he is a damn coward." : : : *Harding to Malcolm Jennings, April 24, 1916, Jennings Papers, Ohio Historical Society*

◢ℜ Few, if any, United States Senators have risen to presidential availability as rapidly as did Warren G. Harding. It was, of course, an invariable quadrennial custom for Ohio, the "Mother of Presidents," to offer one of her sons for the top political office in the nation. Probably no Ohio Senator, especially of the Republican persuasion, had been without presidential whispers in his behalf as soon as he donned his toga. But with Harding, the whispers became murmurs in an unusually short time—by June of 1916, to be exact.

The year was a presidential one, and there was much in store for the brilliant Buckeye orator. His conciliatory talents were needed to help restore Republican unity. For party's sake he accepted the role of keynoter to the 1916 national Republican convention. For party's sake he tempered his militancy with a moderation of the growing anti-German hysteria. And for party's sake—and his own—he disavowed the efforts of some of his rash friends to push him ahead of the more learned and conservative former Senator Theodore E. Burton, who had become Ohio's official favorite son for 1916 presidential bargaining purposes. That Ohio Republicans seemingly wanted Burton for President in 1916, but had been cool toward him for reelection to the Senate in 1914, indicates the degree of warmth of the Burton-for-President movement. Nevertheless, Harding, for party's sake—and his own —modestly supported Burton, and then Charles Evans Hughes, with his usual oratorical chores. This he did in many states, thus winning friends and observing, at first hand, the mistakes that led to Hughes' defeat—mistakes that Harding so skillfully avoided in 1920.

In 1916, the war in Europe became fixed in a long, bloody struggle, and American passions lined up in three factions: one favoring the "Allies," one favoring the Germans, and a third favoring staying out of war. Once more with Harding there came into play his ability to court all sides in a conflict. He had once been a militant in his foreign attitudes, and, no doubt, he still was one in his thoughts. But few people knew of this as he skillfully strove not to offend people with German sympathies and pacific leanings.

There were too many pacifists and pro-German Americans in Ohio and elsewhere in the United States for Harding to indulge in overly belligerent talk about German atrocities, at least before the presidential election of 1916. If he was going to be party keynoter at the Chicago nominating convention in June, 1916—and party officials expected that he was—it would be wise for him to curb his tongue and his feelings. This was, of course, but one of the many adjustments that the junior senator from Ohio would make in 1916 and after so that he and his party might have a political future.

Harding's pro-peace and pro-German adjusting was very deliberately done. When President Wilson, on April 19, 1916, threatened Germany with a suspension of diplomatic relations if assurances were not given for the safety of American travelers, Harding refrained from applauding the President's stand. For this he was rebuked by the *Columbus Sunday Dispatch*, as many rallied behind the President. Privately, however, Harding, in referring to the *Dispatch*'s criticism, admitted that he personally approved of Wilson's warning. It was necessary, he wrote to Malcolm Jennings on April 24, that he refrain from comment because, as keynoter and chairman of the forthcoming Republican convention, he did not want to embarrass the party by a comment that would lose the German-American vote. "I purposely withheld any comments," he wrote Jennings, "because I did not want somebody to elaborate on what the temporary chairman of the Republican Convention had to say. I think you know what my opinion would have been had I chosen to give utterance, but I thought that was an occasion when it would be wise to refrain from commenting. It appears if a man talks he is a damn fool, and if he keeps his mouth shut he is a damn coward." [1]

Harding further showed his adjustability in behalf of the pacific-minded and the pro-Germans by soft-pedaling his real views about preparedness. He would like to have supported a bill in Congress establishing national peacetime conscription, but he found it more politic to remain silent while the supporters of state-militia preparedness argued against those who favored national administration of the problem. "It will be quite out of the question," he wrote Jennings on

April 17, 1916, "to undertake the introduction of any such progressive ideas as you advocate in the present status of the measure. The Senate is in a distressing wrangle over the conflict between the militia and the partisans of the regular army." He thought Jennings' description of the merits of the national plan was "wonderfully valuable," but all he could do about it was to keep it on file for future reference.[2]

As was so often the case with Harding in matters of principle, his thinking was clouded by his politics and prejudices. When, in January, 1916, President Wilson opened the "Preparedness" campaign, the Ohio Senator was quick to challenge the President's sincerity by using "Preparedness" for 1916 re-election purposes. Harding claimed that Wilson was appealing to feelings of fear without showing that there was anything to be afraid of. These remarks backfired when Democratic papers like the *Cleveland Plain Dealer* headlined, "OHIO SENATOR OUT AGAINST PREPAREDNESS,/SAYING IT'S UNNECESSARY."

Harding got his revenge by a personal protest to the *Plain Dealer*'s editor, resulting in the discharging of the headline writer. Then, when Wilson was in fact reelected, Harding sarcastically predicted that Wilson would change his policy and be a better President "now that he has been assured of the most that he can get politically. . . . I think Wilson will now turn to serving the country rather than serving his own political ambitions."[3]

2

A Republican who could thus be discreetly silent on controversial subjects, and who could orate for the party line as effectively as Harding, could not miss the assignment as keynoter and chairman of the June, 1916 Republican convention. In order to qualify, all that he had to do was to find occasions to open the flood gates of his eloquence upon such non-controversial subjects as patriotism and Americanism. That is what Jennings advised, though Harding did not need the encouragement.[4]

The topic for Harding's maiden display of oratory in the Senate was the Philippine Islands. That is how it was billed, and that is what his words seemed to say. But his real purpose was something much closer to home than this far-off, American dependency in the Pacific. It was to talk Americanism and thus qualify Harding as keynoter to the Republican national convention. Observe the following headline from the *Ohio State Journal's* Washington dispatch dated January 27, 1916, the day before the speech was delivered:

CONSIDER HARDING TO SOUND KEYNOTE

Ohio Senator May be Chosen Chairman of the Republican

National Convention

Will Make His First Speech in Senate Today

Opposes Philippine Independence [5]

No headline writer was discharged for this performance. The occasion was twofold. It was to defend the American retention of the islands, which the Democrats, by means of the Jones Bill, proposed to set free; it was also the eve of the birthday of William McKinley, the great proponent of Philippine annexation to the United States. What a splendid chance to propound the great paradox of how annexation meant independence—to wax eloquent about the noble McKinley, who rescued a backward people from the yoke of Spanish tyranny, who shielded them from the other imperialistic autocracies of Europe and Asia, and who prepared the Filipinos for a glorious, self-governing future under the protection of the United States.

There was another subtle virtue in choosing the Philippine topic. It was one thing that Regular and Progressive Republicans agreed about. Who could forget the immortal Roosevelt's support—if not instigation—of McKinley's benevolent imperialism, the brilliant service of the young "Rough Rider" in the war that brought the acquisition of the Islands? [6] To bring up the Philippines was a good tactic to help forget the principles that divided the two. It was the same old Harding patchwork, and it looked beautiful in place of the gaping holes of 1912.

Still another virtue accrued from the Philippine oration. It was an example of an adjustable stance which avoided offending the Germans and instead offended only the Spanish. Harding had no Spanish voters in his constituency—nor, for that matter, did the entire Republican party.

It was a ringing, 100 per cent American, "white man's burden" speech which Harding gave on January 28, 1916, before a politician-studded, Senate chamber audience, in defense of the retention of the Philippines. [7] Service-minded Americans liked to think about the uplift of backward peoples. "We are the first nation on the face of the earth," boasted Harding, "that ever unsheathed the sword on behalf of suffering humanity. . . . Our work in the Philippine Islands in education, in sanitation, in elevation and civilization has been the most magnificent contribution of a nation's unselfishness ever recorded in the history of the world." He disclaimed any similarity between the Philippine revolt and the American Revolutionary War, saying that the latter was for the preservation of an independence already attained, whereas the Philippine uprising was a revolt engineered by agitators who did not know what responsible independence really was. He went so far as to say that the United States had "the first dependable popular self-government on the face of the earth, because the fathers had the inspiration to write civil liberties into our organic law." Harding said that the poor Filipinos need America's help in this regard.

Harding did not hesitate to claim materialistic gain to the United States in this activity, but he did it in a patriotic way. "Here is a nation," he wrote, "with limitless resources; here is a nation excelling in genius; here is a nation unmatched in industry; and everything that is proposed in this body is designed to aid and encourage the widening of American influence and make us a dominant commercial and industrial nation. Well, if that is true, I want to ask what field, other than South America, offers greater attractions than the Orient for expansion of commerce and trade? I fancy that the possession of these rich islands, the Philippine Archipelago, will be very much to our advantage."

There was high ethical and religious justification for the American people to assert their moral superiority in other lands. Harding spoke of "our covenant to the world and to civilization." He spoke of the United States as a great peace-loving nation, "the only one whose voice is heard above the din of conflict in a continental war." "Why not," he asked, "reassert ourselves, not only confident in the possession of the territory which is righteously ours, but make it ornate with an assertion of Americanism that is befitting to so great a nation." The "national heart is right," he said. America was "a nation leading in civilization and in that uplifting work which contributes to the weal of humanity." Such a nation "can no longer limit its influence to its territorial or coast-bound sphere than can the man who stands high in his community, and has the character and the attributes that make him an influence in the activities of the world."

He spoke of the obligations of Christianity in the salvation of souls:

"It seems to me, if it has been our privilege and our boast that we have established and developed the best popular government on the face of the earth, that we ought to go on with the same thought that impelled Him who brought a plan of salvation to the earth. Rather than confine it to the limitations of the Holy Land alone, He gathered His disciples about Him and said, 'Go ye and preach the gospel to all the nations of the earth.'" Harding climaxed with a stirring invocation, "Let us ask ourselves if the time has not come when it is befitting to return to a vigorous, persistent, conscience-founded, determined America, and, clad in our convictions of conscientiousness and righteousness, let us go on, Mr. President and Senators, in our efforts to fulfill the destinies of what I believe to be the best republic on earth."

There was a peculiar twist to Harding's argument that cited the Americanization of immigrants as qualifying us to Americanize the world. "I have a notion, Senators," he said, "that under the uplifting influence of American civilization any of the members of the human race can be brought up to a stature that befits them for American citizenship. We have proof at home. . . . I have myself been the witness of those who come here and hold their heads erect, breathing in the atmosphere of American liberty and opportunity; and, while the influence does not always bring the parent to the full stature that becomes American citizenship, it is invariably true that the next generation is a step higher in the human scale and finds its place fittingly into citizenship and participation in the affairs of the United States of America."

It would be a long time, said Harding, before the Philippines were fit for the independence that the Democrats foolishly offered in the Jones Bill. If America was to teach them democracy, there was much yet to do. "Self-government is one thing and popular self-government is another thing. If we mean to grant the Philippine Islands their independence, it is none of our business what kind of government they have. It may well be an autocracy; it may be a despotism; they may prefer a dictatorship, or they may, and most likely will, attempt a republic like that of China, which recently flashed a moment on the firmament of republics as a sort of triumph of rational over dollar diplomacy, and again faded from the firmament. What business is it of ours if the Filipine people have the inalienable right of independence what kind of government they may choose to have?"

"But we care what kind of government these primitive people have," said Harding. The United States wanted to teach them democracy and had introduced an educational system in which 600,000 children were enrolled in the island schools, and that was a mighty poor guarantee of dependable autocracy. What was needed was 2,000,000 school children "under American education and occupation and sponsorship. Then the pathway will be open for a higher civilization and with it a devotion to the nation that led the way."

3

At least three times more before he was awarded the Republican keynote prize Harding publicly indulged in his politically inspired, Americanistic speechmaking. The first occasion was the widely publicized Lincoln Day address at New Philadelphia, Ohio; the second was on March 11, 1916, at the annual banquet of the Pittsburgh Chamber of Commerce; and the last was on March 21, when he delivered a speech in the Senate on the subject of preparedness. Each time he blasted Democrats, obviously in the mood of a professional politician in a presidential year.

It was politics, politics all the way—the kind that Republicans loved to hear. At New Philadelphia, he taunted the Democrats for their luck in having prosperity for the first time in their experience. "It usually takes only four years to get rid of a Democratic administration by common consent," he told his New Philadelphia listeners. The failure of the Democratic Underwood tariff reduction of 1913 had been concealed by the false prosperity brought on by the war in Europe, which was lasting much longer than he had forecast in his 1914 bid for votes. What a shame, Harding said, to have prosperity "at the cost of the lives of millions of human beings. We don't want that—a tragedy in the old world meaning prosperity in this country." He jeered at President Wilson's announced plan for scientific tariff rates to be set by a new non-political tariff commission in place of the old Republican commission. "You cannot trust Democrats on tariff matters," said Harding. "When the country restores the tariff commission plan it must be a protectionist commission committed to the policy of prosperity for the American people." According to Harding, the only "scientific" tariff rates were "protectionist" rates.[8]

At New Philadelphia and later in Pittsburgh, it was opportune to denounce Democrats for what was going on in Mexico. President

Wilson's Mexican policy of "watchful waiting," in support of a hoped-for consititutional republic under Carranza, came in for some sharp Americanized tail-twisting. Wilson's success in promoting Carranza's triumph over "poor old Huerta," said Harding, was "at the cost of hundreds of American lives." The Ohio Senator had no sympathy with Wilson's concern for a constitutional and democratic Mexican government. In keeping with his belief that only American business methods could redeem any backward country, he told his New Philadelphia audience, "If the flag goes to Mexico we must put it there to show that America means business. We cannot assume responsibility without assuming authority." Harding bitterly accused the President of promoting the very instability that he sought to correct by "grasping the bloody hands of Carranza."

By the time of Harding's Pittsburgh address on March 11, the flag had gone to Mexico, and Harding hoped it would stay there. On March 9, Pancho Villa had made his famous raid on Columbus, New Mexico. The next day American troops, under General John J. Pershing, had invaded Mexico in pursuit. Consequently, when reporters approached him, Harding voiced his pleasure at the invasion of Mexico. "And," he added jubilantly, "if Carranza does not give the consent that has been asked of him, I warn him that we will raise the American flag for an American civilization in Mexico." [9]

Senator Harding did not like the way President Wilson was subordinating the Panama Canal to his Mexican policy. Wilson had offered to waive American claims for tolls exemption in return for a British support of Carranza. This, said Harding, was another surrender of Americanism to an "ephemeral" Mexican President. Wilson has "robbed us of the advantage of American shipping which has in good part inspired the construction of the canal." [10]

It was at Pittsburgh on March 11, 1916 that Harding got one of his biggest boosts to date in national fame. Here he repeated, with business-praising embellishments, the address that he had made to the annual meeting of the National Association of Manufacturers in New York on May 27, 1915. But this time Harding gained a much wider audience because his oration was made a feature article, with a full-page portrait illustration of himself, in the April issue of *Prosperity: The Republican National Magazine* published by the "Republican National Press." As printed in *Prosperity* the speech was entitled, "Commerce and Nationalism: Pioneer of All National Developments and Preserver of National Strength Is Commerce." It was dedicated to the "men who do things."

In this address Harding raised the specter of creeping Socialism and immigrant-inspired national disunity. He described in menacing tones the rapidly increasing Socialist vote. This, he said, has led the Democrats and Progressives, through the direct primary, the initiative, and other appeals to the ignorant masses, to out-socialist the Socialists, and to promote paternalistic legislation and government ownership of public utilities. It was, therefore, high time for the natural leaders of society, that is, the businessmen, to assert their influence. There was danger if they did not do so. "We are a polyglot people, with surface indications of a lack of homogeneousness that might easily develop a national peril." There was need for "a new consecration to unalterable and abiding and glad Americanism. I would like to clarify and emphasize the American ideal, the American aspiration, the American hope, the American resolution, about which we may erect and preserve the altar of righteous and undying American patriotism, and light thereon the unquenchable fires of devotion to flag and country, and illumine the world as they flame with love and passion for our national life." [11]

The Socialism scare came up again in a much-applauded oration in the Senate on March 21, 1916 on the so-called Armor Plant bill to provide for the construction by the national government of a plant to make plate for an enlarged American battle fleet. Harding told his friend, Malcolm Jennings, that he favored this bill at first, but was influenced against it by the radicalism and incompetence of its Democratic supporters.[12] The Democrats, he said, had criticized the selfishness and greed of the "steel monopolist." This aroused the opposition of businessmen, and Harding joined his fellow Republicans in coming to the defense of the steel industry and private enterprise. He maintained that the "wizards of the world of iron and steel" had "made these United States the greatest iron and steel producing nation on earth. . . . The glory of the furnaces made a beacon of American national good fortune." A Socialistic bill like the enactment of the Armor Plant bill would kill the spirit of private enterprise "which made us what we are." "Our capital is uncounted and our credit unlimited and our stockholders, the American people." [13] So furiously did Harding assail the Democrats for their alleged folly that he was again surrounded at the close, as he had been after the Philippine address, by admiring senatorial colleagues who congratulated him for his eloquence.[14]

4

And so the show approached its appointed climax with Harding slated to preside at the Republican national convention of 1916. Mirages were again in order. Harding had been inspiring in the graciousness with which he had toned down his militancy so as to avoid the semblance of German-baiting and warmongering. He had curbed his own desire to denounce German submarine warfare and to promote vigorous nationalistic preparedness. He had shown how to combine the doctrine of tariff-sponsored business and the laissez-faire doctrine of leaving business alone into a smokey blur of 100 per cent Americanism. He knew how to make the Democratic plan of independence for the Philippines appear to be an invitation to anarchy, and how to make the Republican idea of the continued dependence of the islands on the United States seem like the promise of responsible democracy. He could detect a Democratic depression before it began, and, when it did not come, he could predict its inevitability anyhow. He could praise the unity of the American people in one breath, and express fear of the immigrants in the next. He now was to stand before the assembled Republican delegates at Chicago and try to make the reunion of Regulars and Progressives a reality.

Harding was assigned the role as keynoter and chairman of the convention on April 7, 1916. His chief function was to be the leading symbol of a "let's be kind to the Progressives" movement. Charles D. Hilles, chairman of the Republican national committee, made this quite clear in the announcement. He invoked the myth of the 100,000 plurality of Harding in the 1914 Ohio election. "Senator Harding was nominated for the Senate," Hilles told reporters on April 7, 1916, "after the progressive split and elected by a large plurality, which, I believe, fully answers the question of whether he will be acceptable to the progressive element of the party." [15] The opponent of Progressives of 1912 had become, in Hilles' view, the forgiver of Progressives of 1914 and 1916. Hilles stuck to this line all his life. On September 4, 1935 he wrote to Ray Baker Harris, "Senator Harding was well received in the Senate. He had ability, affability, a good voice, a fine presence. He had recently passed a severe test in his own state, for he had presented Mr. Taft's name to the Convention of 1912, and supported him vigorously in that year. Two years later he led the divided party in Ohio to victory. That fact motivated the Committee on Arrangements in choosing him as the temporary chairman keynoter." [16] Hilles did not mention that Harding had lost the governorship in 1910, in a two-party contest, by the same figure of 100,000. Nor did he cite what gentlemen never mentioned in public, the fact that the 1914 plurality was inspired by anti-Catholicism.

In the build-up for the June convention Harding played well his assigned role as forgiver of Progressives. On the afternoon following the announcement of his choice as keynoter he held a press conference in Chicago. "What about Colonel Roosevelt?" he was asked. Harding's well-planned answer was typical. "There is no reason why Theodore Roosevelt should not be consulted if he is back in the Republican party, but the party is too big to trail any man. The principles of the party stand ahead of any candidate or all the candidates together. I am distinctly a party man. We are governed by parties, not by any one person, and I hope we may never be governed by an individual. The salvation of the country rests with the Republican party. I think we all feel that. I think Colonel Roosevelt himself feels it as deeply as any of us. If Colonel Roosevelt wishes to be a member of the Republican party we welcome him, but the Republican party, as I have said, will not trail any man." [17]

In the evening of the same day, April 8, 1916, in the sumptuous quarters of the Hamilton Club in Chicago, Harding gave a full-dress oratorical exhibition of how the reunited Republican party could be the salvation of the nation.[18] The occasion was the anniversary of the Civil War's closing battle of Appomattox. Many of the party dignitaries were present either in the flesh or in the portraits on the wall of this midwestern Republican party shrine. Harding told of an irresistible tide of public opinion that was rising to preserve the nation's security when the end of Europe's war would present it with the peril of renewed industrial competition. For such a crisis the party must be united. Alluding to 1912, he attributed the split to a "needless disagreement over methods of procedure which deserved correction." By this he meant the fatal disputes over the convention delegations, mostly from the South, that were decided in favor of Taft—to the cries of robbery from the Progressives. This flaw in the party organization, he said, had been corrected. The party's national committee had officially reduced the number of delegates from the states by basing Republican representation at future conventions more closely on the size of the party vote cast in each state. It was a generous gesture, because, by making it, Harding admitted gracefully a degree of fault on the Regular side of the dispute.

But, said Harding, never during the party crisis of 1912 had there been any disagreement over fundamental Americanism. As the united party under McKinley, Hanna and Foraker had saved the country in 1896 from a Democratic tariff, so must the reconsecrated party in 1916 save the country from the fatal effects of the Underwood tariff of 1913, which were sure to come upon the close of war in Europe if President Wilson was reelected. That was the most important preparedness of all. "The protective policy is inseparable from any preparedness discussion." "We must be a people with one great ideal, one all encompassing aspiration, one guiding hope, one common interest, one people and one flag. . . . I do not mean to say our party has a monopoly on American patriotism. But I would like for a slogan, 'Made in the United States.' To make it effective we must also have American consumers of American products. I would prosper America first. That's Republican doctrine." As he closed, the applause was deafening; during the next few hours the congratulatory telegrams came pouring in. The party had found a spokesman in whom all Republicans might find confidence.

Nor did Harding and the reunionists forget the patronage so absolutely essential to discipline. In the days before the opening of the convention, he made it quite clear that if local leaders inclined to favor Progressives, and would behave themselves, they would have as much opportunity to get public jobs as the Regulars. He knew, as did every other practical politician, that it was the lack of patronage control that had much to do with the break-up of the Progressive party. The Roosevelt movement—or hysteria—was really directed from the top. It did not have sufficient patronage or grass-roots bases at the village, town, county, and state levels. American local government was idealogically very conservative, and in the Wilson-Roosevelt days, there was little local counterpart to the liberal aspects of the national Progressive movement. Harding had always been a locally conditioned politician and knew the importance of local appointments to local workers.

Harding did not come out bluntly and say that to the localities belonged the spoils. He confined himself to general remarks on local party self-government. Local politicians, however, have a sure instinct in such matters and can read much between the lines that ordinary folks cannot see. Thus it was that, when Harding mentioned local political self-government, he was telling certain of his hearers what they wanted to hear. He did this in the Spring of 1916 as the various local and district Republican candidates maneuvered in their own behalf. He made it quite clear to those who were interested. In a *Cleveland Leader* interview on May 10, 1916, he was quoted as saying "I do not believe in using my office to effect a party choice on nominees. I have had occassion in the past to complain of Washington interference with Ohio affairs and I do not mean in any way to lend myself to such practice." What he was saying was that he had no intention of imperiling local tenures and ambitions by Rooseveltian wild-goose chases.

5

Harding's keynote speech of June 7, 1916 to the national convention [19] was thus important not only for what he said but for what he did not say. There were histrionics of blazing Americanism to conceal the old idealogical differences of days gone by, and to conceal new differences resulting from the war. And there was the unvoiced assumption that back in the localities all was as it had been in regard to courthouse and town-hall politics, with the usual rewards for the politically faithful.

Harding spoke, as he was supposed to do, in pious platitudes, stinging Democrat-baiting, and strident Republican Americanism. That meant a show of regret and contrition for the sins of 1912, a scorn for the Democrats, who could win only when Republicans were divided, and a call upon heaven to witness that the Republicans would never be so foolish again. The Senator did not quite live up to the prediction made to Scobey that he "would not attempt the cross of gold." [20]

It was the same old call for a return to Republican fundamentalism. As in the past, the Republican party and its tariff Americanism were the best hopes for America's future. Only by restoring the protective tariff could the betrayal of American business to foreign competition be remedied. The tariff, Harding solemnly declared, was an absolute essential to our "subsistence," and "subsistence is the first requisite of existence. . . . We have the higher standard of living because of the Republican policy which makes of Americans the best paid workmen in the world. Out of the abundance of employment and higher compensation, together with the beckoning opportunity which offers every reward, we Americans have attracted the laborers of the earth and set new standards here. . . . I prefer a protective and productive tariff which prospers America first. I choose the economic policy which sends the American workingman to the savings banks rather than to the soup houses. I commend the plan under which the healthful glow of prospering business is reflected in every face from the great captain of industry to the schooling child of the daily wage earner."

Harding's Americanism was a grand theme for party "stumpers," and every Republican campaigner received a copy in the party handbook. It gave them the phrases to use in their appeals to Americans in every part of the country. It was thrilling to use and hear these words.

> We believe in American markets for American products, American wages for American workmen, American opportunity for American genius and industry, and American defense for American soil. American citizenship is the reflex of American conditions, and we believe our policies make for a fortunate people for whom moral, material, and educational advancement is the open way. The glory of our progress confirms. The answered aspirations of a new world acclaim. We have taken the ideal form of popular government and applied the policies which had led a continent to the altars of liberty and glorified the Republic. We have justified pride and fortified hope. We need only to preserve and defend and go unfalteringly on. Power is the guarantor of peace and conscience the buckler of everlasting right. Verily, it is good to be an American.

As the Washington *Evening Star* said on June 8, 1916, "Americanism has not been more forcibly stated, even by the man who claims to have invented it."

6

Behind this oratorical barrage of reunionism and Americanism, the practical steps of Republican reconciliation took place. Harding did not dominate this work, but played his part as an important member of the Republican organization. The cautious mood of the convention of 1916 was in striking contrast to the exhilaration and pugnacity of 1912. As the *Columbus Citizen* said, June 8, "Nearly everybody present was prepared not to lose his balance." The seriousness of the situation was deepened by the fact that the Progressives were holding their national convention in Chicago at the same time that the Regulars were. Delegates from each body were in frequent conference and negotiation. On June 7, the first day of each convention, so much fraternization was taking place that it was planned by Senator William E. Borah to follow Harding's keynote address of that day with a motion to create a committee of five Regulars to meet with a similar committee of Progressives. A phone call was made to Roosevelt at Oyster Bay, New York, and he approved of the step.[21]

The important thing, however, was not the calling of a Regular-Progressive conference, but who would make the first open move to have one. The idea was that the first to move would be the loser. Moderates, therefore, on the Regular side prevailed on Borah to hold back his action so as to get the Progressives to take the bait offered by Harding's keynote. This the Progressives did on the morning of June 8. When Harding, as permanent chairman of the Regular convention, announced the Progressive offer, there was a genuine burst of applause for the first time in the proceedings. The Progressives had flinched, and the advantage was now with the Regulars. Harding then recognized a motion by conservative Senator Reed Smoot to appoint a committee to meet with the Progressive committee. This motion passed easily, and Harding appointed a well-balanced committee of conservatives, moderates, and liberals.[22]

As the two committees met and dickered, both conventions proceeded on their way to the adoption of very similar platforms, and then paused on the brink of the great decision as to candidates. While intensive behind-the-scenes maneuverings were going on, it was suddenly reported that Roosevelt had indicated his willingness to accept the conservative Henry Cabot Lodge. This was a shocker for the Progressives, and a thriller for the Regulars. Roosevelt himself had flinched. The angry Progressives indignantly rejected Lodge and, in desperation, named Roosevelt, only to have him decline, after both conventions were over, in favor of the liberal Charles Evans Hughes, whom the Regulars had selected. Thus did reconciliation come about. There were some very crestfallen Progressives in the lobbies.[23]

Harding was as eager on the uptake of Roosevelt's surrender as he was in maneuvering for it. There began a personal and political friendship, keenly watched and gossipped about, that eventually led to talk of paring the two for Republican standard-bearers in 1920— Roosevelt for President and Harding for Vice-President. The first step was for Harding, as convention chairman, to write on June 28 to the accommodating Colonel Roosevelt, applauding "this splendid contribution to the success of . . . Mr. Hughes." This action, said Harding "effectively emphasizes the sincerity of your opposition to the present Administration and gives proof of your unselfishness in your desire to serve our common country. It will re-enlist the devotion of thousands of republicans who have never been lacking in their personal esteem, but were arrayed against you for a considerable period because of party differences. I believe you will have your reward in the high esteem of your fellow countryman." [24]

The Harding-Roosevelt rapproachment did not go unnoticed. When Roosevelt replied in cordial tones, the letter was published and made much of in political circles. The *Ohio State Journal* referred to it on July 8 as "full of pep, energy, and affection." "He finds," said the *Journal* "that nothing short of the word 'Bully' will express his estimation of Harding's letter to him." The *Journal* added that "Senator Harding is equally cordial toward the Colonel."

These reunion developments reveal the very important fact that the initiative in the process of surrender came from the Progressives, not from the Regulars. This was amply borne out in January, 1917 when Harding visited Roosevelt *at Roosevelt's request*. This is how Harding described the affair to Scobey: "My interview with Col. Roosevelt at New York was not of significant importance. I went over at his request and was very glad to have the meeting, and found it a very satisfactory one. He made a rather more favorable impression on me than I have ever had heretofore, but I cannot say as to what impression I left with him. My best guess is that the Colonel is looking forward to a candidacy in 1920, and felt that it might not be unwise to be on friendly terms with me. Later developments have tended to confirm this impression. The most enjoyable part of the interview was the revelation of his thorough understanding of the republican members of the Senate. He had the Progressives down to an ant's heel, called one of them an S.O.B. and suggested that another was impossible." [25]

7

The reunion of Republican Regulars and Progressives in the nomination of Hughes in June, 1916 was one thing; the election of Hughes was something else. It was Hughes' campaign, not Harding's. Indeed it was hardly even the Republican party's campaign. The well-meaning Hughes appointed as national campaign manager a personal friend, William R. Willcox, who proceeded to do almost all the things a campaign manager is expected not to do to win an election. Harding performed his assigned duties in the campaign, speaking not only in Ohio but elsewhere. But the over-all management was so poor that it became a model to be avoided when Harding and his party set about planning the campaign of 1920.

Harding had no great admiration for Hughes' campaigning ability. After the nomination the Ohio Senator commented tartly that campaign manager Willcox was a "fine fellow," but that he "is not a very strong man to direct the campaign." When the fireworks had ended with Hughes' defeat, Harding's tartness was again apparent in his comment to Scobey, "The impression is very general here, as well as in Ohio, that he would have fared much better had he gone to his summer residence after the speech of notification and acceptance, and remained there and retained the halo about his head which came on his exceptional nomination."[26]

There were many flaws in the Hughes-Willcox management of the campaign of 1916.[27] In fact, management was subordinated to the grand idea that the best way to win back the Progressives was for Hughes, a former member of the United States Supreme Court, to inspire unity by the conspicuously judicious example of his high-minded character and perspective. That meant that local political committees were ignored, and national reportage bungled. Hughes sought to give the impression of coming down to earth by taking to the stump and speaking to local gatherings without fusing it all together in a nationally coordinated system of publicity. This was overdone. The candidate rapped Wilson vigorously for not being militant against Germany, while the Wilsonians emphasized the effectiveness of the President's policy of keeping the country out of war. Hughes' militant criticisms then backfired as Wilson was successful in getting Germany to suspend the submarine campaign in respect to its imperiling the lives of Americans. Hughes criticized similarly in regard to Wilson's Mexican "watchful waiting" policy, thus strengthening the impression that the Republicans were warmongers. Hughes' austerity in ignoring the fact that in certain localities the Progressives still resented the bypassing of Roosevelt lost much Progressive support, particularly in California, where Hiram Johnson and his pro-

Roosevelt followers became highly incensed and gave little or no support to the Republican national ticket.

Harding's part in the 1916 effort was entirely loyal. He did his eloquent best, which, of course, was not enough, even to carry his own state. His oratory was in great demand. The *Washington* (D.C.) *Sunday Star*, September 10, listed him among the "big guns" in the Republican "oratory drive." He spent three weeks campaigning in the West as far as Wyoming and Montana. He was summoned to Maine for the early gubernatorial vote in that state, and gave the Republican voters there the benefit of his tariff Americanism. When Maine went its usual Republican way, Harding rejoiced, saying, "As protection was the big issue in Maine, it is evident the Republican party will win largely on that issue." The fact that Maine Progressives were back in the Republican fold seemed to Harding to justify his assumption that tariff Americanism was the most important issue.[28]

Back in Ohio it was similar. Harding keynoted the Republican opening at Dayton, and then stumped up and down the state with frequent visits to New York, Pennsylvania, and New Jersey. At Dayton, on September 25, he warned of the economic disaster in store when peace would return and "the fever of war production" subsided. He sniped at the Adamson Law, which had established the eight-hour-day standard for railroad workers. The industrial paralysis resulting from peace and the Democratic tariff would make labor sorry for their victory. "I warn our people now," he thundered, "if present policies continue, Woodrow Wilson will come to be the five-hours-a-day president—four working days a week with five hours pay, because the lack of our activity will not require longer hours." He, of course, protested that he was an eight-hour-a-day man, citing his policy as a publisher of the Marion *Star*. There were frequent jibes at Wilson's Mexican policy, which he called "throwing out a *de facto* government and supporting de facto [*sic*] anarchy in its place." He recognized the Ohio anti-war sentiment being cultivated by the Democrats by saying that it was "an insult to the intelligence of American voters to tell them that Charles E. Hughes will get us into war." He predicted a 100,000 Ohio majority for Hughes in November.[29]

It did not happen. Ohio Republicans went down to an unprecedented and stunning defeat for a presidential year as Wilson carried the state by a plurality of 89,408, and Cox was elected over Willis by a slim plurality of 6,616. Prosperity, the eight-hour-day (which Hughes criticized Wilson for submitting to), and a desire for peace had carried the country.[30] Harding, himself, after the campaign was over, said that the eight-hour-day was a deciding factor. He told an *Ohio State Journal* reporter, "It was this endorsement of eight hours as a day's work that did more than anything else to carry Ohio for President Wilson. It was in the air everywhere." [31]

The election of 1916 marked a turning point in Harding's views on labor. Since President Wilson had profited by it, so must he and the Republican party. The Ohio Senator was quite frank about this. "It may shock you to know," he wrote Scobey after the vote, "but I mean to translate this vote of the country into an actual eight hour day. The people have voted strongly for such a thing and I purpose to be an active participant in bringing it about." "I am in favor of giving them what they want." He still distrusted the "labor agitators" who, he said, would now push for the six-hour day. "If the reformation goes far enough, nobody will have to work at all. Then we can let God do it." [32]

An important Harding by-product of the 1916 campaign was the gossip about the "Garfield issue," which cast Harding in the role of "dark horse" candidate for the Presidency. This talk had reference to the 1880 Republican national convention when "dark horse" James A. Garfield "stole" the nomination from his fellow Ohioan, John Sherman. It was a strange parallel that in 1916, former Senator Theodore E. Burton occupied the same role in relation to Harding that Sherman had in relation to Garfield. Both Burton and Sherman had high reputations as statesmen, but were generally considered poor vote-getters. Scobey used the term "old grandmother Burton." In 1916, the Ohio Republican machine promoted Burton in the presidential preference primaries with Harding as a delegate pledged to Burton. Nevertheless, there was a strong undercurrent of "Harding for president" feeling, and some of his "fool friends" persisted in raising the question, "Will Harding pull another Garfield?" Testimony to this situation is found in a letter dated April 19, 1916, from Alexis Cope of Columbus to Albert Shaw, editor of the *Review of Reviews*. Said Cope, "The perfunctory character of his [Burton's] candidacy is further evidenced by the fact that many organization Republicans are openly advocating Senator Harding as 'a dark horse.'" [33] People could not easily forget how eagerly in 1914 Republicans had turned from Burton to Harding for Senator.

As a matter of fact, some of Harding's friends had been urging him for the Presidency in this same 1914-1916 period. The two self-appointed "original unterrified, out-spoken discoverers of an absolute sure and certain candidate for the presidency upon the republican ticket in 1916" in the person of the Ohio Senator were Scobey and George B. Christian, Sr., father of the Senator's secretary. Malcolm Jennings and Harry Daugherty were not far behind. They had been nagging ever since the 1914 victory, noting "Harding for President" sentiment in various parts of the country. The Senator labeled such sentiment as "insanity," and its agitators as men of "poorly balanced minds" and candidates for the "asylum" which he intended to build and "fill up with my numerous friends." This asylum would be "well stocked with moisture." He told Scobey that the senatorship was enough, he must make good in that first. "One can spoil everything," he wrote, "by being too ambitious." Besides, there was so much "anxiety and stress and strain" in a nationwide campaign—and so many friends to disappoint in case of failure. He wrote of his "cavorting around in 1915 making speeches until I tumbled to the fact that people were mistaking my speech making endeavors as laying the foundation for a candidacy to succeed Mr. Wilson." He thereupon "cut it out." [34]

And so Harding became a loyal, if not enthusiastic, supporter of Burton for President. The Burton candidacy, he told Scobey, "does not catch on with a hurrah, notwithstanding the fact that everybody respects his commanding ability and looks upon him as the biggest figure in Ohio Republicanism." It lacked the "insane enthusiasm" that characterized the candidacies of Foraker and McKinley in "days gone by." He felt that Root or Hughes had more general support than Burton. However, the ardor of the Senator's "insane" promoters was not dampened. As George Christian, Jr., wrote to Scobey, "The Harding 'dark-horse' sentiment in Washington is strong and you hear expressions wherever you go. He is discouraging it, but that has no effect." [35]

In spite of Harding's disavowals of the Garfieldian presidential "pot shots," they continued to appear in the state and national press right up to convention time. On April 28, 1916, the Ohio State Journal actually cartooned him as "flirting with Miss G.O.P." As the delegates gathered in Chicago, rumors circulated that, in case of continued stalemate, some delegations might turn to Harding. It was also rumored that a "strong delegation of manufacturers and representatives is quietly working to shift things around so that Senator Harding will be nominated." Samuel S. Blythe, popular magazine writer, went so far as to say in the *Cincinnati Times-Star* that, if the delegates could not stop the Theodore Roosevelt movement with Hughes, "the man they have most in mind is Senator Warren G. Harding of Ohio." According to the *Cincinnati Enquirer* of June 6, the Harding boom had gone so far that "campaign buttons are here already for distribution." The *Enquirer* was also responsible for the report that the Cincinnati delegation refused to endorse the unit rule for Ohio's vote for Burton as an "aid to a possible Harding movement." The *Cleveland Plain Dealer* called these delegates "the U-boat crew," who "talk of Root but at heart they would be delighted to vote for Senator Harding." Mary Roberts Rinehart and William Jennings Bryan mentioned the Harding boom, but deprecated his chances. One municipal delegate, James H. Remick, wrote to a Detroit business friend, "Harding's speech this morning was wonderful. Don't miss reading a word of it. I would not at all be surprised to see him the nominee of the Republican Party, and he will be some standard bearer. I think T. R. is practically eliminated." [36]

Harding, of course, repudiated all these reports. This enabled reporters to emphasize his self-sacrifice. On June 8 the *Chicago Herald* quoted the *Detroit Free Press* as saying that "Senator Harding acted an altogether unselfish role in delivering the keynote speech. There had been speculation whether or not his speech might elevate him to the nominateable pedestal. Instead of saying one word that might have done some such thing in his own behalf, the Ohio Senator spoke of harmony, concord, Americanism and all that the word means." The *Cincinnati Times Star* went further and declared that Harding's dignified and important role had made him "one of the coming men in American politics. . . . The convention may not see fit to honor Senator Harding with the nomination. But the distinction will remain with him that contact with the nation's Republicans has vastly increased his influence. Warren G. Harding is today one of the big Republicans in the United States." [37]

The Ohio Senator was not altogether displeased with his own oratorical efforts. To be sure, after the June keynote, he professed to his friend Jennings that "since the rousting [*sic*] I received at Chicago, I no longer harbor any too great self confidence in the matter of speech making." This was probably because of the jibes of Irvin S. Cobb, Heywood Broun, and others. Cobb had likened Harding's spine to that of John Philip Sousa, his profile to that of a "matinee idol," and his motions to those of "Annette Kellerman." Broun called his speech "cheap," adding, "sometimes one could hardly see Harding for the words about him." And a writer to the *Chicago Herald* described his performance as a "gracefully modulated series of quavers, semi-quavers and semi-semi-quavers." However, William Jennings Bryan had called his voice "excellent" and his delivery "splendid," and Arthur M. Evans likened his voice to "a diapason note on a cathedral organ." [38] But in the fall, after campaigning in Pennsylvania, New England, and the Rocky Mountains, he felt much better. He wrote to Mrs. Harding that at Lynn, Massachusetts the crowd waited for him to speak after several others had expounded and then half of them departed. Out in Idaho and Montana, he confided, "I seem to have a better and vastly greater reputation than at home. My speeches seem to be well received." [39]

The campaign of 1916 had, indeed, made Harding a "big Republican," big enough to be thought of seriously for the Presidency in 1920—big enough to be thought of in the same breath, if not the same class, with Charles Evans Hughes. Hughes, off his Supreme Court pedestal, was merely "Wilson with whiskers." He taught Republicans that statesmanship was not enough for a presidential candidate. The haunting thought came to many that they had seen another man on another pedestal who could do better than Hughes. This was Warren Gamaliel Harding, a man who looked like a President and yet acted like a human being and a fellow politician.

In conclusion, it may be said of the political situation of 1916 that, though the Republicans failed with Hughes, they might still hope for success so long as there lived an irrepressible Colonel Roosevelt and an adjustable Senator Harding. And if there were no Roosevelt?

CHAPTER THIRTEEN

Politics and the Americanization of
World War I, 1917–1918

*"If, after the war, we will all be intensely American, it will have been
worth all it cost."* : : : *Harding to the Columbus Elks Club, as
quoted in the "Ohio State Journal," September 21, 1918*

⌐ Harding's ideas of the nation's objectives in 1917 in entering
World War I were highly Americanized. It was not a war for world
democracy but a war for American rights and American security,
especially against those in America who were not yet "truly American." He was referring to unassimilated immigrants and their descendants. These people had to find out how to be American by their part in
the common war effort. As for Germany and the other Central Powers,
Harding stated that after their defeat they should be allowed to have
whatever sort of government they desired.

Harding was propounding a sort of liberalism which the German-
Americans might appreciate. But the idea was entirely opportunistic.
If any principle was involved, it was not freedom for the German
people to choose their own form of government but the promotion of
the patchwork unity of the Republican party.

There can be no doubt that Senator Harding was playing as much
politics during World War I as he could. If there was politics involved
in opposing some of President Wilson's requests, Harding said it was
because the problems involved were not directly concerned with the
war. So far as Harding was concerned, he was justified—whatever
politics he played—by claiming that the Democrats were the original
sinners. The Democrats got all the choice political appointments. "The
present Administration," he told his New York friend J. W. Hibbard in
January of 1918, "seems determined to make it a Democratic war in
many ways. At any rate, the faithful are being rewarded in numbers
beyond my counting." Harding accused Wilson of interfering in local
elections. "The President," he told Frank Scobey on April 2, 1918,

"violated all political decency in his open interference in the Wisconsin campaign and there has been a lot going on here of an extremely partisan character, all of which makes it very difficult to make one's partisan devotion yield to what seems to be a fairly patriotic attitude." In October of 1918, as the President negotiated with Germany for an armistice, Harding saw politics involved. "You need not think that politics is adjourned for a single moment," he wrote E. R. Smith of Warren, Ohio. "There has been political design in the notes which have been sent to Germany concerning arrival at terms of peace." To Scobey he confided, "It is pretty generally felt about here that much of the war correspondence with Germany has been inspired by a desire to influence the elections."

Early in June of 1918, when Wilson called for a suspension of politics in drafting war-tax measures, Harding expressed supreme contempt for Wilson's alleged hypocrisy. He told Jennings that Wilson originally wanted to postpone tax legislation until after the election, but, when the Republicans objected, the President made it look as if it was the Republicans who had sought the postponement. "No greater outrage—no greater piece of hypocrisy was ever pulled off," wrote Harding.[1] When the President asked for a Democratic Congress to be elected in 1918, Harding was extremely angry. This was an example, he said, of Wilson's mad desire for power and for a perpetual dictatorship. As a matter of fact, the President had wielded his power so poorly, Harding said, that it was only Republican support that had made possible the successful conduct of the war.[2]

A particularly savage piece of wartime politicking occurred in Columbus on August 27, 1918, when Harding addressed the Republican state convention and criticized President Wilson for the promise made in the Fourteen Points to reduce trade barriers, i.e., to lower tariffs. Low tariffs had been anathema to Harding throughout his career as editor and politician. Wilson's proposal was, in Harding's view, an attack on Americanism. It was internationalism and, therefore, Socialism. Harding gave it all the unreasonable exaggeration that he could muster before his bewitched listeners: "We gloried in nationality, now we are contemplating internationality. . . . Addressing Congress last winter the President declared for the removal of all barriers of trade. This is the tenet of international faith. The Socialists demand it. But it can not be now. America will never lower her standards, but they cannot be maintained without trade barriers. Let the world advance to ours. The theory of banished barriers is beautiful, the practice is destroying. American labor will never consent. We must have protection to hold us to what we are, and send us to greater eminence." [3]

Whether it was politics or not, Harding performed as the practical patriot, the isolationist who saw America first, America the greatest. President Wilson was the "Presbyterian priest," who saw morality first and America as its servant. Although Americans came to realize that the Wilsonian approach to foreign policy was sounder than isolationism, it was not yet accepted in 1918. Only the brutal course of events could teach Americans what they could not learn from Wilson.

Thus Harding's isolationist position, unpopular though it was to become, was still more representative of the views of the average American than was the foresight of Wilson. Harding, as a successful newspaperman and politician, knew the feelings of the man in the street. Therefore, as he revealed his narrow interpretation of the causes and purposes of the war, he was saying what millions of Americans understood. He had his feet on the ground, and his head was still on his broad shoulders, instead of in the clouds. It is easy to see why his practical-minded fellow Americans, as they listened to his eloquent, obvious, and adjustable phrases, would eventually trust him with the highest office in the land.

Although Harding was burning with indignation against Germany in those heady days of early April, 1917, as he spoke and voted for a war declaration, he stayed pro-German as long as he could. As late as December 12, 1916, when Germany offered to President Wilson to open peace negotiations on the condition, among other things, of a restoration of its colonial possessions, Harding was most enthusiastic. "This is glorious news," he told reporters, "if only it turns out to be true. . . . I hope that peace is in sight and that the German proposals will lead to definite results." He expanded upon the final peace terms which he hoped would provide for world disarmament. However, he advised against the United States seeking to mediate between the opposing forces because "the fellow who tries too soon to bring about peace between combatants often gets swatted himself." [4]

When war became inevitable as the result of Germany's declaration for all-out submarine warfare against United States shipping, fiercely patriotic emotions stirred the people and Harding felt the stirring. His reactions were as common and down-to-earth as those of the average American. When German submarine commanders hit their American targets, Harding was instant in response: "It means war—nothing less." He told a Wheeling audience on his way to Washington, "Germany's desperation has drawn her to give us an affront to which all self-respect and regard for just American rights demand an armed reply." As President Wilson called the new Congress into special session to receive his war message, Senator Harding was totally loyal. His talk to his Wheeling listeners blazed with fighting phrases: "When the world's mad you cannot escape the blows, and I say, when the time comes for action, be for America first, last and all times. . . . Frightfulness, hiding in the depths, aimed death and destruction when none could defend, and today an outraged nation answers—it shall be done. . . . The American soul is aflame with awakened patriotism, and the hour has struck for the reconsecration of our citizenship to the service of our country." [5] Finally, as he cast his senatorial vote for war, he vowed unfaltering allegiance to a newly inspired nation in its resolve to destroy the "maddened power" that was seeking "to dominate the earth." [6]

2

Obviously, for the sake of his own German-American constituents, Harding had to temper his anti-Germanism—but only to a degree. He was disposed to fight against Germany for sinking our ships, but not against the right of Germans to have whatever form of government suited them. On the fighting side he told a Teutonic delegation of anti-war Cincinnatians, who called on him in Washington in support of a referendum on a war declaration against Germany, that he would resign his office before voting for such a proposition. When national honor and the protection of "just American rights" are involved, there was only one response—"by instant resistance, first by protest and then, if necessary, by war declaration by Congress." [7]

But Harding never failed to say nice things about the Germans— when German-Americans were listening. He appreciated the German love of the fatherland. Harding was much concerned about his tactics when a call came in mid-March, 1917 from a group of Cincinnati businessmen to attend an Americanism rally to identify Cincinnati, with its large German-American element, solidly behind the rising war sentiment. "It looks like inviting trouble to go to Cincinnati for such an utterance," he wrote Jennings. "Write me frankly." The result was that when he got to the Queen City on March 31, he was at his oratorical and Americanistic best and said the right things. He showed appreciation for the German-American dilemma, speaking tenderly of their "conflict between sympathy and duty. . . . I know nothing more beautiful in all the world's passions for country than the German love for the fatherland." [8]

Wilson's war message a few days later gave Harding another chance to please his German-American constituents. He interpreted the President's war-for-world-democracy sentiments as an affront to the lovers of the Fatherland. "I am not voting for war in the name of democracy," he told his fellow Senators. "It is none of our business what type of government any nation on this earth may choose to have." "The German people," he said, "evidently are pretty well satisfied with their government." He admired the sense of loyalty of the German people: "I would not ask a better thing for this popular Government of the United States of America than the loyal devotion on the part of every American that the German gives to his Government." [9]

3

Essential to Harding's theory of Americanizing the objectives of World War I were his views on the mixed nationalities in the American population. It was the old isolationism of his nineteenth-century *Marion Star* newspaper days, when he had seen immigration as a menace to the American spirit. By merging all in a common war effort, that source of disunity would be ended. America could find its national soul. It was bombast, pure and simple, but it was thrillingly eloquent in the usual Harding manner, and appealed to the kind of Americans who had come to comprise the people to whom Harding's newspaper and political talent had been dedicated.

Harding was very frank about his polyglot theory. In a 1917 Memorial Day address in Columbus he said, "It is the pitiable truth that under the banner of our boasted freedom, with open gates to the oppressed of the world, we were becoming the haven of a polyglot people instead of the treasured home of a patriotic people. The tumult of the world brought us to a realization and we are now brought to the test of making the preserved nation of 1865 the patriotic nation of 1917 and forever thereafter. Henceforth the man who dons the habiliments of an American and dwells in American opportunity must be American in his heart and be committed to every American cause.

Then shall we be gloriously American at home and invincibly American throughout the world." [10]

The Senator spoke similarly in his April 4, 1917 explanation of his war vote. The war, he told his fellow Senators, would be a great opportunity to build a stronger Americanism. He said that he "doubted if we had that unanimity of sentiment which is necessary for the preservation of this free Government." Americans had reached a stage where, seemingly, they were without a "national soul." The fires of the melting pot seemed to have died down, and the people were divided. He said that he had heard doctrines preached on the floor of the Senate which indicated divisions and selfish interests. It indicated that the country was "becoming a mere collocation of states." Americans had become obsessed with the pursuit of the ease and comfort of their higher standard of living and were thus unfit for self-preservation. Popular government had added to their sense of self-satisfaction without the realization of what would be needed for self-defense. Instead of hyphenated, factional, and sectional Americans with all their petty self-complacencies, hates, and jealousies, there should be "real" Americans capable of giving "a new guarantee of nationality," as Americans in the past had done, when life was simpler and less weakened by ease and comfort. "I hope that out of this great tumult of the world, and our part therein, there will spring from Columbia's loins the real American, believing in popular government, and willing to suffer and sacrifice, if need be, to maintain the rights of that government and the people thereunder. I believe that this is the great essential to the perpetuity of the American republic—the maintenance of rights in confidence, absolutely without selfish interests." Suffering and sacrifice would do what ease and comfort could never do—"put a new soul into a race of American people who can enthusiastically call themselves truly and spiritually and abidingly American people." [11]

Harding's views on the war were strongly conditioned by his belief that the conflict was not popular among Americans. He remembered the emphasis on peace of the campaign of 1916. On August 31, 1917, during a Senate discussion of the war-revenue bill, he bluntly told his fellow senators, "I know full well, sirs, that this is not a popular war." He knew this, he said, because peace had been one of the basic issues in the campaign of 1916. It was "dwelt upon in studied oratory on every stump—not on one side alone, let it be said." The political animus against President Wilson was obvious. [12]

Privately, Harding expressed himself much more vigorously against the idea of warring for world democracy. Such a goal, he told Jennings, was not worth fighting for. For one thing, judging by the way events had been going in the United States under Democratic and Progressive leadership, and with the encouragement of excessive immigration, America was getting too much democracy. "The real solemn truth is," he told Jennings on June 14, 1917, "that we have said so much about democracy in this country that we are on the verge of a chaotic democracy and are developing conditions which seriously cast a doubt upon our ability to defend ourselves." [13]

Another strong consideration in Harding's opposition to Wilson's world-democracy talk was that it sought to promote revolution. Harding did not approve of that, because it worked not just for other nations but might encourage revolutionary thought in the United States. "I do not think we are yet ready for the reformation of the world," he told Jennings, "and we ought not to be encouraged in a pitiable endeavor to instigate revolt against governmental authority at a time when we are soon to see governmental authority in this country put to a more than serious test." [14]

Harding was evidently having nightmares over this propaganda for world democracy. He saw organized labor leading us to the verge of Bolshevism. He thought Jennings out to know that the "representatives of organized labor have said to the President that unless a good dictatorship is immediately established in this country, there will be a universal demand from organized labor for a 40% increase of wages, and in case the demand is not allowed, that these organizations will not attempt to guarantee against a nation-wide revolution." [15] At the end of the year 1917, Harding confessed to Jennings that he found himself "wondering every night what the end is going to be. Many a moment I am convinced that we are doomed to the rule of something similar to the Bolsheviki on the one hand or a very strong military autocracy on the other. You can put it down as an established fact that the result of the war is going to depend on the loyalty and devotion of the laboring force in this country." He hinted darkly about "revelations" in the secret sessions of the Senate Commerce Committee relative to the labor situation in the shipbuilding world. "It has much inclined to drive me into a pessimistic state." [16] By May, 1918 Harding was fearful that the labor influence throughout all the Allied nations would drive America to a "peace without victory" under President Wilson's leadership. Thus did Harding's nineteenth-century distrust of organized labor survive as he saw it sabotaging the nation in World War I.[17]

4

Harding's utilitarian Americanism can be seen at its epitome in his effort to use the aging Theodore Roosevelt to popularize the conflict. The need for an early Atlantic crossing by a few American divisions to boost Allied morale led certain Republicans to believe that the old Rough Rider should ride again. The proposal was sheer politics, with as much intent to promote the Regular-Progressive reunion as to aid the war effort.

The idea of using the war to promote Republican-Progressive re-union was not originated or monopolized by Harding. It was a prime policy of Republican national committee chairman Will Hays. Harding, himself, as has been shown, was the object of the Rooseveltian maneuvering in January, 1917. These overtures continued with the war, and Harding was quick to notice and comment thereon. In September, 1917 he wrote to Scobey, "Undoubtedly the Colonel is thinking politics all the while, and one must accredit him with a very sensitive gauge of public sentiment." A month later Harding confessed to Scobey that it looked like Roosevelt for the election of 1920. "You have to hand it to T. R. He is a real American." At another time Harding wrote, "You can say all you please about him, he has a personality which cannot be put aside and he has the qualities of Americanism which have very largely restored him in the affections of the people." The Senator added facetiously that he and T. R. were getting to be "quite Buddy," but there was no danger of a "seduction." "I mean to maintain my virtue at all hazards."

By March, 1918 Chairman Hays had pushed the reunion so far that Harding was moved to write, "Hays already has under way the complete reconciliation of Taft and Roosevelt. I think one who can perform such a miracle as that gives every promise of thoroughly harmonizing the various factions in the Republican party." [18]

That Senator Harding was the man for the job of getting senatorial backing for the creation of a "Roosevelt division" was recognized and arranged for by the Colonel's friend, Senator Henry Cabot Lodge. In a letter to Roosevelt dated April 23, 1917, Senator Lodge described the arrangements to amend the Senate Army Bill to increase the size of the army so as to allow Roosevelt to raise and command a division. Wrote Lodge, "Harding said the other day that he would like to offer such an amendment and I told [Hiram] Johnson that I thought it was a great deal better that Harding should offer it than either he or I, because we are known to be very close to you—in my case personally and in Johnson's case politically. I am going to try to take it up with them this morning and try to get the amendment in at once." [19]

That Harding eagerly and effectively did his part in promoting the "Roosevelt division" scheme is fully attested by the *Congressional Record*, by Senators, and by Roosevelt himself. On April 28, 1917 Harding, in his usual spread-eagle way, addressed the Senate in behalf of the "Roosevelt amendment" that he had introduced.[20] He said that the immediate and intensive training of a volunteer army, recruited by a former commander-in-chief of the United States Army, opened the way "to provide the earliest possible armed American force to participate in the battles on the western front of Europe. It provides the advance guard of American ideals, bearing the oriflame of New World liberty, New World civilization, and New World humanity, and armed assurance of our everlasting committal to maintained national rights." Millions of Americans, and millions of Europeans, will cheer the acceptance of Roosevelt's valiant tender. "An immediate force of one to four divisions of American volunteers would put new life in every allied trench and a new glow in every allied camp fire on every battle front of Europe. A division tomorrow would exert the strength of 10 divisions next year and add to the morale of the allied armies what shells and guns and assurances of food could not add in many months of most cordial co-operation. The psychic moment awaits." Roosevelt's army would not be a substitute for conscription, but an inspiration that victory was nearer while the conscripted soldiers prepared for action. (Roosevelt's divisions would be taken from an older age group not covered by the conscription law.)

There was another virtue to the Roosevelt proposal, said Harding. It recognized the fact of disunited America and offered an immediate response, while the disunited ones were gradually discovering their duties as Americans. There were those who opposed conscription. There were those who had lived in the lap of luxury who were slow to learn the need for sacrifice to protect America from German aggression. There were those who believed that Europe's madness must be corrected by Europe's efforts, not by America's; there were those who assumed that someone else must do the fighting. "Our own land has its hundreds of thousands impelled by love or hate, and see only the European issue, without a concern for the fate of our own Republic, now inseparable from the peace terms to which Europe must come. Somebody . . . must speak the great peril. A German triumph and our American security are utterly incompatible. . . . Germany must be brought to terms, or the world becomes her dominion."

Harding was saying what he thought so terribly true about the uninspired, undedicated part of America. "Popular realization has not yet come," he lamented. "Duty and sentiment have not yet been clearly separated. The great awakening has not yet come. The pity is that it will never come except in the echoes of national disaster and the convulsive sobs of an American tragedy."

It was starkly realistic and commonsense talk and gave bitter confirmation to many listeners that what should come first was Americanism, American unity, not far-fetched dreams about world democracy. "It may be, in one sense, a war for democracy, though I have already disputed that contention on this floor. I can only consent that incidentally it is a war to prove the capacity of democracy to defend its rights."

Harding's strongly realistic view was convincing to those who preferred voluntary enlistment to conscription. The Roosevelt soldiers would step into the breach at once, while the rest of America came to realize its part. "The Roosevelt volunteer division or divisions will prove the agency, the expression, and the assurance of American interest while we make the resolute preparation, while we commit the American mind, while we consecrate the American spirit. . . . It will be the first manifestation of the American spirit, the first earnest of the American intent." It will guarantee the acceptance and success of conscription of which so many Americans were traditionally suspicious.

In the final draft of the Army Bill which became law, the Roosevelt amendment appeared in a form that left it to the discretion of the President to send the troops to be commanded by the old Rough Rider.[21] President Wilson never did so.

Harding's strategically apt part in managing the Roosevelt amendment to the Army Bill was widely recognized and publicized. When the bill passed the Senate, the *Cleveland Leader* reported the congratulations that poured in on him for the "tactful and masterly manner" which got nineteen Democratic votes as well as almost solid Republican support. When at last, after the conference committee report favoring the measure had been rejected by the House, supported by the Senate, and finally accepted by the House, the *Leader* headlined, "Another Harding Victory." It said that "in many respects it was a great personal victory . . . due largely to his tactful, persistent and persuasive leadership." Roosevelt's telegram of congratulation to Harding was nationally broadcast.[22]

It was a great personal gratification, as well as a political boost, for Harding to find his role of party pacifier producing such practical results. Not only had he received the approval of Roosevelt but he had found partnership with party notables. Senator Lodge, who selected Harding for the assignment in the first place, was thoroughly pleased with Harding's skillful performance. Lodge told Roosevelt so, and added, "I think it would gratify Harding if you were to write him a letter. I am sure he deserves it." Roosevelt did so, and Harding's reply was warmly cordial and vigorously American.

When, at last, the Roosevelt amendment had become law, and the former President had again thanked Harding, the Senator from Ohio, in his reply, wrote in a most forthright manner of his ideas about the disinterest of the American masses in the war, and of how Roosevelt could popularize it for them:

> I hold the conviction that your expeditionary force to Europe along with the mental development of the country incident to its organization, would light the American spirit and immensely popularize the war. We can not disguise the distressing fact that the war is admissably lacking in popularity. If we could get down to a basis where all of us are agreed, we shall develop the unanimity of spirit and cordiality of support which is essential to the success of our great undertaking. I can believe that the righteous defense of our national right, the preservation of our national honor, the guaranteed securities of American lives in lawful pursuits wherever they may be, and the enforced contracts of civilized nations—all these combined will afford us a reason around which to light the campfires of American enthusiasm and unquestionably commit all the people to a war which can have none other but a triumphant ending for this people.

To this, Roosevelt replied, "That's a very interesting letter of yours. I would like to discuss, at some length with you, the points that you raise." He invited Harding to visit him at Oyster Bay. Thus was strengthened a political friendship which was to do much in guiding the destinies of Harding toward the White House.[23]

The political utility to the Republicans of the Roosevelt war buildup was well illustrated by what happened when the Democrats criticized it. Roosevelt had added to Democratic discomfort by a series of articles in the *Kansas City Star* critical of the conduct of the war. This led Democratic Senator William J. Stone of Missouri to denounce these "villainous screeds" as inspired by "dominant Republican leaders" who were "making politics out of the war." Senator Stone allowed himself to go so far as to call Roosevelt "the most seditious man of consequence in America." He charged that "since our entrance into the war Roosevelt has become a menace and obstruction to the successful prosecution of the war." [24]

Stone's attack on the heroic Roosevelt was a godsend to Republican politicians, including Harding. It was called a gross breach of American war unity made possible by Republican support of the war. Harding's comment was especially vindictive. "Up to Monday," he blandly told an *Ohio State Journal* reporter, "the Republicans in the Senate, indeed, in both branches, have submerged partisan views and surrendered well-cherished ideals of legislation in order to most fully support the nation." Stone's attack on Roosevelt "rends that unity which has made possible everything the president has asked." Harding vowed that "it will not be so from this time on." [25]

5

Senator Harding was performing his Republican duties in big-time, nationwide company. His audience included the front-rank leaders of his party—and they recognized in him a political peer. He could maneuver, manipulate, and spellbind any development into a Republican advantage. One of Harding's chief skills had always been the ability to attack the Democrats—and now he could do it in the name of patriotism.

All his life Harding had believed that Democrats were bunglers, depression creators, demagogues, place-hunters, and generally incapable of living up to the responsibilities of power. He applied this belief over and over again in the United States Senate. The Roosevelt division episode proved to him that the Democrats were the same as ever, and could not be counted on to win World War I. They were divided in purpose, politically small-minded, and without military know-how in their leadership. The Republicans, of course, though in a minority, were united, patriotic, capable, and businesslike. They had a great military leader in Roosevelt. They would support the war, win it, and claim credit for themselves. Harding supported this line skillfully and indefatigably throughout the war and into its League of Nations sequel. It did more than any other single thing to make him President of the United States.

An amusing phase of Harding's war politicking was that he denied it. On April 29, 1918, during the debate on the Overman Bill giving President Wilson complete war dictatorial powers, Harding opposed the measure and blandly denied his political bias and that of his Republican colleagues. "I am the last man in the Senate," he piously declared, "who is inclined to find fault with the administration in this hour of trial. . . . I rejoice to say from the minority side of the Chamber that the support of the administration in all its war measures by the minority has been most cordial and almost unanimous." [26]

Harding's Republican superiority complex seemed to justify for him this needling of Democrats in which the Senator took a leading part. An especially sharp thrust was made on June 4, 1917, at Democratic leader Senator J. Hamilton Lewis of Illinois. It was supposed to show that the Democrats were blundering in their political handling of the war. Lewis was accused of putting it up to the people of New Hampshire, in a by-election, whether they were "for the President or the Kaiser." Since New Hampshire was a strongly Republican state, this was especially insulting to followers of the GOP. It aroused Harding's Republicanism, and he took occasion in some senatorial byplay to suggest that "while we are elevating the world, as I hope we may, we shall contribute something to the fortune of our land if, as partisans in our political contest, we are a little more considerate of one another and a little more frank and sincere in addressing our appeals to the constituencies of this land." [27]

Sometimes Harding's needling was not so deftly done. This happened in a Memorial Day address in Columbus, where he attacked—unjustifiably as it proved—the first Liberty Loan campaign. This included the creation of a clown-like image for the vigorous William Gibbs McAdoo, Democratic Secretary of the Treasury. The *Ohio State Journal* reported that Harding had told a group of ladies that the first Liberty Loan campaign was "hysterical and unseemly," and "calculated to give America's enemies the impression that only by such intensive measures could she raise the sinews of war." He contrasted this with the "fascinating devotion of German citizens to their Government." When rebuked in the Senate on June 8 by Senator Lewis for placing "barriers of obstruction against the sale of bonds," and of pandering to the pro-Germans in Ohio, Harding went further and said that the undignified bond-sale ballyhoo was the result of the lack of confidence in Americans by the Democrats, and resulted from trying to tell the people that they were fighting for world democracy instead of self-defense. This kind of talk, he said, was "balderdash." "I say to you that America, with an ability to buy seventeen billions of bonds on any day, is reluctant to buy because of its lack of confidence in the present administration." Jennings rebuked Harding privately for this anti-bond talk.[28]

This criticism of bond-campaign tactics was another of the many occasions in which Harding ridiculed the war-for-world-democracy theme. Harding claimed that both issues—war bond promotion and the claim that the war was for world democracy—were ballyhoo. Such tactics were unworthy of the integrity and common sense of the American people.

> You can not unify the American people in the defense of the American Nation except on the justifiable ground of defending and preserving American national rights . . . the safety of American lives, the assistance of American honor, and our freedom to participate in the commerce of the seas. You can go to the people with that declaration and find an unfailing response in every American heart. I say it now, and I will repeat it again and again, it is not any business of the American people what class of government any nation on earth may have so long as that government respects the requirements of international law and the tenets of civilization. I think it ill becomes the United States of America to measure a man's patriotic devotion in accordance with his determination that the houses of Hohenzollern and Hapsburg shall be destroyed.

Harding even went so far as to say that Democratic Senators Lewis and Reed had said in secret session that there were matters calling for investigation "which would disturb the confidence of the American people of this day in the conduct of the war." Harding was sharply rebuked for this by Reed and forced to admit that there was nothing "unholy" or "scandalous" in what had been discussed in secret.

Harding soon changed his attitude toward Liberty Loan drives. To have denied his country his talent in speech-making would not only have been unpatriotic but highly unpolitical. But he gave it with an inward reluctance. Privately, he admitted he was irked by the task. As he told J. M. Coker, on September 18, 1918, "I find it a duty to participate in the Liberty Loan campaign and am obliged to put aside my personal preferences to perform this evident duty." He told J. W. Hibbard, on September 29, "I do not relish it but it is one of the things a man in public life is called upon to do, whether he likes it or not." [29]

What especially irked Harding about the Liberty Loans was the alleged hypocrisy of the Democrats in getting the glory involved in floating them, when basically the appeal was to the profit-making motive via the high interest rate. As he wrote to Scobey on April 14, 1919 concerning "a Liberty Loan stunt" in Ohio that he did not wish to engage in, "I do not see very much occasion for trying to put patriotic spirit in the Loan Campaign after the Treasury Department has provided for an interest rate of 4¾ percent. That ought to appeal to the selfishness of all the money in the world, regardless of the patriotic devotion which originally impelled and which has made a success of all previous loans." [30]

Sometimes Senator Harding's war needling seemed no more than locally inspired meddling. This was the case with his suggestion to the Secretary of War in regard to the Rainbow Division destined for early combat service in France. This was a unit made up of men from the National Guard of twenty-six states, especially veterans from the Mexican border scuffles of 1914–16. Harding protested against the separation of men from their former company and regimental officers. He claimed broken faith by the federal recruiting officers who, he said, had promised "home associations and maintained comradeship under the command of officers of long standing." Harding hoped that the Rainbow Division would be organized with the "least of grief and disappointment to those who were inspired to enlist through the belief in the fellowship of service in performing a patriotic duty." [31] Army officers, of course, denied the Ohio Senator's request.

6

Among the chief of Harding's *bêtes noires* were dictatorship and price-fixing, that is, after he had gotten over his earlier naïveté on the subjects. No man ever reversed himself as completely as Harding did in these regards. On August 12, 1917 there appeared in the magazine section of the *New York Times* a feature article by Richard Barry entitled "Need of a Dictator Urged By Harding." "What the United

States needs and what it must have if it is to win this war," Harding was quoted as saying, "is a supreme dictator, with the sole control of and sole responsibility for every phase of war activity, and this today means practically every phase of government. More than that; not only does this country need such a dictator, but in my opinion it is sure to have one before the war goes much farther. It is the inevitable logic of events here in Washington." Barry asked, "Would you suggest that congress delegate all its powers to one man?" Harding was quoted in reply, "Practically that, if not actually." Barry then asked, "Does that not mean the complete abandonment of democracy?" To this, Harding was quoted as saying, "Call it what you will, it is the only way to win the war. However, it means that we abandon nothing except the incapacity of all legislative bodies in war time." Harding likened an American dictatorship to a counterfire by which a great prairie conflagration is subdued. Using another figure of speech, Harding was quoted, "We would put on autocracy as a garment only for the period of the war, whereas they [the Germans] wear autocracy as a flesh that clings to their bones." "We have a republic to save. We can't do it with the processes of a republic." That Harding meant Wilson for the role of supreme dictator was specifically admitted in response to Barry's persistent questioning. The responsibility was Wilson's. "If he fails then it is his fault, not ours. If he fails under present conditions it is our fault, not his."

Even as he wrote, Harding was guilty of complete contradiction on the subject of dictatorship in respect to the Food Control Bill giving Food Administrator Herbert C. Hoover price-control powers. On a typed copy of the Barry article in the Harding Papers in the Library of Congress are some penciled notes in Harding's handwriting which read, "Personally I have been enthusiastic over the food control bill. It was part of a necessity created by suggestion. Undeniably something was needed, and orderly government must meet such needs in hours of crisis, else it fails utterly no matter what limitations temporarily have to be broken down." And yet, in the Food Control Bill debate on July 21, 1917, Senator Harding raised the spectre of "creeping Socialism." Price control for the farmers added to wage control as in the Adamson Act for railroad labor, had "laid the first stone in the structure of the socialized State. . . . While we are making the world safe for democracy we are going through processes of revolution or evolution that are likely to leave the world a socialized democracy." The effect was vicious. It meant more wage-fixing. It meant efforts to fix prices on iron, steel, and countless other products. What happened to the law of supply and demand? "No Congress, no political party, no leadership can set aside the abiding laws of economics." (Harding never invoked these laws in his tariff thinking.) What was the war doing to the precious virtues of thrift and self-denial? "The nation which comes to the fore in the great reorganization and reconstruction of the social fabric and the industrial world after peace comes again will be the nation which has taught itself some self-denial, some economy and thrift in its every day affairs." What, indeed, had happened to patriotism? "I venture to say, Mr. President, that if the qualities of American patriotism are such that you must guarantee the American farmer a price for his wheat in the face of a world famine, then there is not patriotism enough in this country to win the war." [32]

On the price-fixing bill, Harding voted with the majority on the passage of the Food Control Bill, asking divine forgiveness as he did so. "I will vote for the food bill and full control," he wrote Jennings, on July 6, "and will thank God if industrial paralysis does not follow, and will also ask him to forgive my official sins." [33] It is difficult to understand Senator Harding's confusion in his expressions, public and private, on this bill.

Of course, the nationalization of the railroads came in for some histrionics from Senator Harding against the methods of a dictatorship. This happened in December, 1917, after the railroad and harbor facilities in the East had been frozen up by the weather and by competitive confusion. On December 26 the President had seized the roads and appointed William G. McAdoo director-general. Harding's reaction was political, and his remarks smacked of McAdoo-Wilson-baiting. The Senator took the ground that the Democrats were up to their old tricks of nagging the railroads and that the government could easily have avoided the seizure by earlier attempts to solve the problem:

It has been the popular thing to hammer the railroads, and one who dared to say a word about the importance of their good fortune was looked upon as a tool of capital. A hundred ills are charged to the railroads that they are no more responsible for than the man in the moon. One effective effort to help them relieve the congestion for which consignees are responsible would have worked wonders, but the export cargoes awaiting transfer to docks or ships and priority orders have paralyzed them; and no government help has been extended. Here in Washington is a striking object lesson of choked yards for which the rail lines are not one whit responsible. There will be relief, of course. It might well have come without the assumption of complete control. But the world is in revolution, or feverish evolution, and let us believe this new course to be the solution which will add to efficiency and enhance our strength.[34]

The big test of Harding's sensibilities on war dictatorship came with the Overman Act, which did, in effect, make President Wilson a dictator. It authorized him to redistribute the functions of any and all executive agencies as he saw fit. As historian F. L. Paxson has said, "Few statutes have in so few words surrendered so much and . . . vested more discretion in the President"—and, he added, few statutes had been more completely accepted as just by public opinion.[35]

As for Harding, he who had once told Richard Barry that "what the United States needs . . . is a supreme dictator," now scourged the President with accusations of incompetence and autocratic ambitions. He cited cases of lack of coordination and bureaucratic subordination in which bureau heads had complained of interference "by numbskulls on Capital Hill." He spoke bluntly: "The chief source of lack of coordination in our war activities is the Executive himself. . . . There have been numberless errors on the part of the department heads and others in authority. It would have been a very simple thing to have corrected these errors by removals and changes such as have recently been made by Executive authority. It would also be possible to have corrected mistaken policies. But the Executive has not seen fit to make that acknowledgment and make all the necessary corrections, and he asks at the hands of Congress this blanket authority in order to say to the people of the Republic that he has been a victim of conditions heretofore that he could not correct, but under the authority granted by this bill he will bring about the necessary changes."

Harding's bitterness was excessive. Congress might as well "complete the program by delegating the taxing and appropriating power, adjourn, and go home." Having proclaimed "our participation in a war for democracy . . . the moment we are involved, we propose to entirely put aside our popular form of government and dwell in America under the most autocratic form of government on the face of the earth." Rather than "create a smoke screen for a retreat from our boasted popular government to the establishment of a complete dictatorship I think I would rather fight a bit, covering the retreat. . . . If any man says to me, 'Well, this is only a change for war,' I warn him now that 99 per cent of the changes effected in this war emergency will continue after the war. . . . I stake my reputation as a prophet or as an observer of American tendencies and say now that you will never see them returned . . . the tremendous task of altering the civil institutions of the United States of America ought to be done in the deliberations and reflections of peace and not in the strains and anxieties of war." On final passage, Harding voted no on this bill.[36]

7

One of the handiest things for Harding and the Republicans to challenge in World War I was the shipping problem. Late in 1918 Harding engineered an investigation of the United States Shipping Board which he hoped would be the sensation of the year. During 1917, as the German submarine toll of merchant ships mounted to fearful proportions and the American "bridge of ships" failed to materialize, public apprehensions neared the hysteria stage. Quarreling between chairman William Denman of the Shipping Board and General George W. Goethals, general manager of the Emergency Fleet Corporation, had dismayed the public, and President Wilson had to transfer both of them to spheres of greater usefulness. The business genius of Edward N. Hurley, who succeeded both Denman and Goethals, had not yet acquired the acumen to publicize the sound steps taken to commandeer ships and shipping yards, and to provide for building new ones.[37]

Tension reached a breaking point in the Senate on December 18, 1917 with Harding leading the Republican criticisms. The *Washington Evening Star* of that day headlined:

U. S. LACKS SHIPS, SENATE ASKS WHY

DEMAND INQUIRY

"High Time Americans Were Informed Of

Shipping Program," Says Harding

A resolution instructing the Senate Commerce Committee, of which Harding was a member, was introduced by Harding and quickly passed. Public hearings were begun at once, and the newspapers came out with scare headlines and stories. "Shipping Board Has Sorrowful Career," flared the *Washington Star* on December 21. "Admiral

Bowles Says Wooden Ship Program A Failure," it reported on December 27.[38]

So far as Harding was concerned, the Commerce Committee's investigation of the Shipping Board was supposed to reveal great Democratic incompetence. Senators brought out arguments against the reversion to wooden ships by order of the Board; against the Board's refusal to promote the concrete ship which was said to be the new commercial mistress of the seas; against the seemingly unconscionable costs of construction of new shipbuilding yards such as the one at Hog Island in Philadelphia. Harding told the Senate, "The Shipping Board has indulged in a system of finance that in ordinary times would drive a sober financier to drink." [39]

Housing, port congestion, government-sponsored war-risk insurance, and many other controversial subjects were attacked in highly publicized Commerce Committee hearings with Republican, and sometimes Democratic, witnesses. They were defended with equal spirit by the Board and its Democratic supporters. Many a senatorial critic, as well as defender, found his name bursting into the headlines. Harding, who had started the affair, was headlined as a star critic when he accompanied his committee to Hog Island on February 25, 1918. Here he showed his optimism, as well as self-satisfaction by remarking, "There is more prudent management of expenditures there now, which, I believe, has been a result of the furor which has been stirred up." On April 13, 1918 Harding spoke in New York at a luncheon given by the National Security League. After summarizing the improvements in merchant fleet efficiency, he warned that "they are vastly insufficient for the needs of effective warfare." [40]

The shipping investigation did not produce its hoped-for, Republican-boosting, Democratic-damning results. The image of Democratic incompetency simply could not be sustained by Republican needling. For every technical criticism there was a technical rebuttal. Gradually the public got the idea that the Board was not so bad after all. But, above all, the public got the idea that the race with the murderous submarine was being won by the United States. In spite of heavy losses, deliveries of precious supplies were made in massive quantities. A system of U.S. Navy convoys was worked out to protect and escort the merchant fleet and foil the submarines. The proof of it all seemed to be the ability of the Allied armies to stop the German offensives of 1918 and to mount an overwhelming and war-winning counter-offensive.[41]

Harding never tired of claiming that his investigation of the Shipping Board was responsible for its reform. On June 10, 1918, in a Senate debate on rules procedures, he said, "It is very certain that we would not have had the ship-production program speeded up and made efficient, if we had not had investigation and discussion." Upon another occasion, April 29, during the debate on the Overman Bill, Harding said it was he, himself, who solved the problem of getting deliveries of steel to one shipbuilding yard. It seems that the head of the yard was complaining bitterly that he could not get steel. Also, it seems that this person had not contacted the War Industries Board, which had charge of deciding priorities in regard to the steel deliveries. Harding made this contact and got a member of the War Industries Board to attend a hearing of the Commerce Committee, where he met Hurley. The two immediately sized up the situation and within forty-eight hours steel deliveries were arranged for.[42]

Back in Ohio, Harding was also able to make his Shipping Board service look good. In August, 1918, when the Ohio political campaign was getting hot, Harding claimed much credit for the improved performance of the Shipping Board and the Fleet Corporation. He told the Republican state convention at Columbus, on August 27, "For thirty years the Republican party had been declaring and striving for a restored merchant marine. . . . But the party now in power maintained its abiding opposition and the war found us without the shipping necessary to carry on war across the broad Atlantic. We hurriedly appropriated hundreds of millions, and yet more hundreds of millions, to do what private enterprise would have accomplished with a relative pittance of encouragement. But there was delay and dispute and well-grounded alarm, with Germany destroying the allied carriers and our own at sea. Finally, by calling the attention of Congress to the growing menace, I unintentionally became sponsor for a resolution to investigate. Partisan intent was charged, but we did investigate, and we stirred to endeavor, and we corrected colossal blunders." [43]

On April 13, 1918, shipping was the subject of one of Harding's best performances before the National Security League, an America First organization. (In 1916 Harding steered clear of the League because it was a leading Preparedness propagandizer). It was a Washington's birthday oration, and Harding was equal to the occasion. His speech was entitled "Shipping," and he took full advantage of his well-known reputation as originator of the Shipping Board investigation. His oration bristled with statistics and even technicalities in regard to the progress of our merchant marine. "We have begun a shipping program which is going to place the flag eminently on the paths of ocean traffic throughout the world." Another year, he said, will witness the "essential paralysis of the submarine ruthlessness and frightfulness." Above all, Harding's speech was studded with purple passages which the Security Leaguers loved to hear. "Suppose," he declared, "that poor, miserable, impotent, and chaotic Russia should never strike another blow. Suppose that Italy, less able to meet the oncoming hordes of the Hun than the other nations at war, should fall. Suppose that noble, heroic, respiritualized France should be destroyed—and nothing else, my countrymen, would take her out of the war. And suppose that brave England should be starved, though we can little believe such a misfortune as that. But should all these things occur, mark you, my countrymen, even then the United States of America must go on." [44]

8

Warnings of "creeping Socialism" and its monster cousin, Bolshevism, continued to be part of Harding's wartime oratory. When a bill was introduced into the Senate in January, 1918 to enable the Federal Trade Commission to curb the skyrocketing price of newsprint, the Ohio Senator was filled with foreboding. Pass this bill, he said, and you will "bury the Republic that we boasted of and put in its place a socialistic order" that will make the United States a "land of paralysis and hopelessness for all time to come." This was "a tendency which will ultimately put the Bolsheviks in control of the United States." [45]

The War Revenue Bill of 1917 and its "revolutionary impositions" on incomes and "excess profits" filled Harding with more fears. What an enormous levy this was against capital—twenty-one twenty-sixths —and one twenty-sixth against the consumer. Capital was in danger. "Tell it to the hundred millions of Americans that not only is Congress not trying to shield capital and wealth, but is assigning to them the burdens of war cost on the one hand and has written the authority to restrict prices and reduce profits on the other." This sympathy of Harding for the tax burden on capitalists was very popular with businessmen. After a Harding speech on December 13, 1917 to the Allentown, Pennsylvania, Chamber of Commerce, in which he used similar figures, Charles M. Schwab of the Bethlehem Steel Corporation asked for further information, and Harding was pleased to oblige. [46]

Yes, he said, as he returned to his Ohio constituents for the election of 1918, "we are far adrift toward the socialized state." He cited the nationalizing of the telegraph and telephone lines. Authority was asked by the President with a hope he would not need to use it. Authority was granted. "In the weeks after the grant of authority was passed, without an emergency arising, without a proclaimed necessity, the seizure was made. Another step taken! Others will follow. No man can mark the halting place. War authority is almost limitless and while the sons of the republic are battling to make the world safe for democracy, the radicals at home are making the republic the realm of state socialism." [47]

It is only fair to Harding to show that his public fulminations about "creeping Socialism" were matched by private convictions along that line. In a January 3, 1918 letter to the Scobeys, he wrote, "The Bolsheviki are getting stronger in America every day, and after the Kaiser is cared for, we can prepare to combat the Maximalists [sic], Bolsheviki and Radical Socialists in our own midst. Busy times ahead." His chief consolation came from Elihu Root, who announced that Russia would soon return to its senses. "Russia has all gone to pot," Harding opined to Scobey. "Democracy has made a miserable failure of it there because the people are not educated to self-government, and the new order following the revolution was inaugurated under the control of the Socialist movement. Elihu Root spoke very hopefully concerning Russia in a recent visit to Washington, and seemed to think that she will come to herself in due time." [48]

9

Senator Harding politicked his way through a great world war and looked good at it—to Republicans. He had fought hard to make America safe for Americans. His doctrine of a war for self-defense was more understandable to the average man than President Wilson's war for world democracy and security. So was his patriotic venture of offering the Roosevelt divisions for the aid of America's war-weary allies. In behalf of Republican loyalty and alleged superiority, he had needled away at alleged Democratic inefficiency. He faced both ways on war dictatorship, criticizing the Democrats for making it necessary. He warned of the danger of Socialism and Bolshevism unless the level-headed, competent Republicans were returned to power. It was good, solid Americanism; it was politics—and he relished it.

CHAPTER FOURTEEN

From the Brink of Political Extinction
to the Portals of National Fame,
1918–1919

"I grow so weary of the conspiracies, insincerities, the petty practices of politics, that I have moments when I am inclined to make a sweeping gesture and tell all of them to 'go to hell.' " : : : *Harding to Malcolm Jennings, November 4, 1919, Jennings Papers, Ohio Historical Society*

From 1918 to 1920 political extinction and political salvation were sometimes not very far apart for Warren Harding. Before the death of Theodore Roosevelt, on January 6, 1919, he had to fight to retain his position as Senator. After the death of Roosevelt he had to fight to keep from being pushed into a hopeless contest for the Republican presidential nomination and thus lose everything. After he decided to seek the Presidency, he had to fight a Leonard Wood faction in Ohio to win his own state's endorsement for the nomination. After he had beaten Wood in Ohio, he had to fight Wood and all the other Republican hopefuls at the Chicago convention. And finally, as Republican nominee, he had to fight the Democrats, but this was the easiest part of all. Always there was a fight with a danger of defeat and political extinction. Small wonder, then, that when he saw people urging him for President with the thought of causing him to lose both the Presidency and the Senatorship, he professed a desire to be rid of the whole political mess—Senatorship, presidential candidacy, and all. He had abundant reasons to know that Ohio politics was a jungle containing many ambitious men who desired to wear his senatorial toga, and force him into political exile.

Who were these rivals of 1918—hoping for Harding's step to falter or his sight to be unwary? First, there was the old Regular, Harry M. Daugherty, eventually to become President Harding's attorney general when chance made him Harding's ally instead of rival for party control. There was the former Bull Mooser of 1912, Walter F. Brown, still of Progressive persuasions but eventually to reach President Coolidge's cabinet via the postmaster-generalship. Next there was the hardy perennial candidate for the Ohio governorship, Frank B. Willis, who was to take Harding's place in the Senate when Harding went on to the White House, but who would have enjoyed the acquisition even under circumstances less fortunate for Harding. Over in Cleveland, with its regional right for senatorial recognition, was banker and former governor Myron T. Herrick, still smarting from his 1905 defeat for reelection to the Ohio governorship. Herrick would eventually settle for the ambassadorship to France. Finally, down in Cincinnati, with its traditional regional rights, was a new political prima donna, state Republican treasurer William Cooper Procter of the great Procter and Gamble soap firm.

Essentially, the problem in 1918 was: Who was to control the Ohio Republican party—the Regulars or the Progressives? The leaders of these two factions were the same pair who had squared off in 1912— Daugherty and Brown. Daugherty had retired from active leadership as chairman of the state central committee, but in 1918 he was still the guiding influence through his satellite, Newton H. Fairbanks of Springfield. Brown was still his old designing and ambitious self, working with a new and powerful ally, Rudolph K. Hynicka, successor to George B. Cox as boss of the Cincinnati and Hamilton county Republican machine.

The personal possibilities in this Ohio power struggle between Daugherty and Brown were many. If Daugherty won, he would be in line for Harding's seat in the Senate, with Harding taking the Vice-Presidency, possibly paired with Theodore Roosevelt, to whom Daugherty was reconciling himself for the Presidency. Of course, if Roosevelt died—and, as will be seen, Daugherty had special occasion to observe how weak the old Colonel was—Harding could then be pushed into the Presidency with Daugherty having anything he wanted, and Willis could have the United States Senatorship that neither Daugherty nor Harding needed any more. On the other hand, if Brown beat Daugherty for party leadership, Daugherty would be through, and so also would be Harding and Willis. Brown could slip into the Senate, some other Progressive into the Ohio governorship, and Hynicka would be free to control Hamilton county politics, and hold the balance of power in Ohio politics. As for the Presidency,

Brown would be satisfied with Roosevelt or perhaps some other non-Ohioan of the Rooseveltian persuasion. Eventually, when Roosevelt died and Harding's power increased, Brown discreetly became a convert to the Harding cause.

A crucial factor in this 1918 Ohio political scramble was the prohibition issue. This was a vital matter to one of Hamilton county's leading industries, the manufacture of beer and liquor, and its German patrons. The Eighteenth Amendment to the United States Constitution was up for ratification by the Ohio legislature, and the Anti-Saloon League was scenting victory as it approached the climax of its most effective crusade. Hynicka and the Hamilton county Republicans were determined to prevent the impending disaster and were therefore glad to join with Walter Brown and other urban Progressive leaders in their political ambitions.

Through this Ohio political jungle Harding managed to pick his way warily, but his fate was still uncertain at the end of the year 1918. He was able to straddle the prohibition problem. He courted the Progressives with a new device, the Ohio Republican advisory committee. But he could not compose the bitter rivalry that existed between Daugherty and Hynicka over the role to be played in Ohio Republican politics by the Cincinnati organization. The Hynicka-Progressive coalition might be quite able to obliterate Harding and his patchwork organization. It all depended on the life of the master of Progressive destinies, Theodore Roosevelt. When T. R. died on January 6, 1919, the coalition had no one to cling to. Then, and only then, was Harding's approach to political oblivion arrested. From then on there would be a road to the pinnacle of American politics, if he was wary and well advised.

2

The adjustable Senator Harding met the crisis of the prohibition amendment with one of his most ingenious maneuvers. Prior to 1917 he had maintained his equilibrium on the slippery issue by announcing that he would vote in the Senate as the people of Ohio voted in state referenda on the question. Therefore, he voted wet on a congressional bill to make the District of Columbia dry because the referenda of 1914 and 1915 had produced wet majorities and helped keep the state party from endorsing the proposed Eighteenth Amendment.

Nevertheless, in 1917 he masterminded certain Eighteenth Amendment tactics so as to catch the approval of both the wets and drys at the same time. Part of this maneuvering was to prepare a clause to be added to the amendment that would require the states to ratify it in five years (later changed to six and then seven years). Many Senators and Cincinnatians believed that such a time limitation would kill the amendment. They therefore supported its submission to the states with the Harding clause attached. The clause was agreed to by Wayne B. Wheeler, general counsel of the Anti-Saloon League, in a personal interview with Harding. Wheeler had plans that would make the seven-year clause harmless.[1]

Let there be no mistaking the fact that Senator Harding was both opposed to national prohibition and in favor of it, depending on whom he was dealing with. In a letter to Scobey, written in the midst of his politicking on the Eighteenth Amendment, he wrote, "I was a participant in writing into the resolution an amendment limiting the pendency of the amendment to six years. My notion is that, if prohibition cannot be made a part of the Federal organic law within that time, it ought to be left to the states to be handled. It belongs there anyhow. But I yielded to the rising tide sufficiently to give my vote in favor of submission." Thus did he sacrifice his own moral judgment about prohibition. "It is well," he told Scobey, "to be on what is manifestly a preferable side ethically and economically, whatever one thinks about the moral question involved." [2]

Quite differently did Harding write to H. B. McConnell, dry editor of the *Cadiz Republican*. In a letter of January 24, 1917 Harding explained his wet voting record as part of his policy of being governed by state referenda on the question: "I am a public servant with a public pledge to be carried out." He recognized that this would alienate the drys, but he added, "In the long run I shall command the respect and esteem of all men who believe in faithfully keeping a campaign pledge." However, he hoped that the drys would win out: "If the people of Ohio should change their attitude in voting on the prohibition question in 1917, I would feel free, under my pledge, to vote in accordance with their later expression of preference and would much more gladly then vote the sentiment of a majority in favor of prohibition than to follow the course which I feel honor bound to pursue at this time." [3]

Having made his arrangements with Wheeler, Harding proceeded on August 1, 1917, to explain to his constituents, via an address in the

Senate, how his plan should please everybody. He declared that he was no prohibitionist, but rather a "temperance man." He viewed the liquor problem not as a moralist but from the "ethical and economic side." Since America was claiming to fight a war for democracy's sake, he believed that the constitutional amendment process enabled this issue to be considered in a democratic manner because every state would have a chance to act on it after consulting with the electorate. He regretted that such a controversial problem should be placed before the people in the midst of the war because it would accentuate their disunity over a matter of personal liberty. However, since the people were so evenly divided, and the drys were so "insistent and intruding," the country was compelled to "reach a decision now," and get the thing out of politics for good. He hoped that each state would limit its ratifying effort to one election, but he was aware that the indomitable Wheeler had maneuvered him into the possibility of two or more such efforts. In later years Harding made himself look very good as he described for the benefit of critics his senatorial wire-pulling on the prohibition question. On May 21, 1919 he wrote to John M. Wehrley of West Manchester, Ohio, "I have been a constant supporter of federal prohibition, indeed I made that measure possible in cooperating with three other members of the Senate who held the balance of power. The four of us decided to submit the federal amendment as the solution of the prohibition question." The Senator did not elaborate further.[4]

Harding wanted to be sure that the wets appreciated his understanding of their point of view. He frankly said that he thought prohibition would not work because the people did not really believe in it. "You cannot make any law stronger," he said, "than the public sentiment which seeks its enforcement. . . . I freely express my doubts about its practicability." However, if the amendment should be ratified, he was in favor of compensating the brewers and distillers for their losses. He was willing, he said, to "join a movement to make it effective through a process of compensation to the business destroyed." The Eighteenth Amendment was passed by Congress and submitted to the states on December 18, 1917.[5]

Privately, Harding came to believe that the prohibition amendment would be adopted. On December 26, 1917 he wrote to his friend, O. S. Rapp, in Marion, "I can believe you are quite right about the country going dry." He added that Rapp had been "amply warned in advance," and should "prepare for the long trail across the desert."[6]

3

Any political advantage to Harding resulting from his prohibition amendment compromises was largely nullified by an ugly division that prohibition caused in the Ohio Republican party. The amendment intensified a bitterness between Ohio wets and drys as the Cincinnati brewery and distillery interests organized to get Ohio to reject prohibition, and the Anti-Saloon League organized to get Ohio to accept it. The break was accentuated by a revival of the Progressive movement, as Walter F. Brown turned his influence to the support of the wets through a political alliance with the powerful Hynicka, boss of the Hamilton county Republicans and Ohio member of the Republican national committee. Leading the dry Republicans was Harry M. Daugherty, who had blocked Brown back in 1912 in the name of party loyalty, and proposed to do so again in 1918. Daugherty correctly assumed that the war had brought a majority of Ohioans to the support of the dry cause. State prohibition was endorsed in the 1918 referendum by a majority of over 25,000 votes.[7] It was Harding's job and intention to gain the support of all these Republican factions, but by the end of the year he had not secured such support, especially not that of Daugherty. If the factionalism persisted into 1919 and 1920, his senatorial tenure would be imperiled.

What Harding needed was a strong political machine—of the kind Mark Hanna had—that could speak in the name of party unity and, incidentally, of Harding himself. After all, he would eventually have to seek reelection to the Senate.

But the Ohio Senator brought himself to this work of politicking and machine-making in his own behalf with great reluctance. He was in danger of committing the error that Senator Foraker had made back in the early 1900s, when "Fire Alarm Joe" had lost his local contacts amidst the comforts of senatorial tenure, thus forfeiting his Ohio political control to Mark Hanna and Roosevelt. Harding was fully and specifically warned about this by his friend Scobey. In urging Harding to maintain an Ohio machine, Scobey reminded him, "I will go back to a little ancient history, and recall to your mind that as long as Senator J. B. Foraker had control of the machinery in Ohio he was there—the minute he let loose of the machinery, he began to slip. You will recall that Senator Mark A. Hanna, after he got hold of the machine, he ran it, and I might say ran it might well—I was on the other side, and I know. But the only thing that made Hanna the great power was his control of the political machinery." [8] Harding had good reason to remember the truth of Scobey's warning (see chapter 8).

Harding explained his reluctance about politicking to Scobey. In the first place, he said, the war was destroying all popular interest in politics. "There is precious little interest in partisan politics," he wrote Scobey in March, 1917, "and we are having a very difficult time to get up enough steam to reorganize the party in Ohio." In the second place, he was a busy man and could ill afford to neglect his senatorial responsibilities. "They are deliberately making me the party boss out in Ohio," he observed, "and while I appreciate the compliment which such an expression of confidence conveys, I realize that it adds great responsibility to those that I must bear and I feel the burden of being told that I must make good." In summary, he said, "the Ohio reorganization is altogether premature." [9]

Harding knew that the greatest difficulty in creating a political machine was caused by the direct primary system. "I recognize full well," he told Scobey, "the advantage of having control of a political organization, and I am really sorry that I can cultivate no fondness for such control. . . . Your ideas are all right but you are living in an age that has long since passed. You are thinking of the time when we held conventions and bosses were able to issue orders and have them faithfully carried out. The primary system will not yield to that sort of control." [10]

4

And so the harried Senator applied himself to constructing such a piece of political machinery as the circumstances would permit. His chief unifying device was the so-called Ohio Republican central advisory committee. It was a faction-soothing, patchwork organization. It was adopted and authorized by the Ohio Republican central committee on December 28, 1916 from a system developed in Indiana by Will H. Hays, who had been able to engineer a GOP-Progressive reconciliation that had brought a Republican victory to the Hoosier state in the presidential election of 1916. The main function of the state advisory committee and its county and congressional district counterparts was to create an opportunity all over the state for Progressives to "come back home," even to hold office if they behaved themselves. Harding was the state chairman of the committee and its temper was like his. As the *Ohio State Journal* said, its main concept was of "a gentle government that harries not the nerves." It reflected the kind of a man that Harding was: "a person of steady thinking," who "never rants or becomes hateful to anyone," who "has an equilibrium of ideas that keeps him in a tranquil mind. . . . A leader upon whom faction can fasten no clampers." [11] To use Harding's words, the committee would "ignore all grievances, factional warfare and personal ambitions. . . . The best way and the only way to get together and stay together." [12] This was simply a way of saying to local politicians that the future of the party was not to be embarrassed by independent Progressivism, and its lack of patronage power. Local politics was being returned to local control. The placid conditions so dear to the ambitions of court-house-minded politicians were being restored. Such men could rejoice that the days of Progressive heroics were over.

The top personnel of the committee were the calm, level-headed fellows who would not quarrel. For the Regulars this meant Harding, former Senator Charles F. Dick, former Governor Myron T. Herrick, Hynicka, Cincinnati businessman William Cooper Procter, and Cleveland's Republican boss, Maurice Maschke. Daugherty was omitted, probably by his own request. For the Progressives, it meant strong and wise men like Walter F. Brown, Myers Y. Cooper, A. L. Garford, and James R. Garfield. It also meant—at least the *State Journal* thought so —that the Regulars were in control and that the reorganization was along the old, tried-and-true lines. It meant emphasis on loyalty to country in time of war. It even meant leaving the tariff alone for a while because of war prosperity. There was no place for "live issues" during the period of the rejuvenation of the Grand Old Party.[13]

It was a time for glad-handing, and the chief glad-hander in charge of the advisory committee's Columbus office was the amiable Rudolph W. Archer of Cleveland, former state treasurer, who had lost his job in the 1916 election. Archer was a sort of junior Harding, whose chief ambition was to be state treasurer again when the Republicans came back to power. Harding had proposed him for the position of field manager for the state advisory committee, and nobody objected to the choice. Together they evolved a plan of Regular-Progressive reconciliation, county by county, and district by district, through the creation of local advisory committees. Together they issued a public statement, describing their method as promoting the "elbow-to-elbow" touch among the Republicans. By July, 1917 everything was established, with Archer in his new office in Columbus and with Charles E. Hard, a Portsmouth newspaperman, as his secretary. Hard's chief function was editing a new weekly called the *Ohio Republican,* designed to send out "canned editorials" or "thought gems" to Republican editors throughout the state. As the *Ohio State Journal* advised, August 5, 1917, "Get on the mailing list now if you want to hear inside political news." [14]

If we are to believe the Republican press, this "elbow-to-elbow" and "canned editorial" campaign of the Ohio state advisory committee was remarkably successful. From May, 1917 to May, 1918 Archer created advisory committees in all of the Ohio congressional districts and in seventy-four counties. [15] There are no records of the committee's procedures, but the sweetness and light of Archer's methods were described facetiously in the *Ohio State Journal* of August 26, 1917:

> Rudy W. Archer . . . has been calling in the leaders of the party organizations in the various counties, especially the counties noted for their persistent and serious Republican factional rows and sending them back armed with the olive branch and loaded to the guards with brotherly love and affection. Perhaps you have wondered at the string of notable Republicans coming to town with no apparent object. This explains it. They drop in at the Neil House lobby and then by a round-about way make their appearance at the state headquarters in the Savings and Trust Building. Then comes the long talk with Pacificator Archer, who impresses upon his callers the importance of taking advantage of this season of political dullness incident to the war, an unusually opportune time for burying past feelings in the party and getting ready to present such a united front in the Democrats when the war is over.

5

The Harding state advisory committee did neither Harding nor the Ohio Republican party much good. Contention was in the air, and the ministrations of Rudy Archer could not stop it. The new war between the wets and the drys over prohibition, and the revived Progressive movement, with its Hynicka-Brown plans for the control of the party, disturbed committee harmony. Harding ended the year 1918 as powerless as he had been at its opening to control this menace to his Senatorship and to the unity of the Ohio Republican party.

The reasons for the swiftly rising effectiveness of the prohibition movement are not hard to find. The emotionalism of war led many to see prohibition as a way of saving the nation's grain supply. To others it was more elevating than petty politics. Certainly the war diverted much public interest from things political. As the fighting in France approached its hoped-for victory, Americans fixed their thoughts on their encamped and embattled sons, brothers, friends, and sweethearts. To match the sacrifices of the "doughboys," the folks at home gave their hearts and money to war-bond drives, Red Cross campaigns, Y.M.C.A. meetings, war-garden work, and many other causes. As the *Cincinnati Enquirer* said on August 11, 1918, the appeals of politics seemed "flat, stale and unprofitable to them amid the tingling episodes of which they are a part." Commentator James W. Faulkner said in September that political news was practically eliminated in favor of "descriptions of how the fellows over there had fought their way across the Vesle River and were advancing to the heights at Juvingay and Cousy-le-Chateau." Moreover, during the weeks immediately before election day the severe influenza epidemic led to the quarantine of public meetings.[16]

But one important set of campaigners was active. That was the group of Anti-Saloon Leaguers who took advantage of the general apathy to promote their prohibition drive.[17]

The political instincts of Warren Harding and his advisor, Harry Daugherty, were sorely tried by this trend toward prohibition in the Buckeye state. Rumblings of the Brown-Hynicka, Progressive-wet alliance raised the old fears of the split that had broken Ohio Republican unity in days gone by and had made the Democrats the dominant party in Ohio ever since 1908. Such a condition in 1918–20 could make Senator Harding a Republican one-termer, and could make Daugherty a has-been.

Throughout 1918 these two men, Harding and Daugherty, watched the approach of Republican disunity with an increasing dismay that, by the end of the year, approached desperation. Basic to their alarm was the fact that it was more and more apparent that the nation was going dry, that a great mass of rural Democrats supported the drys, and that the Republican party would have to endorse prohibition. City saloon interests seemed to encourage bossism and crime, to be careless about "proper" liquor control, and to be unwilling to assume their "share" of taxpaying. This disturbed the commonsense Daugherty, who said he would "rather trust the Republican party if a little bit soused than the Democratic party stone dry." Nevertheless he was impressed with the numbers, respectability, and loyalty of the dry

Republicans who met in Columbus on January 17, 1918, endorsed the Eighteenth Amendment, and complimented Harding for his part in getting it through Congress. "They seemed to be all thorough-going Republicans," Daugherty wrote Harding, "and I am satisfied a day's work was done that will be of great benefit and very lasting. It was a very respectable set of men." He predicted that the voters of Ohio would "go more than 50,000 in favor of Prohibition this Fall, and it will go more than that against us if the Republicans undertake to antagonize those who are in favor of Prohibition." [18] (The actual count in the November, 1918 prohibition balloting was a 25,759 majority for state prohibition). This, of course, frightened Harding as he saw his advisory committee completely bypassed and its "blessings" counteracted. "I am unable," he confessed to his friend, H. H. Timken, "to see myself how the prohibition fight is to be avoided." [19]

On January 17, 1918 Harding acknowledged the impotence of the advisory Committee when he agreed that a meeting of that organization scheduled for January 22 was dangerous. It was best, advised Daugherty, to avoid outbreaks.[20] Daugherty reminded Harding of the famous "forget together" meeting of Regulars and Progressives in 1914. "The circumstances, at present, are entirely different," he said. Considering the pent-up frustrations of the about-to-be dispossessed brewers and distillers of Hynicka's following, it was best to try to forget without getting together. "I am satisfied," he admitted, "that we could not hold such a meeting without the Wet and Dry propositions being brought up. It would be impossible to control it." Daugherty believed that such a control could be best exercised by "a high class banquet" where Harding and two or three others would "make just the right kind of speeches and shut out things that might be considered especially partisan, and depend upon good patriotic speeches helping the party." [21] Harding, of course, agreed because that was the sort of thing he was good at—oratory, patchwork, mirage-making.

As good as a "high-class banquet"—but not to the liking of the dignified Daugherty—was the party circus put on by Harding's advisory committee on June 15, 1918. Discussion was prevented by a spread-eagle speech from Indiana Senator James E. Watson, and by the county-fair atmosphere. The latter consisted of "prize fighting, pig shows, fake bicycle racing, and a lot of other cheap things, with some gambling devices, and charge of fifty cents admission."

And so the two, Harding and Daugherty, agonized politically throughout the spring and part of the summer of 1918. Daugherty brought up the subject of getting Hynicka off the Republican national committee as Ohio's representative, but Harding advised against it because it "could start a rumpus which would have a tendency to seriously rend party unity in Ohio." Besides, the "eastern fellows" were highly pleased with Hynicka's judicious and constructive participation in the national committee meetings. Reluctantly, Daugherty agreed. He admitted that "this is a very hard nut to crack." He compiled figures to show that in the 1917 prohibition referendum the wet majority in Hamilton county was 56,981 and that the dry majority in the rest of the state was 55,744. Harding agreed that this was disturbing, but, characteristically, expressed his sympathy for the "embarrassment of a man who speaks for the organization in Hamilton County." Conferences were held with Hynicka by both Harding and Daugherty. By the end of May, 1918, Harding found Hynicka "very greatly discouraged," but hoped that he and Daugherty would remain "on the most agreeable terms and voting for party success together." [22]

Daugherty, however, gradually became convinced that to conciliate with Hynicka would split the party. Hynicka, in alliance with Brown, represented a minority of the Republican party in the state, and they were trying to blackjack the party into a wet endorsement. "Seventenths of the Republicans of Ohio," Daugherty told Harding May 31, 1918, "now expect the party to declare in favor of Prohibition." Hynicka was more interested in defeating prohibition than in promoting Republican unity. He had allied with Brown of Toledo and the wets in Cuyahoga county to achieve a result not desired by the Republican majority. Therefore, Daugherty said, it was necessary for the majority to stop the plotters. "If it comes to a question of winning in the state and losing in Cuyahoga and Lucas counties, I am for carrying the state." Harding agreed, but he still hoped for peace. "I do not find myself in disagreement with your sentiments," he replied. "It is infinitely more important to win Ohio than any one or group of counties, great or small." The thing to do was to frame a party platform containing a temperance clause and other clauses covering many issues so that "the party does not make a measurement by the temperance yard stick the sole and only qualification for the standing in the party." [23]

Equally dangerous to Ohio Republican integrity, in Daugherty's estimation, was his old nemesis, the Progressives. Brown and his 1912 aide, Robert F. Wolfe of the *Ohio State Journal* and the *Columbus Dispatch*, scenting Republican embarrassment, were on the prowl again. Their object, Daugherty declared on June 3, was "to nominate Roosevelt in 1919," and name a Roosevelt delegation from Ohio to the 1920 Republican national convention. "When that is done," Daugherty pointedly went on, "they expect to elect United States Senators and Governors, and wipe the real Republicans off the face of the earth." Wolfe had formerly supported Democrats after Progressives had weakened the Regulars, and was up to his "old tricks." Daugherty saw only another Democratic victory ahead as a result of this "unscrupulous" plot. "As far as I am concerned," he concluded, "it is no killing matter with me, for I have discovered that I can live and get along under Democratic administrations if other people can, but I am not much inclined to join in and support an organization which is undertaking to supplant administrations which these men themselves are responsible for. Our friends are very angry over the situation; I mean our real friends who are real Republicans." [24]

Things did not turn out quite as badly at the August state Republican convention as the calamity-howling Daugherty predicted. The delegates put on a good, old-fashioned display of party-unifying ballyhoo. The wet-dry showdown finally took place without a bolt, and Harding claimed credit for it. As he told his friend Scobey, "I exercised my best endeavor and prevented the Hamilton County crowd from bolting the convention." What Harding did was to harangue the delegates with a patriotic oration which denounced "creeping Socialism," belittled the blundering Democrats, praised the loyal Republicans, and glorified mighty America with its "new birth of the national soul." Something of the electrifying effect of Harding's eloquence was caught by his friend Colonel George B. Christian, who came down to Columbus from Marion to observe his former neighbor's performance. On the flag-bedecked platform were National Republican Committeeman Will H. Hays and Republican nominee for Governor of Ohio, Frank B. Willis. "I wish I could picture to you," Christian later wrote Harding, "the appearance of the bunch on the stage behind you during one of the climaxes of your talk. Hays and Willis, like all the rest of us, were standing on their tiptoes with their arms raised upward, heads thrown back, yelling like school-boys at a baseball match. No finer compliment and none more deserving was ever paid to an American orator." [25]

Daugherty's influence was also apparent in this August 27 politics-fest. His part was to present a platform containing practically every Progressive plank under the sun—including not only an endorsement of the prohibition amendment, but old age pensions, the eight-hour day for women factory workers, labor representation on school boards, increased state aid to schools, relief of financially burdened cities, woman suffrage, a league of nations, and "all the radical things that you seem to favor," to use Harding's phrase in his September 20 letter to Scobey. The intent was deliberate: to give Brown and Hynicka no right to claim the party as being delivered over to the Anti-Saloon League. "I am not in favor," Daugherty had told Harding, "of making the Prohibition proposition the sole plank or the predominating plank in the platform. Every important question should be touched upon and a short positive stand taken on each. No party can run on one issue any more than an automobile can run on one wheel." [26]

The last leg of the 1918 campaign in Ohio was a weird one—and it did little to improve Harding's political standing. The Republicans won everything but the governorship. Willis lost because he was severely cut in Hamilton county for his blunt support of the drys and for questioning the patriotism of the Queen City Germans. The legislature went Republican and dry. Seemingly the Cincinnati-Hynicka-Brown bolt had been prevented except for the cutting of Willis. The state voted in favor of prohibition by about 25,000 votes. The curtailment of public meetings and the front-page hysteria of the newspapers during the closing weeks of the war had severely dampened the public's interest in politics. [27]

Harding professed to be satisfied with the election, but his standing in the party was by no means improved. The wet-dry issue, he said, was now out of politics because of the adoption of statewide prohibition. The Cincinnatians had not bolted, but had merely retaliated against Willis for his dryness and for the mean things said about their patriotism. Harding never had liked Willis because of the latter's bombastic oratorical manner, and because he made so many patronage promises to become Governor that he would be unable to deliver on most of them.

Nevertheless, Harding was his usual forgiving self and proposed that, since the election was over, everybody could let bygones be bygones. Whereupon there ensued a Harding-Daugherty feud that brought both of them to the brink of enmity and possible political oblivion. Daugherty had called the Cincinnati 1918 election vote against Willis a "bolter's crime," and predicted that "henceforth the fight in Ohio will be against Hamilton county, and on that issue the Republicans will never lose." Harding disagreed. He condoned Hamilton county's vote by citing Willis' provocation. "I do not agree with you," wrote Harding, "that we are always to have a fight in Ohio against Hamilton County." The liquor question has been "more or less eliminated," and he thought "the broadest viewpoint requires us to contemplate every cooperation with Hamilton County which is possible without permitting that county or any other to dominate the politics of the party in Ohio." He proposed to return to Ohio soon and renew the advisory committee because the term of office of its members expired.[28]

Harding's plan to call a December meeting and renew the soothing ministrations of the advisory committee brought a roar of protest from Daugherty, who informed Harding that it would be political suicide. Without specifying details, Daugherty insisted that the Hamilton county wets and the Walter Brown Progressives, whose representatives the conciliatory Harding had put on the advisory committee, planned condemnatory proceedings against Willis for his inept leadership—presumably a reference to his criticizing the war loyalty of Cincinnati Germans. If the meeting were held, Daugherty said, a ruckus would ensue with the exultant drys accusing the unholy alliance of Hynicka and Brown of party disloyalty. In the melee Harding would be unable to obtain harmony. His leadership abilities would be seriously compromised. Stronger men would come to the fore—presumably Brown and Hynicka—and that would be the end of Harding's assurance of reelection to the Senate. It would also be the end, Daugherty hinted, of the plan of the Ohio organization to promote an Ohioan—namely Harding—for the Presidency. Brown was a Roosevelt man (so was Daugherty, but with a preference for a healthy Harding as Vice-President to an ailing T. R.), and Hynicka did not care who ran for President in 1920 so long as he could control Hamilton county and fight to the bitter end to preserve the interest of the Cincinnati wets. Even if Harding did run for President, Hynicka was more willing to use him for bargaining purposes than to try to get him elected. In short, the Daugherty-Harding Ohio political dominance would be shattered.[29]

The distracted Harding gave in and "postponed" the meeting, ascribing the delay to his wife's illness. Nevertheless, he was personally furious with Daugherty. In a letter to his friend Charles E. Hard he claimed that Daugherty "in a veiled way . . . intimated that I was inviting an opposition candidate for my place in the Senate." "I must refuse," he said, "to be intimidated by any such a threat." Harding was also disgusted with Daugherty's intransigeance toward Hamilton county. "I will make no arrangements of any kind in the future with Daugherty," he told Hard, "All this has destroyed my confidence." [30]

Harding did not confine his expression of anger to Hard. He wrote directly to Daugherty. He accused Daugherty of being two-faced in promising to agree to a meeting to revive the advisory committee and then telling Chairman Hays of the national committee that such a meeting would not take place. He bitterly accused Daugherty of putting his personal vendetta with Hynicka above party success. Hynicka and the Cincinnati Republicans had been responsible in the 1916 primaries for Daugherty's loss of the senatorial nomination to Myron T. Herrick. "This disappointment," Harding wrote, "has left you bitter toward the Hamilton County organization. It is not for me to insist that you put your resentment aside, that is wholly a matter for your determination. I only know that we can't have a winning party in Ohio organized in a spirit of reprisal or impelled by the bitterness of disappointment." Harding also rebuked Daugherty for calling him the gullible tool of the so-called Cincinnati black-birds. "The trouble with you, my dear Daugherty," admonished Harding, "is that you appraise my political sense so far below par that you have no confidence in me or my judgement. Pray do not think because I can and do listen in politeness to much that is said to me, that I am always being 'strung.' " [31]

Although Hamilton county was the bane of many Ohio Republican's existence, and made things difficult for Harding down to the very hour of his presidential nomination, the adjustable Ohio senatorial compromiser always assumed the Hynicka machine to be a full partner in the fellowship of Ohio Republican unity. It was wet, but it was also Republican. In a letter to Scobey, December 4, 1918, he described the Hamilton county situation as central to the "tangle over the control of the organization." The problem hinged over the cutting of Willis by the Cincinnatians because he was a dry. "I can sympathize," he told Scobey, "with the feeling up state over Hamilton County's action and I am genuinely sorry that Hamilton County can never be counted upon to support a candidate with sympathy for the Prohibition Amendment. At the same time, on other lines the Hamilton County forces are abiding Republicans and we have got to have them cooperating and coordinating with the party to win real victories in the state." [32]

On the presidential front, Harding was ready to adjust himself to a return of the redoubtable T. R., whose patriotic posturing and blazing war fulminations were winning back much of his popularity. Harding had been adjusting to Roosevelt for a long time, including the campaign of 1916 and the "Roosevelt division" episode in 1917—and so had many others. When the Colonel visited Columbus in the fall of 1918 as a Liberty Bond rallyer, Harding's friend, Mrs. Mary E. Lee of Westerville, reported people in the crowds saying, "It's Harding or Teddy," "It looks like Teddy," "It looks like Harding." [33] In 1937 Daugherty wrote Ray Baker Harris that he had squired "Teddy" through the Liberty Loan performance and discussed with him a Roosevelt-Harding ticket for 1920. Daugherty also noted the Colonel's feebleness, saying that he himself put the completely exhausted T. R. to bed in his hotel room.[34] Harding himself, in November and December, 1918, noted the growing strength of the Roosevelt movement with emphasis on its support financially and by non-Progressives. He told Scobey on November 18, "The Roosevelt candidacy looms greater than any other. I think he has a well-organized and well-financed campaign under way. I note that some of the old stand-pat crowd who never enlist for campaigns without abundant appropriations have been made very busy in promoting his candidacy." On December 4 he added, "The Roosevelt candidacy is being thoroughly organized, is heavily financed, and promises to grow to a very formidable strength." [35] It is important to note that a few weeks before Roosevelt died, Dan R. Hanna, the Cleveland Progressive, had strongly urged on Harding the T. R. candidacy, and that Harding had written Herrick that he (Harding) had assured him (Hanna) that there was "no insurmountable obstacle to my supporting Col. Roosevelt." [36] As Harding told H. A. MacDonald of Salem, Massachusetts in 1920, "The Colonel and I had a perfect understanding and I quite agree that we all would have been for him had he lived." [37]

Obviously, as the year of 1918 ended, Harding's political future in Ohio was unsure. The Ohio Republican party was its old factional self with new contenders for leadership. Harding's advisory committee was in disrepute. Drys, wets, Progressives, Regulars, Hamilton countyites, up-staters, prima donnas like Hynicka, Brown, Daugherty—and Harding himself—constituted a political melange that seemed to be beyond the power of the Marion master of political patchwork and adjustability. If Harding was to survive, even in the matter of retaining his senatorship, he needed the help of developments beyond his control. He got it.

6

In the pre-dawn hours of January 6, 1919 Theodore Roosevelt died in his home at Oyster Bay. Before the day was over, Harding was being talked of throughout the nation as front-runner for the Republican presidential nomination in 1920. In a *New York Tribune* Washington dispatch dated January 6, Carter Field wrote that, in the hushed office conversations concerning the Republican choice for 1920, two names were mentioned most frequently: Senator Warren G. Harding and Major General Leonard Wood. Field cited the Harding-T. R. rapprochement since 1912 and declared that "without any such opposition as the spectacular leadership of Roosevelt might afford," Harding could "easily be nominated." [38] The *New York Times* headlined, "Talk Most of Harding." It said, "Everywhere that his name was mentioned at the Capitol, Senators appeared to be satisfied with the idea of his being put forth as the 1920 candidate. Among radicals and regulars the same feeling was expressed. Harding in one day appeared to have jumped into a prominent place in the consideration of possibilities." [39]

Harding's national reputation for adjustability was paying off. He pleased all sectors of the Republican party: Regulars and Progressives, wets and drys, Ohio and the nation. So said the *Times* as it described how the Ohio Senator "has steered a strictly party career during his first term in the Senate, but he has advanced with the trend of political events which have put progressive theories more to the fore than ever before." The *Times* cited his recent support of the prohibition and woman suffrage amendments to the Constitution. As for the Regulars, they recalled "the way in which Mr. Harding presided over the 1916 Convention; they say he was impartial. They speak of him as possessing statesmanlike qualities." It was also emphasized that the Senator "comes from the state known as the maker of Presidents. The Republican Party more than once had been obliged in a crisis to turn to Ohio." The New York *World* wrote similarly, "He is straight on all leading public issues." He supported "Nationwide Prohibition and Woman Suffrage." [40]

Roosevelt's death on January 6, 1919 solved at one stroke Harding's drive for leadership in Ohio politics. He himself was the first to see this. Before the day was over Harding wrote to Hard, "I think very likely the death of Col. Roosevelt will somewhat change the plans of some Republicans in Ohio, especially in their attitudes toward state organization. I may be very overconfident about the situation, but I think we are going to be able to organize without any serious friction." [41] More specifically and triumphantly he wrote to Scobey, "Of course, the death of Colonel Roosevelt has greatly simplified matters, because it has taken away the inspiration of a number of active forces to try to control the organization." He said that he was especially gratified at a "very agreeable letter from Walter Brown today, expressing his desire to cooperate with me for the good of the party." If Roosevelt had survived, Harding said, Brown "would not have been very anxious to cooperate unless I had worked to his plans. . . . I have never felt perfectly free to give him very full confidence." Harding concluded with the emphatic assurance, "If any trouble arises, I am going to use the steam roller because I feel confident that I have the strength to do it." [42]

Harding was quick to act and left no doubt that he was boss and that the advisory committee, with its conciliatory policy, was to run the Ohio Republican party. At a Columbus meeting on January 15, 1919 of the Republican state central committee, (Newton H. Fairbanks, chairman) and its subordinate agency, the state executive committee (E. M. Fullington, chairman) he was completely victorious. He did, in fact, steamroller his state advisory committee into revived existence with everybody meekly in acquiescence. He picked his own man, George H. Clark, as chairman of the revived committee in place of the retired chairman, R. K. Archer, who had been elected state treasurer in the November, 1918 election. The advisory committee was to be a fully staffed permanent organization with headquarters in Columbus and with authority to do all that would make for the unification of the party and prepare for a Republican victory in 1920. For the first time in its history the Ohio Republican party had a full-time, permanent staff—and Harding was its creator. [43]

The press gave full play to Harding's victory with sly references to his being a candidate for President in 1920. The *Ohio State Journal* headlined, "Republicans United to Back Harding," adding that the Senator "waved aside inquiries about the Presidency as being too early." The Cincinnati papers emphasized the action as a deal between Harding and former Governor Willis. "Willis Bends the Knee to Harding as Leader," headlined the *Enquirer*, and added, "Fourth Nomination for Governorship Offered as Reward to Willis." The *Times-Star* put Willis a bit higher. "Party Unity among Ohio Republicans," said the headlines with the usual references to Harding for President plus the suggestion that the movement originated with Willis so as to create a vacancy for Willis in the Senate. Everywhere it was "Hurrah for Harding." Said the *Cleveland Plain Dealer*, "Willis to Back Harding to Limit. Harding Can Have Support of Ohio Delegation for President If He Wants It." The *Toledo Blade* built up the Harding boom, announcing "Harding Sounds Harmony Keynote." [44]

Equally important in the Harding triumph was the fact that Daugherty had been captured and tamed, and that Harding's idea of uniting all factions had prevailed. Enemies were to be forgiven and gladhanding resumed. Daugherty's desire to fight was completely squelched. He was at last given a berth on the advisory committee along with Walter Brown and his "black bird" friends from Cincinnati. Willis was named, and Fairbanks and Maurice Maschke and many another "good old soul," such as the industrialist John N. Willys of Toledo.[45] On January 24, 1919 the *Cleveland News* announced that Daugherty, who had been said to have "left the ranks of Senator Harding," had changed his mind and would hereafter boost the Senator for the Presidency. By November, 1919 Harding felt that Daugherty had been trimmed down to size. He confided this feeling in a letter to Hard in which he said, "Daugherty has been a typical scrapper for what he thinks to be the right course. I have always felt I could depend on Daugherty, though he did give me a little annoyance during the trying period we passed through last winter." Harding said that he had had many letters from Daugherty and "other members of the group who originally opposed the Advisory Committee and everything seems to be lovely with them." [46]

Something of the effect of Roosevelt's death on Harding's future may be observed by inspecting the Harding-Clark relationship before and after that event. When Harding broached the matter on December 9, 1918, he indicated that he wanted to see Clark, but hesitated to take a drastic step until he could "feel confident of pretty wide support." Clark's reply was quite frank. He told the Senator that life in Washington had made him soft and had caused him to lose control of the Republican party in Ohio. "The time was," wrote Clark, December 16, 1918, "when the situation lay within your very hand to control. Through consideration of others, fear of petty wire-pullers, or disinclination for the strenuous work involved, you hesitated and held back. Opportunity ordinarily knocks but once at the door and is gone. . . . You have in some measure surrendered the prerogatives, privileges, and rewards of that responsibility [of party leadership]. Self styled leaders, discredited and out of favor and faced with the great mass of our party, are permitted to be its candidates and its spokesmen." Clark said he knew the "easy way of Washington official life." He knew "quite well how pleasant all that is, I know equally well how destructive of initiative, energy, and constructive tendency it is." "But there was political house-cleaning to do in the Ohio Republican party. Inside that house is much that is now rubbish and must be thrown out. . . . Outside is much that is rubbish that wants to come in, but the saving feature is that outside that house there is so much of merit that, given opportunity, will come in, that it will make for the saving of the house itself." Clark admitted that it was not pleasant work, that "the natural instinct is to delay—perhaps another day the sun will shine." It was "a man-sized job," and "you, Warren, are coming to the forks of the road. It is for you to pick and choose; one way lies happiness, usefulness, high resolve, and the esteem of a grateful people, the other road follows a straight path back to Ohio, return to civil life and embittered age." And so Clark asked, "After all, my dear Warren, do you really want to see me?" [47]

Harding's reply to Clark on December 20, 1918 was equally frank. It showed that he admitted Clark's charges "of the failure on my part in Ohio," and was resolved to remedy them. "Your letter does not offend me in the least. I see the need of doing things, and mean to do them. Frankly, I have no taste in the line you describe, but I do not mean to be a slacker, and I am willing to pull my full share of the load, if I can have a lead horse like yourself to team with." Even more significant was the fact that he included Daugherty, without mentioning him by name, among those "busy-bodies" who needed to be "house-cleaned" out of party affairs. "There has been blown up a tempest in a teapot, particularly at Columbus, but I do not regard it as a tremendously serious matter. . . . A lot of busy-bodies have an opportunity to work off their surplus energy in 'stewing' when there is really little or nothing to fuss about. Of course I realize that the organization control is at stake; so do other people. This is the issue to be settled. I think it can be done without excessive difficulty." [48]

Harding and Clark had their meetings and talked things over. And as they talked, and thought, the whole situation changed, and made things easy for Harding. Roosevelt died. After that, everybody was for Harding—Clark, Daugherty, "rubbish," "busy-bodies," and all. The central committee met and accepted Harding's proposal for a revived advisory committee with Clark at the head. Clark changed from a Harding skeptic to a Harding enthusiast, setting up headquarters at Columbus and giving full time to his job. Harding's devoted friend Charles E. Hard became the committee secretary. There was no doubt as to who was head of the Ohio Republican party now. As Harding informed Clark on February 1, two days after the central committee action, "You will be interested to know that [E. M.] Fullington [chairman of the state executive committee] and Daugherty very cordially joined in urging you for the place." Harding admitted that central committee chairman Newton H. Fairbanks acquiesced with "rather poor grace" but would "give you cordial support." Fullington was told "in advance" that there was a place for him on the advisory committee's executive staff. Harding cinched everything by sending Clark a check for $1,000, which was the beginning of a successful fund-raising campaign for the sustaining of the morale of the staff, the retirement of the party's debts of $70,000, and the acquisition of a fighting fund for the 1920 campaign.[49]

As Harding moved into a more commanding position in the Ohio Republican party following Roosevelt's death, he showed considerable wisdom in regard to party financing. On the one hand, he deprecated the idea of over-subsidization by wealthy supporters: this led to waste and extravagance. "I am not in accord as to excessive expenditures," he wrote Clark on February 7, 1919. "When we have an abundance of financial resources there is a strong inclination to expend without fitting returns. I know that we wasted large sums in 1916 and we incurred the heavy indebtedness as a result thereof." He said that party treasurer William Cooper Procter, Cincinnati soap millionaire, would be expected to "assume a considerable share of the burden himself." [50]

On the other hand, there was no sense, said Harding, in the impecunious, hard-working members of the Republican organization being underpaid. As he told Clark, "You must not allow indebtedness to interfere with keeping a sufficient financial balance on hand to meet all current expenditures. It is my judgment that nothing so much destroys the spirit of an organization endeavor as to be overdrawn at the bank or indebted to salaried workers without resources to discharge the obligation." In July, when Harding learned that there was not enough money to pay Clark, he declared that "there was nothing more discouraging in all the world than to be undertaking a line of activity without sufficient financial means to carry on the work. It is no less than an outrage that you should be called upon to make expenditures out of your own purse and it is very unfair to you and to the other associates with you that you have not received the salaries supposed to be paid for your own time and neglect of affairs." [51]

Roosevelt's death solved another problem for Harding. This was the acquisition of the support of the leading Ohio Progressive newspaper editors Robert F. Wolfe of the *Ohio State Journal* and Dan R. Hanna of the *Cleveland Leader*. The *Ohio State Journal* had long ago ceased being the stalwart Republican sheet the party fathers had been used to in the late nineteenth and early twentieth centuries. In November and December, 1918 Harding promised certain Republicans to make the financing of a new Columbus Republican journal with statewide circulation a chief item on the agenda of the revived advisory committee. "We are lacking," he told W. A. Stover of Bellevue, "in the good old time Republican organs which were inclined to handle current questions with a good strong wallop."[52] Perhaps the prohibitive expense of such an enterprise, with the need for a press service to overcome the alleged Wolfe monopoly stopped further consideration. But with the magic of T. R. no longer in the headlines, the magic of Harding could manage to find its way into publicity—Wolfe or no Wolfe.

As for Hanna and the *Cleveland Leader*, this Progressive journalist was quick to make his peace with Harding after T. R.'s. death. This was fully arranged early in February, as seen by Harding's explicit instructions to Clark: "I also hope you make it a point to get in touch with Hanna. Hanna wants to be a factor in Ohio politics and is quite capable of giving you both newspaper and financial support, as well as having capacity to command a considerable personal following. He will probably have a good deal to say about the drift of things in Cuyahoga Co. You very much want him to be a cordial backer of your program. He told me he would subscribe to any program which I had decided to adopt in Ohio, but I think it important for you to win his confidence and cooperate and have him support your program rather than mine."[53]

This did not mean that Harding was through with Daugherty, or that the advisory committee became so powerful as to dominate Daugherty—far from it. It meant that Daugherty came to be Harding's most skillful adviser, but always with the understanding—*and the fact*—that Harding was the boss. Republican political power in Ohio in the hour of need came to reside in Harding and Daugherty, not Harding and Clark. Clark and the advisory committee soon slid into a secondary position as the Harding-Daugherty team took command. Daugherty wisely did as Harding required by cooperating with him in a way to bring about a "hopeful situation" in the state. He eventually reported to Harding on July 25, 1919 that he and Clark had "straightened things out in good shape . . . [and] I think we brought about what you have been wanting and I have been trying to help work out for some time. I believe you will see the benefit of it." Harding, of course, was mollified and expressed his gratification. "I felt confident," he replied, "that you would be very effective in bringing this about and I want you to know of my gratitude for the part you have played in creating a more favorable situation. I think if we can have the cooperation of the active forces of the Central Committee with Clark and his organization, and at the same time have sufficient financial resources to carry on a real program, that we can do some real things in Ohio." [54] Eventually as the Harding-Daugherty campaign for the Presidency went into high gear, the advisory committee was left far behind. In fact, it stumbled over its own heels, but did no damage to the major effort.

This blending of the efforts of the astute Daugherty and the glad-handing of Clark and the advisory committee was an excellent example of the adjustable Mr. Harding at his best. It made the unity of the Ohio Republican party a full reality. And its mastermind was Harding, not Daugherty.

7

It is of the highest importance to emphasize that Harding's rise to leadership of the Ohio Republican party following Roosevelt's death did not mean that he was seeking the Presidency of the United States. That was the intention of Daugherty and many of the Ohio Senator's adoring friends—such friends as Marionite O. S. Rapp, who wrote to George Christian, Harding's secretary, concerning Roosevelt's death, "My God! what an opportunity for him now"; or Reverend John Wesley Hill of New York, who told him he "ought to be kicked" if he did not go for the Presidency. Harding estimated that over five hundred well-wishers wrote him urging him to declare for the Presidency.[55] But throughout most of 1919 it was Harding's intention not to run for the Presidency. He said so most emphatically, and gave strong and cogent reasons in support of his feeling.

An amusing example of how Harding brushed off one of his more enthusiastic presidential backers involved the case of E. Mont Reily of Kansas City, Missouri. Reily was a political prognosticator who came out for Harding in the days immediately following Roosevelt's death. On January 20, 1919 Reily addressed a circular letter to Republicans all over the nation representing Harding as the national candidate to succeed Roosevelt. He went into detail about the other presidential possibilities, eliminating them one by one for appropriate reasons. He cited Harding's loyalty in 1912, his "senatorship" victory of 1914, his keynote speech and chairmanship of the national convention in 1916. He used the "Ohio, the Mother of Presidents" argument, listing all the other Ohio "jewels" who had graced the high office. With a side glance at the Hughes campaign of 1916, Reily said Harding was too levelheaded to make blunders like those of Hughes. He represented Harding as a believer in normal things and proposed that the motto of the 1920 campaign be "Harding and back to normal." He turned up in Washington in July, 1919, spreading his gospel among all and sundry.[56]

Harding was embarrassed by Reily's persistence, and regarded him as a "nut." He wrote to Scobey on July 31, 1919, "I have had a regular nut in Washington several days lately who is more foolish about the presidential candidacy for me than you are and he thinks it so easy it is like taking a stick of candy from a helpless child. However, I have not been very greatly tempted by the allurements he has presented. The only problem I have at this moment is to get him out of town so as not to have the subject drilled in my ears from day to day." To another friend, James B. Reynolds, Harding wrote, August 5, 1919, "What is a reasonably modest and reticent public servant going to do when friends like E. Mont Reily come to town and camp on your trail for a week at a time, seeking to get some command to go forth and gain delegates? I am beginning to wonder if I am deficient in some of the ordinary human attributes of the every day politician or very ordinary statesman." [57]

One reason that Harding gave for not wanting the Presidency was that it would be the end of his personal happiness. "I should be unhappy every hour from the time I entered the race until the thing was settled," he told Scobey, January 14, 1919, "and I am sure I should never have any more fun or any real enjoyment in life if I should be so politically fortunate as to win a nomination and election. I had much rather retain my place in the Senate and enjoy the association of friends and some of the joys of living." Seemingly Scobey had a remedy for this. He reminded Harding of a long-standing promise of appointment to the office of "Commissioner of Eugenics." "You must now think," wrote Scobey "that I have lost my cunning if I could not produce some kind of entertainment that would make you throw off the grind of office life." To this Harding replied, facetiously, that the promise of the "Commissionership of Eugenics" had been made so long ago that he doubted Scobey's ability to perform efficiently. "Remember," Harding wrote, "that you are essentially of the same age that I am, I am really growing strong in the conviction that you are swiftly passing the period when you have the capacity to render such efficient service as would be expected of you. I know you are all right in spirit but I doubt if you could carry out a public administration up to the highest expectations." In 1920, when rumors circulated that Scobey was to be Harding's "Colonel House," Scobey wrote to a friend denying it, but added "confidentially, . . . He is going to create a new office for me and that is Commissioner of Eugenics." [58] Inasmuch as there was no such government office as the Commissioner of Eugenics, it is not clear what it might have to do with Harding's "joys of living."

It is interesting to note that Harding was discovering that his speech-making popularity could be a boomerang. He loved to make speeches, but when they threatened to make him a presidential contender, he backed off. As he wrote to Scobey in March, 1919, "Everybody wants a speech. It is a bore. Besides, I am tired. And more, if you make speeches outside your own state you are suspected of being a candidate—and I am not. But I would like your company, and Evaland's [Mrs. Scobey] and I'd like Golf and Bobs and the yellow-legged chickens. . . . I'd like to run away to Texas and be free and let politics and people go to thunder for a couple or three weeks." In April, after a visit to Ohio, he wrote to Mrs. Scobey, "I never went to Ohio with such reluctance in my life." There were a hundred calls for speeches, and, in spite of his desire to take a "whack at Woodrow," he turned them all down, for a while, and then finally gave in. "I was like the woman," he wrote Mrs. Scobey, "who had resisted gold, and precious jewells [sic] and all that and was finally offered a winter's supply of coal and she told the tempter to put it in." [59]

Of course, the chief reason for Harding's not wanting to run for President was that he did not yet have an organization sufficiently strong to run for the national office. It was difficult enough to do as he was doing, to shape up his advisory committee system in order to control the state Republican party and prepare for his reelection to the Senate. As he told Scobey, "I would not think of involving my many good friends in the tremendous tasks of making a Presidential campaign. The sorrow of my political life in the Senate lies in the fact that one who has been honored by his state can never hope to return on one-thousand percent of the political obligations which he has incurred. With this feeling I should be very reluctant indeed to broaden the field of my political activities." [60]

This attitude explains the campaign that Harding *did* conduct in the winter and spring of 1919. It was a series of speeches in Cleveland (the Tippecanoe Club), Columbus, Dayton, Toledo, and Lancaster upon the occasions of McKinley's and Lincoln's birthdays and the memorialization of Theodore Roosevelt before a joint session of the Ohio legislature.[61] Victory Loan addresses in April were also in order.[62] They were full-dress, spread-eagle orations and resulted in much comment on his presidential possibilities. These addresses were studded with glorified Americanism, and were a part of his advisory committee build-up of Republican state unity and his reelection to the Senate rather than bids for the higher position. In fact, he strongly, though privately, resented the extension of the purpose of the campaign beyond his own intentions. When called upon for a statement, he simply said, as he wrote to A. G. Snow of Columbus in March 31, 1919, "I think far more of being a candidate to succeed myself in the Senate than to aspire for any higher position." [63]

Another trap that may have contributed to Harding's wariness about running for President was the fear of becoming the rich man's candidate. The temptation for this is alleged, by E. Mont Reily, to have been made by millionaire Procter in the summer or early fall of 1919. Reily, in his "The Years of Confusion," told of visiting Senator Harding's office in Washington just as Procter was leaving. According to Reily, Harding made the following astonishing remark, "That was Colonel William Cooper Proctor [*sic*], President of the Proctor and Gamble Company and he told me that if I became a candidate for President that he would contribute $600,000 to help bring about my nomination." Harding's reply to Procter's offer was equally amazing, if we are to believe Reily:

> I told Proctor that I was in no wise a candidate, and never expected to be, and I could never think of accepting such a sum from anyone, or permit a committee to do so in my behalf. That such a sum of money should not be connected with any candidate for the great office of President. That it would smell of "big business" in command, and that

any candidate for that office should enter the contest with clean hands, and carry that thought clear through until the people understood his unquestioned position. I also told him that if I accepted such a vast sum, or permitted a committee to do so for me, I felt that I would be compromised and entangled, and if elected should not be permitted to take the oath of President of the United States. Furthermore, any candidate who would accept such a contribution, in the end would either be defeated, or his administration would be wrecked.[64]

In Reily's version of Harding's account of the meeting, Procter then told Harding that he was transferring his loyalty and money to Wood. The Colonel was quoted as saying, "If you do not become a candidate, and accept this sum, I am going to see General Wood and his committee, and contribute this amount to them, as the Republican party must win this election."

How the energy expended in this Ohio senatorial build-up affected Harding in resisting the Presidency was related in a letter to Scobey on February 7. "The strain and incessant alertness," he confided, "incident to meeting several hundred people about exhausted my nervous strength. If I had to go through this sort of thing to be a candidate for the big job, I am sure I should want to surrender before I had begun. Really, my dear Scobey, the winning of such an undertaking is not worth the work and anxiety involved. I do not mean by this that I am utterly lazy and unwilling to shoulder my share of any burden, but I can not for the life of me see why anybody would deliberately shoulder this annoyance and worries and incessant trials incident to a campaign for a nomination and election to the presidency."[65]

Nevertheless, there were those sincere friends of Harding's who went about anyhow in their prideful way promoting Harding as presidential timber. For instance, there was his secretary, George Christian, who loved to get letters along this line and to encourage their writers in a pixie-like way. There was Clevelander Harvey Wood, who heard Harding's Tippecanoe Club speech and wrote to Christian on January 29, 1919, "Take it from me—Gov. is in the lead and I think we can nominate him without very much trouble. His speach [sic] was the best I have ever heard him make and was commented on by the 500 guests at the banquet." Wood reported that "Gov's standing" was excellent among the Illinois and Wisconsin grain dealers contacted in the course of business. He proposed to spread the gospel in Minnesota and the Dakotas, to which Christian replied, "You are in class A of the Nut Club. Keep me posted as you go along as to sentiment." [66]

8

What bothered Harding in this senatorial-presidential maneuvering, was that encouragement for the higher office from some of the professionals was designed to eliminate him from high office. This meant that, by pushing him for the Presidency, ambitious politicians would expect him to relinquish his candidacy for the Senatorship and thus stand a chance of losing both. Harding had no intention of being maneuvered into such a situation. The man under most suspicion in Harding's mind for these sinister intentions was Walter F. Brown, the old Roosevelt 1912 booster, and, more recently, the plotter with Hynicka to displace the Harding-Daugherty control of the Ohio Republican organization.

Harding's suspicions came to a head—though not publicly—at the February 12, 1919 Lincoln Day Republican celebration in Toledo, the home of Walter Brown. At the evening banquet of the day's ceremonies it developed that the toastmaster, and central committee chairman, Newton H. Fairbanks—no enthusiast for Harding—introduced the Senator with fulsome praise and inspirational predictions of Republican victory in 1920. Turning to Harding he said, "If the people are to make a change in administration, we are most desirous of having Ohio counted in permanently in that theatre." Fairbanks then pointed dramatically at the Senator as the assembled Republicans rose to their feet with a rousing cheer.[67] Harding, of course, could not show his displeasure at the banquet table. He proceeded to make his expected inspirational speech. But he was inwardly and profoundly disturbed by Fairbanks' presidential gesture. This could be the kiss of death. He knew the lukewarmness of Fairbanks and others about his leadership. He knew that there were several others who wanted his senatorial seat —Brown, Willis, Herrick, and Procter. He resolved to stop this kind of talk at the very outset, and Charles E. Hard, secretary of the advisory committee, was the first to be told so in no uncertain terms.

On the day following the Toledo meeting, Hard and Harding had it out as they rode back together on the train to Columbus. The bitter mood that Harding was in has been vividly described by Hard in his recollections. "He was insistent," Hard wrote, "that I discontinue these efforts as he was not and would not be a candidate for the Presidential nomination. I insisted that he owed it to the State of Ohio (Mother of Presidents!) to add one more to the list—that it was a State and a party duty. We lost our tempers. He finally said . . . that 'I didn't know a damn thing about it.' To which I replied that if he thought the Republican party had just sent him to the United States Senate that he might find it congenial he 'didn't know a damn thing about it.' " By the time they reached Columbus they had made up. "We had to," Hard laconically explained.[68]

Hard was at no loss for details in giving Harding's reasons for not wanting the Presidency. In the first place, "he did not feel that he was big enough to fill the office of President. There were many Republicans much better qualified." In the second place he could not be nominated. In the third place, "in seeking the Presidential nomination he might imperil—might lose—his chance to be returned to the Senate in 1920." He liked it in the Senate. "It was congenial. Ohio should have pride in having a good Senator as well as a President." Harding protested that his senatorial record was good and that Ohio should be satisfied with it. He was faithful in his committee service. He was well informed on the important measures, "consulted with the wiser and older Senators," and spoke with effect upon proper occasions. He was "building himself into a position of influence and ultimate leadership in the Senate." [69]

It should be added that on occasion Mrs. Harding "sat on" those who were trying to push her husband into the presidential nomination. This she did in the case of Charles E. Hard and E. Mont Reily. To the latter, she said, "I am going to take you to your train at two o'clock and see that you get away! And I do not want you to come back here and talk Warren into running for President, for I do not intend to permit him to run. Because of the condition of his health it would bring a tragedy to us both." The problem was, said Mrs. Harding, the work required in campaigning effectively. "I know that a Presidential campaign means strenuous activity, and a fight from the beginning until the last vote is cast and counted in November." [70]

9

Hard was right—Harding had an obligation to the Ohio Republican party. He had made this thing of patchwork and its endurance depended on him. He could not abandon it. He must fight on confidently, serenely, because his shaky organization depended on him. As Hard said, the Ohio Republican party had not sent him to the Senate "that he might find it congenial." A President was stronger than a Senator and therefore the organization would be stronger with a President of the United States as its head.

This dependence of the Ohio Republican politicians on Harding was vividly illustrated in September, 1919 when Harding let Clark know that he was thinking of withdrawing from heading the advisory committee. On September 4 he wrote that he was so satisfied with Clark's work in leading the Republican party back to the dominant position in Ohio that he wanted to make Clark chairman of the state central committee in place of the do-nothing Fairbanks. Consequently he wrote, "If at any time, you find my retirement necessary to bring about such a result, you have only to suggest it and I will gladly give way to someone who can command a more cordial support." [71]

Clark was horrified. The advisory committee without Harding would leave the Ohio Republican party headless, and the whole organization and its local dynasties would be in danger. "I am half amused and half angry at your suggestion of possible retirement," Clark wrote back. "Great Heavens! You are the one force that is keeping things together in this old state of Ohio. Forget it." [72]

The only direction in which Harding could now go was forward. He had to lead vigorously—and he could never put the possibility of the Presidency behind. He had to do this, even to retain his Ohio senatorship.

10

Suddenly, in the late fall of 1919, Harding's political adversaries struck. They sought to make him choose between the presidential and the senatorial candidacies. Such a choice might easily be politically fatal. If he chose the presidential candidacy, he might be roundly defeated by a stronger candidate such as General Leonard Wood with his great financial backing. If Harding chose the senatorial candidacy and some other Republican became President, the prevailing Republican organization might be displaced. A new Ohio Republican organization might come into existence and make patronage arrangements with a non-Ohio Republican presidential candidate. There would be plenty of new political vacancies with the possible 1920 changeover from the Democrats to the Republicans. It would be much better for the present Ohio organization if Harding could postpone his choice, thus preserving his and Ohio's political bargaining power while sentiment in the Buckeye state and elsewhere was organized for the popular Senator. And that was exactly what Harding was able to do, with the result of a sharp increase of confidence in his leadership and presidential availability.

Harding's opponents were the former "blackbirds," the Brown-Hynicka faction, that had tried in November and December of 1918 to stop his efforts to establish political leadership in Ohio via the revival of the advisory committee. However, this time they operated within the advisory committee because Harding had magnanimously placed on it Brown and Hynicka's henchman, Procter, as part of his policy of unity and forgiveness. The procedure of "the blackbirds" was to prevail on Clark and the committee to adopt a resolution on October 17, 1919 asking the Senator what were his plans in regard to the presidential nomination. The committee followed up the passage of its resolution by having representatives call on Harding in Washington.[73]

It seemed so very innocent. Yet Harding and Daugherty saw in it a sinister plot to overthrow their organization. If Harding accepted the bait and announced his preference for the Senatorship, Brown and his allies would start the ball rolling to capture the Ohio delegates to the nominating convention in 1920 in support of General Leonard Wood for the Presidency. Brown would do this with the aid of the millionaire Procter, who was known to be friendly to Wood, for whose nomination to the Presidency he eventually declared.

In the opinion of Harding and Daugherty this Brown maneuver was a bid to put the Ohio Republican patronage in the hands of Brown and the Progressive faction of the party. With Leonard Wood in the White House, hundreds of Ohio political jobs held by the departing Democrats would be at his and Brown's disposal. Thus would Senator Harding be deprived of his senatorial perquisites and the whole Republican Old Guard machine would be unable to strengthen its power. It would undermine the Ohio Republican party as controlled by Harding in favor of the Progressives. Thus would the Progressives have a patronage basis, the lack of which had been the essential reason for their former failures. Former Governor Frank Willis was of the same opinion. He wrote Harding, November 17, 1919, "a small group of Republicans in Ohio are eager to fix up a party program that will give them the control of the party organization and patronage in

Ohio. . . . This party must not be permitted to get into the hands of those who have not been loyal to its candidates, State or National, who now seek to humiliate you and injure the party in their own selfish ends." [74] Poor Willis might well be concerned, considering his propensity to make so many promises to his supporters.

Daugherty explained this patronage threat to the Old Guard organization in a letter to Harding dated October 24, 1919. What the Brown plotters were trying to do, said Daugherty, was to get Harding to declare for the Senatorship and leave the Presidency open. Brown and the Progressives would then go to work in Ohio to build up a set of district candidates for the Republican nominating convention of 1920 pledged to Wood for President. It was not that they were really for Wood, but that they would have an Ohio delegation that "can be thrown to somebody whenever a trade is made to distribute the patronage in the state." This, declared Daugherty, would embarrass Harding to the point of imperiling his chances for reelection to the Senate because he would not have any jobs to promise. In effect, Brown was willing to sacrifice the Ohio Senatorship to the Democrats so that a Republican President would help him build up a new Progressive Republican organization in Ohio. As Daugherty put it, the Brown people would "have you nominated for senator and have the story out that if you are elected you will have nothing to do with the patronage. . . . They pretend to be friendly with you, but as a matter of fact they would trade you off for a yellow dog at any time if they could go patronage rabbit hunting with the dog." [75]

Harding saw the point quite clearly. The Brown-Wood maneuver would put patronage control in their hands and deprive Harding of it. Therefore, Harding might lose his Senatorship, Wood might win the Presidency, and that would be the end not only for Harding but for the Republican organization that Harding was a part of. This, he wrote to Scobey on October 25, 1919 "was the trick of a dirty political dog." He reproached himself for having been nice to Brown by putting him on the advisory committee "in spite of the advice of my friends who opposed such a course." [76] To Hard he confessed, "I really smiled with rather good humor, and had some fun with myself for having gone so far in placating certain elements of the Party in our state and then finding that I had nursed those who would make political life unpleasant for me, if it were possible to do so." [77]

It was this political jungle-fighting that led Harding to express a desire to get out of the miserable business of politics, even to the point of being willing to give up the Senatorship. As he told Clark, September 12, 1919, "When I contemplate the number of people who strongly pretend to be friends, who are at the same time plotting to undermine me politically, I feel a disgust at the whole proposition which makes me ready to step aside for somebody else." [78] To Jennings he wrote, October 11, 1919, "I not only have no inclination to be considered for the big job, but I am getting to a point where I will be quite content to be retired from the one which I now hold. It is more or less of a dog's life and I could be lots more happy living on a farm out in Ohio and giving a half day's attention to the newspaper shop at Marion." [79] To Massachusetts Senator John W. Weeks he confessed that he "could welcome retirement to private pursuits and be in a position to tell everybody to go jump into the ocean." [80] In the same mood he confided to his friend Colonel George Christian, "I could not surrender party domination and control to a small band of political high binders who have never been friendly to me or those who were good enough to support me in political affairs. I made up my mind that I would rather quit politics than remain in public office by their sufferance." [81] Again he wrote to Jennings, November 4, 1919, saying, "I grow so weary of the conspiracies, insincerities, the petty practices of politics, that I have moments when I am inclined to make a sweeping gesture and tell all of them to 'go to hell.'" [82]

But Harding could not quit. He was a prisoner of his party, of its machinery, and of the loyalty to the many whose political future depended upon his leadership. Daugherty was watching him closely. As Harding considered the Brown-inspired demand for a choice between the senatorial and the presidential nominations, a telegram came October 18 from Daugherty stating tersely, "Do not think their programme helpful to party." As Harding hesitated about the proposal to chose, Daugherty grew impatient. Somebody must call Brown's bluff, Daugherty wrote October 24, "It will take some courage . . . and the right kind of courage always wins." If Harding would not speak in his own behalf, Daugherty said that he would do it himself. He was "much inclined to flinch," but the time had come to fight back in order to "stand by friends and the party." That put it up to Harding who decided to do the manly thing. He replied saying, "I do not intend to allow the organization, or any part of it to stand me up in a corner and tell me what I must do." [83]

Harding's answer to the Brown plotters on the advisory committee, as published October 31, 1919, showed high poise and dignity. He told them that he would run for whichever office suited him and the Republican party of Ohio. He gently rebuked them by questioning the propriety of their asking him to choose between the senatorial and the presidential nominations. Neither he nor anybody else, he said, knew as yet by which candidacy he could contribute more to party success. Personally he was gratified at being honored by presidential urgings from hundreds of friends. But he had invariably told them that he did not aspire to the Presidency and that he hoped to remain in the Senate. When a decision could be made that would assuredly make for party success, he would make it.[84]

Harding was now in a commanding position. He had beaten Brown and the rest of the "high binders" at their own game of politicking, and everybody knew it. When the time came to decide about the Presidency—and it would come very soon—he would make his decision and protect his party from outsiders and their mercenary and plotting supporters. At the same time, of course, he was protecting himself from political extinction. "The little bunch," he triumphantly told Scobey, November 3, 1919, "evidently assumed that I would assent to whatever they suggested without showing any disposition to dispute them. They have learned better, and things seem quite rosy now." The situation in Ohio he said, was now "bully good" and "leaves the way open for me to take such course as I deem best. . . . I am stronger than I have been at any time in the past."[85]

11

These maneuverings marked the return of Harry M. Daugherty to the complete confidence of Warren G. Harding—and that, in turn, meant a powerful influence in the manipulating necessary to gain the presidential nomination for the Ohio Senator. Daugherty had no intention of working merely for Harding's reelection to the Senate. Daugherty saw Harding's chances for the Presidency and did everything he could to improve them.

Daugherty had Harding's confidence for several reasons. One was that their leadership of the party was at stake. The two agreed completely about the danger to all Ohio Republicans ambitious for office from the Brown-Wood-Procter faction. Daugherty had saved the blundering George Clark and the advisory committee from being outfoxed by Brown. Without embarrassing Harding, Daugherty on

November 2, wrote to Christian, "Hereafter in a nice way . . . before any important thing is done I think Harding should (in a nice way I say) tell Clark to talk over things with me." Moreover, Harding was at the time deeply immersed in his senatorial efforts against Wilson and the League of Nations. The task of developing Harding's presidential potential in the country at large was too big for the Senator alone— and Daugherty was eager to go ahead.

With a nod to Christian, Daugherty put the Harding-for-President campaign skillfully under way. Consider the spirit and significance of the rest of the Daugherty-to-Christian letter:

> Now I think we should without Harding knowing about it canvas & keep in touch with the big field. We need say no more [than] that he would not be a candidate for the Presidency. He will of course not say that he is. He don't have now to do much talking or know much. Presidents don't run in this country like assessors you know. He had at home the same troubles that McKinley & Hanna & Taft had. In a way at the right time I will make this clear. This canvas will cost something. It must not cost you or him a cent. I can't take care of it all. I always try to do my full share. I wish you could make up a list of some good friends of Harding's I can see & have discreetly seen who will contribute for this personal use of *canvassing the field*. Publicity & c. We must not let it be known anything is being managed. We must keep our own secrets and thereby avoid jealousy. Write me at once and leave it to me to be discreet. You can tell people who are expected to help in this way to see or write me. It is not necessary to let Clark know anything about it just now. I will keep in touch with him. Write to me as soon as possible. Believe me there is a difficult situation here [Columbus] and will be hereafter . . . Harding can hold up his head now & be not afraid. It is a good thing it all happened.[86]

Consider also the high-priced and determined financial considerations in Daugherty's letter to Scobey in Texas, November 28, 1919:

> The important thing we need now is to start in to raise a fund to pay the necessary expenses. . . . We are moving now at a rapid pace and I want to see thirty to forty men put out over the United States in the next two or three weeks; more after the holidays. Confidentially, you probably know that the legitimate expenses of making a campaign with any chance of winning is from seven hundred and fifty thousand to a million dollars. This is all necessary and legitimate.[87]

Oddly enough, Daugherty did not raise a million dollars; and though the Wood and Lowden men did raise such a sum, it worked to their disadvantage and to Harding's gain.

Consider finally the frank and forthright promises that all who aided Harding would share in the spoils of victory. Again it was Scobey to whom Daugherty made a declaration in order to win the support of the Texas Republican machine, headed by H. F. Mac-Gregor, state committeeman from the Lone Star state:

> I know MacGregor very well. . . . I know his temperament, his ambition, his worth, and the reason for hesitancy on his part as far as committing himself is concerned. I can make it clear to him . . . that Harding had probably the best chance to be nominated. Of course, if MacGregor is with us we win, he and his friends will control the patronage. The game will be played as it should be played. Harding has seen it all played often enough to know how it must be played and that the men who help bring about a big thing like this must be consulted and in control.[88]

Daugherty wound up the Harding victory over Walter Brown and the advisory committee with a flourish. On October 31, 1919 he got the committee to adopt a resolution, written by Daugherty and introduced by Fairbanks, giving fulsome praise to Harding as Senator. The committee, in effect, apologized for trying to force Harding's hand. It said that such a man as Harding was needed in the Senate, but "he should not deny the Republicans of Ohio, if at the proper time they may see fit to do so, the right to use his name for the Presidency." Then, to make sure that everybody understood the full meaning of the resolution, it was added that, if he were not nominated for the Presidency, it "should not prejudice his unopposed nomination by the Republicans of Ohio for a second term as United States Senator." Referring to Hynicka and the Progressives on the committee, Daugherty, who was present at the meeting, wrote Harding, "There was some little squirming. . . . Brown did not act cordially; Garford kept still; Procter said nothing but blushed, Hynicka protested somewhat against the insinuation that he was not always of this mind and jumped on the newspapers. Then all got on the bandwagon." [89] The meekness, as well as the embarrassment with which the committee surrendered, was described by another eyewitness member, Charles D. Simeral of Steubenville. He wrote Harding on November 1, "We had a very nice meeting of the committee: Some folks were evidently smoked out. No one chirped in the final roundup, but our friend Walter was evidently in distress." [90]

Harding's critics got in a little jab at the end of this episode, but it did not matter. The Associated Press report made it look as if he had chosen the Senatorship and given up the Presidency. It read, "Senator Warren G. Harding announced that he is not a candidate for the Republican nomination for the Presidency and asked the committee's support for re-election to the Senate. The Committee adopted a resolution endorsing him for re-election to the Senatorship." This was the very impression of dependence on Brown and the committee that Harding had successfully avoided. His friends sent in clippings and protests, and he admitted to Clark that he "very much" disliked "to be proclaimed to all of the United States as one who was not looked upon with favor at home." But, as he told Simeral, "I do not greatly grieve about it." [91]

As a matter of fact, Daugherty saw to it that Harding's triumph got the proper national coverage. In a release written by him, he rebuked the committee for trying to embarrass the distinguished Senator. Harding, he said, "does not propose at this time to be run out, smoked out or knocked out" of either the Presidency or the Senatorship. Daugherty was proud of this publicity performance in counteracting the Associated Press. He told Christian that his "smoked out, knocked out" phrase was carried in the press throughout the country. "That was the purpose in so writing it." He added, "Things look fine for Harding's future now." [92]

Harding was delighted. "There is a general feeling of satisfaction over the situation," he wrote Daugherty. "I know full well that Brown and others of his particular clique are not at all pleased. You are certainly a very devoted friend for anyone to have. I should like you to know of my very genuine appreciation." [93]

Thus it was that the man who wanted not to become President was in grave danger of losing his desire. Thus it was that he who stood at the brink of political oblivion in 1918 was now on the threshold of national fame.

CHAPTER FIFTEEN

The Americanization of the
League of Nations, 1919

"I think the world today, trembling under the menace of Bolshevism, owes a very large part of that growing menace to the policies and utterances of the Chief Executive of the United States." : : : *Harding in U.S. Senate, January 21, 1919, "Congressional Record," 65 Congress, 3 Session, p. 1808*

"We can carry the banners of America to the new Elysium, even though we have to furl them before we enter." : : : *Harding in U.S. Senate, September 11, 1919, "Congressional Record," 66 Congress, 1 Session, p. 5225*

⳽ Harding's rising role as a Republican strong man and presidential contender required that he use his oratorical and Americanistic talents more and more at the presidential level. This meant that his targets must be Woodrow Wilson and the League of Nations. The result was no intellectual *tour de force*. It was a triumph of the same old Harding spellbinding and mirage-making in the name of Americanism. It did not take many alterations for Warren Harding to transform his tariff Americanism into League of Nations Americanism.

The end of World War I was a great help to Harding in his anti-Democratic politicking. He could now intensify his Wilson-baiting. In the process, Wilson's war for world democracy became a lie, the Fourteen Points for a permanent peace became a promotion of Bolshevism, and the Wilson League of Nations became a threat to American independence.

Gradually, instead of being a mere opponent of the League of Nations, Harding became a presider over a great national forum in which the pros and cons of a new international order were debated before millions of people with the constructive idea of seeking to understand what kind of a league of nations or association was best fitted to America's proper participation in world affairs. It may have been ambivalent, but Harding and hosts of his followers did not think so.

The spirit of the day was contentious. The prize was control of the destiny of the nation—well worth contending for. As a denouncer of Democrats, Harding would be aggressive. Wilson would become the egomaniac, the power-mad dictator, the "Paris visionary," prating about idealism and world peace for domestic political purposes. The GOP would become the restorer of sanity and normalcy, the savior of America, and the true preserver of an honest peace.

Typical of this new mirage-making by Harding was the pretense of Republican non-partisanship. He sought to raise the image of the Republican party to that of transcendent Americanism and whole-hearted support of the war effort. And yet Harding could not try to make his point without immediately destroying it by damning the Democrats. He had done so during the war, and he did it again and again as the war closed and the years of peace succeeded.

The deadly conflict in France and on the ocean was still going on when the Ohio Senator, in his address to the state Republican convention of August 27, 1918, declaimed with his usual eloquence how the Republicans during the war had avoided partisanship in order to help develop "a national soul aflame." Ignoring his wartime, Roosevelt-division politicking, and all the rest, he blandly declared, "We submerged partisan lines for the concord of the republic, and, in Congress and out, the present minority party has given to the president the most cordial and whole-hearted and abiding support ever given to any federal executive by a minority party since the republic began." The Republicans, he said, do not "turn to nagging faultfinding in Congress or on the stump while the flag is imperilled. We will wait our return to power and correct the errors of a party unfitted by teaching, and unsuited because of its dominant elements for the best advancement of our republic." And such Democratic errors: an aircraft-building fiasco, the "saturnalia of extravagance," money "spent vainly in incompetence," "the popular notion of the hour that it is good to dissipate the resources of the country." In view of this "we ought to have accomplished vastly more at half the cost." Moreover, "Democratic party politics hasn't been adjourned for one hour in the control of the government by the administration now in power."

But trust the Republicans. "We are the best fitted to solve the problems to come because the errors are not ours, and we are neither called to apologize nor defend. . . . We only claim the conscience and capacity, already proven, to work out the best solution. We are free from committal to the fundamental changes made in the name of war." After all, it was the Republicans who sparked the investigations of incompetence, and "turned failure into developed might"—and Harding cited his own sponsoring of the shipping board investigation as an example. The ridiculousness of such tongue-twisting while the flag was still "imperilled," was lost upon the Republican convention-eers, who screamed their approval at every period.[1] It was sheer and unadulterated Harding Republican politics.

In fairness to Harding it must be stated that he professed to see in his Wilson-baiting the highest of motives. It was a matter of patriot-ism. As he wrote Daugherty on September 18, 1919 in the midst of the League of Nations wrangle, "I have long since given up any thought of winning political favor by any course in dealing with this wholly patriotic problem."[2] Earlier, Glen C. Webster of Genoa, Ohio, accused him of playing "peanut politics" when the nation required statesman-ship. Harding replied angrily, declaring that he was "quite as cordially in favor of a suitable agency for the promotion of world peace and tranquility as you are . . . who dwell in loftier realms of politics." Moreover, he was doing something about it as evidenced by the constructive revisions being made in the League covenant even by Wilson himself. Harding said that it was not the function of the Senate to give "unvarying and unquestioning support of Woodrow Wilson." Moreover, he declared that it was "not wholly 'petty partisan politics' to devote oneself to the preservation of the things which we Americans have cherished from the immortal beginnings."[3]

The "lie" speech on the war for world democracy was given by Harding on January 21, 1919 in a Senate debate on a measure re-quested by President Wilson providing $100,000,000 for war relief in Europe. Harding tore into Wilson with various allegations, including, of course, those of extravagance and dictatorial ambitions. As for the world democracy call, Harding said Wilson's motive was to avoid offending the German-American vote. War for world democracy would never have been mentioned, said Harding "if it had not been for the politics of the moment, when most men in public life were fearful of offending the so-called German vote in the United States of America; and, instead of announcing we were making war on Germany, which had trespassed upon American national rights, we made the excuse we were making war for democracy, and it has been a lie from the beginning." [4]

To his friends Harding confessed how sickening to him was this Wilsonian cant about world democracy. In a letter on January 24, 1919 to James R. Sheffield of New York, he wrote, "I am particularly interested to know that you approve of what I said concerning the insincerity of our proclaimed warfare to make the world safe for democracy. . . . I have always assumed that we were to charge that abiding hypocrisy to the fact that we were insisting that we make war on the Kaiser to avoid offending large pro-German votes in the United States. . . . It has all been such an astounding fraud, that it wearies one to think of it. Of course, I have always felt if we had been making war for democracy's sake, we would have gotten into it from the very beginning." [5]

As for the Fourteen Points, Harding had not always been as bluntly disdainful of them as he became after the war was over. On January 24, 1918, shortly after the President had made his statement of war aims, former Secretary of the Treasury Leslie M. Shaw had prepared a denunciation of these aims which he wanted Harding to publish in the *Congressional Record*. Shaw was especially severe on point number 3, calling for the removal of trade barriers. This was denounced as Socialistic and as "international free trade." Harding, of course, agreed with Shaw. But, for the moment, he did not think the time opportune for coming out into the open about it. "I do not think," Harding told Shaw, "that it would be prudent to do the things which will have the savor of attempting to take partisan advantage of a crucial situation. If you will allow me to use my judgment in the matter I very much prefer to await the hour when I think the situation justified having your illuminating letter presented to Congress." [6]

The hour to blast the Fourteen Points came on the same occasion that Harding took to denounce Wilson's world democracy talk, the January 21, 1919 senatorial oration on relief for Europe. He contrasted the "average" soldier's idea of what the war was about with Wilson's alleged far-fetched sermonizing. He cited the example of one returned soldier whom he asked "if he was not rejoiced at the American triumph and the victorious fight he had made for the President's 14 points of peace." The soldier answered, said Harding, "like the practical fellow that he was," saying, "Hell, no! I don't know what they are." Harding said, "Why, it is the impression that you were fighting to carry out the ideals of the Chief Executive." The soldier scornfully replied, "My dear sir, of all the soldiers I know upon the battle fields of France, every mother's son of them was fighting to whip Germany and, by the eternal, we did it, and we are glad." [7]

Harding spoke passionately about Wilson's alleged betrayal of the nation's war-built merchant marine. While the shipping board went on with its public building of ships at extravagant prices—$250 a ton —Britain restored her shipbuilding to private enterprise and got vessels out for $90 a ton. She then retired her entire merchant marine from war service "to go seeking and bearing the commerce of the world," while Wilson did nothing but dabble in internationalism and promises of no trade barriers. "What boots it," Harding asked, "what advantage is there to us to have the greatest merchant marine in the world, if under this new idealism, we are to have a compact of nations in the international relationship where there is no competition, no seeking of national eminence, no seeking of American triumph? What was the use of winning the war if one of the greatest gains in the victory, a new U.S. merchant marine was to be abandoned?" [8]

Senator Harding even went so far as to blame President Wilson and his revolution-promoting Fourteen Points for the spread of Bolshevism. "I do not agree with him," he told his fellow Senators, "in his notions of a new internationalism paralyzed by Socialism. I do not agree with him in sowing the seeds he has of a modified and magnified democracy throughout the world. I do not hesitate to say that I think the world today, trembling under the menace of Bolshevism, owes a very large part of that growing menace to the policies and utterances of the Chief Executive of the United States." Harding was referring to the intention of the Fourteen Points to stir up nationalistic revolutions against the enemy governments, and he said so. "I do not forget, Senators," he said, "that in high places in this country, both executive and legislative, we preached the gospel of revolution in the central empires of Europe. We were so eager to make war on constituted authority that we proclaimed revolution as one of the greatest essentials to bringing about peace and tranquility in the world. You lighted a fire there that is difficult to put out now." In some countries there is no righteous mean between "hateful autocracy" and "destroying anarchy and its democracy." In such cases, he bluntly declared, "I choose autocracy." [9]

Still other political crimes did Harding ascribe to President Wilson. One was to attribute deliberate deceit to the President in the emphasis upon peace of his campaign for reelection in 1916. Here are his words as reported in the *Toledo Blade* of February 13 and the *Lancaster Daily Gazette* of February 14, 1919: "We made the country safe for four years of the Democratic party, before we drew our righteous sword. Some day the truth will be written, and it will yield a recital of neglected duty and the unutterable cost in life and treasure through proclaimed aloofness and security when a responsible government knew, absolutely knew, we could not escape involvement, and dwelt in unpreparedness when the very safety of the republic was imperilled." [10]

Then there was the premature armistice and the delayed peacemaking at Paris, which Harding attributed to Wilsonian bungling. Many kinds of alleged evils came from this: the failure to destroy the power of Germany, the destruction of the morale of the American and Allied armies, the spread of Bolshevism. These he told to his Ohio audiences in the spring of 1919. Only the armistice, he said, saved Germany from complete surrender. It came so quickly that the world was dazed in its rejoicing. We were so fevered in our activities that we did not think clearly. And so our magnificent army, which had turned the tide of battle, thought its job had been done. "The armistice destroyed the morale of the armies of the republic." For the job of fighting, "the American soldier was eager to sacrifice and train and suffer and fight. He knew his job. He was enrolled to bring Germany to terms. When that was done, his thoughts turned to the good old U.S.A., to home fires, to home tasks, and to the home folks." [11]

Harding's anti-Wilson appetite was whetted by a belief that the President was inept as a politician. He was egotistical, incapable of consulting with practical people, and overly idealistic. "No one will dispute President Wilson's towering mentality," he told H. H. Timken in February, 1918, "nor can anyone question that he means to play a noble part in the war, but the absolute truth is that he is too much aloof from the leadership of both parties and is unwilling to put himself in touch with the big men of the country whose advice would not be otherwise than helpful to him." [12] Such a man, Harding was convinced, would destroy himself politically. "If we will only allow him to go on in his egotistical way," he told Scobey in December, 1918, "I think he will cease to be a strong factor in American political life." [13] He would be incapable of accepting criticism gracefully in the coming days of political contention as he dealt with problems that should be left out of politics.

Harding used his Wilson-baiting as part of his new role of Ohio's strong man while he strengthened himself politically after the death of Roosevelt on January 6, 1919. As he put George Clark to work on the revitalized advisory committee, he accompanied his announcements with spirited anti-Wilson remarks aimed to unite Republicans against the Democrats. Thus at the January 15, 1919 meeting of the advisory committee he thrilled them with some oratorical pyrotechnics. He took President Wilson to task for his world democracy and Fourteen Point philosophizing, and then praised "the boys" who were fighting for American national rights. "They bared their breasts and they crave and have a right to material fulfillment, not a surrendered sovereignty to have this great republic become an important unit in a socialized and paralyzed internationalism." "Peace must first be riveted and the Bolshevist beast slain. . . . Bolshevism is a menace that must be destroyed, lest it destroy." Then the nation must turn quickly to the solution of its domestic problems so vital to the future. But, he hastened to add, "the task is too big for President Wilson." [14]

Harding not too subtly invoked the shades of Roosevelt and McKinley as much more trustworthy guides to an American foreign policy than Wilson. The Ohio Senator fostered the image of a giant Roosevelt in contrast to the pygmy Wilson in the Roosevelt memorial address to the Ohio legislature on January 29, 1919. Calling Roosevelt America's "bravest defender . . . the most courageous American of all time," Harding described the efforts to enable Roosevelt to take a volunteer army to France in 1917 and how Roosevelt was denied his ambition. (Wilson's name, of course, was not mentioned.) It was good, said Harding, that the old Colonel was forced to remain at home. "I believe he rendered a greater service with voice and pen at home than was possible to perform with his sword in France." More than any other man he helped achieve the greatest objective of the war, "the finding of the American soul." He "smote divided loyalty and hyphenated Americanism at every turn." He "called to the slumbering spirit of the republic and made it American in fact as well as in name." With a side glance at Wilson's allegedly impractical idealism and one-man diplomacy, he cited Roosevelt's great practical achievements in building the Panama Canal and in forcing the Kaiser to back down in the Venezuela affair of 1902–3. Harding declared that there were few American presidents who "sought advice more widely or were more ready to accept it." [15] It seems not to have occurred to Harding that he was describing a similarity rather than a difference.

On the evening of the same day, January 29, 1919, it being McKinley's birthday, Harding was in Dayton for a banquet. Again he placed the image of the pygmy Wilson beside that of a giant Republican by comparing McKinley's Spanish-American War nationalism with Wilson's World War internationalism. We need the McKinley kind, said Harding, in place of the Wilson kind that sacrifices our country. President Wilson was at the Paris Peace Conference at the time. Harding smugly declared, "In the peace conference today we know that France is looking out for France, Italy is looking out for Italy; and if McKinley were alive today he would be working for the United States." [16]

Not everybody could stomach the image of the dictatorial Wilson as portrayed by Harding. One commentator, James W. Faulkner of the *Cincinnati Enquirer*, was quite frank about it when he observed, "With due respect to Senator Harding . . . the people will refuse to believe that, big as he is, Woodrow Wilson could not even think up half the devilment of which he is accused." [17]

2

Thus, as President Wilson undertook, at the Paris Peace Conference, to bring about a stabilized world via the League of Nations, Harding saw the President's every move through the eyes of a politician. Said Harding, while Wilson maneuvered for his world utopia, "Bolshevism grew. The German army, still intact, secretly plotted with it." That is what Harding told his Toledo and Lancaster listeners in February, 1919 as he played his game of Ohio politics. "Not only is Bolshevik destructiveness," he solemnly asserted, "to be countenanced in fallen Russia, but the World will awake pretty soon to the fact that Germany is dominant there and has expanded infinitely more through revolution and delay than it was expected to accomplish by force of armies." [18]

Wilson was criticized for the secrecy with which the Paris Peace Conference was being conducted. "We do not know all that is involved," he said. "I fear the President isn't telling us all that he knows, as he said he would, by cable, else there isn't much doing. I am sure he doesn't want to tell us." [19]

The President was negligent, said Harding. He left his country to drift, ignoring the Republican pleas for domestic reconstruction. He acted like a schoolteacher instead of like a nation's leader. "He has been six years teaching congress, after the manner of a teacher," he told a reporter in Columbus on January 29, 1919 "that it can't do anything except as he orders, and then he runs away at a difficult time and leaves no one to teach and direct in his stead. Such a man is incapable of learning from Congress. We had to goad him to accomplishment in the war. Our criticisms have saved at least a pretense of representative popular government. We of the Republican party offered a comprehensive program of reconstruction long before the armistice, and he ignored us. It lingers in the committee pigeon holes while the country goes to ruin." [20] To Scobey, Harding sourly confided, "He will have no hesitancy in risking the ruin of the country to carry his point at Paris." [21] Harding did not want the President's Paris venture to succeed. He disapproved of the trip, telling Cornelius Cole of Los Angeles, "I rather think he will return to America in a state of great disappointment." [22]

Harding even avoided listening to a pro-League discussion by such a distinguished thinker and Republican as William Howard Taft. It happened that on March 23, 1919 Harding was vacationing in Augusta, Georgia with several Republican Senators including Hale of Maine and Frelinghuysen of New Jersey. Taft was also there, having been scheduled for a pro-League-of-Nations speech in behalf of the League for the Enforcement of Peace, of which he was president. Harding played golf with Taft in the morning, but what happened in the evening was another matter. As Harding wrote to the "Duchess" (Mrs. Harding), "Taft speaks tonight on the League at the Methodist church. We are rather expected to go, but nothing doing. The gang at the hotel is not strong for the League." "The gang" played bridge instead. Next day Harding wrote to the Duchess that "most of the gang went to hear Taft's speech, but they were not carried away." [23] Harding did not believe that Taft was sincere in favoring the League. He told a friend that Taft was using the League as "an avenue of returning to the White House." [24]

There was nothing in Wilson's League of Nations for the United States except pulling chestnuts out of the fire for other people's benefit. "You have the right dope on the league of nations," Harding wrote to Scobey. "I don't think there is anything in it for the United States of America, but it does make us the financial backer of all the bankrupt nations of the earth and pledges us to their preservation and protection for all time to come." [25]

The first official act by Harding against the Wilson League came on March 3, 1919 when he subscribed to the so-called round robin statement of the thirty-three Republican Senators of the expiring Sixty-sixth Congress. This was a brief declaration that the signatories could not accept the Peace Conference's draft of the Covenant of the League of Nations recently published in the American press. (It was a forewarning of what Wilson could expect from the next Congress and its Republican majority.) Reasons for the opposition to the League were not contained in the statement, but previous discussion in the Senate showed that the Republican Senators believed the League was a war promoter instead of a war preventer; that it violated the Constitution; that it imperiled the nation's sovereignty, and therefore its independence. It was implied that President Wilson, who had returned temporarily to the United States from the Peace Conference sessions, should, upon rejoining the diplomats in Paris, bring about adjustments in the League covenant to remedy these fatal defects. Harding had taken no part in the debate preceding the "round robin" declaration.[26]

With this official Republican warrant, Harding was free to call upon his fellow countrymen with Americanistic fervor to resist the false leadership of their President. In a *New York Times* interview, April 3, 1919, he declared the original League draft "doomed here, if not buried in Paris." Again he ridiculed the delay in approaching the important problems of reconstruction, and again he raised the "red scare," with German trimming. "General Foch fixed armistice terms in less than ten days, which rendered Germany impotent as an armed force. We might ask Foch to write a treaty and he could do it quickly and guard our security as he would that of France and Great Britain." The delay was causing many horrible things. "Bolshevik destructiveness" was being "countenanced," and Germany was recouping her power by being the dominant force in Russia. All that was needed to safeguard peace was the "clear and unmistakable interpretation of international law, to which the allied nations would be committed for enforcing. Under such an arrangement there would never be another war unless some madman of the future again undertakes to dominate the world." If that happened all that we would have to do would be to go to war again to strip the madman of his power. "All the Leagues ever dreamed of will never eliminate world politics. . . . One man power by force of arms has been proven impossible again and again. It will not prevail in the rhetoric of peace."

Harding was very serious about the idea that World War I's chief result was the strengthening of the American national soul. Why should Wilson and the rest of the world disrupt the nation's new unity by driving it into internationalism, Socialism, and Bolshevism?

The war, Harding told a large meeting of the American Defense Society in New York on May 18, 1919, solved the immigrant problem. America was not a mongrelized nation any more. With blazing eloquence, he told his enraptured listeners, "We came to the awakening in the World War. With sympathies divided, with prejudices revealed, with divided sentiments menacing not only our tranquility but the nation's very existence, we saw the need of consecration, and we commanded it. We found the need of awakening, and the republic awakened. We found the growing peril and overwhelmed it with patriotism. We saw the need of dedication and consecration and we dedicated and consecrated. We came to realize that no nation could survive half loyal and half disloyal, and we declared loyalty to the Republic. We saw as we never saw before that privileges and advantages of American citizenship call for the duties and devotions of that citizenship, and it was proclaimed by the conscience of the Republic that every man who fattens his existence on American opportunity must be an American in his heart and soul. . . . The United States is 100 per cent American today, and we mean to hold it so henceforth and forever." [27] In Cincinnati it went as follows: "We went into this war a polyglot people without a soul. We have found our soul. We are Americans today and we will be Americans from this time on." [28]

The unreasonableness of imperiling this new American unity by joining Wilson's League was expounded by Harding in an interview published in the Scripps-McRae papers on April 10, 1919. "In my mind," Harding was quoted as saying, "the inevitable effect of membership in any world league of nations will be the submerging of national spirit." (The word "any" may have been reporter's language rather than Harding's.) Referring to pride in national citizenship as greater than pride in family, he went on, "Never was pride in citizenship greater than it is today in the United States. After long years in which perhaps the real flame of our patriotism lay latent, the country has been swept into a new realization of national pride through the struggles and sacrifices of the last two years." It was not clear then, he reasoned, "that in joining such a league we are in danger of surrendering our nationalism, of submerging and smothering the national spirit we have developed, of paralyzing it by merging it in a supernationality. . . . We cannot merge our nation in a supernation and still be free." [29] All the other nations had bartered their support of the League for something selfish. Why should the country be so foolish as to barter away its newfound strength and independence? The United States Senate would never consent to such a thing.[30]

Harding's feeling of political nationalism were much stronger than his feelings of moral responsibility. He was confident that in the end all would agree to enter the League, if we did not surrender anything vital in so doing; a moral commitment was all that was needed. That is what he wrote Charles H. Tolley of Ilion, New York on April 5, 1919. "My notion is," Harding said, "that the League of Nations proposition is going to fail at its source of original consideration. I do not believe that the nations represented at the Peace Conference are going to be able to submit any fundamental constitution of a character to seriously engage the attention of the people of the United States. If the document ultimately agreed upon does not surrender anything vital to American national life and only commits our moral influence to the maintenance of world peace, I fancy there will be very little opposition to it in this country. Anything which savors of surrendering any vital American inheritance will be promptly rejected but, frankly, I do not look for the submission of any such document." [31]

3

Harding gradually tempered his feeling and expressions about a league of nations, but not his animosity toward President Wilson and Wilson's League of Nations. The Senator admitted the existence of much public opinion in favor of a league. This did not mean a surrender to Wilson, but rather some adjustment that the people would accept and that the President would not accept. On April 4, 1919 Harding confided to Daugherty, "Manifestly the public mind has not been ready to accept a flat declaration against any sort of League of Nations." It was Harding's opinion that the process of recognizing the aspiration of humankind for some guaranty of peace, and, at the same time, temperately subjecting it so as not to surrender American nationality, "will ultimately adjust the popular mind to such a program of opposition as is necessary to put an end to Wilson's dreaming." [32] As other Republican Senators expounded more or less radically on the subject, Harding held his tongue, on the grounds, as he said, that it was "a more promising situation to maintain an apparently unprejudiced mind until we can have the treaty and the actual league of nations compact before us." This "leaves one in a better position to impress the public which is willing to be convinced." Daugherty advised reticence on the subject, saying that if the Republicans defeated the league and a war came, the GOP would be blamed. After all, he said, "calves have fits, locusts come back, ingrowing toe-nails or indigestion" occur. Best to try it out for a couple of years so that at the end of that time we could withdraw "if it is desirable and causes no inconvenience." [33] All in all, Harding did not agree with a large section of his correspondents, especially "the perfunctory and the propagandists' letters." But the letters from "those in whom one has learned to place confidence are nearly all against the covenant and the Wilson program." [34]

Harding publicly cultivated the attitude of the open mind as he encouraged the widest possible discussion of the subject of a league. This idea of a national forum had much merit, and Harding came to be its main protagonist and beneficiary. Eventually, when he became a candidate for the Presidency, this role of moderator of a great discussion enabled him to receive the support of many shades of Republican opinion, from extreme opposition to the League by such persons as Hiram Johnson and William E. Borah to ardent support of the League from William Howard Taft and others. Harding's characteristic of counseling on important questions before deciding was never used to better effect than on the League of Nations question.

Harding's appearance of open-mindedness was deliberately publicized. It appeared in the *Cincinnati Enquirer* on April 11, 1919, when he was quoted as saying, "It would not be quite fair to criticize the covenant as we hear about it today. The League of Nations, according to the articles presented, doubtless will undergo many changes before an agreement is reached." When he spoke before a group of Cleveland businessmen on April 23, 1919, C. W. Whitehair of the Union Commerce National Bank wrote congratulating him on his moderation. He admitted to being a strong Republican and desirous of the defeat of the Democrats, but "your self-restraint and kindly way of dealing with the national problem, made a deep impression upon me. . . . I firmly believe that your type of sane, intellectual, self-restrained leadership will bring the people results." Harding modestly replied that he really felt deeply about Wilson's errors and wanted to "cry out against the administration, though I knew the error of doing so at a time when it may seem to be the outburst of partisan cultivation." [35]

Harding advised that those who spoke violently on the League—like Johnson and Borah—not be taken too seriously. They were more interested in building their political fences than in the League. As he told former Governor Willis on May 5, 1919, "We have a fine body of Republicans in the Senate and a much better prospect of unity and harmony than the newspaper reports would seem to indicate. Much of the conflict within our ranks is very largely of an advertising variety and will not develop anything serious when it comes down to voting." Moreover, there was a "tremendous sweep of sentiment throughout the land which is hostile to the present administration," and, Harding said, "there can be no doubt about our party returning to full responsibility in 1920." He advised Willis not to worry about Wilson's League. "We have the strength to defeat the plans of President Wilson in foisting upon us his interwoven league of nations." [36]

To those who urged him to assail the League more vigorously, Harding counseled delay for strategic purposes. To W. T. Spegal of Delaware, Ohio, he wrote, on May 21, 1919. "It may be that you are ready to pass final judgment on this tremendously important question at this time, but I have been watching the actions of our peace commissioners and noting the trend of events at Paris with unusual care and probably with more information available than the average citizen can command, and yet I find myself very much unable to decide definitely concerning many questions which have been raised. My own judgment is that a matter of such supreme importance ought to be given the completest understanding on the part of American citizenship before venturing to reach a final decision. . . . I do want the American people to have a full understanding which is so essential to an intelligent and dependable expression thereon." [37]

To Harding's Kansas City enthusiast, E. Mont Reily, who advised a barnstorming anti-League tour, the Senator replied with similar moderation. The best forum at present for influencing public sentiment was the Senate itself, and "I am reserving my remarks on the League of Nations covenant until we have the question squarely before us." It would be "poor politics and poor tactics," to engage in premature discussions "because the popular mind inclines to look upon this advanced discussion as mere opposition to President Wilson. When we have the treaty before us, it will be a perfectly simple matter to say that we are arguing for the United States of America, whether it is in opposition to President Wilson or to anybody else in the world." [38]

4

Some justification of Harding's counsels for moderation in League discussion seemed to come in June, 1919 with the proposal of the so-called Elihu Root reservations to the League covenant. These were often referred to as the Root-Hays or Root-Lodge reservations, having been prepared by Root in a letter of June 21, 1919 to Henry Cabot Lodge, chairman of the Senate Foreign Relations Committee, after consultation with Republican national chairman Will H. Hays. Root's letter contained a clear-headed and highly constructive, as well as critical, analysis of the League covenant. It recommended United States entry into the League of Nations with certain restrictions designed to preserve her independence and freedom of action. The covenant, said Root, contained a "great deal of high value that the world ought not to lose." He specified what this was: (1) the arrangement to hold conferences of League delegates whenever war threatened; (2) provisions for joint action in matters affecting common interest; (3) agreement for delay in cases of serious dispute; (4) recognition of the rights of nations to self-government; (5) creation of a plan for setting up a trusteeship system in areas formerly ruled by autocratic imperialists. The uncertain conditions in Europe required some immediate stabilizing to end idleness and the danger of the spread of radicalism. However, some changes in the covenant were necessary in behalf of American self-government. They were: (1) some limitations of the obligation under Article 10 for all nations to pledge assistance to nations subject to external aggression; (2) a statement of the right of any nation to withdraw from the League with two years' notice; (3) complete protection of the Monroe Doctrine as defined by the United States. [39]

The importance of Elihu Root in the councils of the Republican Party is vital. Republicans looked to him with near reverence on matters of international law and foreign affairs. Everybody knew of Root's devotion to the ideal of establishing a World Court of International Justice. In 1907, as Secretary of State, he had given practical form to this by his instructions to the American delegates to the Second Hague Peace Conference. In the same year he had engineered the establishment of the Central American Court of Justice. He was past president of the American Society of International Law. In 1913 he was awarded the Nobel Peace Prize of $40,000 and would have made another notable address on world peace in November, 1914 on the presentations of the award, if the outbreak of World War I had not prevented.

The deference with which Republican Senators turned to Root for counsel, while Wilson was in Paris working on the League Covenant, was remarkable. Party leaders consulted with him—Lodge, Hays, Philander C. Knox, Henry L. Stimson, Frank B. Kellogg, Frank B. Brandegee, and others. It was Root who assured Senator Lodge, the key man as head of the Foreign Relations Committee, that the acceptance of the League with reservations was entirely feasible. The failure of President Wilson to use such a superbly qualified counselor as delegate to the Peace Conference was a point of frequent reference in emphasizing Wilson's dogmatism. Ignoring Root and picking the undistinguished Henry White as a Republican delegate was felt to be ridiculous.[40]

Harding instantly approved the Root-Lodge plan to accept the League with reservations. He instructed his Ohio Republican advisory committee, through its secretary, Charles E. Hard, to publicize it throughout the state via the committee's weekly news-sheet, the *Ohio Republican*. On June 24, 1919 Hard reported to his chief, "I shall therefore follow your suggestion and get the matter out in proper form to the editors of the state. . . . I am utilizing the Root letter to Lodge in this issue of the Ohio Republican." In his reply the Senator wrote, "I am glad you are utilizing the Root letter and I think it will be well to include in your publicity stuff to follow up the editorial which you sent me with something similar and wholly along the same lines. . . . I do not think there is anything at all inconsistent in our attitude and shall take occasion to say so at the proper time when I am called to do so here in Washington." [41]

Harding was right. He was selected by Lodge to be a member of the Foreign Relations Committee in the hearings on Wilson's League. After preliminary hearings, he wrote Daugherty on July 25, "My best judgment is that we will finally adopt what has been made public as the Root-Hays program." [42]

Root approached the League of Nations problem as a lawyer and a statesman; Harding approached it as a vote-seeking politician. Both men saw the peace-preserving, international good in the organization.

But Root˙could detect that good, puzzle out its metes and bounds, and then define and contain it. It was a slow, painstaking process of balance and analysis—"leg over leg" work, to use Root's figure of speech. In contrast, Harding's unanalytical mind could not encompass the international nature of the League problem. He could only see it as a nationalist, as a patriot, as an America-firster, conscious of American freedom and independence. Such an outlook did not require definition or explanation, but could have its expression in oratory and in political rhetoric, with a minimal expenditure of intellectual effort. As he wrote to Lucius E. Pinkham of Kansas City, "I do not think the Senate is ever going to consent to ratify the League of Nations Covenant, which subjects us either to Great Britain or to a super-government of the world." [43]

Harding had complete confidence that the people would support his nationalistic approach to the League question through the process of education. As he wrote to Willis on July 25, 1919, "I quite agree with you that the Republican Party need not fear of this being made an issue in 1920. I would be willing to risk my political career on a test between Nationalism and Internationalism at any time, and I feel sure that we may confidently look forward to a great victory next year." [44]

Thus, was Harding—in the Senate, and in Ohio through his advisory committee—disposed to emphasize nationalism to assure people that they could have peace within the League and freedom outside of it. The outside was far more attractive than the inside, and was susceptible to assurances without definitions.

In Ohio the agencies for this process of describing the League to the people, and of discovering their reactions, were Charles E. Hard, the advisory committee, and the *Ohio Republican*. Hard and Harding looked upon their work as one of educating the people away from the internationalist "Wilson League," and toward a league with reservations that preserved nationalism. People in general did not know much about the League, and they were not going to try very hard to find out. Therefore, some show of logic, patriotism, and partial knowledge was all that was necessary.

Something of this non-international state of mind with which Hard, with Harding's approval, approached this mission of education was described in a letter of July 1, 1919. "Two points," wrote Hard, "are impressed upon me locally. First, the support which is being secured for the league of nations gotten, in the main, by the statement that the league is to estop war. This argument will always catch church organizations, and those who have not read the League of Nation's covenant and never intend to. . . . The thinking people are concerned about our nationality, the Monroe Doctrine, the sole right of Congress to declare war of its volition, and matters along these lines, but the great masses of the people know nothing and care nothing of international law or our international obligations: They simply want peace. That is what they have in their minds and, in my judgment, they must be made to realize that the league of nations is more certain to produce war for us as it now stands, than to keep us in peace." [45]

Another point that Hard said was useful in arguing against the Wilson League was that the bankers favored it. The Ohio bankers, of course, got this idea from the New York bankers. "Money is the root of all evil and a tremendous amount of politics," moralized Hard. "Being out of business and having what little financial hay i [sic] have made and in the barn, I can watch without wincing the larger burdens which are being prepared in public sentiment for the shoulders of wealth. Like the churchs [sic] banks should stay out of politics." [46]

To these reflections on the unthinking people, on the Wilson League as a war promoter, and on the Root-Lodge League as a war preventer, Harding gave his blessing. "You have the correct dope on the League of Nations question and you have evidently sent out some bully good stuff to the newspapers of Ohio." Harding then added that they were "getting in shape here in Washington and are going to handle this difficult problem, I think, with satisfaction to the party and to the satisfaction of the country as well." [47]

It took only two months in the summer of 1919 for the Hard-Harding propaganda to convert the Ohio people to an Americanized League. At least that is the way Harding saw it. In midsummer, when the League to Enforce Peace, through its secretary, Felix E. Held, was addressing form letters to "Republicans favoring the League of Nations" with copies of petitions to sign favoring the "Wilson League," Harding described the effort as a dismal failure. On July 30, 1919 he wrote to Hard, "Up to this time we have not had any of the proposed petitions and I am frank to say I very much doubt if there is any considerable development. The preponderance of office mail at the present time is very much in the opposite direction. Scores of people are sending the letters which they have received from Felix Held, along with copies of their reply to him and I can assure you these are of a highly satisfactory character to me." He approved of Hard's suggestion to maintain "a classified list of these petitioners" if and when they did come in.[48]

By September 5, 1919 reports confirmed this favorable trend of Ohio opinion in favor of an Americanized League. Hard wrote on that day that Republican national chairman Hays had wired Ohio Republican advisory committee chairman Clark "asking the present status of public sentiment in Ohio in regard to the League of Nations." Clark replied "that the prevailing sentiment in Ohio was favorable to the entering of the League providing there was sufficient restriction to safeguard American sovereignty and protect our national welfare." He also stated "that public sentiment favored prompt action." [49]

Harding was satisfied. The people of Ohio had found the "truth" about the League and there would be no change but for the better. He congratulated Hard for his work and assured him that there was no need for a senatorial visit to the home state. "If my correspondence is any index to the sentiment of the country," he wrote on September 13, 1919, "I think there has been an overwhelming change in the past sixty days and the sentiment is strongly against the League covenant in the form presented." [50] Ten days later he was even more confident, as he wrote, "I know precisely what the outcome is going to be in the Senate —or at least I think I do—and I am really not concerned about the preponderance of public sentiment because I am confident it is changing all the while toward the right side. I can not see for myself how the Republican party is going to get any of the worse of the existing situation." [51] Of course, as he told Scobey on September 21, "most of the people do not understand the League, but I have a pretty strong conviction that they are coming to an understanding and there is a change of sentiment accordingly." [52]

Climax came in the late summer of 1919 as President Wilson made his famous cross-country appeal to the American people. The first speech was on September 4 in Columbus, where he spoke clearly on the merits of his cause, without undue emotion, on such points as: the healing influence of conferences and cooling-off periods when wars threatened; the need for curbing aggression by the exhibition of its immorality; the effectiveness of world-wide economic boycotts when sanctions became necessary; and the glory of the United States leadership in making the new day possible.[53]

As the day for Wilson's visit drew near, the Harding forces were ready for the attack. George Clark was their leader. He reported to his chief the day before Wilson arrived, "Was in Columbus yesterday laying the ground-work for counter-publicity and other matters in connection with the President's visit there Thursday." [54]

In Senator Harding's estimation President Wilson's appeal to the people was not nearly as effective as his own. From Columbus came the report by Malcolm Jennings that the "Wilson circus" drew a big crowd of curiosity seekers, but that "there was no enthusiasm and not a cheer was raised for him from one end of the parade to the other." Jennings said that Wilson's "adroit, theological speech was cheered sufficiently, but I don't believe that it changed the views of anybody." Harding was glad to get this report and replied that it was in accord with reports from "nearly every section of the country in which he speaks." The Senator characterized the favorable comments of the *Ohio State Journal* as "balderdash." He had assurances from Kansas City and Omaha that Wilson's visits there were "little less than failure." By September 22, Harding was happy to write that "instead of the President's trip changing sentiment in the Senate and strengthening his support, the very opposite effect is noted." "The simple truth is," he wrote Daugherty on the same day, "that he is very much strengthening the situation in the Senate in making sure of modifying the document before it is accepted." [55]

Similar reports of the President's alleged failure came from Reily after Wilson's Kansas City appearance. Reily was on the platform as Wilson spoke, and the next day informed Harding, "There was very little enthusiasm, and not much applause. I was greatly surprised at the lack of all this. He must realize defeat is at hand." Reily believed that the country was "five to one" against Wilson's League. When Hiram Johnson appeared a few days later and denounced the League with super-Americanism, Reily reported that Johnson had a larger crowd and was cheered upon entrance sixteen minutes as compared with only three for Wilson. All of which was most gratifying to Harding, who replied to Reily, "I am glad that Senator Johnson received such a cordial reception in Kansas City. . . . Johnson has really rendered a very great service in his campaign for the direction of public sentiment in the right way, and I am more than pleased that he has been so cordially received in the middle west." [56]

Particularly harsh were Harding's comments on the President's illness which caused a cancellation of the end of the tour. This, Harding told Scobey, was brought on by Wilson's own excessiveness. "I quite agree with your impression," he wrote September 27, 1919, "that the

President did not accomplish very much by his western trip. He has really worked himself into such a frenzy and disappointment that he has made himself ill and has been obliged to cancel the trip. The only perceptible effect of his campaign in the Senate has been to strengthen the opposition to his declaration." The longer the President remained ill, the more confident Harding became of the defeat of the "Wilson League." On October 8, Harding told Scobey, "If the illness of the President continues, I think our proposition will be strengthened because when he ceases to continue in personal command his forces are very much weakened." [57]

An ingenious and, no doubt, sincere turn of Harding's thoughts about Wilson and the League, was the conviction that the President's audiences were less intelligent than usual. That is what he wrote Hard on September 6, 1919, "There is much that the President talks about that is very appealing to everybody and an artist like he is in the use of language, with as little conscience as he exercises in sincerity of utterance, it is an easy thing to make a very attractive presentation of the subject to the unthinking mind." Two days later he wrote similarly to Jennings, "I sometimes wonder how such a speech can catch the assembled multitude, but when one comes to think of it there is the conviction that there are not very many analytical thinkers among the thousands which assembled for such an occasion." [58]

A basic reason for Harding's belief in the inferiority of Wilson's audiences was that internationalism appealed to a lower order of the intellect. Nationalism was a great commonwealth-preserving virtue; internationalism was something vague and not to be trusted. This came out in July upon the occasion of Wilson's message to the Senate in presenting the draft of the treaty of Versailles and the League covenant. As quoted in the *New York Times,* July 11, Harding said, "It was the appeal of the internationalist. It was utterly lacking in ringing Americanism." It also came out in Harding's September 11, 1919 Senate speech in support of the League with reservations:

Nationalism was the vital force that turned the dearly wrought freedom of the republic to a living, impelling power. Nationalism inspired, assured, upbuilded. In nationalism was centered all the hopes, all the confidence, all the aspirations of a developing people. Nationalism has turned the retreating processions of the earth to the onward march to accomplishment, and has been the very shield of democracy wherever its banners are unfurled. . . . It was nationality that conceived the emergence of new nations and the revival of old ones out of the ashes of consuming warfare. Nationality is the call of the heart of liberated peoples, and the dream of those to whom freedom becomes an undying cause. It was the guiding light, the song, the prayer, the consummation for our own people, although we were never assured indissoluble union until the Civil War was fought. Can any red-blooded American consent now, when we have come to understand its priceless value, to merge our nationality into internationality, merely because brotherhood and fraternity and fellowship and peace are soothing and appealing terms? [59]

6

In the precise defining of the structure of an Americanized League of Nations, Senator Harding took no part. The job was masterminded in large measure by Henry Cabot Lodge, on the basis of the Root recommendations. Lodge was the chairman of the Senate Foreign Relations Committee, whose public hearings were widely publicized.[60] The result was the preparation of fourteen reservations that were designed to make the League of Nations safe for American participation, under the primary guidance of Congress, not the President. Article 10, guaranteeing nations against outside aggression, was made subject to congressional determination so far as any action by the United States was concerned. Other League decisions affecting the United States were made dependent on congressional approval, such as the assignment of mandates, the definition of what was a domestic American question, the reduction of armaments, and so on. The Monroe Doctrine was to be interpreted by the United States alone; American assent was withheld from the granting of the Chinese province of Shantung to Japan; and the United States was not bound by any League decision in which any nation cast more than one vote (a provision directed against the British Empire).[61]

The Foreign Relations Committee hearings were largely Senator Lodge's show. He was able to accentuate the Wilson dictatorship image by revealing that neither Secretary of State Robert Lansing nor anyone else had been consulted by Wilson in regard to making the League an inseparable part of the Treaty of Versailles. Lodge also showed that the world-minded Wilson had no knowledge, prior to his arrival in Paris, of the secret treaties made by the other allied powers, which treated many minority peoples as pawns. He enabled minor groups like the Greeks, Serbs, Chinese, Egyptians, and others to voice their protests against being transferred from one imperial master to another. Harding helped in this. Lodge's reservations, though they did not emasculate the League, were phrased with such asperity and with such obliviousness to the moral quality of the League's influence that Wilson rejected them with much indignation. Wilson also claimed that the reservations would require the reconvening of the Peace Conference. In this the President was proved to be wrong. The Lodge reservations were said to be League-preserving and not emasculating, and the leading powers agreed that the Peace Conference did not need to be reconvened. Wilson required the Democratic Senators to vote no on the reservations, though their leader, Gilbert Hitchcock of Nebraska, desired to support them. This lost the support of the "mild reservations" Republicans, who believed in party unity for the 1920 campaign more than in the merits of the League. Hence, on November 19, 1919, in the final vote, the moderates supported Lodge and defeated the treaty without reservations while the Democrats defeated it with reservations.[62]

The most significant part that Harding played in the committee hearings was his encounter with Wilson in a White House conference on August 19–20, 1919 on the question of the moral nature of the League's influence.[63] This revealed in clear-cut lines the difference between the idealistic, world-minded Wilson and the very pragmatic, American-minded Harding. Lodge had elicited from the President the opinion that the obligation assumed by League members under Articles 10 and 11 of the covenant, to protect nations against aggressors, was a moral one. This seemed to the practical-minded politicians a rather easy way to get out of an obligation. And so Harding asked, "If there is nothing more than a moral obligation on the part of any member of the league, what avails [sic] Articles 10 and 11?" This was rather shocking to the President, who rebuked Harding, saying, "Why, Senator, it is surprising that that question should be asked. If we understand an obligation we are bound in the most solemn way to carry it out." Wilson went on to demonstrate the obvious, describing how the revelation of the faith of a great nation in moral principles "steadies the whole world by its promise beforehand that it will stand with other nations of similar judgment to maintain right in the world." Harding's silence was eloquent.

According to Daugherty, Harding's personal encounter with President Wilson was one of the best exposures of the President's obstinacy —at least that was the way it looked in the papers. Daugherty said, "I think you have the old man where the country can see that he was not capable of negotiating a contract of this character or comprehending the effect of it." Referring to the recent ridicule cast on Henry Ford because of anti-Semitic activities, Daugherty added, "I think your questions and his [Wilson's] answers made him look like Ford looked when he got through with his examination." Daugherty urged that somebody should develop Harding's theme in a Senate "speech or two." [64]

7

Although Harding's role in shaping the Lodge reservations was minor, his role in popularizing them was major. It consisted of his oratorical and personal ability to represent the reservations to the League covenant not as carping criticisms made by politicians against their opponents but as constructive Americanizing improvements that would save the League from destruction and assure the retention of world-security benefits that Wilson's overzealousness was losing. As he told Malcolm Jennings privately on September 18, 1919, "There never has been a time when I have not been favorably disposed toward our participation in promoting international action which is designed to establish and maintain the peace of the world. I think such a proposal fairly represents the aspirations of the great majority of the American people, but they do not want it at the excessive cost of surrendered Americanism. . . . I choose to support such a policy as will make it possible for our people to remain proudly American and still contribute of our might and our conscience toward peace and stable democracy throughout the world. This, in short, fairly expressed the attitude of the majority on the Republican side of the Senate—to preserve all of the League proposal which we can with safety to the United States, in the hope that the consciences of the Nations may be directed to perfecting a safe plan of cooperation toward maintained peace." [65]

Harding's ability to blend the Lodge reservations and the League covenant into firm and inspiring Americanism was a blessing to the Republican party. The American people were, of course, by their very nature, Americans first. They were, as a whole, not averse to an American leadership in international progress as long as there was leadership and not entanglement. But they were averse to a long, drawn-out effort of thinking out the pros and cons of the details of the covenant and the reservations. If someone could synthesize them all into a whole that sounded secure and reasonable, they would be satisfied. For the presentation of this kind of popularized synthesis, Harding was superbly qualified.

From the day of the first senatorial debate on the League of Nations to the end of his life, Harding labored vigorously in this role. In his mind there was never the slightest inconsistency in the hundreds of speeches and millions of words that he uttered—be they those he used in the senatorial reservations debate of 1919, the debate on the Wilson League in the presidential campaign of 1920, the conduct of the Washington Conference of 1921–22 for disarmament and Pacific security, the maneuvering toward the withdrawal of American troops from Germany in 1922–23, or his ardent support of American entry into the World Court in the same years.

For the moment analysis must be confined to a description of his September 11, 1919 League of Nations speech upon the opening day of the Senate's consideration of the report of its Foreign Relations Committee and the Lodge reservations.[66] It is of the utmost importance that Harding was the keynote speaker in opening this debate. The Republicans liked his interpretation, and its popular appeal.

Note the contagious self-assurance with which Harding declared that the Republicans were far better able to build an enduring League than were the dictatorial Wilson and his alleged Democratic puppets. As the people learn what is wrong with Wilson and his League, said Harding, they do not learn how to destroy the League but how to conserve and, eventually, how to improve it. Without reservations the covenant of the League was "unthinkable"; with them there was still "a framework on which to build intelligent cooperation. . . . A clearing house for the consciences of people. . . . A semblance of a league on which to build." "If this ratification is made with the reservations . . . there remains the skeleton of a league on which the United States can, if it deems it prudent, proceed in deliberation and calm reflection toward the building of an international relationship which shall be effective in the future." There was no need to perfect it at once. The things that came first were America and its problems. Later on, America would think of the world. When that time came it could really help civilization "by making the covenant of peace everlastingly righteous. . . . Europe needs us infinitely more than we need Europe. . . . We can carry the banners of America to the new Elysium, even though we have to furl them before we enter." Delay would give time for clearer thoughts. "Civilized people are not supposed to move unthinkingly in creating the surpassing covenant of all ages."

A sad thing, said Harding, was that the covenant of the League was the work of an obstinate man who was obsessed with unattainable ideals and theories, a man who would not consult adequately with the Senate. The Senate's responsibilities in the premises were as great as his. "In the most extraordinary and unparalleled wreck in the wake of world-wide war, he consented to counsel and advise with none who have sworn duties to perform, and devoted, essentially alone, his talents and his supreme influence to reformations and restitutions, and the establishment of governments, and the realizations of ambitions and fulfillment of dreams which human struggles and battling principles and heroic sacrifices have not effected since the world began, and never will be realized until the millenial day that marks the beginning of heaven on earth. The situation presented intensely practical problems, and he clung mainly to lofty theories." Harding saw Wilson as a historian who made the mistake of thinking that he could make history as well as write it. "It is easy to understand the perfectly natural and laudable ambition to do the superlative thing which history is waiting to record, which superlative thing was in the historian's mind, but it needed penetrating vision to meet the pressing practical problems which were awaiting solution—and it needed very practical men."

Harding bore down mercilessly on the President's alleged mistakes, listing them one by one. Wilson ignored the secret imperial bargaining of the allied victors who denied the national aspirations of Egyptians, Chinese, Greeks, Slavs, Irish, and Magyars. He failed to get great sea powers like Great Britain and Japan to begin naval reduction. He had unwarranted trust in the moral judgment of selfish League members. He created a supergovernment of the world which would compel the United States to protect the territorial integrity of nations whose subject peoples had national ambitions. He ignored the age-old virtues of nationalism and exaggerated the alleged virtues of a non-existent internationalism. He rejected the mandate of the election of 1918, especially with reference to the known and repeatedly expressed senatorial disagreement with the covenant. He perverted the purposes for which millions of Americans fought in the war from self-defense to the "afterthought" of promoting revolution and world democracy. He sought to involve this nation inextricably and forever in Euro-Asian intrigues through the Armenian mandate.

Harding let his dislike for Wilson carry him to excessive abuse. He tried to shatter Wilson's integrity by claiming that, if he were truly interested in world democracy, the German assault on Belgium should have been "answered with every American gun," and that, if suffering humanity was Wilson's goal, he should have done likewise when the *Lusitania* was sunk. Far more practical and sincere than Wilson's "lofty ideals" was McKinley's action in fighting for the liberation of Cuba and the Philippines in 1898. Harding saw Wilson disuniting the United States by encouraging hyphenated Americanism through sympathy for the ambitions of foreign minorities against their mother countries. Of Wilson's tour in support of the League, Harding said that, if it had political motives and sought "to test popular feeling about putting the presidency permanently in the hands of one equipped to direct the world aright and at the same time merge this republic in a super government of world, he [Harding] welcomed the partisan contest."

On the subject of Americanism, Harding knew how to arouse the national fervor. "I am thinking of America first," he declaimed. "Safety as well as charity begins at home." "Without established American rights there could be no American nation, and we had rather perish than fail to maintain them." "Germany held us in contempt which one militant American voice in authority might have dissolved, but we delayed until two million fighting sons of the republic shot Germany to respectful understanding."

Harding left nothing to the imagination as to why America should be first: it had gone further than any other nation, he declared, in building a sound republic. But it needed much more strengthening before it ventured into world intrigue and perished in the process. "No republic has permanently survived. They have flashed, illumined, and advanced the world, and faded and crumbled." But this should not be America's fate. "I want to be a contributor to the abiding republic. None of us today can be sure that it shall abide for generations to come, but we may hold it unshaken for our day, and pass it on to the next generation preserved in its integrity. This is the unending call of duty to men of every civilization; it is distinctly the American call to duty of every man who believes we have come the nearest to dependable popular government the world has yet witnessed." There should be an America "walking erect, unafraid, concerned about its rights and ready to defend them, proud of its citizens and committed to defend them, and sure of its ideals and strong to support them. We are a hundred million and more to-day, and, if the miracle of the first century of national life may be repeated in the second, the millions of to-day will be the myriads of the future. I like to think, sirs, that out of the discovered soul of the republic and through our preservative actions in this supreme moment of human progress we shall hold the word American the proudest boast of the citizenship in all the world."

Harding's confidence in the rectitude as well as the popularity of his Americanized League position was borne out by the zeal with which he and Hard spread copies of the September 11 speech over Ohio. At Harding's request, Hard had plates made of the speech, and sent them to the leading newspapers in every county of the state. Thousands were printed in Columbus, in addition to several thousands sent by Harding from Washington. These were sent out individually in franked envelopes, and in bundles, to county chairmen with franked mailing tags furnished by the Senator. All in all, said Hard, the speech was given "a very good circulation in Ohio, along newspaper and committee lines." Hard reported "a great number of demands" for the speech. It was received "most favorably here in Ohio and every comment that I have heard on it has been most favorable." Harding himself was quite satisfied. He told Hard on October 3, 1919 that "the distribution of publicity and the transmission of information to the great American public has undoubtedly very greatly altered the existing situation in this country and turned the trend of sentiment in the right direction." [67]

As for joining the League debate personally in Ohio, Harding firmly declined. Hard and Jennings had the situation under control, and there was no need to desert the "true" battlefront, the Senate chambers in Washington. As for the Johnson-Borah wrecking squad, who followed the Wilson itinerary and bespoke the bitter opposition of the irreconcilables, Harding had no sympathy. "I think I have already told you," he wrote Jennings, "that I do not approve of the trailing delegation of the Senate." (This, of course, is not what he told Reily.) The "missionaries" out in the country, he wrote Hard on September 23, 1919, "have been called in and we are all on the job faithfully from this time on." All, that is, except the ultra-isolationist Johnson, who dogged Wilson down to the bitter end in pursuit, Harding said, not of the President or of the League of Nations, but of the presidential nomination in 1920 for himself. As Harding wrote Hard, "I do not quite wish to be charged with the same motives as those which have been impelling the Senator from California." [68] (This, too, is not what he told Reily.)

In the final vote, both the Wilson League and the Americanized League were defeated. But so far as Harding was concerned, that was not the important thing. What was important, he said, was that the President's dictatorship was overthrown, and the balance of power was restored to the American system of government. On the day of the final vote, Harding expressed his sense of victory when he told his fellow Senators, "If there is nothing else significant in the action of this day, you can tell to the people of the United States of America and to the world that the Senate of the United States has once more reasserted its authority and representative government abides." [69]

As might be expected, there was a strong ingredient of anti-foreignism in Harding's views on the League. He approved of the Hiram Johnson reservation directed against the British Empire. This would have exempted the United States from any "election, decision, report or finding" of the League Council or Assembly in which any member and "its self governing dominions, colonies or parts of empire in the aggregate have cast more than one vote." "We are holding off its consideration," Harding told Scobey September 27, "until the last possible moment in the expectation of inducing a number of Senators to join our ranks." [70]

Harding did not like the United States to be subject to the whims and fancies of "insignificant nations" trying to get us to pull chestnuts out of the fire for them. "Frankly," he told E. E. Margraf, "I do not relish the thoughts of an international political body where a lot of insignificant nations have a voting power equal to that of this great republic and which nations are likely to bring before the league all the problems that are based on the enmities and jealousies and rivalries which date back to a period long antedating the Christian era." He feared that "a goodly number of them are looking anxiously to a draft upon American resources in wealth and man-power to settle their problems." [71] Why should America's conscience be bound to the will of "a lot of little European countries?" he asked the Builders' Exchange in Cleveland on December 1, 1919. He was particularly annoyed at the desire of Armenia to be placed under a United States mandate to protect it against Turkey. "That means," he said, "patroling of their country by American troops. My countrymen, let me tell you something. If you ever plant an American soldier in that gateway between the Occident and the Orient, that hotbed of the world, you will never withdraw until the world comes to an end." [72]

9

Nevertheless, Harding predicted that the Americanized League would be adopted early in 1920. At first he worried that the incorporation of so many reservations would be a handicap. He told Scobey so on September 27 as he discussed the Johnson British Empire clause. This, he said, "would open the way for numerous amendments, which would tend to wreck the whole league scheme. A very considerable number of reservationists do not want to adopt such a course." [73] One may well question the sincerity of Harding on this point of too many reservations. The Johnson reservation and fourteen others were endorsed by the Republicans, and did, in fact, prevent an adoption.

However, Harding still believed in a 1920 adoption of an amended League covenant and in a future for that organization. He told Margraf that he had "long been convinced that we ought to make some progress in international cooperation for the prevention of war." The senate Republicans were attempting to "preserve a skeleton of the Covenant . . . so that the conscience of civilized nations may build upon it effectively and prudently in proper reflection and deliberation." [74]

Sincere or not, Harding had convinced himself he was a pro-Leaguer. The real anti-Leaguer was President Woodrow Wilson. "The difficulty with the existing covenant, in the form negotiated, lies in the fact that President Wilson undertook to do the big thing to emblaze his part in history rather than to think of the things which his country might do in making its full contributions to the advancement of civilization." [75] Yes, the League failure was Wilson's fault. As Harding told his friend Judge O. Britt Brown, December 29, 1919, "A very reasonable effort on the part of the Administration forces to affect a compromise would promptly bring about a satisfactory adjustment." [76]

The adjustable Senator Harding had come a long way in the year 1919. He had emerged from the danger of losing the position of Senator to the status of being pushed for the Presidency. He had evolved in the public's view from the attacker of the League of Nations to its savior. Another year and he would go even further.

CHAPTER SIXTEEN

Second-Choice Maneuvering

"The only thing I really worry about is that I am sometimes very much afraid I am going to be nominated and elected. That's an awful thing to contemplate." : : : *Harding to F. E. Scobey, December 30, 1919, Harding Papers, Ohio Historical Society*

Harding's nomination as the Republican candidate for the Presidency at the Chicago national convention was no accident. He was no dark horse, and he was more than the mere favorite son of the Buckeye state. His candidacy was known to political leaders through the nation and was vigorously and skillfully promoted in a well-directed campaign. The primary strategy of Harding's promoters consisted of two basic efforts: (1) to make him a leading second-choice candidate of the convention delegates outside Ohio, and (2) to make him a strong first-choice candidate from his own state.

It is a rule of political arithmetic that the chances for success of an agreed-upon, second-choice candidate for office increase in direct proportion to the number of his first-choice opponents. It was the very nature of Harding's candidacy to encourage a multiplicity of first-choice candidates so that he could concentrate on second-choice promises from all of them. It was also a rule that such a plan be kept quiet, lest other second choices get the same idea and spoil it all. As Harding wrote to C. M. Idleman of Portland, Oregon on March 22, 1920, "I may say to you, confidentially, that we are not revealing all our developing strength because we do not wish to draw too much of the fire of the opposition." [1]

Everybody knows the story of the stalemate at the Republican national convention in June, 1920 when the leading candidates refused to concede to each other, so that eventually the break came and Harding was the beneficiary. But everybody does not know that long before June, 1920, that moment was planned for, and that the phrase "when the break comes," was actually used in the planning. It was used in behalf of Harding as early as December 29, 1919 by W. J.

Smith of Battle Creek, Michigan, who wrote to Harding, "You have many friends in Michigan. When the break comes in the Convention, when there are a number of candidates, you would stand an even show with any candidate whose name is presented to the Convention." [2] It was used on April 2, 1920 when Harding's friend Frank M. Ransbottom of Zanesville, wrote to Henry L. Simons of Minneapolis, "I think he will have the good will of a great many of the instructed delegates, and when the break comes, I shall be disappointed if he is not nominated." [3] It was implied on May 14, 1920, when Fred Blankner of Columbus, in referring to Harding's three chief rivals, Leonard Wood, Frank O. Lowden and Hiram Johnson, told Harding that he thought Wood and Johnson would eliminate each other and the "real contest will be between you and Governor Lowden, which may go a ballot or two when you will get the nomination." [4]

In other words, Harding was a major candidate in a campaign that required considerable secrecy. Nevertheless, he was well known to his fellow Senators, to his fellow Ohioans and to his fellow politicians throughout the nation. He deliberately and skillfully cultivated the friendship of all of these interests and brought his plan to success at the psychological moment. The fact that he was not particularly well-known to the general citizenry of the nation is significant only in that such a condition helped to make his work successful.

2

Before setting about to build up an efficient plan for winning the nomination, Harding had to make up his mind that he wanted to be President of the United States. In his autumn, 1919 contest with the Hynicka-Brown "blackbirds," or Progressives, for control of the Ohio Republican party, the Ohio Senator, with the aid of Daugherty, had foiled the attempt to make him choose between reelection to the Senate and candidacy for the Presidency. But Harding's decision was not a definitive one. He would make his final choice in his own time.[5] (See chapter 14.)

There were very important reasons why he could not put off his decision very long. The compelling reason was that which his friend Hard had told him on the train ride from Toledo to Columbus in February, 1919: that he owed it to his party. There were hundreds of Republicans, city, county, and other local officeholders throughout the state whose tenure depended essentially on the Harding organization helping them against the threat from the Hynicka-Brown faction. There were hundreds more who could expect to move into Democratic vacancies if the State and the nation should revert to Republican control in the election of 1920. These people would work for Harding, if Harding would work for them by running for the Presidency.

This pressure on Harding was the greater because the Hynicka-Brown faction had a new and powerful financial "angel." This was William Cooper Procter, millionaire Cincinnati soap manufacturer, who was disposed to put a goodly share of his fortune into politics with the idea of making General Leonard Wood President of the United States. A political amateur, Procter counted on the help of Walter Brown and Hynicka to offset his own inexperience.

As Warren Harding contemplated these political factors involving his own future and that of the Republican party in Ohio, he conceived a bold idea. If he could detach Walter Brown and his Progressive following from Hynicka and Procter, the chances for reuniting the Ohio Progressive and Regular Republicans and, at the same time, of putting on a vigorous campaign for Harding-for-President would be greatly improved.

Thus Harding's maneuvers against Procter and Hynicka for the support of Brown and the Ohio Progressives were the key to the Senator's decision to seek the presidential nomination. They began with the reports that Brown was responsible for the November 1 dispatch by the Associated Press that Harding had been forced to give up his presidential aspirations by the Ohio advisory committee. The facts were quite the opposite, and the AP dispatch had the effect of weakening Harding in national esteem. Daugherty had rectified the misinformation by his own press release saying that Harding had smoked out his opponents and still retained his choice between the Presidency and reelection to the Senate.[6]

Harding saw in the episode an excellent opportunity to make a sly overture for Brown's support. Both Harding and Clark of the advisory committee had expressed doubts that Brown was the AP's informant. But Harding made the rumor the occasion for suggesting to Clark that it would be a good thing to have a clever man like Brown on Harding's side.

Harding's method was to send Clark two letters dated November 7, 1919.[7] One letter was written for Clark's eyes alone, the other for Brown. As Harding said in letter number one, "The letter which accompanies this note was dictated more or less with the thought that you might want to submit it, in a confidential way, to Walter Brown. I am not insisting that you shall do so, but in consideration of what you wrote concerning him [regarding the AP dispatch], it has occurred to me that perhaps a letter of this sort to you might be shown to him to your advantage at least and probably it will have the good effect of mollifying him in his suspicious of my hostility."

Letter number two of November 7 from Harding to Clark, and designed for Brown's perusal, seemed to be a very innocent epistle of thanks for Clark's handling of the presidential-senatorial choice matter by the advisory committee meeting. But it was really a suggestion that Clark negotiate with Brown for the support of Harding for President. In it Harding told how sincere were his efforts for Republican harmony. He also said that he did not believe the rumors that Brown was responsible for the AP's misinformation. As a matter of fact, Harding went on, he rather liked Brown. (Shades of the War of 1912!) "He is really a very brilliant politician and a man of exceptionally good judgment and I should infinitely prefer to have him a participant in party councils, even though I knew his hand was always against me, than to have him at variance with the party." Harding said he hoped that Clark could enlist Brown in the advisory committee's conciliatory, party-unifying activities.

There was more to the second Harding-Clark letter, of November 7, 1919, than its contents would suggest. No mention was made of patronage, but Harding, by seeking to have Brown as "a participant in party councils," was actually offering Brown—and the Progressives—a share in the patronage that would follow a Republican victory in 1920. Brown himself would thus have a place in the upper echelons of the party.

Clark needed no further urging and proceeded to get the Brown maneuvers under way. Whether he showed the Harding letter to Brown, as Harding suggested, is not known. More likely he conveyed the message to Brown via an emissary—for it is known that such a messenger was sent to see Brown and that his name was George B. Harris, pro-Harding state central committeeman from Cleveland.

Brown himself is the authority for the fact that overtures were brought to him by George Harris. Brown, of course, was at the very moment in touch with Procter. In the Brown correspondence there are five telegrams—two from Wood and three from Procter—beseeching Brown to declare for Wood. The last one, dated December 12, 1919, was from Procter, and read, "I need thee every hour." [8] There is also a letter from Brown to Procter, dated December 2, showing that Brown was aware that Harding wanted his (Brown's) support.[9] Brown related that Harris had called on him on November 30. Harris was, in fact, an emissary from Harding via Clark,[10] who told Brown that Harding did not take seriously Procter's announcement for Wood, and that Harding intended to challenge the Wood candidacy by becoming a candidate himself. Two days later, Brown told Procter, Harris phoned him and invited him to come to Marion for a conference. Brown also told Procter, "I don't know whether I can arrange my plans to see him, and have not concluded that it is worth while."

As a matter of fact, Brown did interview Harding in Marion, and was convinced of the wisdom of supporting Harding instead of Wood for the Presidency. There is no account of what happened at the interview, but in his letter of December 2, 1919, Brown frankly told Procter that Harding was too strong in Ohio, that, indeed, he was too strong in Procter's own county of Hamilton. Harding's ambivalent stand on prohibition had taken care of that. Under the circumstances, Brown said that for him to support Wood would split the Ohio Republican party and elect the Democrats. Brown's words deserve quotation. "In my judgment," he wrote, "there are many members of the Republican organization in Cincinnati who would think it politically unwise to oppose Senator Harding's avowed candidacy." That being the case, "it would be a mistake for me to take any part in the [Wood] campaign, because I may be forced into carrying the brunt of the struggle in the state and accused of trying to break up the party and playing into the hands of the Democrats." (Brown had already done too much of this in 1912 and 1916 to risk trying it again in 1920.) "I cannot permit myself," concluded Brown, "to be drawn into a situation where perhaps almost single-handed I would be obliged to fight half of the Republican friends which I have in the state, and perhaps undo all of the work of conciliation that has been accomplished in the past two years, all in a cause concerning the fundamental soundness of which I have the most serious misgivings." Brown did not mention the patronage side of the deal with Harding. He did not need to.

The Harding-Brown agreement brought great strength to the Harding candidacy. It was the climactic touch in reuniting the Ohio Progressives with the Regular Republicans. It was a near fatal blow to the Procter-Wood challenge. Harding could now declare his candidacy. Two days before he did so, he wrote directly to Brown of his intentions: "I want you to know my contemplated action and I do want you to believe I am very anxious to have your cooperation and support. I was very much interested in our interview at Marion and I was glad to accept, at face value, the many pleasing things you said to me at that time, in spite of the fact that a good many men engaged in political activity in Ohio have endeavored to make me believe that I never could expect any evidences of political friendship at your hands. I have always resisted accepting that belief because I have known of no reason why we should not cooperate together, inasmuch as we are interested in the common cause and there ought to be no grounds on which we can be mutually interes [sic] and fully understood." [11]

This agreement with Brown was later ratified by former Progressive leaders Dan Hanna and A. R. Garford. "I have had some very frank assurances from him," Harding wrote Jennings in January, 1920, "and I have been present at an interview between him and Dan Hanna with Garford and I as witnesses, in which he had made the most unequivocating statements in my behalf and declared that he would support me if I would let him and he would not join in opposition if I refused to let him support me. I can hardly believe the affair was staged. I do not mean by this that he has grown fond of me or has acquired a new confidence in me, but I think he had the political wisdom to see that that's the only course of any promise which he can reasonably pursue." [12] These letters should be read with the usual patronage implications.

Further strength came to the Harding candidacy from assurances that he would be seriously considered outside Ohio. Harry Daugherty took care of this, as he himself told E. Mont Reily of Kansas City. "After canvassing the situation with influential men from all over the country," Daugherty wrote on December 3, 1919, "I advised Senator Harding that he ought to be a candidate." Daugherty said that he had a "very satisfactory talk" with Senator William E. Borah of Idaho. Borah told him that he would support a western man at first, but "thought Harding ought to get into the contest." Daugherty talked "with a dozen of the most influential Senators, including Senator Penrose [of Pennsylvania] who said that there was nothing else for Harding to do but to go in." Daugherty even conferred with George W. Perkins, financial backer of T. R. in 1912, and found that he "is not tied up with Wood, and I am not sure but he may be for Harding." [13]

Yes, there would be strength in the Harding presidential candidacy, if he chose to declare it. There were spirited expressions of trust from solid people. For example, William H. Speer of Jersey City told of the growing disillusionment among the voting public with the militaristic General Wood. "Yours is the crescent and his the declining candidacy." Speer likened the Harding boom to the firmly based, Hanna-sponsored McKinley boom, quoting John Hay's remark to Henry Adams, "There are eels under the rocks that betoken the early collapse of other booms." [14] From one of the wisest of Harding's small-town editor friends, Harry R. Kemerer of Carrolton, Ohio, came similar talk of the fading of Wood, "The district has had enough of the general." He foresaw a completely loyal Harding delegation to the national convention standing undaunted behind their leader. "His friends," Kemerer told Christian, "should see to it that the delegation is, if necessary, for the Senator until Hell freezes over." [15] From Frank Bogardus, an Old Guard Republican wheelhorse, who had a statehouse job in Columbus, came the defy with reference to the Procter-Wood "invasion" of Ohio, "I don't like to see you decorated with the double cross. They can take my job and go to Hell with it before I become a party to the damned thing." [16] Bogardus was one of those who probably would have lost his job if Wood had become President of the United States.

One who well expressed the feelings of state political dependence on Harding of the many subordinate officeholders and officeholding hopefuls was former Governor of Ohio Frank B. Willis, who was to be Harding's successor to the United States Senate. In a letter to Harding of November 17, 1919 he told the Senator that, as "the honored and acknowledged leader of the Republican party in Ohio . . . you owe something to the party." It was an "obligation." Willis' letter was a strong combination of pleading and demanding. "If you do not permit the use of your name as a candidate, the Ohio delegation [to the nominating convention] will be split into petty personal cliques and in the campaign there will be such a factional war as will seriously endanger party success." "Senator," Willis implored, "you and you only can prevent this factional strife, to do so you must be Ohio's candidate for the Presidency." Willis admitted that it would require a personal sacrifice. But "in my opinion you should disregard your personal wish." He did not ask for this "at the point of a gun," he merely pleaded "for the good of the party." He had no doubt that Harding would win the Presidency. [17]

And so it was that Harding decided with profound personal reluctance to run for the Presidency for the sake of Ohio Republican unity and his own political future. As he wrote Reily, November 22, 1919, "The efforts of the Wood supporters to break with the State have made a situation which must be checked if party disruption is to be avoided. Apparently, the only way to effectively check the movement is to permit my friends to use my name as a Presidential candidate in choosing their candidates for delegates to the convention." [18]

There was a strange blend of dignity and naïveté in the Harding-for-President movement. Harding was the latest of the Buckeye statesmen to uphold the ancient role of Ohio's leadership in national politics. Ohio was the "mother" of five or seven Presidents, depending on how one counted. This Ohio leadership had a stabilizing and upbuilding effect on the entire nation. To let it be weakened was to weaken the United States. For Ohio not to try to strengthen the nation every four years with an Ohioan-for-President movement was tantamount to disloyalty, to secession. Daugherty reflected something of this Ohio obsession when he told Ohio Congressman I. R. Foster, in December, 1919, how "certain persons"—meaning Procter and Wood—had thought that "Ohio had seceded and would not be a factor in the next national convention. . . . Some of the old-fashioned Republicans," he avowed, "are of the opinion that Ohio should never secede and should always be a factor in every Republican convention, and especially now when we have such a man who has such a following as Harding has over the United States." [19]

Thus, when Harding made his announcement of presidential candidacy on December 16, 1919, his message breathed that pride in Ohio for its responsibility to the nation. He did not plead for Ohio Republican party unity, he assumed it. He assumed that his supporters meant it when they said that they wanted him for President. This was not the maneuver of a dark horse whose hopes rested on chance. It was the declaration by Ohioans that they had the power and skill to win, not merely for a candidate, but for the welfare of the nation, which depended on a Republican restoration. "One thing must be stated," he warned. "We are all agreed that a thing worth doing at all is worth doing well and with all our might. I could not assent to an enterprise designed merely to control Ohio's representation in the national convention. This undertaking is not without encouragement beyond the borders of our State, and we must play a worthy part, assuring our fellow Republicans of our utter good faith, and that it is ever our belief that party success is of first importance when Republican restoration is so vital to the nation."

It was an Ohio call to Ohio Republicans with Ohio political pride. "I do not forget, however," he said, "that my first obligation politically is to the Republicans of our state, who so generously have honored me, and I cannot ignore the natural and laudable wish to maintain the large part Ohio has taken in the national councils of the party and to invite the attention of Republicans in the nation to the availability of a candidate from our great state." Harding's commitment for Ohio was complete. It was not for mere bargaining purposes. At least, that is what he told publisher Robert F. Wolfe of the *Ohio State Journal* at the time of announcing. "I would dislike," he told Wolfe, "to have anyone believe me so petty or so ready to do a small thing politically as to believe I would enter upon such an enterprise as I have before me, for the sole purpose of bartering the political influence of the great State of Ohio." [20]

Harding always liked to emphasize his duty to those who made possible his rise to fame. "I owe everything," he was quoted in the *Cincinnati Enquirer* as saying, "to the Republicans of Ohio and it is my duty to be governed by their desires in regard to me." [21] To Scobey, he confessed, "Had I abandoned those who are my friends, I would have been guilty of the crime of ingratitude, and then been out with both factions." Daugherty also reminded him of his duty.[22] In May, 1920, as the nomination campaign drew to a close, he reminded Harding of "the great objective, *viz.*, the nomination of an Ohio candidate for the Presidency and the solidifying of the party in Ohio." [23]

Fundamental also was Harding's own political survival. As he wrote to Marshall Sheppey of Toledo at the time of his declaration, "I mean to play the game in the biggest way possible, because my political existence seems to depend more or less thereon." [24]

2

The drive and power of the Harding candidacy became quickly apparent, with Daugherty in the director's booth. "Work, write letters, drive," Daugherty instructed Scobey January 19, 1920. Harding was really the commander and did his own ingenious part. As Daugherty told Reily, December 24, 1919, "I quite agree with you that Harding will not need a guardian; he handles himself fine." [25]

Nevertheless, Daugherty was the manager and, on many important occasions, acted without direct contact with the Senator. "Just remember," he wrote Harding facetiously on December 19, 1919, "you are nothing but a candidate and have no particular rights." Daugherty admitted that he was joking and that this was not the "modest manner in which I generally approach your magnificent presence." But, he added, "Good Lord, let's kid a little while—this is pretty serious. You may be nominated for the Presidency." [26] Harding did not falter in his loyalty to Daugherty. He appreciated Daugherty's political insight and depended on it. "He is much too smart . . . to be intimidated or bamboozled," he told Scobey. "He is vastly much the smartest politician in the bunch and the only one with vision and acquaintance to carry on a nation-wide campaign." Besides, Harding added, "He is the only big fellow in Ohio who doesn't find his system more or less tinctured with jealousy of me." "Daugherty does not own me in any way," Harding assured Scobey, "and I am under no particular spell in my relationship to him. He does have one appealing attribute, namely, that he is cordially for me in the open, and I would rather go to Hell and defeat with an outspoken friend than ascend to the seats of the Mighty by coddling those who are friendly to my face but ready to stab me when I am not looking." [27]

Daugherty put everything he had into the campaign. "I am going now eighteen hours a day," he told Reily December 24. "This is no piker's game," he wrote Scobey, on December 27, 1919, "perhaps I don't know it, having put up every cent for the whole thing until the day after Harding made his announcement." On February 6, 1920, he confessed, "I have never put such strenuous efforts to anything in all my life and I have gone through some experiences." As for finances, he told Reily on April 23, 1920, "I have gone down in my pocket away beyond the stopping point in order to keep this thing going." [28]

It was to be a campaign with an optimum of publicity. This was to be directed by press agent Robert B. Armstrong, who was hired by Daugherty. Armstrong was a Washington correspondent of the *Los Angeles Times*, with headquarters in Washington, and he was ready to accompany Harding on all his trips. Harding was an expert in the business of newspaper publicity, and shaped the program according to his own notions. He told Scobey, January 31, 1920, "We have enlisted a very satisfactory press agent, and I think we are going to have all the publicity that is becoming. It has been my own judgment not to go at it too vigorously in order to reach the high tide of our publicity movement until late in the campaign. Some enterprises make such a booming start that they fizzle out later on." [29] The Harding campaign was to be a skillfully publicized show.

And what a show it was. Daugherty picked December 9, 1919 for a display of Harding strength in Washington on the occasion of a meeting of the Republican national committee. On that day Harding headquarters were opened at the New Willard Hotel amidst the fanfare of a lavish dinner attended by Ohio congressmen, an enthusiastic delegation of Marion boomers, and, of course, Harding himself. The build-up preceeding this had included canvassing Ohio Republican legislators and announcing their support of Harding for President. After this, it was Congressmen who were canvassed with the idea of making them more aware of Harding's appeal. No "trumpets or brass bands"—just good, honest, man-to-man talk. This was the spirit of Daugherty's letter of December 4 to Ohio Congressman I. R. Foster. Foster was to confer with Republican friends who were interested in Harding. Then he was "to see every Republican member of Congress immediately and impress upon each the necessity and great desirability of taking the time to meet Republican members of the National Committee who will be there next week, and chairmen of the State committees . . . and generally influential Republicans over the country, and impress upon them the fact that Harding is the one man that can carry Ohio." [30] Daugherty did his own share of making contacts, but, as he told Christian, "they must be important, if I am to see them at all." [31]

Daugherty's idea was to create a folksy image of Harding, a new McKinley, an old-fashioned, friend-winning personality. "Comparing Harding with McKinley has been on my lips and pen for three months," he wrote Scobey. "I have written a thousand interviews about it and it is a part of a methodical plan over the country to compare Harding with McKinley and a campaign like McKinley's." [32] Tell them, he told Foster, "that he is more like McKinley than any other man that ever lived, and that he will make a thoroughgoing, straight-forward, partisan, courageous Republican President. . . . that he is a likable man whom the people will take to, and there will be some old-fashioned kindliness and wholesome enthusiasm in a campaign with Harding as the candidate like that akin to the candidacy of McKinley and that we have not had since." No more pushy Roosevelts, reserved Tafts, and intellectual Wilsons.

This McKinley image got another boost from Daugherty. He arranged with Harding's friends Beecher W. Waltermire and Hoke Donithen for the preparation of a campaign biography. It was a booklet entitled, "Senator Warren G. Harding," and was sponsored by the Marion Harding-for-President Club. Harding emerged from its pages not only as a new McKinley but as Abraham Lincoln, Theodore Roosevelt, and Sir Galahad. He was the son of a country doctor "who found no night too dark and dreary and no journey too long" over almost impassable roads "to go to the relief of a suffering patient, however poor and unable to pay for the services rendered." He was of "good old colonial stock" with ancestors who fought, bled, and died in the Revolutionary War. As a farm boy he "learned to fell trees, chip wood, split rails, plant and hoe corn and do all things incident to farm life when crops were raised between roots and stumps. . . . No fabled goddess hovered over the chamber when he was born. . . . [He was] just a natural, healthy, robust boy of humble but honest parentage, endowed with the supreme gifts of nature—good, hard, common sense, a rugged constitution, a sunny disposition and a heart full of the milk of human kindness." He was a "boyhood leader," a college man "high in scholarship," an "expert typesetter," proprietor of a prosperous, money-making newspaper, "always a booster, never a knocker," "always conservative and fearless," a bank director, a church trustee, a three-time traveler to Europe, where he spent his time "not on pleasure bent, but to study at close range their systems of government and economic problems" such as the tariff and wages, always returning to the United States "with a deeper love for his own land and a firmer conviction that its form of government is the best which was ever devised by the brain of man." There was the usual praise for loyalty to party in 1912, the 100,000 plurality in 1914, reconciliation with Roosevelt, and special emphasis on his masterly job of presiding over the 1916 convention. He was a convincing orator, never verbose, and appealed "to head and heart, never to passion or prejudice." He was "first of all a patriot," and believed that "the problems which vitally concern us are domestic and not foreign. . . . With the ship of state befogged, a wavering hand at the wheel, anxiety in the cabin, there is need for a commander who can guide us away from the rapids. . . . The record of Warren G. Harding, in public and private life, indicates that he is the logical man of the hour." [33]

The preparation of this Waltermire-written and Daugherty-inspired biography was a prime example of the driving intensity of the Daugherty leadership. This showed in Daugherty's letter to Hoke Donithen, the Marion contact man for this phase of the Harding campaign. On December 30, 1919 Daugherty wrote: "I am very anxious to hurry this matter. There is a great demand for it over the country and we should have it in the hands of Republicans to educate them as to what Harding is, where he came from, and where he should go. Keep driving at this and see Waltermire, of the Utilities Commission, won't you please? Try to see him on Friday of this week, if possible. You can make an appointment with him over the telephone. . . . I know you will do it. I saw Harding yesterday. He said you were a good old horse like I was and would work. I know that things look good. Don't worry but work on." Three days later, Daugherty wrote again: "Your efficiency helps very very much. I understand Waltermire was over to see you yesterday. I hope this work may be completed in the next few days. There is a great demand for this sort of literature." In a week the job was done, and Christian, Harding's secretary, wrote, "I am very glad to know that you and other friends have been of some assistance to Waltimaier [sic] in producing something forceful and effective." Christian added, "Even if W. G. did spend some time hoeing corn I doubt very much the value of his efforts." [34]

The Daugherty-Donithen correspondence revealed another important feature of Daugherty's promotionalism. This was to show Harding to the businessmen of the United States as a fully qualified businessman of his own home town. On December 19 Daugherty instructed Donithen:

Form a committee especially at once to see every business man, in fact, everybody in Marion and have them write strong personal letters urging Harding's availability to everybody in the United States. Let this work start at once. When the Chamber of Commerce resolutions are adopted have the Harding people and his paper see that it is carried in the Associated Press as fully as possible; also see that copies are mailed to every member of the Chamber of Commerce in the United States; every Republican member of Congress; the chairmen of the state central committee; every member of the National Committee. You have the list of members of the National Committee and the list of chairmen of the State Central Committees in the United States. . . . We want particularly to develop Harding as a man who has been in touch with and a part of the business structure of his community and the country. The demand will be for a man with such accomplishments, so in your resolutions make that fact strong.

Daugherty requested that Donithen at once send in a list of the businesses in Marion with which Harding was connected. Donithen did so, listing the Marion County Bank, the Marion Lumber Company, the Home Building Savings and Loan Company, the Pendergast

Company, the Harding Publishing Company, and the Olean Realty Company.[35]

Financially, also, Daugherty was active, with modest results. Frank Whittemore of Akron, he told Harding on December 19, was a "gold nugget and true as steel." In another letter of the same day, he told of a check for $1,000 from Mrs. Annie Norton Battelle of Columbus and of another from the "home folks" at Marion. "I thought I would like to have a woman make the first contribution," he said, "and in due time we will use the fact by publishing it." Daugherty suggested that Harding write her "a nice little note." "She will help some more too," he added. All in all, he concluded, "we are going along and the word is going out to everybody to pull, push, pray and work. That's the motto." However, to Reily, Daugherty professed that financially he was very discouraged. Part of this was because of Harding's own fear of overdoing financial solicitation. "Do not approve of state wide canvass for friends," he wrote to Dr. Charles M. Sawyer on February 1, 1920.[36]

That Daugherty was in command was frankly acknowledged by chairman Fairbanks of the Ohio Republican central commitee. It developed that a meeting of the Republican national committee was scheduled at Chicago at the same time, January 6, 1920, as the Ohio Society of New York's annual banquet, at which Harding was to speak. At first, Daugherty had wanted Fairbanks to go to New York with an Ohio delegation, but later he asked him to go to Chicago instead. Former Governor Willis and the state central committee vice-chairman were to be in Chicago. "But I am afraid," Daugherty wrote Fairbanks, "they cannot handle the situation." To this Fairbanks dutifully replied that he would do as he was bidden. "You are the Director General," he wrote Daugherty, "and I am one of the soldiers whose duty it is to obey orders, and this I am trying to do, so give me any specific directions you have in mind in relation to this work in Chicago, that I may move in accord with your desires and plans." [37]

3

Speechmaking was Harding's forte, and Daugherty recognized it. "I am very comfortable," Daugherty said, "in regard to your speeches. If I was not I would be crazy. I am far more comfortable as to your ability to cope with great public questions and public appearances, petitions and utterances, than I am for you to deal with those who are engaged in intrigue. I will take care of the latter and together we will make a fair combination in this great enterprise." [38] Handling intrigues covered a lot of ground, as we have already seen, and as we will subsequently observe.

Nevertheless, Daugherty was much concerned with the assignment, subject matter, and publicity of and for Harding's speeches. He wanted Harding to keynote in a New York City speech early in January at the Waldorf-Astoria. He wanted three regional keynote speeches in the West. The subjects must be Americanism and defense of the Constitution against subversive influences such as Bolshevism and the League of Nations. Enormous publicity would accompany these performances. This program was followed to the letter, including the Americanism emphasis. According to Daugherty in 1932, he and Harding went over the final manuscript of the Waldorf-Astoria address together. This claim is borne out by Harding's own invitation of December 29, 1919 asking Daugherty to go over it with him. It is also borne out by Daugherty's remark to Reily by letter of December 27 that Harding was to prepare speeches for New York and Cleveland and that "we will go over them on Monday." [39]

These were the days of all days to talk Americanism. A secret foreign enemy was said to be lurking in the land. Some called it Bolshevism, others the "red peril," still others, "bloody anarchism." It began with the 1919 May Day bomb plot and the discovery that thirty-six homemade bombs had been mailed to distinguished anti-radical Americans with the apparent intention that the recipients would be wiped out upon opening their packages. Only two casualties took place: Georgia Senator Thomas W. Hardwick's maid had her hands blown off, and his wife was severely burned. Riots followed as vigilante groups organized to defy radicals and allegedly subversive organizations. A particularly nasty affair took place in Centralia, Washington on Armistice Day, November 11, 1919, when parading World War I veterans were shot at by some organized "Wobblies," (I. W. W. members) who claimed to be acting in self defense. Four veterans were killed and one "Wobbly" emasculated and then lynched. Attorney General A. Mitchell Palmer organized agents to go about discovering the alien "enemies within our gates." Eventually 249 of them were deported. On January 2, 1920, four days before Harding's much-heralded Waldorf-Astoria keynote, mass roundups in thirty-three cities of 4,000 suspected radicals took place. Thousands of persons and many societies vied with each other to declare the virtues of Americanism and the need for self-defense.[40] Harding was one of these.

The temper of Harding's January 6, 1920 campaign keynote speech at the Waldorf-Astoria was not hysterical.[41] It had the effect of a great leader calming his excited listeners. But it was all-American. It was calm, dignified, reassuring, yet fervent, unafraid, inspiring. He avoided the role of the ranting demagogue, but he did not reach anywhere near the level of a highly intelligent analysis of America's problems. He was poised and sincere—and this helped to reassure the commonsense, moderately intelligent, upper-middle-class, and business-minded listeners in his celebrity-studded audience.

Harding interpreted American history to be the revelation of an inspiring evolution into an "ordered liberty" which he called Americanism. It was institutionalized in the Constitution of 1787. By this document "the star of the American republic was set aglow in the world firmament." "On that day," he said, "Americanism began, robed in nationality. . . . On that day America headed the forward procession of civil, human and religious liberty, which ultimately will effect the liberation of all mankind. . . . The world's orderly freedom has come of its inspiration." That was enough for America to contribute to the world. The central thing for us was the restoration of "a sane normalcy" at home. The League of Nations would not make us normal. Those who said that it would were only making the "plea of the patent-medicine fakir whose one remedy will cure every ill." As a matter of fact, he said, "actual peace prevails and commerce has resumed its wonted way." Our country "required no council of foreign powers to point the way of American duty. We wish to counsel, cooperate, and contribute, but we arrogate to ourselves the keeping of the American conscience and every concept of our moral obligations."

In the meantime we must work out our own sensible salvation on practical lines. "It is fine to idealize, but it is very practical to make sure our own house is in perfect order before we attempt the miracle of the Old-World stabilization." He commended the simple virtues of thrift and industry, and legitimate personal aspirations. He commended the desire of the normal American "to lift his children to a little higher plane than mediocrity can bring and which socialism never reaches." We had to educate the poor, deluded foreigner, who was "more a victim than a conspirator." We have failed to counteract the agitators by failing to "teach the American language," by failing "to utter American sympathies," by forgetting the "extent of American fellowship," and by omitting "the revealment of the loftiest ideals of American citizenship." He sought to calm his listeners about "impotent Russia" and its "misapplied and bolshevistic democracy." "Let Russia experiment in her fatuous folly until the world is warned anew by her colossal tragedy. And let every clamorous advocate of the red regime go to Russia and revel in its crimsoned reign. This is law-abiding America."

It was very inspirational. It closed with a credo that was repeated again and again in campaign documents, in orations, in newspapers and magazines—not only by Harding but by others.

> Call it the selfishness of nationality if you will, I think it an inspiration to patriotic devotion—
>> To safeguard America first,
>> To stabilize America first,
>> To prosper America first,
>> To think of America first,
>> To exalt America first,
>> To live for and revere America first.

This atmosphere of red peril helped Harding in courting the labor vote. Militancy in union activity was associated with radicalism, and radicalism meant association with Bolshevism. As the Senator wrote on September 12, 1919 in support of Clark's efforts to promote labor loyalty to the Republican party, "I find it exceedingly gratifying that there are strong Union Labor men who can think soberly about some of the proposed radicalism which is undertaken in these trying days." [42]

4

The most important part of the Harding-for-President boom was the second-choice plan. Obviously Harding would not make much of an impression merely by having the delegates from his own state. There had to be systematic work on a national scale. As Harding told Ransbottom, on February 14, 1920, "If I am to succeed in the political enterprise on which I have ventured I must give essentially all my attention to matters outside our own State. . . . The winning of the Presidential nomination must come from the friends to be made outside our own borders. It is because of this that I am giving so much time to activities outside the State." Harding had many friends throughout the nation, and it was wise to make use of them. "The situation here is very comforting," George Christian told a friend on March 31, 1920. "We find a friendly feeling in each state and I feel confident that the situation will arise in Chicago which will make Harding the logical candidate." [43]

There were at least nine aspirants besides Harding for the Republican nomination. They were:

> General Leonard Wood of the U.S. Army
> Governor Frank O. Lowden of Illinois
> Senator Hiram Johnson of California
> Herbert Hoover of California
> Nicholas Murray Butler of New York
> Senator Howard Sutherland of West Virginia
> Governor Calvin Coolidge of Massachusetts
> Governor William C. Sproul of Pennsylvania
> Senator Miles Poindexter of the State of Washington

Each of these opponents was treated with the technique best adapted to Harding's advantage. Wood and Hoover were fought openly, the other seven were flattered and encouraged in the hope that they would kill each other off and, in the aggregate, keep Wood from getting a majority of delegates, while Harding worked the second-choice game. Even Senator William E. Borah of Idaho and Governor James P. Goodrich of Indiana were patronized for the purpose of gaining the good will of their followers for Harding.

Wood, of course, was the man to beat. His boom, like Harding's, had begun following the death of Theodore Roosevelt on January 6, 1919. Memories persisted of Wood's association with T. R. in the Rough Riders' enterprise of the Spanish-American War, and in the preparedness movement prior to United States entry in World War I. Wood had shared in the martyrdom complex resulting from the denial to both of them a spectacular part in the fighting in Europe. The boom was lavishly financed. It nourished the concept of the need of the country in the reconstruction period for the steadying influence of a practical man whose strength of character and capacity for decisive action was preferred to the deviousness of smooth politicians and pettyfogging Senators.[44]

Harding did not oppose Wood because he was a military man. If the public wanted a general for President, that was all right. But if the public did not want such a man that too was all right. In other words, Harding did not judge the matter on the basis of principles, but on the basis of expediency. Hence, when it became apparent that the public was developing strong scruples on the idea of a military President, Harding made up his mind. At first, Harding dodged the issue. "I confess," he wrote Kemerer of Carrollton on November 11, 1919, "my inability to pass final judgment on this question." He needed a little more time to discover the consensus of public opinion.[45] When a strong feeling began to develop against Wood on the military issue, Harding followed. Thus he wrote H. V. Fisher of New York City on December 23, 1919, that he was persuaded to become a presidential candidate partly "because of the very strong prevailing conviction that the deliberate judgment of the country would not favor a military candidate." [46]

Harding's second-choice handling of the Lowden-for-President boom was crucial. It paved the way for the famous switch of Lowden delegates to Harding on the last day of the June, 1920 convention in Chicago. Harding's sportsmanlike conduct in refusing to enter the Illinois primaries against the state's Governor contrasted sharply with the rashness of the Wood activity in Illinois. The Wood challenge helped make the Illinois endorsement of Lowden far from unanimous. It engendered bitter feelings in loyal Illinoisians. Wood allied with Chicago Mayor William H. Thompson against Lowden and caused Chicago Republican voters to send over 600 Wood delegates to the state convention. Lowden was endorsed by a small majority. The harsh things that were said against Lowden by the heavily financed Wood campaigners help to explain the refusal of Lowden to join with Wood at the climax of the June convention. Lowden turned his delegates over to Harding instead.[47]

Harding's encouragement of the Lowden candidacy was exhibited from the very beginning of the Lowden boom. He knew of the Illinois Republican factionalism between Mayor Thompson and the rest of the state, but, unlike Wood, he rejected the urgings to take advantage of it. Such urgings came from Chicagoan W. S. Sarter, December 10, 1919, "Push, Push, Push for the nomination. You can win over Lowden in his own state. He does not stand very high with the public here." [48]

Harding rejected all such anti-Lowden suggestions. When Harding's Chicago relative, Everett Harding, followed up the Senator's presidential announcement of December 16 with a move to form a Harding-for-President club, Christian wired him to suspend operations at once. Later Harding informed his relative that Lowden was entitled to the support of his own state. The Senator said that he would resent outsiders contesting him in Ohio. "I had much rather," he wrote, "treat Governor Lowden with the courtesy and consideration which is due than to attempt any activities and incur the resentment of him and his friends." On February 27, 1920 he wrote to L. K. Torbet, a candidate for delegate to the Illinois nominating convention, disapproving of any opposition to Lowden in Illinois. He added, "I would delight myself to be a second choice preference among the goodly number of your delegates but I would not want to participate in a direct contest with Governor Lowden for the support of your state." Torbet was sympathetic, "If Illinois cannot furnish the GOP nominee," he wrote, "Ohio must." When Chicago Negro journalist Nahum D. Brascher sent Harding a copy of his editorial favorable to the Harding boom, the Senator wrote similarly, "I have felt I should be content in taking my chances as second-choice of a large percent of the delegation from Illinois." Harding took the same tack in Nebraska and Virginia, writing to the Lowden leaders there—Frank A. Shotwell of Lincoln, Nebraska, and C. Bascom Slemp in Virginia—soliciting second choices in case Lowden's nomination was not successful. Both Shotwell and Slemp said that Harding was viewed with much favor by many delegates in their respective states.[49]

The Harding treatment of the Hiram Johnson boom was equally skillful. The arrangements to support Senator Johnson in California in return for second choices for Harding were direct and forthright. On January 20, 1920 Harding wrote to his former senatorial colleague from California J. H. Rossiter, of San Francisco, assuming that California Republicans were united on Johnson for President. "However," he wrote, "there may come a time when his nomination develops to be an impossibility, in which event I would like to be kindly considered by the men who represent California in the National Convention. . . . There always does come a time in the Convention when the support of the majority narrows down to one man. It is in that particular moment when I would like to have some friends in the California delegation." Harding, therefore, suggested that, if Rossiter was "so inclined and could do so without embarrassment," he would "say the word here and there which would lead to a favorable consideration of my ambitions." Rossiter replied that he would be glad to do this. He described the reunion movement in California behind Johnson to prevent a repetition of the "sad result in 1916" and was glad to report that "we are once again a happy family," except for the "misguided ones who are 'shouting Hoover.'" There would probably be an equal number of Progressives and "Old-line" Republicans in the California delegation. The "real fight," he said, was against Wood and Lowden and, "as the affair developed I believe it would be settled as between Johnson, Harding or Poindexter—all friends of mine." [50]

Former Senator Rossiter did a thorough job for Harding. By the time he was through with the arrangement, the Johnson-Harding second-choice deal was accomplished. He reported to Harding on February 29, 1920, "The delegation as agreed upon will, in major part at least, be strong for you as second choice and I can speak with certainty on this part, as I have discussed the question fully with all of the leaders, including the closest friends of Senator Johnson and when the delegation is organized, you may be sure that I will continue to work along that line." [51]

Daugherty, of course, was in full approval of the Johnson deal. Its specific purpose was to heal the wounds of 1912. "We all like Senator Johnson," wrote Daugherty to Reily on February 6, 1920. "Harding is fond of him and so am I and if Johnson loses the Presidency and Harding wins we will treat him and his friends right. It would be a good way to patch up this old feeling which started in 1912 and help and trust each other." [52] This letter helps to explain Harding's encouragement of Johnson's expression of vigorous anti–League of Nations views.

It should be emphasized that Harding was an anti-Johnsonite to the extent that he thought Johnson was too radical, not only on the League of Nations question, but in appealing to the Bolshevik element, and in being too pro-labor. As he told Scobey, "Johnson will make a very small showing outside the state of California. . . . [He] may appeal to the Bolshevist sentiment of some of the wild and wooly Western states and develop the following, but he will never cut much of a figure in the national convention." Moreover, on certain labor matters Johnson votes "according to the order of Gompers"—meaning president of the American Federation of Labor, Samuel Gompers.[53]

Harding gave further aid and comfort to the Johnson boom by showing his opposition to the bid of Herbert Hoover for California delegates. "I have been well aware," he wrote L. R. Loomis of San Francisco, "of the formidable character of the Hoover movement." But he doubted that a man who had served under Wilson so long during the war had enough Republican qualifications to be a serious contender. Besides, Harding added, "I have a very strong conviction that in its deliberate moments the country does not want a dictatorial and autocratic personality like that we know our friend, Hoover, to possess." Harding told Scobey that, if Hoover becomes President, "we will have a tighter little autocracy than we had under the war administration of President Wilson." There was little chance for Hoover to become the autocrat of the White House if we may believe Rossiter's description of what the Progressive-Regular coalition did to him. "With both factions well represented on the Republican delegation," he assured Harding, "there should be no chance for the Hoover ticket." [54]

Another aid to Harding's designs on Johnson was Johnson's anti-League friend, Senator William E. Borah. In December, 1919, when there seemed to be a possibility that Idaho might push for Borah's nomination, Harding instructed his friend Albert White of Glenn's Ferry, Idaho, to withhold all Harding promotion. "I wish to observe all the properties," Harding wrote. Later, Borah put his influence behind Johnson. This whetted Harding's appetite, although he still kept himself within the bounds of "the proprieties." He wrote to White, April 1, 1920, "Senator Borah, of course, will be strongly for Senator Johnson in the early expressions of the Convention. I think he looks upon me with considerable favor in case it is impossible to nominate Senator Johnson." On the same day, Harding put it very frankly when he wrote to Charles R. Forbes of Spokane, "I think we can count on the friendly attitude of Borah to help things come our way if it is apparent that Johnson can not succeed." By April 18, 1920 White was able to report to Harding, "Your candidacy in this state is now receiving serious consideration by Republican leaders." [55]

Oddly enough, Harding in one instance, contributed involuntarily to the slowing down of the Johnson boom. This happened in the Indiana primaries in May. The conservative Republicans of the Hoosier state believed it would be a calamity for their party to endorse such a radical as Johnson. They, therefore, agreed to concentrate on Wood, with the result that Wood nosed Johnson out, while Lowden and Harding ran a very poor third and fourth. The *Indianapolis Star* commented on the "fine service rendered by those supporters of Lowden and Harding who, at the last moment, sensed the danger of Johnson, and threw their votes to Wood in order to save the good name of the state. If they had not done this act of patriotic sacrifice, the brains and character of Indiana would have been discredited all together today, instead of giving the world an exhibit in wise and courageous patriotism." Harding wryly observed that if the *Star* had only shown a semblance of this post-mortem courtesy during the campaign, he would have been able to make a much better showing.[56]

Harding's support of Johnson was, to some degree, disingenuous. The Ohio Senator indicated to Californians that the second-choice deal was mutual. But in Ohio, it was a requirement that there be no second-choice concentration on anybody. Thus, on May 18, he wrote to Conrad Schweitzer of Los Angeles that six of the Harding delegates in Ohio were pledged to Johnson for second choice. "If the time comes when it is apparent that I have no chance to win, I have no doubt that these six delegates will go to the support of Senator Johnson." Of course, he added that he hoped that that time would not come. On the other hand, Harding specifically prescribed the limitations on the second-choice selection in Ohio when he informed Dr. L. C. Weimer of Dayton that "it would utterly destroy all our chances if the delegation from Ohio were overwhelmingly in favor of any one candidate as second choice." His own notion was that "good politics" required ten second choices for Wood, ten for Lowden, and probably ten more for Senator Johnson. The remainder should be scattered among the other candidates.[57]

Harding's strength on the Pacific coast and in the Rocky Mountain states was vigorously promoted by the activities of Charles R. Forbes of Spokane in relation to the presidential ambitions of Senator Miles Poindexter of the state of Washington. Few took the Poindexter candidacy seriously. Therefore, Harding and Forbes took it very seriously for the purpose of its grist of second choices. Forbes had been a very enthusiastic friend of Harding's ever since 1915 when the two had met in Honolulu. Forbes wrote on December 7, 1919, with characteristic enthusiasm, telling of his plans to promote Harding sentiment in the Northwest. Harding replied on December 16, asking him not to antagonize Poindexter, and made the usual suggestion of cooperating with Poindexter's friends "in a manner to make sure of securing their support at such time as they might become convinced that he can not be made the nominee of the Convention." Harding said that Poindexter was much inclined to be cordial, and would "cooperate with a friendly understanding." Daugherty wrote Forbes to the same effect and was assured that all was under control. Forbes said that not even

Roy Slater, Poindexter's manager, expected the boom to spread. Slater and other "big men" admired Harding very much, and this would do the Ohio Senator much good in the long run. "I am very sure," he wrote Harding December 29, 1919, "that we are going to be able to carry out a very successful Harding program in the Pacific Northwest." This pleased Harding, who urged Forbes to continue in the good work. Forbes spent the winter combining politics with business in Washington, Idaho, Montana, and Oregon, reporting great success in all four states. On March 20, 1920 he wrote Harding, "We know you must succeed, Senator, and we are going to work to that end, no matter how things look." [58]

The New York situation was favorable to the Harding second-choice strategy. Harding's emissary to New York was Fred Starek, a man of some wealth with friendships among politicians and businessmen. He reported that the Republican party in New York state was divided into seven or eight regional organizations, each under a "satrap," whose powers corresponded to Boss Cox's of Cincinnati. Each one was open to "persuasion and conviction, and would not remain behind the candidacy of Columbia University President Nicholas Murray Butler, to whom they were willing to accord initial complimentary votes." Wood and Lowden were not at all popular, and Johnson was too radical for all but a few "hotheads." This "leaves them open to argument respecting their second choices, and therein lies your opportunity, which I consider quite favorable now."

After several months of "observing" the situation, Starek was able to report much improvement in Harding's standing in New York. Herbert Parsons, the liberal New York member of the Republican national committee, was anti-Wood and would not go to Butler. The conservative Chauncey M. Depew would cast a couple of votes for Butler, but "actually he is for you and will vote for you. More than that, he will *work* for you and is doing so already." Starek told how Governor Clement of Vermont came to Depew for advice, and Depew suggested that he back Harding. "This," wrote Starek, "he assured me he will continue to do." Clement, he added, was impressed and would carry the word back home. Harding's old friend Charles D. Hilles, who was a delegate from New York, would, of course, support him after a complimentary vote for Butler. All in all, summarized Starek in April, "it is my dispassionate judgment that the bulk of the New York delegates can be swung over to you," especially since the Wood sentiment seemed to be on the decline. "The fact that you are pursuing a gentlemanly, courteous and dignified course is being commended by people who are watching development." Starek suggested such names as Otto Kahn, Ogden Mills, and others for Harding to write to, and the Senator promised to do so.[59]

Then there was Governor Calvin Coolidge of Massachusetts. Nobody took his presidential boom seriously either, except that Harding, as usual, used it as a springboard for his second-choice promotion. As he told Scobey, on December 30, 1919, "I have a bully good lot of friends there after they have done their duty in supporting Coolidge." Earlier, Russell A. Wood, president of the Republican Presidential Club of Massachusetts, urged Harding to campaign in Massachusetts. Harding replied sharply, declining to do any such thing. "I joined with the country," Harding said, "in rejoicing over the re-election of Governor Coolidge last November, and since Massachusetts evidently means to support him for a Presidential nomination, I would not consent in any way to put a strain in the way of his united support by the old Bay State." Harding had a strange letter from Massachusetts legislator and former mayor of Salem Herman A. MacDonald, apologizing for the Coolidge candidacy and suggesting to Harding that the "greatest number of second choices will eventually win the nomination." He, therefore, offered to write to all Massachusetts delegates urging Harding as their second choice. Harding, of course, accepted MacDonald's offer.[60]

With Senator Howard Sutherland of West Virginia, it was the same. On January 12, 1920 Harding wrote to Olin C. Carter of Middlebourne, saying he did not want to compete with the state's favorite son. Yet eight days later, he told Scobey, "The candidacy of Sutherland is not to be considered seriously. I have been in intimate touch with the leaders in his State and I know the West Virginia situation accurately, and am entirely pleased about it." [61]

Harding gave Pennsylvania Governor Sproul the same encouragement for favorite sons whose chances for being nominated were slim. As the Keystone state was sure to be Republican, there was great incentive for Harding to seek its second-choice favor. The occasion came in the spring of 1920 when Sproul wrote apologizing for not being able to entertain the Ohioan at his home in Chester when Harding was in the vicinity. Mrs. Sproul had done the honors, and the Governor said that she was so charmed by Harding that she had decided to "veto" her husband's presidential ambitions. In his reply, marked "Purely Personal," Harding graciously protested against Mrs.

Sproul's "veto" and added that he had "never held to the belief that a man should be penalized and denied political ambitions outside his state because he has a residence in an overwhelmingly Republican State." "There will be no quarrel," Harding added, "if events should so transpire that you should be the choice of the Chicago convention." [62] No mention, of course, was made of second choices for Harding, but he would get his share when the time came.

In Texas the second choices came to Harding in an unusual way. His loyal friend F. E. Scobey, of San Antonio, started out with the idea of winning the entire Republican state delegation for Harding. Eventually Scobey had to settle for considerably less, as his letter to Harding of May 8, 1920 revealed. At the county convention, he said, he and a Wood man made a deal to be the district's two delegates on a mutual second-choice pledge. Scobey said that he could have controlled the entire district and sent two Harding men from it, but "this chap is a very important man and has five or six state leaders that will be on the delegation for Wood as first choice, and if I had slapped him in the face, I am satisfied that he would have deprived us of this support at the Convention." As it was, by letting him go, "we can get most of the state" by the second-choice method. [63]

Scobey's plan was to get himself named as a Harding delegate to the national convention, and to promote Harding as second choice for the rest of the delegates, who were mostly for Wood, but "are all pretty reasonable fellows." As he told Daugherty, on January 16, 1920, "What we are trying to do is to get the right personnel on this delegation and after the first or second ballot, if we can show that Harding is in the running, I am satisfied we can get the big end of this delegation." H. F. Macgregor, Texas national committeeman, was friendly but cautious. Daugherty encouraged Macgregor with the promise not to set up a state Harding organization because, as he said, "to open headquarters in Texas might discourage the local state organization and might possibly interfere with some plans you have. We are not willing to fuss up the Texas organization." Daugherty and Macgregor had quite an understanding, if one interprets correctly the following Daugherty remarks to the Texan: "I am not worrying about you, nor will I at any time until it is absolutely necessary to jump on you with both feet. I am going to continue to trust you. You understand me and my position." A Texas primary tour was arranged for March, 1920. [64]

The Texas delegation at Chicago was not a Harding delegation, but it was Harding-conditioned. Macgregor had informed Scobey that he expected Harding to put on an aggressive primary campaign. "I can only say," he told Daugherty, "that the country at this time is not looking for a candidate that is afriad." Neither Macgregor nor Daugherty was well pleased with Harding's showing in the primary campaign, especially in Ohio. As convention time approached Daugherty was worried, but told Scobey that "in the ruck the convention might turn to Harding." He strengthened that hope with specific instructions to Scobey as to the handling of the Texas delegates. "As a friend of Senator Harding," wrote Daugherty on May 8, "I am making the request of you that you be at the convention as early as possible—in advance of the opening, if convenient—that we may take council together and assign our various parts. Naturally you will, first of all, look after matters in your own state. We shall want a full and complete understanding of all the circumstances and conditions of your delegates as to their first and second choice, and with respect to all preliminary matters before the Convention. These matters must be intrusted to those best informed. I shall feel free to ask you early and fully advising these facts." [65]

It is important to record that Scobey's influence lined up Harding with the "lily-white" faction in Texas Republican politics. Late in 1915 Harding had promised Scobey that he would talk to Daugherty about bringing the Texan "into the confidence of the National Organization." Scobey was pleased and described his intentions: "I will not hook up with the fellows that are running things here now," he told the Senator on January 6, 1916. "They are crooked and Macgregor knows they are crooked, and if he will give us a square deal and will seat our delegates if we win in a straight fight we can reorganize a decent Republican Party in San Antonio and get control." The trouble with the local organization was that it was "handled by a little crooked Jew and another chap who has no standing, and you can't get twenty-five responsible white men to follow them. . . . We could get up a fine organization here if it was led by respectable white people." Harding was quite understanding. He wrote Scobey on January 20, 1916, "I can understand why you declined to hitch up with any crooked agent of the Republican party." Then he added, sarcastically, "I not only know of your personal high mindedness, but I know full well if there is any crooked business to be done you want to do it yourself." [66]

That was in 1916; in 1920 Scobey worked for Harding on the same conditions, and won out by becoming one of an all-white delegation to Chicago. He found himself in a contest with E. H. R. Green, an adopted Texan and son of the millionairess Hetty Green. It was Green's purpose to promote and finance the selection of a "black-and-tan" Texas Republican delegation, half white, half black. Chief Negro aide to Green was one "goose-necked Bill MacDonald," who had insulted Scobey by circulating stories that his warehouses bore signs reading "no niggers, cockroaches and rats wanted here." Scobey told one of his own political aides in Fort Worth that "we are not going to stand for any negro nomination." "If you boys in Fort Worth," Scobey declared, "can't control that district you ought to have guardians appointed. I wouldn't let any negro run a thing over me." The way to handle the situation was for "you white men to get together and organize every county to get your friends at the precinct meetings to select delegates to the County Convention, and they, in turn will select them to the State Convention and Congressional Convention." Accordingly, everybody did his part. An all-white delegation was sent to Chicago. A contested "black and tan" delegation was set up by "Gooseneck" Bill MacDonald, and was denied admission by the Republican credentials committee.[67]

Harding was a sly one in regard to the vote of the fraternal orders. He was a member of several, including the Elks, the Loyal Order of Moose, and the Knights of Pythias. He knew, of course, that they were non-political and that he should not seek a formal commitment from them. Nevertheless, he came as close to it as he could. On March 24, 1920 Harding wrote to his fellow Moose, Louis Rinkenburgh of Cincinnati, reminding him of a previous address to the brethren and recalling that Rinkenburgh was "conspicuous in the leadership" at that time. "I know, of course," Harding said, "that the Order does not play politics, and I wouldn't have them break the role in my behalf." However, he suggested, "I do not think it would be amiss to have the Brethren know that I am the only member of the Order seeking the Presidential preference vote in Ohio, and I believe the members would be glad to show their friendly attitude to a member of the Order." "Of course," Harding added, "if there is anything inconsistent about this I hope you will drop the matter because I would not want to infract the national ethics in any way." There is no way of knowing how much the brethren cooperated in ths respect. We do know, however, that three days after Harding wrote this letter to Rinkenburgh in Cincinnati, Judge Joseph B. Kelley of Cincinnati told Christian to have Harding write to the national head of the Moose, James J. Davis and get him "busy not only in this county but elsewhere." [68] As for the Knights of Pythias, Harding had the assurance of certain of his brother knights of their support. On April 7, 1920 James J. Walker of Cleveland reported, "In conference with Maurice Maschke yesterday, he asked me what I was doing for you, not only here, but through the state with our Pythian brethren. I told him, as you well know, that I did not need any urging in your behalf." [69] Maschke was the Republican leader of Cleveland.

In some cases Harding's efforts at fence-mending were aided by his being forewarned to stay out of certain local Republican feuds that had reached a state of great bitterness. This was true of Delaware and Oklahoma. Delaware Senator William Saulsbury wrote to Harding, on January 30, 1920, telling of a revolt against the "high dollar" control by Alfred du Pont in Delaware politics. "You may be sure," Harding replied the next day, "that I will not make any misstep but will be fully cautioned by the information which you have placed at my disposal." [70] In Oklahoma there was a feud between James J. McGraw, the state's national committeeman, and Jake Hamon, a rich oil operator and backer of General Wood. Harding replied to his informant, O. E. Harrison, "In view of the fact that I have not edged in any way into the contest and have, therefore, engendered no hostilities, it would seem very probable that the delegates from that state could come to me without any serious embarrassment." [71] Hamon eventually became an ardent Hardingite, especially with his munificent bank roll.

In only one state outside Ohio did Harding abandon his second-choice technique and enter the primaries directly for first choices. This was Indiana, and the results were disastrous. As described earlier in the chapter, the political exigencies in Hoosier Republican politics required sacrificing Harding and Lowden in order to concentrate on Wood to beat Johnson. Harding had hoped that he could "second-choice it" there with Governor Goodrich, the favorite son, but Goodrich did not run. "I really would have preferred," he wrote to an Indiana friend on February 5, "to have Governor Goodrich remain in the race and have the delegation from his State." He asked J. C. Rosser of Crawfordsville to promote his second-choice standing among the Goodrich followers and others. Harding was a poor fourth in the presidential preference primary and managed to salvage a few first-choice delegates from the districts. He consoled himself and his Indiana manager, Judge Vernon W. Van Fleet, by advising, "I think

you ought to have no hesitancy in playing with the Lowden supporters, in order to get as many delegates as possible, and I am sure I
would rather have them go to him than anyone else in the field." [72]

The Indiana experience emphasized the wisdom of Harding's staying out of most of the primaries. He thus escaped the humiliation of
being made a pawn in the rivalry between the "major" candidates as
he had been in Indiana. For example, by staying out of the Michigan
primaries, the Wood vs. Johnson fight was fought out directly between
the two, with the Wood boom receiving a severe jolt. When the
returns favoring Johnson came in, Harding wrote to a friend, "The
Michigan vote made me feel a little more optimistic." Hence his
previous letter of December 24, 1919 to William J. Smith of Battle
Creek requesting second-choice consideration by the Michigan delegates had not been counteracted.[73] He politely declined invitations to
enter primaries in Michigan, Kentucky, Minnesota, Wisconsin, Nebraska, and probably others. He left it to his friends, of whom there
were many, to use their influence to spread second-choice sentiment
among the delegates.[74]

Harding's avoidance of the primaries and his preference for second-choice negotiations, illustrate the disrepute into which the primary had fallen among conservatives and many moderate politicians.
It seemed to them a crude and haphazard way of getting at national
sentiment. They said that the direct primaries promoted financeering,
feuding, and factionalism. Republican candidates were forced to say
things about each other that could be used by the Democrats later.
The primaries helped weaken parties when they should be
strengthened. The bitterness of the Ohio primary, to be described in
the next chapter, gave national publicity to this criticism of the
primaries. So, also, did the exposures by the Kenyon Committee of the
use of money by the Wood and Lowden forces. Thus Harding profited
by not making use of the primary. He never concealed his dislike for
this method of nomination—even though its use and abuse were vital
factors in making him President of the United States.[75]

5

During these 1919 and early 1920 months of presidential preliminaries, the Harding boom was kept in the public eye by the nation-
wide use of his oratorical talents. Harding played the role of spell-

binder as he had never played it before. This time he had a national audience and his own personal national press agent. His central themes were Americanism, anti-Bolshevism, and Wilsonian dictatorship and extravagance. It is significant to note that eight of the speeches included in the 1920 campaign book, *Rededicating America*, were from this period. They were: on January 6 the New York Waldorf-Astoria keynote on "Americanism"; a eulogy of McKinley on January 29 at Niles, Ohio; an address entitled "Auto-Intoxication," emphasizing thrift, to the Baltimore Press Club on February 5; an oration on Abraham Lincoln in Portland, Maine, on February 13; a star-spangled party oration to a Republican rally at Columbus on February 23; a panegyric on private enterprise before the Providence, Rhode Island Chamber of Commerce on February 25; a glorification of Theodore Roosevelt in Topeka, Kansas on March 8; and a "back-to-normal," "save America first" address to the Home Market Club at Boston on May 14. On the next day in the Senate, he delivered a Wilson-blasting speech on the Knox Resolution to declare the war with Germany ended. Early in March, Daugherty, Scobey, and E. Mont Reily put him on display in a tour of Texas, Missouri, Kansas, and Colorado, accompanied by widespread publicity through press agent Armstrong. The Indiana campaign in April was a daily grind.[76]

Harding's reaction to this intensive speechmaking campaign varied from exhiliration to disillusionment. Of his New York Waldorf-Astoria Americanism performance, he was very proud, for, as he told Scobey, "If it will not seem immodest to say it, it was well gotten away with and seemed to make a hit." It pleased him "to have gotten away with it just like some of the really big fellows might have done." [77] Soon, however, the work began to wear on him. He told Colonel Christian on January 19 that he found it "a real task to prepare speeches worth while and at the same time acquaint myself with them for effective deliverance." Nevertheless, this was part of the job, and he was not going to complain. "It is a strenuous life though and utterly lacks the charm of leisure and agreeable associations and complete relaxation." [78]

6

All of this is not to say that Harding had a sure majority of second choices when the Chicago convention assembled in June, 1920. But it is to say that his second choices plus the number of uninstructed delegates exceeded the pledged first choices of any one candidate. Never, he wrote Herrick on May 12, had there been so many unin-structed delegates.[80] Even when his support in the Ohio primaries did not meet expectations, Harding's spirits were sustained by his national standing. It gave him the determination to continue the contest. "I do not pretend," he wrote on May 17 to Bert Buckley in Columbus, "to say what the outcome will be at the present time, but I can assure you we are going on through with the presidential candidacy and from such information as we are able to secure the situation is more promising today than it was at any time prior to the primary fight in the State of Ohio."[81]

It is apparent that the Harding-Daugherty strategy of making the Ohio Senator the leading second-choice candidate for the Presidency had been remarkably effective. Daugherty, Reily, Forbes, and many others had made practical preparations for a switch to Harding that was clearly in the minds of scores of delegates as they went to Chicago. They were ready for "the break," and when it came, they did what they were prepared to do.

CHAPTER SEVENTEEN

The Fight for First Choices in Ohio

"I would rather be the favorite son of the state of Ohio than the billboard favorite of the whole United States." : : : *Harding, as quoted in the "Ohio State Journal," April 14, 1920*

◖ℛ The story of the Ohio Republican primary campaign of 1920 between Harding and his opponents is one of the most dramatic in the history of Buckeye politics. To politically-minded Ohioans, this contest was a war of self-defense by the Ohio Republican party against an enemy invasion. The invader was General Leonard Wood, whose mercenary "hirelings," paid by the millionaire "fifth columinst" William Cooper Procter, of Cincinnati, sought to win Ohio Republican votes by the lavish use of money and send forty-eight Wood delegates to the Republican national convention instead of forty-eight Harding delegates. The defenders were loyal Ohio Republicans, rallying against an outsider in order to protect a candidate from Ohio, "the Mother of Presidents."

The invasion was highly dangerous. It was the third 1919–20 assault of a Republican group calling itself Progressive, seeking to depose Harding from his Senatorship and the Regular Republican organization from its control of state party politics. At stake were the political jobs expected to be available with the overthrow of the Wilson Democrats in the November election. The first attack had been made in October, 1919 when the Progressives, via the state advisory committee, tried to make Harding choose to run for reelection to the Senate instead of for election to the Presidency, and thus lose both. Harding had foiled this by retaining his freedom of choice. The second attack had come in November, 1919 when Procter declared for Wood for President and forced Harding to declare for himself for President. The third attack came in January, 1920 when Procter announced that candidates for Wood delegates to the national nominating convention would run in every Ohio district and in the state at large against Harding candidates.

To Ohio Republican politicians, this third Procter-Wood effort to obtain delegates in Ohio was unfair. It violated the custom that gentlemen do not fight favorite sons in their home states. If there had to be a fight in the primaries at all—and, as we have seen, conservative Republicans objected to the primaries for that very reason—let the fight be in the states which had no favorite sons. Of course, the Wood men were doing this, but they made the mistake of carrying their well-financed campaign into every state with a favorite son. This contrasted with the highly honorable conduct of all the other candidates, who declined to challenge their rivals in their home states.

2

Harding's tactics in resisting the Wood attack in Ohio emphasized the gentleman's code. He did not assail Wood, he merely called attention to the virtues of the code. As we have already seen, he conspicuously declined to enter the primaries in favorite-son states, seeking only their second choices. He conducted a moderately financed campaign, and raised the vital issue of what a primary vote meant when it was overly influenced by heavy expenditures. He appealed to Buckeye Republican loyalty, the virtues of the "Ohio spirit," and party unity. He practiced a policy of letting each district pick its own national convention delegates in its own way, subject only to the condition that they were sincerely for Harding for President.

Harding's assumption that he would not have to campaign much in Ohio was a proud one. On March 24, 1920 he told Scobey that he could not bring himself to make a strong canvass in Ohio because he thought it "beneath the dignity" of the position to which he aspired. He told his friends this because it was a way of assuring them of his appreciation of their loyalty. He emphasized how necessary it was for the folks at home to do their part locally while he was covering the parts of the country which did not know him so well. As he put it to William R. Wilson of Urbana, Ohio on January 15, 1920, "I am hoping things will so adjust themselves in Ohio that it will not require any considerable activity in order to secure a united and cordial delegation from our state. I am hoping for this situation because really we must be giving our attention to fertile fields outside our borders. Presidential nominations naturally come from a very much wider territory than the horizons of one's own state." Later, in a gloomy mood resulting from the Procter-Wood invasion, he confided to A. F. Johnson of Ironton, "In simple truth, I have had a strong feeling all the while that, if I had to go out and make a plea to every section of the state, in order to secure Republican support in Ohio, I am not strongly deserving of the State's backing." After Harding had fought it out with Wood in Ohio, one of his friends commented, "He ought to have had the state without this bruising contest." [1]

Harding liked to talk about the "Ohio spirit." In January, 1920 he wrote to New Yorker Joseph C. Bonner, a former Ohioan, thanking him for a financial contribution, and added, "I haven't any knock for anybody who enters the big game, but I do want to boost the Ohio spirit and Ohio's capacity to meet our exacting situation." [2] To Paul V. Connolly of Cincinnati, who wrote of the feeling among certain Queen City politicians that Harding's candidacy was not serious, the Senator replied reassuringly, "I am hopeful that the Ohio spirit will assert itself in a way satisfactory to me and to the party in Ohio." [3]

One of those imbued with the Harding spirit was a gentleman named Jess W. Smith, friend of Daugherty and, in the spring of 1920, secretary of the Harding-for-President Club in Columbus. On April 7, Smith wrote to Scobey, "The Ohio situation is rapidly shaping itself and we do not fear at all the outcome, although the Wood people are spending a half million dollars in this State, while we have very little money for the State. . . . Our organization here is largely a volunteer organization and our people are waking up very rapidly. . . . In the final analysis when the acid test is applied there will be but one 'all wool' candidate, and that is Harding." [4]

The same spirit of self-confidence showed in Harding's assumption that he need not worry about the modest financial requirements. This was intended to be a contrast to Wood's extravagance. A strong politician can always count on financial aid from loyal supporters who can afford it. But Harding always emphasized that he did not need much. His confidence on this score was well expressed in a December 30, 1919 letter to Scobey. "Don't you be distressed about the financial calls of my campaign," he wrote, "I don't want you to make any contribution in that direction. More than that, I don't want you to solicit any from any of your friends. Such financial support as is needed can be acquired without imposing upon any of my intimate personal friends. Quite apart from this fact, I do not want an extravagant money spending campaign. If a nomination must come through such a process as that, I do not want the thing at all." [5] He told how his 1914 senatorial campaign cost only $4,000. He told the same thing to his brother "Deac," Dr. George T. Harding, when he returned the modest check that had been sent.[6] Harding got a certain thrill out of not needing much money—a thrill that included confidence in loyalty that went beyond material things. On February 21, 1920, he wrote J. E. Mulligan in Tampa, Florida, "I am not carrying on an extended campaign through friendly agents because I am not in a position to engage their activities and properly look after their expenses and becoming compensation for the time. It is a rather disappointing thing to be a candidate without ample sinews of war, but I confess I enjoy it in some ways and am glad to be one aspirant who is operating without large resources. It is pretty hard on some of my friends but one can be sure of friendships which are made manifest when there is no encouragement in a material way for political activity." [7] Harding's aide, Howard D. Mannington, summed it all up rather succinctly when he told Scobey, "If poverty is a virtue, then indeed we should stand very high." [8]

Harding went so far as to declare early in the campaign that the excessive expenditure of money was more of a hindrance than a benefit to the spender. On January 20, 1920 he said so to Scobey. General Wood, he wrote, "is not going to be strong enough to be nominated on the first ballot or any other ballot. Though there is limitless money back of his campaign, it is my deliberate judgment that the crest of the Wood movement has been reached. As a matter of fact, the excessive financial support back of him at the present time is proving the greater hindrance to him at the present time than it is a help." Eventually, when the Wood backers prepared to throw their hundreds of thousands of dollars into Ohio to beat Harding, the Senator became quite philosophical about it. "If there isn't a well grounded sentiment in my behalf in the State," he told Scobey on March 24, "you can be sure that the large expenditure of money which is planned will prove effective in spite of any individual efforts." [9]

Scobey gave a peculiar twist to this modest spending policy of the Harding campaign. His idea was for Harding not to criticize the other candidates for their allegedly mercenary campaigning but to let Hiram Johnson do it. This advice he gave to the chief Harding publicity agent, Robert Armstrong, on March 10, 1920, in commenting on the "barrel of money" Wood was spending in Ohio and Indiana. "Of course," he told Armstrong, "nothing should ever come from the

Harding Camp about the expenditure of our opponents, but with a line up like DuPont, Percy Rockefeller, Dan R. Hanna, Bob Wolf, Wm. Cooper Procter [sic] people ought to know of these vast expenditures. It just occurred to me that if Senator Johnson has already made an attack on these vast sums being expended, you might get his Publicity man or Poindexter [sic] man to work this out through the press. If they won't do it, I believe it would be a good idea to get someone else, but it must be kept away from our Camp as we want to be friendly to all. Take this matter up with Daugherty." Then, on May 20, after the primaries were all over and the money spent, Scobey advised Howard Mannington of Harding's staff "to get out among the delegates the amount of money Wood has been spending in each state, what he did in Ohio, and that he is trying to buy this nomination. Of course, this must not come from Harding sources. Can you not figure some other way to get it out? Let the Johnson fellows do it. They have already made the attack." [10] As the sequel was to show, it was Johnson who made the attack, it was Wood and Johnson who suffered, and it was Harding who benefitted.

Harding, of course, had to have some financial backing for his primary campaign. The man in charge was Carmi Thompson of Cleveland. When Scobey asked George Christian about the subject, the secretary replied, "Can't tell you a thing about finances. That has been left entirely to Carmi Thompson." [11]

3

The basic test of the loyalty of Harding's Ohio backers was that they should have no second choices. Such choices for Harding outside of Ohio were much desired; inside Ohio they were near-treason. This was the rule from the very beginning of Harding's candidacy. On December 16, 1919, Wood-supporter Dan Hanna offered Daugherty a mutual exchange of second-choice pledges for Wood and Harding. Daugherty met the suggestion with a resounding no. "I said I never have a second choice until I have completely lost my first choice." So expounded Daugherty in the first of a series of pungent pronouncements that fixed the steady course of Harding toward the White House. To Harding, on December 19, with unerring insight, he wrote, "This concerted action on the part of all the Wood people to have us declare for Wood for second choice, if agreed to, in the final wind-up of the contest would be fatal, because the friends of other candidates would hold it against us when they voted for a second choice. The proposition originates from no source friendly to you. On any such matters as this please do not commit yourself until we have had a chance to talk." Next day, to complete the assurance, he wrote Ohio State Republican Committee chairman Newton H. Fairbanks, "I am having a devil of a time with these fellows who are insisting upon the Ohio delegation declaring a second choice. Our real second choice should be the nominee of the convention if it is not Harding, and we ought not to talk about second choice until then, and anybody who does is not interested in Harding's nomination. The matter has to be handled diplomatically for they have almost worn me out, but not quite, old fellow, not quite." To this, Fairbanks dutifully replied, "Harding must be First, Second and Last choice." [12]

No counsel ever given Harding by Daugherty was wiser or more timely. To make sure that it was fully understood by all who could read, he made it public. In the *Cincinnati Enquirer* of January 11, and the *Ohio State Journal* of January 12, 1920, Daugherty allowed himself to be quoted, "Our delegates must be the soul of honor and true as steel. . . . If Ohio's cause and Harding's ever goes down, I will go down with it." On January 15, in the *Cleveland Plain Dealer*, he was quoted: "My own second choice for the nomination is the choice of the convention after I regain consciousness should it happen that Harding is not nominated. We are not running the Wood campaign."

Harding saw the point and stuck to it with almost equal firmness. The Wood backers, he told Jennings, offered not to run their candidate in Ohio if Harding would instruct his delegates to name the General for second place. "This means," said Harding, "the bitter ruin of any prospects in the convention and the mere perfunctory support in Ohio besides, and I could not in self-respect contemplate any such barter." And Harding also made it public. Throughout the state, on January 19 and 20, the word was published. To permit a second choice would infer that the first choice was "a mere perfunctory thing. I never would permit my name to go before a national convention with a merely perfunctory or complimentary support by the delegates from Ohio." [13]

There was a refinement in the way Harding and Daugherty toyed with the Wood bargainers. Perhaps it was a matter of dollars and cents. If the Wood men could only get Harding to accept Wood as a second choice in Ohio, it would save them the hundreds of thousands of dollars they eventually had to spend in the state. At any rate, Harding enjoyed the toying. "They are all eager," he told Scobey December 30, 1919, "to enter upon a harmony program conditioned upon our committing ourselves to Wood for second choice. We are letting them dangle this proposition before us for the time being but we do not have any intention of accepting such a proposition." [14]

There was a slight exception to the hardness and fastness of the no-second-choice rule. It has been pointed out that it was part of the placating of Johnson to give a little. Hence it was expedient to give a little to Wood—the suggested formula being 10 for Johnson, 10 for Wood, 10 for Lowden, and the remaining 18 to be scattered. The idea was to prevent a concentration. Further evidence of this came from Fremont and Toledo. C. C. Waltermire wrote that sentiment there was overwhelmingly for Wood as second choice, but that "sentiment will change if we do not press the issue." Harding acquiesced, adding the assurance, "I am confident that we shall ultimately have the moderate cooperation of Mr. Brown in any program which I approve." [15]

Harding was serious about curbing the consideration of Wood for second choice. So was Daugherty, and so was the Ohio Republican Party. The Ohio-Mother-of-Presidents legend was no plaything. It was firmly in the minds of Ohio Republicans as they pledged themselves to pursue the Harding candidacy to the very close. This mood of deadly earnestness never faltered, and helps explain a powerful factor that eventually produced success.

That the Ohio primary law required the declaration by all delegates of second choices was no deterrent. Daugherty met this obstacle by announcing a dummy candidate in the person of the eighty-four year-old General J. Warren Keifer of Springfield, Civil War veteran, former Republican Congressman, and former Speaker of the House. The aged general was either of unstable mind, or he was not properly consulted, for he proved to be somewhat difficult. He was quoted in the *Springfield Morning Sun* of March 2, 1920 as saying that he would not attend the Republican national convention, that the Ohio Republican party was split, and that Harding's chances for getting the nomination were "narrowed." The Harding Republicans were horrified. Keifer was waited upon by persons unknown and persuaded to repudiate his remarks. In the *Sun* of March 7 he was made to say that he "may have stated" his regret that there was a "possibility" of a divided loyalty to Harding, "but otherwise the article is incorrect and misleading." He wished Harding well and was "heartily for his nomination and shall be to the end." His contemplated absence from the national convention should not be attributed to anything except that he thought his presence there was not necessary.[16]

The Wood men and the Democrats denounced the Keifer dummy-second-choice maneuver. "Aut Caesar, Aut nullius," mocked the *Plain Dealer*, February 20, at Harding's "ukase." Procter countered with the announcement of the highly respectable James R. Garfield for his second choice. Daugherty and Harding gave a little, but most of the candidates stayed with Keifer.[17]

The most difficult person to manage on the second-choice problem was Boss Hynicka of Cincinnati. Early in December, 1919 Hynicka proposed to Harding that, in the April primary, "Harding partisans could declare for Wood second choice and Wood partisans could declare for Harding second choice. Let all agree to be bound by the result of the primary election." Harding refused to be caught in such a trap. Here again was the old Cincinnati "blackbird" trickery. As the time approached for a confrontation with Hynicka, Harding was fully prepared to stop the Cincinnati boss's plot. "I will meet him in a tolerant mood," he told Carmi Thompson, "even though I do not intend to make any surrender which may jeopardize my interests." It was perfectly reasonable to permit Hynicka's Cincinnati delegates to file for Wood for second choice. "I can have no objection to that in individual cases, provided such individual cases do not become too numerous. . . . I can consent to no frame-up which is going to unduly emphasize the Wood sentiment in our State." [18]

When called on by Thomas F. Turner of Akron for an explanation of the Keifer dummy-second-choice plan, Harding gave a good one. Ohio was the only state that required a public second-choice expression. Thus a presidential contestant from Ohio "is the only one who is forced to show his hand in playing the game which goes with a convention contest." The Republicans had such a dummy candidate in 1916 when they promoted Burton for President and agreed on Paul Howland of Cleveland for second choice. Howland was not in any sense a candidate, and the thing was done as "a mere perfunctory compliance with the law." There could be nothing seriously wrong with naming Keifer, "because we had to do something of that sort and no one could have been seriously humiliated by complimenting such a fine old veteran." Moreover, he said, "Ohio's Democratic Governor James M. Cox will do the same thing and nobody is going to complain." Above all was the need of unity and firmness in support of an

Ohio man: "I have said publicly and I have said it privately, and I repeat it to you now, that unless Ohio is cordially in favor of my candidacy, I do not have any thought of having my name presented to the convention." [19]

4

The Harding-Daugherty plan for nomination required the presence of strong and unfaltering Harding first-and-last-choice delegates from Ohio at the national convention. There must be no second-choice squeamishness about them. They must be the "soul of honor and true as steel," as Daugherty had said. They must resist the strong temptation to bargain Harding away that was sure to come in the snake-pit atmosphere of the convention.

Within this "true as steel" requirement, the plan was somewhat democratic. There were twenty-two congressional districts, from each of which two delegates were to be chosen subject to Harding's eventual approval. The initiative was local, except that it was supposed to be taken by the "organization," i.e., by the chairmen of the Republican county committees in conference with "Republican leaders." As Harding informed Clarence C. Fravel, of Pataskala in Licking county, "I have said to the various organization heads in Ohio that I wish them to call the Republican leaders in each district to a district conference and see if they could not agree upon candidates for delegates and alternates, so that we shall have but one ticket and avoid any contest." Harding was quite open about this. In a Cleveland speech on March 30, he said frankly, "I asked the district organizations in Ohio to select outstanding Republicans pledged to the approval that the law contemplates. I made but one condition not altogether unreasonable. I said that if they were to stand for election with my name and consent I would like them to be friendly to my candidacy." The language used in his letters to local leaders varied. To Dr. L. C. Weimer of Dayton it was to "the organized forces"; to A. N. Wilcox of Paulding, it was to "a council of the Republicans"; to C. L. Newcomer of Bryan it was to "a group of representative Republicans from the districts interested." Whatever the local initiative was, it was designed to propose only *one* slate—a Harding slate—of two delegates for the Republican voters to endorse on primary election day. Actually, in every county there were two slates because the Wood leaders got another group of Republicans to prepare a Wood slate of two delegates.[20]

The Harding delegate selection process varied between two extremes. In some districts, such as the Seventh (Columbus), the Harding leaders wanted him to pick the delegates. In others, such as the First and the Second (Hamilton county), they insisted on hands off. In the case of the former situation, Harding usually threw the matter back to the localities. But in other cases, even when he was not asked to do so, he suggested candidates of his own. This was the way he handled such distinguished applicants as Harry L. Vail of Cleveland and Walter F. Brown of Toledo.[21]

There was nothing stand-offish about Harding's selection of the Big Four candidates for the positions of delegates-at-large. In his March 30 speech at Cleveland, he proudly admitted to "a bit of personal assumption" when he described how he picked the four biggest men in the Ohio Republican party. He used a formula of geographical distribution plus ex-governors plus Daugherty. "I knew," he said, "Cleveland wanted Myron T. Herrick, and he was promptly certified. I believed Ohio wanted our other ex-governor, Frank B. Willis, and he was certified. Hamilton County Republicans wanted Cincinnati Mayor John B. Galvin and nobody questioned." For fourth choice Harding picked Daugherty, and was very emphatic about it. "I want him elected," Harding said. "It would be a sorry spectacle to see Ohio Republicans punish him for playing the game in the biggest possible way." [22]

There was a combination of two kinds of personal feeling in back of Harding's choice of Daugherty for candidate. One was admiration for his management, and the other was personal vindictiveness toward Hynicka and H. P. Wolfe of the *Ohio State Journal* and the *Columbus Evening Dispatch*. These feelings, he revealed in a letter to Scobey on January 20, 1920. "I took the bull by the horns," he wrote, "and asked Daugherty to stand for the fourth place. This will be very displeasing to Wolfe and Hynicka, and it will probably be very offensive to some former Progressives. However, there was no other honorable course to pursue, and I have decided that if the Republicans of Ohio do not think sufficiently well of my judgment to elect one man for delegate-at-large who is my particular choice, they do not have a sufficient confidence in me to justify supporting me for a Presidential candidacy." [23]

Harding had a hard time with certain Ohio Negroes who insisted on the naming of Fred D. Patterson, Greenfield carriage manufacturer, as one of Harding's Big Four delegate-at-large preferences. The Negro leader was Ralph W. Tyler of the *Cleveland Advocate*. According to Tyler, "the race" will support Patterson. The *Advocate*, "to retain its influence with the race, must support him, but without particularizing which of the other candidates should receive the support of the race." Patterson, he said, was a thoroughgoing Harding man. "I have written him," Tyler said, "telling him to write Warren G. Harding, as his first choice, on his petition, and to have no second choice." Tyler also said that he talked Harding at a Chicago meeting of a national political organization called the Lincoln League. He said further that he could control several delegates from the South. Harding refused and replied to Tyler, describing the factors for the good of the party that required the selection of Herrick, Willis, Galvin, and Daugherty as the Ohio Big Four delegates-at-large. "I can not imagine," Harding went on, "any Republican organization casting its plans for the purpose of defeating any aspirant for delegate-at-large." Tyler thereupon switched to Wood, sending out letters to Ohio Negroes describing how "the Harding managers flatly refused to recognize the race's plea for representation, but the Wood forces did, and left a place vacant on their ticket for Patterson." A Negro Wood-Patterson Club was being organized to ensure Patterson's election as delegate-at-large.[24]

Harding retaliated by selecting a Toledo Negro, Charles A. Cottrill, as his choice for alternate delegate-at-large. This, said Tyler, was the "same old chestnut." It was done, incidentally, at Cottrill's suggestion, and also at Daugherty's. Cottrill's letter to Harding of February 21 pointed out the adverse effect on the colored vote of not naming a Negro delegate-at-large. The best way out of the difficulty was for Harding to write Cottrill a letter describing why he had to pick four white men for the Big Four and asking Cottrill if he would make the sacrifice and accept the alternate appointment. This idea, he said, was "suggested to me by Mr. Daugherty." This procedure, Cottrill also said, "carries the inference that but for the circumstances stated, one of the delegates-at-large would probably have been a member of the colored race."[25]

A bit of overconfidence, which probably cost Daugherty his delegateship but did not hurt Harding very much, was Daugherty's "2:11 A.M." remark predicting that Harding would be selected by a small clique of men in the "wee small hours" of the last day of the national convention, after all the other aspirants had refused to agree on one of their number. It was a tactless thing for Daugherty to say, and caused Harding much embarrassment by emphasizing machine politics rather than popular appeal. The statement was made in New York in the presence of reporters and published in the *New York Times* and other papers on February 21, 1920: "I don't expect Senator Harding to be nominated on the first, second or third ballot, but I think we can well afford to take chances that about eleven minutes after 2 o'clock on Friday morning at the convention when fifteen or twenty men, somewhat weary, are sitting around a table, some one of them will say, 'Who will we nominate?' At that decisive time the friends of Senator Harding can suggest him and abide by the result. I don't know but what I might suggest him myself." [26] David F. Pugh of Columbus said that the remark almost gave him the "blind staggers." Fred Starek in New York wrote that Harding's friends were aghast. The Wood men, he wrote, "are already engaged in designating you as 'the candidate of the Old Guard and the reactionaries.' My, even the Wood people, financed as they are by Wall Street, are referring to you in that way—brazen and impudent it is, to be sure, but they are trying to camouflage the situation, and the [Daugherty] interview helps them do it." It delayed Starek's financial solicitations considerably. People had "thrown the remark into my teeth a score of times," he wrote. Harding admitted that Daugherty had made a mistake, but, as he told J. S. Aydelott of Detroit, "we have to expect to encounter slips here and there in such a large political enterprise." To the public, Harding brushed it off as a joke.[27]

5

The Harding-Wood primary fight for delegates was a bitter one. Wood was said to be the mercenary attacker, and Harding was represented as the gentleman defender, clothed with the armor of righteousness and fair play. The more bitter the public fight became, the better Harding looked, as the people saw their favorite assailed by wild and harsh allegations. The newspapers of city and country were spotted with anti-Harding advertisements, billboards along the highway spread anti-Harding diatribes, and leaflets and cards by the tens of thousands denouncing the Ohio Senator and praising the great General found their way into circulation. The effect was to build up a justification in the minds of people that, even though Harding obtained a plurality of only 14,692 over Wood, and only 39 of the 48 delegates, it was a noble victory to have done that well without resorting to such blatant and mercenary tactics.[28]

An example of an anti-Harding leaflet was one headlined, "Vote as You Shot! Go to the Primaries April 27th, and Vote Against HARDING and DAUGHERTY." It was signed by eight World War I veteran officers of the army, navy, and air force. It featured quotations questioning Harding's patriotism in the war: "Much of the sentiment concerning our part in the war is balderdash"; "I have believed the Liberty Bond campaign hysterical and unseemly." From the *Marion Star* of September 13, 1912 was quoted his editorial, likening Theodore Roosevelt to Benedict Arnold. "A MAN HOLDING SUCH VIEWS SHOULD NOT BE PRESIDENT!" Daugherty's "2:11 A.M." remark was cited.[29] Display advertisements appeared in scores of newspapers and were sponsored by "The Leonard Wood Committee of Ohio, John H. Price, chairman." [30]

The central theme of the Wood-Procter advertising was the need for the steadying influence of a man like General Wood, with his strength of character and capacity for action and decisiveness, as against the deviousness of "smooth" politicians like Daugherty and Harding. The Wood speeches, editorials, and advertising teemed with such phrases as "back stairs conspiracy," "senatorial coterie," "political bossism," "old guard crowd," "stand patters," "need for house cleaning," "gang of high binders," "edicts by Daugherty," and "Mr. Harding's squiggling stand." A particularly catching theme was the "favorite-son ambush," which represented Harding and a lot of other "little" men ganging up on the heroic Wood, forcing him to fight with all of them at the same time. When an anonymous Harding enthusiast came out with a pamphlet entitled "What A Country Boy Did with 200 Pounds of Type," the *Cleveland Plain Dealer* sarcastically urged the author to come forth and reveal himself so as to qualify for "secretary of something in the Harding cabinet." [31]

The chief point of strength in the Wood propaganda was military preparedness. With a backward glance at the half-way, "milk-and-water" measures of preparedness before our entry into World War I, Wood supporters said that anything short of his proposal of compulsory, universal military service was pacifism. Our unpreparedness was the very thing that caused Germany to insult us and require our entry into the hideous slaughter. And that was the cause of all the unnecessary expense and tragedy in preparing to fight after we got into the war. Said the *Cleveland News*, April 1: "The country knows now how long it took to raise and train and equip the army in 1917 and 1918, knows that another time America may not have allies to hold the enemy while she makes ready, knows that the reputation of constant readiness is the best protection against attack, knows that Americans probably would not have been sent to death on the Lusitania and other ships in 1915 and 1916 if America had been as ready to fight then as she was in the summer of 1918."

Wood's practice of making his public appearances in military uniform was no matter of apprehension to his supporters. "Why Assail the Men Who Fought, Senator?", headlined the *News* in answer to Harding's criticism. "Does the olive drab of the United States army disgrace the man who wears it? Is the uniform of the United States navy, or that of the marine corps a livery of shame? Were our soldiers, seamen and marines a detriment or a menace to our country in the war period? Are they a national danger, now that they have returned to civil life? Would there be grave public peril in giving other boys the same training they had?" [32]

Out of the Procter-financed advertising, Wood emerged as a splendid example of manly Americanism. He was as much a super-American and anti-Wilsonian as Harding or anybody else. Wilson had personally spited him, it was claimed. Wood was the victim, not the pawn, of bosses: witness the way in which he had been switched from post to post during World War I and denied a chance to command a division in France, even though it was he who had made wartime conscription an efficient and popular thing. Wood's firm hand in democratizing Cuba was alleged. His handling of strikes in West Virginia, Omaha, Nebraska, and Gary, Indiana was praised as fair to labor. "WOOD IS HERALDED AS CANDIDATE OF PEOPLE," headlined the *Ohio State Journal*, citing his allegedly judicious conduct in regard to strikes. The *Cleveland News* did similarly in an editorial entitled "Why There Is Nothing of the Autocrat in Leonard Wood." Toward the end of the campaign, the papers began to play down Wood's military record, omitting the "general," and showing pictures of him in civilian clothes. A typical Procter advertisement headed by a picture of Wood in "civvies" ran:

LEONARD WOOD

"A Man "Four Square"

Administrator, Statesman, Soldier

Forward-Looking American.

Wood's association with Theodore Roosevelt since the days of the Rough Riders was described. "What Theodore Roosevelt Thought of Leonard Wood," captioned a *Cleveland News* editorial on April 23, 1920. Cartoons showed the spirit of the departed Roosevelt blessing Wood.[33]

The image of a stalwart, steady Wood was contrasted with one of a weakling Harding, quite unable to face the great decisions confronting the nation. "If the country," said the *Cleveland News*, "must face some tremendous choice, if it must impress the world with its steadfast resolution, its unflinching courage, its mastery of fate, then a weak man in the White House might easily prove the source of enormous harm. His inability to do the right thing at the right time might entail terrible consequences in blood and ruin. His littleness might be as harmful as a colossal crime." The weak and frightened Harding was cartooned being awakened by an alarm clock set for "2:11 A.M." Harding's frank and well-known dislike for the direct primary was claimed to reveal his undemocratic, pro-boss leanings. As the campaign progressed, the only doubt was said to be the size of Wood's majority.[34]

But the Harding propaganda-makers were as ingenious as the Procter-Wood variety. The appeal was to Ohio pride against an outsider who was interferring with Ohio customs and traditions. The "Ohio, Mother of Presidents" legend was revived. An excellent example of this was an advertisement published in the *Ravenna Republican* on April 22, 1920. Vividly captioned "Stand By Ohio—The Mother of Presidents," it pictured Harding flanked by Ohioians and Harding-isms: "Senator Harding—Ohio's Choice"; "Do you as an Ohio citizen and voter, want an officer of the regular army from New Hampshire, or a business man from Ohio as President? Be loyal." One paragraph read, "Every Republican President since Lincoln, with one exception, hailed from Ohio. In each instance, the elevation was from humble surroundings—from tanner boy, canal boy, soldier boy. Now Ohio has the opportunity to elevate a printer boy to the White House. The very thought fills one with traditional Buckeye pride and enthusiasm." [35]

It was similar down along the Ohio River. When the Republican central and executive committee of Scioto county met at Portsmouth and resolved on Harding for President, reason number one was that "the Republican party has made Ohio the new Mother of Presidents." History was resorted to and details compiled to reveal that since

Lincoln's day "the Republican Party has *ten* times out of *thirteen* commissioned a man born upon the soil of Ohio to be its standard bearer." As it was in the past, so now must it be today for Republicans "in this, their era and generation to see that Ohio leads, and that again in 1920, as in the secure and glorious past days, *the most distinguished son of Ohio is to lead the Republican Party to victory.*" [36]

Harding made this "Ohio Man" emphasis his main appeal. He used it wherever he went in his own home state. It became a tremendous attraction to the Buckeye mentality. Alluding to the Procter advertising methods, he said, "I would rather be the favorite son of Ohio than the billboard favorite of the whole United States of America." On March 20, 1920 at Norwood, near Cincinnati, he said, "There has always been a great pride in Ohio's conspicuous part in national conventions. We must still play that part." At Cincinnati on March 25, he said, "I am an Ohio Republican always. I glory in the tribute the Republicans of the nation have paid to sons of Ohio. I do not think a day has passed when we [no longer] develop sons of Ohio who are eligible to national preference. . . . The Ohio spirit isn't dead, and no opposition, however well organized, can destroy Ohio pride." At Steubenville on March 28, he told his listeners that "it would be a strange reversal for Ohio to surrender its big part in Republican national politics." At Columbus on April 14, he reminded his Republican audience that "the Republicans of the nation have elected only one President since Abraham Lincoln who did not come from the state of Ohio and it was thought in the state, and outside, that probably an Ohio candidate would add to the assurance of victory in both the state and the nation" in 1920.[37]

Harding's glorification of the "Ohio Man" was very thrilling to Ohio residents. He pointed out that the Ohio call was so compelling that a man must accept it no matter what sacrifice of personal preference was involved. In a remarkable passage in the Columbus speech just quoted, he declared that the Presidency "is the greatest enslavement in the world," and that he really did not desire to be a candidate. "No thoughtful normal man who loves his personal freedom, and who has had opportunity for observations which come with an experience in Washington official life, would have a personal preference to be a candidate for president of the United States." But he said, referring to the Senatorship, Ohio had summoned him to "the most important and the most desirable place in the public service that I think the world can give." Therefore, he had to accept the mandate. "Men who had given me their support said I owed it to the party to permit the use of my own name, and party obligation always appeals to me." With an apology for his lack of modesty, he added, "I was intimately acquainted with the activities of men in the workshops of the nation, and I knew the great undercurrent of thought about the need of restoring party government, and I knew that my convictions and habits and associations fitted me to serve in that undertaking as well as anybody proposed in the United States of America." [38]

Having accepted Ohio's mandate, said the Senator, a vigorous and confident campaign by a united party must be waged. If he was going to be Ohio's proud standard-bearer, he had to resort to the Keifer subterfuge. The second-choice requirement weakened Ohio's ability to unite behind its first choice. The party had spent too much painful effort between 1917 and 1920 rebuilding its unity via the advisory committee system to submit its new strength to artificial risks. As he said in Steubenville, "For three years we have been planning and working here in Ohio to unify and organize to insure Republican success. We have spent time and all our scant resources to that one end. We have invited, even drafted, representatives of all factions into the organization and we thought we had our forces well brought together." Suddenly there came this small outside group of the Procter-Wood persuasion which "sought to deny the Ohio right of a Republican candidacy." With their second-choice wedge, "they offered perfunctory support to compliment me with a favorite son ballot, provided I would pledge the delegates to their candidate after a complimentary ballot. I would not consent to this. It would not be fair dealing [to the Ohio Republican party]. A member of the Senate finds no great elation in a perfunctory compliment. I had no right to barter the judgment and support of an upstanding delegation from Ohio. That would have been personal dictation rather than representative judgment." As for compliments, it was all right to give one to "good old General Keifer," that "grand old man of Ohio," former speaker of the House of Representatives, "civil war hero . . . who has honored his state by his residence therein." In other words, the reunited Ohio Republicans wanted an Ohioan for President and aimed to concentrate on him to the fullest of their political strength. "Frankly," he said, "I little dreamed of opposition in Ohio. I assumed that the restoration of the party to confidence and dominance in Ohio would be so deeply implanted in every Republican breast that every contribution of an awakened spirit would be welcomed by the Republicans of this state, and I said, 'Very well, we will go to the convention; we are assured of a friendly interest beyond our borders.'" If Procter, or anybody else, could do Ohio's part better, it was their privilege to try to be Ohio's standard-bearer. Whoever it is, "we will play Ohio's big part, and we will participate in the convention's decision at the polls in November. That statement has expressed the whole purpose from the very start. We would submit an Ohio proposal to the delegates in representative convention."

Harding made a vigorous defense of Daugherty as the chief architect and promoter of the high Ohio purpose. He attributed the opposition to Daugherty to "a very small thing, but it was big enough for me to meet it decisively." He was referring to Edward C. Turner of Columbus, whom he characterized as a dictator and one who had sought to destroy the Republican party in 1912. Turner had been state attorney general in 1911–12 and had had the job of prosecuting some of the Republican officials whom Governor Harmon had accused of financial irregularities. Daugherty had defended these Republican officials, and had laid the basis for a Turner-Daugherty personal feud. This had been intensified when Turner joined the Roosevelt bolt in 1912. Thus, said Harding, Turner in 1920 was trying to revive an old feud, when all the other Progressives had agreed to let bygones be bygones.[39]

Harding told quite bluntly why he chose to support Daugherty against Turner. He cited "Mr. Daugherty's unselfish and unfailing Republican activities for more than 30 years," and Turner's unreliable conduct and exaggeration of a personal vendetta. Daugherty was "unfailingly a fighting Republican. I would not agree that a presidential contest could be cast on such lines as a personal or factional fight against a man willing to sacrifice his time and his patience on a managerial campaign and I would not think of beginning a campaign by sacrificing a friend, no matter who asked me to do it. . . . It would be a mighty miserable army which shaped the plans of battle on the advice of enemy scouts or the mutineers within the ranks." Harding said he had to reject Turner and his sympathizers, who leaned toward a second choice, because they "would have traded me off before they reached the Indiana line on their way to Chicago. . . . I would rather go to defeat with fidelity to my friends than win a temporary victory through their betrayal." He had a right to say which candidates for delegate he approved if those candidates were to bear the hopes of Harding and the Ohio Republican party at Chicago.

6

There were other phases to Harding's bid for Ohio votes against Wood besides the appeal of the "Ohio Man" against the mercenary Procter. There was Harding the friend of the late Theodore Roosevelt. There was Harding the non-militarist, as against the uniformed General Wood, advocate of compulsory military service. There was Harding the non-dictator, who as President would return power to Congress. There was Harding the friend of a league of nations with reservations, and the foe of the Wilson league. There was Harding the moderate on the Cummins railroad bill, with its anti-strike conciliation service.

Harding loved to dwell on his reconciliation with Theodore Roosevelt, and admitted the bitter feelings of 1912. "I fought him as he fought us. But he and I buried the past without apologies when we came to fuller acquaintance in later life. I called on him at his request four years ago, after the defeat of Justice Hughes. He had returned to the party, he had given cordial support to Justice Hughes; and, recalling the failure of the Hughes campaign and the Republican disappointment throughout the country, the colonel opened the interview by declaring in characteristic fashion, 'Harding, we have got to get together and put the Republican Party back in power to serve this country of ours.' And then and there we agreed to work together and we buried the past and we conferred often thereafter to the time of his death." And Harding added proudly, "God help the political party that stakes its hopes of success in 1920 on its recollections of 1912."

On the issue of militarism, Harding won the loyalty of both factions —for and against. At Steubenville he told the audience they should "make it so that the nation would never again be unmindful of the national defense." This was vague enough for both big and small national defense proponents. So was his desire for "a navy ample to meet any power on the big sea . . . a nation stronger in the air than on the seas. . . . [And] an ample army to preserve the stability of the republic and defend its relations abroad. . . . Military training, voluntary but compulsory . . . [leaving] it to the convenience of the young men of the republic and not making it necessary under Prussian rule in the United States." [41] The part on voluntary military service enabled the Washington county [Marietta] Harding Club to advertise that a three-month voluntary period was better than a six-month compulsory period. Therefore, "if you would keep your boy in civil life, vote for Senator Harding next Tuesday. If you would dress your boy in khakis and have him carry a gun vote otherwise." [42] The *Akron Beacon Journal* on April 24 headlined:

EX-ARMY MEN CONDEMN CAMPAIGN OF

GENERAL WOOD—ORGANIZE HARDING CLUB

Former Army Men Also Condemn Efforts of Makers

of War Supplies to Fasten German System of Military

Training on Their Country.

This appealed to the veterans who were tired of soldiering and to the large mass of civilians with no war records.

Harding's feeling about militarism was amusingly illustrated by an episode in April when he campaigned against Wood in Cleveland. According to Mrs. Harding, they were received with great semimilitary éclat, much to her husband's annoyance. "Our escort," wrote Mrs. Harding to the Scobeys, "consisted of the Chief of Police in his car and twenty-four of Cleveland's 'finest' mounted police on splendid Ky. horses—ten plain clothes secret-service men and Heaven knows what else. At each stop they all lined up to salute, etc. W. G. 'G—d D—d' it, and I, well I was quite thrilled and enjoyed the 'Show.'" [43]

As for the veterans, Harding, at Steubenville, sought the votes of the bonus-seekers, the patrioteers, and the general public, ever concerned with cutting taxes, by the following blanket offering:

Our party, every party, ought to pledge the gratitude of the republic to the sons who responded to its armed defense. Much has been said about what won the war. It is easy to be certain about it. Our armed forces won the war and the nation must never be ungrateful. I cannot speak the details of the four alternatives for grateful expression which the American Legion has worked out. I only know that a compensation based on service is designed to aid farm settlement and encouragment of homes, to facilitate vocational education in addition to the aid already provided for wounded men or to afford cash aid for those in urgent need. I understand the plan contemplates a period of award extending over a term of ten years so that treasury economics may be worked out to avoid distributing burdens not to exceed $160,000,000 a year and I want a grateful congress and a grateful public to applaud. We owe this to the men of America who defended the republic. And I would spread the increased allowances on which the aged civil war veterans depend for their support, for they gave us the preserved union and nation for whose rights the World War Americans fought. And I would stop millions of needless expenditures to bring this about. During the war they established a bureaucracy crowned with an autocracy and this provided commissions to "pass the buck." I'd get back to simple government again.[44]

On the labor front Harding's stance was ambivalent: he was a conservative trying to appear liberal to the laboring man. What liberal votes he lost by this were more than offset by those who were concerned about Bolshevism having too much influence in the ranks of labor. On April 29, at the Akron Goodyear Tire and Rubber Company, he added flattery to his vote-catching repertoire when he spoke to the Goodyear Assembly, a company-dominated organization allegedly representing the workers. Harding told the men that he would be willing to trust a body like that with such questions as the treaty of peace with Germany. "I am willing," he said, "to trust to the wisdom and common sense of the wage earners, and I hope to meet a Goodyear assemblyman in the United States Senate. A man does not have to be a lawyer or a rich man to gain a seat in the Senate. With the training that you get here you would do better than many who go there." [45]

Harding proceeded to regale the workers with an example of the kind of high thinking that he would expect them to exercise about the Wilson League of Nations and its provisions for the alleged reduction of the American standard of living via the International Labor Office. "Do you know one of the reasons why the senate rejected the League of Nations?" he asked his listeners. "I'll tell you. It was because the compact provided for a league of labor. It provided for a council of foreigners for American labor and this council could prescribe for labor throughout the world. My countrymen, the senate of the United States thinks the American standard of labor is the highest and it does not propose to lower that standard to the standards of foreign countries." Evidently Harding thought that this anti-foreigner talk to laborers gained more votes than it lost. "As an American citizen I do object to England having six votes, and Hejjaz [sic] and the United States each having one vote." [46]

Harding's thinking on strikes had always been conservative. The red scare helped him view strike activity, especially against public utilities under government regulation, as an infiltration by Communists. The right to work was part of the Bill of Rights, so far as Harding was concerned, and his business associations strengthened his view. When the strike-forbidding provision in the Cummins railroad bill was before the Senate, Harding's friend, Malcolm Jennings, secretary of the Ohio Manufacturers Association, asked for a copy. Harding replied immediately, saying that he was strongly in favor of the anti–railroad strike clause, and asked Jennings to "make a little canvass of sentiment among men whose judgment you trust." Jennings' friends, of course, were all of the anti-strike persuasion. Hence he replied, telling of the desire of Ohio's manufacturers for an anti-strike law for all public utilities. Jennings embellished his views with overtones of alarm concerning the Boston police strike then in process. This impressed Harding, who agreed with Jennings' fears of revolution against the government. "Clearly," said Harding, "we have a very important duty to perform in providing that government services shall not so organize and affiliate themselves as to paralyze the arm of the law at the time of any great emergency. The Boston situation may be a very costly one and prove very expensive to that city of culture, but it is going to make a wholesome contribution to the country." [47]

Harding was sharply challenged on his vote favoring the Cummins bill anti-strike clause. E. J. Miller, secretary of the Baltimore and Ohio Railroad Local Federation of Newark, Ohio, demanded a public explanation. Harding gave him a sharp one in a letter widely publicized on January 3, 1920. He said that the Cummins bill made so many restrictions on the rates and profits of the railroads that it was not fair to subject the roads to risks by the threat of service interruption through strikes. The bill provided full and fair mediation and conciliation service. Moreover, it was not fair to the public to permit labor so much power as to paralyze commerce and industry. He said that the "long fight to revive the domination of capital, now fairly won, is lost if labor domination is substituted in its stead." [48]

Harding's Miller letter, rebuking the unions, delighted businessmen. Coming at the same time as his January 6, 1920 pro-American, anti-Bolshevik speech at the Waldorf-Astoria, it caught their attention at once. "Tell Harding that I said he will not have to write many more letters like that to get the votes of all businessmen." So said a friend to Harding's western political manager, E. Mont Reily, who was also a Kansas City financial broker and mortgage consultant. C. C. Connell of Lisbon, Ohio reported much favorable comment by men who "pay the freight." O. S. Rapp, Marion lumberman, sent out to his fellow tradesmen a thousand copies of the Miller letter. The Hamilton Club

of Chicago made it a feature in the publication, *The Hamiltonian*. As
Reily said, "The more fellows like Miller try to put you on record, and
the more you answer along this line, the more easily [*sic*] it is going to
be to nominate you." [49]

Thus it was that, at Dayton on April 20, Harding made little progress
in explaining his anti-strike vote so as to please labor. He called the
bill the greatest forward step possible in behalf of workers and the
public. The anti-strike clause did not hamper collective bargaining, he
claimed, but helped it by providing a commission to hear both sides in
a dispute. It provided "full and exact justice to every man in the
railway employ. . . . Righteous claims and rightful aspirations could
be met without resort to force, without employment of the strike."
Citing his own status as a union-recognizing employer, he gave forth a
torrent of words about the virtues of unionism and high wages. "I
think," he expanded, "unionism has wrought a liberation and awakened a conscience which unheeding greed came near destroying." [50]
Almost, it might seem, Harding had become a labor sympathizer
himself.

7

When the votes of the Ohio April 27 primary were counted, it did
not seem like a great Harding victory. He did not get a majority of the
preferential voting. Daugherty was defeated, and the Wood people
had elected nine out of the total delegation of 48. The figures for the
preferential vote were: [51]

Harding	123,257
Wood	108,565
Johnson	16,783
Hoover	10,467

The Johnson and Hoover votes were of the write-in variety.

Nevertheless, it was a great Harding victory—considering the circumstances. At least it was said that Wood had not been able to buy a
majority for himself. Harding could go to the national convention
proud of the fact that in the state of the fiercest fighting and the
greatest expenditure of money he had done so well with so little
expense. And when the Kenyon Committee made its revelation of a

profligate and, in some cases, corrupt use of money, the Harding candidacy was still a respectable if not a powerful one.

The alleged mercenary and military part of the Wood candidacy was a strong force from the very beginning in leading Harding to predict that the General would never be nominated. The people did not want that kind of a man, he thought. At least that is what he wrote Scobey on January 29, 1920 when he said that Wood's popularity had started to decline even "though there is limitless money back of his campaign." Harding then made a statement of remarkable finality: "It is my firm conviction that General Wood will never be nominated. The country is coming to a realization that a military candidate does not fit the present situation. If it were not for this fact I would incline to think that he would capture the convention." [52]

This uncanny sense of things to come grew on Harding as the Wood men spent their "slathers" of money in Ohio. He even predicted the revelations which were eventually to destroy the Wood candidacy. Again it was to Scobey that he made this remarkable prediction. "My judgment is," he wrote on March 24, "that continued revelations are going to put the distinguished military candidate out of any likelihood of a nomination. He may make things impossible for me, but you can be sure he is planning for his own retirement at the same time." [53]

Thus it brought no terrors to Harding when Dan R. Hanna threw his newly acquired paper, the *Cleveland News*, to Wood. "I happen to know," he wrote to Scobey, "that Hanna is one of the financial backers and chief boosters of the Wood movement. In many respects, this is vastly more helpful than harmful in Ohio. We are losing no sleep on that score." Hulbert Taft, publisher of the *Cincinnati Times-Star* agreed with Harding. "Judging on the basis of the thousand word extract they sent us," he wrote to Harding, "I should think it would do you more good than harm." [54]

As the campaign developed, the money from Wood's "millionaire angels" poured in and the Hardingites deplored it. It is "appalling" said W. R. Halley of Columbus, who was trying to get together a modest Harding fund in the state of Ohio. By April 4, Harding estimated that Wood had spent over $300,000, "and the end is not yet." In Wooster, Ohio, Wayne county chairman E. S. Landes reported that the Harding workers in northern Ohio "are mad and getting madder." Landes submitted a copy of one of his own advertisements in which the anti-Harding campaign was attributed to "malicious persons" in control of "so-called Republican political newspapers" whose editor had not supported a Republican candidate for twelve years. This, of course, was Robert F. Wolfe of the *Columbus Dispatch* and the *Ohio State Journal.* In Putnam county, editor George Stauffer of the *Ottawa Gazette* published Woods' paid advertisement and then editorially boosted Harding, calling on the Republicans of Putnam not to be deceived. Stauffer sent a clipping to Harding, who replied that he was "completely and wholly delighted," that it did "better for me than any paid advertising that I could send you if I had the means to pay." To F. B. Maullar of Chillicothe, Harding wrote, attributing the anti-Harding agitation among the Negroes and the railroad workers to Wood subsidies. To Thomas F. Turner of Canton, Harding reported the possession of affidavits frankly stating that "money was contributed by the campaign managers of General Wood for the organization of anti-Harding Clubs." Many of the "Wood bunch," Harding told John F. White of Logan, are not Republicans and have "intruded themselves into our Primary." Such tactics were so despicable, he said, that they would produce their own defeat.[55]

The man who felt the full force of the Wood financial onslaught was Harry Daugherty. It was he who had to finance the counterattack. Carmi Thompson was also involved financially, but not as actively as Daugherty. "I have not been able to raise anything like the amount of money we ought to have," wrote Daugherty to Reily on April 23, 1920. "We are going on notes now to raise the money to carry this through. This Ohio fight is the most expensive thing I have ever seen. I have never seen so much money used in my life as they are putting into this fight here. . . . We are being driven to the limit. . . . When you have to go up against from eighty to a hundred thousand dollars in a single district where money can be used successfully, you know what the danger is. . . . We must win this Ohio fight." [56]

After the battle was over and Harding had not swept Ohio, the monetary argument was given full play in explaining that it was a glorious victory after all. The most laudatory of these offerings was, naturally, from Scobey, who congratulated his friend "on the magnificent fight you put up in Ohio, because I can read between the lines that it was a fight." It seemed to Scobey that the Wood people "had all the money in the world" and that "they bought the machines" in Cincinnati and Cleveland. The most vindictive of the explanations of the Harding "victory" was that of A. F. Johnson of Ironton. "This campaign," he wrote, "has been the meanest, most contemptible that I have ever known or heard of, it was nothing less than a conspiracy

between the military candidate and the devil." If it had been necessary, Johnson said that he would have given up everything in the
world except his "kimona." From James M. Faulkner came lurid
accounts of corruption in the "flop wards" of Cincinnati where, under
Hynicka's orders, the voters "threw the soup" into Harding candidates,
especially Daugherty. Faulkner cited one precinct in which Wood
drew sixty-seven votes and Harding none. Howard Mannington, of
the Washington, D.C. Harding headquarters, said that only one-third
of the Republicans of Ohio had taken part in the election. This was a
dangerously small turnout. Former Progressive David Mead Massie of
Chillicothe claimed that Wood appealed to a "lot of bad motives," and
that "most of the votes against you were in the precincts where the
colored vote is strong." [57]

Particularly interesting, and sometimes pungent, were the opinions
of those who believed that the Harding-Wood Ohio primary revealed
the ridiculousness of the direct-primary method of selecting delegates
to the national convention. Wood had shown the "rich man's primary"
at its worst. The *Ravenna Republican* was of the opinion that "the
presidential preference primary in Ohio particularly is a joke." In
Pomeroy, seat of Meigs county, the *Tribune-Telegraph* called the
primary "a very great and expensive farce. . . . Fewer than one fourth
of the voters of this county turned out at the polls. Half of the people
did not so much as know that there was an election and seemed to
care much less." Down the Ohio River, in Brown county, the *Ripley
Bee* opined, "It cost $1,694.10 to hold the Presidential primary in
Brown County and it was of no earthly use. That money could have
been put to better use on our roads. Cut out the primaries and go back
to the convention plan." All three of these counties were strong for
Harding.[58]

Even in larger constituencies anti-primary talk was heard. Harding's
old advisory committee organ, the *Ohio Republican*, asked of what
use was the primary when the stay-at-home voters outnumbered those
who went to the polls by over 3 to 1, and when the winner got a 1-to-6
minority of the total number of party members. Even the once mili-
tantly Progressive *Akron Beacon Journal* confessed to the primary's
failure. It has "brought to the surface only the small political drift-
wood. No first rate men who can make a living at anything else care to
put in the better part of a year in campaigning for office. . . . We once
selected great men governors of the state and sent to Washington
statesmen instead of politicians. That will never happen again as long

as the primary lasts. . . . One can only point to it as another of those beautiful reforms, perfect in theory, but which in practice has turned out to be an utter and absurd failure." [59]

Harding himself had similar views. He believed that his showing in Ohio on April 27 hurt him in Indiana, and he wished that he had concentrated more on Ohio so as to win a 100 per cent Harding delegation to Chicago. Hence he spoke caustically in Indianapolis on May 1. According to the *Indianapolis Star*, he was loudly applauded when he called the primary "the destroying agency of political parties." Harding declared, "I abhor the primary system myself. How can a man conduct a primary campaign when he can only reasonably expect to appear before five percent of the people of the states? It has come to pass that we now give 99 percent of our attention to making the nominations and only one percent to the election of our candidates. I believe that the time has come for the Republican Party to unite against the common enemy." He said that it was ridiculous for a party to nominate men before they declared their principles in a platform. It should be the other way around so that the nominee should be chosen who best fitted the party principles. He was thankful that that procedure was to be followed at the Chicago convention. [60]

8

As the primaries closed and the convening at Chicago approached, the confidence of the Harding men that the other candidates would kill each other's chances was boldly and specifically asserted. This was in keeping with the strategy of not revealing that intention at first, but presenting it as a plain matter of fact toward the end. From Harding headquarters in Columbus the word went out, written by Daugherty in clear and confident tones in a May 10 press release: "No candidate will have anything like a majority of the delegates on the first ballot, and no candidate will have more friends among the uninstructed delegates. Candidates who have made a fight throughout the country to secure this advantage have failed. That Senator Harding will be the beneficiary of many changes after the first ballot is an assurance that comes from various states, especially those that will doubtless influence the nomination. The prospects for Senator Harding's nomination at Chicago were never brighter." W. R. Halley, publicity agent in Columbus, wanted to make these announcements more frequent to make sure the nation saw them, but Harding demurred on the ground that to overdo it would make it look like bluffing.[61]

Harding himself was even more specific in revealing the secret purpose of his courtship of Lowden. He rejoiced, privately, of course, that the Lowden-Thompson feud revealed far more disunity in Illinois than existed in Ohio. On May 18, he wrote to Daniel C. Brower, chairman of the Montgomery county (Dayton) Republican executive committee, "Governor Lowden has a more difficult situation in Illinois than that with which I am confronted in Ohio." And so he concluded, "There was some disappointment in the State of Ohio, but there is no use dwelling on disappointments. The big thing is to go out and win the larger game. I have no doubt that we are going to make a more than creditable showing and have a very reasonable prospect of achieving a victory." [62]

Equally confident was his letter to E. Mont Reily on May 18: "We have never thought for a moment of dropping the fight in the slightest degree. On the contrary, we have been resolved from the day of the Ohio primaries to go through with it to the big finish. As a matter of fact, it looks much more promising today than at any time since we began the enterprise." [63]

It is evident that Harding's first-choice strength in Ohio and second-choice strength outside Ohio gave him a solid foundation for successful politicking at the national convention. He was by no means a weak candidate for the nomination.

9

The Harding workers never knew it, but the Wood organization was sharply divided about challenging a favorite son with a high-priced, home-state campaign. William Cooper Procter admitted this. When he first began to help finance the General, the Cincinnati soap tycoon had estimated that it would cost about a million dollars to put Wood on a successful campaign. Then, as the work proceeded, there developed a split. Frank H. Hitchcock, once Postmaster-General in the Taft administration, favored staying out of state primaries and emphasizing politicking with the prevailing organizations. The other faction favored going into such primaries full tilt with much public electioneering and newspaper advertising. The result was fatal.

Procter described the split and its unhappy effects in a letter of

April 23, 1920 to his niece. "Owing to the Hitchcock matter," wrote Procter, "and the consequent lack of cooperation in Wood's part, there has been a divided organization, and a great let down in its morale. Naturally this has been reflected into the State organizations with the result that we will not be as successful as we expected and would have been in the primary states. Our campaign was based on winning in the primary states and as a result we have had to reform our lines and modify our plans materially and along lines which I don't like as much, don't feel as competent to play and more doubtful of success." Procter went into detail about the Hitchcock quarrel, describing how it had taken away the "pep" in the Michigan and Illinois primaries and threatened success "in other primary states," such as Ohio. The result was that Procter turned to "trading on Hitchcock's unpopularity with the Hays element of the Republican party." The conclusion was that "Wood's case is critical if not desperate. . . . He is not the *cordial* candidate of the politicians so he will not receive their ready and eager support. We, therefore, have the difficult work of persuading by one means or another, enough powerful politicians that he is still the most available candidate. In other words, he will now have to get his nomination by a favor of the politicians who don't really want him." [64]

It is clear, therefore, that the Wood campaign was breaking down. The Harding men did not know it for certain, but, like the professional political fighters that they were, they bore down on their divided foe with a unity which was to be their salvation.

CHAPTER EIGHTEEN

The Nomination

"Why is it that Galvin is receiving all these ovations?" "Because he is the most courageous man in the convention." : : : *Conversation between Frank B. Willis and a friend, as reported in the "Cincinnati Times-Star," June 14, 1920*

◁{ On the eve of the Republican national convention of 1920, events ran true to Harding's prediction that the "rich man's primary" would destroy the chances of Wood and Lowden. A senatorial investigation had been made of campaign expenditures, with sensational results. The Procter-Wood million-dollar advertising methods were exposed to an astounded public. Even more astounding, the Lowden management was revealed as spotted with corruption. Thus it was that the convention met with talk of scandal in the air, and with a haunting fear that the Republican party might lose its surest victory hopes in years if it named as a candidate one who had bought his nomination. For that reason Senators Harding and Johnson had built-in advantages.

Harding's candidacy had greater advantages than Johnson's. Harding was known as a moderate conservative with slightly Progressive leanings. Johnson was believed to be a radical Progressive. His radical reputation limited the degree to which moderate Progressives would support him. Thus, as the Wood-Lowden forces faltered, when the time came to switch most moderates were inclined to support someone less radical than Hiram Johnson, with his strong anti–League of Nations views, and his stand in favor of government ownership of the railroads. The Harding supporters could then approach the roll calls of the nominating convention with mounting confidence.

A crisis came with the campaign fund revelations of the so-called Kenyon Committee. As might be expected, it was Harry Daugherty who hindsightedly claimed credit for this crucial turn of events, in an effort to magnify his own importance. On March 26, 1920 a motion was made in the Senate by William E. Borah calling for an investigation of primary campaign expenses. Borah accompanied his motion with an eloquent discourse on the evil of money in politics, but the Senators were in no mood, as yet, for immediate action. However, by mid-May senatorial tempers had changed to a state of alarm as the Wood campaign won more and more delegates. Thus, on May 20, 1920 the Borah resolution was passed without opposition, and Senator W. S. Kenyon of Iowa was made chairman of the subcommittee involved. Hearings were held immediately.

Daugherty was not one to hide his light under a bushel. How he allegedly masterminded the creation of the Kenyon Committee is told in his book *Inside Story*. "I met the situation," he wrote, "by a carefully guarded movement in Washington. I got the right man to pour into Senator Borah's ear the truth about this vast expenditure of money in a primary election and suggested that the foundations of the republic were being destroyed by this method of making a President. Borah made an eloquent speech and demanded an immediate investigation by a Senatorial Committee and got it." He made these maneuvers, he said, "to put the fear of God into the hearts of the big interests who were seeking making the enormous gifts to General Wood's cause." [2]

Another and more likely version of the origin of the Kenyon Committee is the claim that Hiram Johnson was the one who got Borah to introduce his resolution. The source of this version is an interview by Ray Baker Harris in Washington, D.C. on February 25, 1935 with Senator Simeon D. Fess, who had been a representative from Ohio in 1920. According to Harris, Fess said of Hiram Johnson, "Being himself an aspirant for the nomination, he looked with a critical eye at the obvious expensiveness of General Wood's campaign organization. Upon his return to Washington Senator Johnson immediately conferred with his closest Senate associate of those days, Senator Borah. Senator Johnson pointed out that both Governor Lowden and General Wood were spending such large sums of money in behalf of their candidates that other aspirants, like the Senator himself, could not hope to compete. The next day Senator Borah introduced in the Senate a resolution calling for an investigation." [3]

Whether or not the creation of the Kenyon Committee was deliberately planned to further the presidential hopes of Johnson or Harding, the passage of the Borah resolution was pushed and applauded by the Hardingites. The wounds inflicted by the Wood mercenaries were still hurting Ohio Republican Regulars. On the day before passage of the resolution the *Cincinnati Enquirer* headlined:

DEMAND

Of Borah Approved

When Harding Forces in Ohio Call For Inquiry

The *Enquirer* report included a public announcement from Harding headquarters in Washington that the formation of the Kenyon Committee "will have the approval of all persons who cherish the principles of our representative form of government, and who believe that the selection of a candidate for the Presidency should be free from the corrupting influences resulting from the expenditure of an excessive amount of money or from money obtained from questionable sources. It is a well known fact that the management of the Harding candidacy at all times has invited the closest scrutiny of all receipts and expenditures." [4]

The Kenyon Committee thereupon proceeded to investigate the Wood and Lowden campaign expenditures, much to the glee of Harding men. The first front-page dose of lurid, anti-Wood, slush-fund headlines appeared in the *Cincinnati Times-Star* on May 27: "COL. PROCTER ADVANCED $500,000 FOR THE GEN. WOOD FUND CAMPAIGN." The next day it was "DAN HANNA AGREED TO RAISE HALF MILLION TO FINANCE WOOD'S CAMPAIGN"; in a smaller item was the headline "HARDING HAD FUND OF OVER $113,000." The disparity between the Wood and Harding funds was conspicuous, especially if one read on to secure the details. By June 4, the alleged Wood totals had reached $1,252,916 and were still mounting. Procter's personal contribution was said to have been $721,000. In a 1921 Chicago lawsuit Procter sued for the repayment of "loans" totaling $745,433. His own "gift" contribution made the grand total $813,200. [5]

Then came Lowden's turn. His total was not so great—only about one-half million dollars. But the ugly specter of gross bribery seemed to emerge from the spending of it. Canceled checks to the amount of $2,500 were found payable to each of two national convention delegates from Missouri pledged to Lowden. It was a grossly improper, if not dishonest, thing to do. The Lowden financial manager tried to say there was a legitimate purpose for these checks, but he could not say exactly what that purpose was. The Thompson Republicans in Chicago gleefully welcomed the exposure and exaggerated it.[6]

And so Lowden got his share of Ohio front-page slush-fund headlines with their pro-Harding implications. "That 'Missouri stuff' is not doing Lowden any good," sneered the *Cincinnati Times-Star*. On May 25, 1920 the *Ohio State Journal* headlined: "$404,984 IN EFFORTS TO NAME LOWDEN." A week later it was:

DELEGATES SHARE LOWDEN FUND

Two Admit Getting $2500 Each. Will Pay It Back

They Say, If Lowden Loses

On June 9, 1920 the *Cincinnati Times-Star* had it as: "Lowden's Candidacy Injured by Missouri Testimony." The Harding supporters rejoiced at the misfortunes of their rivals. "Harding Boosters Gain in Optimism," blared the *Cleveland Plain Dealer* on May 30, 1920. "Harding Gains by Wood Exposures," flaunted the *Enquirer* on May 31. Daugherty capped it all with a ringing statement stressing Harding's emergence from the ordeal unscathed "when other candidates fail." The *Times-Star* of the same day put it neatly when it said that "the Harding organizers show that the Senator held Ohio and that but for the character of the campaign arrayed against him he would have held it by a big majority."

Daugherty's conduct before the Kenyon Committee was masterful. He played out his figures to show their modest and popular nature: Carmi A. Thompson—$13,000; Harry Daugherty—$9,500; and the citizens of Marion—$22,500. These were the highest donations. Others ranged from $100 to $2,500. As to what the money was spent for, Daugherty rattled off items for printing and advertising, expenses of the Columbus, Washington, Indianapolis, and Kansas City headquarters, details on the Ohio campaign, and so on. Someone asked him a leading question: "What about opposition expenditures?" Daugherty shot back, "Don't know. We didn't conduct anything like the campaign made for Wood, because we depended on the unanimous endorsement for Senator Harding from the Ohio Republican organization. You can learn the facts from the Wood men." [7]

The Kenyon Committee revelations seemed to confirm the "rich man's primary" feeling so prevalent in Ohio. The *Cincinnati Times-Star* called the primary a "consummate failure. . . . The Presidential primary system is a matter of dollars and demagogy. You must have one or the other these days if you are going to secure delegates to a national convention. Wood and Lowden had dollars. Johnson had both. But nobody has been nominated." [8]

The *Enquirer* called the Ohio primary a "fiasco." "The public is no more enlightened as to who those choices will be than it was in the old days of district and state conventions. The more than $3,000,000 that has been spent on primary propaganda . . . has revealed no outstanding first-choice people's candidate for either party." The hold of the bosses had been strengthened instead of weakened. The primaries had led to the building up of "machines within machines" and to "the concentration of power by a smaller group of leaders which it allegedly was designed to break." In not a single state primary had a majority of the voters participated. In the Ohio primary barely 20 per cent of the party members had voted. [9]

Out of all this disillusionment, an important and indisputable fact appeared: Warren G. Harding had more friends among the delegates to the approaching Republican national convention than anyone else. That does not mean that he had more first choices—but it does mean that he had more second, third, and fourth choices than anyone else. That was as Harding and Daugherty had been planning. That is what Daugherty said in one of his last preconvention announcements: "Senator Harding's availability is the great asset of his campaign. His campaign has left no bitterness, no rancor, no wounds to be healed. He has incurred no enmities, no animosities to militate against rallying to his support." [10]

2

During the springtime pause of mid-May to June 8, preceding the opening of the Republican national convention, Harding did all that he could to preserve and strengthen his standing as a presidential contender. Judging by the sequel, he seems to have done nothing wrong. His conduct was not that of last-minute desperation but exuded a serene confidence in the successful culmination of plans intelligently conceived and skillfully carried out.

One immediate objective was for Harding to deliver a few strategic speeches in keeping with his reputation for mastery as an orator. He did so in two notable appearances: one was his famous "Back to

Normal" speech to the Home Market Club in Boston on May 14, 1920; the other was a brief statement the next day in the Senate, bringing to a close the debate on the Knox Resolution, which sought formally to end the war with Germany.

The theme of the Boston address was a call for the return of America from the fevered ways of war, extravagance, and unneeded reform to the normal ways of peace. It bristled with references to "tranquility at home," "sober capital," "thoughtful labor," "wholesome common sense," "simple living," "thrifty people," a "becoming restoration," and "rational healthful consumption." He spoke of "America's chance to lead in example and prove to the world the reign of reason in representative popular government where people think who assume to rule." "No overall fad will quicken our thoughtfulness." He thought that "we might try repairs on the old clothes and simplicity for the new." This speech contained that famous alliterative and highly quotable declaration of normalcy:

> America's present need is not heroics, but healing; not nostrums, but normalcy; not revolution, but restoration; not agitation, but adjustment; not surgery, but serenity; not the dramatic, but the dispassionate; not experiment, but equipoise; not submergence in internationality, but sustainment in triumphant nationality.[11]

The Harding speech supporting the Knox Resolution was pure politics. As a presidential contender, he brought the season of senatorial peace discussion to a dramatic close. If President Wilson would not terminate the unwanted experiment in internationality, Harding said, the Senate would. Congress had declared war; the Senate had rejected the Wilson League; and now Congress sought to end the war which had really ended months ago. It took the man who insisted on "my will or none," and cast him aside. Wilson was a defeated dictator, a vanquished Caesar. And "if the President of the United States in his obstinancy refuses to say so, then let Congress assert itself and say that war no longer abides." There had been a time when, by adopting the Lodge reservations, the United States would have entered into a new international relationship "on our own terms as we ought. . . . But we frittered away our day of opportunity to dictate the terms on which we might enter. It ought to have been done in the beginning." And now that the discussion is ended the government of the United States is back to "normal." "We are demonstrating to the people of the United States of America and giving notice to the world that the Chief

Executive alone does not run the Republic . . . that this is still a representative, popular government under the Constitution, that the Senate has equal and coordinate power with the President in the making of treaties, and that neither to-day nor to-morrow shall there ever be a Chief Executive of this Republic who, in the lure of ambition or the intoxication of power, can barter away anything essential to the welfare of the Republic." [12] From Dr. L. C. Weimer and Daniel C. Brower of the Dayton organization came the comment that this speech "has caused the people to appreciate more than ever your real value to the country. The nation must have men who are fearless. . . . Right always prevails. You will win." [13]

Another significant bit of last-minute preparation for Harding was to adjust his thirty-nine-man delegation with an idea of strengthening it in his support. This involved Hynicka and the Hamilton county delegates, all of whom were committed to Harding for first choice and Wood for second. Wood had run very strongly in the Ohio primaries in Hamilton county, with Hynicka secretly backing him, and it was, therefore, logical that Wood should be the second choice of its delegates.[14]

The crucial point for Harding in these last-minute days was Hynicka's desire to have some understanding as to when the Wood second choices were to switch to Wood.[15] There were eleven of these in all, five of which came from Hamilton county. Harding, of course, in keeping with the principle of the Ohio united front, preferred not to think about second choices at all. Hynicka, who had a dim view of Harding's chances, wanted a preconvention conference of the Harding delegates to discuss the matter. As a "realist," Hynicka was ever ready to trade with a winner when the break came. Thus, Hynicka might ruin everything by seeing a break *against* Harding and start a stampede for Wood with second-choice Wood delegates. This, of course, would make impossible a stampede for Harding of second-choice Hardingites. This was exactly what Hynicka tried to do in the convention—and he failed.

Fortunately for Harding there were two kinds of Hamilton county Republicans: the suspicious, cynical, "realistic" Hynicka type, and the John B. Galvin "Harding-to-the-last-ditch" type. Galvin was the popular mayor of Cincinnati, and, as it turned out, he was the one who stopped the Hynicka effort to stampede Ohio second-choicers to Wood. It was one of the wisest moves in Harding's entire political life

to encourage John Galvin. By so doing he had a friend in Hamilton
county politics to protect his candidacy from Hynicka's "realism."

The trouble with Hynicka was that he never got it through his head
that Cincinnati was part of Ohio—Galvin did. *Gemütlichkeit* had long
since shriveled in the Teutonic spirit of Rud Hynicka; but it survived
in the Irish soul of John Galvin. Mayor Galvin was the key man in the
Ohio delegation. By cultivating the friendship of both Galvin and
Hynicka, Harding retained the unity of the Ohio delegation, so that
the break went to Harding for the nomination instead of against him.
Hynicka broke against Harding, but came back after two ballots. If
Harding had taken Daugherty's advice, he would have fought Hynicka and probably have lost the nomination. Hynicka's break would
have been permanent instead of temporary.

Daugherty probably had the right idea about Hynicka's intentions,
but he had the wrong idea about how to handle him. Daugherty
believed that Hynicka was power mad. The Cincinnati boss wanted to
be reelected Ohio's national central committeeman with the power to
eliminate Harding from presidential consideration, from his Senatorship, in short, from Ohio politics. This would make Hynicka the
Republican boss of the entire state. "Hynicka," wrote Daugherty,
"does not want you to be President of the United States, because, in
that event, if he were a member of the national committee, he would
be a mere figurehead. Hynicka does not want you to be United States
Senator because, in that event, and there was a Republican President
of the United States, he would be more or less of a figure-head. So Mr.
Hynicka is against you for both positions." The biggest thing, Daugherty said, that could happen to the United States, so far as Hynicka
was concerned, was for the Cincinnati boss to "get you out of the way,
and in a sense get me out of the way and then take over the party for
good or bad." Daugherty related the repeated "treachery" of Hynicka
and asked Harding to consider the effect of Hynicka's continuation in
the national committeemanship on the leaders as well as the rank and
file of Republicans who were loyal "in season and out." [16]

And what did Harding do? He was his usual conciliatory self. He
kept both Hynicka and Daugherty in the party. He conferred with
Hynicka, and, on June 1, announced his hope that the Ohio delegates
would vote the Cincinnatian to succeed himself as national committeeman.[17] No public statement was made as to second choices, the
assumption being that all would remain loyal to Harding. Thus Har-

ding could go to Chicago with his thirty-nine Ohio delegates seemingly solid for him—Hynicka, Galvin, and all the rest. All that Daugherty could do was to smile outwardly and hope for the best.

It is important to emphasize that Harding approached the Chicago convention in full and strong command of his forces. He was making the decisions. He rejected Daugherty's advice to fight Hynicka openly, yet he did not bow and scrape. He rebuked the Cincinnati boss for past disloyalties and placed party unity above personal feelings. "I am very frank," Harding wrote to Hynicka, "to say that I have had some very keen disappointments over the development in our State, but I am always a Republican and have long since acquired the habit of doing the things which seemed essential to achieve party triumph. If I have any scars, I can hide them sufficiently to do whatever is necessary to promote the campaign cause." [18] To A. R. Johnson of Ironton, whom Harding privately favored for Ohio national committeeman, the Senator explained why party unity required that Hynicka be sternly admonished. Harding said that he had no misunderstanding of the way Hynicka had treated him in the past, especially in supporting Wood in the primary and in wanting to bargain away Harding's presidential chances with a premature use of the Wood second choices. "However," he told Johnson, "we have an enterprise to promote and we must promote it in the best way possible consistent with friendships and honor among friends." [19]

This was the old mirage-making Warren G. Harding at his patchwork best—bringing together two opposite factions. He had once believed in the uniting of the ultimate in opposites, Roosevelt and Foraker. He had failed in this. Now that Harding himself was boss he could force the Hynickas and the Daughertys to tolerate each other. The lions and the tigers (not lambs) had to lie down together. A leader like this might really get to the White House.

Harding did not say that his entire political future was at stake in his fight with Hynicka. But the Democrats did—and publicly. In the *Cleveland Plain Dealer*, columnist W. C. Howells was quite frank about it. He saw the Hynicka plot to take the nine Ohio first choices for Wood and, by adding Ohio second choices for Wood, build the basis for a Wood stampede when the "break" came. "To attack Hynicka," said Howells, "would not only endanger Harding's chances for the presidency but for the senate." [20]

Harding, the publicist and the politician, was in command. He made a big display of magnanimity and of overlooking grievances in a

bit of masterful grandstanding as he arrived in Chicago on June 6. He
was met at the railroad station by Daugherty, went to his headquarters at the Congress Hotel, and called Hynicka. After this meeting with
Hynicka, Harding made a strong and dignified announcement, calling
for Republican party unity, the Ohio spirit. As Harding told a reporter
after arriving: "I am here because the Republicans of Ohio, in a
preferential vote, asked me to become a candidate. When the candidacy first was suggested to me, I told the largest state gathering of
Republicans staged in Ohio in 19 years that I would be guided by
their wishes, and the preference primary election gave to me a vote
that was a call to service. . . . This Ohio mission is not to dictate nor
to demand, nor even to attempt dramatic appeal inside or outside the
convention. It is but to present an Ohio candidacy to the delegates, in
the belief that, in their representative capacity, the delegates will
express party conscience in the platform covenant, and choose a
nominee to represent it best. In that way they will promote party
interests and serve the country best. It would be folly to fit a platform
to a nominee and mark the end of popular government through
political parties." [21]

It was good "Ohio Man" talk, and it was good national Republican
talk. It was what hundreds of delegates recognized as high-class
political appeal. It showed Harding strong, dignified, and in the
limelight.

3

The story of the Republican nominating convention of June 8–12,
1920 at the Coliseum in Chicago has been told many times, but mostly
in highly inaccurate versions. It has often degenerated into a generally
accepted legend originally invented by George Harvey, a professional
publicity maker, editor of the *North American Review,* and publisher
of *Harvey's Weekly.*[22] (He became Harding's choice as ambassador to
England). In this legend Harding became the puppet of the senatorial
clique assembled late at night in a "smoke-filled room" after the
delegates had lost their direction in a confusion of indecisive balloting. The weather was oppressively hot; the delegates were tired, out
of money and out of temper. They wanted to get it over with quickly
and go home. At about 2 o'clock in the morning of Saturday, June 12,
Harding was called to Room 404 of the Blackstone Hotel where
"president-maker" George Harvey and his senatorial guests asked him

if there was anything in his past to prevent him from accepting the nomination. After due consideration he assured the group that he would accept their offer. When the convention delegates reassembled, the "boys" put him over. This legend is far from the truth.

There is one element in the "smoke-filled room" legend that is true —the delegates *were* confused. So were the leaders. Because of the large number of aspirants for the nomination there was no dominant figure. The delegates were afraid of any one leader, as a result of the Wood-Lowden impasse. Mark Sullivan reported this leadership vacuum as the delegates gathered on June 4. Senator Boies Penrose of Pennsylvania, one Republican of confident strength and determined personality, was sick and unable to attend. "An army has been created ready for leadership," Sullivan wrote in the *Cleveland Plain Dealer*, "and the leader is a stricken man." The minor leaders milled about and got nowhere. "They have no program. They don't know what to do. They don't know what to think." Procter, manager of the strongest contender, was almost an outcast. People were afraid to be seen with him—and his tainted millions. "Drifting about, they talk, and talk, and talk. Everyone in Chicago is looking for a sign. It begins to appear more and more likely that the nomination may be settled in one of those 'eleven minutes after 2' conferences." [23] Gus Karger, in the *Cincinnati Times-Star*, put it bluntly, "Nobody knows a damn thing." [24]

A prelude to the nomination confusion was the platform confusion, and this played into the hands of Harding. The convention opened officially on Tuesday, June 8, and the first few days were devoted to preliminaries concerning credentials, procedures, and platforms. Discussion of the platform produced some real fireworks over the League of Nations issue, with the necessity of forming a plank that would placate the Borah-Johnson irreconcilables and the Lodge-Lenroot strong and mild reservationists. The result was a catchall document that appealed to many points of view. [25] This was a real aid to Harding, according to Daugherty, who was thus enabled to spin a web of talk emphasizing Harding's party loyalty and his ability to explain difficult issues to the public's satisfaction. [26]

Personalities also played their part in the convention preliminaries. Harding himself was, of course, conspicuously present in the lobbying and the lunching. His headquarters in the Carnation Room of the Congress Hotel was a mecca for those who sought his genial and imposing presence.

Mrs. Harding did her part well. She was left free to talk to whom-
ever and about whatsoever she pleased. According to Daugherty, she
had a way of making a good impression with her frank, "straight-
forward, honest thinking." She was especially effective, of course, with
the reporters. She told them that she knew that her husband would
win, but personally she had always opposed his running. "Think you'd
like the White House?" "I would not," she answered firmly, "We've a
lovely home in Washington and many warm friends. Being a Senator's
wife suits me. It's pleasanter, quieter, its problems never heartbreak-
ing." In the *Chicago Tribune*, she was quoted as saying, "I am content
to trail in my husband's limelight. But I can't see why anyone should
want to be president in the next four years. I can see but one word
written over the head of my husband, if he is elected, and that word is
'Tragedy.' . . . Of course, now that he is in the race and wants to win,
I must want him to, but down in my heart—I am sorry. . . . I've lived
with my husband for twenty-nine years, and I know him. I'm not
talking for effect, he is all the things that I say he is—and more. The
only reason I want to go to the White House is because it is his
wish." [27]

Another personality that helped was that of former Ohio governor
Frank B. Willis, one of the Ohio Big Four, and deliverer of the
address nominating the Ohio Senator. Willis was the athletic type, big
and broad and capable of a resonant, sharp-toned oratory which
Daugherty said, "would lift the tired delegates out of their seats."
Willis was purposely scheduled toward the end of the long-winded
nominating speeches, in the hope of electrifying the bored delegates.
Evidently he did so, first with the unexpected and rousing opening
remark that every one of the nominees was a great statesman. Willis
not only made the rafters ring with the printer-boy, Senator-statesman
hyperbole, but he played the clown effectively as he departed from his
prepared text, and bending his huge frame over the railing of the
speaker's runway, said, in a confidential manner, "Say, boys—and
girls, too, why not name as the party's candidate . . ." Before he could
mention Harding's name everybody was laughing and cheering because of the reference to the girls. This was all the more effective
because it was the first national election in which women were eligible
to vote in all the states. Yes, Willis knew how to make the delegates
laugh in spite of their being tired, and bored—and confused.[28]

Finally, on the evening of Friday, June 11, the "trial by ballot"
began. The expected deadlock developed at once. In four roll calls

Wood and Lowden maintained first and second places respectively, but showed no signs of making heavy inroads on the scandal-scared supporters of Johnson, Harding, and the minor candidates. The box score [29] on these ballots (493 was a majority) was:

	First	Second	Third	Fourth
Wood	287½	289½	303	314½
Lowden	211½	259½	282½	289
Johnson	133½	146	148	140½
Sproul	54	78½	79½	79½
Butler	69	41	25	20
Harding	65½	59	58½	61½
Coolidge	34	32	27	25

Wood's strength was scattered over more states than that of any other candidate. Harding's 61½ votes on the fourth ballot were distributed as follows:

Colorado	1
Delaware	2
Indiana	3
Louisiana	2
Mississippi	2
New York	2
North Carolina	1
Ohio	39
Texas	4½
Utah	1
West Virginia	4
Total	61½

Then came the night of the smoke-filled rooms and the turn of the tide toward Harding. But the turn was not decided by the alleged senatorial clique as the guests of the egotistical Harvey. To be sure, Harvey was there, as were various Senators, but it was hardly a meeting. It was quite informal, and there was much coming and going. Harding was among the visitors after most of the Senators had left. Some conversation was had with Harding about whether there was any disability that might jeopardize the campaign. Evidently none was brought forth, and most of the conferees seemed to have come to "a kind of weary understanding" that, when the convention resumed, support would start going to Harding. That did not mean, however, that those attending the meeting went out to work for

Harding. They merely diagnosed the situation, sensing a turn toward Harding which might still be stopped. Indeed, some of them hoped it would, and envisaged a move toward Will H. Hays.[30]

E. Mont Reily urged other arguments against the Harvey "smoke-filled room" theory. One was that too much senatorial influence would make him too dependent on the Senators later. Reily said Harding told him that he did not approve the "plan that senators and congress-men alone should handle the patronage from the various states, but that those recommendations should come from the President's per-sonal representatives in the states that know the situations back home." As for Penrose, Reily said that Harding had mortally offended the Pennsylvanian in 1916 by failing to support him in the Roosevelt reconciliation committee. Besides, said Reily, Harding said that he never felt that Penrose represented the "better element" in the Repub-lican party. All in all, summed up Reily, there were only sixteen senatorial delegates at the Chicago convention and fourteen of them voted against Harding up to the last ballot.[31]

4

There was another smoke-filled room on the night of June 11–12 that was of far greater importance in strengthening Harding's position than that of the senatorial clique. This was a gathering of the thirty-nine Ohio delegates for Harding to decide whether or not they should switch to Wood when the balloting resumed on the following morn-ing.

This meeting of Ohio delegates for Harding produced a hero who was later acclaimed as the man who prevented the collapse of the Harding-for-President movement. This was Mayor John B. Galvin of Cincinnati, one of the Big Four Ohio delegates committed to Harding. It was Mayor Galvin's refusal to join his fellow Cincinnatians in deserting Harding that gave heart to the rest of the Ohio Harding delegates to stay with their leader until the end. In Galvin, the man and the hour met when the faith requisite to Harding's triumph was put to the test.

The evidence that puts Mayor Galvin in the hero's role comes from the *Cincinnati Times-Star* of Monday, June 14, 1920 when the dele-gates had returned from Chicago and reporters had had a chance to piece together the story of what had happened.

The central issue of the Galvin episode was the delicate subject of second choices. By official action of the Hamilton county central committee, Galvin and the other four Cincinnati delegates were authorized to vote for Wood for second-choice. But Galvin interpreted his "true-as-steel" loyalty to Harding to mean not to vote for Wood until the very end. Galvin's colleagues, especially Hynicka, were men of lesser faith in Harding's prospects and were disposed to vote for Wood after it seemed apparent to them that the Harding cause was hopeless. On Thursday, June 10, the day before balloting began, Galvin sought, without success, to get assurances from Hynicka that there would be no break in the Harding solidarity.

On Friday, June 11, the night of the smoke-filled rooms, Hynicka was ready for the break. There had been four ballots, and Harding had had his day, the votes having actually declined from 65½ to 61¼. Hynicka so expressed himself as the Ohio Harding delegates caucused. So did Cincinnatian Myers Y. Cooper. Harding was called in, and made a brief talk in which he reminded them of the primary campaign for Ohio Republican unity and the dangers to Republican success if Wood captured party leadership. "I believe that I have a chance," he said, "I believe that the hour is not far off when the tide will swing to me. All I ask is that you give me my chance." A motion was made that the delegates stick to Harding until he released them. Hynicka and Cooper refused, saying that almost as many Republicans in Hamilton county voted for Wood as for Harding.

But Galvin would not budge. "My course of action," he declared, "will be to stick to Senator Harding because I believe he is the logical man for President. He has asked us to give him his chance, and gentlemen, I, for one, am going to give it to him, whether it takes six ballots or sixty." Willis thereupon hugged him unashamedly. Galvin's loyalty had prevented the Ohio Harding delegation from collapsing.

Galvin's stand was heartening, but Hynicka's was alarming. The latter had given the Harding men warning that the time had come to make good on their second choices outside of Ohio. He would support the Senator for one more ballot, and then, if he was not satisfied, he would switch to Wood. Great indeed was the scurrying about by Daugherty, Brown, and even by Harding, as they went to work that night on their pledges. Many a smoke-filled room was visited.

There is not a complete record of all the Harding second-choice work on that night of June 11–12, but there is an indication of how the work was begun that swung New York State to Harding. The Harding nucleus in New York consisted of George W. Aldrich and a fellow delegate from Rochester who voted for Harding from the very beginning of the balloting. Aldrich was one of the New York regional "satraps" referred to by Fred Starek. On June 14, 1920, Aldrich told a *Rochester Times Union* reporter that he had decided to support Harding "after looking over the situation." When the news came to Aldrich on the evening of June 11 that the Harding men needed his help, "heartening words were sent to the Ohio manager." So said the *Times Union* reporter on the basis of his interview. The next morning, before the convention was called to order, the New York delegation caucused to see where it stood. According to New York Senator (and delegate) James W. Wadsworth, it developed "that six delegates, in addition to the two delegates—Aldrich and his colleague—intended to vote for Harding." [32] Further evidence of Aldrich's work for Harding comes from New Yorker, Charles D. Hilles. In a letter to Aldrich of June 28, 1920, Hilles wrote, "I told Senator Harding a week ago that you were responsible for the two votes he got from the New York delegation at the 'go off,' and largely responsible for the accretion thereto." [33] Daugherty claimed that he operated on the New York delegation via Aldrich, who "in turn worked on Wadsworth and the New York delegation with great effectiveness." [34] Needless to say, Aldrich was rewarded for his services. After Harding became President, he awarded Aldrich one of the best plums in the New York state patronage, the collectorship of the Port of New York.

And so, on Saturday, June 12, 1920, the day of the final balloting, Harding had his last chance. There were six more ballots. On each of them Harding made gains: on ballot number five, Harding gained 18—five of them from New York as a result of Aldrich's influence. This was not enough for Hynicka, who thereupon switched his Cincinnati delegates (but not Galvin) to Wood, to the accompaniment of hisses from the convention floor in testimony of a general contempt for his disloyalty to Harding. [35] The hissing at Hynicka's defection was not the only expression of contempt for his lack of faith in Harding. Back in New York City a group of men were watching a Wall Street news ticker. One of them was Harding's friend, Joseph C. Bonner, who, upon observing the switch of Hynicka's four votes to Wood, wired Myron T. Herrick, "Take the 4 Ohio delegates who went wrong in the 6th ballot and drown them in Lake Michigan." Herrick wired back, "Your telegram was duly received and delegates drowned as per request." [36] Hynicka later explained his action with what may have been a very politically realistic reason. On the fifth and sixth ballots, he said, it became evident that a concerted move was being made to slaughter Wood for the benefit of Lowden, with no thought whatever for Harding. He, therefore, switched his four Hamilton county votes from Harding to Wood to stop the Lowden drive and to spur the Harding men on to get more second-choice votes for Harding. He did this, he said, with full consulation with Walter Brown, chief manager for the Senator on the floor of the convention. Hynicka insisted that Harding "knew what was going on, so that there was absolutely no double-dealing treachery or double-crossing." [37]

As it developed, what Hynicka said he was trying to do took place. Harding continued to gain. On ballot number six, he received 89 votes; on ballot number seven, 105, as Brown and his assistants continued to gather in the promised second choices; on ballot number eight, Hynicka and his Cincinnatians were satisfied, and were back in line as Harding's total mounted to 133½. The long-hoped-for break to Harding loomed as the Missouri delegation, at the close, sought to change all its votes to Harding. Thus, according to Hynicka, "my attitude and position there was absolutely just and politically correct." In fact, Hynicka believed it was he, and not Galvin, who was responsible for the break to Harding.[38]

At this point, the panic-stricken Wood, Lowden, and Johnson forces called time out, much to the consternation of Daugherty, who shouted that the voice vote on the recess motion had not carried, in spite of Chairman Lodge's ruling that it had. The purpose of the recess was for the leaders to organize a stop-Harding movement either by enabling Wood and Lowden to come to an agreement, or, lacking that, to engineer an adjournment until Monday, June 14.[39]

Several important conferences took place during this Saturday afternoon stop-Harding recess. One of these was the famous closed-taxi ride by Lowden and Wood through the Chicago streets as each tried vainly to get the other to accept the Vice-Presidency. Another event was a hurried conference between the Lowden and Wood backers to try to accomplish the same thing. During these conferences the greatest single piece of Harding second-choice planning fell into place as Governor Lowden told Wood and his followers that it was arranged to support the Ohio Senator.

The authority for this fact of Lowden's pro-Harding ultimatum to Wood is a four-page letter of June 18, 1920 from Wood's manager, Procter, to A. R. Moore, publisher of the *Pittsburgh Leader*. A copy of this letter is in the Harding Papers.[40] Procter told Moore that he had just read, in the *New York Sun*, Colonel George Harvey's account of the smoke-filled room conference of the night of June 11–12 in which all the agents of the presidential aspirants, except Wood, agreed upon Harding. To show the absurdity of Harvey's story, Procter related the "exact facts." At no time during the night, said Procter, were either he or Wood invited to Harvey's room. The only invitation came on Saturday, June 12 at 2:00 P.M. when Lowden proposed the closed-taxi meeting. For forty-five minutes the two talked. Lowden stated that unless Wood and he got together and agreed on who was to be President and who Vice-President, "the combination was made to nominate Harding." No such agreement could be made. The only thing they could agree on was to seek a postponement until Monday, June 14.

After the return of the two from their ride, Procter conferred with Wood and then went hurriedly to Governor Lowden's room and talked with the Governor and his manager, Alvin T. Hert. The Procter letter continues, "The Governor at once began by stating that it was arranged to nominate Harding and nothing would prevent it unless the Wood and Lowden forces got together." He thought the nomination of Harding would be a great mistake and lead the Republicans to defeat in November. Again the opponents refused to accept each other's vice-presidential offers. Procter then reported back to Wood, got further instructions, and returned with Will H. Hays to Lowden's room, with a proposal to try to avoid the pending Harding stampede by getting an adjournment until Monday. There was some talk of trying to make Hays the nominee. They all agreed to the adjournment plan, but, by the time they could get to Chairman Lodge, the convention had resumed its session and the Harding stampede was on. Hert had pledged to hold his Kentucky delegates for Lowden, but, when he arrived at the Coliseum, it was too late.

While this was going on, Harvey and his friends were in session in the "smoke-filled room," No. 404 in the Blackstone Hotel. According to T. C. Wallen of the *Hartford Courant*, a call was made to J. Henry Roraback, chairman of the Connecticut delegation, that Harvey wanted to see him. Taking his fellow delegate James F. Walsh with him, Roraback went to Room 404, where he was told that pledges had been obtained from 600 delegates to make Hays the nominee. Harvey wanted Roraback to get the Connecticut delegates to switch to Hays. Connecticut was the sixth state in the role call, and, since nothing was to be expected from the first five states, the Connecticut switch would start a stampede to Hays. According to Wallen, Roraback refused "in picturesque language," saying that, though Lowden was his delegation's first choice and they had remained true to him, Harding was their pledged second choice. The convention delegates were all at sea, and the time had come to deliver. "That," said Harvey, "will mean a stampede to Harding." To this Roraback bluntly replied, "Nothing would please me better." The conference was ended. The stampede to Harding was assured.[41]

At 4:46 P.M. Chairman Lodge pounded his gavel to call the delegates to order for ballot number nine. The moment of decision had arrived. Harding, Daugherty, Brown, and other loyal Ohioans had done their job. All second-choicers for Harding had been alerted. When Connecticut was called, Roraback arose and announced, "Connecticut gives one to Johnson and thirteen to Warren G. Harding." Pandemonium broke loose. Harding delegates, seizing a large Harding poster, marched down the aisle in front of the Connecticut delegation amid wild cheering and applause. Myron T. Herrick rushed over to the Connecticut section and extended a hearty handshake to Roraback.[42] Another sensation came on the call for Kansas, when Governor Henry J. Allen, who had put Wood in nomination, announced his state for Harding. This was in fulfillment of second-choice preparations between Daugherty and J. B. Adams of El Dorado that had been going on since January, and between Harding and Kansas Senator Charles Curtis.[43] Kansas was quickly followed by Kentucky, a Lowden state, which also went for Harding. In mounting tumult, New York and other states swung over. As each state was called, Andrew B. Johnson, a young medical student who had stationed himself in the rafters of the Coliseum with 25,000 surreptitiously obtained Harding cards, released them by the handful so that, as the stampede grew, a shower of Harding propaganda cards continued to descend upon the hysterical assemblage.[44] When the totals were announced Harding was in the lead with 375, with Wood 249 and Lowden at 122. Ballot number ten was a ratification by tumult, and Harding became the nominee with 692⅕ votes. The usual motion for nomination by acclamation was carried.[45]

As the tenth ballot proceeded to its uproarious conclusion, an episode took place which showed whom the Ohio delegation considered to be the key man in the victory of their candidate. Willis was in the gallery with friends, and a woman sitting next to him asked, "Why is it that Galvin is receiving all these ovations?" "Because," replied the former governor, "he is the most courageous man in the convention." [46]

It is a point of some interest to speculate on the reasons for the unusual loyalty to Harding of John Galvin, who refused to follow the Hynicka move to Wood on the sixth ballot. It may have been Irish obstinacy, or it may have been a clear-headed understanding of the requirements of loyalty in a complex situation. Galvin believed that second-choice thinking for Wood by Ohio delegates was weak thinking. "I simply did," he said, "what I had pledged I would do when I ran for election in the primaries. I believed from the very first that Harding had a splendid chance because the fight among Wood, Lowden, and Johnson followers was developing into a bitter affair. I did not believe that any of the three could muster the votes necessary for nomination. There seemed to me only one other choice—Harding —whom the congressional investigation in Washington had left absolutely unsmirched. And I felt throughout the convention that it was my duty to stick to him to the very last." [47]

5

Harding's choice for a running-mate had been Senator Irving L. Lenroot of Wisconsin. Lenroot himself is the authority for this fact. He wrote to Reily in August, 1920 that after the final roll call on Harding's nomination Will Hays immediately conferred with the Wisconsin Senator, informing him that, in Lenroot's words, "Harding was very anxious that I accept the nomination for Vice-President." Lenroot, after conferring with his wife, reluctantly accepted. But before they could get to the convention floor, the stampede for Coolidge was on. According to Reily, the choice of Lenroot had been all worked out in Washington before Harding and his managers left for Chicago.

6

It is now in order to summarize the factors that made Warren G. Harding the choice of the 1920 Republican national convention. The circumstances of the "rich man's primaries" and the deadlock of the three leading candidates—Wood, Lowden, and Johnson—are clear enough. Though he was fourth in pledged first-choices, Harding was really not a minor candidate. He was nationally known for many reasons, and there had been talk of his candidacy ever since 1916 when he had been keynoter of the Republican national convention.

He had personal qualities of tremendous appeal. Classically handsome, he looked like a Senator—even a President. He was an effective orator for political purposes; he helped out less eloquent Senators and others in their campaigns; in the midst of the red scare, he spread his America-first messages far and wide. His reputation in preparing party platforms, and his vigor in their support, no matter how ambiguous they were or how much he might disagree with details, was implicit.

His ability to reconcile past quarrels and prevent divergencies of personality was magic. He had the ability to please his one-time archenemy, Theodore Roosevelt, and actually inherit his mantle as a presidential possibility. To receive the trust of former Progressives and, in fact, to supervise a plan of reconciliation in his own state, was a tribute to his charm, if not to the depth of his political principles. To win the approval of both sides in the debates on the League of Nations, prohibition, and woman suffrage was a tribute to the same ambivalence of his nature.

His image as another "Ohio Man," a new McKinley, was important because of the importance of Ohio. The ability to team with the rival managers, adept in promoting that illusion—Daugherty, Walter Brown, Hynicka, Myron T. Herrick—was almost unbelievable. His success in wrenching from such strong and conflicting Ohio characters sufficient support for the plan of no second choices in the Buckeye state and no first choices outside of Ohio was a masterpiece. So was his ability, in the final preconvention days, to use the influence of John B. Galvin to hold Hamilton county in line.

Of the highest importance was his escaping the mercenary exposures which ruined Wood and Lowden. The ability of Harding and Daugherty to sense this flaw, especially in the Wood campaign in Ohio, and to exploit it to the full was evidence of the keenest political insight and public-relations mastery.

CHAPTER NINETEEN

The Return of the Progressives, 1920

"It is very possible that we shall soon come to a condition in this country when a type of old-fashioned Republicanism will be more or less welcome to a majority of our people." : : : *Harding to George D. Simmons, February 3, 1919, Harding Papers, Ohio State Historical Society*

"I have always been a rational Progressive." : : : *Harding to William Allen White, August 12, 1920, Harding Papers, Ohio State Historical Society*

The Republican national convention of 1920 marked the "official" end of the Progressive movement. That is to say, there was no separate Progressive convention as in 1912 and 1916. Also, it was the business of Harding and the Republican organization not only to treat the ex-Progressives as equals but to make considerable display of the process of doing so.

The GOP leaders began the presidential campaign of 1920 in a state of jitters; they ended it in a state of serenity, confidently expecting the unprecedented majority which they received. The central reason for their change of mind was the role of their candidate, Senator Warren G. Harding of Ohio. It was the calm, dignified, friend-winning personality of their candidate and his magic-making oratory which soothed their original fears. His ambivalence on party principles and platforms also helped.

Republicans had reason to feel jittery in the early days of their 1920 campaign. In the previous two presidential runs they had performed miserably. In 1912, they had split wide open and suffered the penalty in the election of a minority Democratic opponent, Woodrow Wilson. In 1916, with Charles Evans Hughes as their candidate, poor management had caused another loss. In the primaries of 1920, they had narrowly escaped division again in the Wood-Lowden-Johnson fight for the nomination. Fear of mistakes was in the air. Old-timers like Henry Cabot Lodge recalled the "Rum, Romanism, and Rebellion" mistake of Reverend Samuel D. Burchard which lost the election of 1884 for James G. Blaine. "I am an old man," Lodge wrote to Senator Harry S. New of Indiana, "and I remember the Burchard luncheon. I am afraid of what somebody else may say." [1]

This fear psychosis accounted in large measure for the decision to conduct the Harding campaign from the candidate's front porch in Marion. "Keep Warren at home," warned Senator Boise Penrose, "he might be asked questions if he went out on a speaking tour and Warren's the kind of damned fool who would try to answer them. Besides he hasn't any opposition." [2] In September, party adviser Richard Washburn Child told Hays, on September 12:

> Don't let them get Harding on tour. . . . Today we are winners. Today the country is absorbing the idea that Harding is a statesman and not a war politician. We are working out a fine, dignified picture, and a fine, dignified policy. Nothing but some calm will allow us to go on building up that effect. A tour will absolutely wreck the attempt. It is full of risks. Cox will say he has smoked us out. We will appear to be in a panic. Factional division will pull and haul on the candidate wherever he goes, and he will get in wrong. There is a great danger of some local frost. Hold the outside speaking to New York, two Great Lake cities, St. Louis —allow no banquets or receptions. Boston is not necessary. We win in New England anyhow. Hold 'em down. This is not an uphill battle requiring panic methods. It is a fight won unless breaks occur. The Republican Party has done some stupid things before you took hold. For Heaven's sake, don't let's be stupid now. [3]

Others felt the same way about the front-porch idea. Said the *Chicago Tribune* editorially, "If Harding doesn't make any fool breaks during the campaign, and he doesn't measure up like a man who would—and more important yet, if he can keep his friends from making too many fool breaks on his behalf—the election looks like a certainty for him." [4]

The jitters eventually subsided. It gradually became clear that the well-poised Harding was foolproof. There would be no "boners" as far as he was concerned. For one thing, every effort was made to be nice to California and the Far West. There would be no recurrence of anything like the Hughes "snub" of Johnson in 1916. As subsequent pages will show, Harding leaned over backward in indulging Hiram Johnson and William E. Borah in their isolationist, anti–League of Nations sentiments. One of Harding's first campaign maneuvers was to recommend to party chairman Hays the selection of Elmer E. Dover of Tacoma, Washington as chief of the GOP headquarters in San

Francisco. Harding made a strong point of Dover's association with Mark Hanna in the campaigns of 1896 and 1900. The veteran Dover was thereupon appointed to the San Francisco post, with the *Chicago Tribune* announcing that it was done "to avoid the blunder of 1916." [5]

Before the campaign was over the Republicans learned to have full confidence in Harding. It became necessary to leave the front porch and appear before farmers in Minnesota, southerners in Oklahoma, and audiences in the East. In the process, he conducted himself magnificently, replying to hecklers with charming frankness and dignity. In October, author Meredith Nicholson caught this feeling when he wrote to his friend "Dearest Bill" Hays, "You know as well as I do that Harding's no great shakes, and that his nomination was against the best thought of your own party. But he won't do anything foolish, and I do believe that he will assemble high grade men for the big job." [6]

There was no one more sure of Harding's foolproofness than Harding himself. When *Cincinnati Times-Star* reporter Gus Karger told him that the Democrats would try to bait him into indiscretion, Harding replied, "There will be a lot of things about which you may have a very reasonable doubt, but there is one thing you can be very certain about throughout the campaign: nobody is going to make me lose my temper and indulge in impulsive utterances." [7]

2

The demands on Harding for reconciling Progressives, Californians, *et al.*, put a premium on political patchwork—and this was the Senator's forte. Indeed, the Republican presidential campaign of 1920 was one of the greatest examples of patchwork politics in American history. Harding had been patching together divergents and opposites ever since he took over the *Daily Star* in 1884 to make profits out of business, and created the *Weekly Star* in 1885 to make profits out of politics. He had patched and politicked all his life and loved it. He had developed the newspaperman's techniques of a column and an advertisement for everyone and offense to nobody until it was part of his personality. He knew how to sublimate it into the Harding friendliness, poise, and oratorical magic that was his equivalent for the bedside manner that he had observed in his father's handling of medical patients.

All through his political life Harding had patched and patched and patched. He had patched Hannaism and Forakerism, Forakerism and Rooseveltianism, Herrick and anti-Herrick men, the Anti-Saloon League and the wets, Progressives and Regulars, Hynicka and Daugherty, Hamilton county and the Ohio cross-words, 100 per cent Americans and pro-Germans, woman suffrage and traditional politics, Johnson-Borah irreconcilables on the League of Nations and the Lodge-Root League reservationists. His patching together of second choices at the nominating convention was a marvel to behold. And he was to do it again and again in the election campaign of 1920, uniting the following diverse factions: the Roosevelt following, the "Penrose gang," the GOP machines in every state, the pros and antis on the ratification of the woman suffrage amendment, the members of the leading fraternal lodges in the country, the jangling elements of the nascent farm bloc, the "lily whites" and the "black-and-tans" on the Negro question, the nationalists and the internationalists with regard to the League of Nations question, the Hooverites and the leave-us-alone business and commercial interests. He could write to a friend on February 3, 1919, "It is very possible that we shall soon come to a condition in this country when a type of old-fashioned Republicanism will be more or less welcome to a majority of our people." A year later he could claim in a letter to William Allen White, "I have always been a rational Progressive." [8]

It helped, of course, that the Republican platform was a convenient straddle on most issues. Harding used it in the usual gospel way in calling for loyalty to it. When interpreters of varying persuasions would heckle and harass, no one could outwit the master of the double talk in mollifying them.

Upon one occasion Harding himself admitted that he was a double-talker. This related to the issue of the direct primary. He was strongly opposed to this device of nominating candidates and said so openly until the time came to court the Progressive prodigals back into the GOP. Then he deliberately suppressed his convictions. He admitted this quite frankly in a private letter to Lafayette Young of Des Moines, writing on June 30, "I really think if the primary is to be accepted as a thing worth while, I ought not to have been the nominee of the Chicago convention. I have some well defined convictions on this subject but I am very reluctant to say some of them because so many of them are fearful that it will stamp me as possessing reactionary tendencies." [9] This was typical of Harding. With all of his personable attractiveness, many of his thoughts could not stand the light of fundamental discussion in the open.

"All Republicans look alike to me," beamed Harding as he returned in triumph to Washington on June 16, 1920 and put his charm to work. On June 18, he breakfasted with Herbert Hoover, lunched with Harry Daugherty, and dined with Will Hays. In between he conferred with Calvin Coolidge, Lowden manager Alvin T. Hert, Wood backer and oil tycoon Jake L. Hamon of Oklahoma, Senator John W. Weeks of Massachusetts (also a Wood man), and New York political leader Charles D. Hilles.[10] Telegrams came and went between him and party notables Walter Brown; Albert J. Beveridge; Senator Medill McCormick and his equally influential wife Ruth; Alexander P. Moore, Johnson backer and editor of the *Pittsburgh Leader*; and dozens of others.[11] Each day was as crowded as the day before. As he told Senator Lawrence C. Phipps of Colorado, "I have been making it a point to get prominent men committed before they have had an opportunity to grieve over the results of the convention." [12] One could not make a "fool break" forgiving everybody.

The fact that the extremes of the Republican party were so far apart held no terrors for the gracious and confident Senator. Perhaps it was true, as conservative Governor Goodrich of Indiana said, "Penrose, Brandegee and Smoot do not belong in the same party with Johnson, Kenyon, Cummins, Capper, La Follette, Borah and others." [13] But such opposites were not too much for Harding's talents. As he told the liberal Raymond Robins, Roosevelt backer in 1912 and 1916: "I am sure you knew that I went as far as it was possible for me to go in making an appeal to the widely divergent elements in our party. It was no easy task and I had the problem of reaching out and inviting all factions and still cling to the things which I could say with the utmost sincerity." [14]

3

Harding's sincerity in reuniting the Regulars and the Progressives for the campaign of 1920 got its supreme test soon after he was nominated when the Democrats published the hateful things the *Marion Star* had said about Roosevelt in 1912.[15] How could a man sincerely seek the support of Roosevelt's friends when his newspaper had bluntly likened T. R. to Benedict Arnold and Aaron Burr. When

Harding's *Star* managing editor, George H. Van Fleet, upon request, sent to Harding the terrible truth in the form of straight quotations from the 1912 *Star*, the only thing Van Fleet could think of to suggest was that Harding had not actually written them and Malcolm Jennings had. Jennings admitted this.[16] The Senator, of course, had to assume responsibility.

But Harding was able to accomplish the impossible. He instructed his Washington press agent, Robert Armstrong, to write to Columbus press agent W. R. Halley for copies of the Roosevelt memorial address by Harding to the Ohio state legislature on January 29, 1919. Armstrong promptly did so with a "rush special delivery" telegram, and the nation was soon serviced with Harding's encomium on the man he had once called a traitor. T. R. was now "the flag's bravest defender," "the most courageous American of all times," "the great patriotic sentinel, pacing the parapet of the republic, alert to danger . . . always unafraid." [17]

4

More important to Harding than this post-mortem T. R. patchwork was the greater patchwork involved in securing the return of the T. R. prodigals who had stood with their leader at Armageddon in the heady days of 1912. In 1916, the Progressives had not run a third ticket, but they had not really "returned." One of the blunders of the Hughes-Willcox campaign of 1916 was the failure to stage a spectacular "return of the prodigals." If they had done so, the Republicans would not have alienated Hiram Johnson, and thus would probably have won California and the election.

Harding and the Republicans really put on a big display of the "return of the prodigals" in 1920. It was one of the central features of the campaign. It was deliberately planned by high party counselors. National Speakers' Bureau chairman and Indiana Senator Harry S. New wrote to Daugherty on July 16, "Two whose names occur to me as those who should be requested directly by the Senator are Mrs. Douglas Robinson and young Colonel Roosevelt. These because one is the sister, the other the son of an ex-President." [18]

And so, one by one, starting with T. R., Jr., the Progressives came trooping in, to the accompaniment of flaring headlines and repeated news items. Before the month of June was over, judging by newspaper coverage, it seemed as if the entire tribe of former Progressives had duly registered their reentry into the GOP. Some came back to the tune of such headlines as the *Chicago Tribune* displayed on June 28:

MOOSE PULLING WITH G. O. P. IN HARDING CHARIOT

Roosevelt's "Best Bets" in Senator's Corral

Said the *Tribune* editorially, "The unification movement which two weeks ago seemed almost insuperable is well nigh complete. Senator Harding has always been noted as a past master in promoting harmony, but his success in bringing together discordant elements within the party has surpassed all expectations." Progressive notables with whom Harding had already conferred were listed: Theodore Roosevelt Jr., Albert J. Beveridge, Kansas Governor Henry J. Allen, Oscar Straus, Miles Poindexter, Medill McCormick, Frank B. Kellogg, and Irving Lenroot. Actually, these Progressives and others had been approaching the Republican shrine since T. R. died in January, 1919.

Obviously most spectacular in this display of bandwagon gladhanding was the early return of Colonel Theodore Roosevelt Jr., a rather impressionable young man who lacked most of the qualities of his father, except his ambition and susceptibility to flattery. In this operation the influence of the former President's friend Walter F. Brown is discernible. Young Roosevelt had left the Chicago convention somewhat miffed at the failure of his favorite, General Wood. However, the foxy Brown carried a message from Harding to the young man suggesting an interview. Roosevelt at once telegraphed in reply, suggesting a meeting on June 25 or 26 at Atlantic City. Harding wired back accepting, but expressed his preference, of course, that Roosevelt see him in Washington. Roosevelt then wrote an apologetic letter to which Harding immediately replied with effusive praise and reference to the Harding-Roosevelt rapproachement following the Hughes defeat in 1916. These letters were then released to the press, and the meeting—at Washington, not Atlantic City—took place. Roosevelt then followed up with two detailed memoranda for Harding's acceptance speech. They concerned the soldier's bonus and a plan of improved employer-employee relationship and profit-sharing along the lines of certain leading industries such as the Endicott-Johnson Shoe Company and the Procter and Gamble Company at Cincinnati. Harding again replied effusively, acknowledging the Roosevelt proposals as "very helpful" and stating that "their reflex" would be found in his acceptance remarks. Eventually, on Acceptance Day in Marion, July 22, Roosevelt was conspicuously placed on the platform and spoke a few enthusiastic words in behalf of the candidate.[19] There was very little evidence of Rooseveltian "reflex" in Harding's acceptance speech.

Some former Progressives were rather annoyed at the young Colonel's haste in jumping on the Harding bandwagon. Such annoyance was reflected in the observations of E. A. Van Valkenburg, editor of the Republican *North American,* who led a diehard, rear-guard action deploring the Harding convention "stampede" of the weary delegates. In a letter of July 25 to Brown he said, "Teddy Jr. has aroused the most violent criticism because of the unseemly haste he displayed in getting on the band wagon." He attached a clipping of his editorial entitled "A Disappointing Result," in which the Harding nomination was lamented. Brown sent both letter and clipping to the Senator.[20]

The names of other members of the Roosevelt family were invoked. As New suggested, T. R.'s sister, Mrs. Corinne Roosevelt Robinson, was coached into being an enthusiastic Harding supporter. She was named a member of the Republican national executive committee, her name being listed prominently in that body's letterhead. In the last six weeks of the campaign she was speaking daily in an extended stumping tour as part of the effort to attract the new women voters. In between, she and Harding exchanged congratulatory letters with special emphasis on the Senator's January 29, 1919 Roosevelt memorial address to the Ohio legislature. Copies of this were distributed by Mrs. Robinson among her friends who resented the Harding *Star* criticisms of her brother in the "political disagreement" of 1912. Mrs. Robinson said she liked Harding's 1919 memorial address more than "almost any other that was made at that time." Help also came from T. R.'s widow, from whom a pro-Harding statement was obtained and circulated in pamphlet form.[21]

Special treatment was also given to prominent T. R. sympathizers. One of these was Hiram Johnson, who had shared the Harding *Star* animadversions in 1912 and who had been supersensitive ever since the Hughes "snub" of 1916, which lost California to the Republican cause. The conversion, indeed, the coddling, of Johnson was considered by the Republican party leaders to be a matter of supreme importance. If Johnson could be induced to campaign in the East, the support of the host of Johnson and Progressive enthusiasts would be assured. To many important Republicans this seemed vital to party victory in the November 2 election.

The deliberate and bare-faced flattery with which Hiram Johnson was courted in the 1920 campaign would be unbelievable if there were not the very words of its authors to prove it. These authors were Harry S. New, director of the party's Speakers' Bureau, Harry M. Daugherty, and Warren G. Harding. On July 16, 1920 New wrote Daugherty the following frank and confidential letter: "There are two or three matters connected with the Speakers' Bureau game that are delicate and of supreme importance concerning which I wish specific and definite information just as early as it can be furnished me and I am putting it up to *you* to see that I have it." The most important of these supremely important matters, wrote New, was that of "three or four high-grade people for whom there is already great demand who ought to be first approached by Senator Harding and his request followed by me as Chairman of the Speakers' Bureau. First among these is Hiram Johnson. You know what a prima donna he is. I may say to you that the demand which comes for him is greater than that for all other speakers combined. He will be of perfectly immense value to us in this campaign. In fact I think indispensable. It is of the most vital importance that we should be able to get him to come East on a trip that will occupy a full month say from September 15th to October 15." New suggested that Harding should not approach Johnson until after the acceptance speech of July 22. By that time the issues will be "complete," and "Johnson will know exactly where he stands and what he is willing to do, and Warren should put it squarely up to him in the way he knows the Johnson family likes to be approached." [22]

Daugherty needed no urging. He immediately forwarded Senator New's letter to Harding with appropriate embellishment. "Tell Johnson," said Daugherty, "you expect him to help pull this ticket through. You know how to pump him, a letter that he will show his wife and then she will help. Say to Johnson by all means he must make two or three speeches in Ohio." [23]

Harding agreed. Five days after his acceptance speech of July 22, he wrote to Johnson, using the flattery that New had suggested. This consisted of thanking Johnson for being so generous in approving the acceptance speech. In his speech Harding had made a point of accepting United States international responsibilities without at the same time impairing American isolationism. Harding blandly wrote that Johnson had made previous utterances along the same line, and that Johnson was, therefore, the official spokesman of the Republican party on foreign relations. For Harding to write this to the fiercely isolationist Johnson was a piece of arrant hypocrisy, considering the concessions to internationalism Harding had already made and was to continue to make. Harding's words must be quoted to reveal his double-talk. Harding wrote that he was so glad that Johnson, by approving the acceptance speech on foreign policy, "understood the necessity of performing a party service in making it possible for the divergent elements of the party to come together, with the assurance of preserved nationality, on the one hand, and a readiness to participate in performing a recognized duty to world civilization, on the other. I did not mean to add to the interpretations which you have already made quite correctly and which will stand as the official utterance on our international relationship." [24] (See chapter xxiii.) If this private truckling to Johnson had been known by the public, Harding would have lost the support of the internationalist wing of the Republican party. Whether this would have lost him the election is debatable.

Harding did more than flatter Johnson—he flattered Johnson's financial backer. This was the wealthy William Kent of Kentfield, California, who had financed the Johnson senatorial campaign in 1916. Word came to Harding in a letter of June 18 from William Seward Scott, secretary of the Republican county central committee in San Francisco, that "it would not be a bad idea for you to write Mr. Kent a personal note soliciting his assistance and co-operation," especially since Kent was a candidate for the Republican nomination to the Senate.

Harding replied that he would do so immediately and, on July 7, sent a letter, telling how anxious he was to harmonize the party and make "all elements feel that they could be a part of the big enterprise," and soliciting Kent's "suggestions and advice." On July 15, Kent replied, making rather detailed proposals about Republican policy and promising to be "a staunch and steady help" to Harding. Kent published his letter, and, if we are to take the judgment of G. S. Arnold of San Francisco, California, Progressives were saved from defection. Wrote Arnold, on July 17, "You letter to William Kent means thousands of votes for the party from Progressive Republicans of California. If the same wisdom had been shown in the 1916 campaign, California would have been unquestionably Republican. Most of the Republicans in California are not of the type known as 'old line,' but the party will be none the less successful if your action in this matter is indicative of the kind of leadership we are to have." [25]

Harding's Kent-Johnson maneuver almost backfired into another California "snub" affair. On June 24, Edward J. Sullivan, manager of the conservative senatorial candidate Samuel M. Shortridge, claimed that Kent supported Wilson in 1916, and that Harding should not interfere in California politics. Harding was able to wriggle out of this predicament by replying that he was taking no sides in the California senatorial primaries.[26]

Helpful in obtaining Progressive converts to Harding was Frank A. Munsey, publisher of several important daily newspapers such as the New York Sun, New York Evening Telegram, Baltimore News, Baltimore American, and the Boston Morning Journal. In 1912, Munsey and his dailies had "bull moosed it" for T. R. In 1920, the Munsey papers still retained the confidence of eastern Progressives. The rapprochement between Harding and Munsey began in December, 1919 when George Christian sought to get former Marionite H. V. Fisher, New York broker, to arrange a Harding-Munsey dinner where the Ohio Senator's "bigness, business qualifications, his executive capacity, banking connections, his poise, etc. might be presented to Munsey in an appropriate manner." How productive the rapprochement was may be judged from the fact that, when Harding was nominated on June 12, Munsey put his papers enthusiastically behind the new nominee. On Sunday, June 13, the day after the nomination, Munsey's Sun and New York Herald led off with a page-one editorial entitled "Harding and Coolidge an Exceptionally Strong Team." Two days later, in a front-page, signed editorial, Munsey lavished great praise on Harding, using the "small town boy makes good" theme, plus the idea of the commonsense leader with his "feet squarely placed on the ground." "We have had two years of hitting the sky. We have had enough for the present." By June 17, Munsey was so proud of what he had done that he phoned Fisher and asked how he liked the Sun's Harding policy. Munsey's zeal for Harding went so far as to place at the candidate's disposal for as long as he liked "his beautiful Bachelor house with his household staff—one of the most delightfully located in the Adirondacks." [27]

An affair that did much to complete the back-to-Harding trek of the Progressives was a dinner at the New York Harvard Club on July 1. It was arranged by Walter Brown (Harvard, 1892) and other alumni. The purpose of the meeting, according to the *New York Times*, was to assure chairman Hays that the Progressives were solidly behind Harding. Among those present were Theodore Roosevelt Jr.; Lawrence F. Abbott of Roosevelt's old magazine the *Outlook*; Henry L. Stoddard, author with Rooseveltian persuasions; E. A. Van Valkenburgh of the *North American*; Porter Emerson Browne, the novelist; Alexander M. Moore of the *Pittsburgh Leader*; and James R. Garfield of Cleveland. Invited but unable to attend, and in full sympathy with the reunion idea, were many old Progressives, including Kansas Governor Henry J. Allen, former Indiana Senator Albert J. Beveridge; New York banker Oscar S. Straus; Theodore Douglas Robinson (T. R.'s brother-in-law); Myers Y. Cooper and A. L. Garford of Ohio; and Dr. Albert Shaw, editor of the *Review of Reviews*. Practically everybody present spoke, and the general theme was that Harding would grow as a candidate, was a broad-minded man, and was attractive to all elements of the population. What most pleased the assemblage was the report that Harding was strongly against one-man government—as per President Wilson. A resolution was adopted pledging support to Harding and Coolidge and endorsing the "enlightened leadership" of chairman Hays. The *Times* made a point of reporting that "all of the leaders of the Progressives who had formerly supported the party had abandoned it." [28]

After this Harvard Club meeting the Progressive return became quite fashionable. Van Valkenburgh of the Philadelphia *North American*, who had previously been disappointed in Harding, wrote to him on July 2 that the Harvard Club meeting "served to clarify the atmosphere and that increasingly we shall have the effective cooperation of most of the old Progressives." Van Valkenburgh was "mighty glad that Walter Brown enjoys your confidence as he is altogether the best person you could have to bridge the gulf between you and the old Roosevelt men." There would be no anti-Harding editorials in the *North American*, assured Moore of the *Pittsburgh Leader*. Van Valkenburgh's future editorials were pro-Harding with a T. R. twist as, on September 2, he cited Roosevelt as the originator of the World Court-Hague Tribunal compromise which Harding incorporated into his views on the League. Moore, head of the Pittsburgh Progressives, took it upon himself to guarantee the loyalty of Beveridge and claimed credit for the return of Hiram Johnson to the fold. "That is one of my jobs completed," he wrote Harding on July 8, following Johnson's announcement. From Hays came the report that one of the editors of the *Outlook* would soon call for an interview in the preparation of an article which will "do a great deal of good." The *Outlook* gradually became ardently pro-Harding, especially on the League of Nations question. This was shown in an article by R. W. Montague on October 6, entitled "Harding's All American Plan." Similarly shepherded by Hays came a writer from the *Metropolitan Magazine* for an article in the issue of October 15. "This will reach the Roosevelt-Wood group effectively," wrote Hays, "as they are largely the clientele of that magazine." Even before the July 1, Harvard Club affair, Albert Shaw had brought his *Review of Reviews* to the Harding cause with a highly laudatory article by Ohio Congressman Simeon D. Fess. Then there was George Harvey, opinionated host of "the smoke-filled room," who was filling *Harvey's Weekly* and *North American Review* with praise of Harding for his stand against the League of Nations. In return, Harding invited his "benefactor" to the "front porch" for "assistance and advice." And the future ambassador to England was not one to refuse.[29]

Most enthusiastic of the Progressives who were willing to return in support of Harding was Chicago social worker Raymond W. Robins, chairman of the Progressive convention of 1916. Robins was the one out-and-out Progressive placed on the Republican national executive committee in 1920. He was an intellectual and a full-time aide to Hays during the preconvention months in directing research in preparation for the framing of the party platform, the composing of Harding's July 22 acceptance speech, and in supplying facts for the subsequent campaign. Five days before the acceptance ceremonies, Robins wrote the candidate of a plan to borrow some of the choice "Hardingisms" from the acceptance speech—in the preparation of which Robins hoped his influence was considerable—for special pamphleteering purposes.[30]

Robins' letter to Harding contained what may be called an intellectual's obituary of the Progressive movement. It premised the idea that the insecurity resulting from the European post-war wreckage, the rise of Bolshevism, and Wilsonian super-idealism required the strengthening of constitutional government in America in support of ordered security and the freedom of private enterprise. This, said Robins, Harding was ideally fitted to bring about:

> The central idea shall be that your candidacy deserves the support of all who believe that respect for and faith in constitutional republican government, with its ordered liberty and just authority safeguarding the

legal rights of all persons and property, and permitting such modifications of the social structure within the Constitution and the law as
changing economics and social conditions demand is the only adequate
answer to Bolshevism and the class hatred and social cleavage which
have wrecked Europe and now challenge America. What the people
want more than all else is a sense of security and freedom under law.
They want to know that they can labor and build and live their own
lives as in the days before the war free from senseless inquisition and
mandates, either of the government or of any class interest. They want
to recover the old good-will and straightforward American spirit of
manly rivalry in the game of life, free from European complications and
domestic spies and censorship. I believe that you can give them this
sense of emancipation from the whole miserable Wilson method of
intoxication through golden promises one day and bitter "morning after
taste" through leaden performance the next.

It would seem from this that Bolshevism and "Wilsonism" had been
helpful cathartics to enable the public to come to the realization that
Progressivism was no longer dangerous, if indeed it was alive at all.

Robins proposed that "around this central principle of fundamentalism as incarnated in your candidacy" and the history of the Republican party, the campaign include an effort to get the special co-operation of the basic groups in American society. He enumerated them:
(1) judges and lawyers, led if possible by Charles Evans Hughes; (2)
religious leaders and laymen desiring the enforcement of the Eighteenth Amendment and the Volstead Act; (3) progressive businessmen
who know that production is a matter of normal self-interest plus good
will and consent; (4) men and women of labor who believe in their
country and own some property, however little; (5) the Roosevelt
Progressives, who believed in him because he instinctively supported
the rights of the whole people as against the special interests of any
class; (6) the Johnson-Borah following, who resented the Treaty of
Versailles as one of vengeance, ruthless force, and economic imperialism.

Akin to Robins in spirit and vision, but far more precise in defining
proposed remedies, were Herbert Hoover and his group of new Progressives. These men—and women—were too young to have fought
with the heroes of the "War of 1912." The buoyant, "pushy" Hoover
and his kind did not "belong." To practical Republican politicians,
including Harding, he had been a *persona non grata* because of his
identification with the Wilson administration during World War I,
which, to Hoover, were times of "rigorous non-partisanship." They

remembered his aberration of 1918, when he supported the President in the congressional campaign of that year. But in 1920, he was quick to rejoin his "lifelong Republican association," and to offer his economic planning approach to Republican responsibilities as he gathered about him a new generation of devoted followers such as Robert A. Taft and the about-to-be-enfranchised women voters.[31] Harding was quick to abandon his 1919 contempt for the young Californian.

Hoover's self-confidence and self-assertiveness may well have been too much for members of the Republican old guard, but not for candidate Harding, whose cordiality extended to all the prodigals, young or old. The Ohio Senator was impressed with Hoover. As a defeated candidate, Hoover was one of the first to congratulate Harding upon his nomination. He was thus one of the first to be invited to confer with Harding, and one of the first to accept. Moreover, Hoover brashly broadcast the results of his conference with Harding as soon as it was over. In a June 18 interview, the eager Hoover told reporters, "I presented the views which I believed were held by a considerable group of independent and progressive Republicans upon various questions." The Senator, he said, wanted to have the views of both the conservative and progressive wings in order to make a strong united front. And there was no longer any danger, Hoover added, that Harding would be dominated, like Wilson, "by any group or coterie." [32]

An important phase of the Harding–Hoover rapprochement was Harding's alleged success in converting Hoover to a belief in the necessity of being a good Republican. He must never consort with the Democrats again as he had with Wilson during the war. Another obstacle to general Republican acceptance of Hoover was the fear that he was too brilliant an efficiency expert to believe in devotion to a political party. And so, in a letter of June 19, Francis B. Loomis of New York congratulated Harding for the brilliant manner in which "you brought the wisdom and necessity of government-by-party to the mind of Herbert Hoover." The statement by Hoover, "after seeing you, was all that could be desired. It will do a great deal of good." "Any man," wrote Loomis, "who could move Hoover to such a splendid and unexpected utterance is certainly the possessor of great powers of argument and persuasion over his fellow men. This is of the essence of real leadership." [33]

Thus the brillant Hoover continued to dwell and grow in Harding's favor throughout the campaign. Basically, this was probably due to

Hoover's conversion to political party–mindedness. It also helped that Hoover was a Californian and fitted in with Harding's need to court the Golden state. Hoover actually reminded Harding of the custom of appointing a Far Westerner—Hoover, perhaps?—to the national executive committee. It also helped that Hoover had great popularity with the new women voters. No doubt, also, Harding liked Hoover's business ability, even though it had been used in the war, as Harding saw it, for Wilson's benefit. Moreover, he had no suspicious Russian views, as had Robins, (Robins was anti-Communist, but also anti-Red-baiting).[34]

Thus it was that, as the campaign developed, Harding showed great preference for Hoover's practical liberal proposals as against the more theoretical ones of Robins. Hoover's ideas were not only practical and progressive but were presented, characteristically enough, with a widespread press coverage. He drew up a summary of his ideas in a letter of September 29 to Mrs. Robert G. Burdette of California, and then skillfully maneuvered Harding into endorsing it. Harding said, in response to Hoover's solicitation, that he was "delighted" to have the Burdette letter published, adding that "if I had been dictating it myself I could not have done it so well, and I am sure I could not have said so effectively the things which you have said in behalf of the Republican cause." [35]

Hoover's Burdette letter, which Harding said he so much admired, was based on the idea that President Wilson's obstinacy required political and representative responsibility to be transferred to the Republican party. Wilson's refusal to compromise had not only delayed world peacemaking but had prevented the development of domestic reconstruction policies that sorely needed attention. In the process the Democrats had lost the public good will, which only the Republicans could now regain. In assuming new responsibility the Republicans must do what the Democrats should have done long ago by the assembling the "best brains in the United States." The Democrats should "have prevented the advanced cost of living, [should] have found solutions for the difficulties of our agricultural industry, [should] have inaugurated constructive methods of resettlement of the land, the development of our industrial employment relationship to protect child life, the solution of our deficient housing, the reorganization of the business administration of the Federal Government, and a host of other domestic questions." The "terrible cost in our daily living," and the "vast unemployment" that will result were testimony of the Democratic failure. Hoover admitted that the Republican platform did not take an "advanced position" on many of these problems, but he was confident that the Republican party had the "skill, the constructive ability and spirit" to meet the nation's necessities.[36]

Among the last of the Progressives to find a spot in the Republican patchwork was Gifford Pinchot, former Governor of Pennsylvania and famous forestry expert, who, in 1910, had split with Taft and Ballinger over the conservation problem. On August 30, from the famous front porch, Harding addressed a group of state governors on the subject of conservation, with emphasis on Theodore Roosevelt's vision of the vast possibilities of our natural resources. It was then that Pinchot made his jump onto the bandwagon with the *Chicago Tribune* headlines proclaiming on August 31:

GIFFORD PINCHOT BACKS HARDING

TO SHIELD THE NATION

Pinchot, with characteristic bluntness, admitted that Harding "was not made to my order, but he is by no means the reactionary that I thought him to be." The thing that made Harding acceptable to Pinchot was that he was not an autocrat like Wilson, but "a regular who supports what his party agrees to and acts with the majority." [37]

Pinchot's record on subordination was not very good, but the Regulars were willing to put up with him if he could be kept in the proper place. For example, C. C. Hamlin of Denver wrote to Hays, "If Pinchot wants to help have him do it in the east—it would be fatal in the west." This view was confirmed in a penciled notation by Hays at the bottom of a letter to him from the Pennsylvanian offering to help. The notation read, "Good man in certain eastern places—not western." After Pinchot's August 31 bandwagon jump, Daugherty advised that "perhaps it would be a good idea to have him keep still." [38]

Another example of the patchwork quality of the Progressive reunion was the way Harding handled Senator Boies Penrose of Pennsylvania. Penrose was the bogey man of the party whom Democrats, and even Republicans far and wide, looked upon as the arch-boss of the party. Typical of the anti-Penrose psychopaths was Progressive editor of the *Pittsburgh Leader* Alexander P. Moore, who on June 29 wrote with consternation to George Christian, noting that "Penrose is coming out every day or so through his secretary with an interview on how the campaign should be run and what Harding should do."

Moore reminded Christian that "the Progressives like Penrose just about as much as they do a rattlesnake," and deplored that "no one can stop Penrose talking if he wants to." All that Harding could do was to inform Moore, "I think you can infer that we are of precisely the same mind that you are but it happens that we are more or less helpless to control the situation." Harding added, "I cannot write about it more but will be glad to tell you about it when I next see you again." [39]

One thing that the Republicans eventually did do about the Penrose-Progressive problem was to get out two official leaflets, one entitled "Why Progressives Support Harding," and the other, "Why Vote for Harding." They were authored by Raymond Robins, who was openly labeled "Chairman, Progressive National Convention, 1916." These pamphlets were officially marked, "Issued by the Republican National Committee." They were conspicuously subtitled "Senator Harding against Class Divisions," "Freedom of Speech and Press," "Progressives for Harding," "Democrats Surrendered to the Profiteers," "Law and Order," and "America First." They were studded with quotes from Harding denouncing "throttled liberties," "the Red Menace," "the red heart of Bolshevism," "the brutal witch-hunting methods of Attorney-General Palmer and Postmaster-General Burleson." They closed with the pious avowal, "To this end in common with an overwhelming majority of those Progressives who supported Theodore Roosevelt and Hiram W. Johnson, I shall work and vote for the election as President of the United States of Warren G. Harding." [40]

There was one exception to the return of the Progressive prodigals to the fold. That was Chicagoan Harold L. Ickes, who made the very moment of Harding's nomination the occasion for his defiant opposition. In his *Autobiography of a Curmudgeon*, Ickes, with refreshing frankness, has told of his Progressive persuasions in 1912 and 1916, of his committal as a delegate for Lowden in 1920, and of his switch to Johnson when Lowden faltered. It was Ickes who, when the motion was passed to make Harding's nomination unanimous, yelled an officially unrecorded "No" at the top of his lungs. To Ickes, Harding was the nominee of "turbulent, grasping, selfish men who were thinking little of their country but much of postmasterships, district attorneyships, and marshalships." He has told how, at the end of the convention, some of the Progressives held their last meeting together —"Robins, Pinchot, Garfield, White, Allen, Richberg, and myself." None of them were happy with the result. "We knew that Harding would be elected. The Progressive party was sunk without a trace.

Progressive principles had been completely abandoned. From the moment of Harding's nomination I knew that I would not support him. I was outraged and disgusted. Here was reaction with a vengeance. The others thought that we either had to go along or go dead. We just couldn't get off the reservation every four years. Someone suggested that we ought to keep in touch with each other and meet from time to time. I had the lists, I had always been the 'come-togeth-erer' and I silently resolved to call it a day. So this was the last meeting of the remnants of the Progressive rear guard that had fought so well in 1912, had faltered in 1914, had broken into full retreat in 1916, and was preparing to follow the sutler's wagon in 1920." [41]

Ickes opposed Harding throughout the campaign of 1920. Although he thought the Democratic and Republican platforms were "twee-dledum and tweedledee," he supported Cox because he had shown by his record as Governor of Ohio that he was a true Progressive. On September 3, Ickes wrote a letter to A. B. Schriver of Winterset, Iowa. He vigorously denied the claim that T. R., if he were alive, would have supported Harding. "The real fact is," said Ickes, "that if Theodore Roosevelt were alive, the Republican gang headed by Senator Penrose would not have dared to nominate such a candidate." The "Penrose, Smoot, Crane gang" had wanted to nominate Harding in 1916, but "did not dare to do so because they knew full well that Theodore Roosevelt was too good a citizen to support such a candidate for the Presidency." In 1916, Hughes had taken the management out of the hands of the "gang" and turned it over to a special campaign committee of Progressive Republicans. Senator Harding, said Ickes, "is completely in the hands of the men whom Colonel Roosevelt stigmatized as 'burglars and porch climbers.' " [42]

A Progressive who came closest to Ickes in disliking Harding's nomination, but who decided to stay loyal "with reservations," was William Allen White, editor of the *Emporia* (Kansas) *Gazette*. White had been a member of the Kansas Republican delegation committed to Wood and had shifted to Harding only because he thought Harding could not make it, and, therefore, the convention would be able to name Hoover. After the nomination Harding included White in the "come and see me" telegrams; but White declined to accept, pleading other commitments. In the correspondence that followed, there took place a friendly but very frank exchange of "man talk," in which White tried to show that he was a Progressive and Harding was not, and warned that he would support Harding only on the ground that he (White) could satisfy himself during the new President's administration that the promises to treat Progressive ideas fairly were sincerely lived up to.[43]

The White-Harding debate gives little comfort to those seeking to find depth in the Progressive and anti-Progressive positions. The sense of patchwork and opportunism in the reconciliation still prevails. The discussion centered around the nature of Progressivism, and neither one did a very good job of definition. One gets the impression of two newspaper prima donnas futilely struggling to think out and define a great ideological conflict, and being able to produce little more than wisecracks and glib phrases.

Harding claimed that "at bottom" there was very little difference between the "so-called reactionaries and the proclaimed progressives," and that what difference existed was "more largely in the habit of thought and form of expression than in fundamentals, and perhaps in temperament." He illustrated his claim by calling White a "red-headed reactionary," and himself a "white-haired progressive." Harding said he was not foolish enough to expect the world to stand still, nor to want it to do so. But he rebuked White for his political instability. "If I am elected," he said, "I hope to assume power supported by a party united on fundamentals, and upon other questions to reach conclusions and party unity in open, fair and considerate discussion and study." He would then be as ready to treat with "men calling themselves Progressives" as with "the more cautious and conservative members of the party." Harding made no effort to define the fundamentals that they were supposed to be united on.

White did no better in handling fundamentals than did Harding. The Kansan accepted Harding's claim that the only difference between them was the "habit of thought" and temperament. "We both recognize the inexorableness of change in the world," he said. "I want to give it a forward push. You want to be sure about it." White admitted that he had been "yipping and kyoodling" in his paper for years. He had been for the income tax when it was supposed to be "rank socialism." He had favored the direct election of Senators when getting it done required the "raping of the very constitution itself." He had been for prohibition and woman suffrage. At present, he said, he was for four constitutional amendments "so radical that if you knew about them you would have me deported when you are elected." He denied that he had been politically disloyal—except for his "gorgeous adventure" with T. R. "I have been as regular as clock work in the fall. It is from December of the even years to August of the next Biennium

that I moult and run wild." Their only differences, White claimed,
were "interprative." And yet, we "oughtn't to belong to the same
party." The best reason for this that White could give was to invoke
the "general theme which impels Providence to put two kinds of bugs
in the human blood; the kind that kills the man, and the kind that kills
the bugs that would kill the man." But, since they were both in the
same party "till death do us part, we might as well make the best of
it."

The discussion eventually degenerated into each calling the other
nice names, kidding each other about Harding's "school-boy Americanism" and the relative efficiency of their newspapers, and promising
to respect one another's sincerity. Harding agreed to try to broaden
his vision, and admonished White to temper his enthusiasm. White
pleased Harding by saying that he had listened to the candidate's
voice on the phonograph "not for what you said, but for the way you
said it." Said White, "One gets a better notion of another man through
his voice." The result was that "I was delighted to find in you a certain
caution, deep earnestness and much conviction . . . one can fool his
reader on the printed page, but it is hard to fool an auditor." The
exchange ended by Harding saying that he would be hurt if White did
not visit him in Marion, and by White telling Harding, "You have
grown every moment since the day of the nomination . . . your
sincerity, your sense of dignity and your steady thoughts have made
themselves felt in the American heart."

White's letters to Harding in 1920 do not square with his remarks
about Harding in 1920, as given by White in his books *Masks in a
Pageant* (1928) and his *Autobiography* (1946). In *Masks*, White said
that in the League of Nations debate "Harding's clarion voice, as
impersonal and mechanically controlable as a phonograph, played a
star part." This implies an insincerity quite lacking in the admiration
he expressed in his 1920 letter for Harding's use of his voice. In
Autobiography, instead of describing how Harding grew in sincerity,
dignity and thoughtfulness, White described him as equivocating,
lacking in conviction, "densely ignorant," and "a poor dub." [44]

5

The return of the Progressive prodigals to the national Republican
fold in 1920 was a serious and pragmatic political necessity; but the
return in Ohio was a comedy. With an "Ohio Man" for the party's

presidential candidate, no Ohio Republican could possibly stay "off the reservation."

The Ohio prodigals returned with varying degrees of dignity. Walter Brown did it best by coming back in full time to be indispensable to the Harding candidacy. As for Wood-supporter William Cooper Procter, he and Harding exchanged the amenities after the convention with gentlemanly aplomb.[45] But the others did not do so well.

Most amusing was the return of Robert F. Wolfe, the man who had committed the once stalwart Republican *Ohio State Journal* and *Columbus Evening Dispatch* to the status of political mavericks. To the victorious Harding, Wolfe presented his compliments—if not apologies—in a formal letter of personal felicitation on June 15. "While I have not always been in a position," wrote Wolfe with some dignity, "to give you the unqualified support to which you perhaps, considering our rather close relations, thought you were entitled, at no time was this, as you know, due to a lack of high personal regard." But, if we are to believe Alexander P. Moore, editor-in-chief of the *Pittsburgh Leader,* Wolfe was somewhat less dignified when he confessed, "How the h—— can you help liking that fellow Harding? He is the sweetest character I have ever known." However, Harding made it easy for Wolfe in a letter which reciprocated his personal regards, but which offered the following fatherly advice, "I have always held a very genuine wish to somewhat inspire you to be a helpful force in making our party dominant in the state and nation. I know that in your heart you wish to return to government under the constitution and I think you will agree with me that there is no other suitable agency at this time except the Republican party." [46]

There was one who raised no shouts of welcome to the returning Wolfe. This was his ancient enemy Harry Daugherty, who never appreciated the maverick role of Wolfe's *Journal* and *Dispatch* during the years of Republican-Progressive tribulation. Thus, Daugherty wrote sardonically to Harding on July 15: "I see you had your interview with Robert. I want to advise you that my information is that I doubt if you are going to get any support from that source." However, Daugherty said, "we do not need Wolfe's support any more." So "let him play his game at present. . . . He can not go straight, he is not true and I know things going on which convince me conclusively of his sympathies and antagonisms. . . . It is a good principle as long as a man tries to save you in politics to give him some rope and chance." [47]

The return of Dan R. Hanna, son of the mighty Marcus, was a bit more manly. He simply swallowed his pride. His first reaction was one of admiration for a masterful job of politicking. On June 13, the day after the nomination, he wired Daugherty, "Old man, I heartily congratulate you and Harding. I wish I had been one of the fifteen tired and perspiring fifteen [sic] that sat around the table at 2:11 A.M. Come down and tell me how you did it." To this, Daugherty replied on the same day that he was sending Harding a copy of Hanna's telegram. "He will be delighted I know. . . . You are a dead game sport and we want your help now." After further amenities via Brown and the telephone, Hanna wrote to Harding, "I don't want a damn thing. (Make a note of that) and will be of any service that *you* think me qualified to perform. I might add that my bad behavior, which was such that any serious minded friend could criticize is ended." Hanna could not refrain from casting some good-natured blame for his misconduct. "I have charged, or credited rather, the final disposition of it to our good disreputable mutual friend Bob Wolfe." However, now that it was all over, "Harry happy, Wolfe contented, and Hynicka satisfied, and you in the state I don't want to see any Democrats get a look in." Typically enough, he wanted Harding to support Brown against Willis in the Ohio senatorial primaries. Harding, though he privately favored Brown, had to decline.[48]

Then there was powerful Ohio national committeeman Rudolph K. Hynicka, the dour, cynical, Republican boss of Cincinnati. Was there a seat on the bandwagon for him? There surely was, even though the public believed that he had twice "betrayed" Harding for Wood, once in the Ohio primaries, and again in the convention balloting on the sixth-ballot switch of his four delegates to Wood.

The anti-Hynicka feeling among many Cincinnati Republicans had reached hysterical proportions. The newspapers were screaming for his scalp. His switch was denounced as "treachery." His abdication as national committeeman was demanded. Otto Pfleger, Harding's Cincinnati primary manager, wanted "to tear Hynicka's head off." Daugherty, of course, agreed. Only the "heroism" of Mayor Galvin had kept the Hynicka defection from becoming a stampede.[49]

Hynicka, however, was defiant. So far as he was concerned it was he, not Galvin, who was the savior of Harding's nomination. By switching from Harding to Wood on the sixth ballot, he had helped stop a stampede to Lowden and had thus made it possible for the Harding men to work on the Lowden delegates for the promised second choices. Harding knew this, Hynicka said, and he was prepared to prove it. He told this to Pfleger in a veiled and threatening manner. "Confidentially," he wrote on June 16, "it is my judgment that Republicans had better refrain from too much discussion of the Chicago Convention tactics." [50]

The indignant Hynicka carried his defiance to the point of demanding further party recognition for his loyalty to Harding—and got it. His demand took the form of a fiery letter to Will Hays on June 18 denouncing the attacks and allegations of treachery. "The motives behind these attacks," he wrote, "are so apparent to those who want to understand that there is no use talking about them. I don't care a tinkers d——m [sic] about them." He insisted upon his right to continue as national committeeman, and practically demanded that Hays appoint him to the Harding notification day committee. His plain-spoken words left no doubt about it:

> Whatever usefulness I might be to the National Committee and to our State in the next campaign will be greatly impaired if any of our folks at home can be led to believe that I have ceased to be in proper touch and standing with National Headquarters. You know how much I care about publicity and having my name "blown in the bottle." I have never asked you or anybody else that I know of, for any recognition of any kind. I have always been willing to "labor in the vineyard" for the good of the cause. If I can be of any help it must be plain in the selection of your committee that I have not lost caste, so to speak. As far as I am concerned I would be perfectly willing to retire from the committee if either you or Senator Harding, or both thought it advisable. You will pardon the abrupt frankness for I know you will understand my position and motives. I leave the whole matter entirely in your hands.[51]

The results of Hynicka's demands were: (1) Hynicka was appointed a member of the notification committee; (2) Hynicka telegraphed Hays on June 23, "Honored by appointment in committee notification arrangement"; and (3) Hynicka continued to "labor in the vineyard."

Something of the feeling of regard for, or fear of, the vindictive Hynicka is found in the Harding Papers. Pfleger, hating Hynicka and his aides as he did, believed that "we can afford to forget their political wrongs and patch up all the sore spots for a united front." Upon reflecting, the angry Hulbert Taft, whose Cincinnati Times-Star had "jumped into him hard" and had editorially demanded Hynicka's resignation from the national committee, urged Harding not to do anything against him. "The main thing is to win the election and you should not do anything that might diminish the Republican majority in Hamilton County." Harding was in full agreement. To Pfleger he wrote resignedly, "I do not wish to write about things which have the savor of anything unpleasant. When a thing is done, I always try to look upon it as done and turn my face to future accomplishments. I am very sure it was this policy which enabled me to secure the nomination at Chicago." [52]

6

The return of the prodigals—at least of the Progressive variety—was not solely Harding's achievement. It had been taking place ever since T. R. had died in January, 1919. Harding had only to be his personable, all-forgiving self, avoid "Hughes blunders," and open his welcoming arms to the Progressive flock.

As the Republican Progressives approached the political campaign of 1920, they were balked not only by the thinness of faith in their own fundamentals but by the failure of their past performances. In the two previous presidential campaigns of 1912 and 1916 they had found their offering duplicated by the Democrats and, fearing to join the "enemy," had contributed to the defeat of both regular Republicans and themselves. They felt this must not happen again, and so they came tailing back to the fold, even though the shepherd was only Warren G. Harding, who had once been their enemy and still did not share their temperaments and their dreams.

CHAPTER TWENTY

Of Managers and Management

"I think Warren Harding will make one of the best Presidents we have ever had. The only thing that worries me is that we don't happen to have any money to advertise this wonderful man to the voters. We received about as much so far as I spend every week advertising a penny stick of Chewing Gum." : : : William Wrigley, Jr., to Ralph V. Sollitt, August 3, 1920, Will H. Hays Papers, Indiana State Library

The Republican campaign of 1920 was a much-managed piece of show business. The proceedings were not always spectacular, but they were always well managed to make a planned effect. The candidate, Warren Gamaliel Harding, was a political showman of the first order —a newspaperman, an advertiser, an orator, and a phrasemaker. He even brought along his own slogan, "Back to Normalcy." Moreover, he was no ham actor; he was a pure professional, incapable of any "fool breaks" that would ruin things, as did the Reverend Burchard's remark about "Rum, Romanism, and Rebellion" in 1884 or the Hughes snub of Hiram Johnson in 1916.

It is important to emphasize that the 1920 election was controlled in accordance with the canons of the new profession of improved public relations. In fact, it is tenable to suggest that the Republican campaign of 1920 was as much a display by public relations experts of their wares and craftmanship as it was of the principles and other offerings of the Republican party and its candidate. In the past, business-minded Republicans had tried to control elections, but their methods frequently jarred public sensibilities. Charges of bossism and corruption had been raised, and the Progressive movement had thrived thereon. "Fool breaks" had occurred. Thus it was that the Republican national management in 1920 was the first to make sure that such things did not happen again. The campaign was to be clean and interesting, *i.e.*, well managed. The platform was dull, and the public, attuned to the phonograph and the motion picture, was no longer thrilled by the average political orator. (Harding, of course, was above the average.) Such political necessities as bossism, party discipline, and the spoils system still existed, but they were to be camouflaged. So the Republican party turned for help to a representative of a new profession—a public relations expert—to manage and entertain the public.

The manager-in-chief was Will H. Hays, chairman of the Republican national committee, a public relations expert with great "know-how." After a couple of years with Harding, Hays was to graduate from managing Republican politics into using his high talents as leader of the nation's motion picture industry. He found a role for every party leader and worker to play—even the ladies. With much counseling and questionnairing, he engineered the building of a platform adapted to the interests of American business and turned it over to a candidate who was himself a master of the art of promotion. The trappings and effects of the stage were used: the front porch, the stump, the bandwagon, the return of the prodigal Progressives, and the grand opening of the notification ceremony.

Hays had a good background of managerial success in politics. He was the inventor of the advisory system that had glad-handed Indiana regulars and Progressives back into harmony in the Hoosier state in 1916 and which Harding had adopted to a similar purpose after the Ohio Republican defeat of that year. Harry Daugherty, of course, was still in the picture, but merely as a respected advisor.

The smoothness with which the campaign proceeded to its victorious national climax was a demonstration of high managerial genius by chairman Hays, a keen efficiency expert who was one of the best in the business. Hays had a far-flung organizational network. His central headquarters was in New York City, with Scott C. Bone, former West Coast newspaperman, as his director of publicity. There were regional centers, such as the one at Chicago, with former Cincinnati Congressman Victor Heintz in charge, and one at San Francisco, under the command of former Ohioan and Hanna aide Elmer Dover. Harding worshiper E. Mont Reily radiated enthusiasm from his Kansas City headquarters. From these and other centers communication lines spread to state and local Republican offices throughout the entire nation. In close coordination with Hays was master advertiser Albert D. Lasker of the Lord and Thomas Company of Chicago.

Some idea of the nature of the Republican facilities available to the nation's voters in 1920 may be gleaned from the voluminous papers in the Hays Collection at the Indiana State Library. These reveal the following bureaus and departments in the New York office: a speakers' bureau systematically coordinating with the state bureaus; a division of regional Republican clubs; a contact office for the congressional and senatorial campaign committees in Washington; a "visiting delegation" bureau for visits to Marion; a colored voters' department; a big division of publicity subdivided into departments and bureaus for motion pictures, display advertising, lithographs, photographs, cartoon-plate service, phonograph records, buttons, billboards, and campaign textbooks. There were departments for women's activities, labor, colleges, and traveling salesmen. Supplies of pamphlets on over one hundred fifty subjects were available in large quantities for the asking. These included the presidential acceptance speech, "Theodore Roosevelt, the Most Courageous American," and "Real Friendship." For women's organizations there was one on "What Republican Women Can Do in the Election Districts." There were anti-Democratic "Stingers," such as "Uncontrolled War Waste," "Billion and the Half Saved by Republican Congress," and "Wanted: A New Business Management for the United States."

Harding's deference to the Hays-Lasker combination highlighted the business-oriented nature of the 1920 Republican campaign appeal. Hays had been working on this for a long time, and businessmen were becoming more and more impressed by his seeming sincerity and thoroughgoing methods. Harding's talk of "back to normalcy" was window dressing; Hays' planning was "the business."

For many months Hays' New York office had been conducting research on the business needs of the country. It was a planning headquarters for post-war reconversion, an issue which President Wilson and the Democrats were said to be failing to cope with in the midst of their alleged world-security dreaming. On September 27, 1919 Hays had opened with the first of a series of confidential form letters to selected American business leaders, seeking their advice about the legislative action needed "to better industrial, economic and social conditions." Wrote Hays, "I am determined to do everything possible to bring to the solution of the problems the best brains in the country," to aid in coming at "wise and sane decisions which will meet present needs." [1]

There seemed to be nothing frothy in Hays' inquiries—they were practical. He specified such problems as: the control of harmful monopolies; corporation regulation; employer-employee relations; federal charters for corporations; deflation of the currency; the high cost of living; employers' accident liability; powers of the Interstate Commerce Commission and the Federal Trade Commission; minimum wages; sickness and unemployment insurance.

It was a big job and required much committee and subcommittee work. Early in January, 1920, Hays had appointed an advisory committee on policies and platforms. It was chaired by Ogden L. Mills, a New York corporation lawyer and Republican state committeeman, and included the nation's leading Republican politicians, with such liberals as Gifford Pinchot and such conservatives as Boies Penrose, plus prominent businessmen and bankers such as John Hays Hammond, Otto Kahn, William Loeb, Jr., and Frank A. Vanderlip. There was a staff of investigators headed by economists Dr. Samuel McCune Lindsay, of Columbia University, and Dr. Jacob H. Hollander, of Johns Hopkins University. Research was conducted through eighteen subcommittees, each in charge of a special subject, ranging from agricultural policies to war risk insurance. Questionnaires were sent out to persons whose views on the selected subjects were deemed significant. Well before convention time in June, 1920, the subcommittee reports were published in a 272-page volume, and each convention delegate had a copy. These reports became, in part, the basis of the Republican platform adopted by the convention. Later the platform was published in the campaign textbook, with copious explanatory insertions and notations from these reports. Many of the reports were printed in full in the textbook.[2]

Harding personally did not like the seeming know-it-all quality of Hays' managerial manner. It reminded him of Wilson, and Harding felt its aspects of economic planning carried the concepts of big business too far. At least, that was the way the Ohio Senator felt in the early days of the Ohio primary fight. On February 4, 1920, he confided to his friend Malcolm Jennings, "I have grown rather weary of Hays and think many of his ideas are as impractical as those of Woodrow Wilson in seeking to regulate the politics of the whole world." However, when Harding became the party's nominee, he curbed his feelings and made the best of things. As he wrote to his *Star* manager in Marion, George Van Fleet, "Hays is really a pretty sensible fellow." In May, 1919, Harding passed on the information to a friend that Hays was being promoted for the Presidency by a "considerable number of influential New Yorkers." Harding professed indifference to the idea.[3]

Harding, of course, had no choice in regard to Hays' leadership. After June 12, 1920, Harding was no longer an "Ohio Man" seeking

Ohio's favor: he was a national candidate and needed a leader with national perspective. That was what Hays had. He had been chosen chairman of the Republican national committee in 1918 for the very purpose of bringing all sections and factions of the party into effective unity in order to win the election of 1920. By June, 1920, Hays had an organization in full operation to seek to accomplish this purpose. Harding had to recognize it, and he cordially did so in his announcement of June 23.[4] This made Hays campaign chairman.

Testimony to the immediacy of Harding's decision on Hays came from the later's advertising aide, Albert D. Lasker. In his *Reminscences,* Lasker wrote that, late in the evening of the day after the nomination, Hays phoned from Marion, saying that he had gone there at Harding's request and that Harding had said that the organization should continue as it was. This meant that Hays wanted Lasker to come to Marion at once as chief propagandist for the party so that the three could confer on campaign policies. Lasker did so and was very favorably impressed with the candidate and his prospects.[5]

The businesslike spirit and manner with which Hays and Mills managed this investigatory work can be observed in documents in the Hays Papers. On January 8, 1920, Mills began a series of lectures in his New York home on "The Economic Problems of Today," to which the members of the advisory committee were invited. As his subcommittees proceeded with their work, Mills kept all Republican aspirants for the presidential nomination supplied with copies of the questionnaires and progress reports. Hays toured the West in January and then reported to his committee on the country's great need for business recovery and the Republican party's responsibility to help provide for it. The candidates were asked for suggestions, as were all the national committeemen. Lowden, in reply, spoke of the constructiveness of the work: "I had no idea of the extent of your activities. I was a member of the National Committee and the executive committee for eight years. . . . And I confess that your report was as much a revelation to me as though I had never served on the committee. I congratulate you with all my heart." [6]

The solid economic worth of the work and the platform resulting from it may be questioned. The document adopted by the convention was the usual combination of anti-Democratic diatribe, Republican glorification, and platitudinous evasion, with the occasional specifics that the contradictory laissez-faire, tariff-promoting nature of Republican thinking required. But it was much to the glory of business, and business had been consulted in the process. The Democrats were blamed for all the strikes and lockouts. The Republicans would prevent such things by intelligent mediation. Taxes and the debt would be reduced, inflation corrected, prices lowered, profiteering ended, the protective tariff principle restored but related to developing world conditions, the merchant marine Americanized, immigration restricted, free speech maintained, lynching wiped out, progress made in legislative budgeting, conservation promoted, women and children protected, housing conditions relieved—all "to the end that our country, happy and prosperous, proud of its past, sure of itself and of its institutions, may look forward with confidence to the future." Foreign policy and the League of Nations were covered in a faction-soothing way that left the subject open to much future discussion.[7]

Harding's function was to take all this and present an oratorical blow-up that made better reading for the vast majority who would never read the platform and who would never even know of the economic reports. This he did at the traditional notification ceremonies on the famous front porch in Marion on July 22.[8]

Harding had plenty of advice in writing his acceptance address. The national advisory committee on policies and platforms, the national committee itself, and the convention had already patched together enough pieces and issued enough subcommittee reports to test the peculiar talents of the Ohio Senator, whose political life heretofore had been a living example of explaining the unexplainable and patching together the unpatchable. For a few days following the nomination, material poured into Marion from Hays, Mills, Lindsay, and Hollander. Hays had led off on June 22 with the proud offering of his voluminous data. "If you deem best to plan your campaign upon the issues of the platform, we can supply you with a great deal of very valuable material from special reports and the replies received from more than 100,000 questionnaires sent out to all the important business and professional interests throughout every section of the country." Harding got it all and put it together, as he said, "by fits and starts and by jerks and jumps upon chips and whetstones." [9]

In Marion, on notification day, a golden glow seemed to rise with a dawning era of hope and prosperity as the candidate stood on his flag-draped porch and accepted the nomination from the impeccable Henry Cabot Lodge. "We stabilize and strive for normalcy," declared

Harding in his calm and reassuring voice. A popular government was about to be returned to the people, an efficient economy to its creators, and a constitution to its owners.

The war of the world was over, and America must steady down. In a time of restiveness, with the red flag waving "in pathetic Russia," America must "not only save herself, but ours must be the appealing voice to sober the world." The discord and misunderstanding at home must end. Employers must understand "the aspirations, the convictions, the yearnings of the millions of American wage-earners." Working men must understand "the problems, the anxieties, the obligations of management and capital." Together labor and capital must understand "their relationships to the people and their obligation to the republic." Out of all this understanding "will come the unanimous committal to economic justice, and in economic justice lies that social justice which is the highest essential to human happiness."

There was no analysis of the platform—for how could it be analyzed? "Our party platform fairly expresses the conscience of Republicans." But there were eye- and ear-catching phrases that "stump" speakers and newspaper editors could snatch for their own uses: "We inflated in haste, we must deflate in deliberation"; "Here is a temple of liberty no storms may shake, here are the altars of freedom no passions shall destroy"; "High wages and reduced cost of living are in utter contradiction unless we have the height of efficiency for wages received"; "The four million defenders of land and sea were worthy of the best traditions of a people never warlike in peace and never pacific in war." At the end there was the stirring peroration: "Have confidence in the Republic! America will go on!"

The Republican management was much pleased with Harding's acceptance speech because he had seemingly used the materials that the advisory committee on policies and platforms had so laboriously prepared. At least, that is what staff director Professor Lindsay and his associate, Professor Hollander, said. When Lindsay saw the preliminary copy on July 19, he was in enthusiastic accord. "It interprets so accurately," he wrote Harding, "both in spirit and substance the platform and platform materials which we laid before the Resolutions Committee of the Convention, that I feel sure you have thereby based your campaign upon very solid foundations." Hollander felt the same way. "My interest," he wrote "has naturally centered on the sections dealing with economic and social matters, and, as to these, nothing could be sounder or more inspiring." [10]

2

The best platform of the new Republican party in 1920 was the personable Harding in contrast with the allegedly remote and austere Wilson. There was good political precedent for personality display, but the Republicans had not been doing it very well for a long time—not since they ran Roosevelt for President in 1904. Taft and Hughes in 1908, 1912, and 1916 were no showpieces. Harding was, and it was repeatedly emphasized by the new management as Hays, in the New York office, gave the idea national coverage. A circular letter was mailed to all Republican newspaper editors, urging them to emphasize the Harding personality, naming both Harding and Coolidge. Hays said, "We are especially anxious that the facts about their splendid individualities and characters be given in every possible way to the country." Victor Heintz, in the Chicago office, said the same thing. "Please do not consider me trivial," he wrote Howard Mannington at the Marion office, "when I say that two of the Senator's greatest assets as a campaigner are his appearance and his affability." From Colorado came the enthusiastic war cry of party stalwart Dr. Hubert Work. "It can now be safely said," Dr. Work wrote to Harding, "that you have attracted immeasureably more interest in the party through it [the acceptance speech] than was accomplished by our platform: in that your personality at once became the platform of the party. If this be true, the most important element of safety has been secured to the party." [11]

In order to facilitate the process of broadcasting the virtues of the Harding personality, Hays enclosed several printed pages of "Suggestions for Public Utterances and Interviews Relative to Harding and Coolidge." This contained hundreds of neat little paragraphs containing easily understood descriptions of almost every virtue under the sun: "born poor," "intensely practical," "cool judgment," "far-sighted," "an ardent patriot," "simple, plain, unassuming," "a splendid type of clean American manhood," and "a man of the people." The "Suggestions" abounded in heart-warming assertions: "In Ohio they love him"; "his employees . . . take their troubles, their joys and their worries to him"; "a vote for Harding means a vote for the home, for the rights of humanity, for the country"; "he has fought for and voted to protect our children"; "he is the man who can lead the country out of the darkness into the light"; "he will live up to the great traditions of the party of Lincoln and McKinley and Roosevelt." [12]

The chief editorial user of this canned Harding personality propaganda was the *National Republican*, the party's national weekly. Its editor, George B. Lockwood, was fully conditioned to take such material for all it was worth. As soon as Lockwood heard of Harding's nomination, he sent a staff correspondent to Marion to get "a human interest story." He then wrote to George Christian that this approach was very important after all these years of Wilson, because the people "are anxious for a regular fellow instead of a stuffed shirt in the presidency." [13]

Some Republicans were not content with merely putting Harding in the class of Lincoln, McKinley, and Roosevelt. They brought George Washington into the line-up. It started with the June 19 *Boston Evening Transcript*, which featured an article entitled "Harding as Washington's Double." Accompanying the article were two portraits; one, a photograph of the famous Stuart portrait of George Washington, the other, a "doctored" photograph of the Stuart portrait, with Harding's face superimposed beneath Washington's wig. The result was merely ludicrous.[13]

More pictorial aid came from the studio of the artist Howard Chandler Christy. It began with a letter to *Pittsburgh Leader* editor Alexander P. Moore from a New York theatrical agent named Howard Shelley, who knew Christy. Shelley reminded Moore of Christy's famous World War I enlistment posters. Why not get Christy, who was an old friend of Harding, to make some posters of Harding "like he did for the war?" Christy's war posters "drew 40,000 men into the Navy alone." After all, went on Shelly, "it would have a splendid patriotic appeal and the Republicans might as well capitalize his patriotic work as the Democrats. . . . Posters by a noted artist who is descended from good old American stock, stock which assisted in founding the nation, would be a big thing to help along the campaign." The idea took hold. Moore passed it along to Christian, who passed it on to Hays, who saw Christy at once. "He was up in the office fifteen minutes after I got your telegram. . . . We have no more enthusiastic man in the organization than he is right now. . . . He is going the limit." The result was a lithograph of Harding, backed by the American flag, and entitled, "AMERICA FIRST." It was posted on billboards throughout the nation.[15]

Harding's acceptance speech of July 22, delivered from the front porch of his Marion residence, was the opening display of an important piece of Republican showmanship. It was part of the build-up of a folksy, home-loving image for the candidate. It gave a quaint, old-time, McKinley-like facade to the proceedings.

The inexpensive, calm, and simple appearance of the front-porch campaign was meant to be a corrective influence for the extravagance and animosity that the Wood and Lowden campaigners had exhibited in the "rich man's primaries" in the spring of 1920. The Wood promoters had been pugilistic and bitterly critical of other good Republicans. The boomerang effect of the public exhibition of mercenary and discordant tactics had been too much for the sensibilities of many office-starved, harmony-seeking GOP loyalists. Suggestions for a new dignity via the front-porch device were contained in much of the advice that Harding received in the early days of his candidacy. This advice came from such distinguished Republicans as Albert J. Beveridge, Albert Shaw, Senators Harry S. New and John W. Weeks, and Charles Stewart Davison of New York City. On the front porch, wrote Shaw, "you can afford to be very deliberate, wholly unruffled and exceedingly good tempered." Harding agreed. As he told John D. Work, "It develops an unfortunate side of our political activities to have a presidential candidate chasing about the country soliciting support. . . . One cannot be his best in conveying his thoughts to the people whose confidence he desires to enlist." Let the undignified Cox do this, and, by so doing, place himself on the defensive in the eyes of people of good taste.[16]

One who saw the relation of the front-porch method to the free-swinging, direct-primary melee of 1920, and described it well, was Myron T. Herrick. During the Harding-Wood Ohio primary fight, Herrick had cringed as he predicted the ruin of the Ohio Republican party as a result of the bitter things Republicans were publicly saying about each other. Of course Herrick, as Ohio delegate-at-large for Harding at the Chicago convention, had supported his man with unfailing courage and splendid dignity in the "no second-choice" strategy. But when it was all over and Harding's nomination had taken place, Herrick sighed with relief, thanked God that "we have the best chance to bring Ohio back again to her position as Mother of Presidents," and wrote Harding a letter.[17]

In this letter Herrick deeply regretted the indignity inflicted by the primaries on two such estimable men as Leonard Wood and Frank Lowden:

We have had a narrow escape, for had either Wood or Lowden been nominated, I am convinced that they could not have been elected. I found a few of my friends among the Wood and Lowden delegates who confessed this to me in the last two or three days when I pressed them hard, but they did not know how to draw away from their chiefs with whom they had enlisted. This, it seems to me, should be the last and final crushing argument against the primaries, for neither Lowden nor Wood spent illegitimately, and we should do all we can to relieve them of the smirch of a money campaign, which, in the eyes of so many people who do not know, has left them in disgrace. It seems to me, from what I see and hear, that our efforts should be directed at once to making adherents of these men, to make them feel that their place in the Party will not be in any sense impaired and that they will share in the administration if they enter at once with the same purpose to win that they had to obtain the nomination.

Herrick advised Harding to do as McKinley had done, "remain at home and make his speeches on his own doorstep." He described how he had advised Hughes to do this in 1916. Hughes was "very much impressed and came very near making that sort of a campaign. Had he done so, the untoward circumstances in California could not have occurred, and he would have been elected." Herrick recalled how in 1896 he had gone to McKinley and advised a stump campaign against the barn-storming Bryan. McKinley declined, saying, "When I make speeches I want to think. I can't roll them off a megaphone, as Bryan does. Furthermore, we can in traveling greet and meet comparatively few people in the country. Therefore, if every day I say something which I have had time to think over carefully, a large majority of voters will read that statement each day, and in the meantime, I will avoid great fatigue." Herrick, therefore, advised Harding "to think of this as a very important matter for the good of your health—and that of the campaign."

Harding agreed with Herrick about the front porch, and cited—most inaccurately—his old difficulties with Hanna. Harding told a *Chicago Tribune* reporter that, in 1897, Hanna had refused him an interview when campaigning in Marion. This hurt the "young editor named Harding, who thought he was some pumpkins in these parts." Hence, "I held aloof, and went on about my business." It of course, was not Hanna's fault—"he told me so later." Harding concluded, "This shows how a man, travelling, can cross his wires without knowing it, and that's the reason I decided on a front porch campaign this summer. I wanted to avoid those crossed wires." However, this was only one of the published reasons attributed to Harding. Upon other occasions he gave more of the McKinley philosophy, as, for example, when the *Chicago Tribune*, on July 1, quoted him as saying, "The country is calling for deliberate utterance, and that is why the front porch appeals so strongly to me." Others felt the same way. Senator Harry S. New of Indiana assured the public, "We are not going to make a whirling dervish of our candidate." Herbert Parsons, national committeeman from New York, advised against "the circus performance of a tour of the country," and in favor of the "full use of the local color of Marion, Ohio." [18]

4

The publicity of the campaign was planned in a big way. Such a plan was not only launched, it was announced with fanfare that it would be launched. A few days after the acceptance ceremonies, a press release came out of Marion telling of the pending inauguration of "a mammoth modern advertising campaign," designed to "sell Harding and Coolidge to the country." It was to be "the biggest advertising drive ever launched in a political campaign. It was to be run by Albert Lasker and William Wrigley, the chewing-gum king. "When Wrigley and Lasker get together," the Marion dispatch to the *New York Times* said, "things happen." What was going to happen was a series of news releases, speeches, newspaper advertising, billboard poster displays, and a slogan. "No newspaper reader will be able to escape breakfast without being confronted by the slogan which will meet his eye again on billboards on his way to work." [19] Harding was to be a "billboard favorite" after all.

The person in charge of national publicity and entertainment creation in Marion was the veteran Munsey-trained newspaperman Judson C. Welliver. He was billed in the *New York Times* as a publicist, former Progressive, and close friend of the late Theodore Roosevelt. His selection, following the June convention, "marks . . . a considerable step in the direction of securing the enthusiastic cooperation of Progressive elements that lined up with Roosevelt in the split of 1916." During World War I he was London correspondent and European manager of Munsey's *New York Sun*. In 1907, he had been sent to Europe by President Roosevelt to study waterway systems, corporation law, and the railroad situation. In 1912, he had written a book entitled *Catching Up With Roosevelt*, which was said to have had a circulation of 10,000,000 copies. It was also said to have been one of the "prize text books" of the Roosevelt 1912 campaign.[20]

Welliver was in a privileged position with respect to press releases in Marion. There were other newspapermen besides Welliver at Marion during the 1920 Harding campaign, and among them were correspondents of the *New York Tribune, Times, Sun, World,* the *Washington Post,* the *Chicago Tribune,* the *Cleveland News,* the *Plain Dealer,* and the *Cincinnati Enquirer.* For the United Press, there was Raymond Clapper; for the Associated Press, Byron Price; and for the International News, J. Bart Campbell. They were not part of Welliver's entourage, and, in large measure, they found their own news and wrote their own stories. But there were certain advantages that Welliver had over them. They did not have a lavishly subsidized local staff. They did not have the access to the candidate and the party machinery which Welliver enjoyed. Above all, they did not have the mandate and the facilities that Welliver had for manufacturing news. Welliver also had the advantage of providing copy for most of the nation's newspapers, because only a few could afford to maintain special correspondents in Marion.

It was Welliver's job to manufacture news in a spectacular fashion, and he had full access to Harding and the party's facilities for that purpose. It is one of the great ironies of the Harding story that, as a newspaperman, he had built the *Marion Daily Star* into a relatively independent institution for the dispensing of news, but that, as a presidential candidate, he was responsible for, and was the beneficiary of, a system of controlled and manufactured news. Yet there are no words critical of Welliver in any of the books by Raymond and Olive Clapper, who wrote of their Marion assignment.[21]

How Welliver manufactured his news is illustrated by many incidents, two of which are presented here in some detail. One was the creating of a story meant to be a statement by Harding but which was transferred instead to Senator J. S. Frelinghuysen of New Jersey. The other concerns Welliver's effort to create a myth about the Democratic candidate, James M. Cox, being a super-boss of the Tammany Hall type.

Late in July, Welliver prepared a statement, to be issued by Harding, calling Cox a puppet of President Wilson. It abounded in quotably caustic phrases and personal quips, saying that the Democrats were "bankrupt in real issues and moral purposes," that Wilson "dictated the San Francisco platform precisely as he wanted it," and that the Democrats "know that the president is about the poorest asset they have." Welliver took the statement to Harding, who rejected it, saying that it was good campaign material, but that it was not in accord with the dignity that should be preserved by a presidential candidate. He recommended that it be attributed to someone else. This was done forthwith, and it appeared in the *Cleveland Plain Dealer* of July 24 as a statement by Senator Frelinghuysen.[22]

Welliver probably never departed more flagrantly from the canons of accurate news reporting, and from his own understanding of the Progressivism which he once espoused, than he did in trying to arrange an interview with Congressman James W. Good of Illinois in order to broadcast his idea of making Cox appear to be one of the greatest boss villains of all time. After consulting with Hays, Welliver told "my dear Jim Good," in a letter of August 11, that he was working "on a line of stuff dealing with this whole proposition of Tammanyizing the nation, and we hope to break it loose before long." He wanted Good to come to Marion with some "illuminating stuff, based on the actual experience of war expenditures as to how these big political organizations graft off the government when they control it. . . . Fix it in your mind so that if you come down here and spill a good interview, you can talk readily and with your accustomed facility and fascination about it. . . . A real animated and punchful discussion of democratic extravagance, adorned with real facts and figures, if spilled here, will get real circulation, and you can provide it." Hays, he added, "is strong for it."[23]

Welliver left little to Good's imagination as to what was necessary to end forever the idea that James M. Cox was a Progressive:

My theory is that Cox was nominated because he was supported by the Tammany machine in New York, the Nugent machine in New Jersey, the Cox machine in Ohio, the Taggart machine in Indiana, the Brennan machine in Illinois and the Wilbur March machine in Iowa. . . . I want any dope you can give me, suggesting how the political machines benefited by the distribution of contracts etc. during the war, and also indicating how the control of administration for the next four years would benefit those organizations in the same way. . . . This is a very serious situation. . . . Cox has been Governor nearly six years out of the past eight years in Ohio, and has built quite a remarkable imitation of Tammany. The cost of government and of government jobs enuring to Mr. Cox's political power has been startling. It is not necessary to suggest the relation of Mr. Murphy's Tammany, or of Mr. Taggart's

Tammany, to this situation. I have been hammering on the proposition that, if the country goes Democratic, it will be ruled four years more by a combination, first of the solid south, and after that the boss ruled democratic states of the north. This is true, and it is a grave situation."

Whether or not Good "spilled" his "facts" as suggested is not clear, but it is clear that Welliver put the Democratic "bogey-man" idea across by cartooning. This was done after consultation with Hays and by arrangement with Albert T. Reid, the Republican party's official cartoonist. Reid was enthusiastic. "It seems to me," wrote Welliver to Scott C. Bone in the national committee's New York headquarters, "that a wide distribution of cartoons, and also of pictures developing the general thought that, if the Democratic party wins, the country will be turned over to the Solid South, plus the democratic machines of New York, New Jersey, Ohio, Indiana, Illinois and the like would be well." This "should be systematically started at once." [24]

Welliver's idea was accepted, and Reid proceeded to do his cartooning best. His anti-Wilson, anti–League of Nations drawings had been gracing the pages of the *National Republican* since early in 1919, and had been used in Republican papers throughout the nation. After the nominations, the images of the heroic Harding and the lowbrowed Cox were joined with those of the sanctimonious Wilson and the loudmouthed "Kunnel Democracy," *i.e.*, the southern Democrats. Early in August, in response to Welliver's suggestions, the new bogeymen appeared. On August 7, Reid portrayed Cox, Taggart, Murphy, and Brennan sitting around a table with a tiger labeled "Tammany" lying on the floor chewing a bone labeled "McAdoo." Murphy was made to say, "Now, think, fellows—one of them slogans like 'He kept us out of war' beats all of your old platform junk to death." Taggart says, "I'll say it does," and Brennan, "That one sure worked." A week later they had a slogan—"Peace, Progress and Prosperity"—with Murphy saying, "I don't know whether that'll work or not, 'Tag'—but this old one sure was a cuckoo," and he pointed to a sign, "He kept us out of war." In the foreground, Cox, attired in child's clothing, is patting the voracious-appearing Tammany tiger and saying, "Nice kitty." On August 28, Cox, as Wilson's chauffeur, was represented as driving a car labeled "U.S." into the mud, while Harding was heroically pointing to the main road. Wilson said, pompously, "Drive on, James, he lacks vision." Soon Samuel M. Gompers, president of the American Federation of Labor, joined the bogeymen, portrayed as a dwarfed shyster seeking to lure a giant named "Labor" into the "Democratic Camp," with a banner flying above it called "International Flag" and the usual Tammany tiger lurking in the background.[25]

Something of the taste exhibited by Reid appeared in a cartoon which had to be publicly repudiated. This was a caricature of Murillo's famous representation of the Immaculate Conception. It was entitled "Having Difficulty in Hanging the Masterpiece." It pictured Cox, "Jimmie," standing on a collapsing stepladder labeled "Public Confidence," trying to hang a painting labeled "Prof. Wilson's League of Nations the Immaculate Conception." The central figure was a bewhiskered Uncle Sam floating on a cloud of dollar bills. His body consisted mostly of a heart labeled "The Heart of the World—U.S." At the bottom of the picture was the inscription "The Greatest He Angel." It appeared, of all places, in the October 23, 1920 issue of *Harvey's Weekly*, the publication of George Harvey.[26]

Had the much-feared "fool break" occurred? The *Boston Post* came out with the editorial challenge, "Is George Harvey Harding's 'Burchard'?" To Harding headquarters came a telegraphed protest from the Philadelphian diocesan publication, the *Catholic Standard and Times*, protesting the "blasphemous and sacreligious cartoon ridiculing the sacred heart and immaculate conception." Official disavowals were sent to Philadelphia by return wire. Harding and Christian were away, but Malcolm Jennings did the honors in Christian's name: "Senator Harding agrees with your opinion as to cartoon. It never had his approval, and he deplores its publication, but is in no wise responsible. The Senator believes in freedom of religious worship. . . ." The cartoon did little harm because it was issued too late in the campaign to get much publicity. After election day, Harvey, himself, made belated apologies.[27]

How pleased Hays was with Reid's vote-catching cartoons was shown in his letter of July 31 to J. Henry Roraback, national committeeman from Connecticut. "The Albert T. Reid cartoon service," Hays wrote, "is going wonderfully well all over the country." [28] One of the most faithful users of the Reid cartoon plates sent out from Republican headquarters was the *Marion Daily Star*.

Reid was not the only cartoonist whose plates flooded the country under the auspices of the Harding management. The famous Jay Northwood Darling ("J. N. Ding") of the *New York Tribune* was one of them, and Grant E. Hamilton, art editor of *Judge* magazine and *Leslie's Weekly*, was another. Scott Bone wrote from the national committee's New York office to Henry Cabot Lodge on September 3, "Our cartoons are reaching thousands of papers and are in demand. In addition to Reid, I am having work from Grant Hamilton of *Judge* and am reproducing the best of Darling's work and striking cartoons from big papers in the west. I am reaching some 4000 papers with plate." [29]

5

One of Welliver's functions was the production of local color. This was a real challenge to him because, to his world-traveled eye, there was not much of it in Marion. He reported to Bone in August that there was a good deal of complaint that not enough "human interest stuff" was getting out of Marion. "The truth is," he added, "that there is some justification in this complaint; the local color stuff is pretty scarce hereabouts." Consequently Welliver had to manufacture some, and he took real pride in doing so. "Tell me," he wrote to H. P. Brown, director of publicity for the state advisory committee of Colorado, "don't you think, under the circumstances, we are getting a pretty good line of publicity out of this village?" [30]

It was Welliver's business to produce local color out of what raw material he could find or manufacture and to send it to the *National Republican* and other appropriate journals. So it was in this manner that the reports and pictures went out: of the subsidized pageantry that the local ladies gave their guests on Woman's Day, October 1; of the colonnade of pillars built by Harding's neighbors on the Mt. Vernon Avenue approaches to his residence; of the Harding portraits in the windows of almost every Marion home. On Sundays he, of course, attended church, sometimes Baptist, sometimes Methodist—it was the broadminded thing to do. Pictures of his speechmaking postures were montaged. On August 4, he was crowned "Prince of the Raisin Festival" by the pulchritudinous visiting queen of the Raisin Festival, Violet Oliver of Fresno, California. Mrs. Harding was also crowned. On August 14, the *National Republican* featured an article by Al Hamilton, an old *Star* employee, entitled "Harding as a Boss," with emphasis on the boss's generous wage policy. In the same issue was a picture of Harding "hauling Old Glory to the masthead" of the flagpole erected on his front lawn for campaign purposes. Incidentally, it was the same flagpole that had graced McKinley's lawn during the front-porch campaign of 1896. Recollections of Harding's teenage schoolteaching and insurance-selling days (of which he was personally never very proud) were offered with much nostalgia. When a sailors' recruiting band from Chicago serenaded before the front porch, Harding's clean, "straight-forward" acknowledgment was billed as coming from one "who abominates gutter methods in a contest for the presidency." The drums of the band were, of course, ostentatiously autographed by the candidate.[31]

Mrs. Harding herself proved to be an excellent subject, providing the domestic touch. As Welliver wrote, "There is going to be a need for this sort of thing right away. I think in the beginning of selling the Harding family to the country, there will be plenty of use for these people." New York headquarters helped him with specific inquiries. He was requested to provide the following information about the candidate's wife: her favorite color; style of hat; whether she wore low or high heels; the way she spent her leisure hours; and whether she preferred the outdoor life. Her vigorous loyalty in the long, uphill fight to make the *Marion Daily Star* a success was a favorite theme. Questions asking how many times Mrs. Harding had been married were answered with the reply that the Senator and his wife accompanied each other on all trips. "Those of us who know the family best are inclined to be envious of the real domestic happiness that prevails." [32]

Headquarters also emphasized the domestic note with requests for material on the candidate's father, Dr. George T. Harding. Pictures were suggested of the Senator at breakfast "with his aged father, portraying the ancestral home atmosphere." Another was desired of the Senator leaving his home "with his aged father to make a call with him on some patient, preferably some old woman." Be sure, the Harding staff photographer was advised, that the call was made "in the ancient buggy which the Senator's father has been using for many years, and which picturizes [*sic*] in good shape." The aged doctor's role as a Civil War veteran was also stressed with photographs of him in full G.A.R. regalia.[33]

There was nothing subtle about playing up the homey theme of the front porch. No front porch in the land was ever enshrined with so much photographed bunting or marked with such a famous flag pole on the lawn. When the *National Property Owners Magazine* requested a picture of Senator and Mrs. Harding seated casually on the front porch, New York headquarters was quick to telegraph the request to Welliver.[34]

Few were more deeply impressed with the home theme of the front porch, and his own part in manufacturing it, than the chewing-gum king, William Wrigley of Chicago. He and advertising king A. D. Lasker visited the front porch on July 27. The next day, after he had returned to Chicago, Wrigley wrote to George Christian, telling how happy the visit had made him. "Yesterday," he wrote, "was one of the greatest days of my life. I do not know when I learned so much, did so much, and had such an absolutely happy time. Hereafter, when I see or hear the word 'home folks' it will mean Marion, and when I see or hear of Marion, it will mean 'home folks'. . . . I think all of us who helped manufacture the publicity punch will never forget the evening. To have known the Senator and Mrs. Harding in their home surroundings is to me a wonderful thing. I was for Harding before I went to Marion—now I fear I shall neglect my business in my anxiety to make others know what I, myself, know." Wrigley was quite pleased with the article in the *Chicago Tribune* which said that he helped get out the *Marion Star*. He confided to Christian that he really got in the way of Harding, "but he did not seem to mind, and I liked it, so we were all happy." He was sending by express a batch of chewing gum, and he hoped the newspaper boys got some of it. He had seen a lot of newspaper correspondents in his time, but never saw "such a bunch of happy ones." Wrigley's enthusiasm for Harding went so far that, according to the *Toledo Blade* of July 28, he said, "Harding is the man of the hour. I think sometimes that a power of which we know nothing guides these things and cares for the nation." [35]

Local color could also be imported. This was the case when some of the great celebrities of stage and screen were brought to Marion on August 24, under the guise of a visit of the "Harding-Coolidge Theatre League." This was one of the productions of Albert Lasker. Something of the big-name spirit of the affair may be observed in the telegram of August 17 from Harding staff man W. A. Grant to Sam P. Gerson of the Garrick Theater in Chicago. Grant said that Hays and Harding had gone over the list of the celebrities invited, and suggested that there should be "more big men from among the actors." "Shubert," he said, "can pull them in. What about Ringling's representation?" [36]

On the morning of the much-heralded day, Pullman cars from New York and Chicago converged on Marion with their famous passengers, including the 110-piece John Hand band from the Windy City. It was a gay day in Marion as the band, playing "Hail, Hail, the Gang's All Here," led the stars from the railroad station to the flag-bedecked porch. Banners pledging the support of the "Harding and Coolidge Theatrical League, 40,000 Strong" and other gaudy displays were conspicuous. At the front porch, Al Jolson, the "Mammy" singer, presided and, before introducing the candidate, sang a campaign song prepared for the occasion:

> We think the country's ready for a man like Teddy,
> One who is a fighter through and through.
> We need another Lincoln to do the nation's thinking,
> And Mr. Harding, we've selected you.

All joined in the chorus:

> Harding, lead the G. O. P.,
> Harding, on to victory!
> We're here to make a fuss,
> Mr. Harding, you're the man for us.

Other stars present, some of whom performed, included the clown Henry E. Dixie, Leo Carillo, Irene Castle, Pearl White, Pauline Frederick, Mary Pickford, DeWolfe Hopper, and Thomas H. Ince. Hays was so impressed by the affair he telegraphed jubilantly to Mrs. Harding, "Thanks for all you and the Senator did yesterday in connection with the Harding-Coolidge Theatrical League. It was simply great. Every one of them is a thousand percent for you." Jolson sent Harding his picture and an autographed copy of his song, and the candidate thanked him for his "bully" souvenirs of "one of our really great days." [37]

Harding's words were not less noted than those of the visiting celebrities, and found their way into the quotable pages of the campaign literature. He said, "I would like the American stage to be like American citizenship, the best in all the world." He jabbed at Wilson for "upstaging." "We have been drifting lately under one-lead activities and I am sure the American people are going to welcome a change of the bill. For the supreme offering, we need the all-star cast, presenting America to all the world." Internationalists who called themselves citizens of the world were ridiculed as Harding assumed a patriotic pose and said, "Frankly, I am not so universal, I rejoice to be an American and love the name, the land, the people and the flag." [38]

Another local importation produced by Lasker, and publicized by

Welliver, was a big-league baseball game. Seldom in the history of sports was a game more "managed" than this one between the Chicago Cubs and the Kerrigan Tailors of Marion.

There was a need for a politically-sponsored, big-league baseball game in Marion because, early in the campaign, Harding had made the mistake of being shown in the movies playing golf. The result was seemingly harmful. Lasker wrote to Walter Friedlander of the Cincinnati Reds baseball club, "It has drawn a perfectly surprising amount of unfavorable reaction from the country. We get hundreds of letters from people saying it's a rich man's game, a mollycoddle game, etc." On July 31, Senator Kenyon wrote to Hays that this sort of thing had better be called off. He told of attending a moving picture show, and, when Harding was shown driving and putting in golf attire, "there was not a hand clap save once." Said Kenyon, "I don't believe the golf business arouses any enthusiasm." Kenyon's letter was sent to Marion, and, at the bottom, Hays wrote, "Confidential—Dear George . . . show this to the Senator. *I want him to see it*—following talk we had." Hays then replied to Kenyon, saying that he realized the golf publicity was bad, and "we are planning to get away from it. It has done real harm in many places." Harding, of course, was glad to cooperate. He played his future golf games in secret. He subscribed to a membership in the Mansfield Country Club and wrote to his friend William S. Cappellar of that city, explaining that he was doing this "so that when I choose to pick up a guest here for a round on your course, I may feel that I may bring them without any embarrassment." [39]

Meanwhile, Lasker arranged his baseball game and had real difficulty doing so. It was easy enough to schedule the Cubs because he was part owner of the club, but he could not get another big league team to oppose the Cubs. He tried the Cleveland Indians, the New York Giants, and the Cincinnati Reds, all of whose owners he knew personally. Lasker was particularly irked at New York Giant manager John J. McGraw, who "kicked it over at the last minute because of his political alinement." Having to settle for the Kerrigan Tailors did not dampen Lasker's determination to get full publicity value for Harding. He wrote to Christian and Welliver, emphasizing the need for big advertising in order to draw a big crowd. Admission should be free, except in the grandstand; the field should be large and the parking space ample.

The affair should be managed to show that it was spontaneous and natural. "The game ostensibly would be paid for by citizens of Mar-

OF MANAGERS AND MANAGEMENT

ion, who, realizing the Senator's love of baseball, had arranged for same." (As a matter of fact, Lasker, Wrigley, and other owners of the Cubs footed the bill.) Lasker even prepared a memo for Welliver which said that, when he and Wrigley visited Marion, "the Senator, who is a great baseball fan, second only to Mrs. Harding, spoke of his love for the game, and how, because of his stay at Marion, he missed that diversion." As a result, the memo continued, Wrigley and Lasker passed Harding's conversation on to William Veeck, president of the Cubs, who thereupon arranged for the Cub stopover. "Just dish it out," Lasker told Welliver, "as you deem best, but I make the suggestion that the above be included in the announcement, so as to bring about the fact that the game was arranged in a normal way." The game "would give our candidate an opportunity to come out in the whole-hearted way he feels in connection with this great American sport, which, we believe will be very favorably received by the country, and certainly would not hurt baseball." [40]

The talents of the well-known sports writer Hugh C. Fullerton were employed to help make the affair seem less staged. Fullerton was informed that Harding had not been a great baseball player, but, he reported, "there has never been a more ardent fan than he." In 1885, Fullerton continued, Harding had played first base "barehanded" in a benefit game for the Johnstown flood survivors. Harding was a stock-holder in the Marion club, which was a member of the Ohio State League, and he attended every home game. He knew such great players as Jake Daubert and Bill Cooper, and could hold his own in any "fan bee" about the merits of such players. He often attended games in Washington "when his work would permit," and even "passed up work for baseball" on occasion. He was happy when Babe Ruth broke his home run record for the year, and "expressed his sincere regret that he was not present to see the 'Babe' do it. Harding likes to see the baseball players hit them out." The writer commented briefly on Harding's liking for golf, but he assured Fullerton that "he is not even what may be called a good player." He and his golf cronies "break no records, but dig up a lot of sod." [41]

Lasker eventually had his baseball game on September 2 at Lincoln Park in Marion, with the Cubs beating the Kerrigan Tailors 3–1. It was a star-studded affair. Among those present were Wrigley, Cub president Bill Veeck, Cub manager Fred Mitchell, and the great pitching "speed king," Grover Cleveland Alexander. Harding, of course, pitched the first ball for the Cubs—the first three, in fact. The candidate made a speech entitled, "Team Play," which gave him a chance to denounce Wilson and the League of Nations in baseball language. "You can't win a ball game with a one-man team. . . . I am opposing one-man play for the nation. . . . The national team, now playing for the United States, played loosely and muffed disappointingly the more domestic affairs, and then struck out at Paris. . . . The contending team tried a squeeze play, and expected to secure six to one against the United States. But the American senate was ready with the ball at the plate, and we are still flying our pennant which we won at home and held respected throughout the world. Hail to the team play of America." [42]

The motion-picture camera was a vital adjunct to these and dozens of other publicity arrangements. The much-publicized scene of the candidate at work in making up the *Marion Star* was one of these. Welliver engineered it. "Please notify your moving picture concern," he wired Grant in Chicago on July 26, "that Harding will do the newspaper office make-up stunt." The "stunt" went off as scheduled for the Chicago movie crew, and, a few days later, was repeated for a crew from New York. Grant went to New York to make the arrangements, receiving another telegram on July 30 to get his moving picture "sharks" on the job the next Monday. Other "stunts" were arranged. August 10 was Ohio primary election for nominating senatorial candidates to compete for Harding's vacancy. Welliver notified Carl Turnage, of the moving-picture crew, that Harding would be the first presidential nominee "to perform his duty as a citizen" in such an election. It would be "pulled off" at noon "in order to get the best possible light." On August 12, it was arranged to have a big Army truck loaded with government supplies come to Harding's house where he would supervise their distribution as part of a campaign "to reduce the high cost of living." At noon there would be a picnic lunch attended by Ohio legislators at which the refreshments would consist of "supplies bought by Senator Harding from the Government stores." Turnage was asked to make reels of these events. [43]

The moving-picture magazines were brought into the Harding campaign. This was done at the urging of one of the top men in the industry, Lewis J. Selznick, head of the Selznick Picture Corporation. Will Hays sent an agent, "R. G. T.," to see Selznick, who was more than cordial. "Mr. Selznick," reported "R. G. T.," "was frank enough to say that he would like some recognition—not financial—in return for active cooperation in giving your candidate and cause publicity through his news weeklies." Selznick wanted to see Hays "and go over the picture publicity situation and to give you his idea," leading up to a meeting with Harding in Marion. "If Selznick goes to Marion," continued "R. G. T.," "it won't be difficult to get the rest of the big men in line, and at heart they are for your ticket because of financial conditions. . . . Make them understand that your vast organization recognizes their vast publicity resources and not only is $$$$$$$$$ [sic]grateful but it looks for their help during the next four years. These men can be made your enduring friends by a little recognition on your part." [44]

6

Beginning on July 31, every day some visiting delegation would be received at the Harding home in Marion, with friendly overtures from the candidate—especially when two or more groups had to share the same day. There were days for all sorts of groups and associations: the farm folk of Richmond and Shelby counties of Ohio; the twenty-second reunion of the 4th Ohio Regiment of the Spanish-American War; a gathering of Ohio newspaper editors; members and alumni of the Ohio legislature; the Ohio Lumberman's Association; the Society of American Indians; delegations from various Ohio counties; blind war veterans; Negro Baptists; miscellaneous groups of schoolteachers; the National Board of Farm Organizations; groups representing American businessmen; delegations representing entire states; a celebration of the signing of the Constitution (September 17); the Knights of Pythias; the Ohio Dental Association; the Men's Glee Club of Bucyrus; and so on. To describe them all would be interminable. Some of the days were "big" days, such as Governor's Day, First Voters' Day, Women's Day (a rejoicing with the ladies over their newly acquired right to vote), and Foreign Voters' Day.[45]

The "days" were, of course, well managed and tightly controlled. Scott C. Bone in New York, Carmi A. Thompson in Chicago, and Howard Mannington in Marion were general co-ordinators. Senator George Sutherland of Utah was general speech writer, although Harding did so much reviewing and revising that he was veritably swamped with work. Welliver was constantly injecting ideas with regard to subject matter and kinds of "days." All speeches had to be censored, that is, drafts sent on ahead, revised, and approved "to prevent any Burchardism," as ex-President Roosevelt's personal secretary William Loeb advised Hays. "Let me impress you," wrote Christian to D. J. T. McCartney of Barnesville, in preparation for a visit, "that whoever your spokesman is he must submit a copy of his written speech here three or four days in advance, and there must be a strict adherence to the speech as finally approved." Delegations also had to be controlled. For example, Women's Day, October 1, had to be handled so as to tone down the League of Women Voters. Colored People's Day was almost managed out of existence because the National Association for the Advancement of Colored People and other advanced civil rights groups injected themselves into the preparation by raising such issues as equality of restaurant and hotel facilities in Marion. The affair was skillfully whittled down to the assembling of religiously minded Negroes, with the Marion Negro Baptist Church providing a tent for accommodating the colored visitors. Foreign Voters' Day, September 18, took a tremendous amount of managing because each nationality wanted a day of its own. After opening maneuvers, the Girl Scouts were finally sidetracked, even though, as Scott Bone said, "there are some strong people behind them." Fortunately the Boy Scouts did not press for a "day," or a hike to Marion, so that Harding could confine himself to solicited inspirational messages from James E. West, chief Boy Scout executive, and from Theodore Roosevelt.[46]

The necessity of managing these "days" so as to obtain the largest crowds in the shortest time, in order to command the greatest amount of news appeal, was illustrated by the handling of First Voters' Day, October 18. The appeal was to the athletically minded youth. The work of organizing was assigned to Peter N. Jans of the "Athletic Committee," which included, as one of its members, the famous Ohio State University football player "Chick" Harley, All-American back in 1916 and 1919. Jans' publicity included a flyer distributed at all football games in Ohio on October 16, urging all schools and colleges to be represented in the athletic parade at Marion the following Monday. A circular had previously been mailed to these schools and colleges, announcing the "America First" rally of young voters and urging each institution to send delegations. Two prizes were offered, one to the school having the largest representation, the other to that which had the best "Athletic Formation." Suggestions for the athletic parade provided for a golf formation, the golfers shouldering golf clubs, and led by a banner reading "A VICTORY DRIVE FOR HARDING AND

COOLIDGE." The baseball formation should consist of the players wearing their uniforms and carrying their bats. Their banner read "HITTING THE BALL FOR HARDING AND COOLIDGE." There were similar provisions for a football formation and a tennis formation. The schools were also urged to bring their bands and a goodly number of girls. "We want the girls in the parade—Bring the *Girls, Girls, Girls.*" [47]

Some attention was given to the so-called intellectual first voters—but not much. Some one suggested that letters be sent to the student Republican clubs at Harvard, Yale, and Princeton. Harding obliged but not in the usual ingratiating way accorded to the "common" man. He wrote to the club chairmen "as an alumnus of a small Ohio college," to young men "favored with the opportunity to attend one of the greatest universities of the country." He was glad that they were Republicans and that they had a sense of public responsibility. But he reminded them that, if they were to be leaders, they "must take from their colleges something more than mere erudition in books and theory. Their associations should make them democratic in spirit, non-sectional in patriotism, wise in the rating of human character, charitable in their judgments and practical in meeting the problems of existence." It did not bother the Republican management when Henry L. Stimson warned Hays that the uproar that the outspoken anti–League of Nations Republicans were making "will lose a lot of the most valuable young material for the party." [48]

First Voters' Day, October 18, went off as scheduled, and a good time was had by all. There were marching bands, along with fife and drum corps; a men's chorus sang "Avalon," and a women's chorus, in white capes and dresses with blue dots and trimming, sang campaign songs. They came from far and near—mostly near—with the Dayton, Ohio delegation of over eight coach-loads winning the award for the biggest group. Harding was in good form as he told his guests that "no like company of new voters ever met together in the morning of their entrance into the the sacred fellowship of representative democracy." He outlined the obligations of citizenship, including going to the polls without compulsion, giving studious attention to public affairs, and, of course, being patriotic. [49]

7

Foreign Voters' Day, September 18, was the culmination of one of the most complicated and wily pieces of management of the entire campaign. It was not founded on the themes of the great American melting pot and the land of opportunity, but upon the dissatisfaction of particular nationalities with Wilson and the Democrats, especially with respect to World War I and its sequel. To be specific, this meant the Greeks, the Italians, the Germans, and the Hungarians. These were the nationalities most adversely affected by the post–World War I peace settlement. It did not mean the Poles, the Czechs, and the Yugoslavs, who were beneficiaries of the peacemaking.

The Republican technique of courting the foreign element alienated by President Wilson was described quite frankly by A. B. Messer of the New York Republican office. Messer took a very realistic attitude toward his work. He agreed that many foreign-born voters approached the problem of the League of Nations and the Treaty of Versailles from a selfish viewpoint. The thing to do was to take advantage of that feeling. "Fortunately," he wrote E. S. Stokes of the New Jersey state republican committee, on August 27, "a great many of these people are not viewing the coming election from a strictly American point of view, or as to whether Mr. Harding and the Republican party are best qualified to serve the people of this country or not. On the contrary they are largely influenced by something growing out of the peace following the great war."

Messer then took up various foreign interests which were offended by Wilson's policies. "The Italian," he said, "feels that he was unjustly discriminated against in the Fiume question and the Adriatic question generally, as indeed he was, and he is very hostile to President Wilson, and the endorsement of Mr. Wilson's stand by Mr. Cox has convinced him that the Democratic party is still hostile to the interests of his native land. You have a very large Italian vote in New Jersey, and it should be cultivated through the Italian organization, reasonably financed by you, working in harmony and conjunction with the National Committee office through its Field Secretaries. We will furnish you with distinguished speakers from outside the state." The Greeks and Hungarians were also offended by Wilson's peace terms. The Greeks felt that more territory, Greek in population and tradition, should have been given to Greece instead of to Turkey and Bulgaria. The Hungarians, "shut off from the coast, reduced to six or seven millions of people, isolated from everyone, feel that the entire weight and blame of the war has been visited upon them. Hardly any of the people of Europe were satisfied with the Peace terms, and lay much of it upon the arrogance, ignorance and pig-headedness of Mr. Wilson, and they should be approached in this coming campaign in such a way as to keep them in their frame of mind regarding the Democratic party which seeks to wage a vigorous campaign for the foreign speaking vote, using the wet issue, the League of Nations and other camouflage to win their point." [50]

The Greek situation was well handled by Judson Welliver's news-feeding activity. One of his first stories concerned a Greek-American delegation that called on Harding in mid-July. These gentlemen informed Harding that they represented 300,000 Greek-American voters, and that they were solidly for Harding "because of his assistance in getting a proper settlement of the question of Thrace." Welliver said that he was giving this to the newspapermen, and that the Greek-language press would give it the widest publicity. [51]

Further evidence of the Republican technique used on the Greek-Americans is seen in an exchange of letters between Senator Lodge and Messer. Lodge called Messer's attention to a Senate resolution in behalf of Greece which, he said, had been "put through by the Republicans with little or no Democratic support." Lodge added that "it was owing to the attitude of the President in resisting the award of Thrace to Greece that any difficulty whatever arose in that direction." Messer assured Lodge that he had the Greek situation well under control, describing himself as the "real editor of the Greek paper Atlantis for over a year, calling at the office of editor Vlasto occasionally and going to banquets with him from time to time. They have supported me as well as any paper in the United States." He referred to a Mr. Moustakis, with whom he was cooperating, and to a "Mr. Theodore Photiades, a prominent banker and importer, who offered his services to stimulate interest and enthusiasm among the Greek merchants." The fact that Photiades and Vlasto were not on good terms "will make it necessary for me to carry on two operations. This is however common among all people of foreign extraction." [52]

How the Republicans applied their wiles to the Italians appears from many sources. Hays explained to Stokes of New Jersey that the organization was "cultivating" the Italians through the Italian-American Republican National League. This organization, said Hays, "will carry on a campaign of publicity through the newspapers, getting out pamphlets, the holding of a nationwide convention in New York, and the cultivation of field secretaries of large Italian colonies in the various states." A big "fiesta" of the Italian-American Republican National League was held in New York September 20–22, under the presidency of Fiorello H. La Guardia, with the delegates from twenty-three states all joining in a message to Harding pledging their support. On September 5, Oscar Durante, editor of *L'Italia*, with a delegation of fellow Chicagoans, visited Harding in Marion in order, according to the *Chicago Tribune*, "to ascertain the attitude of the nominee toward matters affecting Italy, especially Fiume." The Italians left Marion "highly pleased, declaring that Italy would have an understanding friend in President Harding." A month later Welliver, at Marion, was in receipt of *L'Italia* clippings from Durante, quoting former Italian Premier Francesco S. Nitti, as saying that President Wilson's treaties "contain the germs of deep hatred and perhaps new wars." Welliver said that Durante "is doing very useful work," and sent the clippings to the New York office because they "strike me as useful." [53]

A part of this Italian work was to get Enrico Caruso, the great tenor, to come to Marion. The Caruso idea apparently originated with New York banker and art promoter Otto H. Kahn, chairman of the Metropolitan Opera Company, who was informed, "The Caruso matter for the last of September is entirely all right. We will count on you to help to work it out." Lasker also liked the idea; it was a "ten strike." He wrote to Hays to advise the appearance of a Fiume statement to accompany Caruso's intended front-porch concert. "I am delighted," Lasker said, "at the thought that you may be able to get Caruso to come to Marion. Won't you kindly inform me the exact date when arranged, as I feel we can put out a Fiume story which will mean more to us than any one thing we might do in the way of publicity to one group at this time." This statement, Lasker told Welliver, would be to the effect that "if the Senator is elected President, he will put nothing in the way of Fiume joining the Motherland. This will be absolutely consistent with our position of not meddling in European affairs." [54] For some reason the Caruso plan failed, and the Harding propagandists were unable to capitalize on the world-famous tenor's voice.

The Republican organization seemed confident that it had the German-American vote because of Harding's outspoken opposition to the Wilson League and the Treaty of Versailles. Tactful efforts to cultivate this were very much in order. Scott Bone, at the New York office, assured Lodge, "The Germans are largely with us. In fact, the German support in Ohio promises to offset the labor defection. The big German papers like the Staats-Zeitung here, are almost daily attacking

Wilsonism. A very scholarly German editor is doing confidential work for me on the side, not with any direct connection with the committee, and he deprecates the revival of war feelings as affecting the Germans. You will see the practical side of it and understand." [55]

However, when the Germans sought to overdo their case, Harding rejected their overtures. In August, the German-American National Conference, led by George Sylvester Viereck of New York and Dr. H. Gerhard, declared its support of Harding because of his "unalterable opposition to the League of Nations and to the perfidious foreign policy" of President Wilson. Dr. Gerhard then asked for a Marion conference, but was politely advised to stay home. Incidentally, Dr. Gerhard cited J. E. Phillips of Marion as a member of the German-American National Conference. In another case, when one F. F. Schrader of New York alleged undue Republican recognition of Coleman DuPont, whom he called "one of the most subtle German baiters in America," Harding replied that Schrader was a victim of "supersensitiveness." By correspondence, and in the October issue of his magazine, the *American Monthly*, Viereck did his best to flatter Harding for his Ohio pro-German leanings, but the Senator was not one to be caught by such blandishments. Viereck also sought a pledge to pardon Eugene V. Debs, but Harding refused. [56]

The Hungarians seemed no less vigorous for Harding than their fellow malcontents of the Greek, Italian, and German sympathizers. They were so aggressive in seeking a separate visit to the front porch that they were almost on their way to Marion before the distracted managers could impress upon them the fact that they must merge their visit with all the other nationalities on Foreign Voters' Day, September 18. However, the Hungarian-American pilgrimage to Marion on that day seems to have been less a spontaneous outpouring than it was an individual promotion scheme by Dr. Andrew Cherna, editor-in-chief of the Hungarian daily *Szabadsag* (*Liberty*) of Cleveland. According to Max E. Zucher, executive secretary of the foreign division of the Ohio Republican state committee, Dr. Cherna, finding that many of his pilgrims could not afford the trip to Marion, paid their transportation costs. This so encouraged other Hungarian editors that almost half of those visiting Harding on September 18 had their expenses paid. After the visit to Marion, Dr. Cherna continued to finance the efforts of "The Harding for President Hungarian-American League." [57]

So it was that on September 18 Marion took on the festive appearance of an international gala day. Thirty nations in all were represented, their delegates carrying pennants telling of their native country, but each and all were wearing red, white, and blue arm bands for the country of their adoption. Banners were borne by proud hands, declaring "Thirty races, but one country, one flag," "Sons of Italy," "Americans All," and "For America First." Three bands marched in the parade, with the smartly-attired Gugliotta's band of Cleveland the most spirited and conspicuous. Harding used the occasion to emphasize the America First theme and to denounce hyphenism. "America is yours to preserve," he said, "not as a land of groups and classes, races and creeds, but America, the ONE America! the United States, America the Everlasting." He delivered one of his ambivalent talks on American foreign policy. On the one hand, he denounced meddling; on the other, he praised being helpful to world humanity. "How can we have American concord; how can we expect American unity; how can we escape strife, if we in America attempt to meddle in the affairs of Europe and Asia and Africa? . . . It is not alone the menace which lies in involvement abroad; it is the greater danger which lies in conflict among adopted Americans." But on the other hand, being united did not mean "an America blind to the welfare of humanity throughout the world or deaf to the call of world civilizations." [58]

Sometimes, of course, it was necessary to speak against a foreign group, if it was not very numerous, and, as in the case of the Japanese in California, if it was a political necessity to do so. Harding had to meet this problem as preparations were made for a front-porch appearance on September 14 of a delegation of Californians headed by Governor W. D. Stephens of the Golden State.

Harding made it easy for himself and Governor Stephens by getting Daugherty to ask the California Governor to say what he wanted done about the Japanese, so that adequate provisions could be made from the front porch on September 14. On September 5, Stephens wrote Daugherty, "responding to your request that I send you something that may be said to the California delegation on their arrival at Marion." The Governor suggested three statements for Harding to choose from. Each statement pledged Harding to the stoppage by law and international agreement of the immigration of persons "inalienable [sic] to citizenship." Each statement based this pledge on the "impossibility of the assimilation of orientals with occidental people." Harding's speech was in full accord with the Governor's desires, if not with his use of English grammar. "No one can tranquilly contemplate the future of this Republic," Harding said, "without an anxiety for abundant provision for admission to our shores of only the immigrant who can be assimilated and thoroughly imbued with the American spirit. . . . We have the moral, the material and the legal international rights to determine who shall or shall not enter our country and participate in our activities. . . . We favor such modifications of our immigration laws, and such changes in our international understandings, and such a policy relating to those who come among us, as will guarantee to the citizens of this Republic not only assimilability of alien born, but the adoption, by all who come, of American standards, economic and otherwise, and a full consecration to American practices and ideals." Harding added specific promises of adequate tariff protection of California products against those who would "invade our markets and under-bid our farmers." He specified the California fruit industry. There was no doubt about the political intent of these promises. As the *Chicago Tribune* pointed out, with a side glance at the California Republican split of 1916, "There will be no wobbling this year in the G. O. P.," nor would there be any need for a Pacific Coast tour by the candidate.[59]

Harding privately admitted to feelings of concern about the inconsistency of this kind of talk with his concern for the promotion of peace via a League of Nations. But he received impressive support from Cornell University President Jacob Gould Schurman, who was an ardent League advocate. It happened that Schurman had been a member of a good-will delegation of businessmen who visited Japan early in 1920. They had been entertained by Japanese barons, viscounts, and business leaders. In the course of this tour of the islands, Schurman had made several speeches complimenting the Japanese people on their high civilization and suggested that they did not want a stream of Hindu immigrants lowering it any more than the United States wanted a flood of unassimilable Orientals driving farmers out of business and "threatening to dilute the national consistency." This was especially important to the United States in 1920 because "the war had revealed to us fissures in our national consciousness." All these things and more Schurman told Harding, who replied in terms of gratitude. He confessed that the first draft of his speech emphasized the need to "preserve the peace of the world and to deal fairly with all people within and without our boundaries. I had expressed my position, I think, a little more definitely than it appears in the speech, but made some modifications out of regard to the sensitiveness of some of our

California friends, but the two speeches were not in any way in conflict." [60]

One of the most effective "days," considering the buildup to it, and its sequel, was Traveling Salesmen's Day, September 25. This "day" was the climax of a salesmen's campaign to revive the memory of an unfortunate reflection upon their craft made by Cox's *Dayton News* editorial of August 15, 1914, when he was running for reelection to the governorship of Ohio. The Governor's paper had bluntly called the commercial traveler a nuisance and an "unmitigated bore," whom every "sensible business man will do his best to avoid." Respectable executives were said to feel like kicking them out of their offices, and were driven to hiring purchasing agents so as to avoid the contacts. [61]

The traveling salesman did not forget easily, so it was not difficult for the Republican national committee to sponsor a national Harding and Coolidge Traveling Men's League with headquarters in Ohio. A special, pocket-sized leaflet was prepared, entitled, "Travelling Salesmen As Judged by the Two Presidential Candidates." It was embellished by a Reid cartoon entitled "Slightly Difficult Receptions," showing Cox throwing a salesman out of his office, and Harding graciously welcoming one. Cox's belligerent statement was quoted in full beside Harding's kindly telegram of July 26 to the annual meeting of the National Council of Traveling Salesmen. In this, he called the salesmen the "shock troops of every campaign for more and sounder business," who, unlike Cox and the Democrats, "were doing everything they could to get business back to a peace time basis." Another party pamphlet called "The Salesmen's Platform," did similarly, calling the travelers "more sensitive to the pulse of business than . . . the lame ducks and theorists now running the country." Harding had received many letters from business sales departments showing how their salesmen were being encouraged to solicit votes for Harding. Such companies were Marshall Field Company of Chicago, the Pratt Food Company of Philadelphia, and W. S. Ehnie & Brothers, wholesale confectioners of Jacksonville, Illinois. The *Shoe Traveler*, a Chicago publication of the shoe industry, featured the Harding-Cox utterances on salesmen. [62]

Traveling Salesmen's Day, September 25, was a very lively "day" in Marion. It was probably representative of more states than was any other front-porch ceremony. A local Marion Traveling Men's Association was formed to greet the brothers. All trains were met, automobiles provided, and trips around the city conducted. There was the inevitable parade with a jaunty band and spiced-up banners. A long banner with a picture of Lincoln on one end and Harding on the other bore the words, "Senator Harding, We are coming 600,000 strong." Another announced, "The whole d—— [sic] family has agreed on Harding." In his address, Harding gave the salesmen a "pitch" as good as any of their own. "The first travelling men of all civilization became the ambassadors of education and art, the bearers of ideas and the surveyors of the widened fields of human relationships." They were enjoined to travel for the "one big house—this republic of ours—always thinking of America first." [63]

8

The front-porch performances, however, gradually got to be boring, and their publicity value declined. Therefore, the stage managers proposed a remedy—eliminating most of the "days" and concentrating on a few "superdays." This was only partially done. What really happened was the abandonment of the front-porch campaign. The last "day" was First Voters' Day, October 18. From then on, Harding and Cox engaged in a stump-speaking battle, with emphasis on the League of Nations.

The front-porch managers came to take themselves too seriously. Something of the exaggeration of these self-important publicity experts was indicated by the September 8 letter to Hays from Lasker's chief counselor, Richard Washburn Child. Child saw the campaign at Marion beginning to sag and warned Hays of dire consequences unless things were sparked up:

> As I see it, we are winners unless there be breaks or sags. But mark it well, Will—I see a real danger in the possibility of an anti-climax to the porch campaign. We have about forty five days to go, and it would be serious, if the porch campaign part of the period did not assume increasing bigness and pungency. Mere frequency of visiting delegations is even undesirable unless they represent big things and give us a chance to say big things. Heretofore it has been enough for this organization here to sit behind a cigar and wait for delegations to apply. Except for a few occasions, which have been definitely "worked up," I do not think much of the results. Inconsequential occasions give no inspiration to a candidate. . . . The delegation business *must not drift.* It must be stage managed by men of capacity. . . . Hereafter let's avoid the petty delegations and picayune occasions, and get big publicity

material. If we don't the middle of October will see the campaign, without any fault of the candidate, sag like an old empty hammock.[64]

Child was wrong. By the middle of October, Harding had left the porch for the stump as the vigor of the debate on the League of Nations had reached climactic proportions. What Child failed to realize was that the front porch, by mid-October, had already exhausted its campaign value. The multitudinous other forms and phases of Harding advertising were in full play. Straw votes, overdone and misleading as they were, showed an increasing trend to Harding. Betting odds everywhere favored Harding. Local Republican managers began to demand local appearances of the candidates, more for their own prestige than for the candidates. In other words, coat-tailing was in process, and, in view of Harding's advantage, it could be indulged in to a limited degree.[65]

9

Human interest coverage on Harding took in a wide range, judging by five publications sponsored by Welliver and his colleagues. These were: (1) a series of newspaper articles on Harding by "The Girl Next Door," i.e., by Eleanor Margaret Freeland, a Marion schoolteacher; (2) Joe Mitchell Chapple's *Warren Harding: The Man*; (3) C. C. Philbrick's *What a Country Boy Did with 200 Pounds of Type*; (4) Jack Warwick's "Growing up with Harding"; and (5) Frederick E. Schortemeier's *Rededicating America: Life and Speeches of Warren G. Harding*.

Of the Freeland series, Welliver said, "These stories are absolutely the best stuff that has gone out of the town from the women's side." [66] They were originally published in the *Cleveland Sunday News-Leader* starting on July 18, and were later syndicated. They received the high sponsorship of former Senator Theodore Burton of Cleveland, who wrote in Miss Freeland's behalf to Harding. They appeared in the *Detroit Free-Press*, the *Springfield* (Mass.) *Republican*, the *Boston Post*, the *Chicago Daily News*, the *Baltimore Sun*, the *Buffalo News*, the *Portland Oregonian*, the *Washington Star*, and the *Des Moines Capital*. They were a "pantry window" approach to the big events taking place across the lawn. The "girls" of Marion, in their "fluffy ruffles," took long walks just to go past the Harding home.

There was the groceryman's opinion that Wood should have a place on Harding's cabinet. There were the fierce-looking policemen who kept souvenir hunters from snipping twigs off the Harding shrubbery. There was that "jam town" breakfast of ham and eggs, fried potatoes, and hot biscuits with "dandy jam"—all for sixty cents. " 'Now in Washington,' said a new staff worker, 'a breakfast like that'—and he rolled his eyes and held up his hands and couldn't say another word." Miss Freeland's style was quite folksy. "Oh, I am sure you would like to hear about the inside of Mrs. Harding's house." And then came the tidbits about "nice little cretonne curtains . . . on the windows," simple upholstered furniture—nothing fussy. "Just wait until she gets to the White House and she won't do a thing to those fussy glass chandeliers that seem to take up most of the ceiling, and those terrible old-fashioned looking pictures that clutter up the walls, and all the rest of the queer looking junk." In the notification ceremonies the candidate was introduced by "a Mr. Lodge," and he said "those beautiful words about 'us women,' and as I saw tears in other eyes I just didn't care a bit." A reference to Mrs. Harding's waffles evidently brought so many inquiries for the recipe that Miss Freeland "ran over and asked Bernice for it." (Bernice was the Hardings' maid.) And, of course, there was the man from West Virginia who called his newly-born twin sons "Warren" and "Harding," It was a great season for Marion, said "The Girl Next Door." "Some old guy once said, 'All roads lead to Rome.' Well Rome hasn't a thing on Marion." [67]

What the Republican organization thought of Chapple's book is indicated by the fact that it put copies in the hands of 3,800 editors of "Smaller Republican papers." [68] Chapple, an adopted Bostonian, was the editor of a patriotic periodical called the *National Magazine*. He was also a Redpath Chautauqua worker and the author of novels entitled *The Minor Chord, Heart Throbs, Heart Songs, Heart Letters*, and *Heart Chord*. His opus on Harding was written "as a friend would speak of a friend." It was widely advertised as "The Book of the Hour," "An Imposing Biography of a Real American Boy and Man," "A Great Book—Tense, Virile and True Blue," "All American," and "A Man's Book for Your Boy after you have been inspired by it." James J. Davis, Harding's future Secretary of Labor, was so impressed by it that he thought he ought to "get the people of America, especially the working man to read it." He said he was going to buy "a large number" of copies and send them to men with whom he used to work in the steel mills. As director general of the Moose, Davis was also glad that a fellow Moose wrote it. "Dear Joe," he wrote, "Senator Harding secured the right man to do the right job." Chapple agreed, and quoted one correspondent who said, "The book has a melodic sweetness that could not be given in any campaign book or to any other candidate." [69]

Indeed, Chapple's book fairly reeked with "melodic sweetness." He started Harding out in life in a chapter entitled, "A Blue-Eyed Babe in Blooming Grove," and carried him to the role of "Champion of Americanism." In a crashing conclusion, Chapple declared that "Young America, with its red blooded hopes; first voters with their visions; American manhood and womanhood in their struggles and triumphs; veterans in the sunset of life will declare by ballot and support . . . the conviction that Warren G. Harding is the measure of a man to be chosen President of the United States." In between, Harding emerged as a veritable demigod, a brilliant college student, a "business genius," one who realized "the richness of Hellenic ideals," the choice of "the deep sober judgment" of the convention of 1920, a fit successor of the beloved Roosevelt whose "spirit . . . goes marching on." [70]

Chapple devoted the entire October issue of his *National Magazine* to the campaign, calling it the Harding number. It was "loaded," he wrote the Senator, "with hot stuff for the last blast before election. It reveals you as you are, a cool-headed, common sense friend and American to the core." He asked Harding to write a letter, as if to a friend "as Lincoln did to his friends, showing you in your true form and modesty." Harding obliged with a note, saying "We are just plain folks, like so many of the American people, though we do have earnest convictions and high aspirations for our common country." Harding added, "The people of the United States are going to vote very deliberately this time, and they are not going to be blinded by the chaff of the campaign." [71]

C. C. Philbrick was editor of a Columbus publication called the *Week*, which was one of the original "Harding for President" publications—partly as a protest against the so-called Wolfe-controlled Columbus papers, the *Evening Dispatch* and the *Ohio State Journal*. Philbrick was more knowledgeable about his subject than was Chapple, but it was written in the style of a Horatio Alger story. He was the young man with plenty of pep who was able to pay off the company's mortgage at the last minute and, from then on, was able to "ride out the storm tossed sea of financial trouble." When dirty rival journalists insulted him, he shook his fist under their noses and threatened to "lick the everlasting dickens" out of them. Marion became a prosperous city "largely through Harding's efforts." He met his payrolls on time. His family life was happy. "Mrs. Harding never lost her fine spirit of comradeship and implicit faith" in her husband. He was a man's man worthy of Theodore Roosevelt's confidence, a supporter of the famous colonel's desire to fight for his country in World War I. He was an inspiration to the young men of his time who "may find not only inspiration to combat the obstacles in their pathway, but may well emulate him in no fear of luring the 'Moving Finger' 'back to cancel half a line.' "

The syndicated series entitled, "Growing up with Harding," by Harding's boyhood pal Jack Warwick, was copyrighted by the *New York Post* and ran daily in the Scripps papers for several weeks during July and August. Warwick had been one of Harding's partners in acquiring the *Marion Daily Star* in 1884, and had stayed with him in various capacities, though not as a partner, until 1904, when he joined the staff of the *Toledo Blade*. Warwick's writing did not have the weird tints of the Freeland, Chapple, or Philbrick productions. In fact, it had considerable accuracy and was more moderate in tone. Both Hays and Warwick sent copies for Harding to correct.[73] Warwick's version of the Harding story also had Horatio Alger overtones, but with greater authenticity. It had a certain dignified quality and a gentlemanliness in telling the truth without being maudlin. Yet it was sentimental. The enthusiastic young printers did actually sleep with their project, stick their own type, assemble their own forms, cut their "boiler plate," nurse their wheezy press engines, and glory in the printed product. Harding coaxed the advertisers with the magic of his personality, and he forgave his help when they went on drunken sprees. Warren Harding and Florence Kling held clandestine meetings, while the townfolk encouraged their romance against the wrath of Florence's father, Amos Kling, the richest man in town, who had little faith in his daughter's sense and less in Harding's future. Aylmer Rhoades, "the best reporter I ever had," in Harding's words, kept a constant eye on the courthouse lest it collapse in his absence. Warwick, himself, got homesick for Caledonia, and once knelt in prayer with Mrs. Dr. Harding beside the fevered form of one of his own children. Mother Harding returned home, singing quietly in her happiness in a life of ministering to others.[74]

Schortemeier's *Rededicating America* was a documentary. There was a foreword by Hays, and an inspirational biography by Shortemeier, who was secretary of the Indiana Republican state committee. It contained the text of twenty-one Harding speeches, with appropriate subtitles to make for easier reading. The speeches selected were all of a patriotic nature: his acceptance speech; two of his Senate efforts on the League of Nations; his Waldorf-Astoria address of January 6, 1920, entitled "Americanism;" a series on George Washington, Abraham Lincoln, Ulysses S. Grant, William McKinley, and Theodore Roosevelt; and various business-slanted efforts, including the "Back to Normalcy" address in Boston, May 11, 1920 and one opposing the excess-profits tax.[75]

10

Characteristic of the Hays-Harding management was the influence of Lasker and his firm, Lord and Thomas. Here was an agency that could sell anything and anybody. They had done it with Wrigley's chewing gum; they had done it with Lucky Strike cigarettes—"Reach for a Lucky instead of a sweet"; with soap—"Keep that school girl complexion"; with breakfast food—"Grains that are shot from guns." They proposed to do it with Warren Gamaliel Harding.[76]

A key to the Lasker touch, of course, was slogans. For Harding, it was decreed that the slogan should be "Let's have done with wiggle and wobble." This was supposed to suggest the hypocrisy of Wilson promising to keep Americans out of war in 1916, getting them into war in 1917, out again in 1918, and in again, possibly, with his League of Nations. The persistence with which Lasker proceeded to administer this slogan was overwhelming. He was not merely a part of the Hays-Harding machine—he was a machine all by himself. There were no committees to be consulted, no New York offices; there was Lasker, and Lasker alone.

His first step with "Wiggle and Wobble" was to go straight to the candidate and get its instant adoption. The proof of this is indisputable. On August 16, Lasker wrote to Scott Bone, director of publicity at the New York headquarters. "The candidate," he informed Bone, "has agreed to include the slogan in his speech of August 28th on the League of Nations." Lasker minced no words in describing this to Bone. "The important thing I want to get to you is: that the candidate will include the thought of the slogan in his speech and will make the closing words of his speech thus: 'Let's be done with Wiggle and Wobble. Steady America! Let's assure good fortune to all.'" He pointed out that billboards were already going up featuring the slogan, and Harding's use of it would enable "the papers to get the slogan, 'Let's be done with Wiggle and Wobble' to lift and work around." That Harding did his part is without question. His August 28 League of Nations address contained the following words in its closing paragraph, "Let us be done with wiggling and wobbling. Steady, America, let us assure good fortune to all." [77]

An amusing thing about Lasker was his order that his decree to Harding about the use of "wiggle and wobble" should be handled so as to be certain it looked as if it were not decreed. It must be casual, natural. Everything Lasker ordered had to look sincere and spontaneous. (Remember the Cubs baseball game in Marion.) Thus did he instruct Welliver in Marion as of August 20, "We want it to appear that when the candidate wrote this sentence in his speech, it was merely a passing sentence that he injected, but that it was so forceful that it was spontaneously picked up. If you deem it wise, when the speech is delivered, to do anything with the local correspondents, in this spirit, of course, use your own judgment! But if you do call their attention to it, kindly do so in such a way that they won't know that the publicity end of the campaign had anything to do with the expression, and the thought appearing in the speech." To make sure that Welliver realized how serious it all was, Lasker reminded him that the billboards, slogan and all, would go up by October 1. Lasker was still not satisfied. Four days later he telegraphed Christian, "Even at risk of being a nuisance, want to remind you to see that slogan is included in Saturday's speech." [78]

Opposition to "wiggle and wobble" did not phase Lasker. Senator John W. Weeks of Massachusetts telegraphed Hays, "Reported here that Wiggle and Wobble is to be used as campaign slogan. Cannot find anyone who believes that this should be done and I feel there are many reasons why it should not be." Hays immediately got Lasker on the phone, and what Lasker told Hays may well be inferred from what he proceeded to write Hays in a letter: "Regarding your phone message on 'WIGGLE AND WOBBLE,' Don't worry, I will put it over with editorial cooperation and speaker's cooperation if I can get it; if I can't I will put it over without it. . . . I shall have to rely on the force of the display advertising in the weekly magazines like the Saturday Evening Post and the bill posting. These two media alone will put it over." That this was done the pages of the *Post* and the *Literary Digest* amply reveal.[79]

As a matter of fact, since the New York office objected to the use of "wiggle and wobble," it became a matter of principle for the Chicago office to use it. Lasker made the defiant announcemment to Hays on September 3: "Raymond Robbins told me yesterday he had received no notice to use 'WIGGLE AND WOBBLE,' but that he would surely use it after this." [80] Also, the official party letterheads were immediately amended by the addition of a purple stamp reading "NO COUNTRY ON EARTH BUT OURS COULD SURVIVE YEARS WIGGLING AND WOBBLING." [81]

Eventually, even the New York office was converted to "wiggle and wobble"—at least chairman Hays was. In a form letter of September 18 to all the Republican workers in the country, he urged a continuation of the good work that had been indicated so far. Their leader, said Hays, was magnificent—"as faithful as Washington, as humble as Lincoln, as unafraid as Roosevelt." He closed by saying, "I know you will not forget to make every possible use of those lines from Senator Harding's speech of August twenty eighth: 'Steady America! Let us assure good fortune to all. Let us be done with wiggling and wobbling.' " [82]

On and on went Lasker in his "wiggle and wobble" campaign. He got it into a cartoon series via the pugnacious editor of the Hearst papers, Arthur Brisbane. Lasker bluntly informed Hays of the Brisbane arrangement, which, he said, would be of "infinite value." He enclosed a letter from Brisbane describing the effort "to popularize Aunt Wobble and Uncle Wiggle" through a cartoon series in the *New York Journal* by Frederick Burr Opper, creator of the comic strips "Happy Hooligan" and "Alphonse and Gaston." [83]

The quality of the Opper cartoon contribution to the circulation of "wiggle and wobble" propaganda may be judged by two that appeared in the *Cleveland News* on September 11 and September 20. The series was entitled "Jimmy and His War Bride," "Jimmy" being Harding's Democratic opponent, James M. Cox, and his bride, shown as a very ugly crone, being the "League of Nations" whom "Jimmy" had been forced to marry by the bride's father, Woodrow Wilson. In every cartoon the mismated pair had fourteen ugly children in line, seeming to indicate the articles of the League of Nations Covenant— or could it be Wilson's Fourteen Points? Each child had a number, and number 10, referring to the controversial League Article X, was always clad in black. In the September 11 cartoon, "Jimmy's" wife, the "League of Nations," was portrayed dancing with a leering John Bull to the tune of "Rule Brittania," and saying to him, "If my husband gets elected we shall expect you to dine with us regularly." To this, John

Bull replied, "What's your telephone number?" In the midst of it all were the very shocked "Aunt Wiggle" and "Uncle Wobble," the former saying, "Land's Sakes," and the latter "Wa'al I'll be darned." The September 20 cartoon showed an educated donkey "Dopo," the Democratic party, reviewing a parade of pairs and trios of performers running around him in a circle. Each pair or trio carried a banner, the first one reading "Wiggle and Wobble," and the rest of them such terms as "Middle and Muddle," "Stuff and Nonsense," "Hem and Haw," "Flub and Dub," and "Bunk, Punk and Junk."

There may have been disgust in some Republican quarters with the Lasker-Brisbane-Opper contributions, but not in the case of chairman Hays. He instructed his Chicago office to show Lasker all the party literature so that the advertising man could know what to illustrate. "He has evidenced," wrote Hays, "a most keen political insight in some of the advertisements he has prepared." Lasker himself liked best the one illustrating the conversion to the Republican cause of a Democratic businessman, Charles Sumner Bird, who wanted to subscribe $1,000 to the campaign so as to help get business out of the clutches of Democratic bunglers. This, Lasker proudly proclaimed, was another "ten-strike." "It subtly covers the matter of financial subscriptions in such a way that no matter what Cox does to agitate the subject, or whether you subsequently raise the limit, this will fit it by showing the character of the subscriptions we get." More of the same kind of subtlety was Lasker's deliberate effort to make his display advertising appear less lavish than that put out by the Democrats. "I would like the Democrats," he wrote, "to use the bigger space thereby letting it show on the surface that they are spending infinitely more money than we are." [84]

An outstanding piece of Republican spectacularism was the use of the name and influence of aviator Captain Edward V. Rickenbacker, hero of World War I and "Ace of Aces" in the downing of German planes. The idea, as proposed by Walter A. Clennin, Chicago publisher's representative, was for the popular "Captain Eddie" to take his 94th Pursuit Squadron, which he had commanded in France, on a series of flights from July 4 to November 2 to cover every state in the union. Harding was to plan his itinerary with this in mind, flying with Rickenbacker from place to place. "You would be as safe in his machine," Clennin told Harding, "as you would be riding across country in a railroad train . . . and you could speak in every city of importance of the United States . . . and . . . would give you the biggest plurality ever given to any candidate going into office." Lasker was all for it. A conference of Hays, Lasker, and Rickenbacker was arranged in Chicago in mid-August "to close the deal." [85]

In his recent autobiography, Captain Rickenbacker has a slightly different version of this plan which may help to explain why it did not go through. The original idea was to obtain a $500,000 DH-4 airplane. "We can buy an airplane," Rickenbacker told Hays and Lasker, "and I'll fly him back and forth between your national headquarters in Chicago and his front porch." According to Captain Rickenbacker, the Republican managers "bought the idea immediately. A flying candidate! I made arrangements to buy a DH-4 and designed some modifications for it. One was the installation of a little canopy over the rear seat for my distinguished passenger. The total bill would run to about $500,000. But before I could buy the plane, the Democrats accused the Republicans of having a five million dollar slush fund, and in the face of this adverse publicity, Hays and Lasker decided that the party had better not spend half a million flying Harding around." [86]

Whatever the explanation of the Hays-Rickenbacker "deal," the Republicans found the Captain very useful in playing the soldier theme against the Wilson League of Nations. An arrangement was made with the *Cleveland News* to publish a series of anti-League articles. In this series Rickenbacker made it appear that the League would make American soldiers fight and die for useless causes. "What is there to nerve men against death in the thought that by his death he will help one of these foreign countries retain a territory as big as Long Island and prevent another country from getting it? . . . Does a man die gladly for anything so foreign and so sordid?" It was unfair to him and to his mother. "No soldier can be for a covenant that is so cruel to her whom he loves best." Rickenbacker contrasted the soldiers who had fought for our freedom with those who would give our freedom away. "What does the soldier find on his return from France? It is incredible. He finds a large number of Americans trying through a league of nations to give away the very freedom and independence which he risked his life to preserve." [87]

11

While the national campaign went forward, the Ohio management subsided into localistic futility. The old Ohio advisory committee system, which had worked so faithfully over the years to patch together the Ohio factions and to produce the appeal of Harding as a new "Ohio Man" was needed no longer. The advisory committee chairman, George H. Clark, was still in his Columbus office, chafing for something to do to help produce a great triumph in November. On June 19, Clark's *Ohio Republican* brought forth its "Victory No. 100" issue with banner headlines, above pictures of Harding and Coolidge, which read, "Ohio, New Mother of Presidents, Has Another McKinley in Harding." The text declared:

> Ohio, "Mother of Presidents" is coming again into her own. Harding is due to be added to Grant, Hayes, Garfield, Benjamin Harrison, McKinley and Taft, and to William Henry Harrison, who resided upon her soil when elected to the presidency. . . . "America first; Ohio first in America"—is the slogan of every generation of Buckeye Republicans. . . . State pride, conferred obligation, and party necessity all make it imperative that the electoral vote of Ohio—the pivotal state—be swept into the Republican column in November.

But, alas, there was little for poor Clark to do. Ohio was the least of Hays' worries. Letter after letter came to Hays and Harding from Clark's office, complaining about being neglected. Eventually, on August 6, Clark became so frustrated that he wrote to Harding declaring that there was "something the matter with the National Committee. It does not function on policy or detail." Harding passed this on to Hays without comment. Hays, in turn, relayed it to Victor Heintz and Ralph Sollitt—with a comment. At the bottom of the letter was inscribed, in Hays' handwriting, "Vic-Ralph Read and do not worry. W. H. H." [88]

12

How much this managing, front-porching, advising, counseling, and vote-influencing actually produced in the way of votes for Harding cannot be measured. Some said that Harding could have been elected without it because the country was tired of Wilson. Others said that such managing was required in order to keep the opposition from monopolizing the headlines and thus winning votes. Still others claimed that the public relations folks were an overly aggressive lot who knew a good thing when they saw it, and thus put on a grandstand display of their professional wares especially for their own benefit. Whatever the explanation, it is apparent that not only was Harding a much-managed candidate but the public was a much-managed public, and that they enjoyed it.

CHAPTER TWENTY-ONE

How to Make Friends and Win Elections, 1920

"Permit calling attention to the most clannish vote now known—that of the MOOSE ORDER. This vote has elected DAVIS, Mayor [of] Cleveland, THREE TIMES. IT NOMINATED HIM, IT HOLDS THE BALANCE OF POWER IN OHIO. And most everywhere else. . . . MAYOR BRUENING of Baltimore . . . is an ORATOR, and if permitted to campaign in MOOSE SECTIONS of Ohio would Increase the G.O.P. Majority." : : : *Mimeographed circular from "Doc Waddell," in Harding Papers, Ohio State Historical Society.*

Harding's high talents in political adjustability were, of course, given full play in 1920 by his activity in making contact with an unusually large number of people. Although Harding was not too adept at handling the special problems of labor, he was especially effective in the areas of prohibition, the woman suffrage movement, the farm vote, and what may be called the aspects of religious and fraternal affiliation.

2

Harding's powers of political agility were at their best in his ability to cope with prohibition. He was aided by the finest contact man in the field: Wayne B. Wheeler, general counsel of the Anti-Saloon League. From 1900 to 1910 Harding had managed to straddle the local-option stages of the controversy to the satisfaction of both the Anti-Saloon League and the liquor interests. When the League sought to dry up the entire state via referenda, Harding stayed wet when the referenda went wet; but he switched to the drys during the war, when the people and the Republican party went dry.[1] In the Senate debate on national dryness via the Eighteenth Amendment, he was able to please the drys by voting yes in the final adoption, and to please the wets (1) by authoring the seven-year ratification limitation, (2) by proposing the compensation of brewers and distillers for their losses,

(3) by expressing doubts as to Prohibition's enforceability, and (4) by dropping hints about the eventual repeal of the amendment.[2] Finally, as presidential candidate, he met the issue of strict or loose enforcement, *i.e.*, the prohibition or non-prohibition of light wines and beer, by a masterpiece of evasion in his acceptance speech: "There is divided opinion respecting the eighteenth amendment and the laws to make it operative, but there can be no difference of opinion about honest law enforcement. . . . Modification or repeal is the right of a free people, whenever the deliberate and intelligent public sentiment commands, but perversion and evasion mark the paths to the failure of government itself." [3] Neither in this speech, nor in any other speech, did Harding say whether he himself favored modification or repeal. He thus avoided being labeled wet or dry, whereas his opponent, Cox, frankly admitted to being wet.

The crucial point of evaluation was Harding's failure to say whether or not he favored repeal or modification of the Volstead Act, which defined as intoxicating any beverage containing one-half of one per cent or more of alcohol. The wets claimed that this definition was ridiculous because it barred the manufacture and consumption of light wines and beers. Harding was challenged many times to say flatly whether or not he favored a revision of the act to permit the manufacture and sale of light wines and beers, but he repeatedly refused to be definite. He would say that he was in favor of law enforcement, but this evaded the point of what kind of law he wanted.

One who frankly described the reason why Harding evaded the issue of Volstead Act revision was Cincinnatian Charles M. Dean, secretary of the First Harding Club of Ohio. In a letter of July 15 to Daugherty, Dean wrote, "It is a wellknown fact that if the wet and dry issue is kept out of the campaign Harding's plurality in Hamilton County will be from 30,000 to 40,000. We can then tell the wets that the Chicago platform ignored this question as an issue and it is a matter to be handled by Congress. If however he is obliged to take a strong stand against any modification of the Volstead Act we have a hard fight in front of us. I have taken the stand that until Senator Harding brings in the issue we will keep quiet and gather support wherever we can. . . . These facts ought to convince anybody that some one is going to make trouble for Harding down here if he has the slightest opportunity." The letter was forwarded to Christian with the simple request, "Have the Senator read the enclosed letter from Charlie Dean." No amplifications were needed.[4]

Try as they might, the pro-Volstead prohibitionists could not get Harding to commit himself one way or the other on the question of the revision of the law. The candidate simply failed to answer the questions asked him. The first to ask him was R. D. Hinkle, editor of the *Christian Herald*, who wired Harding July 29, saying hundreds of people wanted to know "categorically whether you will favor or oppose repeal or modification of the 18th amendment or Volstead Act." Harding blandly replied, "There is no ambiguity in my statement on this question in the formal speech of Acceptance." [5] This was not only ambiguity, it was complete evasion.

Another who put Harding to the Volstead Act test was Virgil G. Hinshaw, Prohibition party candidate for President. On August 26, Hinshaw telegraphed Harding asking him to join William Howard Taft and William Jennings Bryan in declaring opposition to any increase of alcohol limit in the Volstead Act. Harding again dodged the issue of what was an intoxicating beverage, this time via a letter from Howard Mannington, who wrote that Harding had voted for the Volstead Act "and has not regretted or apologized for that vote." The Senator, said Mannington, proposed to support the law, and would not "support any movement which would re-establish the traffic in intoxication beverages." Harding had no intention of discussing in private correspondence the merit of a "measure not yet formulated." He proposed to "stand upon the platform of his party and his own public record." [6]

Harding, on October 11, again evaded a candid answer on what was an intoxicating beverage. Professor Henry Beach Carré, of the Vanderbilt University School of Religion and secretary of a "special committee" of the Anti-Saloon League, wired Harding asking categorically, "Will you, if elected, favor or oppose modification of the Volstead Act to permit the manufacture or sale of beer or wines or the increase in alcoholic content thus rendering the enforcement of the Eighteenth Amendment more difficult." Harding's reply was as evasive as ever, "My recorded vote for the submission of the Eighteenth Amendment and the law to enforce it answers your telegram. I stand by the record made in the public service." [7]

Harding dodged on the Volstead Act to the very end of the campaign. On October 25, he publicly answered social worker Frederick D. Smith that he "stood by" his vote on the Eighteenth Amendment. He would not "recall" this vote, and he "opposed the re-establishment of the traffic in intoxicating liquors." He thus begged the question that

Smith had asked about amending the Volstead Act, *i.e.,* the redefinition of what was an intoxicating liquor. This same evasion occurred in a letter of October 20 to Senator Charles Curtis of Kansas. He would oppose, he said, for the rest of his public career "the restoration of the traffic in intoxicating liquors," adding that "this is as clear cut a statement as any honest man should desire." [8]

Harding was sustained in this prohibition evasiveness by the most powerful prohibition agency in the United States, the Anti-Saloon League. The League did not want Harding to say that he favored the retention of the prohibition of light wines and beers because, if he did so, he might lose the votes of the wet states, lose the election, and thus forfeit the drastic prohibition that the drys had managed to get via the Volstead law. It was a case of Harding's not acting too dry in order to keep the country very dry. One who suggested this idea to Harding was his friend Wayne B. Wheeler. On September 30, Wheeler wrote to Harding, "I wired you last night concerning certain appeals that are being sent to you from temperance workers most of them third party prohibitionists, to get a further statement from you on prohibition. If a very strong statement is given it is to be used as a fire-brand in New Jersey, New York and other wet centers while Cox remains non-committal or practically so. You know the purpose of this." [9]

The Harding straddle was further promoted by Wheeler in counseling the meeting in Washington of the National Legislative Conference of twenty-three national temperance and prohibition organizations. Wheeler's part in this involved sending Harding telegrams on the Volstead Act that could be answered evasively. Wheeler told Harding on September 23 that he had actually framed telegrams after several hours of heated discussion with "our opponents" who wanted a more radical and pointed question. Harding was asked by a committee headed by H. H. Russell, "Do you stand by your record as indicated by your vote on the Eighteenth Amendment and on the Volstead Act for enforcement?" It was a leading question, enabling Harding to give an evasive answer. Cox, however, was asked pointedly "whether he favored the Volstead Act." This was a non-evasive question which the radicals also wanted to ask Harding. Harding piously replied as Wheeler expected, saying, "My record stands and I stand by it. I did not know that there was any question about it." Cox saw the hypocrisy of his being asked a non-evasive question and refused to answer. He insisted on identical questions which were later asked in evasive terms, with Cox able to answer as evasively as Harding had done.

Cox, in his public protest against the conference's unfairness, said that the tricky phraseology of the first telegrams was Wheeler's doing—an allegation which was denied indignantly. His denial, as the letter to Hays of September 23, just quoted, shows, was a falsehood.[10]

The records show that Wheeler was seeking to control the phrasing of *all* questions by the committee as well as the answers of Harding thereto. On September 17, *five days before the telegrams were actually sent,* Wheeler telegraphed Harding, "Think it is important for you to answer Carré's letter stating that your record vote on the Eighteenth Amendment and the law to enforce it speaks for itself and that you stand squarely for the enforcement of all law." Carré's letter to Harding, if there was one, has not been found, but it is obvious from Wheeler's intimation of its content that it was like the telegram written by Wheeler for Carré to send later. And it is also obvious that the tone of Harding's reply had the vigorously evasive nature that Wheeler suggested.[11]

The prohibition radicals finally got to Harding with a blunt telegram, but it did not do any good. Harding and Wheeler were ready. It took the form of an inquiry from Charles Canlon, president of the "World Prohibition Federation." It asked Harding the specific, non-evasive question, "Will you use your official authority and influence to prevent repeal or weaken Volstead law?" It was immediately followed by a telegram from Wheeler advising Harding, in effect, *not* to answer the Canlon telegram. It read, "If any telegram was sent in reply to yours it does not represent the Legislative Conference or the Temperance Council or the Anti-Saloon League or W.C.T.U." In his reply to Canlon, Harding, therefore, declined to make "declarations of supposititious questions." [12]

The Harding-Wheeler game of deception was deliberate and complete. The candidate's mailing department made use of Wheeler in helping the cause along. When personal inquiries came about the Volstead law, the secretaries would reply as they did to Mrs. Margaret Twinem Bisbee of Minneapolis, "His attitude in this connection has been pronounced as satisfactory by Mr. Wayne B. Wheeler of the Anti-Saloon League." [13]

Another phase of Harding's evasiveness on the Volstead law was to emphasize that he was seeking an executive office, not a legislative one. As such, it was his job to execute the law and not to make it. It was "unthinkable," he solemnly avowed, "for an executive not to enforce the law." Enforcement, he told a delegation of women in

Marion, "is an executive responsibility and must be undertaken by the executive without regard for his personal approval or disapproval of the law which it was the will of the people to enact." This fitted in with Harding's much-belabored concept of being a consultative leader rather than the dictatorial leader he felt Wilson to be.[14]

The hypocrisy of the drys is obvious. They wanted Harding not to arouse the ire of the wets, and then they denounced Cox for being wet. Cox talked about law enforcement and the Volstead Act in the same evasive way as did Harding, but the drys mucked up Cox's past to make him out a veritable devil. For example, there was Clarence True Wilson's article in the August, 1920 issue of the magazine *The Voice,* which was the organ of the Board of Temperance, Prohibition, and Public Morals of the Methodist Episcopal church. Wilson was national secretary of the Temperance Society of the Methodist church. In this article Wilson praised Harding for going "far to redeem a bad situation" by his acceptance speech, but he called Cox a "dripping wet." Wilson said that for three terms as Governor of Ohio, "Cox has been loose, low and liquid on the drink issue, the champion of the liquor interests of Cincinnati, the advocate of the laxest enforcement regime that Ohio has ever known. . . . It would take an imagination swelled out of proportion and disorganized to chaos to imagine law and order, prohibition or moral reform getting any aid or comfort out of him as President." Wilson blamed Cox for the Dempsey-Willard prizefight in Toledo on July 4, 1919. Toledo, he said, was selected "because the plug-uglies who bruised each other up for the amusement of a crowd and grovels in such things, knew they had nothing to fear from the Governor of that state." [15]

Thus, while Harding acquiesced in Wheeler's call not to exempt light wines and beers from prohibition in order to keep states like New Jersey dry and Republican, he rejected the pleadings of the Senator from that state, Walter E. Edge, for him to favor such exemption in order to keep New Jersey wet and Republican. As New Jersey Deputy Attorney General Emerson Richards told Edge, "If Harding is to be labeled 'dry' and Cox 'wet' there is absolutely no use wasting time in making a campaign in New Jersey." Thus Cox was labeled wet and Harding was not labeled at all, so that New Jersey would go for Harding, as it did in November.[16]

While he was seeking to escape labels, Harding had some explaining to do because of his past record of owning stock in the Marion Brewery Company. There were dozens of inquiries, and a set form of response. This stressed his loyalty as a local newspaper editor and public-spirited citizen to all new enterprises that came to Marion. He was expected to show confidence in all "worthy" projects and to encourage others to do so. He thus took three shares of the brewery stock as payment for advertising and promotion. The brewery was a small one, was not successful, and was now out of existence. The impression given to all inquirers was that of self-sacrifice—the venture being an example of one of the many enterprises into which Marion-ites put their money and from which they got no returns. These claims were not kept secret, and were given considerable airing in the press.[17]

3

Adjustability—and plenty of it—was the keynote of Harding's handling of the woman suffrage problem. For a man who was as unprogressive as Harding, and who was so outspokenly lukewarm about the women's favorite crusade, to emerge as the great beneficiary of the first national ballot-casting by women was no small achievement. Of course, he needed assistance from the Republican national committee, eight of whose twenty-two members were women, including the vice-chairman, Mrs. Harriet Taylor Upton.

There was no enthusiasm in Warren Harding's senatorial acceptance of woman suffrage. His thinking depended on what the states did with the Nineteenth Amendment. As in the case of his vote for the Eighteenth Amendment, his action was a reference of the issue to the states, not a personal endorsement of the measure on its merits. Not until mid-June, 1920, when he had become his party's nominee for the Presidency, did he publicly endorse the reform. By that time the embattled ladies, and their male cohorts, had come within one state of getting the required three-fourths (36) of the state ratifications. Women were about to get the vote, and it was up to Harding to get most of them to vote Republican.

The pressure from the women brought candidate Harding into conflicting adjustments. According to the ladies, it was his business to take vigorous command and get the ratification of the thirty-sixth state. According to Harding, if he was too vigorous in this, it would be a violation of one of the fundamental rules of American politics—the right of states to make their own judgments about amendments to the national Constitution without undue outside pressure. How Harding managed to adjust himself both to the women and the believers in states' rights is a fascinating story.

First to pressure the Republican candidate to get him to intervene actively in state ratification of the Nineteenth Amendment was the indefatigable vice-chairman of the Republican national committee, and president of the Ohio Woman Suffrage Association, Mrs. Harriet Taylor Upton of Warren, Ohio. Convinced that, so far in the history of American politics, the men had not done very well and that the hope of things political depended on the participation, trust, and confidence of the women voters, she first exercised her new prerogative by telegraphing Harding and writing to Chairman Hays that they must publicly ask the governor of Vermont and/or the governor of Connecticut to call their respective legislatures into special session to act on the Nineteenth Amendment. She included in her advice to Hays a vague hint of resigning if things did not go to suit her. She also included some sharp reflections on Harding. She said that she had telegraphed her Vermont-Connecticut proposal to him and that he had replied evasively, saying that he was "joining in every effort" to get ratification. "The man does not know," said the impatient Mrs. Upton, "that his very political success rests on the fact of being the person to bring this about. We do not want him to join in with anybody. He must do it himself and for himself. Can you get the word to him in any way so not to hurt his feelings?" Hays told her to get her own word to Harding—which she forthwith proceeded to do, her first letter, she said, being sent "by Express and marked 'Personal' in red ink." [18]

In her first red-ink letter to candidate Harding, Mrs. Upton practically took over the ratification campaign. The Senator was informed that he could not be elected unless he obtained the ratification of the Nineteenth Amendment by the thirty-sixth state. If he did not do so, the Democrats would, and the grateful women would thereupon elect their deliverer, James M. Cox, President of the United States. "Now that I am on the national committee," she declared, "I feel a conscientious responsibility to see that the ticket is elected, and I am telling you from the bottom of my heart that I truly believe the Republicans will not win this fall unless you get the thirty-sixth state." There was no doubt about this, said the newly elected first national committeewoman: "I know much more about it than you do. I know the woman feeling throughout the West much better than you do, and much better than any of the men who surround you do. I do not know much, but I do know the woman situation and the woman logic." In her next letter Mrs. Upton was more insistent. Republican Vermont was the state to concentrate on, so as to beat the Democrats in their campaign to make Democratic Tennessee the thirty-sixth state to ratify. She therefore begged the Senator to tell Governor Clement of Vermont "The positive truth—namely that your election depends on the Reps getting the 36th state and that getting depends upon him. . . . How I could work and with such hope if Vt. could come in in ten days." [19]

Mrs. Upton soon learned who was running the Republican party, and how much she knew about politics. In a neat piece of publicity manipulation Harding managed to show himself as being in favor of Vermont or Connecticut becoming the thirty-sixth state, but as being blocked by the governors thereof. However, he did not offend the governors, whose right to defend the states from precipitate action he graciously acknowledged. Both governors were conservatives and had acquired a dislike for the lady militants ever since representatives of the National Woman's Party had insulted the Republican party and had, in the governors' view, disgraced both their sex and their cause by picketing the Republican national convention in Chicago.[20] This made them "suffragettes," and put them in the same class with that horrible Englishwoman, Emmaline Pankhurst, who was shocking the sensibilities of her countrymen in behalf of equal suffrage. Harding himself had rebuffed the militants in a Washington interview on June 22, 1920, saying he would not "tresspass on the rights of the states . . . or . . . assume to wield a club." But on July 1 he received Governor Clement at Marion and announced that he hoped the Governor would call the Vermont legislature. Governor Clement, on the other hand, spoke of his reluctance to call the legislature. Nevertheless, Mrs. Upton rejoiced. She wrote Harding on July 2 that she could hardly eat her breakfast because of the glorious news that the Vermont governor would call the legislature and that "he wanted to do it for your sake." This enabled Harding to assume the hero's role, though he replied to Mrs. Upton that the Governor had not really promised to call the legislature, but "I feel that ultimately he is going to do so." [21] The Governor did not.

The Harding luck continued. In spite of Mrs. Upton's disillusionment, Harding was still the hero. Governor Clement decided not to call his legislature because he said it had been high-pressured by the women in a manner similar to the tactics used to force ratification of the income tax and the Prohibition amendments. It may have been good reasoning, but Mrs. Upton did not see it. "Now, I realize," she wrote to Harding, "that what you say is true. You cannot club Governor Clement, but somebody has got to club him or somebody under him." She confessed she knew nothing about how to "club" governors, and she suggested that they put a man on the job. By July 13, Mrs. Upton was so furious at the Vermont governor that hints of resignation from her office again fell from her feverish pen. "This is the worst thing that could possibly happen to us," she wrote Hays. "Women are now pressing me to retire from the chairmanship because the party refuses to demand Governor Clement's action. . . . I am in a very uncomfortable place. Suffrage is my religion and the Republican party is the religion of my father and my husband. There was no reason why I could not have worked for both." Her advice was for somebody to "get Governor Clement to go away and let the Lieutenant Governor call the session." She enclosed a telegram from Carrie Chapman Catt, president of the National American Woman's Suffrage Association, which said, among other things, "Might as well go home and save your self respect. . . . No self respecting woman can serve the Party under the circumstances." And the smiling Harding looked on and sympathized with sincere regrets. "I had hoped," he said for publication, "that Governor Clement would convene the Vermont legislature." [22]

From this time on everything that Harding did on the suffrage question was right, so far as Mrs. Upton and the "respectable" part of the women suffrage movement was concerned. When the National Woman's Party, i.e., the "suffragettes," blamed Harding, in a circular letter, for his alleged do-nothing, states' rights doctrine about ratification, Harding replied publicly on July 14, with much spirit. "My patience is sorely tried sometimes," he said, "over the persistent misrepresentation of the Republican party." The GOP, he claimed, had a vastly better record on woman suffrage than had the Democrats. "It was a Republican Senate and a Republican House which submitted the 19th Amendment to the states after a Democratic Senate had refused to do so. Of the 35 states which had ratified, 29 were Republican. Only one Republican state had declined to ratify and seven Democratic states had declined. In the Senate vote on the 19th Amendment there were 36 Republicans and 20 Democrats in favor of it, and eight Republicans and 17 Democrats against it." Under such circumstances, he declared, "it is simply amazing that Democratic managers should now have the audacity to be assuming that they are the friends on whom the cause must depend if it is to succeed." He would rejoice, he said, if Tennessee or any other state ratified, but he would not interfere with their legislatures. Mrs. Upton was impressed. The statement had strength, she wrote Harding. "It was dignified and spirited—firm." Her opinion of the "suffragettes" was not high. "We regulars hate the militants. They have done us untold harm." [23]

Things fell the same happy way for Harding when, two days later, Connecticut was lost to the women's cause. Harding had been asked by the *Hartford Times* whether he intended to ask Governor Holcomb to call his legislature. Harding curtly and publicly telegraphed back, "I answer no." This time Mrs. Upton was more co-operative. She who had once declared that the loss of Vermont would defeat Harding, and that the "women are not as attached to the party as are men," now counseled with a delegation of Connecticut women, who came to see her in Columbus. She took them to Marion, where Harding urged them to be loyal to the party. After this visit, she wrote Harding, "the Connecticut women came down to Columbus very much disgruntled and went home satisfied in every way with what was done for them, feeling kind towards me, which was important since I have an official position, enthusiastic over you and your treatment of them; determined to make the Connecticut women see it as you showed it to them; resolved to take up their affiliation with the Party and to give up the fact of fighting longer in Connecticut. What you did and the way you did it was exactly right." [24]

Do nothing, or do little, Harding's final triumph in courting the women's suffrage sympathies came on acceptance day, July 22, on the Marion front porch. Here, in glowing terms, he took the ground that woman suffrage was not really a radical thing. He spoke of womankind in all its "glory," its "inspiration," its "uplifting force," as "about to be enfranchised." It was his earnest hope that the thirty-sixth state be added to the list to make this possible. He elaborated on the benign influence this would have on American life. "It will bring women educated in our schools, trained in our customs and habits of thoughts, and sharers of our problems. It will bring the alert mind, the awakened conscience, the sure intuition, the abhorrence of tyranny or oppression, the wide and tender sympathy that distinguish the women of America. Surely there can be no danger there." Mrs. Upton was again gratified. "You said exactly the right thing about suffrage," she wrote, adding that such approval should satisfy those who "feel that we are hard to please." [25]

Harding was not really worried about the thirty-sixth state to ratify the Nineteenth Amendment. He confessed this in response to a letter on June 22 from Mary G. Hay, chairman of the Republican Woman's Executive Committee of New York City. Mrs. Hay said that the women were "very bitter over the fact that we have not succeeded in getting ratification of the Suffrage Amendment." The Republicans should "finish the job." "If that can be done at once, you will have the women vote largely Republican." Harding was not impressed. He replied on July 7, saying, "I do not think the proposition is sufficiently promising to justify a zealous bit of interference." The same feeling—that the ladies were to be tolerated but not taken too seriously—was evident in the telegram Hays sent to Christian on July 3 about preparing a word of greeting for Harding to send to the women via *Good Housekeeping* magazine. "The greeting," instructed Hays, "need not express any particular view on any particular subject but rather that he is looking to the women of America to take a responsible part in party work." [26]

Hence it was not as calamitous as Mrs. Upton thought that the thirty-sixth state came to be a Democratic state instead of a Republican one. But the men had to put up with the ladies' agitations. As the time approached for the Tennessee legislature to assemble, the eager women sent forth their agents to the Nashville battlefront. The gentlemen of the party, including Harding, professed a real desire to help. But the stake was small: the Republicans were in a minority in both houses of the legislature. The issue between the Republican party and the ladies was even smaller. The women wanted the unanimous vote of the Republican minority. Hays and Harding were willing to settle for a majority of said minority, and that is what they got.

There seems to have been nothing devious about the Republican procedures with regard to Tennessee. Hays presented the problem to a special session of his executive committee in Columbus. Telegrams were sent on July 21 to each of the Tennessee Republican legislators urging them to vote for ratification of the Nineteenth Amendment. On the same day Harding wired Mrs. Catt of the National Woman Suffrage Association in Nashville that "if any of the Republican members of the Tennessee Assembly should ask my opinion as to their course, I would cordially recommend an immediate favorable action." He followed this up with a message to John C. Houk, Tennessee Republican state committee chairman, declaring the hope that the Republican legislators would vote to ratify. Later he asked Houk to poll the legislators and then advise him whether he needed any more help. That was as far as he was willing to go. When Winfield Jones, chairman of the militant Harding-Coolidge Republican League Number One, Washington, D.C., asked Harding to send a personal telegram to each Republican legislator, he declined, citing states' rights considerations. He wired similarly to Mrs. Catt and Mrs. Upton.[27]

When the Tennessee legislature met early in August, 1920, the states' rights people began to exert counterpressure on Harding. On August 5, the Tennessee Constitution League asked both Harding and Cox to cease pressuring the state legislature. One of the states' rights leaders, Judge G. N. Tillman, wrote Harding privately that the Tennessee constitution contained an "inhibition" against the right of the special session of the legislature to ratify the Nineteenth Amendment because it had been elected before the amendment was submitted to the states. Harding replied that he believed in the right of every legislator to follow his own conscience, and if such legislators believed that the Tennessee constitution forbade ratification by this legislature, they should vote accordingly. Armed with this statement, and with a telegram from Christian permitting the public use of the Harding letter, if quoted in full, Judge Tillman appeared before a joint legislative committee and read it. This was immediately published in the local papers, much to the consternation of the suffrage ladies, and much to the joy of their opponents, many of whom disliked enlarging the suffrage so as to include Negro women. The crestfallen Mrs. Upton wired Harding, "You fell into their trap," and urged that there was still time to bring pressure to bear upon susceptible Republican legislators. Mrs. Catt was so wroth that, on August 17, the day before the final vote, she wired Hays that Harding had ruined everything, and that ratification was lost unless Harding's letter to Tillman was repudiated. Her telegram read, "Harding's letter to Tillman in morning paper interview has lost us votes and unless counteracted will bring defeat—the world will lay entire responsibility for defeat upon Harding—immediate action is necessary." [28]

Mrs. Catt had overplayed her hand. Harding had not ruined everything; he had saved the Republican party. Certainly Hays did not repudiate Harding. There was no need to do so. Hays could see that Harding had pleased both sides of the local Republican thinking on the constitutionality of Tennessee's ratification. In the Tillman letter he urged those who had constitutional scruples to be faithful to them. At the same time, through Tennessee state committeeman Houk, he told Republicans who did not have such scruples that they could "serve both party and country by effecting ratification." The result was that Tennessee became the thirty-sixth state to ratify, with the support of a majority of Republican and Democratic legislators. (The Republican vote was 15–11 in the lower house of the legislature.) After it was all over Harding summarized his position in a letter to general manager H. C. Adler of the *Chattanooga Times*, "I am committed personally and by edict to a support of Equal Suffrage but I would not willingly urge any member of the state legislature to violate his oath to support the constitution of his State, in carrying out this policy. I do not assume to have authority over the actions of the Republican office holders and I do not wish to trespass on matters of state policy." [29]

Everybody was satisfied by the Tennessee ratification. Another "fool break" had been avoided. The women were satisfied because Harding had helped to bring the victory. On the day of triumph, August 18, the relieved Mrs. Upton wired Harding, "Republicans holding the ballot [balance] of power today made ratification possible. Strong state leaders stood back of us." On the same day even the militant "suffragettes" gave Harding some credit, when Alice Paul, president of the National Woman's Party, wired Harding on behalf of her organization, "I wish to express our deep appreciation of your cooperation in the campaign for the ratification of suffrage. Your aid has been of great help in winning the large Republican vote in the Tennessee legislature." [30] Tennessee Republicans (and even Democrats) were satisfied because Harding had respected states' rights. The Republican party in general was happy because it could claim that a majority of Tennessee Republican legislators in a Democratic state had maintained the record of the Republicans, who had provided for more state ratifications than had the Democrats. One has but to consider that, in November, Tennessee went Republican. The adjustable Mr. Harding had "done it again."

4

It would be a mistake to describe the Republican campaign for the women's votes merely in terms of the jockeying of the candidate and the organization with the militant and non-militant woman suffrage leaders. There was another approach to the women's votes. That was to the women in general. The average woman was not a part of the suffrage movement. She found the vote suddenly conferred upon her, and proceeded to use it pretty much under the same public-relations influences as any voter would be expected to do. The Republican management, therefore, showed much more interest in appealing to the average women than it did to the woman suffrage movement leaders.

Characteristic of this Republican public-relations appeal to the women in general was a piece of stage management especially designed for female consumption. This was the arrangement of a special day for the ladies, and special promises by the Republican candidate of new government services for women's and children's welfare.

Women's Day, October 1, was the occasion set aside for this display of Republican wares for women. The masterminds of the affair were the top public-relations expert of the party, Albert D. Lasker and his chief consultant, Richard Washburn Child. The managerial approach was well described by Lasker in a note to Hays on September 4. "Dick Child," he wrote, "got me on the telephone this morning regarding a day which he wants to arrange for Marion, and which he and I both consider possibly the most important day, other than returned soldiers' day, that we will have in Marion. It is the day when the women are to come and when the candidate will deliver his social legislation speech. . . . We will have to do a lot of special work on this." [31]

Women's Day was a highly managed affair. It was designed to avoid the appearance of beng too aristocratic or too militant. Mrs. Upton was especially concerned about its not appearing too aristocratic. Memories of the Hughes campaign floated through her mind as she recalled the "Billion Dollar Special" of 1916, which, the women claimed, lost the election for Charles Evans Hughes. This was a campaign train which toured the West and was sponsored by such eastern members of the "Four Hundred" as Mrs. Payne Whitney, Mrs. Cornelius Vanderbilt, and Mrs. Elizabeth Stotesbury. Thus, Mrs. Upton evidenced her midwestern, middle-class sensibilities in her telegraphed warning to Harding on September 13: "Please make no arrangement about a reception of a delegation of women until you hear from me. We must be very painstaking about this thing. We better not have it at all than to have any recurrence of the billion dollar train of four years ago." [32]

On the other hand, the Lasker-Child approach was to ensure a truly conservative ladylike tone to Women's Day. October 1 was not to be Suffragettes' Day, but rather, "respectable" Women's Day. That was why Lasker told Hays that his first step was to enlist the services of a very special woman, Mrs. Douglas Robinson, the sister of former President Theodore Roosevelt.

Mrs. Robinson was respectability incarnate. She was not only a sister of the great T. R. but the widow of a New York real estate, banking, and insurance magnate. Her function was to enlist in the cause other women of the same respectability, or, as Lasker put it, to invite to go to Marion from various parts of the country, "fifteen, twenty or a hundred women of achievement." Lasker was quite specific about this. Most of them, he said, "should not be suffragists or women who have made their names in politics, but women in business, particularly employers of large numbers of laborers. There should be also women labor leaders, one or two authors like Mary Roberts Rhinehart [sic], the deans of colleges, Ethel Barrymore et al. And at the Marion end they should be met by the respectable women folk of the city all organized and subsidized to act as hostesses to their distinguished guests." [33]

And so, as Women's Day approached, the atmosphere of respectable womanhood was preserved. Of course, Mrs. Upton, as vice-chairman of the national Republican committee, was officially in charge. Certainly she was of the "proper" type, even though she had acquired a record of "mild militancy" during her twenty years or more as president of the Ohio Woman Suffrage Association. At any rate, she was entirely of Lasker's and Child's opinion to make Women's Day a respectable affair. "Child's extremely anxious," she wired Hays a week before the great day, "that no other group women interfere with program on arrangement which satisfies all concerned and wants you and me to use our influence to prevent any interference from other women interested, which might upset delicate adjustment." [34] Lasker was so concerned about the possibility of the suffragettes deciding on a demonstration that he made it his business to be present, "so as to insure," he wrote Hays, "that there will be no heckling and that nothing goes wrong." [35] Mrs. Upton's concerns about heckling took a slightly different direction. She became very agitated about the right of the women to see a copy of Harding's front-porch address before it was delivered. It took a letter from Harding himself, describing that the practice of issuing advance copies was a phase of press-release work, to subdue Mrs. Upton's sensitiveness on this score. [36]

There was no heckling in Marion on Women's Day—or, as it was also called, Social Justice Day. Only the "best" people were there. Mrs.

Robinson headed the list. It was an affair of the wives of governors and senators—Mrs. William C. Sproul of Pennsylvania, Mrs. James P. Goodrich of Indiana, Mrs. Ernest Bamberger of Utah, and Mrs. Harry S. New, also of Indiana. Mrs. Leonard Wood was present, as were Mary Roberts Rinehart, Florence Kelley, Mrs. Nicholas Longworth, and Mrs. Gifford Pinchot. (There is no record of the possible reason for Mrs. Longworth's conversion.) Other notables were Mrs. Lena Lake Forest, national president of the Business and Professional Women, and Mrs. Minnie E. Keyes, right worthy grand secretary of the Grand Chapter of the Order of Eastern Star. To call the role was to present a list of the leading women of America—except that there were no Whitneys, Vanderbilts, or Stotesburys.[37]

To greet their famous guests, the ladies of Marion put on a well-managed show. The visiting notables were chauffeured in hired limousines, dined at the Marion Hotel, and were entertained at the Columbia Theater. For the climax they were paraded through the streets, escorted by richly uniformed bands and lavishly decorated floats representing great women in world and United States history. All the best women's clubs of Marion helped in this effort—the Marion Federation of Women's Clubs, Round Table, Bayview Reading Circle, the Ben Hur Literary Society, King's Daughters, Pythian Sisters, the Wayside Rose Rebekahs, the D.A.R., the Marion Steam Shovel Girls, and so on.

On the festive porch, waiting for them, was the candidate, prepared to give one of the historic speeches of the campaign—a speech describing the new days of social justice that were to come. Harding spoke in characteristically glowing phrases of the need for the protection of motherhood, of the "right of wholesome maternity," of equal pay for equal work, the eight-hour day, the extension of the Children's Bureau, the suppression of child labor, the enforcement of prohibition, and the prevention of lynching. This was the speech in which Harding came out for the creation of the new cabinet department of public welfare. It was also printed in considerable numbers and given wide circulation.[38]

Perhaps, in the atmosphere of flowers and ballyhoo, the ladies did not notice it, but Harding's emphasis was much more on the side of administrative efficiency than on the principles of humanitarianism:

There can be no more efficient way of advancing a humanitarian program than by adapting the machinery of our federal government to the purposes we desire to attain. While others may have their eyes fixed upon some particular piece of legislation or some particular policy of social justice which calls for the sympathetic interest of us all, I say, without hesitation, that our primary consideration must be the machinery of administration. . . . It is almost useless for us to go on expanding our energies in advancing humanitarian policies which we wish to put into effect until we have prepared to create an administrative center for the application of our program. At present social welfare bureaus and undertakings are scattered hopelessly through the departments. . . . The picture is one of inefficiency and of wasted funds. . . . Let's make social justice real and functioning, rather than visionary and inefficient.

Harding also urged his listeners to be sure to avoid the pitfalls of government paternalism.

This moderated concern for social welfare, which went far less deep than the words seemed to say, was best revealed in his comments on the League of Nations. We must have, he told the women, an association of nations, not a nation-sacrificing League, that would take "our sons and husbands for sacrifice at the call of an extra constitutional body like the Paris League."

5

Harding adjusted himself to the farm voters with his usual facility. This was because he early sought the counsel of one of the leading apostles and publicists of the new type of businessman-farmer, Henry C. Wallace of Des Moines, Iowa. Wallace was president of the Wallace Publishing Company and editor of *Wallace's Farmer*, a weekly devoted to "Good Farming, Clear Thinking, Right Living for Thinking Farmers." He was recommended to Harding early in July by Senator William S. Kenyon of Iowa when the candidate was planning a conference of the "best minds" to guide his thinking on farm affairs. Kenyon told Harding that there was nobody in the Republican organization who had any comprehension of the agricultural problem. Wallace's weekly, said Kenyon, "has the absolute confidence of all the farmer element of the country west." It was "gospel" to them. Wallace "is a sturdy Scotchman, staunch, level-headed, and knows the agricultural problems. . . . I am sure he would give you most valuable suggestions along this line, and you can absolutely count on him." [39]

Harding really needed a practical, up-to-date farm adviser. His agricultural thinking was considerably retarded and constricted by his

Ohio environment. Back in February, 1919, he had written to Uri C. Welton of Burton, Ohio endorsing the latter's opinion that "the farmers don't need either farm loans or farm agents." Wrote Harding, "This has been my conviction for some time—a conviction which has come of such knowledge as I have of the Ohio farmers." [40]

The nature of the Wallace influence among midwestern farmers was solid. It was also inspirational in the sense of promoting alertness and efficiency. It was defensive in the sense of seeking to protect a high standard of rural living. If there was a price problem, it was that farm prices had not been as high as they should have been during the war, and that they were likely to be the first to suffer in the readjustments of peacetime. Farmers did not propose to be the victims of any government policy that sought to reduce the high cost of living at their expense. Wallace supplied the columns of his *Farmer* with advice and warnings. He told them that Food Administrator Hoover had "short-changed" them during the war until they had sacrificed precious soil fertility in their patriotic production of grain and livestock. He stormed at anti-profiteering "price drives" by politically ambitious Attorney General A. Mitchell Palmer, with the farmer being the chief sufferer.

There were such factors as the rising price of farm land, the rise in wages caused by organized labor and its strikes, the drifting of workers away from the farms, the continuing high cost of living for the farmers in the things they had to buy such as clothing, education, luxuries, marketing and storage services, and loans. Deflation and restricted foreign markets took their toll. The urban-minded Democrats had no policy or vision to correct these inequities, and the farmer therefore proposed to extract from the Republicans something more assuring. [41] Said Wallace in his February 13, 1920 *Farmer*, "The farmer is getting tired of being made the goat. . . . This does not mean that he promises to make a disturbance, or try to overturn the government, or start a new political party, or confiscate property. . . . It means simply that . . . he sees it is time for him to study the business game and see how to play it for himself. . . . He is tired of being double-crossed not only by other business interests but by people who are in positions of authority in government. . . . There is no national agricultural policy and therefore nothing left for the farmer to do but to make a fight for prices that will enable them to maintain a sustaining agriculture, and, failing that, to look after Number One." [42]

By allying with Wallace, Harding found himself in favor with the latest and most powerful farm organization, the American Farm Bureau Federation, which was born in the spring of 1920. Wallace himself was instrumental in getting the Federation organized, and praised its work repeatedly in the *Farmer*. Presided over by Wallace's friend and fellow Iowan James R. Howard, this dynamic and conservative organization was dedicated to effective efforts at sustaining the farmers' standard of living by the promotion of farm co-operatives, improved farm management, and the elimination of favoritism toward business, banks, railroads, and other interests in such a way as to hamper the farmers in their right for a just profit based on costs of production. The orientation of the Federation was distinctly pro-Republican. President Wilson had, in a White House interview with Howard and others, rebuffed their statistics about the high cost of living not being primarily caused by prices charged by farm producers.[43]

Before Wallace was approached for advice both he and Howard showed a predisposition to favor the Republicans. In his June 18 *Farmer*, Wallace said that the agricultural plank in the party platform was the "most intelligent and straight forward yet adopted at a national political convention." This may have been because he was one of the 179 members of the Advisory Committee on Politics and Platform, and had answered staff-director Lindsay's questionnaire. At any rate, Wallace, as an apostle of scientific agriculture, thought it was especially noteworthy that the party obligated itself to the statistical study of farm prices and production costs, and that it denounced price-fixing and price drives. He liked the tariff plank and the idea of the enlarged home market, and also the road-aid plank which favored help to states on the basis of constructing farm-to-market roads rather than a coast-to-coast highway. The Democratic platform lacked these things. Howard was more personal about his Republican preference. He liked Harding. "I am with him heart and soul," he told a friend, July 12. "My impression is that we farmers will get a square deal." He was glad Harding was an "old fashioned protectionist for the tariff."[44]

It was not until Wallace took a more direct hand in counseling Harding that the candidate's utterances and party pamphlets began to look as if they had been phrased by a farmer. Harding's acceptance speech still had the tone of the library and the office dictaphone as it cited the farm origins of the party and listed grievances such as price discrimination, unfair tax appraisals, the need of cooperatives to help farmers "reap the just measure of reward merited by their arduous toil." [45] It would be different when Wallace started visiting Marion and Judson Welliver began writing up dispatches.

Before the Wallace influence was felt, the political exchanges between the Republicans and the Democrats on agricultural issues had been of the old-fashioned slug-fest type. The Democrats thought that they had found a ghost from Harding's past involving his praise of "dollar wheat." This was a reference to a point made by Senator Harding during a 1917 debate on the "food bill" when the Senator had allowed himself to reminisce about the "good old days" when farmers could sell wheat for a dollar a bushel and make a profit. For 1920 campaign purposes the Democrats took Harding's remarks out of context, as the Senator tried to point out on several occasions. In retaliation, Harding sought to capitalize on a Cox remark promising to appoint a "dirt farmer" as Secretary of Agriculture. Harding pointed out that it was GOP tradition to have such a man in the cabinet, citing "Uncle Jim" Wilson, an Iowa farmer who had served as Secretary of Agriculture continuously for sixteen years under McKinley, Roosevelt, and Taft, whereas Woodrow Wilson had appointed a college president, David F. Houston (Texas A. & M., University of Texas, Washington University), and publicist Edward T. Meredith as his agricultural aides.[46]

The raising of the tone of discussion to the level of farm economics was immediately discernible as soon as Wallace had had his first conference with Harding on July 26. It was skillfully done, with Judson Welliver as stage manager of an interview with Wallace, who was represented as the same kind of "dirt farmer" as "Uncle Jim" Wilson had been. It was even hinted that Wallace might be the next Secretary of Agriculture. Welliver reported to the Republican publicity director, Scott Bone, in New York that he was "particularly pleased" with this interview.

The Wallace interview, as prepared by Welliver, was really a glimpse into the economic nature of the farmers' difficulties as Wallace had described them to Harding. The farmers, said Wallace, had suffered fearfully as the result of the overproduction of livestock during the war. Equally serious was the rise in tenancy as owners sold their acres to speculators who rented instead of cultivating. The inevitable result was that these tenants turned to an overproduction of grain, with harmful results to land fertility that might have been prevented by a greater balance between grain and livestock. In the process, grain prices were falling without a corresponding fall in the price of farmers' purchases or a reduction in the cost of marketing farm products. "The margin between the farmers' price and the consumers' price is today greater than it ever was and vastly greater than it ought to be. It must be reduced." The chief remedy was the lengthening of the time element in borrowing to enable tenants to achieve this balance and acquire ownership at the same time. Cooperative marketing and purchasing were also suggested. What was needed was the introduction of experts to analyze the problem and make suitable adjustments along the line of farm credit and cooperation. Harding was complimented for his understanding of this complex situation and his vision of what must be done about it. In contrast was the ignorance of President Wilson and the Democrats of the problem and their unwillingness to engage the experts necessary to discover sound policy.[47]

The upshot of the Harding-Wallace conference of July 26 was the preparation and submission by Wallace of data for a forthcoming address on agriculture. This would enable the farmers to realize that the new administration could seek to introduce a sound policy of encouraging balanced prosperity. It was Wallace's opinion that the announcement of this policy should not be made to any one or more of the various farm relief organizations that were nagging him. He must speak to farmers, not to organizations. Wallace preferred the Iowa State Fair as the occasion for his farm address, but it was eventually agreed to make it at the Minnesota State Fair on September 8. In several letters Wallace warned Harding not to honor any particular organization or leader with an official declaration of farm policy because each had its own formula for meeting agricultural problems, some radical, some conservative. Wallace cited numbers of these, offering his own private opinion, as, for instance, his belief that Millard R. Meyers of the Farmers' National Grain Dealers Association was an "off ox" because he wanted cooperatives to have a monopoly in grain marketing. Wallace also insisted that the address be concentrated on agriculture alone, and not include any other subject, especially the League of Nations, which would detract from the full effect on the farmers of a full discussion of the agricultural problems. Wallace counseled further regarding the pamphleteering and condensation of the address, so that all farmers would have access to it or to a version thereof.[48]

Above all, Wallace wrote the speech—or, more accurately, submitted the "framework" of the speech—for Harding's consideration. The submission was made by letter on August 1, in which Wallace wrote, "I am availing myself of your permission to hand you herewith the framework of about the sort of an agricultural talk I would make under similar conditions. I don't know that you will find in it much in the way of material help, but if it should be even suggestive I shall feel glad." (The text of the submission is not available). The next day he wrote apologizing for the appearance of having "overstressed the idea that we are really riding for a bad fall and that we must as quickly as possible adopt a national agricultural policy." He supported his views, however, with some clippings of editorials from the *Manufacturers' Record*, "one of the greatest trade papers in the entire world." Harding was not worried about the pessimistic possibilities for the future of agriculture as alleged by Wallace. Harding always had had a dim view of the future of anything under Democratic control, and here was an excellent opportunity to make political capital of Democratic ineptitude in the agricultural area. He therefore at once referred the "framework" to Dr. Hubert Work, head of the national committee's agricultural department. It was completely acceptable. On August 18, Work wired Hays, "I have just read the material on agriculture Wallace has submitted to Harding. Also asked [C. V.] Gregory, the leading agricultural editor of Illinois, to read it and give me his opinion. He handed it back and said, 'If that is delivered it will elect Harding.' In addition to the text, the writer has caught Harding's manner and phrasing. It is a presidential vision for farmers. I hope it may be used as written." [49]

Documentation of the use of the Wallace "framework" by Harding and his speechmaking aides has not been found. Considering Harding's way of writing by "fits and starts" amidst his crowded front-porch activity, it is not surprising that this is so. Nevertheless, it can be said that the speech was changed from the Wallace pessimism about the future of farming to one of constructive optimism, a change made with Wallace's cooperation. The Iowan eventually withdrew his pessimistic ideas as he saw Harding taking hold of the essential truth of the new scientific approach to agriculture. He conferred with Harding again on August 17, and the two parted with a much more optimistic meeting of minds. Thus, Wallace wrote Harding on August 18 with words of encouragement, "As I said to you last night, it seems to me of vital importance that the major part of what you say on this particular subject shall be said in such a way as to convince your hearers and those who read it afterward, that you have a thorough grasp on the agricultural situation in all of its bigness; that you are thinking not only of the problems of the farmer, but of the problems of the consumer; that you realize that the very existence of our nation depends upon a sound, self-sustaining system of agriculture. Once you make this perfectly plain there will be no disposition to pester you with the details. The President of the United States of course cannot deal with the details of all of these great matters. He must consider them in the largest aspects." [50]

Harding's Minnesota speech [51] was a lecture in farm economics spiced with epigrams, patriotic appeal, and praise of the farming way of life. It set up the premise that farming had become a "commercial, scientific operation with Mother Nature to share in the accomplishment of a modern life and know a participation in modern rewards." Then, following the Wallace line, Harding told of the war-induced unbalancing of grain and livestock production with the resulting overproduction of grain, the growth of tenancy, the depletion of the soil, and the need of a government reconstruction policy to encourage a restoration of balanced and diversified cultivation. With the Democrats incapable of conceiving a policy, the United States was in danger of becoming no longer a self-sustaining nation. This would mean the beginning of that decline and fall that had marked the pages of history in the days of Rome. Intelligently striving for the prevention of this fate were the great new farm organizations that were enabling farmers to use the methods of solidarity and efficiency like those that business and labor had found successful. He cited the cooperatives of the California fruit growers, the marketing improvements of the grain growers of the northwest, and all but cited by name the American Farm Bureau Federation when he said that the "farmers of the corn belt are rapidly perfecting the most powerful organization we know in the country."

As for government policy, according to Harding, it should be helpful but not paternalistic. The individualistic farmers did not want government interference. All that was necessary was as fair a chance and as just a consideration for agriculture as ought to be given to a basic industry. That meant farm representation on already existing federal commissions dealing with trade and finance, where farmers had always been ignored. It meant the protection against legalistic interference with the right of farmers to form their own marketing and consuming cooperatives, corresponding to the rights of business to form corporations. It meant statistical analysis to discover how to prevent violent price fluctuations that no other interests were subject to. It meant the end of wartime price-fixing. Of vital importance was the establishment of long-term credits to enable tenants and owners to change from overproduction of grain to an improved balance between crop cultivation and the raising of livestock. Finally, it meant improved railroad efficiency and service, and a restoration of high tariffs to offset dumping from abroad and to give the farmers full benefit of the home market.

The Harding-Wallace address of September 8, 1920 may be said to be the first semi-official forecast of the intention of government to approach the American agricultural situation via the price-supply problem. The author of the basic economic approach shown in the address was Henry C. Wallace, and on him were to fall the responsibilities of the application of his tenets as Harding's Secretary of Agriculture. Experience revealed that the application of such tenets was inadequate, and it became the lot of his son, Henry A. Wallace, to correct these inadequacies by bolder actions than either his father or Harding could tolerate. But inadequate as the Harding-Wallace agricultural program was to prove to be, they were facing in a new and "proper" direction.

The Minnesota speech having been delivered, there ensued a publicity campaign in which the country was supplied with pamphlets, leaflets, condensations, elaborations, newspaper copy, and farm magazine advertisements, all aimed to show farmers that at last here was a candidate who knew the farm problem. Publisher Wallace was indefatigable. He had already advised on the Minnesota speechwriting, and news releases. Printed copies of the speech were supplied by him to all farm newspapers and magazines. It was issued in pamphlet form, as Wallace told Harding, "for very wide circulation." He missed no details. In the advertisements sent out to over a hundred farm papers, he ran a coupon to be used by the reader in requesting a copy of Harding's speech. With each copy of the speech it was planned to enclose Wallace's own personal message in the form of a leaflet entitled a "Heart to Heart Talk to Farmers." This was designed to assure the farmers that Harding and the Republican party were to be trusted. Furthermore, Wallace spent a day in Chicago getting out a twelve-page folder and a four-page leaflet destined for circulation among farmers. That being done, he wrote Harding on September 10, "I think I have done about all the good I can do there. I have prepared and have in the hands of the printers about all the agricultural campaign stuff we can use except a weekly news-letter." This he proceeded to prepare back home in Des Moines, sending the issues regularly to 3,500 different papers. "I can get it out more promptly here than in Chicago, and it is much more convenient for me." [52] Wallace seemed to be able to devote an inexhaustible supply of energy to Harding's cause.

Meanwhile, the national committee's "department of agriculture," directed by Dr. Work, cooperated with Wallace. On October 3, Work, in a letter to Harding, summarized what had been done "in preparing the farmer vote for November 2nd." State organizations, limited to farmers, had been created in thirty states in such a way as to appeal to all farmer-uplift associations with the idea of preventing growing antagonism resulting from the spread of the radical Non-Partisan League. The only place where there was any defection to the League, Work claimed, was in South Dakota. The rest of the department's activity was modestly briefed:

> Page advertisements have been carried in eighty three of the leading farm journals. A news letter for farmers has been regularly sent to 2,500 weekly newspapers of rural circulation. More than ten millions of pamphlets have been prepared for farmers including the briefed Minnesota speech and have been distributed. Five thousand individual requests for the speech have been supplied from this department directly. An automobile, school-house campaign of farmer speakers is being arranged through county chairmen by personal letters which I expect to be effective. . . . The attitude of the farmers is apparently all we could desire at this time. We have outlined a very definite policy towards those who own the soil and farm it. It has become a moral obligation, a national necessity and a party expedient that we keep faith with our agricultural population and retain the confidence of these five millions of people. [53]

The Wallace influence was not the sole factor in the Harding campaign for the farm vote, but it had permeated the campaign and was appreciated. The page advertising to which Work referred bristled with price statistics. A page entitled "A Square Deal for the Farmers" showed how, from 1919 to 1920, prices had declined: number 2 corn, down 29 per cent; steers, 4 per cent; hogs, 33 per cent; and wool, 25 per cent; whereas the consumers were paying 24 per cent more for food articles in 1920 than in 1919. Metal products had increased in price by 20.9 per cent; lumber, 79 per cent; house furnishing goods, 47.89 per cent. What a terrible reflection this was made to be on the Democrats, who were held responsible.[54] In an official national committee pamphlet entitled "Why the Farmers Should Vote the Republican Ticket," five reasons were given, clearly adapted from the Minnesota speech. On October 2, Harding made another agricultural speech at Wilson's Corner in Ohio. It, too, bristled with economic arguments and statistics—obviously Welliver-inspired. The end of child and woman labor on the farms was demanded, the insidious increase of farm tenancy and soil depletion was cited, cooperative marketing extolled, the price disparity between farm and city decried—apples, for which the farmer got one cent a pound, were selling for twenty-five cents a pound in New York City—the greater illiteracy on the farm was deplored with statistics of the appalling number of one-teacher rural schools. The Democrats got the blame for it all.[55]

This is not to specify how much gain the Harding-Wallace agricultural propaganda produced in election-winning votes. Nor is it to consider and evaluate the Democratic rebuttal. But it is to demonstrate Harding's remarkable job of adjustment to farm realities as represented by the best of the agricultural thinkers. How much Harding appreciated the Wallace influence was abundantly evidenced in his letter to the Iowan on November 1, the day before election. "I want to take this opportunity," Harding wrote Wallace, "to tell you how deeply grateful I am for the assistance you have given me, and to say to you again that if the verdict on Tuesday is what we are expecting it to be I shall very much want your assistance in making good the promises which we have made to the American people." [56]

6

Harding's great advantage in the field of religious and fraternal organizations was that he was a joiner. When people wrote, as many did, asking about a particular organization, he could say that he was already a member, or that he was not eligible, or that he would be glad to be a member, or that he believed in the freedoms and responsibilities of being a member. When the campaign began he was a member of the Trinity Baptist Church of Marion, of the Elks, Moose, Knights of Pythias, the Sons of Veterans, the Concatenated Order of Hoo Hoo, and an Entered Apprentice of the Masons. Before the campaign ended he had added membership in the S.A.R., and he was a Master Mason.

In rare cases Harding assumed an attitude of righteous hostility to certain organizations. When L. H. Highley of Butler, Indiana, president of the No-Tobacco League of America and editor of the *No-Tobacco Journal*, wrote, "Cigars is bad enough," in an article on the bad example Harding was setting for the boys of America by permitting himself to be photographed smoking a cigarette, Harding proceeded to dictate a sermon on tolerance: "In this world we can only strive for perfection and never quite hope to attain it," and so on. When "Mrs. V. B. W." of Marion, Ohio—of all places—wrote asking, "Are you a godly man [who] . . . despises liquor and the saloon, cigarettes and vice of every description," he replied sharply, "You are a resident of the community in which I have spent practically all my natural life, and you have every opportunity of investigation among the people who have known me all these years." He suggested that "Mrs. V. B. W." apply her recommended code of conduct to herself and "seek Divine Guidance in prayer." When Hilda W. Korsgren, chief recorder of the Guardians of Liberty, wrote, asking for a comment on an enclosed clipping from the *Torch* citing Harding's stenographer, Kathryn Lawler, as being slated to be his presidential aide, thus continuing, with a "female Jesuit," the Roman Catholic influence in the White House long exercised by President Wilson's private secretary, Joseph Tumulty, Harding permitted Miss Lawler to reply in her own words. Denying that any selections for future positions had been made, the indignant young lady added, "Having enjoyed the privilege of serving Senator Harding in the capacity of his confidential secretary for six years, it is not unreasonable to assume that I shall continue to hold with him the same relationship after his election to the presidency." [57]

Harding was rather patient with other cranks. Dr. E. W. Gossett of Hot Springs, Arkansas wrote on July 19 that he had always been a Democrat, that he did not like the Roman influence in the White House via Tumulty, and felt that, since "you are of Baptist persuasion, I feel like you would protect our nation from the old 'beast.' " In reply to this, George Christian said that he was glad to note that he was a Democrat, that "we are getting much help from Democrats," and that "you are quite right in your information that the Senator is a member of the Baptist Church." [58]

Then there were those who wanted to know whether the Hardings, like the Democratic candidate, James M. Cox, were divorcees. To this the secretary replied that the Senator was not, but that Mrs. Harding was. He told of the "unfortunate circumstances" of Mrs. Harding's marriage to Henry De Wolfe, who became an alcoholic and failed to provide for his family. A divorce had become necessary, and "some years after the divorce," she and Mr. Harding were married. "In this community," it was added, "the facts are thoroughly understood and . . . no people in it are more highly respected than Senator and Mrs. Harding." [59]

Harding did not have to be very adjustable to become a Mason during the campaign. The rule that Masons are not to invite others to join was seemingly violated in his case. Urgings from Masons high and low—mostly high—poured into his office. They came from John H. Wishar, editor of the *Trestle Board,* Masonic publication of the Pacific coast; from William B. Melish of Cincinnati, past grand master of the Encampment of the Knights Templars of the United States; from J. A. Huriga, past master of the Urbana (Ill.) Lodge No. 157; from R. R. Sutton of the Claremore (Okla.) Lodge No. 53; from C. E. Messler, editor of the Bronx (N.Y.) *Masonic Digest*; from B. Woods, editor of the *Masonic Review of New York.* They emphasized, as did Charles M. Dean, executive secretary of the First Harding Club of Ohio (Robert A. Taft, secretary), that the Democrats were laying stress on the fact that Cox was a Master Mason and Harding was not. They pointed out, as did George B. Hische, vice president of the *Masonic Chronicle* of Chicago, that it would "prove a help to your candidacy to put you right with our kind of folks." "You are the right kind of material to be a Mason," wrote Melish. "Wide publicity of the fact that he is a Master Mason would do a great deal of good in the campaign," wrote William Noble of Oklahoma City to Christian. After Harding had remedied the difficulty, Wishar wrote that he was glad to learn that the Senator had "eliminated a source of constant criticism." Harding's Masonic membership "will do him no harm . . . it means that his plurality will be even larger than before . . . that he will have with him the support of a great thinking class of citizens." Huriga said, "It will be of a benefit to you when you become President of the United States. You will find great use for your Masonry there where you never found it before." Another, Gerald L. Burchard of Brooklyn, New York, made a rather indelicate hint in the suggestion that President Taft had taken the degrees in one night "and never entered the lodge again." [60]

Some of Harding's Masonic advice was anti-Catholic. Fred O. Schwenck of Cincinnati, in suggesting that Harding's belated entry into the brotherhood be widely publicized, urged Christian to call the Senator's attention to the September issue of the magazine published by the Oriental Consistory A.A.S.R. 32nd Degree of Chicago, a clipping from which was enclosed. This was a straight quote from the *National Catholic Register* saying that "God has doubly blessed the Catholic Church of America by placing one of its most faithful sons at the right hand of President Wilson," via Joseph Tumulty, member of the Knights of Columbus who, next to Wilson, "wields this greatest political power of any man in America." Every Catholic was urged to "awake to his duty and stand by his church and President Wilson." [61]

In explaining Harding's lack of full Masonic affiliation, his office staff was very frank. It pointed out that years ago Harding was made an Entered Apprentice but was blackballed because of the "enmity of one man directed not against him, but through him at another member of his family." Since then Harding had hesitated to push himself farther "for fear it might be conceived that he was trying to establish his membership for political purposes." In answer to confidential inquiries from Chicago party headquarters as to whether the blackballing was due to his "bad reputation" and whether the office should answer letters "plainly or avoid the question," the Marion office replied that there was "nothing of an objectionable nature." Other letters from Marion said the blackballing was due to newspaper rivalry. Then there was the telegram on October 28, from W. W. Corwin, of St. Clairsville, Ohio that it was very widely circulated that Harding was stopped in Masonry "because he had negro blood. Telegraph answer to C. E. Timberlake." Mr. Timberlake was informed, "No truth . . . the question was never raised in the Lodge." All responses stated that Harding "holds the Order and its work in high esteem," or words to that effect. These letters were, of course, written "under the bond." [62]

It was Marion Lodge No. 70 F. & A. M. that solved Harding's Masonic membership problem. He was raised to the "Sublime Degree of Master Mason" on August 27, 1920. How it was accomplished was explained in a form letter prepared for inquirers by the local Masonic secretary. Speaking of the blackballer, "a Democrat," the secretary wrote, "Pressure was brought to bear upon this man who waived all objection, and Mr. Harding is now a Master Mason in good standing in this Marion Lodge. Marion is proud of him, Marion Lodge is proud to have him a member, and he is proud of both the city of Marion and Marion Lodge." In closing, the secretary assured his correspondents,

"I say to you in all candor that he is the man for President at this time, as he will not be a one man President, or will he aspire to become a world president. If you want four more years of what we now have, it is promised by the Hon. James M. Cox." The pressure was now applied to one more step, viz., the Order of the Eastern Star. This came from W. S. Andres (Doc Waddell) of Columbus, who wrote, "Soon as possible give your petitions (you and wife) to Eastern Star of Marion." Andres added, "From what I've seen and know and feel *Ohio* will give you 200,000. We all love you!" Thus did Harding become a Blue Lodge Mason in good standing—and the publicity went out far and wide via the Masonic magazines.[63]

Membership in patriotic organizations helped. One of these was the Sons of Veterans. How useful this was is shown by the campaign conducted by Victor Heintz of the Chicago national committee office. Heintz had a full list of the 50,000 or more members and had sent to the Republican state chairman the names of the most "prominent and energetic" ones in their respective states. The idea was, said Heintz, that, since the Senator is such "an enthusiastic member," it would be in order to circularize them with a message from him. "Won't you please," he wrote Christian on September 3, "tell him that the membership list is available and that we are ready to shoot?" [64]

Harding's joining the Sons of the American Revolution was the result of stories of his ancestry going back to the wrong side of the Revolutionary War. It was probably the Senator's garrulous father who was responsible for the gossip afloat that his son's line went back via Warren's mother, to the Tory Governor William Tryon of North Carolina.[65] At any rate, on July 15, Lewis K. Torbet of the Union League Club of Chicago wrote to Howard Mannington, one of Harding's campaign aides, saying that he had picked up a "story of Harding's ancestors, especially on his mother's side." Torbet did not give details, but he went on to say, "If the Senator is a Son of the American Revolution and you will give me his National number, I will follow up. Please let me have at your earliest convenience his line on both Paternal and Maternal side, with anything of special interest of each line." Mannington was quick in response. Next day he wrote Torbet, "I know what it is you refer to. You may class it as an unqualifiable falsehood. I am enclosing a brief biography of the Senator, which will show you lineage. Negotiations are now under way by the Sons of the American Revolution to make him an honorary member of that order." Three days later, July 19, W. L. Curry, secretary of the Ohio S. A. R., was pleased to accept the Senator's application and to designate him as a full fledged member of the General Francis Marion Chapter. His number was 34134. In welcoming him into the fellowship, secretary Curry commented, "We are all 100% Americans and believe that 'blood will tell.'" [66]

Harding got much more of the "fraternity vote" by discreet handling. His favorite lodge was the Benevolent and Protective Order of the Elks, for whom he had delivered many an eloquent address for departed brothers on memorial occasions. It happened that on July 29 there appeared in the *Cincinnati Times-Star* an item quoting Harding's letter of sympathy to former Clevelander Henry S. Stowe (misspelled Shawe), a resident of the Elks National Home in Bedford, Virginia, under treatment for failing eyesight. Stowe had been an ardent promoter of Harding's political fortunes in the Cleveland area. The originator of this news item was Harding's loyal admirer and brother in Elkdom John Galvin, mayor of Cincinnati, who heard about the letter from his fellow Elks. As Galvin told Christian, the story "appealed to me as so full of feeling, to say nothing of Elk sentiment, that I was deeply touched." Galvin therefore gave it to the *Times-Star* reporter and the story was published. "I believe," Galvin added, "if you could have your publicity people have this little story copied in the newspapers over the country generally it would do a whole lot of good. I know it would touch the hearts of all Elks, and I believe it would touch everybody for the splendid humanity shown by the Senator in his treatment of Mr. Shawe [Stowe]. . . . Personally I think it just beautiful and wonderful, and I love him more than ever for it . . . I leave it to you to get the necessary publicity over the country on it. It is just these little touches of nature that make the whole world kin, that are sometimes the most effective in a political campaign." [67]

Another way to get the Elk vote was to write a letter on Americanism to the "Exaltic Ruler of the Mother Lodge No. 1" in New York City. This was done at the prompting of John J. Lyons, member of the lodge, and candidate for secretary of state in New York, and who incidently was also chairman of a delegation of foreign-born citizens who visited the front porch on Foreign Voters' Day, September 18. Before Lyons left Marion that day, he had prepared a typed memorandum of his request for Harding's message, and a copy of the message itself. Harding said that he was writing "as a loyal and unofficial member of the Order and not as a candidate seeking to

make political capital." He went on to say that he was proud of the
Elks because of its Americanism as evidenced in the fact that it was
not a "secret order." "It is peculiarly an American organization, of
American inception, with American ideas, its ritual and its duties
conducted in American language, welcoming to its ranks the best
among us, whether native born or merging from the polyglot melting
pot. . . . It knows neither race nor creed . . . it harbors no seeds of
disloyalty or treason or lawlessness or anarchy." It was a typical
product of "this wonderful land of magnificent opportunity." At the
end of his memorandum, Lyon wrote, "In behalf of the State of New
York Mr. Lyons assured Senator Harding that the state would be
carried by a Republican plurality of 400,000, and that even Manhattan
would be carried by him for the first time in its history." [68]

The Moose order also helped. This was because of its director-general, James J. Davis, Harding's future Secretary of Labor. Davis had a
way about him, as has been previously shown from his buying of
several copies of Chapple's biography of Harding for distribution
among the steelworkers. Here is how Davis got Harding to send a
message for insertion in the *Mooseheart Weekly*, endorsing Mooseheart, "Moosedom's Shrine of Childhood" in Mooseheart, Illinois. "I
have talked with you many times about Mooseheart," wrote Davis,
"and if I gather your thoughts correctly they can be summed up in the
following:

'Thru Mooseheart, the Moose are showing the world how to educate
children. Mooseheart is a combination of all that is good in the school
and home. It appeals to me because of the service it is doing our
country in turning out good American citizens who will take an active
part in its life and be real men and women of tomorrow.'

If you object to this, let me know, and I will wire them to keep it out
of the paper." Who was Harding to object to such a help from a fellow
Moose? The message appeared on the front page of the October 30,
1920 *Mooseheart Weekly* under the heading, "A Statement of Senator
Warren G. Harding." [69]

Further evidence of Moosedom's help came from two other members, John J. Lentz of Columbus and W. S. Andres (Doc Waddell) of
Columbus and Cincinnati. According to Lentz's own statement, he
was a member of the Moose board of governors and traveled into
many states, "for the American Insurance Union and the Moose."
Lentz was president of the American Insurance Union. He was a

Democrat and delegate to the Democratic national convention, but he liked Harding. He told the Senator that "the many visitors here at Mooseheart are exceedingly proud of your nomination and you will find the six hundred thousand members of the Moose more helpful in your campaign." True, wrote Lentz, "I am a Democrat, but what I am saying in my trip about you personally, as anxious inquirers approach me, will do you no harm." He also said that director-general Davis, at a meeting of 2,000 Moose officials, made reference to Harding's "Moosemanship." As for "Doc Waddell," he got out a mimeographed Moose newsletter from the Moose Temple in Cincinnati. The letters were spotted with pro-Harding notes, one of which concerned Baltimore Mayor William F. Bruening, a "Past Supreme Dictator" of the order. "BRUENING," wrote Doc Waddell, "is an Orator, and if permitted to campaign in MOOSE SECTIONS of OHIO would increase the G.O.P. Majority." To this Harding replied in a letter to Lentz, dated June 29, "It is a very pleasing thing to know that many of the brethren in the Order are interested in my good fortune." [70]

For promptness in their fraternal loyalty to Harding no lodge outdid the Concatenated Order of Hoo Hoo. This was a lumber-merchants' organization, and the leader for Harding was Chicagoan Bolling Arthur Johnson, editor and publisher of the *Lumber World Review*. In the June 25 issue of the *Review* was a three-and-a-half-page article by Johnson entitled "An Intimate Picture of Senator Warren G. Harding and a Printing—for the First Time—of the Fact that Mr. Harding is a Lumberman—and Member of the Concatenated Order of Hoo Hoo." It was illustrated by a photograph of the Senator's application for membership. The purpose of the Hoo Hoo campaign, Johnson wrote Harding, was "to organize the lumberman of the United States and put them in a marching order to help put over your election this fall." The lumber industry was the second largest in the nation—so Johnson said—and he offered to make a four-page pamphlet to send to his list of "37,000 high class manufacturers and retailers of lumber." He also invited Harding to address the lumbermen's national convention. The upshot of it all was that Harding's office thanked Johnson for his offer, declining with thanks the honor of addressing the Hoo Hoo in convention assembled, and asked him to take his article and mailing list to the Chicago publicity department of the party.[71]

Harding was a bit careless with the Knights of Pythias. On August 27, George B. Donavin of Columbus urged Christian to get Harding to seek membership in the D.O.K.K., a higher branch of the Pythians.

Christian replied that, if Harding did so, it might be misunderstood. Whereupon Donavin replied snippishly that Cox had come to a meeting of the Pythians which started a membership revival by which Cox gained a great many votes.[72]

As in 1914, Harding received some help from the anti-Roman Catholics, but not in the feverish tempo in which he was elected senator. Many such letters and circulars he ignored or replied to evasively. But the letters showed that many anti-Catholics were lining up for him. Such were the Patriotic Knights of American Liberty, dedicated to "help save America from Romish Autocracy"; the Sons and Daughters of Washington, who desired to "PUT A MASON IN THE WHITE HOUSE"; and the Knights of Luther, who sponsored the Converted Catholic Publishing Company of Toledo, Ohio. But in some cases Harding's answers, though evasive, were friendly and left bigoted allegations unchallenged. For example, the Guardians of Liberty were still in the field and were vigorously pro-Harding and anti-Catholic. The Guardian president, Lieutenant General Nelson A. Miles, sent Harding a copy of the June, 1920 number of the Guardians' magazine with the section marked rejoicing at Harding's nomination. In another page, unmarked, was a paragraph lauding the work of Brother Guardian George H. Lyttle in 1914 by which "Warren G. Harding was elected United States Senator from Ohio instead of a devout papist and K. C." To this Harding replied personally to General Miles acknowledging receipt of the magazine "in which you make very pleasing and agreeable reference to the Republican nomination made at Chicago." Harding thanked the General for "your great courtesy and consideration in the way you have handled this matter." Then there was William Lloyd Clark of Milan, Illinois, head of the Truth and Light Publishing House, who wanted to know several things, including whether or not Harding would maintain "an absolutely secular form of government," prevent sectarian use of public property, favor government inspection of convents, monasteries, and Houses of the Good Shepherd, and retain a "Roman Catholic as your private secretary?" In his reply Christian said "the Senator stands upon the constitutional declaration for divorcement of church and state, with fullest religious liberty for all the people." As for inspecting monasteries, this was not a matter "within the purview of the national authority, but it is a matter which he has never had occasion to investigate." That was all the letter said, but its friendly tone could be construed as anti-Catholic after all.[73]

Harding was more careful about the Catholic vote on the question of the Smith-Towner Bill, which would have set up a department of education, with its secretary having cabinet rank. This was opposed by the Catholics as dangerous to the administration of parochial schools. Harding agreed with the Catholics on this. One of his secretaries wrote to Mrs. Katharine E. Roesinger of Indianapolis, saying that Harding had "always been especially zealous in resisting anything that looked like an attack upon the freedom of religious worship or observance." He believed parents should be encouraged to send their children to whatever schools they choose. And he was also of the belief that "parochial schools have, so far as his knowledge and observation go, been both efficient and patriotic." On September 2, on the occasion of a front-porch visit of delegates of the National Education Association and the American Federation of Teachers, Harding politely refused their request for an endorsement of the Smith-Towner proposal.[74]

Harding had some adjusting to do with the Jews who claimed that anti-Semitism was his motivation in voting against confirmation of President Wilson's appointment of Louis Brandeis to the Supreme Court. Jewish newspapers were quick to raise the outcry as soon as Harding was nominated, the papers of Cleveland, the *Jewish Daily World* and the *Jewish Daily Forward*, in the lead. This alarmed Cleveland Republican leader Maurice Maschke, who said that the anti-Semitic story was being circulated all over the country. Chicagoan L. W. Landman reported active propaganda, emanating from the Jewish Lodge B'nai Brith, that Harding was a "Jew hater." Landman admitted that the Americanized non-Yiddish Jews took no notice of it, but that "there are over a million other Jews who will." Both suggested the invitation to Marion of distinguished Jews. They mentioned Oscar Straus, Jacob Schiff, and Louis Marshall of New York, and Julius Rosenwald of Chicago.[75]

Republican adjustment was of various kinds. Visits of distinguished Jews to the front porch were encouraged. The Marion office reported on July 3 that Oscar Straus "called the other day and pledged Harding his enthusiastic support." Rabbi Louis Wolsey of Cleveland arranged to call on September 14. On July 15, Harding made plans to attend the dedication of the Marion lodge of the B'nai Brith and the event was publicized in the *New York Times* of July 19. Harding was quoted as saying, among other things, that he hoped "all Americans would catch the spirit of the organization in campaigning against ignorance, intolerance, defamation and everything else aimed to rend the concord of citizenship." Joseph David, manager of the Investment Company of Cleveland, reminded Harding that the father of William R. Weidenthal, editor of the *Jewish Independent*, had been a supporter of the Senator in prior campaigns, and suggested a letter to the son, which Harding immediately wrote. David followed up by arranging for publication in the Jewish papers of a message by Harding to the Jewish Relief Society. In the last issue before election, the *Jewish Review and Observer* (October 29), appeared a long letter by David containing a quotation from Harding on the theme that "national morality cannot exist without the support of religious principles." An accompanying letter by Cleveland Rabbi A. H. Silver urged his people not to believe the anti-Semitic charges against Harding. The liberal Rabbi Stephen S. Wise of the Free Synagogue in New York was so disgusted with the Democratic use of this attitude of some Jews that he publicly announced that, although he was going to vote for Cox, it was only fair to Harding to declare that thinking Jews knew that Harding no more opposed Brandeis because he was Jewish than did Wilson appoint him because he was Jewish.[76]

When individual Jews inquired about the Brandeis story, a form letter was sent out explaining that Harding's vote was not for religious reasons, but "because of the conviction that his [Brandeis'] extremely radical tendencies did not adapt him to a position on the Supreme Bench of the United States." [77]

On the Jewish journalistic front, aid came from Leo Wise, editor of the *American Israelite*, which was the national Jewish journal claiming to have the largest circulation and to be the oldest and most influential Jewish newspaper in the United States. On July 16, Wise wrote that he was receiving numerous letters complaining of "Harding's mental attitude toward Jews as Jews." Wise said that the impression was gaining lodgment in Jewish minds all over the country, and suggested that Harding see a representative of the *American Israelite* and prepare a statement for national circulation. Harding accepted the offer, and an arrangement was made, galley proof submitted and corrected, and the statement published as an editorial in Wise's paper on October 7, under the title "Keep Religion Out of Politics." The editorial regretted that a number of Jewish newspapers, "especially those promoted in the Yiddish jargon," had been representing Harding as entertaining anti-Jewish prejudices as evidenced by his opposition to Brandeis. "Such claims are absurd." Harding's opposition was attributed to the belief that Brandeis' political convictions were incompatible with American government and economic institutions. An interesting sequel to this affair was that the *American Israelite* asked Republican headquarters for $500 for this editorial. On October 26, Victor Heintz, of Chicago headquarters, telegraphed Christian, "*American Israelite* of Cincinnati say they editorially published article with Harding's OK understanding they would receive five hundred dollars. Please give me all information you have on this subject as they are complaining of receiving nothing." Christian telegraphed Heintz that "Senator Harding knows nothing of the text of your message relative to editorial." [78]

An effective way to win Jewish favor was to show sympathy for Jewish misfortunes in other lands. For example, there were the war refugees in Ukrainia whom the National Citizens Committee of New Americans was seeking to gather together for relocation in the United States. On August 2, the *New York Times* published Harding's letter to Henry Green, general director of the committee, expressing the hope that the mission would be successful, and that "the unfortunates of war's storms may early find a new haven of peace and safety where they may enjoy tranquility after the terrible trials through which they have passed." This letter was published in several Jewish papers. A similar expression by Harding was published in the October 31 *New York Times* and other papers. It featured a letter by Harding to Judge Gustav Hartman of New York, head of the Independent Order of Brith Abraham, "the largest Jewish fraternal organization in the world." On October 16, Judge Hartman had telegraphed Harding thanking him for his message telling of his abhorrence of the slaughtering of Jews as reported from various parts of the world. This gave Harding an opportunity to state for publication his appreciation of the noble qualities of the long-suffering Jew. "I am especially earnest," he told the judge "in my protest against the frequent reversions to barbarity in the treatment of the Jewish citizens of many lands, a people who have commanded always my admiration by their genius, industry, endurance, patience and persistence, the virtues and devotion of their domestic lives, their broad charity and philanthropy and their obedience to the laws under which they live." [79]

A much-publicized affair was the attendance on October 27 of the candidate and Mrs. Harding at the Silver Jubilee of the Cleveland Independent Aid Society. This was an organization to help acclimate Jewish immigrants. Harding took occasion in his address to say some felicitous words not only about the highly developed Jewish sense of charity but about the Zionist movement. According to the *Plain Dealer*, he said that he understood why people of Jewish faith wanted to establish their own fatherland. It was because, he said, they had been "buffeted from nation to nation for centuries." Only the United States made them feel welcome.

7

All in all, candidate Harding made many adjustments in his efforts to win votes. Sometimes, as in the case of Wallace and the farmers, he set his sights high. In others, such as the Guardians of Liberty and the anti-Catholics, he was careless. He was devious with regard to revision of the Volstead Act, cautious in responding to pressure from the women's groups for state ratifications of the suffrage amendment, and ingratiating with fraternal organizations. But the "big game" required many methods and well-chosen weapons. In every case he did his adjusting with the appearance of the well-known Harding candor and sincerity that carried conviction to most of his listeners.

CHAPTER TWENTY-TWO

Negro Rights and the White Backlash *

"I believe in equality before the law. You can't give rights to the white man and deny them to the black man. But while I stand for that great, great principle, I do not mean that the white man and the black man must be forced to associate together in the acceptance of their rights." : : : *Harding address in Oklahoma City, October 9, 1920, as reported in the "Daily Oklahoman," October 10, 1920*

The greatest indignity suffered by Harding in his career was the allegation made during the campaign of 1920 that he had Negro forebears. This was part of the white backlash reactions that were stirred by the moderate concessions made by Harding and the Republicans to the rising Negro rights movement. To be attacked for racial reasons was not a new experience for either Harding or the Republicans. The whites, especially Democratic ones, had been backlashing since antislavery days. The Hardings had been punished with "nigger talk" ever since they espoused antislavery sentiments in a Democratic section of Ohio in pre–Civil War times. It has been standard treatment in certain sections of society, especially in Civil War and Reconstruction times, for Republicans to be called "nigger worshippers" because of their interest in civil rights.

Warren Harding's interest in the rights of Negroes was, in 1920, based on his desire for their votes, especially since there were more Negro voters than ever before. It was a matter of simple statistics that the potential Negro vote in the North from 1917 to 1920 had more than doubled. The great increase came not only from the enfranchisement of the Negro women by the adoption of the Nineteenth Amendment but from the migration to the North during World War I of many thousands of southern Negroes to work in the production stimulated by the conflict. Immigration of cheap labor from Europe was cut off during the war and, therefore, the work force had to be supplemented by southern Negroes.[1]

* A version of this chapter appeared, under the same title, as an article in *Ohio History*, 75:85–107, 184–85.

Increased tension resulted. This came not merely from an increase in numbers of Negroes in the North but from an increase in the Negroes' desire to help remedy their own grievances. The bars of racial restriction were not as great in the North as they were in the South, and Negroes, as a result, were sure to be more active in the direction of securing more equality in political, civil, and even social rights. Many who had served in the armed forces during the war returned home with new ideas and hopes stirring in their minds and spirits. Negro rights societies increased in number and militancy. So did Negro newspapers. In 1910 the National Association for the Advancement of Colored People was born, with its exhilirating idea that the Negroes could not expect to attain more equal rights unless they themselves actively and intelligently sought to get them. Increased lynching after World War I drove the N.A.A.C.P. and other Negro organizations to vigorous counteraction in the direction of federal legislation.[2]

As the signs of increased Negro militancy became apparent to whites, there arose the inevitable backlash. Whites, who had never indulged in the unthinkable possibility of Negro equality, were suddenly confronted with it, and they did not like it. The return of 400,000 Negro soldiers to civilian life had explosive possibilities. An upsurge of lynchings followed. The "Red Summer" of 1919 saw race riots in some twenty-five American cities, north and south.[3] Therefore, as the Republican party and Harding made adjustments to meet the requirements of retaining the loyalty of the traditionally Republican, and now more numerous, Negroes, the defenders of white supremacy made themselves heard. The race problem, which, by a certain gentleman's code of honor, was not supposed to be a part of politics, became such in the minds of many people. Candidate Warren G. Harding was caught in this new political issue. He was required to be more evasive than forthright on the Negro question.

Evasiveness was not difficult for Harding. In his 1920 campaign he and his fellow Republican leaders sought to appease the Negro desire for equality in politics and civil rights in two ways. One was to make displays of devotion to the general principle of racial equality in rights and opportunities without getting down to specifics. These displays were made in such controlled circumstances as the shaping of the Republican platform, Harding's acceptance day address, and the well-managed and subsidized ceremonies of Colored Voters' Day at Marion on September 10. Much maneuvering was necessary in these affairs in order to keep the militants quiet. The second form of evasion was to encourage a protest movement in behalf of the liberties of the citizens of the Negro republic of Haiti. These liberties seemingly were being subverted by the American occupation of the Caribbean island, a process originated by the Democratic administration in 1915. Wilson's Haitian policy, and its support by Democratic vice-presidential candidate Franklin D. Roosevelt, gave Harding an opportunity to play politics.

Even though Harding maneuvered and evaded in the direction of equal rights for Negroes, he was the victim of a strong backlash movement by "lily-white" Democrats in the North and in the border states. As the campaign closed, some of the more desperate Democrats launched two attacks on Harding. One was a claim that his equal rights talk was a threat to white supremacy. The other was an attempt by certain Democrats to represent Harding himself as a Negro.

2

The first Republican adjustment to the Negro rights demands took place at the June, 1920 nominating convention at Chicago with the insertion of an antilynching plank in the party platform. The Negroes wanted more than that—at least the five Negroes appointed to the platform committee did. They presented a resolution asking not only for an antilynching plank but for other statements pledging the party to favor (1) a force act assuring the right to vote to all Negroes in the South, and elsewhere, as provided for in the Fourteenth and Fifteenth amendments to the United States Constitution; (2) a civil rights act assuring the abolition of segregation and discrimination because of color; and (3) a general commitment that the United States should be made safe for democracy at home before it undertook to work for that goal in foreign lands. When the committee accepted only the anti-lynching plank, the Negro delegates tried to introduce the rejected ones in the convention itself. They were ruled out of order. They therefore had to be content with a declaration entitled "Lynching," which read, "We urge Congress to consider the most effective means to end lynching in this country which continues to be a terrible blot on our American civilization." [4]

More adjustment to Negro demands was necessary, and the man to do it, of course, was the candidate. Harding went farther toward

Negro equality than the platform, but not as far as many Negroe thought he had. However, he went much farther than the "lily whites and the backlashers could tolerate.

Strong pressure for racial equality came from Cleveland Negroe who were being courted by the local Republican organization. Har ding was asked by editor-in-chief Ormond A. Forte of the militan *Cleveland Advocate* if he would: abolish color discrimination in th government deparments; get rid of the "Taft Southern Policy" o appointing only lily-white Republicans in the South; follow the Four teenth Amendment, requiring a cut of southern representation in Con gress when Negroes were deprived of the vote. Pressure for racia equality was also brought by Cleveland Republican leader Mauric Maschke, who informed Harding that the Cleveland Negroes wer anxious to repair "the damage" done by their opposition to Harding i the primary campaign. Harding rebuked Maschke for encouraging th Negroes so much.[5]

Nevertheless, in his July 22 acceptance speech, Harding did mucl to attract Negro support. His words went beyond the antilynchin stage. In fact, they were so characteristically eloquent and expressiv in behalf of Negro equality that the impressionable Negro could—anc did—think that they meant the coming of a new day of Jubilee. "N majority," said Harding, "shall abridge the rights of a minority. . . . believe the Negro citizens of America should be guaranteed th enjoyment of all their rights, that they have earned their full measur of citizenship bestowed, that their sacrifices in blood on the battle fields of the republic have entitled them to all of freedom and oppor tunity, all of sympathy and aid that the American spirit of fairness anc justice demands."[6]

By following up these promises of Negro equality with the appoint ment of Negro leaders to high places in Republican party councils, the Republicans could ensure the enthusiastic propagation of the nev doctrine of Negro equality by the Negroes themselves—always, o course, with the understanding that they did not go too far, *i.e.* agitate for integration. One of those so favored was the Atlanta Georgia, Negro attorney Henry Lincoln Johnson. The influential John son was given two appointments, one as a delegate to the nationa convention, the other as a member from Georgia of the powerfu Republican national committee. Johnson became an ardent exponen of Harding's type of Negro-rights promotion. He represented th candidate's acceptance remarks as being on a par with Abrahan

Lincoln's Emancipation Proclamation. To the Negro Methodist pastor Reverend J. G. Robinson of Philadelphia, Johnson wrote, "The Senator spoke to our souls in matchless words in his letter of acceptance and filled with joy every downcast Negro heart with his assurance of his remembrance of our travails, and his purpose, so far as the president's power lies, to allay them." [7]

The other Negro appointment to the Republican hierarchy was Mrs. Lethia C. Fleming, wife of Cleveland city councilman Thomas W. Fleming. She also was given two positions high in the Republican hierarchy. The first was to be one of the five women members of the Republican national executive committee, and the other was to be chairman of the Colored Women's Bureau of the Republican national committee. We do not have examples of her utterances in behalf of Negro rights, but we do have Harding's testimony as to her high qualities as a Republican. In recommending Mrs. Fleming to Maurice Maschke for the appointments, Harding wrote, on June 16, that her "intelligence is equal to any woman. She is tactful, prepossessing in appearance, charming and acquainted with politics." [8]

3

On the basis of the moderate Negro rights statements of the Republican platform and the Harding acceptance speech, the Republicans launched a program of publicity designed to keep things moderate and general, and to curb the militants who wanted more specifics. This was done by three well-managed enterprises: (1) the sponsoring of Negro Republican clubs throughout the North by Johnson's Negro Voters' Bureau: (2) the preparation and circulation of special party pamphlets designed for Negro voters; and (3) the staging of Colored Voters' Day at Marion on September 10.

Henry Lincoln Johnson's club work stressed not only the creation and enlargement of Negro Republican clubs but the sending to each of them of a mimeographed form letter, on official Republican national committee letterheads, urging them to pass resolutions of endorsement of Harding and Coolidge. The letter was simple and graphic. It opened with a brief statement saying that "everyone admits that lynching and mob-violence are the chief aggravations of the colored man in the United States." Beneath this were two columns. The righthand column was headed, "What the Republican Party

Says," and contained three well-spaced quotations of the Republican platform on lynching, Harding's acceptance day remarks, and a statement by Calvin Coolidge on Negro constitutional rights. The lefthand column was headed, "What the Democratic Platform Says," and was largely blank, except that for the Democratic platform was the word "NOTHING," for Governor Cox the words "ABSOLUTELY NOTHING," and for Franklin Delano Roosevelt the statement "NOT ONE WORD."

Johnson was very proud of this form letter. At the bottom of a copy sent to Marion was the hand-written note, "Kind Senator Harding: Just for your information, every important meeting of colored people in the 'voting states' is passing sweeping endorsements of your candidacy in response to requests indicated above." To this, Harding's office replied that the Senator was gratified that the colored people were so generally endorsing his candidacy with the aid of the "clean, concise and convincing contrast of the platforms and candidates relative to the rights of colored people." [9]

Johnson's campaign pamphlets were rousing publications. Harding was represented as the successor to Abraham Lincoln and William Lloyd Garrison. The Democratic party was castigated with a revival of "bloody-shirt" talk, and was represented as based on too much southern white political influence and the disfranchisement of the Negro. Democratic hypocrisy was cited in their support of world democracy abroad and non-democracy in the South; in their talk of endorsement of the Eighteenth Amendment and the nullification of the Fourteenth and Fifteenth amendments. Anti-Negro statements by southern leaders were quoted. In a heavily leaded, boxed paragraph was Senator Ben Tillman's remark, "We stuffed ballot boxes, we shot Negroes: we are not ashamed of it." A Congressman Taylor was similarly represented as saying, "The Democratic party is a white man's party in the North, as well as in the South." Discrimination and "Jim Crow" treatment by the Democrats in the Army, in the offices at Washington, and in the reception of veterans were minutely detailed. There was a special pamphlet written by Negro Major John R. Lynch, U.S. Army Retired, which went deeper. It assailed the Democrats for the sin of instilling an inferiority complex in Negroes so that they could not understand the higher issues at stake in the election. "He enters the campaign handicapped for the consideration of great issues," wrote Major Lynch. Always the Democrats were scored as the Negroes' "life-long enemy." Always the Democrats cited the bitter past and present; nothing was said of the Negro future. There were no specific promises about the full meaning of the equality that was to come.[10]

Grand climax of the Johnson campaign was Colored Voters' Day, September 10, 1920 at Marion. This affair was a piece of "front porch" politicking designed to win Negro voters. The program was carefully managed. It was heavily financed and skillfully prepared so as to discourage the militant Negroes from coming, and to encourage the moderates to come in great numbers.

There were many sources of Negro militancy with whom the Johnson-Harding moderates had to deal in keeping Colored Voters' Day under control. One of these groups was composed of Cleveland Negro radicals who were making real progress in getting into the city government. Republican leaders felt that the way to handle them would be to leave them alone. When they saw the nature of the Colored Voters' Day preparation, they lost interest and stayed out of it. Then there was the N.A.A.C.P. Harding was able to cope with this organization by the Haiti maneuver. Finally there was the most dangerous of all the militant organizations: the Equal Rights League, and its executive secretary, William Monroe Trotter of Boston.

Henry Lincoln Johnson was fully aware of the danger of Trotter and the Equal Rights League. He made it quite clear, at the outset of the preparations for Colored Voters' Day, that there should be no pilgrimage to Marion by that organization. On August 9, he explained his views to Harry M. Daugherty. What he wanted, he told Daugherty, was a visit to Marion of a few carefully selected moderate Negroes who would not raise any embarrassing questions. This kind of people, wrote Johnson, was "alright":

They are just a part of the great majority of the colored people of the United States who want to see the Senator only to assure him of their enthusiastic and loyal support. When it comes to the Equal Rights League, it may be made up of Monroe Trotter of Boston and some other wild-eyed people like that. They may produce some embarrassment. So before you make any dates may I beg that you let me advise with you so that no mistakes whatever will be made? We do not want any colored people to come to see the Senator with question marks. The platform declaration and the unmatched declarations of Senator Harding and Governor Coolidge not only satisfies but enthuses the colored Republican voters of the United States and we do not want to be bothered with any more delegations coming up and asking how a man stands about things.[11]

Johnson had his way. Trotter attended the Colored Voters' Day ceremonies, but he was entirely surrounded and contained by the group of moderate Negroes which Johnson managed to assemble. This group consisted mostly of the Negroes of two Baptist conventions which happened to be meeting in Indianapolis and Columbus on September 10. Negroes who would have to come from more remote parts of the country were kept from coming by the simple device of refusing to pay their expenses. For example, the Reverend J. G. Robinson of Philadelphia, head of the Convocational Council of the African Methodist Episcopal church, wanted to bring a big delegation of Negro Methodists to Marion for the September 10 demonstration. "Let me know," he wrote Johnson on August 28, "if the National Committee will assist me with my delegation—R. R. fare only?" Johnson very bluntly set Reverend Robinson's mind at ease on this proposition. "I should rather advise," he wrote, "against such a pilgrimage for the reasons: (a) the terrible expense involved and the absolute inability of the National Committee to finance such an excursion; (b) the lack of need of such an undertaking." [12]

The Negro Methodists may have been kept away from Colored Voters' Day by the denial of railroad fare, but that was emphatically not the case of the Negro Baptists who were meeting at Indianapolis and Columbus. These places were near enough to Marion to make the expense less onerous on the Republican party financial coffers. The Republican involvement was clearly demonstrated by a letter of August 23 from Harry Daugherty in Columbus to Howard Mannington of Harding's staff in Marion. This letter showed that the Republicans not only paid the railroad expenses of the two sets of Negro Baptists but helped defray the expenses of at least one of the religious conventions. In his letter Daugherty said, speaking of the Columbus convention: "Am asking Rev. J. F. Hughes, General Manager of the National Negro Baptist Association, to call on you tomorrow A. M. This is the big association you know. Yesterday I told you to see if Hughes thought he could arrange to have those in Indianapolis to come also. This will involve the expense of two special trains. Whatever you, Carmi Thompson and Senator New [of Chicago headquarters] work out is alright with me. I have done all I can about it. Confidentially I have secured for Hughes and paid him $1000 to help some of the expenses of this convention." [13]

A danger that lurked in the background of the preparations for Colored Voters' Day was the "Jim Crow" status of Marion's hotel and restaurant facilities. Harding was amply warned on this in a friendly way by former Senator Theodore E. Burton, and in a challenging way, by Ralph W. Tyler, of the *Cleveland Advocate*. Burton said that a leading Cleveland colored Methodist minister, who recently visited Marion, was denied access to any drugstore or restaurant in the city and that, in consequence, there could be no Negro endorsement of Harding in Cleveland. Tyler wrote Christian along the same lines, acknowledged that it was not Harding's fault, but insisted that it would hurt Harding's candidacy for his hometown to engage in practices "diametrically opposite to the Senator's pronouncement for justice for the race as American citizens." Tyler proposed that Christian try to get the Marion "civic associations" to agree to suspend "Jim Crowism" for the duration of the campaign. Harding, in his reply to Burton, said that this was the first time he had ever heard of any lack of consideration and fair treatment of anybody in Marion, but there was nothing he could do about it. He felt sure that the committee on arrangements would provide for equal opportunity "even though that involved some phases of segregation." "You know," he added, "that racial prejudice is a thing which can not be set at naught." The result was that there were no Cleveland Negro visitors to Marion on Colored Voters' Day.[14]

The result was also a smoothly arranged, segregated affair. It was punctuated with religious fervor, but dominated by moderation. No episode took place to reveal to the public eye the fact of the prevalence of "Jim Crowism" on Colored Voters' Day. "We have made arrangements," wrote Mannington to Johnson, "with a local colored church to feed these people and they will erect a big tent, where all visitors can be properly and adequately fed." He hoped that there would be a "goodly crowd," perhaps a thousand people, so that the church would not lose money on the venture. It is doubtful that there were that many present, but, whatever the number, there were three things apparent from the arrangement program prepared by Mannington and given to the master of ceremonies, D. R. Crissinger. One was that the assemblage was overwhelmingly religious. Another was that they visited Harding in four separate groups: the Baptists from Columbus who arrived at Harding's home at 8:15 A.M., and returned to Columbus by the 10:00 A.M. train; the Baptists from Indianapolis, who saw Harding at 1:00 P.M.; a Methodist group which called late in the afternoon; and a delegation from the "National Race Congress" which saw the candidate at 11:00 A.M. The third point of interest was the complete segregation of the Negroes as per item no. 5 in Manning-ton's mimeographed instructions: "All delegations must be told where they can be subsisted, that is, by the A. M. E. Church of Marion, wherever they will serve dinner and supper, and all should be especially directed to go there." A copy of these instructions was given to J. W. Thompson, Marion chief of police.[15]

The main ceremony took place at the front porch at two o'clock. It was marked by climax and anticlimax. According to the *New York Times* report, the affair "had all the fervency of a camp meeting." A colored band from Columbus escorted the visitors to the porch, playing "Harding Will Shine Tonight." At the porch, Henry Lincoln Johnson took charge, and told the candidate that they were not present to ask him questions because they knew what he thought. To make the formal presentation of the Baptist brethren, Johnson called on William H. Lewis, former assistant attorney-general under Taft. Lewis likewise said there would be no questions: "We seek no pledges. Your life, your high character, your public services are pledge enough. Your splendid pronouncement in your speech of acceptance that the colored citizens should be guaranteed the enjoyment of all their rights and entitled to freedom and opportunity, because they had measured up to the requirements of citizenship by their sacrifices on the battlefields of the republic, gives courage and inspiration." Lewis' remarks were punctuated with exclamations from the audience of "Hallelujah," "Amen," and "You tell it."

Then, with awesome effect, there appeared before them General John J. Pershing, who happened to be Harding's guest. He was introduced to the thunderstruck assemblage and gave his inspirational blessings, praising the Negroes for their service to their country during the war. Mrs. Fleming was also introduced. She spoke with excellent poise on behalf of the Negro women, praising Harding for his part in bringing them the vote.[16]

And then, at the grand climax, the candidate himself appeared. He spoke in words of friendly dignity, not as an evangel of liberty, but in a tone of fatherly moderation. His central theme was the great progress the Negroes had made since the days of slavery and the noble part they had played in America's progress and in America's wars. He knew of their trials, the disgraceful lynchings, the irksome discriminations. He knew also of their restraint under great provocation. He praised them for this, but he also reminded them that continued progress was possible only in a land of ordered freedom and opportunity such as America. He reminded them that such progress was not possible in the land of the new slavery under the Bolshevik dictatorship of violent Russia. He enjoined them to work hard, obey the law, and avoid violence. He knew they would understand the basic truth behind his counsels of moderation: "The American Negro has the good sense to know this truth, has the good sense, clear head, and brave heart to live it; and I proclaim it to all the world that he has met the test and did not and will not fail America." [17]

Harding's references to violence in his Colored Voters' Day address need to be understood in the context of the public feeling of the red scare days of 1920. He was warning not so much about the violence of lynching as he was about the violence of the race riots of 1919. His words were: "Brutal and unlawful violence whether it proceeds from those who break the law or from those who take the law into their own hands, can only be dealt with in one way by true Americans, whether they be of your blood or of mine." This was small comfort to the militants, who saw in it the inference that the blame for the riots was as much the Negro's as the white's. It was great comfort to the whites, who saw the law supporting the status quo which was so favorable to them.

What the militant Negroes thought of this performance, as the subdued assemblage dispersed at the end of the day, is not recorded; at least it has not been discovered. The militant Trotter of the Equal Rights League was present, but he had no part in the public speechmaking. He had his say, but it was behind closed doors. There are at least two versions of what was said about the Equal Rights League's special emphasis on segregation. One was the Associated Press correspondent who reported: "One of those who conferred with the Senator was William Monroe Trotter of Boston, Executive Secretary of the National Equal Rights League, who asked that segregation of Negro employees of the Federal Government be abolished. He declared afterward that the Senator had given the request appreciative consideration." The other version of what happened is taken from the *Union*, a Cincinnati Negro newspaper. It stated that the conference was attended by Trotter and the president and vice-president of the Equal Rights League, N. S. Taylor and M. A. N. Shaw. They asked for federal action against lynching, denial of the vote, abolition of segregated travel, and the end of segregation in the executive department of the national government. "Senator Harding promised a careful study of the Congressional measures to the end of correction of the abuses. He declared emphatically against federal segregation and said, 'If the U.S. cannot prevent segregation in its own service we are not in any sense a democracy.' The League officers expressed to him satisfaction with the candidate's acceptance speech statement. Taylor, Shaw and Trotter said league officers would support Harding vigorously." [18]

4

If any of the militant Negroes still thought that Harding's Negro equality talk was what they wanted it to be, their hopes ended with his final campaign utterance on the subject. This occurred in Oklahoma City on October 9. There were other, more important subjects on his mind at this time, as, for instance, the League of Nations, on which he had expanded with unusual effect at Des Moines on October 7. But some party managers were saying that there was a chance to swing Oklahoma over into the Republican column. A speech was, therefore, scheduled for the capital of the Sooner state. It was obviously necessary to reassure the race-minded voters of this commonwealth of the essential moderation of his Negro rights idea.

Harding's Oklahoma stand on race relations included two points: (1) an assertion in favor of the separate-but-equal doctrine; and (2) a repudiation of the idea of the use of the force of the federal government in enabling the Negroes to vote.

Harding was forewarned and prepared on the subject. The morning issue of the October 9 *Daily Oklahoman* had asked him three sets of questions, two of which dealt with race relations.[19] One set was, "Do you or do you not favor race segregation? Do you or do you not favor separate cars for the white and black race; separate schools, restaurants, amusement places, etc.?" Harding's answer was a general assertion of "race equality before the law," but a specific endorsement of segregation. He said, "I can't come here and answer that for you. It is too serious a problem for some of us who don't know it as you do in your daily lives. But I wouldn't be fit to be president of the United States if I didn't tell you the same things here in the south that I tell in the north. I believe in race equality before the law. You can't give one right to a white man and deny it to a black man. But I want you to know that I do not mean that white people and black people shall be forced to associate together in accepting their equal rights at the hands of the nation."

On the subject of Negro voting, the *Daily Oklahoman* wanted to know whether he favored a revival of the attempt to pass the Lodge Force Bill of 1890 authorizing "the use of federal force if necessary to supervise elections in southern states, thereby guaranteeing the full vote of the great negro population of the south?" Harding's answer was a ringing no. "Let me tell you," he declared, "that the Force Bill has been dead for a quarter of a century. I'm only a normal American citizen, and a normal man couldn't resurrect the dead if he wanted to."

Such talk pleased southerners, but not the militant Negroes of the North. The latter made known their displeasure. On October 20, Trotter telegraphed from Westfield, Indiana that the Equal Rights League was disturbed. He requested to know whether Harding's Oklahoma speech "alters your statements to League at Marion or interprets their meaning." H. M. Harris of Washington, D.C. telegraphed in behalf of thirteen Negro rights advocates that Negro "disappointment is general." Harris demanded to know "if you are president whether you will stand on your pronouncement in Marion or in Oklahoma." To Trotter and Harris, Christian answered blandly that there was no conflict in Harding's various speeches, and no change in his position.[20]

Evidently there was widespread knowledge among the Negroes of Harding's segregationist stand in Oklahoma. At least the Republican organization said there was, and they took steps to stop its spread. The candidate was asked to say nothing more about it. On October 11, Senator New, head of the Chicago Republican publicity bureau, telegraphed Christian, "Please say to chief much excitement today among colored element over Oklahoma City answer. Avoid any further reference of any kind if possible." [21]

There was little or no knowledge of Harding's Oklahoma race remarks among northern whites. The press had much talk about Harding's desire to carry Democratic Oklahoma for the Republicans, but that was as far as it went. For example, the October 9 speech was represented in the *New York Times* of the next day as having dealt with oil and the League of Nations. No reference was made to the Negro part of his speech.

Not all Negro opinion was offended by the Oklahoma address. One Negro publisher was actually pleased by it. This was R. B. Montgomery of Minneapolis, editor and publisher of the *National Advocate*, "the leading Negro journal of the North West." "We have never heard such language," wrote Montgomery, on October 25, "from a Christian gentleman like yourself since the days of Abraham Lincoln, who was a friend to all the people. Thousands of Negro papers throughout the United States are supporting you and your coleague [*sic*] for the next President of the United States." [22]

There were many Negroes who could not see any difference between Harding and Trotter on the race question. This came from the ancient tradition that the Republican party was the Negroes' savior. Thought did not strain in the minds of some Negroes toward analysis of men's speeches. Even if the time came, as it always did, when the Negroes could not get all they expected, they would reason quite naturally that all race progress came from the Republicans. There was no hope from the Democrats because of their southern element. Typical of this kind of thinking was W. P. Dabney, editor of the Cincinnati Negro weekly, the *Union*. Dabney at all times boomed and boosted equally for Harding and Trotter. Dabney's October headlines for Harding were expansive: "Harding's Creed for Humanity"! "HARDING, DAVIS, WILLIS and the Entire Republican Ticket Must be Elected, then there will be an end of the segregation policies that have so disgraced a land consecrated to LIBERTY." For Trotter, the Negro editor was similarly expansive: "GAME AS A LION, LITTERED AND REARED IN THE JUNGLES OF DARKEST AFRICA." After Trotter had come and gone Dabney recorded, "He is anti-segregationist, anti-jim crowist, and the volleys fired by him against racial discrimination and its condonation by some of our servile people will bear good results." [23]

5

In 1920, the N.A.A.C.P. did not give the cause of Negro rights the vigorous support which it has in recent years. Perhaps what caused it to focus on the lynching problem and the situation in Haiti was the atmosphere of white resentment resulting from the race riots of 1919. In 1920, its most active leader, so far as the national political campaign was concerned, was field secretary James Weldon Johnson, whose chief concerns were with lynching and Haiti. On August 9, at the request of the N.A.A.C.P. board of directors, he and a few of his colleagues had visited Harding in Marion and presented him some questions involving lynching, federal aid to education, the United States occupation of Haiti, the right to vote, and certain aspects of segregation. According to Johnson, Harding told his callers that he agreed with them in principle about these things, but that "from the point of view of practical politics, he could not make them the subject of specific and detailed statements in a public address." Subsequent nudging from Johnson did not budge the Senator.[24]

However, developments in the Caribbean soon brought a meeting of minds between Johnson and Harding on Haiti. It happened that Haiti was one of the subjects discussed at the August 9 conference, and it also happened that Johnson was an expert on the matter. Indeed, on August 28, there appeared in the *Nation* the first of his exposure articles condemning the United States occupation of that island and the alleged mistreatment of its Negro inhabitants. Johnson sent Harding a copy of the August 28 article and promised "to show up exactly what the Washington Administration had done in Haiti." Three more articles followed weekly in the *Nation*, and Harding was supplied with copies.[25]

Whether by design or by accident, Harding soon injected himself into the Haiti problem in such a way as to be highly pleasing to Johnson and his N.A.A.C.P. colleagues. The Senator did this on September 17 in a speech blaming the "rape of Haiti" on vice-presidential candidate and Assistant Secretary of the Navy Franklin D. Roosevelt, who had publicly boasted that he had written the constitution of Haiti. Harding did not quote Johnson, but the spirit of his criticism was as sharp as Johnson's, and his few facts cited were among the many cited by Johnson. Harding's phrase was "thousands of native Haitians have been killed by American Marines and . . . many of our own gallant men have been sacrificed." Johnson's phrase was "the slaughter of three thousand and practically unarmed Haitians, with the incidentally needless death of a score of American boys." [26]

Whatever the connection was between Harding and Johnson on the Haitian question, the two of them certainly started some fireworks. Secretary of the Navy Daniels denied the charges, Roosevelt called them the "merest dribble," and Harding apologized in regard to personal charges, but added, "This does not in any way abate my opinion as to the policy of your Administration in dealing with Haiti and Santo Domingo." Then came the allegations by navy and army officers concerning the specifics of alleged American atrocities in Haiti. These were from Rear Admiral Harry S. Knapp, General John A. Lejeune, marine corps commandant in Haiti, and Brigadier General George Barnett, former marine corps commandant in Haiti. Civilian commentators also added their gory contributions. The result was that on October 15 Secretary Daniels ordered an official inquiry, and by October 19 a full board of inquiry was holding sessions.[27]

There was instant rejoicing of the N.A.A.C.P. and congratulations to Harding. When Daniels and Roosevelt started squirming, Johnson wrote on September 21, "I see that you have finally gotten under the skin of the Wilson administration. You have smoked them out and got them on the run and I hope that you will keep them running." He added, "You may depend upon the reliability of the facts given in the information which I sent you." Then, on October 14, when Daniels ordered his investigation, Mary White Ovington, chairman of the board of the N.A.A.C.P., exultingly wired Harding, "The N.A.A.C.P. congratulates you upon the result of inquiry into the unconstitutional and brutal invasion of Haiti." A few days later, Negro attorney Samuel B. Hill of Washington, D.C. recorded his gratitude feelingly as he wrote George Christian, "May the God of our fathers preserve and keep the Senator for the benefit of America and her people without harm." [28]

The Harding-Republican moderation on the Negro rights issue was well advised; it kept the "lily-white" backlash down to size. If Harding had yielded to the integrationists, he would have damaged his appeal to race-minded whites. The fact is that south of the Mason and Dixon line, where the backlash was greatest, there was a gain in the Republican vote in 1920 over the 1916 vote of from 41.5 per cent to 46.5 per cent.[29]

Harding's moderation consisted of three main factors: (1) concentrating his courting of Negro voters upon Negroes in the North; (2) favoring Negro political and civil equality on a segregated basis; and (3) confining specifics to such matters as opposition to lynching and the alleged Democratic fiasco in Haiti.

But there was a backlash movement against Harding himself, immeasurable as its effect on voters north and south might have been. As the campaign waned and Democratic prospects for success seemed to wane also, the Democrats, north as well as south, challenged their opponents with two devices. One was the charge that Republicans were endangering white supremacy; the other was an attempt to smear Harding with allegations that he had Negro forebears.

Ohio became a minor storm center on the integration issue. The Democrats could not raise the question of Negro equality in the nation at large because Harding had repudiated such designs in his

Oklahoma address. But Buckeye Democrats were hinting about the opposition to Negro equality in Ohio. In a circular letter sent out on September 16 from Columbus, Governor of Arkansas Charles H. Brough told of his conferring with W. W. Durbin, chairman of the Ohio Democratic state executive committee. Durbin told him that the *Toledo Pioneer* was "urging race equality and urging the Negroes to unite at the polls." This led Brough to include Harding in his criticisms. "It is current knowledge here in the Middle West," wrote the Arkansas governor, "that if Senator Harding and the Republicans triumph, an effort will be made to pass a Force Bill, which will mean Federal bayonets to supervise Southern elections." The Governor also said that Harding's Colored Voters' Day speech of September 10 led Trotter to speak to the Columbus Negro Baptist Convention in favor of equal rights in hotels, restaurants, and elevators and to assert "the oneness of the white and black races." [30]

In mid-October Durbin and the Ohio Democrats came out boldly with the release by the state executive committee of a circular entitled "A Timely Warning to the White Men and Women of Ohio." The circular claimed that the recent great influx into Ohio of southern Negroes plus the enfranchisement of women threatened to give Negroes the balance of power in Ohio politics. Central to their concern was their fear of the Republican candidate for Governor, Harry L. Davis. As mayor of Cleveland Davis had appointed twenty-seven Negroes to the city police force and had placed other Negroes in lucrative positions, the aggregate annual salaries of which exceeded $350,000. It was claimed that in some cities the crowding of Negroes had brought about serious consequences by their moving into residential districts and depressing the value of the properties therein. Referring to certain Negro newspapers, the circular declared, "We find them openly predicting that full social equality will be ensured them by the election of Republican candidates." One of these, the *Toledo Pioneer* of September 11, had editorially urged its readers to vote for Davis and other Republican candidates for the legislature so that a law would be passed "making it a felony to discriminate against a negro on account of his race." [31]

The Durbin circular gave Harding his share of the blame for this rise of integrationist agitation. Citing his acceptance speech and his Oklahoma address, it claimed that the *Toledo Pioneer* and the *Cleveland Advocate* informed their readers "that the Republican nominee for President, if elected would make himself a champion of that cause." Further details emphasized that these illiterate and ill-paid newcomers were "haunted by aspirations for social equality." The encouragement given by the Republicans "of such ambitions can only result in greatly magnifying the evils we are facing." [32]

Reference to the pages of the *Cleveland Advocate* for 1920 does not confirm the Democratic allegations of specifics by Harding on Negro integration. The talk was in that direction, but it was toned down in the face of overwhelming opposition. It did so in respect to Harding's segregation speech in Oklahoma. In April the *Advocate*, in supporting Wood against Harding in the primaries, editorially had condemned Harding, saying that his association with "lily-white Republicans in the South stamps him as a man opposed to EQUAL JUSTICE for the race." Yet when Harding, as nominee, made his segregation remarks at Oklahoma City in October, the *Advocate* ardently supported him, and was willing to let people make their own interpretations. "There are many," said the editor, "who feel that the statement is upstanding while there seems [*sic*] to be equally as many who regard it as unfortunate. Some are saying that the remarks inject a quasi-social issue, which has nothing to do with political matters, while others declare that it means the Senator favors 'jim-crow' cars. Sober thinkers seem to be willing to give it the benefit of the doubt, and accept the many other upstanding utterances as demonstrating the attitude of the candidate if he is elected President." *Advocate* writer Tyler expressed this feeling of resignation in another issue of the paper. "It is quite likely," he wrote on September 25, "that Senator Harding's advocacy of patience, and desistence from forcing what the race conceives its just dues, will meet the approbation of those who are always optimistic even in the face of the most disheartening discrimination, preaching patience rather than radicalism, at all times." [33]

A most interesting phase of the backlash *against* Harding came when certain "lily-whites" discovered a leaflet originally published in Cleveland *in support of Harding*. This leaflet contained a montage of nine pictures—three were of Harding, Frank B. Willis (Ohio candidate for United States Senator), and Harry L. Davis (candidate for Ohio Governor). These were flanked by photos of six Republican Negro candidates for the Ohio legislature. The leaflet was entitled "EQUALITY FOR ALL," and contained, at the bottom, a quotation from Harding's Oklahoma City speech stating, "I want you to know that I believe in equality before the law. That is one of the guarantees of the American Constitution. You can not give one right to a white man and deny the same right to a black man." *The sentences stating that these rights should be enjoyed in a segregated manner were omitted.* The leaflet was issued by Walter L. Brown of Cleveland, and contained the union label.[34]

Democratic segregationists north and south seized upon this leaflet, republished it, and gave it wide circulation to prove that Harding was an integrationist. It was referred to critically in a *Cincinnati Times-Star* editorial on October 29. The writer said, "For a week or more local Democrats have been circulating a card on which are portraits of the Republican candidates for President, Governor and Senator. Grouped around them are pictures of the Negro Republican candidates for the Legislature." One horrified lady, Mrs. E. Taylor of Mt. Victory, Ohio, wrote Harding, imploring him to say that it was not true. She enclosed a copy of the leaflet on which she wrote, "is it true Mr. Harding is it true oh i can not believe it." On October 26, another much disturbed gentleman, Frank E. Linny of Greensboro, North Carolina, chairman of the state Republican committee, telegraphed in consternation that the Democrats were about to circulate that leaflet. Linny's letter concluded, "Answer giving facts." Two Oklahoma Republicans sent in copies of the leaflet, one commenting that it was an example of "the dirty gutter politics" of Democrats. There seem to be no copies of replies to these letters in the Harding Papers.[35]

7

Charges of the Harding family's alleged Negro ancestry had been circulating for almost one hundred years. On October 22, 1920 George Christian, writing to Samuel C. McClure, publisher of the *Youngstown Telegram*, in reply to inquiries, said that the Negro ancestry charge was an "ancient lie which has been revived by the opposition." Christian said that it went back to a chance and malicious remark during an abolition of slavery campaign nearly a hundred years ago. He added, of course, that it had no basis in fact and that Harding had "always refused to dignify it by denial and attention." [36]

It is apparent that Harding was the object of such allegations, made with slanderous intent, throughout his life. The first reference to the Negro ancestry charges that has been uncovered is found in the *Marion Independent* of May 20, 1887. The *Independent* was Marion's first Republican newspaper. The development of the rival Republican

Marion Star, under Warren Harding's editorship, produced a verbal war between the two papers. The *Independent's* editor, George Crawford, was jealous of Harding and feared the *Star's* rivalry in the contest for official spokesmanship of the Republican party. As was the custom in those days, Crawford and Harding engaged in the exchange of mud-slinging epithets. On May 20, the *Independent* called the *Star* a "smut machine," and its editor a "kink-haired youth." The next day the enraged Harding fired back and notified the "retailer of Harding's genealogy" that he was a "lying dog" and "a miserable coward." On May 24, the *Independent* brought the exchange to an end by making a half-hearted apology. In the process the Democratic *Mirror*, on May 23, printed all the charges and countercharges, and mocked the *Independent's* apology as a "beautiful. . . specimen of crawfishing."

In none of his political campaigns did Harding seem to be exempt from these mixed-blood attacks. At least that is what the editor of the Philadelphia *Public Ledger* implied in the midst of the October, 1920 muckfest. "Such an effort to slay Senator Harding," said the editor, "has been in *progress* ever since his nomination. In fact, it has been tried repeatedly in his previous campaigns in Ohio. We have long known of the facts in this office, but have felt that there was no public good to be accomplished by open comment." [37]

The Republican national committee became officially aware of the situation in August and was ready with authentic genealogical data if and when needed. On August 20, West Virginia Senator Howard Sutherland wrote Hays that Democratic candidate Cox had told the game warden of that state "that either the grandmother or great grandmother of Senator Harding was a Negress." After some exchange of correspondence, Hays promised Sutherland that he would follow up the matter and "take the vigorous steps you mentioned if necessary." [38] What these steps were was not mentioned in the Hays Papers, but it is evident from the Harding Papers that one step was to get the facts on Harding's ancestry from the accepted family genealogist. This authority on Harding's ancestry was John C. Harding of Chicago, who wrote to his senatorial relative on October 16 that he was loaning "a book containing the Harding genealogy" to the Republican national committee, "who were seeking authentic information to overcome certain propaganda . . . used to some extent by your opponent." In his reply Harding made one of the few references to the Negro slander so far discovered. "It was fortunate," the Senator said, "that you were able to furnish the data requested, although I do not as yet know what use will be made of it. I have always been averse to dignifying this talk with attention or denial, but if finally deemed necessary we will stamp it as the unmitigated lie it is." [39]

For a while, the anti-Harding mixed-blood gossip circulated via underground methods. For example, there was a one-page mimeographed sheet entitled "Genealogy of Warren G. Harding of Marion, Ohio," and authorized by "Prof. William E. Chancellor of Wooster University, Wooster, Ohio." This came to be called the "Harding Family Tree," and read as follows:

Geo. Tryon Harding Great Grandfather (BLACK)	Ann Roberts Great Grandmother (BLACK)
Charles A. Harding Grandfather (BLACK)	Mary Ann Crawford Grandmother (WHITE)
George Tryon Harding, 2nd. Father (MULATTO)	Phoebe Dickerson Mother (WHITE)
Warren G. Harding Son	

No children have been born to Harding.

One of the senders of this sheet, A. A. Graham, of Kansas, said it had appeared "on the lines of the Rock Island railroad in southwestern Kansas." [40]

There were others. Mrs. S. B. Williams of Columbus wrote with indignation, telling of having attended a political meeting at Memorial Hall. "I saw a man," she said, "with a copy of something reading it to a younger man. So womanlike I listened, and here he was reading what he said was a copy of the Court Records of Marion, trying to prove to the younger man that you had negro blood." [41] George Clark of the Ohio Republican advisory committee called this "moonlighting." He told of "paid emissaries . . . going from house to house spreading vile slanders. . . . From vest pockets are drawn statements which dare not be printed in the open." [42] The *Youngstown Telegram* of November 1 carried a story telling how, for weeks, a whispering campaign had been going on in the border states supported by handbills and anonymous circulars that "appeared mysteriously between night and morning. . . . Women who answered rings of the doorbell late at night were told hastily and emphatically by persons who seemed respectable enough that Senator Harding's blood was not pure white." Particularly vicious was a paper strip attached to a picture of Harding's father, seemingly of dark complexion, the strip reading, "KEEP WHITE [picture of a house] WHITE VOTE FOR [picture of a rooster]." [43]

Many showed deep concern about the effect of the mixed-blood taunts. Traveling man Don Cox of Coshocton wrote with much agitation that people were telling him "that no matter how anxious they might be to vote for you they positively would not do so "BECAUSE YOU HAVE NIGGER BLOOD IN YOU." "For God's sake," he implored, "get busy stamping it out." H. H. Abee of Hickey, North Carolina told of people circulating these stories and wanted to know if such persons should be arrested. "Rush answers," wrote Abee. Franklin Williams of Cambridge, Ohio reported that there were many voters who say that they "will not vote for a nigger President." He added that there are stories that "you are chasing around with another woman." S. A. Ringer of Ada, Ohio, said that the *Pathfinder* magazine printed that "you are one fourth negro." "As a result," added Ringer, "thousands of voters, especially the women voters, may be caused to vote against you." W. W. Cowen of St. Clairsville, Ohio reported a story that "Harding was stopped in Masonry because he had negro blood." "If this charge is not true," wrote James Curren of Cincinnati, "why don't you protest. If not you will lose quite a lot of votes." These are only a few of the many references in the Harding Papers to the Negro reports. To most of them, Harding's office replied that they were not true, "baseless lies," "mendacious slanders," and so forth. [44]

Chief villain in the backlash campaign of anti-Harding genealogical slander was William Estabrook Chancellor, author of the previously cited "Harding Family Tree." This strange person claimed to have the highest credentials for his "facts" about Harding. He was professor of economics, politics, and social science at Wooster College, author of several books including *Our Presidents and Their Office*, and apparently one-time superintendent of schools in Washington, D.C. Above all, he was an ardent Democrat. Earlier in the campaign, in a letter to the *Plain Dealer*, he had praised Wilson and the League of Nations and criticized Harding for his anti-internationalism. He had inciden-

tally shown his anti-Semitic feelings by claiming that the high com-
missars of the Soviet Union were all Jews seeking revenge for the
pogroms and other discriminations of the past. Now, as the campaign
closed, he applied his alleged high scientific qualifications to the
production of "proof" of Harding's Negro ancestry. Chancellor later
denied his authorship, claiming that a Republican of the same name
was responsible.[45]

Among the products of Chancellor's "researches" were posters that
certain Democrats were willing to finance and release for circulation
to help save the country, as they said, from a Negro President and his
radical pro-Negro ideas. One of these, dated October 18, 1920, was
addressed "To the Men and Women of America AN OPEN LETTER." [46] It
was said to be the result of several weeks of touring the country area
of Harding's youth, and of Chancellor's interviews with hundreds of
people. The poster stated that the Hardings had never been accepted
as white people. Warren Harding himself "was not a white man." He
was said to represent "the results of social equality through free race
relations." Referring to Harding's Central College days at Iberia,
Chancellor wrote, "Everyone without exception says that Warren
Gamaliel Harding was always considered a colored boy and nick-
named accordingly."

Chancellor offered in support of these allegations four notarized
affidavits which he said he collected from former residents of the
Blooming Grove area, whom he interviewed in Marion and Akron.
These affidavits were printed in full. From these folks he obtained "the
common report" of "lifelong residents" of the area centering around
Blooming Grove. He claimed that he himself was an ethnologist
trained in scientific methods.

The statements in these affidavits were very specific. Harding's
father-in-law, Amos H. Kling, was represented as having stumped the
thirteenth state senatorial district in 1899, opposing his son-in-law's
candidacy for the senate on the grounds that Harding was a colored
man. Kling was quoted as having declared on the streets of Marion at
the time of his daughter's marriage that she was marrying a Negro.
Another affidavit raked up the story of the murder, in 1849, of Amos
D. Smith by David Butler because Smith called Mrs. Butler a Negress.
Mrs. Butler was a granddaughter of Amos Harding, and a cousin of
Warren Harding's grandfather.

Suddenly, in the last days of the campaign, the slander stories burst out on the front pages of some of the nation's leading Republican newspapers. The strategy was to show that the scurrilous Chancellor and his Democratic backers had gone too far in their dirty work.

Leading off was the Republican *Dayton Journal.* On October 29, the *Journal,* in a frenzy of outrage, blasted forth with full-spread, front-page headlines five rows deep:

THE VILE SLANDERERS OF SENATOR HARDING AND HIS FAMILY
WILL SEEK THEIR SKUNK HOLES 'ERE TODAYS SUN SHALL
HAVE SET
THE MOST DAMNABLE CONSPIRACY IN HISTORY OF AMERICAN POLITICS

Over half of the front page was given to an open letter "To the Men and Women of Dayton" by editor E. G. Burkam. It told of the circulation "in cowardly secrecy" of "thousands upon thousands of typrwritten mimeographed and even printed statements usually under the heading of 'Harding's Family Tree.'" "These vile circulars," wrote the editor, "declare that Warren G. Harding has Negro blood in his veins." These allegations "ARE A LIE. Warren G. Harding has the blood of but one race in his veins—that of the white race—the pure inheritance of a fine line of ancestors, of good men and women." The next day the entire front page of the *Journal* was given to statements of rebuttal under the headlines:

The Whole Vile Structure of the Slanderers Crumbles
Under the Avalanche of Evidence

The Democrats countered with their own charges of falsehood, saying that the racial attack on Harding originated with the Republicans of Ohio in their own primary campaign.[47]

Across the nation swept the news of the attacks on Harding's ancestry. Even the stately *New York Times* gave the slanders front-page headlines. It was there reported that Professor Chancellor had been dismissed from the Wooster College faculty for his alleged authorship of the circulars. Republican press agents thereupon rushed to the defense of their candidate with reams of genealogical copy about the Harding family. The *Times* called upon genealogist Charles A. Hanna to enter the lists. Others traced the name of Harding back to the Domesday Book of 1086.[48] Genealogical antiquity momentarily had front-page billing.

More posters were produced. When Republican reporters besieged the ousted Professor Chancellor, they got him so confused that he was quoted in the *Dayton Journal* as having denied that he was the author of the anti-Harding posters. Thereupon, another set of posters came out, sponsored by the Democrats. One of them, "The Truth Will Out!", was issued from Columbus "By Order of Democratic Ex. Com.," and signed by chairman Ira Andrews and secretary Frank Lowther.[49] In this the professor was quoted as saying that he had not denied his authorship of the Negro stories, and that he was suing the Dayton *Journal* for saying that he had. Even Republican national chairman Will Hays was threatened with a lawsuit if he did not withdraw his attacks on Chancellor's genealogical reputability.

Republican posters to counteract Democratic posters appeared. One of them, entitled "The Harding stock," was issued by the Ohio Republican state executive committee. It contained a chart of the Harding descent from the time of Stephen Harding, the "blacksmith of Providence." [50] This Republican production reeked with boldness and bravado. Long residence in America, it said, has not robbed the Hardings of "the characteristics so pronounced in the Celt and the German." "The blue and gray eyes of the Hardings of today are a legacy from the Scotch-Irish blood that entered the family through the Crawfords." In Harding's veins "flow the blood of English, German, Welsh, Irish and Dutch." And this blood "has been spent on battlefields where the stake was justice and independence." The Hardings were represented as the chief victims of the Wyoming Indian Massacre of July 3, 1778. " 'Remember the Fate of the Hardings' was the cry which rang through the Wyoming valley as a party of settlers sallied forth to wreak vengeance on the blood thirsty savages." Lord Hardinge, British Viceroy of India from 1910–1916, was said to be "undoubtedly a relative of the Ohio Senator."

On Marion street corners things got pretty hot. On November 1, in front of a cigar store, Harding's father, Dr. George, approached Democratic Judge W. S. Spencer and loudly accused him of responsibility for circulating the Negro-blood stories. A friend of Dr. Harding repeated the charges. "You're a liar," shouted the judge. The doctor's friend thereupon punched the judge in the face. "Hit him again," shouted the crowd, and the judge was knocked to the sidewalk. The affair ended with Dr. Harding assisting the judge into the near-by courthouse.[51]

8

Obviously, in the hysteria of the closing days of the campaign the discussion of Negro rights had moved far away from the merits of the issue. Whether Harding gained or lost in the melee cannot be decided. It was said that the mixed-blood charges hurt him most in the border states, costing him votes that might have gone into the Republican column. Possibly so. However, his segregation comments at Oklahoma City probably helped counteract this loss. It is impossible, statistically, to measure the effect of the many factors influencing the voters' choices.

The 1920 presidential election statistics show a definite gain in the border states for the Republican party over the returns for 1916. Assuming the border states to be Arkansas, Delaware, Kentucky, Missouri, North Carolina, Tennessee, Maryland, Virginia, and West Virginia—five of them went Republican in 1920 (Delaware, Maryland, Missouri, Tennessee, and West Virginia), whereas only two went Republican in 1916 (Delaware and West Virginia). Of the total votes of the border states awarded to the Republican and Democratic candidates, 51 per cent went to the Republicans in 1920 as against 45 per cent in 1916. In other southern states the same trend in favor of the Republicans was to be observed. For one thing, Oklahoma supported Harding 243,415 to 215,521, as against 148,113 to 97,233 for Wilson in 1916. Taking the South as a whole (including the border states), the figures are: 46.5 per cent Republican in 1920 as against 41.5 per cent in 1916.[52]

A full-scale analysis of all the reasons for Republican gains in the South in 1920 cannot be undertaken in this volume, but it can be pointed out that Harding's Negro policy did not offset those factors which caused such an increase in Republican votes in the South. It is evident that, to some degree, the injection of the mixed-blood issue softened the backlash against Harding. An example of this was his ever-loyal brother in Moosedom, James J. Davis. "It's very seldom," wrote the enraged director-general of the Loyal Order of the Moose, "I go off on a tangent, but if I could have gotten a hold of that professor that's circulating that stuff on you, I'm sure I'd have punched his snout and punched it hard, but I guess it's best that we never met."[53] Equally indignant but more restrained were the dignified publishers of the *Cincinnati Times-Star*, Charles P. Taft and

Hulbert Taft. These gentlemen made a front-page news item out of "The Truth about Harding's Ancestry." The Democratic charges were headlined as falsehoods and "Sneaking Propaganda." In a signed editorial they declared that the Democratic tactics had "turned the clock back fifty years." [54] In Tennessee, the Democratic *Chattanooga Times* not only refused to print the Chancellor material but gave strong support to the Tafts' handling of the charges against Harding.[55] And there was the ever-critical journalist Robert Scripps, who, according to Samuel Hopkins Adams, wrote, "Tell him we don't care whether it is true or not. We won't touch it." [56]

In conclusion, on the merits of Negro rights Harding had made little progress. As in so many other problems, he had done more for the party than for the people. He was essentially two-faced on this issue. In the North he talked Negro rights but avoided specifics, taking advantage of the non-militancy of the Negro religious leaders, the anti–race riot feeling, the red scare mood of the general public, and the willingness of the N.A.A.C.P. to be satisfied with proposed reforms on the lynching question and on United States Haitian policy. In the South he soft-pedaled the race question and gave specific assurances of continued segregation. Nevertheless, he had prepared the way for two specific reforms, minimal though they were: antilynching legislation, and withdrawal of the Marines from Haiti. He received praise from some, but not all, Negro leaders, and he was severely attacked by white racists.

CHAPTER TWENTY-THREE

Campaign Forum on the League of Nations

"Opinions must be reconciled and harmonized if we are to have any international association at all." : : : *Harding in Des Moines address, October 7, 1920*

"Everyplace I went I found them a unit against article 10 of the League of Nations and feeling very friendly towards 'Harding's League of Nations' as they put it." : : : *"W. B. W." in New York to Harry Daugherty, September 1, 1920, Harding Papers, Ohio Historical Society*

A key to an understanding of Harding's campaign position on the League of Nations is that he desired to make the proposed terms of the League covenant discussable. President Wilson, in the preliminaries of the League movement, had not made them so. With the conviction of an intellectual and moralist dealing with a complex problem, Wilson presented his covenant as a *fait accompli*. Criticism, seemingly asked for in all sincerity, was met by a disposition to concede only a minimum, on the ground that much criticism was unworthy because politically inspired. And yet he made the fatal political mistake of failing to realize his moral responsibility to recognize, after the Republican victory in the congressional election of 1918, competent Republican counsel in league-making. To have failed to appoint to his peacemaking delegation one or more Republican experts on foreign affairs of the caliber of Elihu Root, William Howard Taft, or Charles Evans Hughes was unpardonable.

It was a time for a leader to bring the American people into his confidence when dealing with a great new subject like the League and its international commitments. For this, Harding was much better qualified than was Woodrow Wilson. Under the President's guidance a pattern had been set that seemed to make the League open for discussion only to those in the President's inner circles. One of these circles consisted of those who enjoyed Wilson's confidence. Another was composed of the diplomats at the Paris Conference, with its requirements of secrecy. With Harding, however, there was a choice. He was willing to consider the possibilities of another type of league, or of "an association," or the League itself—with reservations.

Thus, freedom of discussion itself became an important issue in the campaign of 1920, much to the disadvantage of the Democrats, bound as they were to the Wilson League. The common man did not appreciate the need for, and the niceties of, the diplomatic secrecy to which Wilson had had to submit. He loved open discussion, especially about a League that affected his much cherished Americanism. Wilson's moral and international preachments during the war about world security and world democracy had not taken hold of his mind or heart.

In a political sense, Harding's opposition to the Wilson League was more practically based than was Cox's support of that League. The Wilson-Cox singlemindedness, or obstinacy, lost them the backing of the proponents of other means of American relationships to world affairs. There were those who would accept the League with strong reservations, and others with mild reservations. Still others were for a renegotiation of the entire matter, or desire a world court as arbiter in justiciable disputes. There were those who talked of an international association, without being definite as to what they meant. Some felt that general disarmament was an obtainable objective. Always there was strong feeling about the protection of American sovereignty and independence. Not even Hiram Johnson and William E. Borah were totally isolationist in regard to "common sense" international relations.

Harding's first problem was to get the Republican supporters of different views to stick together. He had to make sure that no single faction got the upper hand with its particular brand of foreign relationship. When former Governor of Colorado Herbert S. Hadley suggested the idea of codifying international law under the auspices and enforcement of a world court, which Harding later specified, the candidate replied that he was going to go into the subject matter of foreign policy, but that he had to be vague for a while until he had the party united. "It is a very particular business," he declared, "to harmonize the party this year and I am going to do my best to bring it about." [1]

This broad-based, party-unifying approach to foreign affairs was not Harding's invention: it was a mandate from the Republican party platform. Fortunately, the foreign-policy plank had been prepared by one of the most broadminded elder statesmen in the party—Elihu Root. This was engineered by Henry Cabot Lodge and was in line with Lodge's tactics of emphasizing Republican competence in the foreign affairs field, in contrast with President Wilson's failure to consult with the "best minds" in the Republican party. In the 1919 Senate investigations, Lodge had consulted with Root in laying the foundations of the reservations approach to the League in the 1919 investigations, and he did it again in the Republican convention in June of 1920. Lodge came to the convention armed with the Root plank, which he was able to get adopted.[2]

Essentially, the Root plank asserted the premise that internationalism and Americanism were compatible. There could be an association of nations with the United States in it and without imperiling American independence. "We believe," it said, "that such an international association must be based on international justice." World peace would thus be furthered by the creation and recognition of international law, its interpretation by a world court, and the requirement of international conferences and cooling-off periods in times of crisis. It was specifically stated that "all this can be done without the compromise of national independence, without depriving the people of the United States in advance of the right to determine for themselves what is just and fair when the occasion arises, and without involving them as participants and not as peace-makers in a multitude of quarrels, the merits of which they are unable to judge."

A bit of denouncing of Democrats was added for irreconcilable and isolationistic consumption. The Wilson League, the platform said, "contains stipulations, not only intolerable for an independent people, but certain to produce the injustice, hostility, and controversy among nations which it is proposed to prevent." The League covenant repudiated "the time-honored policies in favor of peace declared by Washington, Jefferson and Monroe, and pursued by all American administrations for more than a century, and it governed the universal sentiment of America for generations past in favor of international law and arbitration, and it rested the hope of the future upon mere expediency and negotiations." Wilson's arbitrary ignoring of the opinion of a majority of the Senate, "which shares with him in the treaty making power," was condemned. "The Senators performed their duty faithfully. We approve their conduct and honor their courage and fidelity."[3]

2

Harding's first task in getting Republican unity in international policy was to appease the irreconcilables. During the Senate ratification debate in 1919 they had been against the Wilson League with or without reservations. The question in the 1920 campaign was what kind of league, association, or world court they would support. It was assumed that they would not be irreconcilable to something Republican. It was assumed that they would be full supporters of whatever international policy the Republican party should agree upon.

Harding's technique was to confer upon the leader of the irreconcilables the honor of being the first to announce official Republican policy on international relations. This, of course, was California Senator Hiram Johnson, and the honor which Harding conferred upon him was taken with all the seriousness that was one of Johnson's outstanding characteristics. It was done with the sole and deliberate intention of bringing Johnson's Progressive followers into the Republican camp.[4]

Harding disliked what he believed was Johnson's personal politicking in the League debate. In 1919 Harding was of the private opinion that the outspoken Johnson and the equally bellicose Senator William E. Borah were using the League issue to seek "publicity and political favor."[5] They had made Wilson's "swing around the circle" in behalf of the League of Nations an occasion to launch a counterdrive in which they thundered their Americanism and denounced Wilsonian internationalism. Harding, of course, had been as guilty of this in his senatorial and other fulminations. But that was when he was merely a Senator from Ohio wanting to be reelected. Now he was a candidate for the Presidency of the United States, and a spokesman for the entire Republican party. It was thus in order for him to give Johnson a full treatment of flattery and cajolery.

The statement, which Johnson made and which Harding elevated into official Republican policy, was released to the public on July 7. The occasion was the action of the Democratic national convention in nominating James M. Cox for President on a platform of the endorsement of the Wilson League of Nations. As leader of the Progressives, Johnson made it clear that his support must go to Harding and the anti-League position of the Republican party. "The overshadowing question of the campaign," Johnson said, "is whether we enter the maelstrom of European and Asiatic politics and diplomacy and become a pawn of the cynical imperialism of the Old World, or whether America shall live her life in her own way, independent, unfettered, mindful always of her obligations to humanity and civilization but free to act as each crisis shall arise, and maintaining always the policy of Washington, Jefferson and Monroe, of friendship with all nations, entangling alliances with none." [6]

Harding's conciliatory desire to preserve party unity on the League question was well revealed in his handling of this statement of Johnson. Although sharply anti-foreign, it had enough of a glimmer of recognition of American "obligations to humanity and civilization" to enable Harding to credit Johnson with a more balanced attitude than his earlier irreconcilability had shown. At least that is what he could say to Johnson. At the same time, Harding could take the much-better-balanced Root plank of the Republican platform and elaborate upon it to the general public in his July 22 acceptance speech. Having thus impressed the public with the broad Root-based view, he could cajole Johnson privately by telling him that the view was Johnson-based.

Thus did the wily Harding speak for internationalism and Americanism on acceptance day. Using the Republican platform, Harding elaborated on the compatibility of the two approaches. "I can speak unreservedly," he said, "of the American aspiration and the Republican committal for an association of nations, cooperating in sublime accord, to attain and preserve peace through justice rather than force, determined to add to security through international law, so clarified that no misconstruction can be possible without affronting world honor." He spoke feelingly of the need of reduced armaments throughout the world. This could be done without sacrificing American sovereignty and independence in a "world super-government." "No surrender of rights to a world council or its military alliance, no assumed mandatory, however appealing, ever shall summon the sons of this republic to war. Their supreme sacrifice shall only be asked for America and its call of honor. There is a sanctity in the right we will not delegate." [7]

Johnson was quick to take the cue. "Mr. Harding's position," he said, following the acceptance speech, "has made Republican success certain and his election assured." He gloried in the Americanism of it, and allowed himself to say that after Harding was in office "we may proceed deliberately, reflectively to a world relationship that would hold us free from menacing involvements."[8]

This made it easy for Harding. He proceeded—privately, of course —to give Johnson credit for the whole idea of the balance of Americanism and internationalism. It was a very nice way of telling the Old Irreconcilable of 1919 that he was no longer considered to be irreconcilable. In a letter of July 27, Harding said that he was so glad that Johnson understood the necessity of performing "a party service in making it possible for the divergent elements of the party to come together, with the assurance of preserved nationality, on the one hand, and a readiness to participate in performing a recognized duty to world civilization on the other." Then Harding penned those words of the highest flattery: "I did not mean to add to the interpretation which you have already made quite correctly and which will stand as the official utterances of our international relationship."[9] There is no little irony in the thought of Harding and Johnson clasping hands as leaders of American internationalism.

Meanwhile, others high in the Republican hierarchy were at work on Johnson's vanity, encouraging him to think of himself as a party leader. One of them was the new Progressive member of the national committee and friend of Johnson, Raymond Robins. Robins' letter to Johnson has not been available, but, according to Johnson's reply to that letter (as quoted in Robins' letter to Will Hays on August 11), Robins had asked Johnson and his friends to "indicate our [Johnson's] appreciation and support of Harding's acceptance of the issue on our terms." Johnson, of course, replied that he had already done so, and thereupon proceeded to lay down what he considered "our terms" to be. They were to oppose the Wilson League, and to be general about any substitute offered. There was to be no "Harding League of Nations" in place of a "Wilson League of Nations." "No man has sufficient ability and wit, over night, to fashion in detail a league of nations and any such attempt will be shot full of holes." Moreover, Johnson required that there should not be even a "league with reservations." All that Harding had to do was to "say that he will scrap the Wilson League, make peace, and then discuss another world covenant designed to prevent war, and to accomplish disarmament, but refusing to go into details."

These "terms" of Johnson approving "another world covenant" were quoted at length in Robins' letter to Hays of August 11. After quoting Johnson, Robins added, "In my judgment the above is a vital matter for holding the Johnson-Borah following. Can it not be brought to the consideration of Senator Harding?" The answer is to be found in the fact that the letter now reposes in the Harding Papers with the following notation by Hays: "W. G. H.—Not sure—W. H. H." [10]

As a matter of fact, Harding and Johnson were already ahead of Robins and Hays in agreeing to work together on the international issue. Johnson had received Harding's July 27 "You are our spokesman" letter, and, on August 9, had replied to it with his characteristic fervor: "I was delighted to have your note of July 27th. Of course I'm going into the campaign with all the vigor I possess. I haven't any doubt of your success." Johnson went on with the same suggestions, and sometimes in the same words, that he used in his letter to Robins, only much more humbly. "I'm sure you'll pardon a suggestion," he said, as he made his point about not specifying details in "your plan for international co-operation." "No man has wit enough, none is sufficiently wise, over night to devise a plan of international cooperation, which cannot the next morning be shot full of holes. . . . We will scrap the Wilson League of Nations, declare a state of peace as you indicate in your speech of Acceptance, and thereafter, as you have clearly put it, we will perform in our own way our recognized duty to world civilization." [11]

3

Here was Warren Harding again in his old patchwork, mirage-making, party-unifying role. This time he was dealing with something of vaster import than unifying public opinion through a newspaper, or holding the Ohio Republican party together with oratory and personality. The future of the nation and the world was at stake, and, in the long run, it required more than politicking to cope with it. But politicking is all it got, so far as Harding was concerned.

One of those who was shocked by the incongruity of the Harding-Johnson alliance was Herbert Hoover, who characteristically had no hesitation in saying so. On September 21, Harding had asked Hoover to help in the patching, by giving "a word of encouragement in support of our ticket" to his friends in California. Hoover replied that he was embarrassed by Harding's failure to contradict Johnson's isolationism. "The many people I am in contact with there," wrote Hoover, "agree that the difficulty lies in Senator Johnson's repeated distortions of your statements, because the League is a more vivid issue there than in most parts of the country. . . . Of the straight Republican vote, the majority are strongly for 'a' League, and it amounts to a conscientious issue of such importance that, on the uncontradicted basis of Senator Johnson's interpretations of the position of yourself and the party on the League, many will regretfully vote for governor Cox." Hoover cited three Republican newspaper editors who declined to "accept my assurances so long as Johnson's interpretations are allowed to stand." Hoover therefore phrased a paragraph for Harding to include in his forthcoming Woman Voters' Day speech of October 1 in which Harding would say specifically that the issue was not between "the" League and "no" League, but between "the" League and "a League or association erected on the basis that the Republican party had contended for from the beginning." This would keep everybody loyal without engaging in "polemics" with Johnson. Something had to be done to correct the constant repetition that "Senator Harding says the League is dead," that "Senator Harding has scrapped the League." People had come to believe that "the Republican party has no sincere intention." [12]

Harding made no such "correction." He proceeded to add Hoover to his flattery list. In his reply he first emphasized party unity and evasion of controversy. "You realize," he told Hoover, "the unwisdom of making specific or detailed commitments upon the subject, because if I am elected I shall be called upon to deal with conflicting views and commitments and to harmonize them so as to secure anything like an effective result." Then came the flattery. Harding noted that Hoover was following the suggestion made earlier of engaging in a campaign speaking tour to present the plans of the Republican party to put the government on a business basis. "No one can be so helpful in this regard as yourself. The whole country recognizes your supereminent ability as an organizer and director of large affairs." This was in line with an earlier comment, on August 7, "I want you to feel that you are a part of the big enterprise and that I am always anxious to have your enquiries and advice." [13]

Harding had gone a long way from his first impressions of Hoover's political abilities. Only a few months before, on February 4, he had expressed to Malcolm Jennings the opinion that the sentiment for Hoover was "ephemeral." "I am sure," Harding wrote, "he will never be considered by the Republican party. If the Democratic party wants to take him up, well and good." [14] Harding's political adjustability was never to be overestimated.

On at least one occasion there was a public confrontation on the League when Harding was asked whether he agreed with anti-League Johnson or pro-League Taft. His answer was a politician's master-piece, and, to his mind, entirely consistent: that he was presiding over a discussion. It was in Cleveland, on October 27 at Gray's Armory, where he had finished another of his orations on Americanism mixed with internationalism. A heckler arose and asked, "Do you stand with Johnson or do you stand with Taft?" Harding's answer was that, as a candidate for President, he did not ask that Johnson or Taft should agree with him. "That," he said, alluding to President Wilson's alleged non-consultative method of forcing his League on the people, "is what I'm rebelling against." He pointed out that that there were many sincere and divergent views about the proper form of America's relationship to the world, and it could not be hoped that a specific program could be evolved and all elements harmonized in a political campaign. "I have said," he concluded, "to Johnson, Taft, Hoover and Wickersham, and now I say it to you, I want to find a program back of which Americans can unite." [15]

There was at least one point of deception in Harding's answer. He did not tell his Cleveland listeners that he had privately told Johnson that the Californian's statement in July was the Republican party's "official utterance on our international relationship."

4

Having brought the chief isolationist into camp, Harding could now swing the emphasis of the League discussion back in the direction of the internationalists. It was the big thing to do. It was done with the big minds of the party and with big publicity. It was important to show the Republican party to be bigger than the Johnson faction, bigger than the Democrats and their false League of Nations bigness, bigger on foreign policy than ever before. That was the build-up for the biggest day in the front-porch campaign—International Relations Day, August 28, 1920.

It is important to emphasize that there were two contrasting dimen-sions to this display of Republican internationalism. One was to enlist the finest minds in the party to give Harding the benefit of their wisdom. The other was to give the event the widest publicity to impress the entire nation with the broadmindedness of the Republican party. It meant counselors of the stature of the brilliant Herbert Hoover and the party sage, Elihu Root, on the one hand, and public relations experts like Albert D. Lasker and Judson Welliver on the other.

It was high time for a Republican demonstration on internationalism. The concessions that Harding had made to Johnson and the irreconcilables had brought a chorus of protest from the world-minded wing of the party. They were infuriated by the cocky Johnson's arrogant assertion of party loyalty, while at the same time he blasted the Wilson League with all the ridicule at his command. When Harding let the fiery Californian's defiance go unchallenged, internationalist leaders began to think that Harding himself had abandoned the League. The candidate was flooded with letters and telegrams of protest, and his office was besieged by those who felt strongly about it. The voices of protest came from Republicans of the highest standing. They included Herbert Hoover, university presidents Jacob Gould Schurman of Cornell and Nicholas Murray Butler of Columbia, former national committee chairman, Charles D. Hilles, Wall Street financier Thomas D. Lamont, Senators Weeks and Lodge of Massachusetts, Senator Walter E. Edge of New Jersey, Speaker of the House Frederick H. Gillette, and former President William Howard Taft.

The reasoning of these distinguished gentlemen gave an excellent composite of the thinking of the internationalist wing of the Republican party. Of course there was Hoover, who, in an 800-word telegram, took the view that the failure of the League would bring world economic and political chaos which the Germans and the Russian Bolsheviks would be delighted to produce. American political and economic interests abroad were "unalterably affected" by the already established League. United States influence was especially needed on the Reparations Commission to prevent injury to international economic stability. The decline of American farm prices in the face of world food needs was caused in part by America's failure to have proper representation in Europe. Such considerations were far more important than the matter of national pride involved in article 10, which the irresponsible Johnsonites, "the worst forces in American public life," were raving about. This sort of thing would lead the "independent and thinking progressive vote" to refuse to take part in the election, and, in the long run, lead to the disintegration of the Republican party.[16]

President Schurman had a similarly enlarged idea of the need of the influence of the United States to prevent world chaos. He cited the many serious situations where the United States could do so much good. It should: stop the Japanese "stealing" of Shantung; moderate the vindictiveness of England and France in saddling Germany with impossible reparations; halt the perversion by the same nations of the League mandate system into crass imperialism; and accomplish the removal from the covenant of article 10 so as to substitute in its place moral influences and sanctions against all kinds of political and economic aggression. The nations needed a world court and arbitral tribunals for settling justiciable disputes, and "automatic conferences" for adjusting non-justiciable ones.[17]

Financier Lamont took the practical approach. The League of Nations was in existence, and therefore, it would be foolish to set up a rival organization headed by the United States. The League was already moving the people away from the "old world of alliances and armament," toward a new world where frontiers did not have to bristle with arms for self-defense. There were agencies for the referral of international disputes and the retarding of war fever. The United States had nothing better to offer; indeed, its refraining from support of the League meant the scrapping of the whole thing and the reversion to the old days of selfishness, rivalry, bitterness, and the arming of nations to the teeth. Lamont stressed, as did Hoover and Schurman, that catering to the old-fashioned bombast of the Johnson group was alienating the intellectual element in the party: "those young Republican and Independent voters all over the country" who believed in the application of thought to world problems.[18]

It is obvious that Hoover, Schurman, and Lamont saw, with deep insight, the need for a more stabilized world, and that they had the wisdom, and even the practical sense, to know the policies and procedures required to achieve one. They were, however, willing to temporize with the Hardings of their day, who preferred political unity to international unity. Neither they nor Harding realized what they were losing in order to make such little gain.

Other commentators did not burden Harding with analytical advice, but they produced rather cogent internationalist considerations. President Butler of Columbia University said that Johnson and Borah were not as popular in the West as they claimed, and that they were cunningly making it look as if the Republican party was dependent on them, when, actually, the reverse was the case.[19] Taft emphasized two points: (1) that America's former allies, especially England, were willing to make the concessions desired in America's League reservations; and (2) that if Cox was elected, he would refuse the necessary reservations and thus never get Senate ratification.[20] Lodge and Hilles were much more interested in meeting pro-League sentiment in the early Maine election so as to make the most of the role that "as Maine goes so goes the nation." [21]

Two other straws which showed the way the wind was blowing in favor of the internationalist view were the reception, by the public, of the publication of Harding's interview with David Lawrence on July 27 and the inclusion, the next day, of the pro-League platform in the New York State Republican platform. These events and their effect were described to Harding by President Schurman in the August 22 letter previously quoted. Schurman said that, when the Harding-Lawrence interview was published revealing "that what your policy actually contemplated was a revision of the treaty and modification of the covenant of the League to meet the views both of the United States and other nations, a general feeling of relief was perceptible among the members of the Republican party and, indeed, among Americans generally in this part of the country." [22] As for the League plank of the New York Republican convention, it left no room for doubt. "Believing that it is the paramount issue of the American people to-day," the New Yorkers resolved, "we favor the league of nations plank as contained in the national platform which declares for a league with such reservations as shall in every way protect the sovereignty and independence of the United States and always retain in congress alone the power to declare war." The national platform used no such specific language and the New York resolution was a most liberal interpretation thereof.[23]

To each of these advisers, Harding wrote more or less perfunctory notes of acknowledgment and thanks. The letters emphasized the need for party unity, for common sense, for compromise, for give and take. They assumed an optimism that all had not been lost, that, under the Republicans, prosperity and happiness would always spread their wings over a busy and contented people.

A reply that showed Harding most clearly the prisoner of party-uniting compromise in formulating a world policy instead of being a free man in his own choices was the one he made to Speaker Gillette. This gentleman had expressed disappointment that Harding, in his acceptance speech, had not said that he, as President, would submit the League covenant to the Senate with reservations. As Senator in 1919 Harding had, of course, voted to accept the League with reservations. If President Wilson had been agreeable, the United States would have joined the League forthwith. But it was different now in 1920. Harding was not as free as he had been as an Ohio Senator. He had to speak for all the party in all the states, and they were not all like Ohio or like Gillette's Massachusetts. "If I had chosen the course I preferred," Harding wrote Gillette, "very likely I should have followed the program suggested in your letter, but the situation which we contemplate now is not precisely the one which had to be met in the Senate, and I am inclined to think, after fullest reflection, that I took the course which is best inclined to unite our party. Of course, one can only do the best he knows how. It was impossible to harmonize my advisers on this subject and ultimately I took the course which seemed to me best. So far as I am personally concerned, I have no regrets to offer, but I should, of course, be very sorry if I adopted a policy which should in any way prove a hindrance to party success." [24]

5

An important thing to do in these preparations for the August 28 International Relations Day was to emphasize Harding's willingness to seek advice. Advising was news. It was in such complete contrast to the alleged Wilsonian and Democratic way of secret agreements secretly arrived at. Four days before the event, the word went out that Harding was rounding out a season of many-sided consultations. "Harding to Hear from Friend and Foe of the League," headlined the *Chicago Tribune*. It was reported that he had conferred with such friends of the League as Charles Evans Hughes, former Senator Sutherland of Utah, and Henry P. Davison, chairman of the board of the World League of Red Cross Societies. There were visits also by anti-Leaguers Colonel George Harvey and Ira A. Bennett, editor of the *Washington Post*. Many others came and went as Harding listened, questioned, thought, and wrote. "This," predicted Lasker, "probably will be the most important speech he will make during the whole campaign." In Marion the lights of Headquarters House on Mt. Vernon Avenue burned late as Welliver's typists, mailing clerks, and messenger boys prepared to deluge the nation with copy. Press associations were alerted for the great event. "I strongly advise," telegraphed Welliver to Bone in New York on August 25, "that most urgent representation be made to all press associations that this is the most important speech of the campaign and should be carried everywhere in full." [25]

How efficiently it was all arranged. Lasker had every detail under control—speed writing, advanced copies, press releases, billboard and magazine advertising, and the bringing of distinguished visitors to Marion. On August 18, Lasker informed campaign publicity manager Scott Bone in New York that Harding would finish his speech by August 23 so that before nightfall advanced printed copies would be brought to Chicago by messenger on the night train. On the morning of the twenty-fourth the Chicago office would start sending press releases to the "far points." On the twenty-fifth they would go to the "nearer points." All would reach their newspaper destinations forty-eight hours before the speech "in order that Republican editors may have a chance to thoroughly digest it and get their bearings." Lasker had arranged that Harding should use the slogan, "Let's be done with Wiggle and Wobble," so as to synchronize with the billboard advertising being set up throughout the nations. Advertisements of Harding's new internationalism to reach "22,000,000 women's circulation" were being readied for such magazines as the *Ladies' Home Journal* and the *Pictorial Review*. Copy was submitted to Harding for his approval:

> Harding promises you a compact of nations with the entanglements left out—a compact which will safeguard your business and your home.

Lasker had gone a bit too far. As they finally appeared in the October *Ladies' Home Journal* the words were:

> Harding is for peace, at home and abroad. Therefore, he fought against those Treaty commitments that would involve your country in European wars. He voted to recall your soldiers from Russia. He fought for the safety of your sons and the peace of your home.

As for distinguished visitors, letters were prepared for Harding to sign and send out. "I certainly hope," wrote Lasker to Christian in Marion, on August 24, "there has been no delay in sending out these invitations, as it is the crux of our publicity that these parties begin calling as soon as possible. I received an inquiry from the chairman [Hays] yesterday on the subject, and I hope to receive a wire from you, advising me when the invitations went out and to whom so that I can report to the chairman." [26]

Suddenly, on August 26, with two days to go, advice came from the greatest Republican of them all. A messenger arrived in Marion fresh from Europe with news from the long-silent Elihu Root. The messenger was Ohio's former Governor, Myron T. Herrick, who had it straight from Root what should be the outlines of a new plan for world peace. At least Herrick thought he had it straight. Root would be home, Herrick was quoted as saying, "very shortly, and I anticipate that his return will be followed by announcements of very important accomplishments that will go far toward clarifying the entire international situation." Herrick declined to elaborate on details, but he talked enough to the *Chicago Tribune* reporter to enable the latter to refer to "the plan for the international tribunal which Mr. Root is helping to build at The Hague as an adjunct to the League of Nations." The reporter added, "It is considered probable that some reference to a new league of nations, with the tribunal of justice as its foundation, will be made by the Senator in his address Saturday." Herrick emphasized the need for such a new league by claiming that the old League with its "military alliance provided under Article X" had shown its futility by its failure to prevent the Russo-Polish war then in process.[27]

Herrick's advice seemed to be just in time. The Republican substitute for the League of Nations had been discovered. It was a new Hague Tribunal, the World Court of International Justice, as an "adjunct to the league of nations"—the new World Court whose constitution the wise and experienced Root was carefully preparing with the help of others wise and experienced.

Nobody knows exactly what Harding and Herrick talked about on August 26 in the house on Mt. Vernon Avenue. But it is known that, two days later, in his much-heralded pronouncement on the League of Nations, Harding did make the recommendation predicted two days before, of a "new league of nations, with the tribunal of justice as its foundation." [28] His proposal was to "put teeth" into the new Hague Tribunal, or World Court, by means of an amended League covenant. It was not a very workable proposal, but only the absent Root could know this, and he had not, of course, been properly consulted. Whether Harding changed his copy from that already sent out to Lasker is not important. The publicity was the thing. Actually, Harding had information on the world court long before he talked with Herrick.

6

Harding's "World Court with teeth" proposal was, and remained, the central pronouncement on international relations for the entire campaign. After denouncing Wilson's League as based on "might instead of right" and as having failed to prevent the current Russo-Polish war, he proposed "an association of, or a league of free nations animated by considerations of right and justice. . . . This is proposing no new thing. This country is already a member of such a society—the Hague tribunal—which, unlike the league of Versailles, is still functioning, and within a few weeks will resume its committee sessions under the chairmanship of an American representative. . . . What once seemed at The Hague to be a mere academic discussion has become a positive, outstanding need of facing terrifying realities. This makes vastly easier the task of so strengthening The Hague tribunal or to render its just decrees either acceptable or enforceable."

It was said that the Hague tribunal "lacks teeth," according to Harding: "Very well, then lets put teeth into it. If, in the failed league of Versailles, there can be found machinery which the tribunal can use properly and advantageously, by all means let it be appropriated. I would even go further. I would take and combine all that is good and excise all that is bad from both organizations. This statement is broad enough to include the suggestion that if the league, which has heretofore riveted our considerations and apprehensions, has been so entwined and interwoven into the peace of Europe, that its good must be preserved in order to stabilize the peace of that continent, then it can be amended or revised so that we may still have a remnant of world aspirations in 1918 bonded into the world's highest conception of helpful cooperation in the ultimate realization." Such "an international association for conference and a world court whose verdicts upon justiciable questions, this country in common with all nations would be both willing and able to uphold. The decision of such a court or the recommendations of such a conference could be accepted without sacrificing on our part or asking any other power to sacrifice one iota of its nationality."

Harding supported his World Court proposal with other arguments.

He reminded his hearers that Prime Minister Lloyd George of England had expressed his willingness to make changes in the League covenant in order to obtain the cooperation of the United States. He cited Viscount Grey of Falloden as saying that "the Americans must be told that if they will only join the league they can practically name their own terms. . . . The Americans should be entrusted with the task of drafting a reconstruction scheme . . . the reconstruction of the league, which would be consonant with the feeling not of one, but of all parties in America." If this involved the reconvening of the entire "convention" for the redrafting of its covenant, this would be a "very slight" objection. Harding therefore suggested the "calling into real conference the ablest and most experienced minds of this country, from whatever walks of life they may be derived and without regard to party affiliations, to formulate a definite, practical plan along the lines already indicated for the consideration of the controlling foreign powers."

There should be no delay, said Harding. "I should give very earnest and practically undivided attention to this very vital subject from the day of my election and I should ask others to do likewise as a matter of public and patriotic duty. Indeed, I should hope to have behind me, after the decision on the national referendum we are soon to have, a country wholly united in earnest endeavor to achieve a true solution of the problem."

7

Harding's world court speech of August 28 was an umbrella speech. It covered the internationalists without losing the company of the isolationists. After it, all shades of Republican opinion on the key issue of international relations could, and did, come in under its protection. Favorable reaction from Republicans was universal. All sides enthused over it—internationalists, isolationists, the "Organization." Harding himself was pleased, relaxing as the messages of approval poured in. "From all I can hear," he wrote Alexander Moore of the *Pittsburgh Leader* on September 3, "matters are clearing up beautifully." He hoped "H. W. J." (Hiram Johnson) would be pleased.[29] "We have come now to the point," he wrote Lodge, "where nearly every one is ready to agree that the Versailles covenant can easily be amended or reconstructed. With that understanding I think we are going to get along famously well from this time on." Harding now felt free to go to work on speeches relating to secondary, but nonetheless important, problems such as labor and agriculture.[30]

The happiness of the "Organization" was unbounded. Hays telegraphed Hoover, Taft, and Wood that he wanted them to read the Harding speech with care. "Really masterpiece," he wired. To the public Hays said of Harding, "He is the masterly leader. He has spoken without truculence or prejudice. His voice now leads the statesmanship of America. We are through with Democratic wiggling and wobbling at home and abroad." Daugherty echoed with equally extravagant acclaim. Said he, "It will be recognized hereafter, as the great pronouncement of the campaign. . . . It is the substitution of a practical working program to preserve peace, for the strange hybrid of autocracy and idealism that is the Wilson league of nations." [31]

The internationalists liked it. Jacob Gould Schurman wired congratulations, saying, "The substance is extraordinarily good, the style fine, very fine, and the presentation very masterly and convincing. Your position will win the country." Paul D. Cravath wrote Hays, "All things considered, I think Senator Harding took about the right position. . . . It has removed a great deal of misapprehension. I hope Senator Harding will stand pat on the speech until Root returns." Business leader John Hays Hammond said it would satisfy those who feared "the 'Chinese Wall' policy of isolationism." George W. Wickersham, Attorney General under President Taft, who was in favor of adopting the League covenant without reservations, said, "I am in full accord with what Senator Harding said in his address of August 28. . . . Senator Harding does not wholly and finally reject the league. He recognizes that it may become so entwined and interwoven in the peace of Europe that its good work and its unobjectionable provisions must be preserved in order to stabilize the peace of that continent. . . . When President Harding, working in accord with a Republican congress, takes up the work of placing upon a firm, just and sane foundation the relation of this country to the other nations of the world, I am confident that the logic of accomplished fact will lead to the adoption of the league, so modified as to remove all just doubts as to its undue effect upon American rights and interests." Charles Evans Hughes gave his blessing, using Harding's own words: "We shall be able to retain all that is good in the proposed covenant, while we shall adequately protect ourselves from what is ill-advised . . . and in a sensible manner we shall do our full share in securing so far as has been possible, international justice and abiding peace." [32]

As for Henry Cabot Lodge, who lived in a continuing state of anxiety lest somebody repeat the Burchard blunder of 1884 and offend the isolationists, he was so pleased with Harding's speech that he hoped the Senator and everybody else would remain silent on the question for the rest of the campaign. He wrote to Senator Harry S. New of Indiana on September 28, "All we have to do is to hold steady and stand by Harding's speech of August 28th which is the most important issue. The policy he then laid down has met with general acceptance and has driven nobody away; on the contrary, I think it has strengthened him." But Lodge was worried. Root was about to return home, and a welcoming luncheon was scheduled in October. Knowing Root's views as to the impracticability of Harding's "world court with teeth" proposal, Lodge feared that Root might be too critical. "I am a little nervous about that luncheon in New York," he wrote, "which I heard of only day before yesterday. His [Root's] making a speech is all right, but I am an old man and I remember the Burchard luncheon. I am afraid of what somebody else may say on that occasion. Hughes has taken a perfectly sound ground in his speech of a week ago Saturday and made one of the ablest arguments on Article X I have ever seen anywhere, but I am not at all clear as to what Root may say. Undoubtedly he will support Harding, but he evidently is all tied up with this court and the court is tied up with the League. If we can only keep as we are for the next five weeks we are going to win a great victory." A thing that Lodge liked about the world court idea was that one did not have to go into details about it.[33]

8

Harding made sure that the isolationists would appreciate the coverage of his August 28 umbrella speech by two devices. One was to include the usual denunciations of the Wilson League, and the other was to write confidential letters to his friends assuring them that he was not selling America short.

For the benefit of Johnson, Borah, and company, Harding drew on his collections of choice Americanisms. Article 10 would deprive people of the right to seek political freedom as the American colonies did in 1776. The Council of the League was an alliance of great selfish powers, designed to impose its will on "the helpless peoples of the world." The Democrats were in favor of joining the alliance. Said Harding, "I am not."

This enabled the fiery Johnson to snatch the familiar phrases of patriotism and to proclaim loudly, "Senator Harding has scrapped the League. . . . He declares, as we have all declared, in favor of arbitration treaties, and the Hague tribunal. . . . Governor Cox says he favors going into the league. Senator Harding now emphatically answers he favors staying out. The long fight is over. . . . The league is dead." Then, under the spell of Harding's non-provocativeness, Johnson bent a little. In the midst of one of his "the League is dead" diatribes to the California Republican convention on September 21, he admitted that "every normal man" wanted to promote peace, and that this could be done "in one way or another in the future," and leave each international crisis to be met by itself.[34]

The voice of Borah also was heard amidst the bandwagon chorus: "If Harding is elected, whatever else happens or does not happen as to a league, Article No. 10 is to be eliminated. The issue is plain, clear-cut and stupendous. . . . He makes it clear that we will never expressly nor implicitly agree to preserve the territorial integrity of the nations of the world. He declares furthermore, that no American soldier shall be sent to Europe for any such purpose. . . . No foreign tribunal shall bind us either legally or morally." [35]

One who believed Harding's "world court with teeth" speech was the isolationist and former Progressive, Raymond Robins. "Your great, clear and satisfying statement made today," wired Robins, "is a clarion call for American nationalism and will win fighting support for the Republican ticket from genuine Americans throughout the land. For every internationalist vote we lose by it, we gain four America first voters because of it." [36]

Two other unyielding isolationists were snared by Harding's ambivalence of August 28. One was the truculent Senator Frank B. Brandegee of Connecticut, who wired, on the same day, "Glory Halleluja, God reigns and the government at Washingtons still lives." The bemused Harding showed his gratitude by writing to Brandegee's friend L. A. Coolidge, "Brandegee's telegram reached me August 28. Glad to know you were with him when it was dictated." [37]

Harding took no chances of losing the confidence of Brandegee and other bitter-end opponents of the Wilson League. On September 6, the candidate wrote to John Hays Hammond, "Remember me to both Brandegee and Harvey. Tell them both that I have my problems with callers of divergent minds about what I really have in mind as to foreign relations, but they can be very cordially assured that there is no change in base and will be none." However, Brandegee remained suspicious. He got wind of a plan of Hoover and Taft to join with Elihu Root upon the latter's return from Europe "to patch up the whole business" of the League and come to a "complete understanding with the gentlemen of high finance." "A word to the wise is sufficient," added Brandegee, "I hope you have heard from Harvey by this time." Harding got Brandegee's meaning, and hastened to assure him, "I am glad to have your warning, but please believe that I am wary if not wise, and there will be no secret understanding and no hidden alliances to embarrass us after the campaign closes." [38]

A similar exchange of confidences was made between Harding and the anti-Leaguer Senator Philander C. Knox of Pennsylvania on September 16; Knox wired Harding that the world court proposal was a "clever plan" by Root "to put us in Wilson's League by the back door. I hope and I know you will not commit yourself to it without the fullest consideration." Harding wired back, "Please have faith in my prudence." This elicited a response from Knox acknowledging "the greatest confidence in your discretion, but I am not going to cease to yell fire when I see what I believe to be a conflagration on the horizon." Harding then slowed the pace a little and wrote to Knox, "I am only distressed because you seem to think I am so utterly lacking in sticking qualities. Maybe you will get to know me better some day." Knox finally closed the exchange with a letter written, as he said, while he could still "sass back." "You have bluffed me often," he wrote, "but hanged if I will stand for any sentiment that I have intimated that you 'are utterly lacking in sticking qualities.' Those are the qualities of which I well know." [39]

People from the opposite end of the League-opinion spectrum were also skeptical. Supporters of Cox and Wilson, like the *New York Times*, called Harding two-faced, contradictory, and confused. From Tom B. Spalding in Lebanon, Kentucky, came a message superscribed on a pamphlet containing Harding's August 28 speech:

> Mr. Harding: On the League of Nations,
> You wire in and you wire out,
> And leave the people all in doubt.
> As to whether the snake that made the track
> Was going north or coming back.[40]

One friend of Harding's was more good-natured about it than the Kentucky skeptic. This was Gus Karger, *Cincinnati Times-Star* corre-

spondent. The day after the world court speech, Karger wrote that he
hoped for the best, but he was not quite sure whether Harding was
"coming or going." The trouble was that both isolationists and internationalists approved of the speech. Karger said he would feel much
better about it "if you would just keep Harvey and Johnson and a few
other irreconcilables from cheering so vociferously." [41]

<h2>9</h2>

Bountiful proof that Harding's world court speech of August 28
produced immediate and favorable results was the Republican landslide in the Maine gubernatorial election of September 14. By common consent between the Maine Democrats and Republicans, the one
and only issue was made to be the Wilson League versus the world
court and an association of nations. Neither side espoused isolationism.

First proof of the internationalist nature of the Maine election came
from Senator Frederick Hale of that state. "We, all of us," Hale wrote
to Harding on September 20, "took the ground that you have taken,
that we must have an Association of Nations." According to Hale,
Calvin Coolidge, speaking in Portland, "referred particularly to the
statement in your speech of August 28th that if the League speech
were found to be so bound up with the Treaty, that we could not get
away from it, we could adopt Viscount Gray's suggestion and amend
it as we saw fit and then go in." The drive, Hale said, was made
"against the League as put up to us by President Wilson and especially Article 10." Senator Hale said that he was "very sure the feeling
in the state is entirely in favor of a League of Nations. . . . I do not
think that I am exaggerating at all in stating that at least 90% of the
people of the state of Maine want and expect us to go into an
Association of Nations for the preservation of peace and we have
every confidence that that is what you will get for us." [42]

Corroboration of Senator Hale's statements came from Lodge, who
campaigned vigorously in Maine. Lodge told Harding on September
15 that he talked "entirely" about the League, "which was what they
asked me to do." "State issues," he said, "were never mentioned. All
our speakers and all the Democratic speakers discussed the League, to
the exclusion of everything else." He quoted Maine Governor Carl E.
Millikin as saying, "The President has demanded a solemn referendum

on the League. Whatever happens elsewhere, he is going to get it in Maine." Lodge then analyzed the Republican election majority which was "simply phenomenal." The largest Republican majority Maine ever had was 46,000 in 1896; the 1920 majority was over 66,000. All of which, said Lodge, means that the rank and file of the Republican party "are entirely in favor of a world court." To this, Harding replied with thanks, saying, "I am for a court, either under the original plan or, as a part of any new compact which we may make with foreign countries." They all disagreed with those who said that the world court was a backdoor entrance to the Wilson League. In an earlier letter to Harding, Lodge showed the same state of mind in the Republican primaries in New Hampshire, where Senator George Moses, a bitter-end opponent of the League in 1919, was renominated by a two-to-one majority on a platform favoring Harding's world court idea.[43]

10

Other extremely effective devices for holding the isolationists in line with the new August 28 internationalism involved a pair of typical Harding points of finesse. One was to promise to engage in no more specifics in the international direction. The other was to accentuate the ambivalence of his own utterances by pleasing the isolationist with sharper language against the Wilson League, but at the same time to encourage the internationalists by retaining and repeating his world court–international association talk.

Harding's pledge of nonspecifics was, of course, made to everybody, but it was especially useful in the let's-be-nice-to-Johnson policy. Johnson told Harding that he liked the August 28 performance because it put more "pep and enthusiasm into the fight" to arouse the people in this increasing opposition to the Wilson League. Harding replied that he was glad for Johnson's support. He told Johnson not to worry about the varied interpretations made of the recent speech. Harding was trying, he said, not to be too specific because to do so "would be a very dangerous undertaking." They must all agree about Americanism. Harding waxed into real Johnsonian enthusiasm on the subject. "We are going to be heartily agreed about clinging everlastingly to American independence, and hold ourselves adamant against the surrender which was contemplated in the negotiations of the President. I do not pretend to specifically point out exactly what I propose to do and think it practical to do, because the big task of the present is to make it reasonably possible for our party to unite in opposition to the surrender which threatened in the course pursued by the President." Harding made the usual appeal to Johnson's vanity by reporting that he was "daily being bombarded" with requests for the Californian's appearance in the East. However, Harding was glad that Johnson was going "into action with your heavy guns" on the Coast.[44] During October, Johnson came roaring east, much to the consternation of the internationalist wing of the party.

As the final month of the campaign opened to the din of pro- and anti-League talk, the demands came from each side for Harding's help, and he gave it to each of them. At Des Moines, on October 7, the candidate detailed the process of (1) killing the Wilson League and (2) promoting an international association. "The Democrats," he said, "want to know if we mean to scrap the League." Harding laughed and said that it was already scrapped by the stubborn action of Wilson in insisting that it be ratified without dotting an *i* or crossing a *t*. The American people had no patience with such a betrayal of American independence. "I do not want to clarify these obligations, I want to turn my back on them. It is not interpretation, but rejection, that I am seeking. My position is that the proposed league strikes a deadly blow at our constitutional integrity and surrenders to a dangerous extent our independence of action." [45]

Harding then said the words that the internationalists loved to hear. The very fact that the United States was isolated from, and unprejudiced about, world affairs qualified it to "formulate a plan and point the way" to world peace. "I am in favor of doing our full part in the rehabilitation of the world and in securing humanity against the horror and tragedy of future war." With a sharp jibe at Wilson's "autocratic assumption of personal wisdom, which will neither take counsel nor learn from experience," Harding solemnly promised "to formulate a plan of international cooperation, which will contribute to the security and peace of the world without sacrificing or dangerously diluting our power to direct our own actions." Discussion and consultation by thinking people, not the Wilsonian dictatorship, must guide our judgment, he declared. "I should not be fit to hold the high office of President if I did not frankly say that it is a task which I have no intention of undertaking alone. There are many and conflicting opinions among the people and among the members of the senate upon the subject. These opinions must be reconciled and harmonized if we are to have international association for peace at all. . . . I shall advise with the best minds in the United States, and especially I shall consult in advance with the senate, with whom, by the terms of the constitution, I shall indeed be bound to counsel and without whose consent no such international association can be formed." [46]

Harding was even more encouraging to the internationalists in an interview with R. W. Montague published in the *Outlook* of October 6. In this he emphasized that the "best minds" would be chosen "without regard to party affiliation." He had no doubt that "the acceptance of our proposals by the five principal nations would . . . be followed promptly by the acceptance on the part of the minor members of the alliance." He pledged, "I should give very earnest and practically undivided attention to this very vital subject from the day of my election, and I should ask others to do likewise as a matter of public and patriotic duty." As a result, he said, "I should hope to have behind me, after the decision in the national referendum we are soon to have, a country wholly united in earnest endeavor to achieve a true solution of this problem upon which the future civilization so largely depends." Montague was entranced with the prospects. He envisioned a commission composed of Democrats like John W. Davis, Republicans like Root, and "say one irreconcilable like Borah," formulating a plan truly representative of a united American people.

The Republican follow-up of the Des Moines address was excellent. It sought to please all shades of opinion on the League. Before the campaign train got back to Marion, statements were being issued. In a dispatch from "On Board Harding Train" came a report: (1) that Harding would never agree to article 10 of the League covenant, depriving Congress of the right to declare war; (2) "he does not oppose 'a' league, but rather 'the' league as negotiated at Paris," which had already been scrapped by Wilson in his refusal to accept reservations; (3) he favored "any association of nations" that would maintain peace without sacrifice of American rights; and (4) he took satisfaction in admitting that he had no specific plan at present for an association of nations; the matter being "too big for one man to solve," he would eventually "take counsel with the best minds of the country regardless of their party affiliation." The next day there was another bulletin to the same effect. [47]

And so it went for the rest of the campaign, as Harding taunted his critics with his necessity of having to be repetitious. On October 15, at

Indianapolis, he spoke of his opposition to the Wilson League and to article 10—"How many times must we say NO?" Then he quoted his words of August 28, and the need for future counsel by the "best minds." It was so again at Louisville, at Baltimore, at Buffalo, and on the train over and over again.[48]

A neat turn to Harding's international talk was his sentimentalizing of it for the benefit of the women, now voting in a national election for the first time in all states. This was deliberate. "I am planning a speech," he wrote Herrick on September 11, "having direct relation to the sentimental idea of the league of nations, and which will perhaps have its effect upon the women." On the same day he explained it more fully to Allen T. Treadway, indicating how the sentimental way was the right approach to feminine sympathies. "I am preparing a speech," he wrote, "aimed at this sentimental view of the covenant, in which I hope to appeal to the reason of the class of voters of both sexes to which you refer." [49]

Other efforts to win over the female voter involved the League clause concerned with the suppression of the traffic in women and children. One of the Lodge reservations dealt with this, with the idea that the control should be subject to American approval—presumably lest it not be strong enough. In a letter to Thomas C. Brown, director of publicity of the Ohio Republican executive committee, Harding's office called attention to a *Star* editorial on the subject, and suggested similar action by his committee. "It will certainly make a strong appeal to the women voters," Harding wrote.[50]

On September 16, this sentimental appeal was officially issued as a "message to all Republican women's organizations" to be "sent to them the country over." It was in the form of a letter from Harding to Mrs. Ray F. Zucker, president of the Women's Harding and Coolidge Club of New York City. "American women," he said, "must realize that the League of Nations as presented by a Democratic Administration would not mean peace for us, but would mean American boys living in army tents overseas, and asked to die in causes in which they have no heart. Such a league as the American people have rejected would mean mandates undertaken in far away places. Such a league as has been devised by bungling hands would not mean peace and amity with the world, but entanglement, stress and the return of the bodies of our men who had been called across the ocean on strange, un-American errands. . . . Let us establish a workable relationship. We do not want one which is fair in promise, while it fails to prevent useless bloodshed to which our own men's veins would contribute." [51] On October 1, at the well-staged Woman Voters' Day on the Marion front porch, Harding found many topics on which to sentimentalize for the ladies, but he managed to refer to the League subject when he told his guests that we must have an association of nations that will never take "our sons and husbands for sacrifice at the call of an extra-constitutional body like the Paris league." [52]

For the male voters there was the impression of calm reason, of the subjection of decisions to judicious thought, consultation, and a sharing of views, and of deference to Congress. Albert Shaw of the *Review of Reviews*, noted this campaign atmosphere of "almost judicial calm." Shaw was so thankful for the August 28 address, which he hoped Harding would redeliver occasionally as he went about. The intellectuals, said Shaw, did not want Harding to provide all the answers about the specific form of world organization. "It is quite enough to have your assurance that you will give all of us who are thoughtful and reasonably entitled to discuss these matters, an opportunity to have our views considered when the time comes for making necessary decisions." [53] When Harding reached the White House, advised President John Grier Hibben of Princeton University, he should "appoint a commission of the most enlightened and experienced minds of the country on international affairs." [54]

Reference of the League problem to the "best minds" in calmer times was what Harding really wanted and pledged—to the people who wanted such promises. "I have a very clear idea of what I think we can do and should do," he wrote to attorney S. O. Levinson of Chicago, "in working out an international agreement, but, as a candidate of a party, I do not want to make my plan an issue in a campaign which I am waging upon the theory that international agreements ought to be made a concrete agreement of the executive and the congress." Always he had in his mind the example of Wilson's alleged one-man folly. As he wrote to Julian Street of Norfolk, Connecticut, "It must appear as clearly to you as it does to me that one of the reasons for the failure of the Wilson League is that it was dictated in advance by one man without much consultation. I am not ready to take the position . . . of constructing a one-man program and trying to force it upon the country." Harding presented the same view to law professor Herbert S. Hadley of Boulder, Colorado: "I will not present myself as a substitute for President Wilson as a one-man government. What I have tried to impress upon the people is our purpose to enlist the ablest brains we could command inspired by the great heart of America to cooperate with the best and wisest of foreign leaders of thought and action in the formulation of an agreement which would satisfy our highest ideals and still leave unimpaired our National independence of action and maintenance of the institutions which we have erected as a free people." [55]

11

One of the most striking—and to some people, unfortunate—phases of Harding's League-forum idea was his simultaneous encouragement of the internationally minded intellectuals, culminating in the "Appeal of the Thirty-One Eminent Americans," and of the crude attempts to smear the League made by Arthur Brisbane in the Hearst papers.

The instigator of the "Thirty-One Eminent Americans" movement was President Jacob Gould Schurman of Cornell University. Schurman was a member of the Republican national committee's advisory committee on policies and platforms. He was in direct correspondence with Harding throughout the campaign, always approving of the utterances on the League question showing international leanings. On September 9, Schurman was in New York City preparing for a September 18 conference of the presidents of the leading colleges and universities in the East. He conferred with national committee chairman Hays and other Republican notables. He hoped that the conference would lead to a successful campaign among professors and other teachers, including the clergy of the country, in behalf of "the supreme issue of the present campaign." Schurman was planning to leave the cloistered halls of learning at Ithaca to devote his entire time to this movement. He asked Harding for a letter to be read at the September 18 conference.[56]

Harding was in full accord with Schurman and, on September 15, sent the requested message describing his views on the "supreme issue of the campaign," to be read to the college presidents. His views were very broad indeed. He mentioned not only a world association of nations with an international court of justice "based on international law and built on the Hague Tribunal," but cited Viscount Gray's proposal that the United States "be entrusted with drafting a reconstruction scheme." Since the "enlightened leadership of Europe wishes us to do this . . . to refuse would be a dereliction. . . . We have an opportunity to do a great service to the world if we will but undertake this effort which the world wishes us to undertake." This, he said, was the most elaborate system of international involvement yet proposed by Harding. Schurman reported a favorable reaction by the college presidents and later by the learned Elihu Root, who was quoted as saying, "with great postiveness that the man must be 'ignorant or insincere' who would undertake to say in advance what should be done in Europe and that he did not see how you could go farther than you have gone in announcing your league policy." [57]

The September 18 meeting of college presidents and others was held, and a committee of three—Schurman, President A. Lawrence Lowell of Harvard, and Herbert Hoover—appointed to draft a statement for circulation to college faculties. Harding gave the proceedings his blessing in a letter to Schurman, saying he was glad to know that the preparation of the statement was in such capable hands. The actual first draft of a statement was made by New York attorney Paul D. Cravath, who had a distinguished war record as a member of the "House Mission" to the Inter-Allied War Conference of December, 1917, and as counsel of the "American Mission" to the Inter-Allied Council on War Purchases and Finance in 1918. For this latter service Cravath had been awarded the Distinguished Service Medal by General Pershing. [58]

According to Schurman, interest flagged until Harding made his Des Moines address on October 7. This "cleared the political atmosphere" for the committee, which found the address "very satisfactory," though it was "grossly misrepresented" in the New York press. The committee then met, with the addition of Root, Hughes, Wickersham, and Cravath acting as secretary. Everybody made suggestions, and it was all finally turned over to Root to draft a final statement. This was to be not only for the benefit of college and university men, but for "all friends of the ideal of a league or association of nations who might be hesitating to vote the Republican ticket." Other distinguished "friends of a league" were being readied to sign the Root statement and the Republican national headquarters was preparing to circulate it. "Of course," Schurman informed Harding, "the first current of energy comes from you. And I am conscious that it grows increasingly powerful and effective. In these last speeches of yours from Iowa to Oklahoma the issue has become more incisive and your own arguments more telling and convincing." [59]

While the intellectuals pondered, the isolationists were in full cry.

The Des Moines speech, which had so pleased the internationalists, was rejoiced over by the isolationists as a body blow to the League. The *New York Times* headlined, "HARDING REJECTS THE LEAGUE OUTRIGHT." Borah was headlined as declaring that Harding's speech was "great." It was further lavishly headlined that "JOHNSON WILL NOW ENTER CAMPAIGN." Johnson surely did, on Harding's invitation, and he was soon burning up the trail in fierce denunciation of the Wilson League, and with ardent praise of Harding. He was ably assisted by the Democratic *New York Times* and its slanted headlines: "JOHNSON SURE OF HARDING" (October 14); "JOHNSON IN CLEVELAND SEEKS LEAGUE REJECTION" (October 15); "UNDER WHICH FLAG—JOHNSON IN NEW YORK CITY" (October 21); "JOHNSON REBUKES THE 31 SIGNERS" (October 23); "JOHNSON OPPOSES ROOT" (October 24); "JOHNSON SAYS HARDING IS AGAINST THE LEAGUE" (October 27). Above all, on October 8 Herbert Parsons, former New York Republican national committeeman and chairman of the New York county Republican committee, resigned as a member of that committee and announced that he would vote for Cox. "The only likelihood that the United States will, under Harding, enter the League," Parsons snarled, "is that he will find it impossible to erect an association or a new League, and so will have to crawl into this one." The country needed Cox, and "aggressive positive leadership, not the self confessed ignorance of Harding. No straddler will do." [60]

The internationalists claimed that they could not understand it. Harding had made an international speech at Des Moines, not an isolationist one. Cravath was much upset. On October 8, he wrote Hays bitterly, lamenting the unanimity with which the New York newspapers had given the Des Moines address "the complexion of a further recession in the direction of a policy of isolation, if not a surrender to the extreme position of Johnson and Borah." This was the more shocking because, in Cravath's opinion, the Des Moines address was Harding's "most satisfactory utterance on the subject of international cooperation to promote peace." "By and large," Cravath said, Harding's position was quite satisfactory "if only it were understood by the public as we understand it." He saw thousands of liberal votes going to Cox because Johnson and Borah went about saying Harding meant to scrap the League, when Harding actually was saying he would only scrap the "Wilson League." Many other young liberals felt similarly and wrote to Hays. One of them was Henry L. Stimson, member of Elihu Root's law firm, and former Secretary of War. "The trouble is not with the speech, but with the headlines which misrepresent it," complained Stimson to Hays. "They confirm the impression that he [Harding] is going over to Borah and Johnson." Stimson too saw young Republican liberals deserting to Cox in droves. "The result will be," he prophesied, "that while we win the election we will lose a lot of the most valuable young material for the party." [61]

One of the earliest to raise the alarm was Speaker Gillette, who was especially concerned about losing the women's vote. He wrote to Harding before the Des Moines address, "I am sorry to find some of our best New England women, Republican to the core in the past, are working for Cox because of the League. We don't need their votes this fall, but we mustn't lose them permanently." [62]

As usual, the warning voice of Hoover was heard. On October 11, he wired Harding, "I wish to urge upon you to stem the tide of Republican desertion being brought by the general Democratic conspiracy to misrepresent your and the party's attitude on the League. If there are not to be more Parsons incidents, it is vital that it should be made clear that the issue is not no league against the league, but a league better calculated to serve this country and the world." [63]

Columbia University president Nicholas Murray Butler added his note of alarm at the defection of many liberals. "Every speech made by Johnson or Borah," he wrote to Charles D. Hilles, "drives hundreds of Republican votes to Cox and weakens the intelligent and reflective element in the party. . . . Those who are coming in to take their places are Sinn Feiners, pro-Germans, and radicals of various sorts, who are not Republicans in principle and who will not stay with us very long." The party was losing a lot of women votes too. Oh, yes, Butler said, the Republicans will win the election. But that is because "we have so large a margin of safety to draw upon and the campaign is so nearly over." [64]

Hays and his office men answered all these letters sympathetically and turned them over to Harding, who wrote likewise. "They were all very much pleased with the letters you wrote them," wrote Hays on October 16. To Henry L. Stoddard of the New York *Evening Mail*, Harding lamented the dereliction of the press. "There is really nothing to say about the Des Moines, Iowa, speech," he wrote, "except that the newspapers were not quite frank in reporting it. What they reported was probably accurate enough, but they took only the emphatic opposition to Article X, and said nothing about the constructive proposition which I invariably offer in following the announcement of the Wilson League." He promised Stoddard and others to keep on hammering away on his August 28 theme of a world court and an association of nations.[65]

And so, on October 15, the "Appeal of the Thirty-One Eminent Americans," written by Root for "from 20 to 25 signers," came out with the blessings of Harding and Hays. The signatures of the intelligentsia were arranged alphabetically from Lyman Abbott to Stanford University President Ray Lyman Wilbur, with Root, Hoover, Hughes, Cravath, William Allen White, and a bevy of college presidents in between—Butler of Columbia, Brookings of Washington University, Dabney of Cincinnati, Faunce of Brown, Goodnow of Johns Hopkins, Hibben of Princeton, Hopkins of Dartmouth, Lowell of Harvard, MacCracken of LaFayette and others. The appeal was premised on the assumption that the Wilson League was a war league, but amended as Harding proposed in behalf of a world court and an association, was a peace league. "The conditions of Europe make it essential that the stabilizing effect of the treaty already made between the European Powers shall not be lost by this, and that the necessary changes be made by changing the terms of the treaty rather than by beginning entirely anew." Attacks on article 10 were deliberately soft-pedaled. As Root told Cravath in his October 9 letter of submission, "I enclose the paper I have prepared for signature, including mine. I have refrained from saying many bad things about Article X, because they might make it difficult for others." [66]

While Johnson went about denouncing the "Thirty-one," the machinery of the Republican party was put fully behind them. In the first place, Republican League policy was officially amended in the direction of internationalism. On October 10, Dr. Lindsay, staff director of Hays' advisory committee on policies and platform, mailed Harding a statement containing alterations of the "Memorandum on Republican Ideals and Policies Concerning the League or Association of Nations." These revisions, according to Hays, "make it stronger." Next day, October 11, a telegram was sent to Harding's speech adviser, Richard Washburn Child, which shows what these changes were. The telegram read, "In view of the misunderstanding or misrepresentation of our position on the League of Nations here in the East, President Schurman, Paul D. Cravath and Dr. Lindsay feel that it is very desirable to have Senator Harding emphasize the affirmative side of our platform declaration for an association of Nations along the lines of the latter part of the memorandum on Republican Ideals and

Policies Concerning the League or association of nations which Dr. Lindsay gave you yesterday and had already mailed to Marion." [67]

On October 14, the day of the issuance of the appeal, further pressure was brought to bear on Harding from Republican headquarters to cue him as to what to say. Hays wired Child that the appeal was coming, and that he hoped Harding would say that he welcomed it: "Statement going out here in the morning by Doctor Schurman and others will please this section of country. If candidate is asked about it they will be glad if he would say that he welcomed the support of the group of thirty distinguished advocates of international cooperation to promote peace. He will know just what to say. Things moving pretty well here." What Harding was to say had been spelled out by staff director Lindsay. In an office memorandum, he informed Hays, "Mr. Cravath and I think that you ought to advise Senator Harding that the Root statement will be released for tomorrow morning's papers, and that you might suggest that he comment on it somewhat as follows: 'I welcome the support of the group of thirty distinguished advocates of international cooperation to promote peace, whose statement was published this morning. Their statement clearly defines what I conceive to be the issues regarding covenant of the League of Nations and correctly interprets my attitude.'" Dr. Lindsay added that Harding had said substantially the same thing in a letter to Cravath.[68]

Harding did not need to be told what to say. He said it in his own, or Child's, language in a speech on October 15 at Seymour, Indiana. "I note," he said, "that a considerable number of notable and influential friends of an association of nations—the leaders of thought in that aspiration—have pointed out the hopelessness of the Democratic proposal and have frankly said the hope of real accomplishment lies in Republican success. This is not surprising. It develops no inconsistency. It only emphasizes the correctness of our platform and the growing approval of the construction put upon it throughout the campaign." [69]

How useful the appeal could be to Harding was shown by the official distribution of copies thereof to places where it would do the most good. For example, there came to the Marion office an inquiry from William F. Kriebel of the Tuxedo Club of Philadelphia. "Each and every member of our organization," wrote Kriebel, "is a Republican voter and furthermore they are in favor of a League of Nations." Harding was away on tour at the time, but one of his staff was ready for the inquiry. He enclosed a copy of the appeal, citing four of its distinguished signers—Root, Hoover, Lowell, and Hughes—and "twenty seven other men of the highest ability in our American public life announcing that they would support Senator Harding for the presidency and upon the issue of the League of Nations." [70]

12

The antithesis, intellectually, of the Thirty-one, was Arthur Brisbane, a journalist whose writings appealed to those who could not think very clearly, to those who could best be attracted merely by waving the American flag and prating about how un-American the League of Nations was. Harding liked Brisbane's pungent style of writing. "You have such a marked faculty for convincing expression," Harding wrote on August 30, "that it delights me to know you are saying some of the things which I find in your column." [71] Harding did not say that he liked, or approved, of everything that Brisbane wrote, but he never told Brisbane what it was that might have provoked displeasure. Brisbane kept on in his vulgar way, blasting the League of Nations and sending in his clippings and suggestions.

Brisbane's coverage was very wide. His daily editorial column entitled "Today," appeared on the front pages of the Hearst papers from coast to coast, including the *New York Evening Journal*, the *New York American*, the *Washington Times*, the *Chicago Herald & Examiner*, the *San Francisco Examiner*, and the *Los Angeles Examiner*, among others. He eventually sold some of his anti-League copy to Hays. Brisbane's attitude toward the common people, upon whom he had so much effect, was indicated by a remark he made to Harding in a letter dated August 11. "The great public," he said, "of whom Watson of Georgia remarked, 'It is impossible to exaggerate their stupidity,' is firmly convinced that a Peace League must mean PEACE. It has got to be made clear that a Peace League such as they plan to saddle on this country would mean WAR." [72]

In mid-August Brisbane sent Harding a set of his anti-League editorial clippings and articles of which he was very proud, and which Harding said he was glad to receive. "I have been noting with very great interest and satisfaction many of the things you have been saying and I want you to know of my very great appreciation." [73] One of the articles which Brisbane included was an anti-League statement intended for his column on August 16. It told in lurid simplicity of two gassed war veterans who hanged themselves to be relieved of their agony. "If those men had lived until next November they probably would have told young Americans NOT yet gassed, and their fathers and mothers, that it would be a good idea to have the United States decide about drafting Americans for service in Europe and not leave the decision to any peace league or combination of European nations." [74] One of the clippings was from a "Today" column on the Brisbane theme that the Peace League was a War League. The Wilson talk about breaking the heart of the world by not joining the League was called "baby talk." European nations had fought for centuries like a "crowd of bandits seeking spoil." "If two sets of barbarians in the Balkans, savages that have not outgrown murder and banditry after thousands of years, start cutting each others throats . . . is it this country's business? . . . Don't believe all you hear." [75]

The Republican national committee also liked Brisbane's style. By his own admission he was especially effective with the Jews, and so the committee asked him to write an advertisement to be published in the Yiddish language in the New York City Yiddish papers. "I am writing," he told Harding, "in such a way, I hope, as to make the Jewish women see and understand what the League of Nations really is. Briefly, I shall point out to them that in the name of the League of Nations the Democrats sent guns and bullets to Poland. And those guns and bullets are now used to murder the defenceless Jews. I think I can convince Jewish mothers that they don't want the League of Nations with its perpetual war. . . . The Jewish people in New York know me and I think they have some confidence in what I say." In another letter to Harding, Brisbane said that he was going to tell the Jews "that, in war, no matter who fights, the Jew is always murdered." [76]

Brisbane's anti-League message was so contagious that it found its way into the columns of the pro-League *New York Times* and other journals that, as he told Harding, "have opposed you but are willing to take money for your advertising." He boasted to Harding of one particular insertion which cost $25,000, and which he got his brother-in-law, Courtland Smith, to pay for. As it appeared in a full page of the *Times* of October 31, Brisbane's advertisement featured pictures of Harding and Coolidge, flanked by pictures of their mothers. The headlines ran, "Good Mothers Have Good Sons." Under this caption, the argument was, "When you vote for Harding and Coolidge, typical sons of noble American mothers, you will vote to maintain the independence of the United States. You will vote against war by dictation from abroad. You will vote as Washington, Jefferson, Lincoln and other great Americans talked when they lived, and as they would vote if they could return and vote with you." [77]

Similar in quality to Brisbane's type of anti-League help for Harding was that of the Senator's future Secretary of Labor, director-general of the Moose James J. Davis. On October 15, Davis wrote to Hays (copy to Christian), describing how he was "cracking out a few" against the Wilson League. Davis said that it was the Labor Council of the League that "rings the bell with the working man," because the United States had only 4 votes in 128. "My point of view is," he added, "will the ivory gatherer of Siam, the rice picker of China, or the diamond laborer of South Africa help us to raise our standard of living?" Davis did not discuss the standard of living of the rice pickers *et al.* He merely concluded his remarks with two more of his best "cracks" against the League. One was the jingle with which, he said, he always ended his speeches:

> He kept us out of War; kept us out of Peace;
> Kept us out of Mexico—mixed us up with Greece,
> Kept us out of Sugar, kept us out of Shoes—
> He joined the League of Nations and wants us to pay the dues.
> He kept us out of everything and you bet we'll remember
> To do some keeping out ourselves on the second of November.
> Harding in the Home—Coolidge in the Constitution.
> America first—November 2nd.

In the margin, he suggested the following alternative for line 3—"or Booze as the crowd will stand." "You understand," he added. Davis' final "crack" was in prose. He described how, when he was recorder in Madison County, Indiana, the banker would bring in mortgages, deeds, and notes to be recorded. They "used to call a note with 25 signatures but only one good man on it a Stud Horse Note. That's what the League is—Stud Horse agreement—only one signature good and that's the U.S.A." [78]

13

Harding and the Republican party had conducted a skillful and useful campaign on the League of Nations. They had made the subject open for discussion in the broadest, if sometimes crudest, sense. They operated on the premise that the American people deserved more understanding of what reasonable alternatives there were to the Wilson League. As the discussion developed, it became apparent that there were indeed such reasonable alternatives as disarmament, an association, and a world court. Certainly the Republicans brought into the discussion a greater and wider participation by the "best minds" than had the Democrats. And they also had to admit into the discussion the ultra-Americanistic, emotional exaggerations of the followers of Johnson, Borah, Brisbane, and James J. Davis.

Could the combination of such incongruous opposites make for disarmament, a world court, a league, or an association of nations for the preservation of world peace? The answer is that, so far as Harding was concerned, that was not the main point. He was seeking a victory, not primarily for world peace but for party unity—and only incidentally for the freedom of discussion about League alternatives. It may have been another piece of Harding patchwork, but, for the moment, party unity was all that mattered.

This mood of party first and world peace later was well reflected in the post-election remarks attributed to Harding by Samuel Colcord. In his 1921 book, entitled *The Great Deception—Bringing Into the Light the Real Meaning and Mandate of the Harding Vote as to Peace*, Colcord quoted Harding as saying, "Few have realized the great importance and the difficulties of the task which confronted me in the campaign. I found two great opposing elements in the party, and it was my supreme task to bring them together. It was vitally necessary to do that if, as President, I am to render any great service to the cause of peace, to which I am so deeply devoted." Then, said Colcord, Harding made a most appealing and "forceful spread of his arms and palms," and added, "That was my task. I had to reach out to both of these groups and unite them and I have done it." And then, commented Colcord, "when I told him what I saw in that gesture, he showed that he appreciated my understanding." [79]

CHAPTER TWENTY-FOUR

Labor and Capital

"I hold that the advancement of labor's cause in America challenges all the world. . . . The progress is the miracle of American opportunity." : : : *From Harding's Marion address on Labor Day, September 6, 1920. "Speeches of Harding . . . to October 1, 1920," p. 123*

"We are the great business nation of the world. . . . Here in America we have developed the most proficient and most efficient types of business organization and administration in the world; they have shown the greatest capacity for administrative vision." : : : *From Harding's front-porch address to businessmen, September 11, 1920. "Speeches of Harding . . . to October 1, 1920," pp. 146, 151*

The image of Harding as a friend of business and management did not need a campaign build-up. Ever since Will Hays had taken charge of the Republican national committee in 1918, ever since Ogden Mills and Professors Lindsay and Hollander of the advisory committee on policies and platforms had undertaken their researching and questionnaires regarding the business needs of the country, the business leaders of the nation knew that the Republican party was in good hands.[1] The national convention was handed a set of reports that bristled with statistics, efficiency, and assurances of the recovery of business sanity. The platforms and the candidates were endorsement of the return to normalcy.[2]

But it was not so with labor. The campaign of 1920 was another act in Harding's life-long play of a conservative trying to appear liberal to the laboring man. Try as he might, he could not conceal from labor the fact that he was the businessmen's darling. As a campaigner he sought to please both sides. But it is certain that, while businessmen, financiers, industrialists—*i.e.*, organized capital—almost universally applauded him and sought his election, no such thing could be said of organized labor. That is not to say that the "labor vote" was universally against Harding, because the "labor vote" was not the same as the "union vote." But it is to say that the unions, especially the

American Federation of Labor, were, in general, opposed to him and that most union members probably voted against him.

Harding simply could not live down his past right-to-work record on labor. In fact, he did not try overly hard to do so. Ever since December, 1919, when he had announced his presidential candidacy, he had spoken to dozens of business organizations, chambers of commerce, and the like, but never to a labor union audience. The nearest that he got to a labor group was on April 29, 1920 in Akron, when he spoke ingratiatingly to the Goodyear Assembly of the Goodyear Tire and Rubber Company.[3] All these prenomination speeches were conditioned by the antiforeign, "red scare" atmosphere of 1919 and the 1920's. Harding seemed oppressed with a certain suspicion and distrust of labor. Upon occasion he felt the need to warn that "unionism must not be permitted to enslave."[4] In his Waldorf-Astoria Americanism address of January 6, 1920 he remarked that "there isn't room anywhere in these United States for anyone who preaches destruction of the government." In his January 20 McKinley memorial speech he condemned the Wilson administration for keeping "step to the Bolshevist anthem." At Baltimore on February 5 he told the Press Club that "every man in America who doesn't subscribe heartily and loyally to the Constitution ought to go to Russia or some other land of tragic experiment." To the Lincoln Club in Portland, Maine, on February 13, he said, "Class legislation is likewise a perversion of liberty and class domination puts an end to liberty's justice." He was referring to "labor legislation," as he did at a Republican rally in Columbus ten days later, when he said, "For the American wage-earner the problem is more pressing, because there is the attempted development of class consciousness, which is always a peril to popular government." "Creeping Socialism" always seemed to lurk in the background. This appeared in his February 25 address to the Providence Chamber of Commerce: "I believe the republic is more endangered by the invasion of public service by the peaceful socialists than it is threatened by the radical who seeks destruction by force." Only rarely did Harding see a flaw in the businessman, and then he would couple him with the erring laboring man. It was so before the Home Market Club in Boston on May 14, when he lamented how much "sober capital must make appeal to intoxicated wealth, and thoughtful labor must appeal to the radical who has no thought of the morrow."[5] Harding's distrust of labor was abiding. In his published letter of January 3, 1920 to railroad labor leader E. J. Miller, previously cited, he revealed his belief that the right to strike on public utilities put society at the mercy of the unions.[6] To Jennings, on November 19, 1919, he wrote darkly of secret information about the unions that he had picked up during the war investigations. "You are quite right," he assured Jennings, "in your declaration that neither farmers nor labor men ought to have any right to organize to plunder the remainder of the human forces." [7]

There was a bit of the "divide and conquer" technique in Harding's thinking about labor unions. He believed that railroad laborers were divided into moderates and radicals, and that the right to work of the moderates should be defended against the desires of the radicals to strike. This was illustrated by an exchange of letters with Hays in 1920. On January 15 Hays called Harding's attention to a case on the Chicago and Eastern Illinois Railroad, as reported by its general manager, F. G. Nicholson. In the fall of 1918 Nicholson had promoted J. F. Ford, chairman of the local chapter of the Order of Railway Conductors, to be supervisor of safety and fire prevention. When a strike occurred on the Chicago and Eastern Illinois, Ford volunteered to work as a strikebreaker. He was tried by his union, defended by the older employees, and exonerated largely because he had an insurance policy whose benefits he did not wish to lose by resigning from the union. Nicholson said that he had talked with the older men who had been through the Pullman strike of 1894, and "without exception, they say that they will not go through a similar occurrence, that they will protect their runs and positions." Nicholson blamed the "younger men, who are the radical element," for continually creating dissension. Hays, in passing the correspondence on to Harding, remarked, "I want you to read this and get this first hand information of what may ultimately be expected from conservative laboring men." Harding, in reply, showed that he was fully in accord with the idea of using the conservatives in unions to break the influence of the radicals. "This is information," wrote Harding, "very much worth having and it does indicate a dependably conservative thought of the worthy working men upon which we may rely in getting back to a state of dependability. . . . Clearly, when we come to the final test in the conflict between radicalism and rationalism we are going to find a very strong support among those who toil for daily wages." [8]

Part of Harding's trouble in the area of labor was that, without counsel, he could not always focus upon the most realistic solution to new and different problems. In other words, it may be said that his facility at oratory and rhetoric led him to self-indulgence. What he needed was a labor-minded Henry C. Wallace. When Harding tried to arrive at a conservative position with regard to labor, he came up with a rather unusual proposal.

This was Harding's suggestion of a plan for labor to buy out management. He proposed such a plan on January 8, 1920 at a banquet meeting in Cleveland of the American Electric Railway Association. For a long time the streetcar operators of America had been harassed by the three-cent-fare agitation based on the premise that higher fares robbed the public while undeserved dividends went to holders of watered securities. Closely allied to the three-cent-fare proposition was the idea of municipal ownership of public utilities. This, of course, was also aimed at watered-security holders. At the Cleveland meeting the streetcar owners knew that they could expect a sympathetic and entertaining performance by the eloquent Ohio Senator. They got one.

Whether he was sincere or not, Harding had his labor-purchase scheme all worked out in his mind. Assuming that the electric railways had been badgered unmercifully by a profit-destroying government, agreeing that the public needed continuous service and the workingman high wages, and ignoring the inroads of the automobile on the streetcar business, Harding offered "a really constructive plan of labor's very own." First, he estimated that there were 300,000 electric railway workers in the United States. If they would organize and assess each member $100 a year for ten years, they could raise $300,000,000, issue bonds for $600,000,000, and by proper investment come to "own one-ninth of all the lines in the United States." The two million railroad workers could do similarly. In ten years they could raise $200,000,000 and buy one-eighth of the railroads. Such a system of collective buying would "transform the so-called laboring classes to the capitalistic class, and the very process of attainment will add to the sturdiness of citizenship. In collective power it is as easy to own mines or railways as it is to buy 'flivvers,' if only capable leadership is turned to constructive endeavor." [9]

After he was nominated for the Presidency, Harding's utterances on labor-management were not quite so fantastic, nor did they emphasize the right to work or the curbing of the right to strike. Rather, they pieced together the elements of a new era made up of the restoration of the old capitalism, plus a new good-will relationship between labor and management and a removal of the danger of Socialism by removing the Democrats from power. Private initiative would thus resume its accustomed vigor and productivity.

It was all very simple. "The world needs production," Harding declared in the *Old Colony Magazine* early in July. "It needs work, more work and still more work. Production will stabilize the world's exchanges." Everything will come out all right "if every man concerned with the production of the necessary goods required to maintain life comfortably and happily in our modern American sense will stop talking, stop agitating and get down to work." [10] In his acceptance address on July 22 he said, "I want, somehow, to appeal to the sons and daughters of the Republic, to every producer, to join hand and brain in production, more production, patriotic production, because patriotic production is no less a defense of our best civilization than that of armed force." [11]

Harding's talk about production had a somewhat hidden meaning for many businessmen. They saw in it a rebuke to labor for not matching the wartime wage increases with increased efficiency. Harding said in his acceptance speech that he wanted the higher wages to abide "on one condition." This was "that the wage earner will give full return for the wage received. It is the best assurance we can have for a reduced cost of living." [12] He showed this same concern in a speech at Jackson, Ohio, on October 20, when he said that he wanted all Americans to share in tariff prosperity including "those American laborers who do their part by giving a 100 per cent efficiency in their productive effort." To many businessmen this involved the alleged propensity of labor to sabotage production. It was alluded to sharply in the *Credit Guide* for August 3, which congratulated Harding for his acceptance speech reference to the need for labor efficiency. "It is believed," said the *Guide*, "that Labor is beginning to appreciate its shortcomings." It went on to quote its president, Julius H. Reiter, as saying, "In every branch of industry Labor is producing less than formerly, and is receiving more pay for it." More caustic was B. C. Forbes in his *Forbes* magazine on August 21: "Labor has been notoriously, scandalously and injuriously indifferent, lazy and arrogant during the last three years. Higher and still higher wages, instead of encouraging honest effort, too often brought less effort and more arrogancy . . . workers are now producing more and are becoming less bellicose. It is not uncommon to find that the laying off of ten percent of a force results in an increase of total production." [13]

Words of calm and assurance for the future of the American economy seemed to flow from Harding's inspiring and imposing presence as wisdom from an oracle. Over half of the front-porch acceptance address dealt with that subject. "Profiteering is a crime of commission, under-production is a crime of omission." "We must stabilize and strive for normalcy, else the inevitable reaction will bring its train of sufferings, disappointments and reversals." "The insistent call is for labor, management, and capital to reach understanding. . . . I want the employers in industry to understand the aspirations, the convictions, the yearnings of the millions of American wage earners, and I want the wage earners to understand the problems, the anxieties, the obligations of management and capital, and all of them must understand their relationship to the people and their obligations to the Republic. Out of this understanding will come the unanimous committal to economic justice, and in economic justice lies that social justice which is the highest essential to human happiness." "We do not oppose but approve collective bargaining, because that is an outstanding right, but we are unalterably insistent that its exercise must not destroy the equally sacred rights of the individual, in his necessary pursuit of livelihood. Any American has the right to quit his employment, so has every American the right to seek employment. The group must not endanger the individual, and we must discourage groups preying upon one another." "The strike against the Government is properly denied, for Government service involves none of the elements of profit which relate to competitive enterprize."

The evils of the high cost of living, inflation, and taxation would be corrected. "We will attempt intelligent and courageous deflation, and strike at government borrowing which enlarges the evil, and we will attack the high cost of government with every energy and facility which attends Republican capacity. We promise that relief which will attend the halting of waste and extravagance, and the renewal of the practice of public economy, not alone because it will relieve tax burdens, but because it will be an example to stimulate thrift and economy in private life." [14]

Not even the revelation of past inconsistencies could disturb Harding's composure. James C. Feeny, former president of the Washington, D.C. Central Labor Union, publicly reminded him of his one-time opposition to, and contempt for, the Adamson eight-hour-a-day bill of 1916 for railroad workers, and claimed that Hughes had lost the election of 1916 because of a similar attitude. Feeny added that if Harding had nothing good to say in behalf of labor unions it was better for him to say nothing at all. In his public reply via a letter to Feeny, Harding, with a great show of honesty, admitted that the Republicans had made a mistake in 1916, and were not going to make it again in 1920. This time, he said, they were going to make a strong appeal to the confidence of the "thinking American wage earner." Harding said that he could do this because he himself had once been a wage worker, and had become the employer of workers. This enabled him to understand their point of view. The days of rivalry and bickering between labor and management were over. "Tell your friends," wrote Harding, "that as President, I will be ever ready to hear the grievances and to know ultimately concerning the problems of the great mass of American wage earners. It is not possible to do all that they want, but I mean to do my part in reaching that understanding which I think is essential to the tranquillity of the country." [15]

3

As the campaign progressed, the image of Harding as the benign friend of labor was enhanced by three outstanding devices. One was to develop the theme of "cooperation as the key to industrial relationship," as publicity-man Welliver phrased it. Another was to emphasize the Esch-Cummins Transportation Act of 1920 as labor's "Bill of Rights," and the third was the old argument of a high tariff to protect the American worker from the competition of cheap labor in other lands.

None of these devices can be said to have made much impression on the so-called labor vote. But that was not their prime intention. The "labor" vote was a rather amorphous thing, and not as deliverable as the expression implies. The true intention was to create an impression for the "general voter" that Harding had an enlightened attitude toward labor. The general public in 1920 was either indifferent to "labor" or looked upon it with slightly red-tinted glasses. It was thus easier for it to see enlightenment in a labor policy that "labor" itself did not necessarily appreciate.

Co-operation as the key to industrial peace was a theme that lent itself to Warren Harding's peculiarly persuasive, mirage-making talents. Against the luridly depicted background of the possibilities of economic ruin, he could appeal to the better nature of all classes to seek to understand each other and keep society producing. He could

always start from the premise of the public uneasiness at the seemingly ever-pending industrial paralysis that might come from the
ever-threatening coal strikes as John L. Lewis and the United Mine
Workers sought to improve the standard of living of the miners.
"Surely," he told Sherman Rogers in an interview published in the
August 18 *Outlook*, and in the press generally, "the events of the past
few months have conclusively proven that the inability of management to secure sufficient capital to carry on its business to capacity
leads to certain industrial paralysis that affects not only the railway
system but every industry and department of economic life in the
entire country." He invoked the prospects of industrial stagnation,
inability of farmers to market crops, widespread unemployment, in
short, "ruin of the entire economic fabric."

He could then turn his words to the higher realms of the virtues of
mutual understanding. "We have entered a new era in the relationship
between management, the workers, and the public." In the past, he
said, capital has cared not for the good will of the workers, and the
workers have been ignorant of the risks and responsibilities of the
employees. Mutual understanding "would beyond doubt dissipate a
majority of the industrial troubles facing us today." Harding did not
propose anything definite, but he was sure that he was right because
of his "unbounded confidence in the American people." "The light of
truth must be thrown on all industrial disagreements that threaten the
happiness and prosperity of the country."

On Labor Day, September 6, Harding offered another utopia for the
establishment of management-labor mutuality and understanding. Before an audience mostly of railroad laborers brought in on free passes
issued by their employers, he laid an oratorical wreath on the old
order of quarreling over subsistence wages. "We will never return to
old pre-war conditions. . . . I wish the existing high scale of wages to
remain." Progress had been "the miracle of American opportunity."
The chief trouble was that labor did not always accompany its increase of wages with an increase of production. How to bring about
such increase? Very simple. Employers must teach workmen "to know
a pride in the thing done. There ought to be inspiration to skill, and
glory in accomplishment." He was thinking of his own newspaper
plant and the profit-sharing program. "To be specific," he said, "the
need of today is the extension by employers of the principle that each
job in the big plant is a little business of its own." Workingmen "go
crazy from lack of self-expression in modern factories. They ought to

be taught by employers the significance of the job—unit costs, relations to other operations, the ways to greater efficiency. In a word, the employer owes it to his men to make them feel that each job is a little business of its own. In this way, as some one has said, the job stops being an enemy of the man and becomes his associate and friend, and the success achieved opens the way for his looked-for advancement." [16]

Akin to this kind of utopian thinking in labor relations was his glorification of the Esch-Cummins Transportations Act passed by a Republican Congress in 1920. This was a many-sided law designed to substitute an enlightened system of railroad operation under benevolent government regulation in place of the wartime government ownership and operation. The Interstate Commerce Commission was empowered to prepare a tentative plan for the consolidation of the railroads into a relatively small number of competing systems. Rates were to be regulated with an idea to guarantee the roads an adequate return on their investments. A revolving fund was to be created out of all earnings above 6 per cent to assist roads making less than that. A system of railroad boards of labor adjustments, capped by a national Railroad Labor Board, was created to hear all labor disputes and determine the reasonableness of wages. The idea was to prevent strikes, though they were not forbidden.[17]

There was some crafty organizational maneuvering in regard to Harding's praise of the Esch-Cummins law. It was used to try to offset his antistrike remarks on the so-called Cummins bill, which the Senate had passed with Harding's enthusiastic support. The lower house of Congress had stricken out the antistrike clause so that, when the bill was enacted under the label of the Esch-Cummins law, it had only the voluntary labor board system instead of the outlawing of strikes. The campaign strategy was to make Harding appear as the great champion of the voluntary Esch-Cummins method rather than the supporter of the compulsory antistrike system which he really wanted.

It was Will Hays who masterminded the transformation of Harding from an antistrike proponent into a voluntary mediation-service glorifier. Word came to Hays that during the Ohio spring primary in 1920 the Harding organization had gotten out a pamphlet entitled "Senator Warren G. Harding on the Cummins Bill." It was a copy of the E. J. Miller letter of January 3, 1920 (see chapter 17.) containing a "good manly" statement of the reasons why the railroads and the public should not be made subject to the workingmen's right to strike. It was pleasing to management and useful in counteracting the appeal that

General Leonard Wood was trying to make to win the labor vote. Numerous requests for copies were made by industrial leaders. Hays saw the danger of the continued circulation of the pamphlet during the summer and fall of 1920. He therefore, on August 13, wrote to W. R. Halley of the Ohio Republican executive committee asking in effect that the circulation be placed under the supervision of the national committee so the the preparation of Harding's role as a supporter of the Esch-Cummins law could be built up. "The literature for the present," Hays told Halley, "is dwelling on the Esch-Cummins bill, which is the basis of the black lists of the Plumb plan supporters of the A. F. of L. The senator's vote on the Cummins bill will be answered when the issue is raised." Hays was referring to the fact that the American Federation of Labor had endorsed the government ownership of the railroads (the Plumb plan) as a substitute for the Esch-Cummins private ownership law. This would enable Harding and the Republicans to avoid taking an antistrike position and would allow them instead to take a free enterprise stand against government ownership of the railroads. "The pamphlet is good," Hays assured Halley, but it would be used only when the proper people asked for it.[18]

Hays' plan worked admirably. By the time the A. F. of L. and other labor protagonists began to remind Harding of his antistrike remarks, an image of Harding as a great friend of private enterprise, as a defender of the uninterrupted service of the railroads in behalf of the public, and as a constructive proponent of voluntary labor mediation and peacemaking had been created.

Thus was the candidate enabled to proceed with his oratory that sought to make the Esch-Cummins law the railroad workers' "Bill of Rights," a "new charter of freedom," "the greatest forward step taken by any government in the world." It provided, he said in his Labor Day address, "full, complete and instant justice for the railway wage-earner; justice on appeal and hearing, without having to fight or measure strength; justice without inconveniencing the American people or hindering their transportation, or suspending railway activities. . . . No labor in the world today is so fortunately situated as that on the American railroads." Harding hoped that it would lead "the way to the ultimate solution of all industrial conflicts." It was the ideal solution for the rights of owners and workers. It saved the nation from the evils of "creeping Socialism." It allegedly rescued the nation from the complete collapse of service and securities caused by the wartime government ownership. He regretted that so many workingmen considered the law as hostile to labor, unjust to unionism, and "subservient to capital." He hoped that experience with the conciliation service of the adjustment boards and the central Railroad Labor Board would enable labor to discover that the law was "unimpeachally fair." "I wish," he said, "I could say the thing which would add to the faith of the millions of railway workers" in their government. There was so much that they could be proud of in the thought that they were taking part in the "practical working out of that harmonized relationship which is our security for today and our best promise for the future." [19] All of this, of course, was played up in special party pamphlets entitled "What Is the Esch-Cummins Act?" and "Putting the Railroads to Work." Labor should know, these pamphlets said, that there were "no guarantees of profit and no compulsory arbitration." [20]

4

Harding had to wait a little before he could use his tariff argument on the railroad workers or anybody else. That is to say that the tariff plank in the Republican platform was against him. It was an internationally minded plank, and Harding had nothing to do with its formation. But he had plenty to do with its modification—indeed, with its cancellation. This was the one and only area in which Harding went against his party platform and his party counselors. Business was not so keen any more on the protective tariff, but it was always useful to dangle before labor.

It is of the highest importance to emphasize that, while Harding was fulfilling the international requirements of the Republican platform in the League of Nations, he crushed the internationalism of the platform's world-trade provisions. If the original intentions of the Republican party as expressed in those provisions had been adhered to in the campaign of 1920, the emergency tariff of 1921 and the Fordney-McCumber tariff of 1922 might never have been enacted. Certainly, a party committed to some degree of internationalism in both foreign affairs and foreign trade would have hardly dared to have contradicted itself as the Republicans did in enacting the high-tariff legislation of the 1920s. By injecting the tariff into the closing weeks of the campaign, Harding made pledges that revived the tariff isolationists and set the pace for a super-protective pattern of legislation for an entire decade. Harding himself must therefore be given a large share of the blame that made the Republican leaders incapable of tempering their policies on trade, finance, and foreign affairs that had so much to do with the domestic, and European, financial collapse of 1929.

Harding's infatuation with the protective tariff has been abundantly demonstrated in previous pages. One of the most tenacious ideas of this old tariff-American war-horse was that the basic reason for the existence of the Republican party was to protect the American standard of living from foreign competition. This is not to say that Harding made the tariff a key issue in the campaign. As he good-naturedly admitted in Wheeling, West Virginia on September 28, "Some say it isn't an issue. Even if it were not, I'd cling to it out of gratitude, for it made us what we are today." [21] Nor did his belaboring the subject make any real difference in winning votes. Probably for that very reason he insisted on his favorite dogma, and probably for the same reason his party counselors let him have his say. But when the American Protective Tariff League insisted upon campaign-plan alterations in favor of more tariff Americanism, the League found in Harding a willing friend and powerful influence in making the required adjustment.

The tariff plank in the Republican platform of 1920 had world-minded implications. To be sure, it was ambiguous, but it provided that future tariffs should be dependent on two factors: (1) world trade conditions and (2) the home market—if and when the latter became a prime consideration. It read as follows:

> The uncertain and unsettled condition of international balances, the abnormal economic and trade situation of the world, and the impossibility of forecasting accurately even for the near future, preclude the formation of a definite program to meet conditions a year hence. But the Republican party reaffirms its belief in the protective principle and pledges itself to a revision of the tariff as soon as conditions shall make it necessary for the preservation of the home market for American labor, agriculture and industry.[22]

This softening of the Republicans on the tariff was deliberately done. It was the result of the researches made by Professors Samuel McCune Lindsay (Columbia) and Jacob H. Hollander (Johns Hopkins), staff director and associate staff director respectively of the

Republican national committee's advisory committee on policies and platform. This was part of the work supervised by their superior, Ogden L. Mills, chairman of the executive committee of the advisory committee, whose questionnaires had been in circulation ever since early in 1920. In May, 1920 these learned gentlemen had submitted a most scholarly report entitled "International Trade and Credits." This showed that, as a result of World War I, the United States had become a creditor nation with a credit account against foreign nations of $12,000,000,000 and a diminishing excess of exports over imports. This excess was expected to continue at least until 1923 and possibly throughout the remainder of the 1920's. Eventually, however, the report said, "As a creditor nation we must have an excess of imports over exports to pay the creditor nation its interest." Without actually using the word "tariff" the professors were demonstrating that high tariffs would impede the payment of interest to American creditors.[23] The softened tariff plank of the platform was the obvious result.

The man who took the offensive against the Lindsay-Hollander report was Wilbur F. Wakeman, treasurer and general secretary of the American Protective Tariff League and a longtime friend of Harding. It was Wakeman who paid part of Harding's hotel expenses at the 1920 Chicago convention. Wakeman even publicized this fact. In the July 2, 1920 issue of the League's weekly newspaper, the American Economist, Wakeman wrote, "The Honorable Warren G. Harding and Mrs. Harding were the guests of the American Protective Tariff League throughout the Republican National Convention." [24] A reason for the League's solicitude for Harding was expressed by its president, A. H. Heisy of Newark, Ohio, who wrote to George Christian on June 18, "Of course you know the Protective Tariff League secured rooms for the Senator, at the La Salle, to give him the necessary rest, which was unobtainable at the Congress Hotel." [25] Harding, of course, was grateful for their concern and said so in a June 29 note to Wakeman: "You know how much I appreciate your thoughtfulness at Chicago." Wakeman also offered Harding the facilities of his summer cottage at Eltington Beach in New Jersey.[26]

The occasion for Wakeman's attack on the Lindsay-Hollander report on the need for an excess of imports over exports was his discovery of this tariff-reducing proposition in the galley proof of the campaign textbook. On August 10, in a state of great alarm, Wakeman wired Harding from New York: "Am confidentially informed that republican textbook is weak on tariff question STOP That it is saturated with the questionnaires of Ogden L. Mills STOP [Wakeman was one of the 174 members of Mills' committee] That it is not up to the platform or to your own declarations STOP Hope that I am wrongly informed STOP If Text Book is satisfactory to you it will be satisfactory to us STOP Delay of publication would be better than explanatory and defensive campaign STOP Hope for success inspires this telegram." It happened that, when Wakeman's message reached Harding's office, party chairman Hays was there. Hays was surprised, and it was written at the bottom of the telegram, presumably in Christian's handwriting, "Hays is here. Some mistake. Go around and read it." This message was at once wired to Wakeman with authorization to visit Republican headquarters in New York.[27]

Wakeman was not mistaken. He went to the New York office and found his suspicions confirmed. He wired back to Harding, "Editors of text book seem more interested in foreign obligations than American prosperity STOP Page three eighty nine reads as follows as a creditor nation we must have an excess of imports over exports dash to pay the creditor nations the interest STOP Recommend that complete proofs be carefully read, scrutinized and corrected by men of great editorial experience and men of undoubted Americanism STOP If we cannot have strong declaration for adequate protective tariff cut out dangerous paragraphs trending to free trade." [28]

Wakeman was not very welcome at Republican headquarters, but he got the revision in favor of the tariff that he wanted from the "free trade professors." As he wrote Harding on August 17, "Pursuant to Mr. Christian's telegram of August 11, I had a long and warm conference with Professor Lindsay and Professor Hollander which at first felt like the refrigerator of the literati of Internationalists. The two Free Trade professors simply put up an argument in favor of the sentence quoted in my telegram 'we must have an excess of imports over exports—to pay the creditor nation its interest,' and the context of the chapter led to this deduction." [29]

The surrender of the "free trade professors" to Wakeman in behalf of tariff-Americanism was made in writing. In a letter of August 12 Professor Lindsay agreed to the changes that "you thought objectionable and believed would give unnecessary offense to many of our friends and might injure the great Republican victory for which we are all working." To be specific, wrote Lindsay, "I have stricken out these words [about the necessity for an excess of imports over the exports] and all of the following lines to the end of the paragraph."

The paragraph was written out in full, and instead of the import-export statement, it read with eloquent evasiveness: "In the post-war period as a creditor nation we must take into account certain new factors in the unsettled condition of international balances which constituted the present abnormal economic and trade situations of the entire world. . . ." This, concluded Lindsay, is entirely consistent with the tariff declaration of the Republican platform and "leaves our candidate for President, Vice-President, Senate and House entirely free and unembarrassed in the development of their position on the tariff." [30] Lindsay might have added that the report in its entirety was still an antitariff report but that its language was too technical for anybody but an economics expert to understand.

Wakeman got one more concession to his tariff-Americanism demands. This consisted of the addition at the very end of the campaign textbook, after all of the appendix material, of a three-page article entitled "Senator Harding and the Tariff Issue." This was an amazing preparation, making everything both confusing and compatible. It quoted the Republican platform on the tariff. It declared, "the two things go together, international trade and tariff, and always have had to be considered together, now more than ever since we are a creditor nation." Three alternatives were suggested: (1) cancel the $12 billion debt; (2) demand its payment in gold "over a series of years," thus avoiding "dumping"; and (3) draw up a "wise tariff policy of protection of our essential American industries so skillfully adjusted that we can absorb European merchandise in which they will pay their debts without harm to our labor standards, our industries or our agriculture." The article closed with a two-page quotation from Harding's 1916 national convention keynote speech in which the Senator was at his all-American, tariff-thumping best.[31]

Wakeman was highly pleased. These changes, he wrote Harding, "will take precedence over the scholastic deductions of the Staff Director and assistant Staff Director on Policies and Platform." He believed that "we have been saved from an awful mistake," such as had lost the Republicans the election in 1916. After all, he said, "The *most important element* of this campaign is to avoid mistakes." As for the textbook, "it would have been better to have no text-book than as written, for the opposition would have magnified Chapter XXI on International Trade and Credits into a California trip by Hon. Charles E. Hughes." [32]

The road was now clear for high-tariff promotion, with Wakeman and the American Protective Tariff League leading the way. Special League broadsides under the title of "The Defender" poured forth, subtitled "AMERICAN INDUSTRY WILL BE SLAUGHTERED By Oriental Competition Unless Protection Is Restored," and "Why Commercial Travelers Are Protectionists." Then, "to supplement the Republican Text-Book," Wakeman promised to use a tariff primer once issued by former Secretary of the Treasury Leslie Shaw. "Naturally this matter will be out ahead of the text-book and will fortify the speakers and editors." [33]

Harding, too, went full speed ahead on the tariff. No sooner had Professor Lindsay surrendered his economic thinking to Wakeman's tariff-thumping than Harding came out openly declaring the tariff to be an issue. On the very day, August 12, of the Lindsay-Wakeman agreement, Harding was at it. It involved the matter of California versus Sicilian lemons. California state senator Frank P. Flint had written Harding how the low tariff, Italian subsidies, inflation, and increasing United States freight rates were threatening the California lemon producers. "Fifteen thousand California fruit growers," wired Flint, "look to the Republican Presidential candidate for hope of relief." They did not look in vain. Harding replied publicly on August 12, saying that the magnificent California fruit industries should not be sacrificed for the benefit of other countries. It was not only lemons but fruit in general, wool, and all other American productions that needed help. "We can't maintain American production at home if we are going to buy our goods abroad." The Democrats, especially Franklin D. Roosevelt, picked up the issue at once, making much fun about the Republicans "picking a lemon." Roosevelt said the tariff was a dead issue to American people. Harding took the bait and solemnly declared, on August 14, "Mark my words, this will be an issue. People can smile now, but you will hear a lot of shouting about this tariff before this campaign is over." [34]

Issue or not, there was, indeed, plenty of tariff-shouting during the rest of the campaign, with Harding doing more than his share of it. Labor Day was a natural time for workingmen to be told of what they owed to the tariff. This was a chance to rededicate the Republican party to its founding principles, which included the tariffs of the 1860's. Harding had learned nothing on the subject since his nineteenth-century baptism in tariff-Americanism. After freeing the slaves, declared the candidate, "the Republican party instantly turned to insuring conditions to afford the abundance of employment. I believe in the protective policy which prospers America first and exalts American standards of wage and American standards of living high above the Old World. . . . If we buy abroad, we will slacken production at home, and slackened production means diminished employment, and growing idleness and all attending disappointments." [35]

Again, economic wisdom seemed to flow from Harding's lips for those who did not understand economics. On September 8 in his Minnesota State Fair agricultural address, with the obvious approval of Henry C. Wallace, Harding expounded on the home market argument for the tariff. "If we are to build up a self-sustaining agriculture here at home, the farmer must be protected from unfair competition from those countries where agriculture is still being exploited and where the standards of living on the farm are much lower than here." Harding admitted that in the past the argument for tariffs on farm products was not so good because Americans were a great surplus-producing people. This made them mere paper duties. But, with dubious logic, he assumed that, since consumption was now absorbing normal agricultural production, "the American farmer has a right to insist that in our trade relations with other countries he shall have the same consideration that is accorded to other industries and we mean to protect them all. So long as America can produce the funds we need I am in favor of buying from America first." He cited as one of our rivals, "the Argentine, whose rich soil is being exploited in heedless fashion." [36]

As the days went by, Harding enlarged his list of America's economic enemies. To a California delegation on September 14, he cited the menace of wheat from Canada, cane sugar from the tropical islands, beet sugar from Europe, rice from the Far East, beans and peas from Manchuria. "It will be necessary to give full and adequate tariff protection to those industries." [37]

Harding's tariff address at Baltimore on September 27 was really astonishing, for it was written by none other than "free trade" Professor Jacob H. Hollander. There is no doubt about this, as is shown by comparison of the draft prepared by Hollander as found in the Harding Papers along with the speech delivered by Harding. Hollander was very proud of his "Memorandum," which Harding used practically verbatim. "I have sought," the professor wrote to Mannington when submitting the manuscript, "to develop the points of particular appeal at this time to Baltimore and to Maryland, and which are likely to help swing the state into the Republican column. . . . Maryland is my native state and my whole life, personal and professional—has been spent there. So it has been possible to write *con amore.*" [38]

A most significant feature of the Harding-Hollander Baltimore address was how flatly it contradicted the original Lindsay-Hollander report, to the Republican advisory committee, on "International Trade and Credit." No longer were there learned demonstrations of the need for an excess of imports over exports to pay the interest due American creditors. It was a complete turnabout emphasizing the need of protection against such imports. The key words are completely explicit:

> A flood of imports from debtor countries intent upon stimulating their productive output, and aided, even though undesignedly, by an unfavorable foreign exchange, would be a bitter experience for the creditor country. We mean to deal considerately, we want to help, but we do not mean to paralyze America to effect a restoration. It would be incomparably better for our credits to remain uncollected, and our balances to be waived than for liquidation to take the form of an undermining flood of imports—whether products of factory, mine or farm—that would cripple American industry, degrade American labor and weaken our whole economic fabric. From any such invasions we have a right to be saved.

The speaker went on to tell of Maryland's heroic war efforts to become more industrially self-reliant. Now Maryland asked for fair play, "that the government which has sanctioned their rise and encouraged their growth shall not now be passive witness to their undoing by an abrupt competitive invasion, whether in the form of 'dumping' or stimulated foreign production, which they are neither mature nor strong enough to resist, and which America does not mean to ask that they shall resist. Prosper America First." There were further exhortations about building up America's merchant marine.[39] No wonder Maryland went for Harding in November.

By the end of the campaign Harding had completely overthrown the Lindsay-Hollander tariff soft-pedalers. He commited his party fully to high-tariff restoration. The nation was told over and over again that dumping of foreign surpluses would bring economic paralysis. "If you allow foreign nations," he propounded in Hammond, Indiana on October 6, "to dump their products in the United States in the aftermath of war, you paralyze American productivity and destroy our own good fortune." [40] To the Southern Tariff Congress meeting in New Orleans on October 11 he sent a stirring message of encouragement: "No section of our country needs so much as at this time the application of the principle of the protective tariff, and if, as seems from the convention, this fact is coming home to the people of the South, I shall be sincerely rejoiced." [41] In his late October stumping in Ohio at Jackson, Cincinnati, Cleveland, and Columbus, he invariably mixed the tariff with his League of Nations talk.[42] In the last week of the campaign, he boldly promised a quick adoption of a new high-tariff law. He did this in a telegram of October 25 to Paul Ewert of the Joplin, Missouri chamber of commerce, who had asked protection for the faltering local zinc-ore industry. "When the Republican Party is restored to control of the government after March 4 next," Harding wired, "there will be a prompt return to the American system of protection for American industry." [43]

Thus did Harding, with the aid of the American Protective Tariff League, restore the tariff to Republican respectability in the campaign of 1920 and prepare for the Fordney-McCumber tariff of 1922. Considering the unhappy effect of this tariff upon the American economy in the 1920s, and its contribution to the collapse of 1929, it would have been wiser for the party managers to have heeded Professors Lindsay and Hollander, and for the professors to have remained faithful to their intellectual principles and convictions.

5

The Harding image of friendship for labor was promoted by many labor leaders. Among these was William L. Hutcheson, head of the United Brotherhood of Carpenters and Joiners, who had been quick to announce his support of Harding in June, 1920. Hutcheson never believed in the nonpartisan political action approach of Samuel Gompers and the American Federation of Labor which was shaping up in the Progressive era, and which was to lead the Federation to oppose Harding in the campaign of 1920. Harding encouraged this division between Gompers and Hutcheson by personally inviting the latter to be present with him on the platform in the Marion Labor Day ceremonies of September 6. Hutcheson gladly accepted and warmly endorsed Harding's Labor Day message.[44] Harding also encouraged the right-wing steel workers organization, the Amalgamated Association of Iron, Steel, and Tin Workers, through his warm friendship with James J. Davis. Harding's friend John J. Lentz told Harding that "Jim Davis is as good a friend as you have in this country. . . . With his long life connection with labor unions, he will be able to give you something more than nice pointers." The Harding-Davis correspondence, especially in regard to the Moose vote, shows that Harding did as Lentz advised. This friendship also paid off in the endorsement of Harding by the Amalgamated early in September. The Amalgamated had been very cool to the steel strike of 1919 dominated by the so-called radical element led by the National Committee for Organizing the Iron and Steel Workers.[45]

There was other labor support for Harding. A laborite backing him was Terrence O'Conner, president of the International Longshoreman's Association. O'Conner's announcement for Harding was made after a conference in Marion with Harding, and was regarded by publicity man Welliver as "rather the most important labor development that has been uncovered here." "O'Conner" he said, "is body and soul for Harding and will do anything he can." [46] Then there was the pro-Harding Railway Employees Harding-for-President Club. This was largely the product of Harry L. Fidler, "special representative" for labor at the Chicago headquarters of the Republican national committee. It arranged for the paid railway-labor delegation at the Labor Day front-porch ceremonies. (Free passes on the railroads had many times been a great boon to Harding.) Fidler was a former official of the Brotherhood of Locomotive Engineers. He and his "labor editor, E. C. R. Humphries, also got out a "Labor Publicity Sheet," boosting Harding and blasting Democrats.[47] On October 31 wide publicity was given to a declaration of "Thirty-nine officials" of the skilled trades, congratulating Harding for his enlightened labor policy in the *Star* plant and for his protesting against the expulsion of five Socialists from the New York legislature. The "Thirty-nine" included Fidler, who sponsored the declaration, many A. F. of L. field agents, representatives of the railroad conductors, switchmen, station agents, and telegraphers, as well as various building-trade agents and others of the pottery workers, lake seamen, bricklayers, photo-engravers, sheet-metal workers, painters and decorators, cigar makers, and so on.[48]

The Harding Papers contain many letters from alleged pro-labor men offering to deliver the votes of their friends. Harding did not rush out to welcome them, but he usually instructed Daugherty to look them over and give them what encouragement seemed wise. For example, there was Harding's fellow Moose and friend W. S. "Doc Waddell" Andres of Columbus and Cincinnati, who, on June 20, sent in a list of "characters," mostly ex-Democrats, who were disgusted with

Wilson and Cox for reasons not clearly stated. "Doc" mentioned "Pop" Downey, father of prize-fighters Bryan and Anthony Downey. "Properly got to—the DOWNEYS would be a Good Help on WEST SIDE in COLUMBUS." A prize-fighter pilgrimage to the front porch was suggested. There was G. M. Grant, who was touring the country in the interest of "Business Men who want Chinese immigrated." Grant's son was with "Billy James, Theatrical Man" of Columbus. "Much good," wrote "Doc," "can be accomplished playing to these UNITS. G. M. GRANT is one of the shrewdest 'Live Wires' I know." Others were named. Harding handled this by writing to Daugherty, on July 8, "May be some merit in his suggestions. It is possible the labor workers mentioned in his letter are of real value. Waddell, himself, can kick up a lot of dust. I do not pretend to pass judgment on the good he can accomplish for us. Of course, I could not well do otherwise than write him that I was submitting his letter to you and would recommend favorable consideration of him." [49]

Similar treatment was given to other labor mavericks. On July 23, Daugherty wrote Harding concerning John L. Lewis of the United Mine Workers. "He wants to see you," said Daugherty, "and if he is not trying some game you ought to see him." [50] There was Clyde Reed of the railway postal clerks, who suggested special treatment of their men. Daugherty wrote, on August 9, "I know Clyde Reed and we have a man put on at my suggestion to look after these men. I think we can take care of them nicely." [51] Another was Ben E. Chapin, editor of the *Railway Employee* (Newark, New Jersey), who wrote Harding on August 4 describing a campaign of denunciation of the Plumb Plan in that paper. Chapin's paper claimed to have "the largest circulation of any railroad labor journal in America supported by individual subscriptions." It had much advertising from railroad supply houses. Its editorials and cartoons depicted Plumb plan supporters as radicals with incendiary torches and bombs attacking the working men's saving banks which had invested 47 per cent of their assets in railroad securities. Harding told Daugherty that he was writing to Chapin "asking him to arrange to drop in to see me when opportunity is favorable." [52]

Another way to get labor to support Harding's cause indirectly was to encourage the formation of third parties. The idea was to keep radical opponents of Harding from supporting Cox. Efforts along this line were suggested on August 18 by Mannington in a letter to George H. Clark of the advisory committee. "If there is any practical way," wrote Mannington, "of securing the entry of the Socialists and of a separate labor ticket it would be well worth the effort. The thing which I fear is that there are large numbers of radicals in Ohio who, while not wishing to vote the Democratic ticket, will never under any circumstances vote the Republican ticket. With only two tickets in the field these men will vote the Democratic ticket. A Socialist ticket and a labor ticket would keep these radical votes away from the Democrats. Is it practicable to do anything along these lines?" Whether or not Harding's friends had anything to do with the preparation of the Socialist and Single Tax tickets in Ohio is not known. The results were miniscule and insignificant, the Socialist vote for Debs being 42,880 and the Single Tax vote 1,497, with Harding's plurality 174,909.[53] Even in the national figures the third party vote was only about 1,300,000 in a Harding plurality of over 7,000,000.

6

While Harding and his friends were building up for him a pro-labor image, strong elements in the union movement were trying to tear it down. Most important of these were Samuel Gompers and the American Federation of Labor.

A central feature of the A. F. of L. position in 1920 was the creation of the "National Non-Partisan Political Campaign Committee," in fulfillment of instructions of the 1919 national convention and of the Farmer-Labor Conference of December 13, 1919. This was dedicated to the duty of defeating "labor's enemies." All locals were called upon to create district committees for the purpose. How much district organizing was conducted is not clear, but it is obvious from the publications of the national A. F. of L. and of the *Cleveland Federationist* that Harding and the Republican party were deemed "labor enemies," and that "non-partisanism" meant that all labor-union men should oppose Harding regardless of their previous political affiliation.[54]

Upon strategic occasions President Samuel Gompers of the A. F. of L., his subordinates, and his publications set the pace for the "Non-Partisan" movement with pronunciamentos against Harding and the Republicans. The national platform of the two parties received the attention of the "Non-Partisan Campaign Committee," with the Republican document bearing the brunt of its attack. The conclusion was that "the Republican platform is defiant in its defense of the enemies of Labor. The Republican convention turned its back upon Labor." With particular reference to the Esch-Cummins Act, condemnation was made of the anti-strike implications involved in the creation of governmental machinery "for the coercion of Labor and for the suppression and limitation of its proper and normal activities." [55]

Harding was given harsh treatment by Gompers and the *Federationist* throughout the rest of the campaign. The September, 1920 issue of the *Federationist* contained a resumé of the legislative records of the two candidates with Cox emerging as a labor-minded candidate for his Progressivism as Governor of Ohio, and Harding looking rather bad as a United States Senator for his support of the anti-strike clause of the Cummins bill, as well as his approval of the Esch-Cummins bill. Harding's acceptance speech was ridiculed for its platitudinous passages about "understanding" between labor and management, his concept of "group citizenship," and his conditional attitude toward collective bargaining. The public was reminded of Harding's having said that Congress had been "intimidated" by labor into passing the Adamson eight-hour law, and that "the surrender of Congress to the behests of an outside body wielding political power affecting national legislation through its influence at the polls, has had a most disastrous effect upon our institutions." His Miller anti-strike letter of January 3, 1920 was given the usual condemnation.[56]

Vigorous attacks on Harding in the closing weeks of the campaign came from Gompers and his cohorts. In the October *Federationist* the A. F. of L. president paid his respects to Harding's "normalcy" utterances. "Normalcy" was made to mean "going backward," as against Cox's progressiveness which meant "going forward." In the November issue, above pictures of Harding and Cox were the headlines "Look Here, Upon This Picture, and on This: For President: Cox or Harding. Read! Think! Choose!" There followed a listing of the candidates' voting records, with Harding labeled "surely, uniformly, unfalteringly on the side of reaction." There was also a stinging rebuke for Harding in the form of a reprint of an article by Norman Hapgood in the October *Yale Review*. "To a Republican friend of peculiar candor," wrote the author, "I put the question: 'When you vote for Harding, what will you be voting for?' 'For the class into which I was born,' he replied, 'and for government by the stronger elements in society. Also I shall be voting against a sentimental and socialistic attitude toward labor.'" The labor campaign closed with contemptuous charges—previously denied—that Harding was a stockholder in Marion's leading industries, which were said to be notoriously scab-dominated. The resolution in support of Harding by the Typographical Union of Marion was denounced as a frame-up. No other union in Marion in affiliation with the local Central Labor Union was said to have endorsed it.[57]

A particularly intimate discussion of Harding's alleged labor views was printed in a series of four articles by Walter Liggett in the *Columbus Labor News* from September 30 to October 21, 1920. Liggett claimed that Harding and Cox had a "gentleman's agreement" to use the League of Nations as a "red herring" to divert the attention of the people from more vital issues. Harding was quoted as saying in an interview with Liggett that he did not fear Gompers because "everyone knows that Mr. Gompers is a Democrat—a British free trader in fact,—and he cannot swing any considerable portion of labor to support his political views." Harding described in detail his "closed union shop" practice in the *Marion Daily Star*, but went on to deny that the closed shop should be a guiding principle for labor in general. Laboring men were more interested in their home life and social affairs than in the promotion of unions. Liggett wound up his series by calling Harding an "ultra-reactionary" with a "benign feudalistic attitude toward labor and life—and foreign affairs—that typifies the old school millionaire." He had no consciousness of the "new" dignity of labor. For labor to organize so as to make its power felt in the political field was "class government." "I doubt," concluded Liggett, "if a man ever was put forward as the president of a great republic more economically and historically illiterate than Senator Harding. . . . He considers Marion, Ohio a sort of modern Utopia." He was "vacant-minded," a "figurehead," a prima donna. When Harding was in the White House, "the Morgans, the Schwabs, the Rockefellers and the Garys will remain behind and pull the strings."[58]

Harding's reaction to these labor attacks was serene. Seldom did he dignify them with pointed rebuttal. He did not allow himself to get on the defensive. In his speeches he presented what he believed to be a positive program and attitude toward labor. He created an image of benign dignity and mastery. As in his utterances on agriculture, on the League of Nations, and on business policy, he avoided contention over specifics. People who saw no basic conflicts in American society had a vision of peace and security in a man who could win the confidence of the important leaders of American life.

7

Although, as has been said, Harding as a friend of business and management did not need a build-up, he got one anyhow. How gratified businessmen were at his nomination was succinctly expressed by New Jersey Senator Walter E. Edge on June 25, when he wrote, "There is a sigh of relief among businessmen which says in effect: 'Thank the Lord we can settle down to a consideration of some of our domestic problems: we can take an account of stock, as it were and get caught up with ourselves and we will cease chasing rainbows and trying to rule the world.' " [59] Less eloquent, but probably more authoritative, was the investors' consultant firm of Dow, Jones, and Company, which canvassed the investing public of the leading United States cities and reported, on June 16, in the *Wall Street Journal* that Harding's nomination had been received "with universal favor by investors." Harding's election was viewed as close to a certainty and would bring about a "common sense constructive administration." Similar views came from the *Manufacturer's News*, the *Bache Review*, *Moody's Investors Service*, and *Forbes*. On August 21, B. C. Forbes wrote, "The business community, as a rule, assumes that the Republican candidate will be elected and that his administration will be more conducive to business confidence." [60]

A quality in Harding that pleased the conservative mind was his consultative nature. This was contrasted with the alleged egotistical, super-intellectual President Wilson. The *Literary Digest* of June 26 said that "Senator New (Rep.), of Indiana rejoices that 'Harding is no master mind.' " The *Argonaut*, a Pacific Coast business journal, commented, June 19: "By no means a master mind, he is a man of intelligence, of sympathy, and he possesses in a large endowment the pure gold of common sense . . . accessible, open-minded, seeks information and counsel. He does not pretend to hold all brains under his own hat." It would be safe to assume "that we shall have as heads of departments not Danielses, Bakers, and Burlesons, but the best intellects and highest patriotism that the public life of the country affords." The *Magazine of Wall Street* on June 26 opined that "the test of his ability as President would probably be, not his own intellectual genius or power of personal leadership, but his skill in the selection of assistants and in coordinating political factions." Herbert Kaufman, editor of *McClure's*, said in his July issue, "It will take a group of wise men, bold men, brave men—experts in the law of the land and the laws of nations—authorities in production and transportation, cutters of Gordian knots, proven captains of big affairs, to get us safely past the immediate future. We want no more amateurs or theorists at the Capital. Washington is the last place to hatch ability . . . we should have recognized cocks of their respective walks representing our manifold interests." *Leslie's Weekly* for July 10 said that "the country has become so exasperated and alarmed over the Wilsonian penchant for surrounding himself with nonentities that it wants to know what the prospects are for getting the national business once more into competent hands. Mr. Harding will have a wealth of good material to draw from."

This promise and attitude of consultation was made and exhibited by Harding on many occasions, always with the "Wilson dictatorship" in mind. In his July 22 acceptance speech he used it skillfully to emphasize the virtues of party and Congressional action in producing popular confidence. "In a citizenship of more than a hundred million," he said, "it is impossible to reach agreement upon all questions." Political parties were necessary to "reach a consensus of opinion." The Constitution guaranteed this. "No man is big enough to run this Republic. There never has been one. Such domination was never intended. Tranquility, stability, dependability—all are assured in party sponsorship." "Our vision includes more than a Chief Executive; we believe in a Cabinet of highest capacity, equal to the responsibilities which our system contemplates, in whose councils the Vice-President . . . shall be asked to participate. The same vision includes a cordial understanding and co-ordinated activities with a House of Congress, fresh from the people." And, of course, the Senate had already proven its ability to "save this Republic its independent nationality." [61]

This same spirit of counseling was evident when prominent businessmen offered advice. When Joseph W. Harriman, president of New York's Harriman National Bank, presented a five-page technical essay on how the Liberty Bonds were "strangling our credit system," Harding replied that Harriman's suggestions involved "an idea so big and a vision so impressive that I want, as you may well imagine, to have some time to study it and think it over. . . . I have very little opportunity for studying those questions as they come up in new form and therefore it is all the more important to me to have good friends and sound advisors like yourself to put them before me in concrete form." [62]

There was New York banker and art connoisseur Otto H. Kahn, who sent Harding voluminous material on the need for tax revision. This included copies of his testimony before the Senate Committee on Reconstruction and Production and copies of his books entitled *Impressions from a Journey in Europe* and *Two Years of Faulty Taxation*. These volumes developed learnedly the author's views on the need for the abolition or reduction of the excess-profits tax, the high income taxes, and the inheritance tax. Kahn wanted a national sales tax. In reply Harding wrote that he was "going to require the best thought in the country to bring about a satisfactory and righteous solution" of the tax problem, and would "like to feel that I shall be able to call for your advice and suggestions at any time. It is very gratifying to know that men of capacity are eager to serve, and serve unselfishly." [63] Similar statements were sent to Charles G. Dawes and Herbert Hoover.[64]

It was easier to preach the gospel of consultation when asked to do so by conventions and associations. When the National Association of Retail Clothiers asked for a message, Harding wired that "in this period of interest and uncertainty in the country the serious consideration of the best minds functioning individually and collectively in constructive endeavors was needed to bring us to the realization of our worthiest ideals." [65] To the National Association of Advertising Specialty Manufacturers in convention assembled, he wired his wish to "save the taxpayers' money and create an administrative government of which the American people can be proud by applying principles of American business sense to government and drafting the most capable men in America for that task." [66] When the editor of the *American Bar Journal* asked for his blessing, Harding gave it gladly saying, "We confront problems that demand the cool and understanding attention of the best constructive minds in the Nation. . . . The American Bar . . . must contribute to the development of those safe and effective measures which will serve the country at this time." [67]

8

Harding had the full confidence of businessmen because, to them, it seemed that he put first things first—that is to say, the speedy restoration of the nation to a peacetime economy. That is what he said in his acceptance speech. "I promise you," he said, "formal and effective peace so quickly as a Republican Congress can pass its declarations for a Republican executive to sign. Then we may turn to our readjustment at home and proceed deliberately and reflectively to that hoped-for world relationship, which shall satisfy both conscience and aspirations and still hold us free from menacing involvement." [68] There were problems of world relationship, but first there was peace and adjustment at home. "I had rather have industrial and social peace at home," he said, on August 14 in one of his first front-porch speeches, "than command the international peace of all the world." [69] It was in fulfillment of the simple statement in the party platform: "We pledge ourselves to a carefully planned readjustment to a peace-time basis." [70]

It was the simplicity of it that business liked. The government would return to its role of minimum activity so far as business was concerned. That meant simply (1) to curb waste and extravagance, (2) to reduce taxation, and (3) to introduce more businesslike procedures into government affairs.

It was good politics to talk about Democratic extravagance. Harding had always been at his best in Democrat-baiting, and he exploited his new opportunity to the full. His campaign speeches crackled with anti-extravagance jibes. "Willful folly," "bungling hands," "saturnalia of extravagance," "the ineffective prodigals of the world," "blunders in every direction," "paralysis and perversion," "useless jobs"—these were but a few of the terms drawn from Harding's oratorical arsenal in his blasts upon the Wilson administration. On August 25 in another front-porch oration, he described how the Republican Congress elected in 1918 trimmed a billion dollars—"mark you, I said a billion" —from supply bills presented by the former Democratic Congress, and had refused to pass any "pork barrel" legislation. Thus was the government able to emerge with a $1,000,000,000 surplus instead of an $1,400,000,000 deficit.[71] In a well-staged "Businessmen's Day" in Marion on September 10 he dramatically described how the American people had paid for the eight years of inefficiency of the Democratic party: "It has engaged in prodigal waste. The American people pay. It has kept its overstuffed bureaus and departments, many of which are doing overlapping work, in a prime condition of reckless inefficiency. The American people pay. It has a record in the appointment of campaign-contributor diplomats who have been without previous experience in foreign affairs. The American people pay. It has engaged in all kinds of costly, bungling experiments of government management and ownership of enterprises which other management could do better. The American people pay. . . ." [72]

As for taxation, Harding, to the delight of businessmen, bore down hard on the excess-profits tax. On July 18 he told a *New York Times* reporter, "No country can go on toward an assured industrial future with a tax on excess profits. Experience has shown that it is inevitably passed on to the consumer." [73] A few days later in the acceptance address, he was more cautious in his language, proposing that the war-emergency taxes be "revised to the needs of peace, and in the interest of equity in the distribution of the burden." [74] This evasiveness moved Alexander Moore of the *Pittsburgh Leader* to words of intense admiration. "I think you are a wonder," Moore wrote on August 3. "You dealt with the excess profit tax question like a modern Richelieu. I knew something had to be said on this question on account of intense interest in it—*and you said it*—and said it better than I thought possible. There was just enough said to cover the matter perfectly." [75]

The ground was well prepared for Harding on the matter of improved business procedures in governmental affairs—especially in respect to the creation of a national budget bureau. The Republican Congress had passed the McCormick-Good Budget bill which the party textbook of 1920 said provided for "the most constructive budget system ever formulated." President Wilson had vetoed the bill and an amended form had been filibustered to death by Democratic Senators. It provided for presidential submission to each new Congress of estimates of expenditures and receipts for past, present, and future, of recommendations for new taxes, loans, and financial policies. There would be a budget bureau, a general accounting office, and a comptroller-general to administer its provisions. The Republican platform commended Congress for its passage of the bill and condemned the President for his veto. This party textbook also contained chapters by the Mills-Lindsay-Hollander advisory committee entitled "Democratic Waste and Extravagances Since the Armistice," "Facts about Our National Deficit and Our National Debt," "Republican Program of National Economy, Retrenchment and Reorganization," and other heavily documented reports mostly critical of the Democrats.[76] These were supplemented with campaign flyers luridly entitled "A Billion a

Month Twenty Billion in All—What the Democrats Did with the Stupendous Mass of Wealth Taken From the People to Fight the War."

Harding, of course, followed up this budget platforming with vigorous promotion. He included future recommendations for the reorganization of the federal administrative machinery on more businesslike lines. This gave him an opportunity to engage in praise of the American businessman and to enlarge on the need for expert counsel from their ranks. This was the theme of his Businessmen's Day speech at Marion of September 10: "We must go to men who know for advice in administrative improvement. . . . we must organize our administrative government upon the basis of American business so that the faith of the American people in the common sense of the Republican Party to put America into shape again shall not have been misplaced. . . . The government is the people's business, and they will not see it broken down. . . . We are looking forward with relief to an end of mismanagement. . . . Here in America we have developed the most efficient types of business organization in the world; they have shown the greatest capacity for administrative vision. We mean to call that administrative quality and fitness into the service of the government, and establish an advance in government business, not merely talk about government progress."[78] One of the more widely circulated magazine articles on the subject was that which appeared in the November *World's Work* entitled "Less Government in Business and More Business in Government."

9

There was something seemingly indestructible in the image of Harding as the friend of business and labor, because it was a part of the unchallengeable image of Harding as the friend of everybody—of Harding as the personification of security. A nation, once reluctantly at war, was back to the common sense of peace again, and proposed to stay that way. It was resolved to feel safe, and it wanted a President who looked safe and talked safe—and was safe.

A man who could thus be the keystone in a fixation of safety could not err. He was foolproof. Incidents which might break a candidate in lighter times would be harmless in this mood of a required resumption of normalcy. Such incidents occurred and left Harding unscathed, not only because of the suavity of his glossy manner of explanation, but because the people saw in him one who, like themselves, had had his moments of error, but who now knew the requisites of peace and was firmly resolved to live by them.

There were several incidents that could have been "fool breaks," but they faded into insignificance in the atmosphere of safety and security. To be quoted as calling a lie the claim that the war for world democracy did Harding no harm because there was no general or profound belief that it was not a lie. Harding was openly attacked by the A. F. of L. for sneering at the Adamson Law and claiming that it was the result of the intimidation of Congress by labor, but it aroused little furore, perhaps because of the red-scare atmosphere of the times.[79] The same can be said of his January 3, 1920 Miller letter defending his support of the anti-strike clause in the Cummins bill.[80] The sacrilegious Reid cartoon in the October 23 *Harvey's Weekly* aroused little interest. No slush-fund exposures marred the Harding record although Cox tried to smear Harding with claims of fabulous outlays by rich Republicans. These were investigated by the Kenyon Committee during the campaign without spectacular revelations.[81]

The nearest that Harding came to a "Burchard blunder" or a Hughes *faux pas* was the publication on September 21 by the *New York Times* of a letter by Harding favoring the recognition of Soviet Russia by the United States. The letter was dated April 10, 1920, and was in answer to an inquiry from Stanley Washburn of Lakewood, New Jersey. In this letter Harding told Washburn, "I have never at any time changed my views concerning Bolshevism, but I think we are coming to a point where there is no other course to pursue than recognize the de facto existence of the government of Russia." When confronted with the letter, Harding told the *Times* to verify its existence with Washburn, and then added that, whatever he had said on April, 1920, he was in line with his party platform adopted in June, 1920. The *Times* represented him as saying that he "was opposed to recognition of any Government in Russia until it shows capacity for observing honor among nations." Two days later the *Times* quoted Washburn as making an emphatic denial that he said or believed that Harding favored Russian recognition. Nothing was said by Washburn about whether Harding had written the letter of April 10. Washburn's statement, said the *Times*, was made "through the Republican National Committee."

If one is to believe a statement made by Washburn in 1950 to the

Oral History Research Project of Columbia University, Harding did in fact write the letter of April 10, 1920 favoring the recognition of Russia. In this statement Washburn was very uncomplimentary to Harding and represented the candidate as a dolt who did not know what he was doing. Washburn said that he wanted to go out to Ohio and use the letter in General Wood's primary campaign against Harding, but was persuaded against doing so by Mrs. Washburn, who said that such a use of a confidential letter would be dishonorable. Shortly after Harding's nomination, said Washburn, John Hays Hammond asked him to come to Washington to "talk to Warren" and "try to explain to him the Russian situation." Daugherty was present at the proceedings. Hammond was quoted as saying, "Warren, I want you to pay attention to Stanley about the Russian situation." Reference was made to the April 10 letter. Daugherty snapped, "What letter?" When it was described to him, "Daugherty turned on Warren like a wolf. 'Did you write this man a letter like that?'" Harding replied by turning to Washburn and saying, "Why, did I write you a letter like this?" Washburn said, "You certainly did. It was on Senate stationery and you signed it. As a matter of fact I've got the letter signed by you." Harding then said, "Major, I don't know the first thing about Russia. Won't you write me a memo?" Washburn wanted to know who would read it. To this Daugherty replied, "Brother, I'm going to read it. You can send that man a copy," pointing to Harding.

If Washburn was telling the truth, Harding was a lucky man. If the April 10 letter had been injected into the Ohio primary campaign, Harding might have lost more votes and delegates to Wood. His standing at the June convention would probably have been fatally impaired. By delaying Washburn's revelation until late September, Daugherty and the national committee took the sting out of the exposure. By that time the image of the dignified, confident, well-poised Harding was exposure-proof.

According to the Wall Street betting odds and other statistical prognostications, by late September Harding's election was a certainty. The Maine election had pointed the way. On September 23, Moody's Investment Service Letter No. 619 predicted that Harding would get between 360 and 399 electoral votes. (The official final count was 404.) Therefore, concluded Moody's, "in so far as politics is a factor in finance we should be bulls on the future of finance and of big business." The betting odds zoomed. They had begun in July at 2–1 for Harding and hovered near that ratio until there was the assurance of no strong third-party action. By mid-August they were 3–1, but dropped back to 2–1 when the woman-suffrage amendment was adopted. After the Maine election the ratio climbed rapidly upward until, on election day, it was at the fantastic figure of 10–1, with no takers.[82]

And so the Republican campaign of 1920 ended as it began—with business confident and satisfied—only more so. The labor movement was hostile to Harding's candidacy—but labor was divided. Harding's anti-strike record and right-to-work belief had been toned down to a "philosophy" of harmony between labor and management through good will and understanding in an effort to present the candidate as having appeal for both sides. Harding had said the right things about the platform and its orientation toward business, but he had injected a vigorous tariff promotionalism which probably had a considerable effect on the average voter, who did not understand the growing needs of reduced trade restrictions in a world of nations more complicated and interdependent than ever before. The suave and dignified Harding made a stronger impression on the public mind with his positive talk of budgets and the need for stronger participation by business in government than could the commonplace Cox, who was saddled with Wilsonian obstinacy and superidealism.

CHAPTER TWENTY-FIVE

Referendum—for What?

"If there is any doubt as to what the people of the country think on this vital matter [the League of Nations], the clear and single way out is to submit it for determination at the next election to the voters of the nation, to give the next election the form of a great and solemn referendum, a referendum as to the part the United States is to play in completing the settlements of the war and in the prevention in the future of such outrages as Germany attempted to perpetrate." : : : Woodrow Wilson to Homer S. Cummings on January 8, 1920, as quoted in the "New York Times," January 9, 1920*

"I found two great opposing elements in the party, and it was my supreme task to being them together. It was vitally necessary to do that if, as President, I am to render any great service to the cause of peace. . . . I had to reach out to both of these groups and unite them and I have done it." : : : Harding, as quoted in Samuel Colcord, "The Great Deception Bringing into Light the Real Meaning of the Harding Vote as to Peace," p. 63*

The vote count following the election of November 2, 1920 disclosed an overwhelming victory for Harding and the Republicans. The party had rolled up a 60 per cent national popular vote, the greatest in its history—indeed, the greatest in all post–Civil War politics. Another record was the achievement of a majority of 172 seats in the House of Representatives. In the Senate the GOP retained every seat held in that body and gained ten more at the expense of the Democrats. The Solid South was broken when Tennessee cast a majority for Harding and Coolidge. The Republican percentage rose through the South, and in most of the North. Oklahoma went Republican, as did Boston and New York.[1]

The greatest single reason for the Republican victory was the return of the Progressives. This would have been accomplished in 1916 if Hughes and the Republicans had not made the "fool break" of alienating Hiram Johnson. Harding was not only "break proof," but he deliberately sought to flatter Johnson. Harding was at his all-forgiving best in wooing Progressives back to the fold in 1920. Ever since 1914 he had been smiting Progressives at their most vulnerable point, *i.e.*, their lack of local patronage. World War I may have cooled the ardor of Progressives for their principles, and brought a new warlike ardor for national victory in the field of battle, but politically they had already been cooled by their lack of the "loaves and fishes," which meant so much to the rank and file of office-seekers. The advisory committee system, "invented" by Will H. Hays in the 1916 Indiana campaign and developed by Harding in Ohio from 1917 to 1919, was a grass-roots institution designed for the forgiving of Progressives—and that meant jobs to Progressives throughout the states if they would behave themselves.

To be sure, Progressive Walter Brown and his Cincinnati "black-bird" allies almost stole the patronage ball from Harding in 1918–19, but the death of Roosevelt early in 1919 enabled Harding to keep possession of his advisory system and speak the language of forgiveness and patronage to a national party audience. By enlisting Harry Daugherty to stand firm for party discipline to please conservatives, and by inducing Walter Brown to counsel Progressives to be "sensible," Harding became a power in state and national politics as his system was discovered by the "Daughertys" and "Browns" of other areas. Harding's personable qualities, his oratory, and his attractiveness to conservative businessmen added gloss to his appeal, but behind him was a workable system of politics founded on the unifying effect of the assurance that loyal party workers should receive their rewards.

The success of Harding and Daugherty in 1919–20 in fashioning the network of second choices for the presidential nomination was a natural extension of this system of Progressive-conservative alliance for the restoration of party unity. Each agreement with local Republican leaders was an implied contract that two things should go together: a recognition of local patronage, and an understanding that normal political progressiveness would be backed by all Republicans. Throughout the North and West, and in parts of the South, there had come to Republican leaders of both Progressive and conservative persuasion the realization that progressiveness should not be the monopoly of Democrats and thus be the nemesis of divided Republicans. Let there be unity in the acceptance of the progress of the recent years, and in the facing toward the future and the steps of progress that the times required. The temperamental Roosevelt was dead, but the need for progress could never die. It was the sensible thing to do, and Harding preached it.

Hence it was that the Republican leaders who joined with Harding in the second-choice maneuvering that led to his nomination, and who followed him through the campaigning that ensued, were satisfied about progressivism because they hoped that it would not be an issue any more. Although many conservatives regretted the "mad" primary system, it could not be repealed. Therefore it had to become part of normal party organizational practices, if for no other reason than to keep the Democrats from being its sole beneficiaries. Similar views prevailed in regard to the reforms of prohibition and women's suffrage. These should be made the most of by conservative temperaments in behalf of law enforcement—not repeal—lest the overly progressive alienate by their own rashness. As for future progress, was it not soundly progressive to have the Harding-Republican endorsement of the new, economically oriented Wallace farm program, the McCormick-Good Budget Bill, departmental reorganization, "enlightened" railroad control, the Lodge-Root-Harding association of nations–world court proposals?

Progressive-conservative reunion was augmented by the arts and devices of skilled management of the Will H. Hays variety. There was an ever-present, though beneath-the-surface, consciousness of the need to avoid the alleged blunders of the Hughes-Willcox campaign of 1916, when the distinguished candidate conducted himself aggressively but with insufficient coordination with the national committee and its local adjuncts. Hence there was the well-centralized but widely circulated publicity motif of the front porch with Judson Welliver skillfully feeding copy to national press services. And when that wore out, there was the "break proof" Harding stumping the country north, east, west and south, exuding good will, charm, and ambivalence. There were political outposts in New York, Chicago, Kansas City—and, above all, in San Francisco, with Elmer Dover doing his best to keep the Hoover, the Johnson, and the conservative California Republicans happy.

There were hints that the Hays management was overdone, that is, that he was a public relations enthusiast creating a tremendous immediate majority, instead of building a party following based on fundamental party principles. The circus atmosphere of the Marion "days" suggests this: the Cubs–Kerrigan Tailors baseball game, the Al Jolson theatrical troupe, the football-minded First Voters' Day, the Baptist Negro Day, and so on. If that is so, the campaign might have been more of a referendum for ballyhoo than for party preference. Management did not care about the loss of intellectuals disgusted with Harding's ambivalence.

An important factor in viewing the election of 1920 is the so-called isolationist sentiment of the American people. This operated in favor of Harding with respect to the labor vote and the question of the League of Nations. In so far as isolationism was a product of the red-scare atmosphere of 1919 and the 1920s, it caused many Americans to be as disinterested and suspicious of the assumed Bolshevik influence in militant labor unionism as they were of the "internationalism" of the League of Nations.

But red-scare isolationism had another foundation. This was the reluctance with which many Americans had given their support to the entrance of their country into World War I. Some have called the American participation in this war a "reluctant crusade." [2] Frequent reference has been made in these pages to Harding's statements on the unpopularity of the conflict, which he attributed to the "polyglot" nature of the nation's population, a result of immigration. Whatever the reason for this lack of interest in foreign involvement, it cannot be denied that the argument "he kept us out of war" had much to do with the votes for President Wilson in his reelection in 1916. Hence, after the war was over and everybody had done his patriotic bit to help win it, there was a certain resentment against the President for seemingly having deceived the people. Wilson's promise of peace, this time by means of the League of Nations, was the forfeit. Harding and the Republicans, of course, encouraged this for political purposes. This feeling existed not only in the German-Americans but in the neo-pacifistic sentiment of many who did not yet know the one-world involvement that later came to be understood as the result of World War II.

In accounting for the tremendous Republican majority of the 1920 election, one cannot overemphasize the ambivalent nature of Warren G. Harding. There has been lengthy discussion of the "forum philosophy" of his stand on the League of Nations. Granting his peculiar endowments of dignity, oratorical Americanism, and genial good will, the forum idea was a powerfully effective device in drawing many shades of opinion to his support. There was much merit in the assumption that the people must, through open discussion, have a clearer understanding of what they were getting into internationally than

President Wilson had made possible. However, a "forum philosophy" could be a straddle. That could be true, not because Harding premised his forum idea on the assumption that the Republican party had to be united before it could have a foreign policy, but because, after his victory of 1920, he might not live up to his promise of enabling the "best minds" to make a satisfactory kind of peace-preserving association of nations. This question will have to be probed by an analysis of his record as President of the United States.

Harding's ambivalence has been demonstrated in many respects. In the question of adopting the Nineteenth Amendment, he was willing to forego pushing for ratification by Republican states, and instead let a Democratic state, Tennessee, become the thirty-sixth state to ratify; Harding was content with an appeal to the state's Republican minority to voluntarily show its loyalty to the party and to the rights of women. On prohibition he shied away from a commitment to the alteration of the Volstead law, thus pleasing the drys, but not encouraging them enough to anger the wets. His groping toward an enlightened agricultural policy, happily under the influence of the able Henry C. Wallace, was favored by the better farming class. On labor he took advantage of the red scare and nourished a labor-management mutual understanding that caught off guard those who did not realize or appreciate the need for more militancy in labor union organization and action. On race relations he exploited the ancient belief by Negroes that the Republicans were their saviors and the Democrats their enemies. In the North he emphasized the advancement into equal rights; in the South he let it be known that no integration was involved. He used the Haiti question to mollify the N.A.A.C.P. On the League of Nations, his simultaneous waving of the American flag on Article 10 and the furling of it in his promotion of an association of nations and a world court are classic. What other man could join hands politically with Arthur Brisbane on one side and Elihu Root on the other? His injection of tariff-Americanism into the campaign, while the Republican platform contained a world trade promotion plank, was another exercise in ambivalence.

2

In conclusion, the political career of Warren G. Harding up to 1920 reveals a man whose growth in political and economic matters was confined to his evolution from a booster of progress for Marion, Ohio to a promoter of the limited view of "Prosper America First." Ambitious, hard-working, talented, articulate, and friendly, he came in the early 1880s to a burgeoning midwestern town which was in the throes of becoming a modern industrial and commercial city. In this small-city businessman's Arcadia, he became its leading publicist as he edited and published the *Marion Daily Star*, the hallmark of the genuineness of the new city's durability. Marion got its pavements, its streetcars, and its water supply with the enthusiastic promotionalism of the *Star*. The newspaper's credo was:

> Talk about Marion—
>
> Write about Marion—
>
> Be friendly to everybody—
>
> Sell all you can—
>
> Buy all you can at home—
>
> Buy all you can at home—
>
> Support your town newspaper—
>
> Advertise.[3]

And Marion prospered, as did Warren Harding.

A man as articulate and ambitious as young Harding could not be confined to a crossroads city in Ohio any more than could his similarly ambitious father, Dr. George T. Harding, be confined to the crossroads towns of Blooming Grove or Caledonia, Ohio. Soon it was the entire state of Ohio in whose promising political destinies Warren Harding could find identity.

Harding entered Ohio politics with strong localistic conditioning. In Ohio, as in all American states, party organization was basically state inspired via a system of county and district committees leading to the state central committee at the top. At times there were conflicts as state leaders—such as Senator John Sherman and Mark Hanna—contended for national prominence. During the 1890s, with the aid of locally supported Senator Joseph B. Foraker, Harding endeared himself to the state and local machines in spite of the opposition of both Sherman and Hanna. In fact, Harding conducted his political career so skillfully that he finally earned the respect of the prominent Hanna. In the process a political ambivalence became part of the Harding style, based on the idea that, in state party versus national party, "politics should be reconciled" if unity against Democrats was to be preserved.

During the decade 1900–1910, Harding, as state senator and as candidate for governor, fought for Republican unity in Ohio at a time when bossism, corruption, and Progressivism were on the rise. He mistakenly judged that machine unity could stop Progressive inroads. The result was that a Democratic-Progressive coalition, centering around moderate-reform Governor Judson Harmon, gained ascendancy in Ohio politics and temporarily barred Harding's advance. However, the revelation of his oratorical talents led him to be recognized as the one Ohio Republican who could lead the Ohio GOP to victory if and when the Democratic-Progressive alliance became unsatisfactory to the Progressives because of lack of patronage.

Harding's basic political principles during these years included no sincere appreciation of the merits of Progressivism, and its emphasis on direct democracy (*i.e.*, the old committee system based on convention action rather than mass primaries) insured the participation of more responsible leadership.

Harding's idealogical principles as a politician were often narrow. They consisted essentially of tariff-Americanism and a combination imperialist-protective attitude toward other nations. Both were based on a lack of knowledge—the first, of the principles of economics; the second, of world history and international relations. His tariff ideas were a simple extension of Marion, Ohio boosterism. He would protect America first with the simple device of tariff walls behind which buying and selling in the United States would bring business to the highest goals of prosperity. Harding's interpretation of American history told him that the phenomenal growth of the American economy was basically the result of tariff protection. Harding had no grasp of any economic factors which might have tempered his isolationism. His narrow view also extended to foreign relations, as seen in his newspaper editorials urging annexation by the United States of Samoa, Puerto Rico, and the Philippines—along with Cuba and Mexico.

Harding's entry into national politics in 1914, via the United States Senate, was largely circumstantial. The scholarly, conservative, but unattractive incumbent, Theodore E. Burton of Cleveland, withdrew from seeking renomination because it was felt that the more popular Harding could win back the Progressive vote lost in the Wilson-Taft-Roosevelt presidential fight of 1912. The Progressives were stopped in 1914 because they had no T. R. coattails on which to hang. Harding thus became the Republican nominee for United States Senator and won a 100,000 majority on the basis of two issues. One was a typical, spellbinding campaign of patriotic tariff-Americanism, denouncing President Wilson. The other was a vicious anti-Catholic crusade, led by the Guardians of Liberty, against Harding's opponent, the Progressive Democrat, Timothy Hogan, on the sole grounds of the latter's religion. Harding gave the anti-Catholics secret support and emerged seemingly as a potential savior of the Republican party because of his large majority.

After he became Senator, Harding's prospects depended on his oratorical magic, on the managerial aptitudes of both himself and Harry Daugherty, and on the eventual disillusionment of the electorate by Wilson's foreign policies. Harding improved his standing on a national level with his business-oriented, tariff-American oratory, his patriotic support of the war, and his constant badgering of the Democrats.

In Ohio, Harding did a workmanlike job of systematizing the conservative-Progressive reconciliation via his advisory committee organization. He ran the risk of having it captured by the Progressive part of the coalition as long as Theodore Roosevelt lived and planned for the nomination in 1920. But when Roosevelt died in January of 1919, Harding, aided by Harry Daugherty, began a powerful "let's be loyal to Ohio, the Mother of Presidents" movement that raised the Buckeye Senator to become a frontrunner in the candidate jockeying of 1920. Skillful politicking and the Wood-Lowden "rich man's primary" debacle did the rest. Harding became the leading second choice of his party and profited therefrom by the proliferation of first-place candidacies. Harding's nomination was not pure accident. It was a case of canny politicians anticipating the accident, and being ready to profit by it when it happened.

The election which ensued was even better planned and managed, The mistakes of 1916 were deliberately avoided, and the candidate was given full play for his talents. His victory was more of an acclamation and an approbation of Harding himself than it was a referendum on the issues.

3

In what sense, then, was the election of 1920 a referendum? It was certainly not a fight over a league of nations, since the public was willing to let this issue wait upon the decisions of nationally eminent figures. But it was a referendum by the public against the idea of a strong federal government, an idea which, begun under Theodore Roosevelt, was felt by the public to have been carried too far by the Wilson administration. Added to this factor was a lingering resentment over "Mr. Wilson's War," and the return to the Republican ranks of the patronage-starved Progressives. Finally, there was the steady, implacable, and eloquent candidate—so carefully managed by his political coaches to avoid any "fool breaks." The result was an overwhelming majority, the largest in the history of the Republican party, which made Warren Gamaliel Harding the President of the United States.

4

Now that he was President, Harding would face challenges far beyond the ones he had met in his Horatio Alger rise to national prominence. For the next two and one-half years he would have to resolve such problems as the need for a new foreign policy; a readjustment in the transportation system to cope with the arrival of the automobile; new policies for an expanding industrial network; the need for programs to stem the rising cost of living; the public's dissatisfaction with Prohibition; and the pressure to make permanent the Progressive-Regular coalition. These and many other concerns would demand another sort of Harding—a man who would try to meet their combined pressure only at terrible personal cost.

CHAPTER ONE

1. Warren Harding had an account of his father's early training in the Marion *Daily Star* (hereinafter cited as *Star*), June 15, 1895. There are several catalogues of this medical school in the Western Reserve Historical Society. The institution had several names, and is now inactive.

2. "Eye Witness," *Chicago Tribune*, August 19, 1920, p. 5.

3. The bases for the genealogical facts on Harding include the following works of Wilbur J. Harding: Genealogical Chart, 1567–1905 (n.p.), a copy of which is in the Harding Museum, 380 Mt. Vernon Avenue, Marion, Ohio; *The Hardings: A Genealogical Register of the Descendants of John Harding* (Kenwood Park, Iowa, 1907); *The Hardings in America* (Keystone, Iowa: The Harding Printing Co., 1925). Also important are: Lawrence Brainerd, "President Warren Gamaliel Harding," *New England Historical and Genealogical Register* (October, 1923), pp. 243–49; Veryl E. Harding, *Four Centuries of the Harding Family* (Beaver City, Nebraska, 1958); Clara Gardiner Miller, "Ancestry of President Harding in Relation to the Hardings of Wyoming Valley and Clifford, Pa.," *Proceedings and Collections of the Wyoming Historical and Genealogical Society* (1930), pp. 1–46.

4. *Toledo Blade*, November 3, 1920.

5. H. J. Eckley and W. T. Perry, *History of Carroll and Harrison Counties, Ohio* (Chicago: Lewis Publishing Co., 1921), p. 549. The authors, in dealing with Sam F. Dickerson of Harrison County, state, "He is a direct descendant of Joshua Dickerson who was born in 1634 in Monmouth County, New Jersey, being the second male child to be born in that county."

6. *The "Old Northwest" Genealogical Quarterly*, X, No. 1 (January, 1907), 56. This is an article [anonymous] on Thomas Dickerson, 1764–1852, of Fayette County, Pennsylvania. He was the son of Joshua Dickerson who is referred to as follows: "As Joshua Dickerson had flown [*sic*] first from Jersey to the Potomac, so, with his family he was first to scale the Alleghenies and settle down in what is now Fayette County, Pennsylvania, on Dickerson Run, near what was later called East Liberty. This migration occurred in 1771 or 1772."

7. "Eye Witness," *Chicago Tribune*, August 19, 1920, p. 5.

8. The numbering of the modern George Tryon Hardings is confusing. Numerically, George Tryon Harding I was a son of Amos. That would make Warren Harding's father George Tryon Harding II, and Warren's brother, George Tryon Harding III. However, in the sense of their all being physicians, except Amos' son, the George Tryon Hardings are today correctly numbered.

9. The house in which Warren Harding was born no longer stands, but the site is marked. The most authentic information about the location is to be found in *Star*, November 14, 1960: "The little old house where Mr. Harding was born, Nov. 2, 1865, just four miles southeast of Galion, at Blooming Grove, no longer stands. On the site is a clump of bushes, growing in the large front yard of the larger home of what always has been known as the Harding farm." A large picture entitled "Birthplace of Warren G. Harding" is in the possession of the Galion Historical Society.

10. References to Phoebe Harding's attendance at the "Medical College in Cleveland" are in *Marion Independent*, November 23, 1893 and *Marion Democratic Mirror*, November 8, 1883. Her medical practice is frequently mentioned in the *Star*, on September 3, 1889; June 7, 1894; January 22, 1896; July 19, 1897.

11. Jack Warwick, "Growing up with Harding," *Northwest Ohio Quarterly* (hereinafter cited as *NOQ*) XXVIII (Winter, 1955–56), 14, 16, 17.

12. *Marion Democratic Mirror*, December 7, 1876.

13. *The History of Marion County, Ohio* (Leggett, Conway & Co., 1883), p. 708.

14. *Star*, January 11, 1899.

15. *Marion Democratic Mirror*, December 17, 1874.

16. Marion County Recorders Office, Town Plat Book No. 1, p. 235.

17. "Eye Witness," *Chicago Tribune*, August 20, 1920, p. 6.

18. Warwick, "Growing up with Harding," *NOQ* XXVIII: 15.

19. Charity Remsburg to Ray Baker Harris, June 6, 1938, Harris Papers, Ohio Historical Society.

20. "Eye Witness," *Chicago Tribune*, August 18, 1920, p. 7.

21. George L. Edmunds, "My Boy Warren: The Father's Story of the President Elect and His Success System," *McClure's* (March, 1921), p. 23.

22. Warwick, "Growing up with Harding," *NOQ* XXVIII: 14.

23. The *Spectator's* career is briefly summarized in the *Mt. Gilead Union Register*, May 6, 1886. There is a copy of the April 22, 1882 issue (Vol. 1, No. 2) in the Ohio Historical Society.

24. In 1882 the faculty of Ohio Central College consisted of three persons: Reverend John P. Robb, A. M., president and professor of philosophy; Albert C. Jones, A. B., dean and professor of ancient languages and literature; and Reverend A. C. Crist, A. M., professor of mathematics and natural science. There were three "courses": the "Academic Course," priced at $7.00 a term; the "English course" for $6.00 a term; and the "Collegiate Course" for $8.00 a term. *Spectator*, April 22, 1882, p. 4.

25. Herbert Corey in *Cincinnati Times-Star*, August 17–September 2, 1920.

26. Ray Baker Harris, "Background and Youth of the Seventh Ohio President," *Ohio State Archaeological and Historical Society Quarterly*, 52:274.

27. Joe Mitchell Chapple, *Life and Times of Warren G. Harding* (Boston: Chapple Publishing Co., 1924), p. 39.

28. "Eye Witness," *Chicago Tribune*, August 30, 1920, p. 6.

29. Herbert Corey in *Cincinnati Times-Star*, September 2, 1920, p. 6.

30. J. Wilbur Jacoby, *History of Marion County, Ohio* (Chicago, 1907), chaps. 9 and 10.

31. *Star*, May 27, 1915, p. 5.

32. Jacoby, *Marion County*, pp. 143–44, 265–66.

33. *Ibid.*, pp. 144–46; *Star*, June 15, 1885.

34. Harris, "Background and Youth," p. 274.

35. *Star*, May 4, 1882, May 5, 1883; *Marion Democratic Mirror*, March 13, 27, April 24, 1884.

36. *Marion Democratic Mirror*, January 10, 1884.

37. *Marion Democratic Mirror*, October 9, 1884.

38. Willis Fletcher Johnson, *The Life of Warren G. Harding* (Philadelphia: John C. Winston Company, 1923), pp. 25–26.

39. Warwick, "Growing up with Harding," *NOQ* XXVIII:20–21.

40. *Ibid.*, *NOQ* XXX, No. 2 (Summer, 1958), 118.

CHAPTER TWO

1. Randolph C. Downes, "A Newspaper's Childhood: The Marion Daily Star from Hume to Harding, 1877–1884," *NOQ* XXXVI, No. 3 (Summer, 1964), 134–45.

2. Warwick, "Growing up with Harding, *NOQ* XXVIII:24.

3. Edmunds, "My Boy Warren," *McClure's* (March, 1921), p. 50.

4. Warwick, "Growing up with Harding," *NOQ* XXVIII, 15; Sherman A. Cuneo, *From Printer to President* (Philadelphia: Dorrance, 1922), pp. 24–25.

5. *Star*, November 29, 1884.

6. *Star*, June 15, 1895.

7. Warwick, "Growing up with Harding," *NOQ* XXVIII:24.

8. Corey in *Cincinnati Times-Star*, August 29, 1920, p. 6.

9. *Star*, June 15, 1895.

10. Warwick, "Growing up with Harding," *NOQ* XXX:121.

11. Corey in *Cincinnati Times-Star*, August 29, 1920, p. 6.

12. Warwick, "Growing up with Harding," *NOQ* XXX:125.

13. *Ibid.*, pp. 172–73.

14. Cuneo, *From Printer to President*, pp. 49–50.

15. Warwick, "Growing up with Harding," *NOQ* XXXI, No. 2 (Spring, 1959), 89.

16. *Ibid.*, *NOQ* XXX:124.

17. "The Railways and Prosperity." Address by Warren G. Harding at the annual dinner of the Railway Business Association, December 10, 1914. In pamphlet collection of the Ohio Historical Society.

18. Warwick, "Growing up with Harding," *NOQ* XXX:131–32.

19. *Star*, August 27, 1904.

20. "The Railways and Prosperity."

21. *Star*, December 3, 4, 5, 8, 10, 11, 16, 1886; January 21, 22, 28, 18, February 21, 1887; November 16, 1888.

22. Norman Thomas, who spent his youth in Marion, wrote to Ray Baker Harris, on September 17, 1957: "A great deal that Mrs. Harding did was done to make that crabbed character, her father, Amos Kling, recognize that in her second marriage, she had chosen a good man. He had made her life a misery for her when she came home after her first marriage and practically disowned her when she married Harding" (Ray Baker Harris Collection, Ohio Historical Society).

23. *Star*, July 8, 1891.

24. One of these invitations is on display at the Harding Museum in Marion.

25. Warwick, "Growing up with Harding," *NOQ* XXXI (Spring, 1959), 81–85.

CHAPTER THREE

1. *Star*, December 1, 1884; February 5, 1885; December 4, 1886.
2. *Ibid.*, December 12, 1889.
3. *Ibid.*, August 22, 1887; September 26, 1891.
4. Warwick, "Growing up with Harding," *NOQ* XXX:127.
5. *Marion Weekly Star*, June 6, July 18, October 24, 1885; August 1, 1885.
6. *Marion Semi-Weekly Independent*, April 6, 9, 1886; January 12, 1889; April 29, 1892; September 1, 1893; October 12, 1894; *Star*, April 7, December 7, 1886; May 21, 1887; August 28, 1893.
7. *Star*, February 7, 1897.
8. Warwick, "Growing up with Harding," XXX:126–27.
9. E. H. Roseboom and F. P. Weisenburger, *A History of Ohio* (Columbus: Ohio Archaeological and Historical Society, 1953), p. 245.
10. *Star*, March 12, 1889; March 8, 1890.
11. *Star*, August 6, 13, 20, 21, 1895.
12. *Star*, September 3, 7, 1895.
13. *Star*, September 14, November 20, 1896; July 6, 1897.
14. *Star*, March 7, 1888; November 2, 1891.
15. *Star*, March 22, 1894.
16. *Star*, February 8, 1889.
17. *Star*, January 11, 1895.

CHAPTER FOUR

1. *Star*, April 28, 1886; April 12, 1897; January 20, 1890.
2. *Star*, June 17, 1887; August 22, 1893; August 3, 6, 1894; January 9, 1896.
3. *Star*, November 17, December 4, 1894; October 3, December 4, 6, 1895, January 13, 14, 1896; December 24, 26, 1894; December 2, 1895; October 7, 1896; January 9, 1897.
4. *Star*, August 10, 1896.
5. *Star*, September 30, 1893.
6. *Star*, December 19, 1896; January 9, 1897; letter from Daytona, Florida, dated March 10, 1898 and published in *Star* on March 12, 1898 under title "Joys and Comforts of a Winter in Florida—Observations by W.G.H."
7. *Star*, November 1, 1900; December 19, 1899.

CHAPTER FIVE

1. *Star*, July 20, 1885.
2. Typed copy of an article from the Carthage, Missouri *Evening Press*, October 7, 1912, in Harris Collection, Ohio Historical Society, Columbus, Ohio.
3. *Star*, September 25, 1888.

4. *Star*, October 12, 1888.

5. *Star*, February 26, 1894.

6. *Star*, January 11, April 2, 1894.

7. *Star*, July 9, 10, June 8, 1896.

8. *Star*, June 24, 30, July 14, 21, 22, August 5, 12, 21, 26, 27, September 17, October 13, 14, 15, 21, 1896.

9. *Star*, November 5, 1896.

10. For an exhaustive account of the Haymarket riot, see Henry David, *The History of the Haymarket Affair* (New York: Farrar and Rinehart, 1930).

11. *Star*, November 7, 1893; November 24, 1894; January 5, 1895; June 24, 1896.

12. For a full account of the Homestead strike, see Norman Joseph Ware, *Labor in Modern Industrial Society* (Boston and New York: Heath, 1935).

13. For a good account of the Pullman strike, see William Horace Carmadine, *The Pullman Strike* (Chicago: Kerr, 1894).

14. *Star*, April 13, September 24, 1896.

CHAPTER SIX

1. John Sherman, *Recollections of Forty Years in the House, Senate and Cabinet: An Autobiography* (Chicago and New York: Werner Co., 1895), II, 1158–59.

2. See chap. iii, sec. 3.

3. *Star*, December 19, 1891.

4. Andrew Wallace Crandall, *The Early History of the Republican Party, 1854–1856* (Boston: Badger, 1930); George H. Mayer, *The Republican Party, 1854–1864* (New York: Oxford, 1964), chap. 2.

5. *Star*, June 28, 1887, June 19, 1888; May 27, 1890; November 5, 1891.

6. James E. Watson, *As I Knew Them* (Indianapolis: Bobbs-Merrill, 1936), pp. 289–90; Everett Walters, *Joseph Benson Foraker, An Uncompromising Republican* (Columbus: Ohio State Archaeological and Historical Society, 1941), pp. 248–50.

7. *Star*, April 29, 1892; Walters, *Foraker*, p. 105.

8. *Star*, June 9, November 12, 1892; Walters, *Foraker*, pp. 105–7.

9. *Star*, July 23, August 3, 1895; Walters, *Foraker*, pp. 107–10.

10. *Star*, October 28, 1895.

11. *Star*, January 16, 1896.

12. *Star*, June 27, October 17, 1896.

13. Herbert Croly, *Marcus Alonzo Hanna, His Life and Works* (New York: Macmillan Co., 1912), pp. 228–41.

14. *Star*, February 8, 10, 1897.

15. *Star*, June 23, 1897.

16. *Star*, November 3, 1897.

17. *Star*, January 4, 1898.

18. J. L. Hampton to Harding, July 19, 1899, Harding Papers, Box 705, No. 648. Notations are based on the arrangement of the Harding Papers as they were originally deposited with the Ohio Historical Society. The Harding Papers have

since undergone a rearrangement, and a code in the Manuscript Division of the Ohio Historical Society makes possible an easy transfer from the original numbered references to their present arrangement.

19. Hampton to Harding, June 14, 1920, Harding Papers, Box 594, Folder 4434-2, No. 271153.

20. *Marion Transcript*, January 12, 17, 1898.

21. *Star*, July 15, 17, 1899.

22. *Star*, July 18, 1899.

23. F. O. Batch to Harding, September 1, 1899, Harding Papers, Box 705-7, No. 501; *Bellefontaine Republican*, September 12, 1899.

24. John H. Smick to Harding, September 1, 1899, Harding Papers, Box 705-7, No. 864; *Kenton News-Republican*, September 9, 1899.

25. J. W. Tilton to Harding, September 23, 1899, Harding Papers, Box 705-7, No. 896; F. O. Batch to Harding, September 28, 1899, Box 705-7, No. 502; John H. Smick to Harding, October 1, Box 705-7, No. 865; Samuel G. McClure to Harding, August 21, 1899, Box 705-7, No. 836; McClure to Harding, September 15, 1899, Box 705-7, No. 734.

26. *Marysville Tribune*, August 16, 1899.

27. Mark Hanna to Harding, November 3, 1899 (telegram), Harding Papers, Box 705-8, No. 642.

28. *Annual Report of the Secretary of State . . . for 1899* (Columbus: Heer, 1899), p. 195. (Cited hereinafter as *Ohio Election Statistics*.)

CHAPTER SEVEN

1. The full text of the Cox Ripper Bill is in the *Cincinnati Times-Star*, January 15, 1900, p. 1, and the *Cincinnati Enquirer*, January 16, 1900, p. 5.

2. *Cleveland Plain Dealer*, February 16, 1900.

3. *Cincinnati Enquirer*, February 16, 1900.

4. Mark Hanna to Harding, February 9, 1900, Harding Papers, Box 706-5, No. 1117.

5. J. B. Foraker to Harding, February 9, 1900, Harding Papers, Box 706-4, No. 1048.

6. For background of the Pugh-Kibler Code proposal, see *Ohio State Journal*, February 2, 1902, p. 3; S. P. Orth, "Municipal Situation in Ohio," *Forum*, XXXII (June, 1902), 430-37. See also Robert H. Bremner, "The Civic Revival in Ohio, The Fight Against Privilege in Cleveland and Toledo, 1899-1912" (Ph.D. dissertation, Ohio State University, 1943), pp. 156-58.

7. *Columbus Evening Dispatch*, March 27, April 6, 1900.

8. *Cleveland Plain Dealer*, April 12, 1900.

9. Franklin Rubrecht to Harding, April 11, 1899 [1900], Harding Papers, Box 705-5, No. 1752.

10. George M. McPeck to Harding, April 7, 1900, Harding Papers, Box 707-1, No. 1163; *Ohio Laws*, vol. 94 (1900), pp. 649-50.

11. F. O. Batch to Harding, April 9, 1900, Harding Papers, Box 707-1, No. 946; *Senate Journal*, 64th General Assembly, p. 585, 754; *Ohio Laws*, vol. 94 (1900), p. 165.

12. J. W. Johnson to Harding, April 13, 1900, Harding Papers, Box 707–2, No. 1070; *Ohio Laws*, pp. 364–67.

13. *Ohio Laws*, vol. 94 (1900), pp. 400–401. In his campaign for reelection in 1901, Harding was criticized for promoting the passage of this law; *Star*, October 26, 29, November 2, 1901.

14. *Ohio State Journal*, March 10, 1900, p. 3.

15. *Columbus Evening Dispatch*, February 11, 14, March 4, 10, 1900.

16. W. Clay Huston to Harding, February 16, 1900, Harding Papers, Box 706–5, No. 1115.

17. *Star*, April 19, 1900.

18. *Ohio State Journal*, April 26, 1900.

19. Charles F. Dick to Harding, September 8, 1900, Harding Papers, Box 707–10, No. 1572.

20. F. O. Batch to Harding, September 13, 1900, Harding Papers, Box 707–9, No. 1381; September 26, 1900, Box 707–9, No. 1384; October 13, 1900, Box 707–10, No. 1418; November 10, 1900, Box 707–11, 1387; F. E. Coon to Harding, September 29, 1900, Box 707–9, No. 1449; J. W. Tilton to Harding, October 10, 1900, Box 707–10, No. 887; J. L. Moore to Harding, October 15, 1900, Box 707–10, No. 1572.

21. Charles C. Lemert to Harding, December 12, 1900, Harding Papers, Box 707–12, No. 1577.

22. Charles C. Lemert to Harding, May 31, 1901, Harding Papers, Box 708–6, No. 2586; June 8, 1901, Box 708–7, No. 2531, June 16, 1901, Box 708–8, No. 2584; F. N. Sinks to Harding, June 18, 1901, Harding Papers, Box 708–8, No. 2817.

23. *Cleveland Plain Dealer*, June 24, 25, 26, 1901; *Ohio State Journal*, July 10, 1901; Hoyt Landon Warner, *Progressivism in Ohio*, (Columbus: Ohio State University Press, 1964), pp. 99–101.

24. *Star*, April 10, July 1, 10, October 8, 12, 1901.

25. J. B. Foraker to Harding, November 15, 1901, Harding Papers, Box 709–8, No. 2000.

26. *Columbus Citizen*, January 14, 1902.

27. Versions of Harding's McKinley memorial speech are in the *Columbus Citizen*, January 29, 1902, the *Columbus Evening Dispatch*, January 29, 1902, the *Ohio State Journal*, January 30, 1902, and the *Cincinnati Times-Star*, January 30, 1902.

28. *Springfield Press-Republic*, February 13, 1902.

29. *Cleveland Leader*, January 30, 1902.

30. *Columbus Evening Dispatch*, November 17, December 20, 1901; January 5, 1902; *Ohio State Journal*, November 19, December 20, 1905.

31. George H. Chamberlain to Harding, December 11, 1901, Box 709–4, No. 3506; F. B. Archer to Harding, November 27, 1901, Box 709–9, No. 1853; Archer to Harding, December 8, 1901, Box 709–10, No. 1854; D. H. Moore to Harding, December 5, 1901, Box 709–10, No. 2120; Moore to Harding, December 9, 1901, Box 709–10, No. 2119; Moore to Harding, December 12, 1901, Box 709–1, No. 3749; Moore to Harding, December 24, Box 709–12, No. 3757. All in Harding Papers.

32. D. H. Moore to Harding, Harding Papers: December 5, 1901, Box 709–10, No. 2120; December 9, 1901, Box 709–10, No. 2119.

33. Mark Hanna to Harding, Harding Papers: November 20, 1901, Box 709–9, No. 2057; November 23, 1901, Box 709–9, No. 2048.

34. *Columbus Evening Dispatch*, January 6, 1902.

35. *Columbus Evening Dispatch*, April 2, 1902.

36. *Star*, April 10, 11, 1902; *Columbus Evening Dispatch*, April 10, 1902; *Ohio State Journal*, April 11, 1902. Warner, *Progressivism in Ohio*, p. 100.

37. *State of Ohio*, ex. rel. *Sheets v. Beacom*, 66 *Ohio Reports*, 491 (1902); *State of Ohio*, ex. rel. *Knisely* v. *Jones*, 66 *Ohio Reports* 453 (1902). Warner, *Progressivism in Ohio*, pp. 105–9.

38. *Ohio State Journal*, July 1, 5, 27, 28, 30, August 16, 1902; *Columbus Evening Dispatch*, July 9, 10, 11, 12, 13, 16, 21, 27, August 14, 21, 25, 27, 1902; *Commercial Tribune* (Cincinnati), August 16, 19, 26, 1902; *Cincinnati Times-Star*, August 16, 1902; Robert H. Bremner, "George K. Nash" in Ohio Historical Society, *The Governors of Ohio* (Columbus: Ohio Historical Society, 1954), p. 138; Warner, *Progressivism in Ohio*, p. 110.

39. *Star*, August 11, 1902.

40. Nicholas Longworth to Harding, July 23, 1902, Harding Papers, Box 711–2, No. 3180.

41. *Star*, August 18, 1902.

42. *Ohio State Journal*, August 26, 28, 1902.

43. *Columbus Evening Dispatch*, September 17, 1902.

44. Warner, *Progressivism in Ohio*, p. 112.

45. *Star*, September 1, 1902.

46. H. E. Owen to Harding, September 18, 1902, Harding Papers, Box 711–3, No. 23186.

47. *Columbus Citizen*, September 20, 1902; *Columbus Evening Dispatch*, September 20, 1902.

48. Hanna to Harding, September 8, 1902, Harding Papers, unclassified.

49. *Ohio State Journal*, September 25, 1902; *Columbus Evening Dispatch*, September 24, 1902.

50. *Columbus Citizen*, September 25, 1902; *Columbus Evening Dispatch*, September 25, 1902.

51. George K. Nash to Harding, October 12, 1902, Harding Papers, Box 711–5, No. 3260.

52. Nicholas Longworth to Harding, November 10, 1902, Harding Papers, Box 711–6, No. 3173.

53. Lewis C. Laylin to Harding, November 10, 1902, Harding Papers, Box 711–6, No. 3125.

CHAPTER EIGHT

1. Mark Hanna to Myron T. Herrick, January 30, 1904, Herrick Papers, Container 9, Folder 1, Western Reserve Historical Society. This letter was said by Herrick to be the last ever written by Hanna. *Cleveland Leader*, February 17, 23, 1904.

2. All of the above may be found in the Harding Papers. Henry M. Stowe to Harding: May 1, 1902, Box 710–8, No. 3370; May 12, 1902, Box 710–8, No.

3369; May 14, Box 710–8, No. 3367; October 24, Box 711–5, No. 3350; R. B. Brown (*Zanesville Courier*) to Harding, January 16, 1902 [1903], Box 710–2, No. 2946; J. H. Chew (*Xenia Gazette*) to Harding, January 17, 1903, Box 712–2, No. 8815; F. B. Patrick (*Urbana Daily News and Republican*) to Harding, January 17, 1903, Box 712–2, No. 9150; P. E. Bissell (*Conneaut Evening News*) to Harding, January 17, 1903, Box 712–2, No. 8760; L. H. Brush (East Liverpool) to Harding, January 17, 1903, Box 712–2, No. 8762; S. A. Cuneo (Upper Sandusky) to Harding, January 21, 1903, Box 712–3, No. 8811; F. L. Hopley (*Bucyrus Evening Telegraph*), to Harding, October, 1902, Box 711–5, No. 3151; F. O. Padgett (*Danville Tri-County Leader*) to Harding, January 17, 1903, Box 712–2, No. 9149; C. A. Warren (*Springfield Press-Republic*) to Harding, February 11, 1903, Box 712–5, No. 9218; W. Clay Huston to Harding, March 14, 1903, Box 710–5, No. 23890; F. B. Archer (Alliance) to Harding, November 15, 1902, Box 711–6, No. 4695; J. W. Rhodes (Steubenville) to Harding, January 17, 1903, Box 712–2, No. 9172; Henry E. Sheets (Shelby) to Harding, January 17, 1903, Box 712–2, No. 9241; George A. Love (*Greenfield Republican*) to Harding, February 28, 1903, Box 710–4, No. 23431; John J. Crowley (Marion) to Harding, January 20, 1903, Box 712–2, No. 8813; George B. Donavin (Delaware) to Harding, February 16, 1903, Box 712–6, No. 8842; F. E. Smiley (*East Liverpool Crisis*) to Harding, January 23, 1903, Box 712–3, No. 5158.

3. Harding to J. B. Foraker, January 12, 1903, Foraker Papers, Box 24, Historical and Philosophical Society of Ohio; Foraker to Harding, January 14, 1903 (telegram), Harding Papers, Box 712–1, No. 8844; Nash to Harding, January 24, 1903, Harding Papers, Box 712–3, No. 9116.

4. James M. Faulkner to Harding, April 23, 1903, Harding Papers, Box 712–10, No. 8857.

5. *Columbus Evening Dispatch*, April 14, 19, 22, 23, 1903.

6. *Chicago Tribune*, August 25, 1920.

7. *Ibid.*

8. Julius Fleischmann to Harding, November 3, 1903 (telegram) Harding Papers, Box 714–1, No. 7930; Hanna to Harding, November 14, 1903, Box 714–4, No. 8019.

9. S. A. McNeil to Harding, October 14, 1903, Harding Papers, Box 713–11.

10. *Star*, September 9, 12, 17, October 3, 7, 28, 1903.

11. *Ohio State Journal*, September 20, 1903.

12. *Columbus Evening Dispatch*, October 11, 1903.

13. *Cincinnati Times-Star*, October 30, 1903.

14. C. C. Dewstoe to Theodore E. Burton, February 17, 1904, Papers of Theodore E. Burton, Western Reserve Historical Society.

15. Myron T. Herrick to James R. Garfield, February 24, 1904, Herrick Papers, Container 36, Letter Book, p. 179, Western Reserve Historical Society.

16. Herrick to George B. Cox, February 23, 1904, Herrick Papers, Container 36, Letter Book, p. 194.

17. Herrick to H. H. Kohlsaat, February 23, 1904, Herrick Papers, Container 36, Letter book, p. 213.

18. Dewstoe to Theodore E. Burton, February 17, 1904, Burton Papers.

19. Herrick to R. B. Bokom, March 3, 1904, Herrick Papers, Container 36, Letter Book, p. 233.

20. Herrick to Theodore Roosevelt, March 10, 1904, Herrick Papers, Container 36, Letter Book, p. 254.

21. *Ohio State Journal*, May 19, 1904.

22. *Ohio Election Statistics*, 1904, pp. 492–93, 494–517.

23. All of the above may be found in the Harding Papers. Julius W. Whiting to Harding, September 7, 1904, Harding Papers, Box 715–9, No. 15763; J. A. Towney to Harding, August 22, 1904, Box 715–7, No. 15664; Towney to Harding, September 8, 1904, Box 715–8, No. 15728; Albert Douglas to Harding, September 24, 1904, Box 715–9, No. 15279; S. D. Crites to Harding, June 11, 1904, Box 715–6, No. 15240; Critics to Harding, August 3, 1904, Box 715–6, No. 15241; D. H. Moore to Harding, August 6, 1904, Box 715–7, No. 15510; Carl A. Albrecht to Harding, November 12, Box 715–10, No. 5216; A. G. Comings to Harding, November 10, 1904, Box 715–10, No. 7206; Frederick Landis to Harding, September 13, 1904, Box 715–8, No. 15442; Clay Huston to Harding, November 10, 1904, Box 715–10, No. 5250; S. A. McNeil to Harding, November 10, 1904, Box 715–10, No. 5283.

24. James K. Mercer, *Representative Men of Ohio, 1904–1908* (Columbus: Heer, 1908), p. 40; *Cleveland Plain Dealer*, April 26, 1904.

25. *Ibid.*

26. Mercer, *Representative Men of Ohio*, pp. 34–35, 51, 55; *Ohio Laws*, vol. 95 (1904), p. 92; *Columbus Evening Dispatch*, October 20, 1904; T. Bentley Mott, *Myron T. Herrick, Friend of France and Autobiographical Biography* (Garden City, N.Y.: Doubleday Doran, 1929), p. 81; Justin Stewart, *Wayne Wheeler Dry Boss: An Uncensored Biography of Wayne B. Wheeler* (New York: Revel, 1928), pp. 66–69.

27. Herrick to A. D. Alderman, January 10, 1905, Herrick Papers, Container 36, Letter Book, May 13, 1904—January 13, 1905, p. 395.

28. Herrick to Charles W. Fairbanks, January 26, 1905, Herrick Papers, Container 36, Letter Book, May 13, 1904—January 23, 1905, p. 511.

29. Herrick to Elmer Dover, January 7, 1905, Herrick Papers, Container 36, *op. cit.*, p. 375.

30. Herrick to Charles F. Dick, January 23, 1905, Herrick Papers, Container 36, *op. cit.*, p. 30.

31. Herrick to Dover, January 23, 1905, Herrick Papers, Container 36, *op. cit.*, p. 31.

32. *Ibid.*

33. *Ohio State Journal*, November 13, 1904; *Cincinnati Enquirer*, November 13, 1904. No copies of the Herrick "literary bureau" press sheets have been found, but they are referred to in the following papers: *Warren County Record*, December 23, 1904; *Mendon Herald*, December 23, 1904; *Green County Press*, December 23, 1904; *Carrollton Republican Standard*, December 23, 1904 and January 6, 1905; *Elyria Republican*, January 5, 1905; *Van Wert Republican*, January 5, 1905. Editorials from these papers were prepared in specially printed and typed circulars, Harding Papers, Box 715–12, No. 5215 and Box 716–2, No. 7600.

34. Circular letter by Charles F. Dick, January 19, 1905, Harding Papers, Box 716–5, No. 7244; same dated January 27, 1905, Box 716–7, No. 7392.

35. *Logan Journal Gazette*, December 29, 1904, January 5, 12, 19, February 9, 1905; *Hocking Republican* (Logan), January 12, 19, 1905.

36. Herrick to J. C. Duncan, January 28, 1905, Herrick Papers, Container 36, Letter Book, January 23, 1905–April 19, 1905, p. 86.

37. *Toledo Blade*, February 13, 1905; *Toledo News-Bee*, February 13, 1905; Scott Bonham to Harding, February 14, 1905, Harding Papers, Box 717–4, No. 6296.

38. Herrick to Dick, February 14, 1905, Herrick Papers, Container 36, Letter Book, January 23, 1905 to April 19, 1905, p. 167.

39. Herrick to Dover, February 14, 1905, Herrick Papers, Container 36, Letter Book, January 23, 1905 to April 19, 1905, p. 193.

40. F. E. Scobey to Harding, January 19, 1905, Harding Papers, Box 716–5, No. 6940; Edwin D. Barry to Scobey, January 21, 1905, Box 716–6, No. 7145; Barry to Harding, January 21, 1905, Box 716–6, No. 7141.

41. *Columbus Citizen*, January 2, 1905, *Ohio State Journal*, January 2, 1905; *Cincinnati Enquirer*, January 2, 1905.

42. Harding to Foraker, January 11, 1905, Foraker Papers, Box 24, Historical and Philosophical Society of Ohio.

43. All of the above may be found in the Harding Papers. J. Q. A. Campbell to Harding, January 21, 1905, Box 716–6, No. 7195; F. E. Scobey to Harding, February 1, 1905, Box 717–1, No. 7960; Silas E. Hurin to Harding, January 29, 1905, Box 716–8, No. 6671; Dr. B. B. Morrow to Harding, January 27, 1905, Box 716–7, No. 7482; F. L. Dustman to Harding, January 5, 1905, Box 716–2, No. 5244; A. H. Norcross to Harding, January 6, 1905, Box 716–2, No. 7542; Duston Kemble to Harding, January 6, 1905, Box 716–2, No. 2726; W. B. Hearn to Harding, January 6, 1905, Box 716–2, No. 7379; S. E. Davidson to Harding, January 17, 1905, Box 716–5, No. 6494; J. E. Kelly to Harding, January 25, 1905, Box 716–1, No. 7432; R. Archer to Harding, January 26, 1905, Box 716–7, No. 7084; H. O. Goodrich to Harding, January 30, 1905, Box 716–8, No. 7311.

44. W. L. Miller to Harding, January 7, 1905, Box 716–2, No. 7660; Hurin to Harding, January 16, 1905, Box 716–5, No. 6657; Howard to Harding, January 13, 1905, Box 716–4, No. 6665; Howard to Harding, February 4, 1905, Box 717–2, No. 7759; Mulholland to Harding, January 3, 1903, Box 716–1, No. 5289. All in Harding Papers.

45. Wheeler to Harding, January 4, 1905, Box 716–1, No. 5348; Wheeler to Harding, January 16, 1905, Box 716–5, No. 7043; Baker to Harding, February 3, 1905, Box 717–1, No. 7155; Baker to Harding, February 4, 1905, Box 717–2, No. 7151. All in Harding Papers.

46. Harding to Foraker, January 18, 1905, Foraker Papers, Box 24, Historical and Philosophical Society of Ohio; Foraker to Harding, January 20, 1905, Harding Papers, Box 716–6, No. 7275; Baker to Harding, February 3, 1905, Harding Papers, Box 717–1, No. 7154.

47. Garretson to Harding, January 30, 1905, Harding Papers, Box 716–8, No. 7201; telegram from *Cincinnati Post*, Box 716–8, No. 7204.

48. Webber to Harding, Harding Papers, February 2, 1905, Harding Papers, Box 717–1, No. 7763.

49. Jennings to Harding, Harding Papers, April 11, 1905, Box 717–9, No. 7465.

50. Freshwater to Harding, Harding Papers, August 9, 1905, Box 718–4, No. 7257.

51. *Ohio State Journal*, September 18, 1905; *Citizen and Gazette* (Urbana), October 27, 1905; *Marietta Daily Leader*, November 1, 1905; *The Leader* (Pomeroy), November 9, 1905.

52. *Ohio State Journal*, October 8, 1905.

53. *Ohio State Journal*, October 22, 1905.

54. *Star*, October 22, 1905.

55. *Ohio Election Statistics*, 1905, pp. 119–20.

56. Anonymous, undated note, Harding Papers, Box 718–7, No. 7770.

57. *Star*, January 18, 19, 25, 1906.

58. For Foraker's views on the Hepburn Bill, see Walters, *Foraker*, pp. 215, 253–54. A good understanding of the Hepburn Bill debate can be obtained from Joseph Benson Foraker, *Notes of a Busy Life*, II (Cincinnati: Stewart D. Kidd Co.), 207–27, and from Ripley, *Railroad, Rates and Regulations* (New York: Longmans Green, 1916), pp. 494–521.

59. *Star*, March 24, 1906.

60. *Cincinnati Enquirer*, September 13, 1906; Walters, *Foraker*, pp. 257–58; *Marion Daily Star*, September 13, 1906.

61. *Dayton Daily News*, September 11, 1906; *Columbus Citizen*, September 12, 1906.

62. Charles F. Dick to Harding, September 28, 1906, Box 719–5, No. 11317; John R. Malloy to Harding, October 5, 1906, Box 719–5, No. 11445; R. K. Hynicka to Malloy, October 6, Box 719–6, No. 11446; Herbert L. Jones to Harding, October 25, 1906, Box 719–6, No. 11576; John Whiting to Harding, October 17, 1906, Box 719–6, No. 11496; Albert Douglas to Harding, November 6, 1906, Box 719–7, No. 11326 (all of the preceding may be found in Harding Papers); *Ohio State Journal*, October 21, 1906, editorial section; *Cincinnati Enquirer*, October 18, 19, 1906; *Cincinnati Times-Star*, October 18, 1906; *Commercial Tribune* (Cincinnati), October 18, 1906.

63. Thompson to Harding, November 8, 1906, Harding Papers, Box 719–7, No. 11575; James to Harding, November 8, 1906, Box 719–7, No. 12243.

64. Walters, *Foraker*, pp. 266–67.

65. "Eye Witness," *Chicago Tribune*, August 25, 1920.

66. *Star*, June 6, August 12, November 23, 30, December 23, 1907; January 3, 4, 6, 13, 15, 21, 22, 1908.

67. Harding to Foraker, January 24, 1908, Foraker Papers, Historical and Philosophical Society of Ohio.

68. Jennings to Harding, [ca. 1908] Harding Papers, Box 720–7, No. 13847.

69. Harding to Foraker, August 20, 1914. Typed copy in Harris Collection in Ohio Historical Society; the original is in the Manuscript Division of the Library of Congress.

70. Fullington to Harding, January 24, 1908, Harding Papers, Box 720–7, No. 13810.

71. Mouser to Harding, December 26, 1907, Box 720–6, No. 13914; January 22, 1908, Box 720–7, No. 13889; January 27, 1908, Box 720–7, No. 13884. All in Harding Papers.

72. Harding to Foraker, May 1, 1910 (typed copy), Harris Collection, Ohio Historical Society, Original in Manuscript Division, Library of Congress.

73. *Ohio Election Statistics*, 1908, pp. 130, 185–86, 191–92.

74. *Ohio State Journal*, October 28, 1908.

75. All of the above may be found in the Harding Papers. Kennedy to Harding, December 24, 1909, Box 720–11, No. 21254; Mallory to Harding, March 22, 1910, Box 721–3, No. 21633; Culp to Harding, July 12, 1910, Box 721–4, No. 21741; Frost to Harding, July 28, 1910, Box 722–1, No. 14757; Templin to Harding, July

30, 1910, Box 722–10, No. 15042; Pavey to Harding, July 28, 1910, Box 722–2, No. 14950.

76. Warner, *Progressivism in Ohio*, pp. 223–25.

77. Waldorf to Harding, July 28, 1910, Harding Papers, Box 722–5, No. 14599.

78. Scobey to Harding, January 14, 1905, Harding Papers, Box 716–4, No. 7662; Scobey to Jennings, January 22, 1905, Scobey to Jennings, Box 716–6, No. 6949–6950; Scobey to Harding, September 15, 1910, Scobey to Harding, Box 723–5, No. 21796. All in Harding Papers.

79. Sheets to Harding, July 31, 1910, Harding Papers, Box 722–11, No. 14508.

80. Scobey to Harding, no date, Harding Papers, Box 722–11, No. 14512; Scobey to Harding, September 15, 1910, Harding Papers, Box 723–5, No. 21796.

81. *Ohio State Journal*, January 30, April 22, 1910; McConica to Harding, April 30, 1910, Harding Papers, Box 721–3, No. 21521.

82. *Star*, January 2, 1910.

83. Circular letter, no date, Harding Papers, Box 723–7, No. 21619; circular letter to delegates, June 1, 1910, Box 721–3, No. 14370.

84. *Ohio State Journal*, February 4, 8, 9, 10, 11, March 4, 6, 1910.

85. *Ohio State Journal*, July 24, 1910.

86. Walters, *Foraker*, pp. 273–87.

87. Foraker to Harding, July 15, 1910, Foraker Papers, Ohio Historical and Philosophical Society; Harding to Foraker, July 14, 1910.

88. Garretson to Taft, July 28, 1910, Charles D. Hilles Papers, Yale University; Vorys to Taft, July 27, 1910 (by telegram and wireless), Hilles Papers. Written on this telegram were the words "wired Harding 7–28–10."

89. The details of the Cox maneuvers are given in a six-page letter from Joseph Garretson to Taft, July 28, 1910 in the Hilles Papers. The convention proceedings and votes were reported in the *Cincinnati Enquirer*, July 28, 1910.

90. J. W. Heintzman to Malcolm Jennings, July 28, 1910, Harding Papers, Box 722–2, No. 14849.

91. *Sun* (New York), October 18, 1910. Further evidence of the do-nothingness of Cox and the alleged business indifference to Harding in 1910 may be found in the following letters in the Hilles Papers; J. W. Hill to Taft, October 21, 1910; A. T. Vorys to Hilles, October 22, 1910; S. J. Flickinger to Hilles, October 25, 1910; Hilles Memorandum to Taft, October 31, 1910; Vorys to Taft, November 3, 1910.

92. *Ohio State Journal*, July 31, 1910, editorial section.

93. Ellis to Taft, July 30, 1910, Hilles Papers.

94. McNamara to Taft, July 29, 1910, Hilles Papers, Watson to Hilles, October 29, 1910.

95. *Ohio State Journal*, September 25, 1910, editorial section, October 9, 1910; *News-Democrat* (Canton), September 24, 1910; Warner, *Progressivism in Ohio*, pp. 258–62.

96. *Ohio State Journal*, September 24, 29, October 1, 4, 8, 16, 20, 23, 25, 29, 30, November 3, 1910; *Cleveland Leader*, October 27, 1910; *Star*, October 11, 27, 28, 31, 1910.

97. *Ohio State Journal*, October 11, 1910.

98. See chap. vii.

99. *Star*, November 3, 1910.

100. See chap. vii.

101. *Star*, November 3, 1910.

102. Foraker, *Notes of a Busy Life*, p. 433; *Ohio State Journal*, October 25, 26, November 4, 6, 9, 1910; Foraker to Harding, November 22, 1910, Foraker Papers, Ohio Historical and Philosophical Society. See also A. M. Bickel to Taft, November 3, 1910, Hilles Papers.

103. Miller to Taft, October 25, 1910, Hilles Papers; Boyle to Hilles, October 20, 1910; Vorys to Taft, October 28, 1910; Watson to Hilles, November 10, 1910.

104. Laylin to Taft, September 28, 1910, Hilles Papers.

105. Hamilton to Taft, November 18, 1910, Hilles Papers.

106. Flickinger to Hilles, November 4, 1910, Hilles Papers.

107. Walker to Harding, June 29, 1912, Harding Papers, Box 724–8, No. 16942.

108. Hilles to Vorys, November 19, 1910, Hilles Papers.

109. Jennings to Hilles, August 1, 1911, Hilles Papers.

110. Harding to Taft, November 23, 1910, Taft Papers, Library of Congress, File 134, Box 340, Presidential Series, No. 2.

111. Harding to Julian Street, n.d., a letter printed in *Christian Science Monitor*, November 30, 1960. The original is in the Blumhaven Library in Philadelphia.

112. *Star*, November 9, 1910.

113. Foraker to Harding, November 22, 1910, Foraker Papers, Historical and Philosophical Society of Ohio.

114. Willis to Harding, November 24, 1910, Harding Papers, Box 723–6, No. 21870.

115. Gongwer to Harding, November 9, 1910, Harding Papers, Box 723–7, No. 71844.

CHAPTER NINE

1. In these years both Harding and Jennings wrote editorials for the *Star*. With a few exceptions, it is difficult to distinguish between the two. In 1920 the authorship of two anti- Roosevelt-Johnson *Star* editorials of 1912 were acknowledged by Jennings to have been written by him. These appeared in the *Star* on August 30 and September 13, 1912. Jennings to Harding, June 28, 1920, Harding Papers, Box 597, Folder 4441–2, No. 272236.

2. *Ohio State Journal*, January 16, 1911; *Star*, January 20, 1911.

3. *Cleveland Plain Dealer*, February 12, 1911; *Ohio State Journal*, February 12, 1911.

4. *Star*, January 20, 1912.

5. *Ohio State Journal*, January 31, 1912.

6. *Star*, November 29, 1911, January 4, 12, June 28, August 12, 30, September 13, 1912. At least two of these editorials, dated August 30 and September 13, were written by Malcolm Jennings, who admitted this in his letter to Harding of June 28, 1920, Harding Papers, Box 597, Folder 4441–2, No. 272236.

7. *Star*, February 18, June 20, 1912.

8. *Star*, February 18, May 6, September 15, 1911, January 20, May 23, 1912.

9. *Star*, May 31, November 7, 1912.

10. *Ohio State Journal*, January 31, 1912.

11. Manuscript by George B. Harris, "The Ohio Republican State Convention of 1912 and Its Effect on United States History." Mr. Harris was a delegate to the convention. See also Warner, *Progressivism in Ohio*, p. 381.

12. *Star*, June 5, 1912.

13. Hilles to Taft memorandum, May 25, 1912, Taft Papers, Library of Congress, Presidential Series, File 134, Box 340. On the Harding-Taft platforms, see same box, Harding to Taft, June 5, 1912, Harding to Forster, June 5, 1912, Harding to Hilles, June 7, 1912, and memorandum dated June 8, 1912. See also Hilles to Dr. Nicholas Murray Butler, June 7, 1912, Hilles Papers, Letter Box 19A, p. 72, Box 170. Butler helped draft the platform of the Republican National Convention and used Harding's platform in so doing.

14. *Columbus Sunday Dispatch*, June 2, 1912; *Columbus Citizen*, June 1, 1912.

15. *Ohio State Journal*, June 5, 1912.

16. Manuscript by Arthur L. Garford, "Recollections of a Rumpus," accompanying a letter by his secretary, Clarence Maris, to Garford, June 7, 1912, Garford Papers, Ohio Historical Society.

17. Harding to Hilles, April 2, 1912, Hilles Papers, Box 91; Hilles to Harding, April 4, 1912, Letter Book 13, p. 75, Box 167; Harding to Hilles, April 8, 1912, Box 93; Hilles to Harding, April 10, 1912, Letter Book 14, p. 214, Box 167 (all in Hilles Papers); Taft to Harding, June 5, 1912; Harding to Taft, June 6, 1912; Harding to Taft (telegram), June 7, 1912; Harding to Taft, June 7, 1912; copy of Harding's speech nominating Taft; Harding to Forster (telegram), June 14, 1912; Taft to Harding, June 15, 1912 (carbon copy of letter) (all in Taft Papers, Presidential Series 2, File 134, Box 340).

18. *Cleveland Leader*, June 5, 1912.

19. *Canton Evening Repository*, October 22, 1912.

20. *Star*, June 11, August 21, 1912.

21. This summary is based on the *Cleveland Leader* and the *Ohio State Journal* for the week of June 18 to 24, 1912. See also Henry F. Pringle, *Theodore Roosevelt* (New York: Harcourt, Brace and Co., 1931), pp. 543–71; Pringle, *Taft*, II, 796–814; G. E. Mowry, *Roosevelt and the Progressive Movement*, pp. 220–55.

22. *Ohio State Journal*, June 23, 1912.

23. *Ibid.*

24. *Ohio State Journal*, June 25, 1912.

25. Alice Roosevelt Longworth, *Crowded Hours* (New York and London: Charles Scribner's Sons, Inc., 1933), pp. 202–3.

26. *Report of the Secretary of State of Ohio* (1912) (Springfield, Ohio: Springfield Publishing Co., 1913), pp. 326–29.

27. *Columbus Evening Dispatch*, July 2, 1912; *Ohio State Journal*, July 3, 1912.

28. *Ohio State Journal*, July 3, 1912.

29. *Ibid.*

30. *Ohio State Journal*, August 1, 4, 1912 (editorial section).

31. *Ohio State Journal*, July 30, August 4, 8, 9, 1912.

32. *Ohio State Journal*, August 11, 1912; Warner, *Progressivism in Ohio*, pp. 372–73.

33. *Ohio State Journal,* August 11, 1912.

34. R. B. Brown to Harding, August 12, 1912, Harding Papers, Box 724–10, No. 16724.

35. *Star,* August 12, 1912; *Ohio State Journal,* August 14, 24, September 1, 1912.

36. *Star,* November 6, 7, 8, 1912.

37. *Star,* November 7, 1912.

38. Daugherty to Harding, January 13, 1913, Harding Papers, Box 725–5, No. 16610.

39. Memorandum dated March 16, 1912, Taft Papers, Presidential Series No. 2, File 3527.

40. Daugherty to Thompson, August 27, 1912, Taft Papers, *loc. cit.*

41. *Ibid.*

42. Daugherty to Thompson, September 11, 1912, Taft Papers, *loc cit.*

43. Taft to Daugherty, September 16, 1912 (carbon), Taft Papers, *loc. cit.*

44. Hilles to Daugherty, September 13, 1912, Hilles Papers, Letter Book 26, pp. 82, 114, Box 174.

45. Laylin to Harding, November 14, 1912, Harding Papers, Box 725–2, No. 22271.

46. Daugherty to Harding, November 16, 1912, Harding Papers, Box 725–3, No. 16805.

47. *Star,* September 4, 1912.

48. *Star,* April 8, 12, May 3, 23, August 3, November 22, December 6, 12, 24, 1913.

49. *Star,* April 12, June 30, September 1, 1913.

50. *Star,* January 29, May 29, July 9, August 12, September 26, October 25, 29, 1913.

CHAPTER TEN

1. *Columbus Evening Dispatch,* January 8, 1914; *Ohio State Journal,* February 24, 26, 27, 28, March 1, 1914; *Cleveland Leader,* February 27, 1914; *Star,* February 25, 26, 27, 28, 1914; Warner, *Progressivism in Ohio,* p. 468.

2. Warner, *Progressivism in Ohio,* pp. 357, 378; *Ohio State Journal,* May 14, 1912; Hilles to A. T. Vorys, February 19, 1912, Hilles Papers, Letter Book 6, p. 258, Box 163; Hilles to Laylin, February 21, 1912, Hilles Papers, Letter Book 6, p. 410, Box 163; Warner, *Progressivism in Ohio,* p. 475; Hanna to Perkins, March 8, 1914, Walter Brown Papers, Ohio Historical Society.

3. Hampton to Harding, April 10, 1914, Harding Papers, Box 726–6, No. 20853.

4. Harding to Scobey, June 18, 1914, F. E. Scobey Papers, Ohio Historical Society, Box 1, No. 3.

5. Forest Crissey, *Theodore E. Burton* (Cleveland: World Publishing Co., 1956), pp. 118–21, 229–30; *Columbus Evening Dispatch,* November 23, 27, 1913.

6. *Columbus Evening Dispatch,* November 23, 1913; Burton to George L. Drake, April 17, 1914, Burton Papers; Charles E. Grosvenor to Burton, April 2, 1914; Burton to Grosvenor, April 6, 1914; Burton to L. A. Sears, April 17, 1914; Burton to Job J. Lehman, April 16, 1914; *Star,* December 20, 1913.

7. *Cleveland Leader*, January 8, February 13, 1914; *Star*, February 27, 1914.

8. Crissey, *Theodore E. Burton*, pp. 237, 297; *Columbus Evening Dispatch*, April 10, 1914.

9. *Star*, April 7, 1914.

10. *Cleveland Leader*, May 16, 1914; *Columbus Evening Dispatch*, April 12, 1914, *Cincinnati Times-Star*, April 11, 1919.

11. Harding to Foraker, August 20, 1914, typed copy of original in the Library of Congress, Harris Collection, Ohio Historical Society.

12. "Eye Witness," *Chicago Tribune*, August 25, 1920.

13. *Ohio State Journal*, May 24, editorial section, May 26, 27, 1914; *Cincinnati Times-Star*, May 27, 1914; *Star*, May 28, 1914; N. R. Howard to Ray Baker Harris, January 10, 1933, Harris Collection.

14. *Ohio State Journal*, May 29, August 9, editorial section, 1914.

15. Harding to Scobey, June 18, 1914, Scobey Papers, Box 1, No. 3; *Cleveland Leader*, July 19, 1914.

16. *Ohio State Journal*, June 14, August 9, editorial section, 1914; *Cleveland Leader*, July 13, 16, 25, August 5, 1914; *Cincinnati Times-Star*, May 28, 1914.

17. *Star*, August 8, Part 2, 1914.

18. Houghton Sulky Company, Circular Letter, July 20, 1914, Harding Papers, Box 726–3, No. 22893; Marion Steam Shovel Company, Circular Letter, August 5, 1914, Box 716–6, no number.

19. Costain to Harding, August 3, 1914, Harding Papers, Box 726–5, No. 23277; *ibid.*, August 4, 1914, Box 726–5, No. 23280. For information on the railroad depression, see J. E. Milligan to Harding, July 23, 1914, Box 726–3, No. 22979.

20. Carney to S. A. Stack, July 30, 1914, Harding Papers, Box 726–4, No. 22858.

21. Stack to Harding, August 2, 1914, Harding Papers, Box 726–5, No. 22851; August 10, 1914, Box 726–8, No. 22893.

22. Hamilton to Harding, July 22, 1914, Harding Papers, Box 726–3, No. 22971.

23. *Ibid.*

24. Houghton to Harding, August 12, 1914, Harding Papers, Box 726–8, No. 23192.

25. There are 8 letters from Gilkey from June 2 to August 7, 1914. They are in Box 726–3, Nos. 22940, 22942, 22943, 22946; Box 726–5, No. 23259; Box 726–6, No. 25256; Box 726–7, No. 23260, 23264. There are seven letters from Hampton, dated from July 1 to August 5, 1914. They are in Boxes, 726–3, Nos. 22950, 22954, 22958, 22961, 22966; Box 726–6, No. 23242.

26. *Annual Statistical Report of the Secretary of State to the Governor . . . of Ohio for the Year Ending November 15, 1914,* (Springfield, Ohio: Springfield Publishing Co., 1915) pp. 564–65, 569.

27. *Akron Beacon-Journal*, August 13, 1914; *Cleveland Leader*, August 13, 1914; *Ohio State Journal*, August 13, 1914.

28. *Cleveland Leader*, August 16, 1914.

29. *Ohio State Journal*, August 19, 20, 21, 25, 26, 27, 1914.

30. *Ohio State Journal*, September 27, October 20, 25, 30, 1914.

31. Harding to Scobey, December 4, 1916, Scobey Papers, Box 1, No. 97.

32. All of the above may be found in the Harding Papers: Harding to Mrs. Upton, June 17, 1914 (typed copy), Box 703, Folder 703–10, No. 153639; Mrs. Upton to Harding, August 28, 1914, Box 727–2, No. 22900; Harding to Mrs. Upton, September 2, 1914 (carbon), Box 727–4, No. 22847; *ibid.*, September 12, 1914 (carbon), Box 727–5, No. 22528; Baker to Harding, August 22, 1914, Box 727–1, No. 22412.

33. *Ohio State Journal,* September 27, 1914.

34. Harding Campaign Book of 1914, in the possession of Don L. Tobin of Columbus, Ohio.

35. *Ohio State Journal,* October 8, 24, 27, 29, November 1, 1914.

36. *Star,* September 23, 1914.

37. *Ohio State Journal,* September 27, 1914.

38. *Ohio State Journal,* October 13, 17, 20, 21, 23, 1914.

39. Harding to Jennings, October 5, 1914, Jennings Papers.

40. *Ohio Statistics,* 1912, p. 324; 1914, pp. 262, 274. The 1914 vote for Senator and Governor was:

Senatorial vote			Gubernatorial vote		
Harding	(Rep.)	526,115	Willis	(Rep.)	523,074
Hogan	(Dem.)	423,742	Cox	(Dem.)	493,804
Garford	(Prog.)	67,509	Garfield	(Prog.)	60,904
Hutchins	(Soc.)	52,803	Wilkins	(Soc.)	51,441
Total		1,010,169	Total		1,129,223

41. Foraker to Kurtz, October 29, 1914, (typed copy of original in the Library of Congress), Harris Collection; Harding to Scobey, September 28, 1914, Scobey, Papers, Box 1, No. 13.

42. *Accuser* to Harding, September 5, 1914, Harding Papers, Box 727–4, No. 22803; Harding to Long, September 12, 1914 (carbon), Box 727–4, No. 22802; Middleton to Harding, September 15, 1914, Box 727–6, No. 22192. No copies of the *Accuser* have been found.

43. Harding to Jennings, February 10, 1917, Jennings Papers.

44. *Menace,* August 15, November 14, 21, 1914.

45. *Catholic Columbian,* October 30, 1914.

46. *Toledo Record,* October 30, 1914. Rev. Washington Gladden of the First Congregational Church of Columbus described and deplored Rev. Rutledge's anti-Catholic campaign in *Harper's Weekly,* July 18, 1914, p. 55, and September 12, 1914, p. 255. The religious issue in the Ohio campaign of 1914 was mentioned by Samuel G. Blythe in an article in the *Saturday Evening Post,* July 25, 1914, p. 7.

47. Humphreys to Harding, October 15, 1914, Harding Papers, Box 728–2, No. 23084. The anti-Catholic letters are scattered through the Harding Papers from Box 726–4 to 728–4.

48. *Star,* November 11, 1914.

CHAPTER ELEVEN

1. "The Railways and Prosperity," Address by Warren G. Harding at the Annual Dinner of the Railway Business Association, December 10, 1914. Pamphlet collection of the Ohio Historical Society.

2. *New York World*, January 8, 1915, business section.

3. Arthur S. Link, *Wilson and the Progressive Era, 1910–1917* (New York: Harper's, 1954), p. 68.

4. *New York World*, January 8, 1915, business section.

5. Arthur S. Link, *Wilson, The New Freedom* (Princeton: Princeton University Press, 1956), pp. 442–44.

6. *New York World*, January 8, 1915, business section.

7. "The American Railways and Prosperity."

8. *Columbus Evening Dispatch*, March 25, 1915; *Columbus Citizen*, March 25, 1915.

9. *Star*, March 26, April 8, 26, 1915.

10. *Star*, March 26, 1915.

11. *Columbus Evening Dispatch*, March 26, 1915.

12. *Star*, April 29, 1915.

13. Frederick E. Schortemeier (ed.) *Rededicating America: Life and Recent Speeches of Warren G. Harding* (Indianapolis: Bobbs-Merrill, 1920), pp. 149–63. This speech is misdated 1916. For verification of its 1915 date, see *Boston Post*, April 28, 1915; *Boston Globe*, April 28, 1915, *Boston Herald*, April 28, 1915; *Boston Transcript*, April 28, 1915; *Star*, April 28, 1915; *Ohio State Journal*, April 28, 1915.

14. The full text is in *Star*, May 27, 1915.

15. *Ohio State Journal*, October 14, 1915.

16. *Columbus Citizen*, March 25, 1915; *Ohio State Journal*, March 27, 1915; *Star*, August 4, September 1, 23, November 13, 1915.

17. *Ohio State Journal*, June 25, 1915.

18. *Star*, July 16, 1915.

19. *U.S. Statutes at Large*, vol. 38, Part I (Washington, D.C.: Government Printing Office, 1915), pp. 1164–85.

20. *Star*, June 17, September 15, October 18, 1915.

21. *San Antonio Express*, January 20, 1915.

22. *Ohio State Journal*, January 20, 1915; *New York Times*, January 20, 1915.

23. *Star*, September 28, 1915.

24. *Star*, July 3, 1915.

25. *Star*, June 3, 1915.

26. See also the editorial "Cuba Will Yet Be Ours," in *Star*, October 7, 1915.

27. Harding to Scobey, August 15, 1916, Scobey Papers, Box 1, No. 91; Harding to Scobey, January 27, 1915, Box 1, No. 33.

28. *Star*, September 15, November 16, 1915.

29. *Cleveland Leader*, May 13, 1915; *Cleveland Plain Dealer*, May 14, 1915.

30. *Star*, May 18, November 2, 1915.

CHAPTER TWELVE

1. *Columbus Sunday Dispatch*, April 23, 1916; Harding to Jennings, April 24, 1916, Jennings Papers.

2. Harding to Jennings, April 17, 1916, Jennings Papers.

3. *Plain Dealer*, February 4, 1916, p. 10; Harding to Scobey, February 19, 1916, Scobey Papers, Box 1, No. 71–72; Harding to Scobey, November 21, 1916, Scobey Papers, Box 1, No. 95.

4. Harding to Jennings, February 29, 1916, Jennings Papers.

5. *Ohio State Journal*, January 28, 1916.

6. Frank Freidel, *The Splendid Little War* (Boston: Little-Brown, 1958) pp. 64–68, 108, 143–73, Walter Millis, *The Martial Spirit: A Study of Our War With Spain* (Boston and New York: Houghton Mifflin, 1931), pp. 217–19, 244–49, 267, 270–73, 275–76, 280, 283, 290–91, 297–98. See Theodore Roosevelt, *The Rough Riders* (New York: Scribners, 1899).

7. *Congressional Record*, 64 Congress, 1 Session, January 28, 1916, pp. 1679–1681; Schortemeier, (ed.), *Rededicating America*, pp. 230–39.

8. *Ohio Democrat and Times* (New Philadelphia), February 17, 1916; *Canton Sunday Repository*, February 13, 1916.

9. *Pittsburgh Dispatch*, March 12, 1916; *Pittsburgh Sunday Post*, March 12, 1916.

10. *Canton Sunday Repository*, February 13, 1916.

11. Warren G. Harding, "Commerce and Nationalism: Pioneer of All National Development and Preserver of National Strength Is Commerce," *Prosperity: The Republican National Magazine* (April, 1916), pp. 25–27.

12. Harding to Jennings, March 29, 1916, Jennings Papers.

13. *Congressional Record*, 64 Congress, 1 Session, March 21, 1916, pp. 4535–37.

14. *Cleveland Leader*, March 27, 1916.

15. *Ohio State Journal*, April 8, 1916.

16. Hilles to Harris, September 4, 1935 in Harris Collection, Ohio Historical Society.

17. *Cleveland Leader*, April 9, 1916.

18. *Ohio State Journal*, April 9, 1916; *Cleveland Leader*, April 9, 1916; *New York Times*, April 9, 1916, section 1; *American Economist*, April 10, 1916.

19. *Republican Campaign Textbook*, 1916, pp. 19–29.

20. Harding to Scobey, April 14, 1916, Scobey Papers, Box 1, No. 81.

21. Eugene H. Roseboom, *A History of Presidential Elections* (New York: Macmillan, 1957), p. 382; *Cleveland Leader*, June 5, 8, 1916.

22. *Cleveland Leader*, June 9, 1916; *New York Times*, June 9, 1916.

23. Roseboom, *Presidential Elections*, pp. 380–83; *Ohio State Journal*, June 9, 1916; *Cleveland Leader*, June 5, 6, 1916; *New York Times*, June 9, 1916.

24. Harding to Roosevelt, June 28, 1916 (photostat copy) in Harris collection.

25. Harding to Scobey, January 23, 1917, Scobey Papers, Box 1, No. 109.

26. Harding to Scobey, July 22, 1916, Scobey Papers, Box 1, No. 89; Harding to Scobey, December 4, 1916, Scobey Papers, Box 1, No. 97.

27. Dexter Perkins, *Charles Evans Hughes and American Democratic Statesmanship* (Boston: Little-Brown, 1956), pp. 50–70; Merle J. Pusey, *Charles Evans Hughes* (New York: Macmillan, 1951), pp. 335–59.

28. *Ohio State Journal*, September 8, 11, 1916; Harding to Scobey, September 20, 1916, Scobey Papers, Box 1, No. 94.

29. *Ohio State Journal*, September 26, October 13, 20, November 1, 3; *Cleveland Leader*, September 26, 1916.

30. Roseboom, *Presidential Elections*, pp. 384–88; Pusey, *Hughes*, I, pp. 335–59; *Ohio Statistics* (1917), p. 239.

31. *Ohio State Journal*, November 28, 1916; Willis' defeat was no surprise to Harding, who said that the Governor had "made such a mess of it." He had predicted Willis' defeat early in 1916 in a letter to Jennings (Harding to Jennings, January 28, 1916, Jennings Papers).

32. Harding to Scobey, November 21, 1916, Scobey Papers, Box 1, No. 95; Harding to Scobey, December 4, 1916, Scobey Papers, Box 1, No. 98.

33. Cope to Shaw, April 19, 1916, Harris Collection; Scobey to Malcolm Jennings, December 8, 1914, Scobey Papers, Box 1, No. 29.

34. All of the above may be found in the Scobey Papers. Scobey to Harding, November 9, 1914, Box 1, No. 20; Harding to Scobey, November 25, 1914, Box 1, No. 25; Scobey to Harding, March 30, 1915, Box 1, No. 37; Scobey to Christian, Jr., April 19, 1915, Box 1, No. 40; Christian, Sr., to Scobey, May 15, 1915, Box 1, No. 41; Scobey to Christian, Jr., May 20, 1915, Box 1, No. 42; Harding to Scobey, July 12, 1915, Box 1, No. 43; Harding to Scobey, September 6, 1915, Box 1, No. 48; Harding to Scobey, December 13, 1915, Box 1, No. 53.

35. Harding to Scobey, September 6, 1915, Box 1, No. 48; Harding to Scobey, December 13, 1915, Box 1, No. 53; Christian, Jr., to Scobey, May 17, 1916, Box 1, No. 83. All in Scobey Papers.

36. *Ohio State Journal*, April 6, editorial section, April 11, 13, 15, 27, 29, May 7, 20, 28, 1916; *Columbus Evening Dispatch*, June 6, 8, 1916; *Cleveland Plain Dealer*, May 31, June 4, 1916; *Cleveland Leader*, April 11, May 21, June 3, 8, 1916; *Cincinnati Enquirer*, June 7, 8, 1916; *Cincinnati Times-Star*, April 14, June 6, 1916; *Washington* (D.C.) *Evening-Star*, June 6, 1916; *Literary Digest*, April 29, 1916, p. 1206; June 3, 1916, p. 1620; J. H. Remick to A. A. Schantz, June 7, 1916, as quoted in Dorothy V. Martin, "An Impression of Harding in 1916," in Ohio State Archaeological and Historical Society *Quarterly*, Vol. 62 (1953), p. 179.

37. *Cincinnati Times-Star*, June 9, 12, 1916.

38. *Chicago Herald*, June 8, 1916; *Cincinnati Enquirer*, June 8, 1916; *New York Times*, June 8, 1916; *New York Tribune*, June 8, 1916.

39. Harding in New England to Mrs. Harding, October, 1916; Harding in Ogden, Utah to Mrs. Harding, October 5, 1916; both in Harding Papers, unclassified.

CHAPTER THIRTEEN

1. Harding to Scobey, March 13, 1917, Scobey Papers, Box 1, No. 113; Harding to Scobey, August 3, 1917, Scobey Papers, Box 1, No. 127; Harding to Scobey, January 3, 1918, Scobey Papers, Box 1, No. 147; Harding to Scobey, February 19, 1916, Scobey Papers, Box 1, No. 72. Harding to H. E. Taylor, June 20, 1918 (carbon), Harding Papers, Temporary Box 2, Folder T, No. 320279; Harding to Hibbard, January 16, 1918 (carbon), Harding Papers, Temporary Box 7, No. 318800; Harding to Scobey, April 2, 1918 (carbon), Harding Papers, Temporary Box 4, Folder Scobey 1, No. 320956; Harding to Scobey, October 22, 1918 (carbon), Harding Papers, Temporary Box 7, Folder Scobey 2, No. 321015; Harding to E. R. Smith, October 22, 1918 (carbon), Harding Papers, Temporary Box 2, Folder S., No. 320210; Harding to Jennings, June 6, 1918, Jennings Papers.

2. *Ohio State Journal*, October 26, 1918.

3. Schortemeier (ed.), *Rededicating America*, pp. 170–81.

4. *Ohio State Journal*, December 13, 1916; *Cleveland Leader*, December 13, 1916.

5. *Wheeling Register*, April 2, 1917; *Ohio State Journal*, April 3, 1917.

6. *Congressional Record*, 65 Congress, 1 Session, April 4, 1917, pp. 253–54.

7. *Ohio State Journal*, March 5, March 27, 1917, sports section.

8. Harding to Jennings, March 12, 1917; Jennings to Harding, March 13, 1917, Jennings Papers; *Ohio State Journal*, April 1, 1917; *Cincinnati Enquirer*, April 1, 1917.

9. *Congressional Record*, 65 Congress, 1 Session, April 4, 1917, pp. 253–54.

10. *Ohio State Journal*, May 31, 1917; *Cleveland Leader*, May 31, 1917; *New York Times*, May 31, 1917.

11. *Congressional Record*, 65 Congress, 1 Session, April 4, 1917, pp. 253–54.

12. *Congressional Record*, 65 Congress, 1 Session, August 31, 1917, p. 6470.

13. Harding to Jennings, June 14, 1917, Jennings Papers.

14. *Ibid.*

15. *Ibid.*

16. Harding to Jennings, December 31, 1917, Jennings Papers.

17. Harding to Jennings, March 8, 1918, Jennings Papers.

18. All of the above may be found in Scobey Papers. Harding to Scobey, May 7, 1917, Box 1, No. 122; Harding to Scobey, September 13, 1917, Box 1, No. 132; Harding to Scobey, October 19, 1917, Box 1, No. 141; Harding to Scobey, March 9, 1918, Box 1, No. 150.

19. Lodge to Roosevelt, April 23, 1917 (photostat of original in Library of Congress), Harris Collection.

20. *Congressional Record*, 65 Congress, 1 Session, April 28, 1917, pp. 1491–92.

21. *U.S. Statutes at Large*, Vol. 40, Part 1, pp. 76–83.

22. *Cleveland Leader*, April 30, May 13, 18, 1917; *Ohio State Journal*, May 1, 1917.

23. Copies of the Harding, Roosevelt, Lodge correspondence on this subject are in the Harris Collection in the Ohio Historical Society. It consists of: Roosevelt to Harding (typed copy of a telegram), Roosevelt to Harding (carbon copy), April 30, 1917; Harding to Roosevelt (carbon copy), May 7, 1917.

24. *Congressional Record*, 65 Congress, 2 Session, January 21, 1918, p. 1083.

25. *Ohio State Journal*, January 23, 1918.

26. *Congressional Record*, 65 Congress, 2 Session, April 29, 1918, pp. 5747–50.

27. *Congressional Record*, 65 Congress, 1 Session, June 4, 1917, pp. 3256–57.

28. *Congressional Record*, 65 Congress, 1 Session, June 8, 1917, pp. 3324–28; *Ohio State Journal*, June 9, 1917; Jennings to Harding, June 18, 1917, Jennings Papers.

29. Harding to Coker, September 18, 1918 (carbon), Harding Papers, Temporary Box 5, No. 317959; Harding to Hibbard, September 29, 1918, Temporary Box 7, No. 318808.

30. Harding to Scobey, April 14, 1919 (carbon), Harding Papers, Temporary Box 4, Folder Scobey 1, No. 321064.

31. *Ohio State Journal*, August 19, 1917.

32. *Congressional Record*, 65 Congress, 1 Session, July 19, 20, 1917, pp. 5269, 5325–26.

33. Harding to Jennings, July 6, 1917, Jennings Papers.

34. *New York Times*, December 28, 1917; F. L. Paxson, *American Democracy and the World War* (Boston: Houghton-Mifflin, 1939), II, 22–24, 212–14.

35. Paxson, *American Democracy and the World War*, II, 222–26.

36. *Congressional Record*, 65 Congress, 2 Session, April 29, 1918, pp. 5747–50.

37. Paxson, *American Democracy and the World War*, II, 66–76; Edward N. Hurley, *The Bridge to France* (Philadelphia: Lippincott, 1927), pp. vi, viii, 16–67.

38. *Washington Evening Star*, December 20, 21, 24, 27, 1917; *New York Times*, December 19, 1917.

39. *Congressional Record*, 65 Congress, 2 Session, March 6, 1918, p. 3086.

40. *New York Times*, February 26, April 14 (section 1), 1918; see also *Hearings before Senate Committee on Commerce*, 65 Congress, 2 Session, Resolution 170.

41. Hurley, *Bridge to France*, pp. viii, 9.

42. *Congressional Record*, 65 Congress, 2 Session, April 29, 1918, p. 5747; June 10, 1918, p. 7567.

43. Schortemeier (ed.), *Rededicating America*, pp. 175–76.

44. *New York Times*, April 14, 1918; *Ohio State Journal*, April 14, 1918, Sports section; Paxson, *American Democracy and the World War*, II, 52, 384, 429–30.

45. *Congressional Record*, 65 Congress, 2 Session, January 11, 1918, pp. 821–25; January 15, 1918.

46. *Congressional Record*, 65 Congress, 1 Session, August 31, 1917, pp. 6469–73; September 10, 1917, p. 6886; Paxson, *American Democracy and the World War*, II, 143–58; Schwab to Harding, December 21, 1917, Harding Papers, Temporary Box 2, Folder S, No. 320130; Harding to Schwab, December 26, 1917, Temporary Box 2, Folder S, No. 320129.

47. *Ohio State Journal*, August 28, 1918.

48. Harding to Scobey, Scobey Papers, Box 1: September 13, 1917 (No. 132); January 3, 1918 (No. 147).

CHAPTER FOURTEEN

1. *Ohio Statistics*, 1915, pp. 221–22; *ibid.*, 1916, pp. 243–46; *Congressional Record*, 64 Congress, 2 Session, December 14, 1916, pp. 334–35; January 9, 1917, p. 1066; *Cleveland Leader*, December 15, 19, 1916; *Columbus Evening Dispatch*, December 28, 29, 1916; *Columbus Citizen*, December 28, 1916; *Ohio State Journal*, January 14, 1917. The Harding-Wheeler conference on the seven-year clause was described by Wheeler in the *New York Times*, March 31, 1926.

2. Harding to Scobey, August 3, 1917, Scobey Papers, Box 1, No. 127.

3. Harding to H. B. McConnell, January 24, 1917, from the collection of Milton Ronsheim, publisher, *Cadiz Republican*, Cadiz, Ohio.

4. *Congressional Record*, 65 Congress, 1 Session, August 1, 1917, p. 5648; *Cincinnati Times-Star*, August 1, 1917; Harding to Wehrley, May 21, 1919, Harding Papers (carbon, unclassified).

5. *Congressional Record*, 65 Congress, 1 Session, December 3, 1917, pp. 478, 490, 529.

6. Rapp to Harding, December 18, 1917, Harding Papers, Temporary Box 2, No. 319957; Harding to Rapp, December 26, 1917, *loc. cit.*, No. 319956.

7. *Ohio Election Statistics for 1918* (1919), pp. 253–54.

8. Scobey to Harding, March 28, 1918, Scobey Papers, Box 1, No. 153.

9. Harding to Scobey, Scobey Papers: March 12, 1917, Box 1, No. 112; April 5, 1917, Box 1, No. 115; April 16, 1917, Box 1, No. 117.

10. Harding to Scobey, April 2, 1918, Scobey Papers, Box 1, No. 157.

11. *Ohio State Journal*, April 2, May 3, 1917.

12. *Ibid.*, May 4, 1917.

13. *Ibid.*, January 31, April 1, 1917.

14. *Ibid.*, March 30, May 4, June 26, 1917; *Cleveland Leader*, May 4, 6, 10, June 10, July 3, 1917. A complete file of the *Ohio Republican* has not been found.

15. *Ohio State Journal*, May 28, 1918. *National Republican*, August 10, 1918 said that advisory committees had been organized in Ohio in all counties except five or six.

16. *Cincinnati Enquirer*, August 11, September 8, 1918.

17. Justin Steuart, *Wayne Wheeler, Dry Boss: An Uncensored Biography of Wayne B. Wheeler* (New York: Revel, 1928), pp. 99–115.

18. Daugherty to Harding, January 17, 1918, Harding Papers, Box 686, Folder 4945–3, No. 314125.

19. *Ohio Election Statistics for 1918* (1919), p. 253–54. Harding to Timken, February 8, 1918 (carbon), Harding Papers, Temporary Box 2, Folder T, No. 320310.

20. Daugherty to Harding, January 17, 1918, Harding Papers, Box 686, Folder 4945–3, No. 314125.

21. *Ibid.*, June 24, 1918, Harding Papers, Box 685, Folder 4945–2. No. 314085.

22. All of the above may be found in the Harding Papers. Harding to Daugherty, February 16, 1918 (carbon), Box 686, Folder 4945–3, No. 314113; Daugherty to Harding, April 11, 1918, Box 686, Folder 4945–3, No. 314121; Harding to Daugherty, April 16, 1918 (carbon), Box 686, Folder 4945–3, No. 314120; Daugherty to Harding, April 17, 1918, Box 686, Folder 4945–3, No. 314101; Harding to Daugherty, April 19, 1918, Box 686, Folder 4945–3, No. 314100; Daugherty to Harding, May 23, 1918, Box 685, Folder 4945–2, No. 314098; Harding to Daugherty, May 25, 1918 (carbon), Box 685, No. 314097.

23. Daugherty to Harding, May 31, 1918, Box 685, Folder 4945–2, No. 314095; Harding to Daugherty, June 3, 1918 (carbon), Box 685, Folder 4945–2, No. 314094. Both in Harding Papers.

24. Daugherty to Harding, June 3, 1918, Harding Papers, Box 685, Folder 4945–2, No. 314088.

25. Harding to Scobey, September 20, 1918 (carbon), Harding Papers, Temporary Box 4, Folder Scobey 1, No. 321006; Christian to Harding, September 27, Temporary Box 5, No. 318128; Schortemeier, *op. cit.*, pp. 170–81.

26. *Cincinnati Enquirer*, August 27, 28, 29, September 1, 1918; Daugherty to Harding, June 8, 1918, Harding Papers, Box 685, Folder 4945–2, No. 314092.

27. *Ohio Election Statistics for 1918* (1919), pp. 241–552.

28. Daugherty to Harding, November 18, 1918, Harding Papers, Box 686, Folder 4945–4, No. 314296; Harding to Daugherty, November 23, 1918 (carbon), Box 686, Folder 4945–4, No. 314294.

29. All of the above may be found in the Harding Papers. Daugherty to Harding, November 26, 1918, Box 686, Folder 4945–4, No. 413288; Harding to Daugherty, November 27, 1918 (carbon), Box 686, Folder 4945–4, No. 314286; Harding to Daugherty, November 29, 1918 (carbon), Box 686, Folder 4945–4, No. 314290; Daugherty to Harding, November 29, 1918, Box 686, Folder 4945–4, No. 314281; Daugherty to Harding, December 7, 1918, Box 686, Folder 4945–4, No. 314284; Daugherty to Harding, December 10, 1918, Box 686, Folder 4945–4, No. 314280; Harding to Daugherty; December 12, 1918 (carbon), Box 686, Folder 4945–4, No. 314277; Daugherty to Harding, December 17, 1918, Box 686, Folder 4945–4, No. 314271.

30. Harding to Hard [December, 1918], Hard Papers, Ohio Historical Society. This is a five-page letter with page 1 missing. The contents show that it was written in December, 1918.

31. Harding to Daugherty, December 20, 1918 (carbon), Box 686, Folder 4945–4, No. 314266; Daugherty to Harding, December 30, 1918, Box 686, Folder 4945–4, No. 314257. Both in Harding Papers.

32. Harding to Scobey, December 4, 1918 (carbon), Harding Papers, Temporary Box 4, Folder Scobey 1, No. 321027.

33. Mrs. Lee to Harding, October 7, 1918, Lee Papers, Ohio Historical Society.

34. Daugherty to Harris, May 4, 1937, Harris Collection, Ohio Historical Society.

35. Harding to Scobey, November 18, 1918 (carbon), Temporary Box 4, Folder Scobey 1, No. 321022; Harding to Scobey, December 4, 1918, Temporary Box 4, Folder Scobey 1, No. 321027. Both in Harding Papers.

36. Harding to Herrick, January 3, 1920 (carbon), Harding Papers, January 3, 1919, Box 686, Folder 4954–1, No. 314931.

37. Harding to MacDonald, January 13, 1920 (carbon), Harding Papers, Box 689, Folder 4961–1, No. 315501.

38. *New York Tribune,* January 7, 1919.

39. *New York Times,* January 7, 1919.

40. *Ibid.; World* (New York), January 7, 1919. See also *Cincinnati Enquirer,* January 7, 1919; *Cleveland Plain Dealer,* January 8, 1919; *Ohio State Journal,* January 9, 1919.

41. Harding to Hard, January 6, 1919, Hard Papers.

42. Harding to Scobey, January 14, 1919 (carbon), Harding Papers, Temporary Box 4, Folder Scobey 1, No. 321042.

43. The text of the January 15, 1919 resolution reviving the Ohio Republican Advisory Committee is in a letter of Harding to Charles D. Simeral, January 21, 1919 (carbon), Harding Papers (unclassified).

44. *Ohio State Journal,* January 16, 1919; *Cincinnati Enquirer,* January 16, 1919; *Cincinnati Times-Star,* January 15, 1919; *Cleveland Plain Dealer,* January 16, 1919; *Toledo Blade,* January 16, 1919.

45. The members of the new Republican State Advisory Committee were listed in the *Columbus Evening Dispatch,* January 29, 1919, and the *Ohio State Journal,* January 30, 1919.

46. Harding to Hard, November 13, 1919, Hard Papers.

47. Harding to Clark, December 9, 1918 (carbon); Clark to Harding, December 16, 1918. Both in Harding Papers, unclassified.

48. Harding to Clark, December 20, 1918, Harding Papers (carbon, unclassified).

49. Harding to Clark, February 1, 1919 (carbon); Harding to Clark, February 2, 1919; Clark to Harding, February 5, 1919; Harding to Clark, February 7, 1919 (carbon). All in Harding Papers, unclassified.

50. Harding to George Clark, February 7, 1919, Harding Papers (Wolfe accession, September, 1967).

51. Harding to George Clark, July 18, 1919, Harding Papers (Wolfe accession, September, 1967).

52. Smith to Harding, November 28, 1918; Harding to Smith, November 30, 1918 (carbon); Smith to Simeon D. Fess, December 19, 1918 (carbon); Harding to Smith, December 31, 1919 (carbon); Harding to W. A. Stover, February 6, 1919 (carbon). All in Harding Papers, unclassified.

53. Harding to Clark, February 7, 1919, Harding Papers (Wolfe accession, September, 1967).

54. Harding to Daugherty, June 14, 1919 (carbon), Box 686, Folder 4945–3, No. 314179; Daugherty to Harding, July 25, 1919, Box 686, Folder 4645–3, No. 314167; Harding to Daugherty, July 30, 1919 (carbon), Box 686, Folder 4945–3. No. 314165. All in Harding Papers.

55. Rapp to Christian, January 25, 1919, Harding Papers, Temporary Box 2, Folder R, No. 319965; Christian to Harding, November 16, 1919, Harding Papers, Temporary Box 2, Folder S, No. 318939; Harding to Jennings, October 11, 1919, Jennings Papers.

56. Circular letter by Reily, January 20, 1919, Reily Papers, Manuscript Divison, New York Public Library.

57. Harding to Scobey, July 31, 1919, Harding Papers (carbon), Temporary Box 4, Folder Scobey 2, No. 321089; Harding to Reynolds, August 5, 1919, Harding Papers (carbon, unclassified).

58. Harding to Scobey, January 14, 1919 (carbon), Harding Papers, Temporary Box 4, Folder Scobey 1, No. 321042; Scobey to Harding, February 1, 1919, Harding Papers, Temporary Box 4, Folder Scobey 1, No. 321045; Harding to Scobey, February 7, 1919, Harding Papers, Temporary Box 4, Folder Scobey 1, No. 321047; Scobey to Dr. Donald C. Balfour, Rochester, Minn., January 19, 1920, Scobey Papers, Box 2, No. 359.

59. Harding to Scobey, March 10, 1919, Scobey Papers, Box 2, No. 245–246; Harding to Mrs. Scobey, April 18, 1919, Scobey Papers, Box 2, No. 260–261.

60. Harding to Scobey, January 14, 1919, Scobey Papers, Box 2.

61. The texts of these Harding speeches are to be found in the following sources: McKinley oration in Cleveland, January 28, 1919 in *Cleveland News*, January 29, 1919; Roosevelt Memorial oration to the Ohio Legislature, January 29, 1919 in the *Ohio State Journal*, January 30, 1919 and in Schortemeier (ed.), *Rededicating America*, pp. 115–22; McKinley oration in Dayton, January 29, 1919 in *Dayton Herald*, January 30, 1919; Lincoln oration in Toledo, February 12, 1919 in *Ohio State Journal*, February 13, 1919, and *Toledo Times*, February 13, 1919; Lincoln oration in Lancaster, February 13, 1919 in *Lancaster Daily Gazette*, February 14, 1919.

62. *Youngstown Vindicator*, April 23, 1919.

63. Harding to Snow, March 31, 1919, Harding Papers (carbon, unclassified).

64. Reily, "Years of Confusion," pp. 124–25.

65. Harding to Scobey, February 7, 1919 (carbon), Harding Papers, Temporary Box 4, Folder Scobey 1, No. 321047. There are many more letters to others in the Harding Papers, expressing similar sentiments in the matter of opposing the presidential nomination and preferring the Senate. See Harding to F. H. Sterrett, February 24, 1919 and Harding to A. W. Thomas, September 3, 1919, Harding Papers (unclassified).

66. Wood to Christian, January 29, 1919, Harding Papers (unclassified); Christian to Wood, January 31, 1919, Harding Papers (carbon, unclassified).

67. *Ohio State Journal*, February 13, 1919.

68. Charles E. Hard, "The Man Who Did Not Want to Become President," *NOQ*, (Summer, 1959), p. 121. See also Hard, "Reminiscences," (manuscript in Ohio Historical Society), pp. 71–72.

69. Hard, "The Man Who Did Not Want to Become President," p. 122.

70. Reily, "Years of Confusion," p. 190.

71. Harding to Clark, September 4, 1919, Harding Papers (carbon, unclassified).

72. Clark to Harding, September 6, 1919, Harding Papers (unclassified).

73. *Cincinnati Enquirer*, October 18, 1919; *Ohio State Journal*, October 18, 1919; *Columbus Evening Dispatch*, October 18, 1919; *New York Times*, October 18, 1919.

74. Willis to Harding, November 17, 1919, Harding Papers (unclassified).

75. Daugherty to Harding, October 24, 1919, Harding Papers, Box 685, Folder 4945–2, No. 314058.

76. Harding to Scobey, October 25, 1919 (carbon), Harding Papers, Temporary Box 4, Folder Scobey 2, No. 321116.

77. Harding to Hard, October 25, 1919, Hard Papers.

78. Harding to Clark, September 12, 1919, Harding Papers (carbon, unclassified).

79. Harding to Jennings, October 11, 1919, Jennings Papers.

80. Harding to Weeks, August 17, 1919 (carbon), Harding Papers, Temporary Box 3, Folder W, Part 1, No. 320607.

81. Harding to Christian, November 3, 1919 (carbon), Harding Papers, Temporary Box 5, Folder C (George B. Christian), No. 318110.

82. Harding to Jennings, November 4, 1919, Jennings Papers.

83. Daugherty to Harding, October 18, 1919 (telegram), Box 686, Folder 4945–3, No. 314629; Daugherty to Harding, October 24, 1919, Box 685, Folder 4945–2, No. 314058; Harding to Daugherty, October 28, 1919 (carbon), Box 685, Folder 4945–2, No. 314657. All in Harding Papers.

84. Harding to George H. Clark, October 30, 1919, Hard Papers. Carbon copy in Harding Papers (unclassified).

85. Harding to Scobey, November 3, 1919 (carbon), Harding Papers, Temporary Box 4, Folder Scobey 2, No. 321122.

86. Daugherty to Christian, November 2, 1919, Harding Papers, Box 685, Folder 4945–2, No. 314050.

87. Daugherty to Scobey, November 28, 1919, Scobey Papers, Box 2, No. 327.

88. Daugherty to Scobey, December 4, 1919, Scobey Papers, Box 2, No. 328.

89. Daugherty to Harding, October 31, 1919, Harding Papers, Box 685, Folder 4945–2, No. 314062.

90. Simeral to Harding, November 1, 1919, Harding Papers (unclassified).

91. *Pittsburgh Gazette Times*, November 1, 1919; Harding to Clark, November 7, 1919, Harding Papers (carbon, unclassified); Harding to Simeral, November 3, 1919 (carbon, unclassified).

92. Press release (carbon), Harding Papers, Box 685, Folder 4945–2, No. 314064; Daugherty to Christian, November 4, Harding Papers, Box 685, Folder 4945–2, No. 314046.

93. Harding to Daugherty, November 3, 1919 (carbon), Harding Papers, Box 685, Folder 4945–2, No. 314061.

CHAPTER FIFTEEN

1. Schortemeier (ed.), *Rededicating America*, pp. 170–81.

2. Harding to Daugherty, September 18, 1919 (carbon), Harding Papers, Box 686, Folder 4945–3, No. 314141.

3. Webster to Harding, March 18, 1919, Harding Papers (unclassified); Harding to Webster, March 28, 1919, Harding Papers (unclassified).

4. *Congressional Record*, 65 Congress, 3 Session, January 21, 1919, p. 1808.

5. Harding to Sheffield, January 24, 1919, Papers of James R. Sheffield, Yale University.

6. Shaw to Harding, January 24, 1918, Harding Papers, Temporary Box 2, Folder S, No. 320163; Harding to Shaw, February 8, 1918 (carbon), Folder S. No. 320161.

7. *Congressional Record*, 65 Congress, 3 Session, January 21, 1919, p. 1808.

8. *Congressional Record*, 65 Congress, 3 Session, January 21, 1919, p. 1811.

9. *Congressional Record*, 65 Congress, 3 Session, January 21, 1919, p. 1808.

10. *Toledo Blade*, February 13, 1919; *Toledo Times*, February 13, 1919; *Toledo News-Bee*, February 13, 1919; *Lancaster Daily Gazette*, February 14, 1919.

11. *Lancaster Daily Gazette*, February 14, 1919.

12. Harding to Timken, February 6, 1918 (carbon), Harding Papers, Temporary Box 2, Folder T, No. 320310.

13. Harding to Scobey, December 4, 1918 (carbon), Harding Papers, Temporary Box 4, Folder Scobey 1, No. 321027.

14. *Columbus Evening Dispatch*, January 15, 1919; *Columbus Citizen*, January 15, 1919; *Cincinnati Enquirer*, January 16, 1919.

15. Schortemeier (ed.), *Rededicating America*, pp. 115–22; *Ohio State Journal*, January 30, February 2, 1919.

16. *Dayton Journal*, January 30, 1919.

17. *Cincinnati Enquirer*, January 24, 1919.

18. *Toledo Blade*, February 13, 1919; *Toledo Times*, February 13, 1919; *Toledo News-Bee*, February 13, 1919; *Lancaster Daily Gazette*, February 14, 1919.

19. *Lancaster Daily Gazette*, February 14, 1919.

20. *Ohio State Journal*, January 29, 1919.

21. Harding to Scobey, March 5, 1919 (carbon), Harding Papers, Temporary Box 4, Folder Scobey 1, No. 321056.

22. Harding to Cole, December 18, 1918 (carbon), Harding Papers, Temporary Box 5, Folder C, No. 317951.

23. Harding to Mrs. Harding, March 23 and 24, 1919 (holograph, unclassified).

24. Harding to George C. Dyer, March 3, 1919 (carbon), Harding Papers, Temporary Box 4, Folder D, No. 318200.

25. Harding to Scobey, May 13, 1919, Scobey Papers, Box 2, No. 203.

26. Denna F. Fleming, *The United States and the League of Nations, 1918–1920* (New York and London: Putnams, 1932), pp. 65–69, 153–57.

27. *New York Times*, May 19, 1919.

28. *Cincinnati Enquirer*, April 25, 1919.

29. *Columbus Citizen*, April 10, 1919.

30. *New York Times*, May 18, 1919, section 4.

31. Harding to Tolley, April 5, 1919, Harding Papers (carbon, unclassified).

32. Harding to Daugherty, April 4, 1919 (carbon), Harding Papers, Box 686, Folder 4945–4, No. 314209.

33. Harding to Scobey, June 4, 1919 (carbon), Temporary Box 4, Folder Scobey 1, No. 321074; Daugherty to Harding, July 3, 1919, Box 686, Folder 4945–3, No. 314177. Both in Harding Papers.

34. Harding to Daugherty, July 25, 1919 (carbon), Harding Papers, Box 686, Folder 4945–3, No. 314169.

35. Harding to Whitehair, April 24, 1919, Harding Papers (carbon, unclassified).

36. Harding to Willis, May 17, 1919, Harding Papers (carbon, unclassified).

37. Harding to Spegal, May 21, 1919, Harding Papers (carbon, unclassified).

38. Harding to Reily, June 24, 1919, Harding Papers (carbon, unclassified).

39. Philip C. Jessup, *Elihu Root* (New York: Dodd Mead, 1937), Vol. II, pp. 373–75.

40. *Ibid.*, pp. 376–99.

41. Hard to Harding, June 24, 1919 (carbon), Hard Papers; Harding to Hard, June 28, 1919. There are no pertinent copies of the *Ohio Republican* available.

42. Harding to Daugherty, July 25, 1919 (carbon), Harding Papers, Box 686, Folder 4945–3, No. 314169.

43. Harding to Pinkham, July 2, 1919 (carbon), Harding Papers, Temporary Box 6, Folder P, No. 319885.

44. Harding to Willis, July 25, 1919 (carbon), Harding Papers, Temporary Box 3, Folder W, Part 2, No. 326684.

45. Hard to Harding, July 1, 1919 (carbon), Hard Papers.

46. *Ibid.*

47. Harding to Hard, July 8, 1919, Hard Papers.

48. Held to Hard, July 22, 1919, Hard Papers; Harding to Hard, July 30, 1919.

49. Hard to Harding, September 5, 1919 (carbon), Hard Papers.

50. Harding to Hard, September 13, 1919, Hard Papers.

51. Harding to Hard, September 23, 1919, Hard Papers.

52. Harding to Scobey, September 2, 1919 (carbon), Harding Papers, Temporary Box 4, Folder Scobey 2, No. 321099.

53. Fleming, *United States and the League of Nations*, pp. 348–57.

54. Clark to Harding, September 3, 1919, Harding Papers (unclassified).

55. Jennings to Harding, September 5, 1919 (carbon), Jennings Papers; Harding to Jennings, September 12, 1919; Harding to Jennings, September 22, 1919 (carbon); Harding to Daugherty, September 22, 1919 (carbon), Harding Papers, Box 686, Folder 4645–3, No. 314143.

56. Reily to Harding, September 8, 1919, (unclassified); Reily to Harding, September 15, 1919 (unclassified); Harding to Reily, September 20, 1919 (carbon, unclassified). All in Harding Papers.

57. Harding to Scobey, September 27, 1919 (carbon), Harding Papers, Temporary Box 4, Folder Scobey 2, No. 321105; Harding to Scobey, October 8, 1919 (carbon), Folder Scobey 2, No. 321111. Both in Harding Papers.

58. Harding to Hard, September 6, 1919, Hard Papers; Harding to Jennings, September 8, 1919, Jennings Papers.

59. Schortemeier (ed.), *Rededicating America*, pp. 94–95; *Congressional Record*, 66, Congress, 1 Session, September 11, 1919, p. 5224.

60. *Hearings before the Committee on Foreign Relations of the United States on the Treaty of Peace with Germany, Signed at Versailles on June 28, 1919* (66 Congress, 1 Session, Senate Document No. 106, Washington: G.P.O., 1919), Serial No. 7605.

61. Fleming, *United States and the League of Nations*, pp. 419–33.

62. John A. Garraty, *Henry Cabot Lodge* (New York: Knopf, 1943), pp. 376–78; John M. Blum, *Wilson and the Politics of Morality* (Boston: Little, Brown, 1956), pp. 181–82; Fleming, *United States and the League of Nations*, p. 396.

63. *Hearings on the Treaty of Peace with Germany*, pp. 515–16, 535–36. See also *Washington Evening Post*, August 19, 20, 1919.

64. Daugherty to Harding, August 20, 1919, Harding Papers, Box 685, Folder 4945–2, No. 314074.

65. Harding to Jennings, September 18, 1919, Jennings Papers.

66. Schortemeier (ed.), *Rededicating America*, pp. 62–102; *Congressional Record*, 66 Congress, 1 Session, September 11, 1919, pp. 5219–5225.

67. Harding to Hard, October 3, 1919, Hard Papers.

68. Harding to Jennings, September 12, 1919, Jennings Papers; Harding to Hard, September 22, October 3, 1919, Hard Papers.

69. *Congressional Record*, 66 Congress, 1 Session, November 19, 1919, p. 8792.

70. Harding to Scobey, September 27, 1919 (carbon), Harding Papers, Temporary Box 4, Folder Scobey 2, No. 321105; Harding to Scobey, October 8, 1919 (carbon), Harding Papers, Folder Scobey 2, No. 321111; Fleming, *United States and the League of Nations*, p. 431.

71. Harding to Margraf, November 5, 1919 (carbon), Harding Papers, Temporary Box 6, Folder M, No. 319313.

72. *Cleveland Plain Dealer*, December 2, 1919.

73. Harding to Scobey, September 27, 1919 (carbon), Harding Papers, Temporary Box 4, Folder Scobey 2, No. 321105.

74. Harding to Margraf, November 5, 1919 (carbon), Harding Papers, Temporary Box 6, Folder M, No. 319313.

75. *Ibid.*

76. Harding to Brown, December 29, 1919 (carbon), Harding Papers, Box 684, No. 313492.

CHAPTER SIXTEEN

1. Harding to Idleman, March 26, 1920 (carbon), Harding Papers, Box 688, Folder 4957–1, No. 315110.

2. W. J. Smith to Harding, December 24, 1919, Harding Papers, Box 690, Folder 4976–1, No. 316414.

3. Ransbottom to Simons, April 2, 1920 (carbon), Harding Papers, Box 690, Folder 4975–1, No. 316344.

4. Blankner to Harding, May 14, 1920, Harding Papers, Box 684, No. 313372.

5. See chap. xiv.

6. See chap. xiv.

7. Carbon copies of the two letters of November 7, 1919 from Harding to Clark are in the unclassified section of the Harding Papers.

8. The five telegrams are in the Walter Brown Papers in the Ohio Historical Society: Wood to Brown, November 1, 1919; Procter to Brown, November 29, 1919; Procter to Brown, December 3, 1919; Wood to Brown, December 4, 1919; Procter to Brown, December 12, 1919.

9. Brown to Procter, December 2, 1919 (carbon), Brown Papers.

10. George W. Harris told the author that, in interviewing Brown, he was, in fact, acting at Harding's request.

11. Harding to Brown, December 15, 1919, Brown Papers.

12. Harding to Jennings, January 12, 1920, Jennings Papers.

13. Daugherty to Reily, December 3, 1919, Daugherty-Reily Papers in Ohio Historical Society; *ibid.*, December 16, 1919.

14. Speer to Harding, November 5, 1919, Harding Papers, Box 690, Folder 4976–1, No. 316442.

15. Kemerer to Christian, November 8, 1919, Harding Papers, Box 688, Folder 4958–1, No. 315223.

16. Bogardus to Harding, November 14, 1919, Harding Papers, No. 313439.

17. Willis to Harding, November 17, 1919, Harding Papers (unclassified).

18. Harding to Reily, November 22, 1919, Harding Papers (carbon, unclassified).

19. Daugherty to Foster, December 4, 1919 (carbon), Harding Papers, Box 685, Folder 4945–2, No. 314039.

20. *Cincinnati Enquirer*, December 17, 1919; Harding to Wolfe, December 15, 1919, Harding Papers (carbon, unclassified).

21. *Cincinnati Enquirer*, December 3, 1919.

22. Harding to Scobey, December 16, 1919 (carbon), Harding Papers, Temporary Box 4, Folder Scobey 2, No. 321134.

23. Daugherty to Harding, May 20, 1920, Harding Papers, Box 685, Folder 4945–1, No. 313912.

24. Harding to Sheppy, December 16, 1919 (carbon), Harding Papers, Box 690, Folder 4975–1, No. 316280.

25. Daugherty to Scobey, January 19, 1920, Scobey Papers, Box 2, No. 358; Daugherty to Reily, December 24, 1919, Daugherty-Reily Papers, Ohio Historical Society.

26. Daugherty to Harding, December 19, 1919, Harding Papers, Box 685, Folder 4945–2, No. 314014.

27. Harding to Scobey, December 30, 1919 (carbon), Temporary Box 4, Folder Scobey 2, No. 321138; Harding to Scobey, January 20, 1920 (carbon), Temporary Box 4, Folder Scobey 2, No. 321146. Both in Harding Papers.

28. Daugherty to Reily, December 24, 1919, February 6, April 23, 1920, Daugherty-Reily Papers; Daugherty to Scobey, December 27, 1919, Scobey Papers, Box 2, No. 344.

29. Harding to Scobey, January 31, 1920 (carbon), Harding Papers, Temporary Box 4, Folder Scobey 2, No. 321161.

30. *Ohio State Journal*, December 10, 1919; *Toledo Times*, December 10, 1919; O. S. Rapp, of Marion, to Harding, December 30, 1919, Harding Papers, Box 690, Folder 4970–1, No. 315981; Daugherty to Foster, December 4, 1919 (carbon), Harding Papers, Box 685, Folder 494–2, No. 314039.

31. Daugherty to Christian, December 26, 1919, Harding Papers, Box 685, Folder 4945–1, No. 313970.

32. Daugherty to Scobey, January 22, 1920, Scobey Papers, Box 2, No. 370.

33. "Senator Warren G. Harding," pamphlet published by Harding for President Club (undated), Pamphlet Collection, Ohio Historical Society.

34. Daugherty to Hoke Donithen, December 30, 1919, January 2, 1920; Christian to Donithen, January 9, 1920, Hoke Donithen Papers, Ohio Historical Society.

35. Daugherty to Donithen, December 19, 1919, Donithen Papers.

36. Daugherty to Harding, December 19, 1919 (two letters), Harding Papers, Box 685, Folder 4945–2, No. 314015, 314017; Daugherty to Reily, January 26, April 23, 1920, Daugherty-Reily Papers.

37. Daugherty to Fairbanks, December 21, 1919, Fairbanks Papers, Ohio Historical Society; Fairbanks to Daugherty, January 1, 1920. See *Cincinnati Enquirer*, December 10, 1919.

38. Daugherty to Harding, December 26, 1919, Harding Papers, Box 685, Folder 4945–1, No. 313991.

39. Daugherty to Harding, December 23, 1919, Harding Papers, Box 685, Folder 4945–2, No. 314012; Harding to Daugherty, December 24, 1919, Harding Papers, Box 685, Folder 4945–1, No. 313964; Daugherty to Reily, December 27, 1919, Daugherty-Reily Letters; Harry M. Daugherty and Thomas Dixon, *Inside Story of the Harding Tragedy*, (New York: Churchill Co., 1932), p. 16.

40. Robert K. Murray, *Red Scare, A Study of National Hysteria, 1919–1920* (Minneapolis: University of Minnesota Press, 1955), pp. 70, 98, 104, 182–83, 217.

41. Schortemeier, *op. cit.*, pp. 103–114.

42. Harding to George Clark, February 7, 1919, Harding Papers (Wolfe accession, September, 1967).

43. Harding to Ransbottom, February 14, 1920 (carbon), Harding Papers, Box 690, Folder 4970–1, No. 315976; Christian to J. J. Garberson, March 31, 1920 (carbon), Harding Papers, Box 687, Folder 4951–1, No. 314614.

44. Herman Hagedorn, *Leonard Wood: A Biography* (New York and London: Harper, 1931), II, pp. 331–32; Wesley M. Bagby, "The 'Smoke filled room' and

the Nomination of Warren G. Harding," *Mississippi Valley Historical Review*, XLI, No. 4, (March, 1955) 657–58; Ray Baker Harris, *Warren G. Harding, An Account of His Nomination for the Presidency by the Republican Convention of 1920* (Booklet, privately published, 1957) pp. 9–10.

45. Harding to Kemerer, November 11, 1919 (carbon), Harding Papers, Box 688, Folder 4958–1, No. 315219.

46. Harding to Fisher, December 23, 1919 (carbon), Harding Papers, Box 687, Folder 4949–1, No. 314500.

47. William T. Hutchinson, *Lowden of Illinois, The Life Of Frank O. Lowden* (Chicago: University of Chicago Press, 1957), II, pp. 442–47.

48. Sarter to Harding, December 10, 1919, Harding Papers (unclassified).

49. All of the above may be found in the Harding Papers. Everett Harding to W. G. Harding, December 18, 1919, Box 687, Folder 4953–1, No. 314775; Christian to Harding, December 18, 1919 (telegram), Box 687, Folder 4953–1, No. 314770; W. G. Harding to Everett Harding, January 26, 1920 (carbon), Box 687, Folder 4953–1, No. 314772; Torbet to Harding, February 16, 1920, Box 691, Folder 4982–1, No. 316758; Harding to Torbet, February 27, 1920 (carbon), Box 691, Folder 4982–1, No. 316754; Brascher to Harding, January 8, 1920, Box 684, Folder 4938–1, No. 313484; Harding to Brascher, January 12, 1920 (carbon), Box 684, Folder 4938–1, No. 313483; Shotwell to Harding, January 12, 1920, Box 690, Folder 4975–1, No. 316290; Harding to Shotwell, January 15, 1920 (carbon), Box 690, Folder 4975–1, No. 316292; Shotwell to Harding, January 28, 1920, Box 690, Folder 4975–1, No. 316291; Harding to Shotwell (carbon), Box 690, Folder 4975–1, No. 316290; Slemp to Harding, March 13, 1929, Box 690, Folder 4975–1, No. 316347; Harding to Slemp, March 16, 1920 (carbon), Folder 4975–1, No. 316349.

50. Harding to Rossiter, January 20, 1920 (carbon), Box 690, Folder 4972–1, No. 316124; Rossiter to Harding, February 13, 1920, Box 690, Folder 4972–1, No. 316158; Harding to Rossiter, February 18, 1920 (carbon), Box 690, Folder 4972–1, No. 316158. All in Harding Papers.

51. Rossiter to Harding, February 29, 1920. Harding Papers, Box 696, Folder 4972–1, No. 316163.

52. Daugherty to Reily, February 6, 1920, Daugherty-Reily Papers.

53. Harding to Scobey, January 20, 1920 (carbon), Harding Papers, Temporary Box 4, Folder Scobey 2, No. 321146.

54. Harding to Loomis, January 13, 1920 (carbon), Box 687, Folder 4950–1, No. 314534; Harding to Scobey, January 20, 1920 (carbon), Temporary Box 4, Folder Scobey 2, No. 321146; Rossiter to Harding, February 29, 1920, Box 696, Folder 4972–1, No. 316163. All in Harding Papers.

55. Harding to Albert White, December 26, 1919 (carbon), Box 692, Folder 4986–1, No. 317188; Harding to White, April 1, 1920 (carbon), Box 692, Folder 4986–1, No. 317222; White to Harding, April 18, 1920, Box 692, Folder 4986–1, No. 317124; Harding to Forbes, April 1, 1920 (carbon), Box 687, Folder 4950–1, No. 314534. All in Harding Papers.

56. *Indianapolis Star*, May 6, 1920; Harding to V. W. Van Fleet, May 8, 1920 (carbon), Harding Papers, Box 691, Folder 4984–1, No. 316909.

57. Harding to Schweitzer, May 18, 1920 (carbon), Harding Papers, Box 690, Folder 4974–1, No. 316257; Harding to Weimer, January 23, 1920 (carbon), Box 692, Folder 4986–1, No. 317095.

58. There are 13 letters in the Harding Papers among Forbes, Harding, and Daugherty from December 7, 1919 to April 1, 1920, including two undated ones. They are in Box 687, Folder 4950–1. Their dates and numbers are: December 7, 1919, No. 314521; December 16, 1919, No. 314516; December 29, 1919 (to Harding), No. 314512; December 29, 1919 (to Daugherty), No. 314514; February 17, 1920, No. 314525; February 25, 1920, No. 314531; February 28, 1920 (2 letters), Nos. 314524, 314533; March 16, 1920, No. 314525; March 20, 1920, No. 314536; April 1, 1920, No. 314534; no date (2 letters), Nos. 314529, 314530. See also Harding to D. W. Locke of Everett, Washington, February 3, 1920, Box 688, Folder 4959–1, No. 315376.

59. The Harding-Starek correspondence is voluminous, covering the period from February 14 to May 6, 1920. It is in Harding Papers, Box 691, Folder 4978–1. The dates and numbers are: February 14, 1920, No. 31601; February 15, 1920, No. 316508; February 18, 1920, No. 316500; February 22, 1920, No. 316487; February 23, 1920, No. 316483; April 6, 1920, No. 316430; April 7, 1920, No. 316538; May 3, 1920, No. 316519; May 4, 1920, No. 316544; May 6, 1920, No. 316518.

60. All of the above may be found in the Harding Papers. Harding to Scobey, December 30, 1919 (carbon), Temporary Box 4, Folder Scobey 2, No. 321138; Harding to Russell A. Wood, December 16, 1919 (carbon), Box 692, Folder 4988–1, No. 317362; MacDonald to Harding, December 30, 1919, Box 689, Folder 4961–1, No. 315505; Harding to MacDonald (carbon), January 2, 1920, Box 689, Folder 4961–1, No. 315504; MacDonald to Harding, January 7, 1920, Box 689, Folder 4961–1, No. 315503; Harding to MacDonald, January 13, 1920 (carbon), Box 689, Folder 4961–1, No. 315501.

61. Harding to Carter, January 12, 1920 (carbon), Box 684, No. 313665; Harding to Scobey, January 20, 1920 (carbon), Temporary Box 4, Folder Scobey 2, No. 321146. Both in Harding Papers.

62. Sproul to Harding, March 5, 1920, Harding Papers (unclassified); Harding to Sproul, April 4, 1920 (carbon, unclassified).

63. Scobey to Harding, January 20, 1920, Temporary Box 4, Folder Scobey 2, No. 321160; Scobey to Harding, May 4, 1920, Temporary Box 4, Folder Scobey 2, No. 321183. Both in Harding Papers.

64. Scobey to Daugherty, January 16, 1920, Box 2, No. 356; Daugherty to Macgregor, February 1, 1920, Box 2, No. 381; Scobey to Daugherty, February 23, 1920, Box 2, No. 398. All in Scobey Papers.

65. Daugherty to Scobey, May 7, 1920, Box 2, No. 440; Daugherty to Scobey, May 8, 1920, Box 2, No. 443. Both in Scobey Papers.

66. Harding to Scobey, December 13, 1915, Box 1, No. 54; Scobey to Harding, January 6, 1916, Box 1, No. 57; Scobey to Daugherty, January 8, 1916, Box 1, No. 60; Harding to Scobey, January 26, 1916, Box 1, No. 64. All in Scobey Papers.

67. All of the above may be found in the Scobey Papers. H. F. Macgregor to Daugherty, February 21, 1920, Box 2, No. 395; Scobey to J. A. Arnold, Ft. Worth, March 13, 1920, Box 2, No. 408; Scobey to Albert B. Fall, March 19, 1920, Box 2, No. 415; Scobey to Harding, May 1, 1920, Box 2, No. 434; Scobey to Daugherty, May 12, 1920, Box 2, No. 442; Scobey to Howard Mannington, May 20, 1920, Box 2, No. 448; Scobey to Richard Lynch, Youngstown, October 11, 1920, Box 2, No. 451.

68. Harding to Rinkenburgh, March 24, 1920 (carbon), Harding Papers, Box 690, Folder 4971–1, No. 316104.

69. Walker to Harding, April 7, 1920, Harding Papers, Box 692, Folder 4985–1, No. 317000.

70. Saulsbury to Harding, January 30, 1920, Box 690, Folder 4973–1, No. 316216; Harding to Saulsbury, January 31, 1920, Box 690, Folder 4973–1, No. 316215. Both in Harding Papers.

71. Harrison to Harding, January 31, 1920, Box 687, Folder 4953–1, No. 314853; Harding to Harrison, February 3, 1920 (carbon), Box 687, Folder 4953–1, No. 314851. Both in Harding Papers.

72. All of the above may be found in the Harding Papers. Harding to Arthur P. Copeland, February 5, 1920 (carbon), Box 685, Folder 4942–1, No. 313777; Harding to Rosser, January 13, 1920 (carbon), Box 690, Folder 4972–1, No. 316145; Van Fleet to Harding, May 5, 1920, Box 691, Folder 4984–1, No. 316907; Harding to Van Fleet, May 7, 1920 (carbon), Box 691, Folder 4984–1, No. 316905.

73. Harding to O. S. Rapp, April 10, 1920 (carbon), Box 690, Folder 4970–1, No. 315961; Harding to W. J. Smith, December 24, 1919 (carbon, unclassified). Both in Harding Papers.

74. For second choice maneuvering in Michigan, see Harding to Henry W. Rose (Detroit), February 9, March 18, 1920 (carbon), Harding Papers, Box 690, Folder 4972–1, Nos. 316151, 316165; Harding to Truman H. Newberry (Grand Rapids), March 16, 1920 (carbon), Harding Papers, Temporary Box 5, Folder N, No. 319716. For second choicing in Kentucky, see H. G. Garrett (Winchester) to Harding, January 24, 1920, Harding Papers, Box 687, Folder 4951–1, No. 314623; Harding to Garrett, January 26, 1920 (carbon), Harding Papers, Box 687, Folder 4951–1, No. 314622; Harding to W. T. Short (Richmond), February 9, 1920 (carbon), Harding Papers, Box 685, Folder 4945–1, No. 313952. For second choicing in Minnesota, Harding's chief emissary was F. M. Ransbottom, and the resident agent was Henry L. Simons of Minneapolis, chairman of the Third District Committee. Simons gave meticulous reports on Minnesota developments and provided a full list of state delegates to the Chicago convention for Harding to write to. The Simons correspondence is voluminous, and is contained mostly in Harding Papers, Box 690, Folder 4975–1, Nos. 315964–316346. Some of the Simons originals are owned by Stephen Brown, 2515 Edison Avenue, Zanesville, Ohio. For second choicing in Arizona, see Daugherty to F. R. Stewart (Phoenix), December 24, 1920 (carbon), Harding Papers, Box 685, Folder 4945–1, No. 313960; Stewart to Harding, February 23, 1920, Harding Papers, Box 691, Folder 4978–1, No. 316582; Harding to Stewart, February 26, 1920 (carbon), Harding Papers, Box 691, Folder 4978–1, No. 316591; Stewart to Harding, March 2, 1920, Harding Papers, Box 691, Folder 4978–1, No. 316590; Stewart to Harding, March 8, 1920, Harding Papers, Folder 4978–1, No. 316587; Stewart to Harding, March 22, 1920, Harding Papers, Box 691, Folder 4978–1, No. 316577; Harding to Stewart, April 4, 1920 (carbon), Harding Papers, Box 691, Folder 4978–1, No. 316761; Stewart to Harding, April 5, 1920, Harding Papers, Box 691, Folder 4978–1, No. 316602.

75. Harding to Henry B. Joy (Detroit), May 11, 1920 (carbon), Box 688, Folder 4957–1, No. 315186; Harding to J. S. Aydelotte, May 18, 1920 (carbon), Box 683, Folder 4933–1, No. 313271; Harding to L. C. Breuning, May 18, 1920 (carbon), Box 684, Folder 4938–1, No. 313445. All in Harding Papers.

76. Schortemeier (ed.), *Rededicating America*, pp. 103–14, 125–35, 218–22, 145–48, 170–81, 198–205, 123–24, 223–29; *Congressional Record*, 66 Congress, 2 Session, May 15, 1920, pp. 7098–7100; Daugherty to Reily, January 26, 1920, Daugherty-Reily Papers.

77. Harding to Scobey, January 12, 1920 (carbon), Harding Papers, Temporary Box 4, Folder Scobey 2, No. 321143.

78. Harding to Col. Christian, January 19, 1920 (carbon), Temporary Box 5, Folder C-G. B. Christian, No. 318097.

79. Harding to V. W. Van Fleet, May 7, 1920 (carbon), Harding Papers, Box 691, Folder 4984–1, No. 316905.

80. Harding to Herrick, May 12, 1920 (carbon), Harding Papers, Box 688, Folder 4945–1, No. 314951.

81. Harding to Buckley, May 17, 1920 (carbon), Box 684, Folder 4939–1, No. 313613.

CHAPTER SEVENTEEN

1. Harding to Scobey, March 24, 1920 (carbon), Harding Papers, Temporary Box 4, Folder Scobey 2, No. 321172; Harding to Wilson, January 15, 1920 (carbon), Harding Papers, Box 692, Folder 4987–1, No. 317285; Harding to Johnson, April 11, 1920 (carbon), Harding Papers, Box 688, Folder 4957–1, No. 315145; *Cincinnati Enquirer*, May 2, 1920.

2. Harding to Bonner, December 18, 1919 (carbon), Harding Papers, Box 684, Folder 4937–1, No. 313424.

3. Harding to Connolly, January 26, 1920 (carbon), Harding Papers, Box 685, Folder 4942–1, No. 313766.

4. Jess W. Smith to Scobey, April 7, 1920, Scobey Papers, Box 2, No. 429.

5. Harding to Scobey, December 30, 1919 (carbon), Harding Papers, Temporary Box 4, Folder Scobey 2, No. 321138.

6. Harding to Dr. George T. Harding, March 25, 1920 (carbon), Harding Papers, Temporary Box 7, Folder Harding, No. 318956.

7. Harding to Mulligan, February 21, 1920 (carbon), Harding Papers, Box 689, Folder 4965–1, No. 315739.

8. Mannington to Scobey, March 22, 1920, Scobey Papers, Box 2, No. 423.

9. Harding to Scobey, January 20, 1920 (carbon), Temporary Box 4, Folder Scobey 2, No. 321146; Harding to Scobey, March 24, 1920 (carbon), Temporary Box 4, Folder Scobey 2, No. 321172. Both in Harding Papers.

10. Scobey to Robert Armstrong, March 10, 1920, Scobey Papers Box 2, No. 401, Scobey to Howard D. Mannington, May 20, 1920, Box 2, No. 448.

11. Christian to Scobey, January 26, 1920 (carbon), Harding Papers, Temporary Box 4, Folder Scobey 2, No. 321158.

12. Daugherty to Harding, December 16, 1919, Harding Papers, Box 685, Folder 4945–1, No. 313968; Daugherty to Harding, December 20, 1919, Harding Papers, Box 4945–2, No. 314017; Daugherty to Fairbanks, December 20, 1919, Fairbanks Papers, Fairbanks to Daugherty, December 22, 1919, Fairbanks Papers.

13. Harding to Jennings, January 20, 1920, Jennings Papers; see also Harding to Scobey, January 20, 1920 (carbon), Harding Papers, Temporary Box 4, Folder Scobey 2, No. 321146; *Columbus Evening Dispatch*, January 19, 1920; *Cincinnati Times-Star*, January 19, 1920; *Cincinnati Enquirer*, January 20, 1920; *Ohio State Journal*, January 20, 1920; *Cleveland News*, January 20, 1920.

14. Harding to Scobey, December 30, 1919 (carbon), Harding Papers, Temporary Box 4, Folder Scobey 2, No. 321138.

15. Harding to L. C. Weimer, January 23, 1920 (carbon), Box 692, Folder 4986–1, No. 317095; Waltermire to Harding, January 29, 1920, Harding Papers (unclassified); Harding to Waltermire, January 23, 1920 (carbon, unclassified). All in Harding Papers.

16. In addition to the *Springfield Morning Sun*, see *Ohio State Journal*, March 3, 1920; *Cleveland News*, March 4, 1920; *Columbus Evening Dispatch*, March 3, 1920; *Cincinnati Enquirer*, March 7, 1920.

17. *Cleveland Plain Dealer*, February 20, 23, 25, 28, 1920; *Cleveland News*, February 24, 25, 26, 27, 28, 1920; *Columbus Evening Dispatch*, February 24, 25, 28, 1920; *Cincinnati Enquirer*, February 24, 1920; *Cincinnati Times-Star*, February 25, 27, 1920.

18. Hynicka to Harding, December 3, 1919, Temporary Box 2, Folder H, No. 318945; Harding to Thompson, December 23, 1919 (carbon), Box 691, Folder 498–1, No. 316701. Both in Harding Papers.

19. Harding to Turner, February 26, 1920 (carbon), Harding Papers, Box 691, Folder 4982–1, No. 316808.

20. Harding to Fravel, January 23, 1920 (carbon), Harding Papers, Box 687, Folder 4950–1, No. 314548; Harding to Weimer, January 5, 1920 (carbon), Harding Papers, Box 692, Folder 4986–1, No. 317098; Harding to Wilcox, December 16, 1919 (carbon), Harding Papers, Box 692, Folder 4987–1, No. 317300; Harding to Newcomer, December 13, 1919 (carbon), Harding Papers, Box 689, Folder 4966–1, No. 315763; *Cleveland Plain Dealer*, March 31, 1920; *Cincinnati Enquirer*, March 31, 1920.

21. For delegate selection in the seventh district (Columbus), see W. E. Halley to Harding, January 20, 1920, Harding Papers, Box 687, Folder 4951–1, No. 314734; Harding to Halley, January 22, 1920 (carbon), Harding Papers, Box 687, Folder 4951–1, No. 314742; Halley to Harding, January 24, 1920, Harding Papers, Box 687, Folder 4951–1, No. 314735. For the first and second districts (Cincinnati), see George W. Tibbles and George T. Poor to Harding, February 21, 1920, Harding Papers, Box 688, Folder 4956–1, No. 315100. For Vail and the Cleveland district, see Harding to Mayor Harry L. Davis, January 19, 1920 (carbon), Harding Papers, Box 685, Folder 4944–1, No. 313880; Vail to Harding, (n.d.), Harding Papers, Box 685, Folder 4944–1, No. 313882. For Brown and the Toledo district, see Harding to Frank E. Calkins, February 14, 1920 (carbon), Harding Papers, Box 684, Folder 4940–1, No. 313678. For others, see Harding to O. S. White, March 2, 1920 (carbon), Harding Papers, Box 692, Folder 4986–1, No. 317184; Harding to G. W. Wilber (Marysville), January 19, 1920 (carbon), Harding Papers, Box 692, Folder 4987–1, No. 317289; Harding to B. F. Wirt (Youngstown), February 17, 1920 (carbon), Harding Papers, Box 692, Folder 4987–1, No. 317271; Harding to Grant E. Mouser (Marion), January 31, 1920 (carbon), Harding Papers, Box 689, Folder 4964–1, No. 315639; Harding to H. L. Gordon (Cincinnati), December 31, 1920 (carbon), Harding Papers, Box 687, Folder 4951–1, No. 314686.

22. *Cleveland Plain Dealer*, March 31, 1920; *Cincinnati Enquirer*, March 31, 1920.

23. Harding to Scobey, January 20, 1920 (carbon), Harding Papers, Temporary Box 4, Folder Scobey 2, No. 321146.

24. All of the above may be found in the Harding Papers. Harding to Tyler, February 4, 1920 (carbon), Box 691, Folder 4982–1, No. 316820; Harding to Tyler, February 9, 1920 (carbon), Box 691, Folder 4982–1, No. 316822; Tyler to Harding, February 17 and 19, 1920, Box 691, Folder 4982–1, Nos. 316826, 316830; Tyler to Dr. Ernest Cox (Columbus) March 2, 1920, Box 684, Folder 4940–1, No. 313565.

25. Cottrill to Harding, February 21, 1920, Harding Papers, Box 685, Folder 4943–1, No. 313800.

26. *New York Times*, February 21, 1920.

27. Pugh to Harding, February 27, 1920 (carbon), Harding Papers, Box 689, Folder 4968–1, No. 315944; Starek to Harding, February 23, 1920, Harding Papers, Box 691, Folder 4978–1, No. 316413; Starek to Harding, April 6 and 7, Harding Papers, Box 691, Folder 4978–1, Nos. 316530, 316538; Harding to Aydelotte, March 17, 1920 (carbon), Harding Papers, Box 683, Folder 4933–1, No. 313236; *Ohio State Journal,* April 14, 1920.

28. Columbia University Oral History Research Project, "Reminiscences of A. D. Lasker."

29. Leaflet, Harding Papers, Box 688, Folder 4954–1, No. 314954; another copy in Box 690, Folder 4971–1, No. 316103.

30. A series of Wood advertisements is in *Columbus Labor News,* March 25, April 8, 15, 22, 1920.

31. Reily, "Years of Confusion," pp. 157–61, 162, 168; *Cleveland News,* March 5, 7, 1920; *Cleveland Plain Dealer,* March 27, 1920; *Columbus Evening Dispatch,* March 5, April 2, 9, 15, 1920; *Ohio State Journal,* March 9, 28, April 7, 8, 1920; *New York Times,* March 6, 1920.

32. *Cleveland News,* April 1, 1920.

33. Hagedorn, *Wood,* II, 330–36; *Cleveland News,* April 22, 23, 26, 1920; *Ohio State Journal,* March 6, April 3, 15, 1920.

34. *Cleveland News,* April 24, 1920; *Ohio State Journal,* March 27, April 8, 24, 1920.

35. *Ravenna Republican,* April 26, 1920.

36. "Resolution Adopted at Portsmouth, December 13, 1919, Calling Upon Senator Harding to Become Ohio's Candidate for the Presidency," Harding Papers, Box 684, No. 313341.

37. *Ohio State Journal,* April 14, 1920; *Cincinnati Enquirer,* March 30, 31, 1920; *Steubenville Herald-Star,* March 29, 1920.

38. *Ohio State Journal,* April 14, 1920.

39. Turner's point of view is given in the *Cleveland News,* February 25, 1920; *Cincinnati Times-Star,* February 25, 1920; *Columbus Evening Dispatch,* February 24, 1920; *Ohio State Journal,* February 15, 25, March 9, 1920.

40. *Ohio State Journal,* April 14, 1920.

41. *Steubenville Herald-Star,* March 29, 1920.

42. *Marietta Daily Times,* April 22, 1920.

43. Mrs. Harding to the Scobeys, (n.d.), Scobey Papers, Box 2, No. 351.

44. *Steubenville Herald-Star,* March 29, 1920.

45. *Akron Beacon-Journal,* April 29, 1920.

46. *Ibid.*

47. Harding to Jennings, September 8, 1920; Jennings to Harding, September 10, 1920 (carbon); Harding to Jennings, September 12, 1920; all in Jennings Papers. See also Reily, "Years of Confusion," pp. 172, 173.

48. *New York Times,* January 3, 1920. The Cummins bill was finally enacted into law as the Transportation Act (Esch-Cummins Act) of 1920. It returned the railroads to private ownership and sought to stabilize the transportation problem by encouraging consolidation of lines, standardization of profits, plus the creation of a labor board to help prevent strikes. Compulsory arbitration of labor disputes, originally a part of the Cummins bill, was not included in the final version.

49. All of the above may be found in the Harding Papers. Reily to Harding, January 3, 1920, Box 690, Folder 4970–1, No. 316070; Connell to Harding, January 6, 1920, Box 685, Folder 4942–1, No. 313782; Rapp to Harding, April 14, 1920, Box 690, Folder 4970–1, No. 315955; C. C. Waltermire to Harding, January 24, 1920, Box 692, Folder 4985–1, No. 317028.

50. Dayton Journal, April 21, 1920.

51. *Ohio Election Statistics* (1920), pp. 632–33.

52. Harding to Scobey, January 20, 1920 (carbon), Harding Papers, Temporary Box 4, Folder Scobey 2, No. 321146.

53. Harding to Scobey, March 24, 1920 (carbon), Harding Papers, Temporary Box 4, Folder Scobey 2, No. 321172.

54. Harding to Scobey, December 30, 1920 (carbon), Temporary Box 4, Folder Scobey 2, No. 321138; Taft to Harding, December 12, 1919, Box 691, Folder 4980–1, No. 316641. Both in Harding Papers.

55. All of the above may be found in the Harding Papers. John B. Kelley to Christian, January 31, 1920, Box 688, Folder 4958–1, No. 315207; W. R. Halley to Harding, March 24, 1920, Box 687, Folder 4952–1, No. 314752; Harding to Blankner, April 4, 1920 (carbon), Box 684, Folder 4936–1, No. 313381; Landes to Christian, March 24, 1920, Box 688, Folder 4959–1, No. 315319; Harding to Stauffer, April 1, 1920 (carbon), Folder 4978–1, No. 316546; Harding to Maullar, March 22, 1920 (carbon), Box 689, Folder 4960–1, No. 315485; Harding to Turner, March 24, 1920 (carbon), Box 691, Folder 4982–1, No. 316814; Harding to White, March 24, 1920, Box 692, Folder 4986–1, No. 317175.

56. Daugherty to Reily, April 23, 1920, Daugherty-Reily Papers.

57. Scobey to Harding, April 30, 1920, Harding Papers, Temporary Box 4, File Scobey 2, No. 321179; Johnson to Harding, April 30, 1920, Harding Papers, Box 688, Folder 4957–1, No. 315148; Faulkner in the *Cincinnati Enquirer,* May 2, 1920; Mannington to Horace Potter, April 29, 1920, Box 689, Folder 4961–1, No. 315918; Massie to Harding, May 4, 1920, Box 689, Folder 4961, No. 315931.

58. *Tribune-Telegraph* (Pomeroy), April 28, 1920; *Ripley Bee,* May 12, 1920.

59. Ohio Republican quoted in *Ohio State Journal,* May 9, 1920; *Akron Beacon Journal,* May 1, 1920.

60. *Indianapolis Star,* May 2, 1920.

61. Halley to Harding, May 11, 1920, Harding Papers, Box 594, Folder 4434–1, No. 271657; *Columbus Citizen,* May 10, 1920; *Cincinnati Times-Star,* May 11, 1920.

62. Harding to Brower, May 18, 1920 (carbon), Harding Papers, Box 684, Folder 4937–1, No. 313532.

63. Harding to Reily, May 18, 1920 (carbon), Box 690, Folder 4970–1, No. 316001.

64. Procter to M. E. J., December 18, 1919, April 23, 1920, in A. C. Denison (ed.), *Letters of William Cooper Procter* (Cincinnati: The MacDonald Printer's Co., 1957), pp. 118, 120–21.

CHAPTER EIGHTEEN

1. *Congressional Record,* 66 Congress, 2 Session, March 26, 1920, pp. 4853–59. The Kenyon committee hearings are in *U.S. Congress Subcommittee of the Committee on Privileges and Elections, 66 Congress, 2 Session, Hearings Pursuant*

to Senate Resolution No. 357 . . . To Investigate the Campaign Expenses of Various Presidential Candidates in All Political Parties, 2 vols. (Washington, D.C., 1921).

2. Daugherty and Dixon, Inside Story, p. 30.

3. Report of Interview of Senator Simeon D. Fess by Ray Baker Harris, February 25, 1935, in Harris Collection, Ohio Historical Society.

4. Cincinnati Enquirer, May 19, 1920.

5. Cincinnati Times-Star, May 27, 28, 1920. Cincinnati Enquirer, May 28, 1920; Cleveland News, June 4, 1920; Hagedorn, Wood, II, pp. 349–51; New York Times, June 23, 1921, p. 29.

6. William T. Hutchinson, Lowden of Illinois—The Life of Frank O. Lowden (Chicago: University of Chicago Press, 1957), Vol. 2, pp. 452–56.

7. Cincinnati Enquirer, May 28, 1920.

8. Cincinnati Times-Star, May 29, 1920.

9. Cincinnati Enquirer, May 29, 1920.

10. Cincinnati Enquirer, May 31, 1920.

11. Schortemeier (ed.), Rededicating America, pp. 223–29.

12. Congressional Record, 66 Congress, 2 Session, May 15, 1920, pp. 7098–99.

13. Weimer and Brower to Harding, May 27, 1920 (telegram), Harding Papers, Box 692, Folder 4986–1, No. 317119.

14. C. M. Dean (Cincinnati) to Christian, March 27, 1920, Harding Papers, Box 686, Folder 4946–1, No. 314302.

15. All of the above may be found in the Harding Papers. Hynicka to Harding, May 6, 1920, Box 688, Folder 4956–1, No. 315103; Harding to Hynicka, May 8, 1920 (carbon), Box 688, Folder 4956–1, No. 315104; Hynicka to Harding, May 17, 1920, Box 688, Folder 4956–1, No. 315109; Harding to Hynicka, May 18, 1920 (carbon), Box 688, Folder 4956–1, No. 315107.

16. Daugherty to Harding, May 20, 1920, Harding Papers, Box 685, Folder 4945–1, No. 313909.

17. Ohio State Journal, June 2, 1919; Cincinnati Times-Star, June 3, 1919.

18. Harding to Hynicka, May 8, 1920 (carbon), Harding Papers, Box 688, Folder 4956–1, No. 315102.

19. Harding to Johnson, May 6, 1920 (carbon), Box 688, Folder 4957–1, No. 315147; Harding to Johnson, May 17, 1920 (carbon), Box 688, Folder 4957–1, No. 315155. Both in Harding Papers.

20. Cleveland Plain Dealer, June 3, 1920.

21. Cincinnati Enquirer, June 7, 1920.

22. Willis Fletcher Johnson, George Harvey, A Passionate Patriot (Boston and New York: Houghton Mifflin, 1929), pp. 273–78.

23. Cleveland Plain Dealer, June 4, 1920.

24. Cincinnati Times-Star, June 5, 1920.

25. Official Report of the Proceedings of the 17th Republican National Convention Held in Chicago in 1920 (New York, 1920), pp. 96–97 (hereinafter cited as Official Proceedings).

26. Daugherty to Ray Baker Harris, June 29, 1938, Harris Collection.

27. Daugherty and Dixon, Inside Story, pp. 37–38; Chicago Tribune, June 11, 1920.

28. Daugherty and Dixon, *Inside Story*, p. 42; *Official Proceedings*, pp. 168–70.

29. *Official Proceedings*, pp. 184–85, 187–88, 190–91, 193–94.

30. Bagby, "The 'Smoke-Filled Room,'" pp. 662–64; Ray Baker Harris, *Warren G. Harding: An Account of His Nomination*, pp. 15–18.

31. Reily, "Years of Confusion," pp. 161–62.

32. Wadsworth to Ray Baker Harris, October 8, 1932, Harris Collection. Wadsworth's recollections were slightly inaccurate. On the fifth ballot only five New York delegates voted for Harding. Not until the eighth ballot did Harding get eight New York votes. On the ninth ballot there were sixty-six, and on the tenth (final) there were sixty-eight. *Official Proceedings*, pp. 214, 220.

33. Hilles to Aldrich, June 28, 1920, George W. Aldrich Papers, Rochester Public Library.

34. Daugherty to Harris, September 13, 1939, Harris Collection.

35. *Official Proceedings*, pp. 200–201, 201–2, 205–6, 210–11, 213–14, 220–21; Hynicka to Otto Pfleger, June 16, 1920, Harding Papers, Box 601, Folder 4457–1, No. 274995.

36. Bonner to Herrick, June 23, 1920 (telegram), Box 565, Folder 4337–2, No. 257133; Herrick to Bonner, June 23, 1920 (telegram), Box 565, Folder 4337–2, No. 257133; Herrick to Bonner, June 23, 1920 (telegram), Box 565, Folder 4337–2, No. 257135. All in Harding Papers.

37. Hynicka to Otto Pfleger, June 16, 1920, Harding Papers, Box 601, Folder 4457–1, No. 274995.

38. Bagby, "The 'Smoke-Filled Room,'" p. 665; Harris, *Warren G. Harding: An Account of His Nomination*, pp. 19–22.

39. Bagby, p. 666; Daugherty to Ray Baker Harris, June 29, 1938, Harris Collection; *New York Times*, June 13, 1920; *New York Tribune*, June 13, 1920.

40. Procter to Moore, June 18, 1920 (carbon), Harding Papers, Temporary Box 6, Folder M, No. 319528.

41. Wallen's account is found in several clippings from the *Hartford Courant* attached to his letter to Harding, June 28, 1920, Harding Papers, Box 508, Folder 4053–1, No. 234602.

42. *Ibid.*

43. Adams to Harding, June 16, 1920, Harding Papers, Box 534, Folder 4199–1, No. 243858.

44. Johnson to Harding, August 10, 1920, Box 519, Folder 4135–1, No. 238104; Harding to Johnson, August 13, 1920, Box 519, Folder 4135–1, No. 238105. Both in Harding Papers.

45. Bagby, "The 'Smoke-Filled Room,'" p. 668; Daugherty and Dixon, *Inside Story*, pp. 54–55; Daugherty to Harris, May 24, 1934, Harris Collection; *New York Times*, June 13, 1920; *New York Tribune*, June 13, 1920.

46. *Cincinnati Times-Star*, June 14, 1920.

47. *Ibid.*

CHAPTER NINETEEN

1. Lodge to New, September 28, 1920, New Papers, Indiana State Library.

2. Walter Davenport, *Power and Glory, The Life of Boies Penrose* (New York: Putnam, 1931), p. 232.

3. Child to Hays, September 12, 1920, Hays Papers, Indiana State Library.

4. *Chicago Tribune,* June 15, 1920.

5. Harding to Hays, June 24, 1920, Hays Papers; *Chicago Tribune,* July 10, 1920.

6. Nicholson to Hays, October 1, 1920, Hays Papers.

7. Karger to Harding, August 13, 1920, Box 636, Folder 4587–1, No. 291326; Harding to Karger, August 16, 1920 (carbon), Box 636, Folder 4587–1, No. 291327. Both in Harding Papers.

8. Harding to George D. Simmons, February 3, 1919, (unclassified); Harding to White, August 12, 1920 (carbon), Box 536, Folder 4219–1, No. 244707. Both in Harding Papers.

9. Harding to Young, June 30, 1920 (carbon), Harding Papers, Box 533, Folder 4191–1, No. 243853.

10. *Chicago Tribune,* June 18, 19, 1920.

11. There is a batch of 36 telegrams for the days June 16–23, 1920 in the Harding Papers, Box 521, Folder 4140–1, No. 238971–239007.

12. Harding to Phipps, June 22, 1920 (carbon), Harding Papers, Box 506, Folder 4026–1, No. 233797.

13. Goodrich to Harding, September 14, 1920, Harding Papers, Box 527, Folder 4159–1, No. 241516.

14. Harding to Robins, July 26, 1920 (carbon), Harding Papers, Box 579, Folder 4382–1, No. 263665.

15. See chapter 9; *Star,* August 30, September 13, 1912.

16. Van Fleet to Harding, June 18, 1920, Box 608, Folder 4478–1, No. 278492; Jennings to Harding, June 28, 1920, Box 597, Folder 4441–2, No. 272236. Both in Harding Papers.

17. Armstrong to Halley, June 17, 1920 (telegram copy), Harding Papers, Box 594, Folder 4434–1, No. 271062; Schortemeier, (ed.), *Rededicating America,* pp. 115–22.

18. New to Daugherty, July 19, 1920, Harding Papers (unclassified), No. 183930.

19. Roosevelt to Harding, June 18, 1920 (telegram), Harding Papers, Box 579, Folder 4383–1, No. 263764; Harding to Roosevelt, June 19, 1920 (telegram copy), Harding Papers, Box 579, Folder 4383–1, No. 263765; Roosevelt to Harding (n.d.), Harding Papers, Box 579, Folder 4383–1, No. 263768; Harding to Roosevelt, June 23, 1920 (carbon), Harding Papers, Box 579, Folder 4383–1, No. 263766; Roosevelt to Harding, July 5, 1920, Harding Papers, Box 579, Folder 4383–1, No. 263772; Harding to Roosevelt, July 16, 1920 (carbon), Harding Papers, Box 579, Folder 4383–1, No. 263775; *Chicago Tribune,* June 24, 1920.

20. *Philadelphia North American,* June 14, 1920; Van Valkenburgh to Brown, July 24, 1920, Harding Papers, Box 588, Folder 4415–1, No. 267928.

21. All of the above may be found in the Harding Papers. Mrs. Robinson to Harding, July 14, 1920, Box 579, Folder 4382–1, No. 263680; Harding to Mrs. Robinson, July 26, 1920 (carbon), Box 579, Folder 4382–1, No. 263684; Mrs. Robinson to Harding, October 13, 1920, Box 579, Folder 4382–1, No. 263675; Harding to Dr. Dell N. Ross, October 2, 1920 (carbon), Box 618, Folder 4516–1, No. 283000.

22. New to Daugherty, July 16, 1920, Harding Papers (unclassified), No. 183930.

23. Daugherty to Harding, July 19, 1920, Harding Papers (unclassified), No. 183929.

24. Harding to Johnson, July 27, 1920 (carbon), Harding Papers, Box 502, Folder 3997–1, No. 232043.

25. All of the above may be found in the Harding Papers. Scott to Harding, June 18, 1920, Box 504, Folder 4006–1, No. 232862; Harding to Scott, July 7, 1920 (carbon) Box 504, Folder 4006–1, No. 232865; Harding to Kent, July 7, 1920 (carbon) Box 502, Folder 3998–1, No. 232128; Kent to Harding, July 15, 1920, Box 502, Folder 3998–1, No. 232126; Arnold to Harding, July 17, 1920, Box 500, Folder 3988–1, No. 230917.

26. Sullivan to Harding, July 24, 1920, Box 504, Folder 4007–1, No. 233037; Harding to Sullivan, July 31, 1920 (carbon), Box 504, Folder 4007–1, No. 233039. Both in Harding Papers.

27. Christian to Fisher, December 24, 1919 (carbon), Harding Papers, Box 687, Folder 4949–1, No. 314505; *The Sun* and *New York Herald*, June 13, 14, 15, 16, 17, 18, 1920; Fisher to Harding, June 17, 1920, Harding Papers, Box 570, Folder 4350–2, No. 259492; Harding to Fisher, June 25, 1920 (carbon), Harding Papers, Box 570, Folder 4350–2, No. 259494; John E. Milholland, Wadhams, N.Y. to Harding, July 23, 1920, Harding Papers, Box 701, Folder 701–1, No. 152337.

28. *New York Times*, July 2, 1920.

29. Van Valkenburgh to Harding, July 2, 1920, Harding Papers, Box 619, Folder 4520–1, No. 283442; Moore to Harding, July 8, Harding Papers, 1920, Box 616, Folder 4510–1, No. 282466; Moore to Harding, July 26, Harding Papers, 1920, Box 616, Folder 4510–1, No. 282454; Hays to Christian, July 28, 1920, Harding Papers, Box 579, Folder 4382–1, No. 263724; Hays to Harding, August 3, 1920, Harding Papers, Box 653, Folder 4692–3, No. 299357; Shaw to Harding, June 22, 1920, Harding Papers, Box 580, Folder 4386–1, No. 264235; Harding to Shaw, June 23, 1920 (carbon), Harding Papers, Box 580, Folder 4386–1, No. 264236; Harding to Harvey, August 17, 1920, Harding Papers, Box 572, Folder 4356–2, No. 266398; *The Outlook*, October 6, 1920, p. 235, October 13, 1920, p. 280; *Review of Reviews*, (July 1920), pp. 35–41.

30. Robins to Harding, July 17, 1920, Harding Papers, Box 579, Folder 4382–1, No. 263661; there is a copy of this letter in the Hays Papers.

31. Herbert Hoover, *The Ordeal of Woodrow Wilson* (New York: McGraw-Hill, 1958), p. 295; *Columbus Sunday Dispatch*, March 14, 1920. See also R. K. Hynicka to Hays, March 18, 1920, Hays Papers, for Robert Taft's part in the Hoover movement.

32. Hoover to Harding (undated telegram), Harding Papers, Box 519, Folder 4133–4, No. 237980; Harding to Hoover, June 15, 1920 (carbon), Harding Papers, Box 573, Folder 4360–1, No. 260904; *Chicago Tribune*, June 19, 1920.

33. Loomis to Harding, June 19, 1920, Harding Papers, Box 575, Folder 4364–1, No. 262071.

34. Hoover to Harding, June 20, 1920, Box 573, Folder 4360–2, No. 260918; Robins to Harding, August 1, 1920, Box 523, Folder 4145–1, No. 239688; Harding to Robins, August 5, 1920 (carbon), Box 523, Folder 4145–1, No. 239689. All in Harding Papers.

35. Hoover to Harding, October 4, 1920, Box 573, Folder 4360–1, No. 260907; Harding to Hoover, October 12, 1920 (carbon), Box 573, Folder 4360–1, No. 260906; Harding to Hoover, October 27, 1920 (telegram carbon), Box 573, Folder 4360–1, No. 260909. All in Harding Papers.

36. Hoover to Mrs. Robert A. Burdette, September 29, 1920 (typed copy), Hays Papers.

37. *Chicago Tribune*, August 31, 1920; *Star*, August 31, 1920; *Cincinnati Enquirer*, October 5, 1920.

38. Hamlin to Hays, September 2, 1920, Hays Papers; Pinchot to Hays, September 13, 1920, Hays Papers; Daugherty to Harding, September 5, 1920, Harding Papers (unclassified).

39. Moore to Christian, June 29, 1920, Box 616, Folder 4510–1, No. 282450; Harding to Moore, July 2, 1920 (carbon), Box 616, Folder 4510–1, No. 282452. Both in Harding Papers.

40. Pamphlets in Harding Papers, Box 526, Folder 4150–3, No. 240735.

41. Harold L. Ickes, *The Autobiography of a Curmudgeon* (New York: Reynal and Hitchcock, 1943), pp. 229–34.

42. Ickes to Schriver, September 3, 1920, Harding Papers, Box 553, Folder 4191–1, No. 243704.

43. The Harding-White correspondence from June 28, 1920 to October 5, 1920 is in Box 536, Folder 4219–1 of the Harding Papers: White to Harding, June 28, No. 244695; Harding to White (carbon), June 30, No. 244694; White to Harding, July 10, No. 244710; Harding to White, August 12 (carbon), No. 244707; White to Harding, August 25, No. 244699; Harding to White (carbon), September 5, No. 244696; White to Harding, September 10, No. 244705; Harding to White (carbon), September 14, No. 244704; White to Harding, October 5, No. 244703.

44. William Allen White, *Masks in a Pageant* (New York: Macmillan, 1939), p. 401; *ibid.*, *The Autobiography of William Allen White* (New York: Macmillan, 1946), p. 596.

45. Harding to Procter, June 15, 1920 (carbon), Box 602, Folder 4459–1, No. 275238; Procter to Harding, June 22, 1920, Box 602, Folder 4459–1, No. 275240; Harding to Procter, June 23, 1920 (carbon), Box 602, Folder 4459–1, No. 275241. All in Harding Papers.

46. Wolfe to Harding, June 15, 1920, Box 607, Folder 4476–1, No. 278164; Moore to Harding, July 15, 1920, Box 616, Folder 4510–1, No. 282447; Harding to Wolfe, June 25, 1920 (carbon), Box 607, Folder 4476–1, No. 278162. All in Harding Papers.

47. Daugherty to Harding, July 15, 1920, Harding Papers (unclassified), No. 184121.

48. All of the above may be found in the Harding Papers. D. R. Hanna to Daugherty, June 13, 1920 (telegram), Harding Papers, Box 518, Folder 4132–1, No. 237499; Daugherty to Hanna, June 13, 1920 (telegram carbon), Box 518, Folder 4132–1, No. 237500; Hanna to Harding, June 22, 1920, Box 594, Folder 4434–2, No. 271171; Harding's secretary to Hanna, June 22, 1920 (carbon), Box 594, Folder 4434–2, No. 271169; Hanna to Harding, June 26, 1920, Box 594, Folder 4434–2, No. 271175; *ibid.*, July 3, 1920, Box 594, Folder 4434–2, No. 271118; Harding to Hanna, July 6, 1920 (carbon), July 6, 1920, Box 594, Folder 4434–2, No. 271180; July 7, 1920, Box 594, Folder 4434–2, No. 277182; Brown to Harding, June 22, 1920 (telegram), Box 594, Folder 4434–2, No. 271174.

49. Clippings from *Cincinnati Enquirer* and *Cincinnati Times-Star* in Box 601, Folder 4451–1, No. 275129; Pfleger to Harding, June 18, 1920, Box 601, Folder 4457–1, No. 274994; W. F. Porter to Harding, June 14, 1920, Box 601, Folder 4451–1, No. 275126. All in Harding Papers.

50. Hynicka to Pfleger, June 16, 1920, Harding Papers, Box 601, Folder 4457–1, No. 274995.

51. Hynicka to Hays, June 18, 23, 1950 (telegrams), Hays Papers.

52. All of the above may be found in the Harding Papers. Pfleger to Harding, June 14, 1920, Box 601, Folder 4457–1, No. 274986; Hulbert Taft to Harding, June 26, 1920, Box 606, Folder 4471–1, No. 277095; Harding to Taft, June 30, 1920 (carbon), Box 606, Folder 4471–1, No. 277093; Harding to Pfleger, June 25, 1920, Box 601, Folder 4457–1, No. 274990.

CHAPTER TWENTY

1. Form letters dated September 26 and 27, 1919 in Hays Papers.

2. *Republican Campaign Text-Book* (1920) (issued by the Republican National Committee, 1920).

3. Harding to Jennings, February 4, 1920, Jennings Papers; Harding to Van Fleet, June 30, 1920 (carbon), Harding Papers, Box 608, Folder 4478–1, No. 278497. See also Harding to P. J. O'Keefe, June 23, 1920 (carbon), Harding Papers, Box 572, Folder 4142–1, No. 239331; Harding to J. C. Rossen, May 9, 1919, Harding Papers (carbon, unclassified).

4. *Chicago Tribune*, June 23, 1920.

5. "The Reminiscences of Albert Davis Lasker," from interviews by Allen Nevins and Deal Albertson from November, 1949 to June, 1950 in Oral History Research Office, Butler Library, Columbia University.

6. Hays to Advisory Committee, January 28, 1920, Hays Papers; Lowden to Hays, February 2, 1920, Hays Papers. The Hays Papers are full of correspondence relating to this business-minded activity. A sampling of this may be seen in such letters as: Mills to Otto Kahn, January 6, 1920; Mills to Hays, January 8, 1920; Mills to Harding, February 6, 26, March 4, 10, 16, 1920; Hays to Penrose, January 27, 1920.

7. *Republican Campaign Text-Book*, pp. 107–94.

8. *Ibid.*, pp. 35–53; *Speeches of Senator Warren G. Harding . . . from His Acceptance of the Nomination to October 1, 1920* (hereinafter referred to as *Speeches of Harding*) (issued by the Republican National Committee, Toledo, Ohio), pp. 20–37; Schortemeier, (ed.), *Rededicating America*, pp. 34–61.

9. Hays to Harding, June 22, 1920, Hays Papers (carbon); Mills to Hays, June 14, 1920, Hays Papers; Lindsay to Harding, July 7, 13, 1920, Hays Papers; Harding to T. O. Marvin, Boston, July 16, 1920 (carbon), Harding Papers, Box 545, Folder 4271–1, No. 248169.

10. Lindsay to Harding, July 19, 1920, Box 575, Folder 4368–1, No. 261915; Hollander to Harding, July 19, 1920, Box 573, Folder 4366–1, No. 260824. Both in Harding Papers.

11. Hays to Republican editors, July 22, 1920, Box 674, Folder 4873–1, No. 309068; Heintz to Mannington, July 21, 1920, Box 518, Folder 4133–2, No. 237842; Work to Harding, July 29, 1920, Box 507, Folder 4031–1, No. 233972. All in Harding Papers.

12. "Suggestions for Public Utterances and Interviews Relative to Harding and Coolidge," Box 674, Folder 4873–1, No. 309069.

13. Lockwood to Armstrong, June 16, 1920, Harding Papers, Box 636, Folder 4590–1, No. 291613.

14. Clipping from *Photo Era* in Harding Papers, Box 568, Folder 4343–2, No. 258429.

15. All of the above may be found in the Harding Papers. Shelley to Moore, July 13, 1920, Box 616, Folder 4510–1, No. 282445; Moore to Christian, July 15, 1920, Box 616, Folder 4510–1, No. 212444; Christian to Moore, July 17, 1920, Box 616, Folder 4510–1, No. 282457; Christian to Hays, August 6, 1920, Box 653, Folder 4692–3, No. 299380; Hays to Christian, August 7, 1920, Box 653, Folder 4692–3, No. 299355; Hays to Christian, August 13, 1920, Box 653, Folder 4692–3, No. 299319; Christian to Hays, August 14, 1920, Box 653, Folder 4692–3, No. 299320.

16. All of the above may be found in the Harding Papers. Beveridge to Harding, July 6, 1920, Box 526, Folder 4154–1, No. 240997; Shaw to Harding, September 23, 1920, Box 580, Folder 4386–1, No. 264238; New to Harding, June 18, 1920, Box 529, Folder 4166–1, No. 242294; Weeks to Harding, June 15, 1920, Box 546, Folder 4277–1, No. 248872; Davison to Harding, August 19, 1920, Box 568, Folder 4345–2, No. 258765; Harding to Works, July 2, 1920 (carbon), Box 505, Folder 4010–2, No. 233330.

17. Herrick to Harding, June 14, 1920 (carbon), Herrick Papers, Western Reserve Historical Society. See Herrick to Hays, July 3, 1920 (carbon), in which Herrick congratulates Hays on the handling of the campaign and closes by saying, "I feel that we have had a narrow escape."

18. *Chicago Tribune*, July 1, August 18, 25, 1920; Parsons to Hays, June 15, 1920, Hays Papers.

19. *New York Times*, July 21, 1920; *Toledo Blade*, July 28, 1920.

20. *New York Times*, July 24, 1920; *Star*, July 23, 1920.

21. Olive Ewing Clapper, *Washington Tapestry* (New York: McGraw-Hill, 1946), p. 57; Olive Clapper, *One Lucky Woman* (New York: Doubleday Page, 1961), p. 85; Raymond Clapper, *Watching the World* (New York: McGraw-Hill, 1944), pp. 11–12.

22. Welliver to Bone, July 24, 1920, Hays Papers; *Cleveland Plain Dealer*, July 24, 1920.

23. Welliver to Good, August 11, 1920, Harding Papers, Box 518, Folder 4132–1, No. 237560.

24. Welliver to Bone, July 19, 1920, Hays Papers.

25. *National Republican*, August 7, 14, 28, October 23, 1920.

26. *Harvey's Weekly*, October 23, 1920, p. 27.

27. Clipping from *Boston Post*, Harding Papers, Box 545, Folder 4271–2, No. 248230; *Catholic Standard and Times* to Harding, October 27, 1920 (telegram), Box 617, Folder 4495–1, No. 280348; Jennings to Hays, October 27, 1920, Box 652, Folder 4692–1; *Harvey's Weekly*, November 6, 1920, pp. 2–3.

28. Hays to Roraback, July 31, 1920 (carbon), Hays Papers.

29. Bone to Lodge, September 3, 1920 (carbon), Hays Papers.

30. Welliver to Bone, August 17, 1920, Hays Papers; Welliver to Brown, August 6, 1920, Harding Papers, Box 588, Folder 4414–2, No. 267900.

31. *National Republican*, August 7, 14, September 18, 25, October 16, 1920; *Star*, October 1, 1920; *Cincinnati Enquirer*, September 5, 1920; *New York Times*, July 20, 1920.

32. Welliver to Hays, July 19, 1920; Hays Papers, Bone to Welliver, September 3, 1920, Hays Papers; *National Republican*, August 21, 1920; "p" on Harding's staff to G. W. Clemons, Greensburg, Indiana, October 23, 1920, Box 527, Folder 4155–1, No. 241200.

33. "R. G. T." of the New York headquarters to William A. Grant, photographer at Harding headquarters, August 25, 1920, Hays Papers; *National Republican*, October 16, 1920.

34. Bone to Welliver, August 29, 1920 (telegram carbon), Hays Papers.

35. Wrigley to Christian, July 28, 1920, Harding Papers, Box 526, Folder 4150–4, No. 240854; *Toledo Blade*, July 28, 1920.

36. Grant to Gerson, August 17, 1920 (copy of telegram), Harding Papers, Box 518, Folder 4132–1, No. 237496.

37. *Star*, August 24, 1920; Hays to Mrs. Harding, August 25, 1920 (carbon of telegram), Hays Papers; Harding to Jolson, September 13, 1920 (carbon), Harding Papers, Box 574, Folder 4363–1, No. 261347.

38. *Speeches of Harding*, pp. 67–70.

39. All of the above may be found in the Harding Papers. Lasker to Friedlander, August 7, 1920 (carbon), Box 520, Folder 4137–1, No. 238380; Kenyon to Hays, July 31, 1920, Box 653, Folder 4692–3, No. 299311; Hays to Kenyon, August 3, 1920 (carbon), Box 653, Folder 4692–3, No. 299313; Harding to Cappeller, July 31, 1920 (carbon), Box 589, Folder 4417–1, No. 268278.

40. All of the above may be found in the Harding Papers. Lasker to Christian, July 28, 1920, Harding Papers, Box 520, Folder 4137–1, No. 238378; Lasker to Christian, August 7, 1920, Box 520, Folder 4137–1, No. 238879; Lasker to Friedlander, August 7, 1920, Box 520, Folder 4137–1, No. 238880; Lasker to Welliver, August 19, 1920, Box 520, Folder 4137–1, No. 238366; Lasker to Welliver, August 20, 1920, Box 520, Folder 4137–1, No. 238363.

41. "H. S. N." to Fullerton, July 29, 1920 (carbon), Harding Papers, Box 560, Folder 4321–1, No. 255064.

42. *Star*, September 2, 3, 1920; *Speeches of Harding*, pp. 107–8.

43. Welliver to Grant, July 26, 1920 (carbon of telegram), Box 518, Folder 4132–2, No. 237622; Welliver to Grant, July 30, 1920 (carbon of telegram), Box 571, Folder 4354–1, No. 260037; Welliver to Turnage, August 6, 1920 (carbon), Box 606, Folder 4472–1, No. 277429. All in Harding Papers.

44. "R. G. T." to Hays, August 27, 1920, Hays Papers.

45. The best source for direct reports on the front-porch campaign is in the *Star*, whose reporters chronicled the events of each affair from the July 31 opening to the last "day" on October 18.

46. All of the above may be found in the Harding Papers. Hays to Christian, July 12, 1920, Box 653, Folder 4692–4, No. 299443; Welliver to Bone, August 3, 1920 (carbon), Box 652, Folder 4691–1, No. 299095; Welliver to Thompson, August 23, 1920 (carbon), Box 524, Folder 4147–1, No. 240275; Christian to McCartney, August 20, 1920, Box 599, Folder 4450–1, No. 273725; Harding to John C. Harding (carbon), Box 518, Folder 4133–2, No. 227712; "Memorandum for Mr. Hays," from Loeb, July 7, 1920, Box 572, Folder 4357–2; Bone to Christian, October 8, 1920, Box 565, Folder 4337–1, No. 257099; West to Harding, July 13, 1920, Box 583, Folder 4397–1, No. 265644; Harding to West, July 19, 1920 (carbon), Box 583, Folder 4397–1, No. 265649; Harding to T. Roosevelt, Jr., October 23, 1920 (telegram carbon), Box 579, Folder 4382–1, No. 263762.

47. "Athletic Committee," form letter and circular, October 13–14, 1920, Harding Papers, Box 519, Folder 4135–1, No. 238064.

48. All of the above may be found in the Harding Papers. Harding to John E. Hamlin (Harvard), October 19, 1920 (carbon), Box 583, Folder 4396–1, No.

265483; Harding to Edwin V. Hale (Yale), October 19, 1920 (carbon), Box 583, Folder 4396–1, No. 265485; Harding to Charles Denby, Jr. (Princeton), October 19, 1920 (carbon), Box 583, Folder 4396–1, No. 265487; Stimson to Hays, October 8, 1920, Hays Papers.

49. *Star*, October 18, 1920.

50. Messer to Stokes, August 27, 1920 (carbon), Hays Papers.

51. Welliver to Bone, July 24, 1920 (carbon), Harding Papers, Box 514, Folder 4127–1, No. 236500.

52. Messer to Lodge, August 30, 1920, Hays Papers; Lodge to Messer, August 31, 1920, Hays Papers.

53. Hays to Stokes, August 18, 1920 (carbon), Harding Papers; *New York Times*, September 6, 21, 1920; *Chicago Tribune*, September 6, 1920.

54. Welliver to Bone, October 3, 1920, Hays Papers; "hg" to Kahn, August 27, 1920, Hays Papers; Lasker to Hays, August 21, 24, 1920, Hays Papers; Kahn to Hays, August 23, 1920, Harding Papers, Box 574, Folder 4364–1, No. 261404; Hays to Harding, August 27, 1920, Harding Papers, Box 574, Folder 4364–1, No. 261408.

55. Bone to Lodge, September 3, 1920, Hays Papers.

56. *New York Times*, September 4, 1920. All other quotations from Harding Papers: Gerhard to Harding, August 25, 1920, Box 518, Folder 4132–1, No. 237481; Schrader to Harding, July 31, 1920, Box 580, Folder 4385–2, No. 264077; Harding to Schrader, August 5, 1920 (carbon), Box 580, Folder 4385–2, No. 264082; Vortriede to Harding, August 31, 1920, Box 582, Folder 4395–1, No. 265295; Vortriede to Harding, September 5, 1920 (telegram), Box 582, Folder 4395–1, No. 265243; Harding to Vortriede, September 6, 1920 (carbon), Box 582, Folder 4395–1, No. 265242; Jennings to Vortriede, September 10, 1920 (carbon), Box 582, Folder 4395–1, No. 265294; Vortriede to Harding, October 1, 1920, Box 582, Folder 4395–1, No. 265237; Vortriede to Harding, October 15, 1920, Box 582, Folder 4395–1, No. 265259; Harding to Vortriede, October 20, 1920, Box 582, Folder 4395–1, No. 205257.

57. The Cherna correspondence with Marion headquarters is voluminous and is found in Harding Papers, Box 589, Folder 4417–2, No. 268405–268421; Zucher to Harding, October 21, 1920, Box 608, Folder 4477–2, No. 278374.

58. *Star*, September 18, 1920; *Speeches of Harding*, pp. 187–92.

59. Governor W. D. Stephens to Daugherty, September 5, 1920, Harding Papers (unclassified), No. 183980–1; Daugherty to Harding, September 11, 1920, Harding Papers (unclassified), No. 183979; *Speeches of Harding*, pp. 169–71; *Chicago Tribune*, September 15, 1920.

60. Schurman to Harding, September 16, 1920, Box 580, Folder 4385–2, No. 264108; Harding to Schurman, September 21, 1920, Box 580, Folder 4385–2, No. 264110. Both in Harding Papers.

61. See *Jim Jam Jems*, a monthly for traveling salesmen, published in Bismarck, North Dakota, (October, 1920), pp. 56–60.

62. All of the above can be found in Harding Papers. "Traveling Salesmen As Judged by the Two Presidential Candidates," pamphlet issued by the National Harding and Coolidge Traveling Men's League and the Western Division Headquarters of the Republican National Committee," Harding Papers, Box 526, Folder 4150–3, No. 240752; "The Salesman's Platform," pamphlet issued by Republican National Committee, The New York Division. Harding Papers, Box 623, Folder

4534–1, No. 285198; W. S. Hypes, General Sales Manager of Marshall Field & Co. to Harding, June 14, 1920, Box 519, Folder 4133–4, No. 238056; Harding to Hypes, July 13, 1920 (telegram carbon), Box 519, Folder 4133–4, No. 238046; Hypes to Harding, July 14, 1920 (telegram), Box 519, Folder 4133–4, No. 238047; W. H. Schuman, General Sales Manager of Pratt Food Co. to Jerry H. Carson, September 20, 1920, Box 589, Folder 4417–1, No. 268300; Carson to Harding, September 26, 1920, Box 589, Folder 4417–1, No. 268299; Christian to Carson, September 29, 1920 (carbon), Box 589, Folder 4417–1, No. 268303; W. H. Ehnie & Brothers, printed circular, October 16, 1920, Box 517, Folder 4130–1, No. 237237; J. Kalesky, Chicago shoe salesman, to Harding, November 1, 1920, Box 519, Folder 4136–1, No. 238184.

63. *Star*, September 25, 1920; *Speeches of Harding*, pp. 212–18.

64. Child to Hays, September 8, 1920, Hays Papers.

65. The evolution of Wall Street betting from 2–1 to 10–1 for Harding may be traced in the *New York Times*, July 7, 10, 15, 21, August 21, September 15, 21, October 19, 27, 28, 29, 30, 31, November 1, 2, 1920.

66. Welliver to Bone, August 6, 1920, Hays Papers; Bone to Welliver, August 25, 1920, Hays Papers.

67. The account of Miss Freeland's work is distilled from the columns of the *Cleveland Sunday News-Leader*, beginning with the issue of July 18, 1920.

68. Bone to J. T. Adams of the Chicago GOP headquarters, August 19, 1920, Hays Papers.

69. Advertising material for Chapple's book is in Harding Papers, Box 543, Folder 4265–1, No. 247258; Davis to Harding, July 26, 1920, Harding Papers, Box 516, Folder 4129–1, No. 237002.

70. Joe Mitchell Chapple, *Warren G. Harding: The Man* (Boston: Chapple Publishing Co., 1920).

71. Chapple to Harding, October 5, 1920, Box 543, Folder 4265–1, No. 247263; Harding to Chapple, October 12, 1920, Box 543, Folder 4265–1, No. 247262. Both in Harding Papers.

72. [C. D. Philbrick], *What a Country Boy Did with 200 Pounds of Type*, (Columbus: McClelland & Co., 1920). The book was originally written to support Harding in the Spring primaries but New York headquarters bought up copies for use in the later campaign. See "S.W.V." to George H. Clark, September 1, 1920, Hays Papers.

73. Hays to Harding, August 14, 1920 (telegram), Box 652, Folder 4689–2, No. 299301; Warwick to Harding, August 18, 1920, Box 607, Folder 4474–1, No. 277642. Both in Harding Papers.

74. Warwick, "Growing up with Harding," *NOQ* (Winter, 1955–56), pp. 10–25; *NOQ* (Summer, 1958), pp. 116–36; *NOQ* (Spring, 1959), pp. 72–93. Warwick's article was reprinted in pamphlet form by the Harding Memorial Association of Marion, Ohio in 1965, in connection with the Harding Centennial.

75. Schortemeier (ed.), *Rededicating America*, pp. 34–217, 223–29, 250–56.

76. For the Lasker story, see John Gunther, *Taken at the Flood: The Story of Albert D. Lasker* (New York: Harper, 1960).

77. Lasker to Bone, August 18, 1920, Hays Papers; *Speeches of Harding*, p. 97.

78. Lasker to Welliver, August 20, 1920, Box 520, Folder 4137–1, No. 238363; Lasker to Christian, August 24, 1920, Box 520, Folder 4137–1, No. 238351. Both in Harding Papers.

79. Weeks to Hays, September 3, 1920 (telegram), Hays Papers; Lasker to Hays, September 3, 1920, Hays Papers; *Saturday Evening Post* (October 9, 1920), p. 176; (October 16, 1920), p. 130; (October 30, 1920), p. 25; *Literary Digest* (October 9, 1920), p. 107; (October 30, 1920), p. 99.

80. Lasker to Hays, September 3, 1920, Hays Papers.

81. Victor Heintz to Charles E. Hard, September 29, 1920, Hard Papers.

82. A copy of this form letter from Hays was sent to Harding, Harding Papers, Box 652, Folder 4692–1, No. 299193.

83. Brisbane to Lasker, September 3, 1920, Hays Papers.

84. Hays to J. T. Adams, September 3, 1920 (carbon), Hays Papers; Lasker to Hays, August 30, 1920, Hays Papers; Lasker to Hayes, September 4, 1920, Hays Papers.

85. All of the above can be found in the Harding Papers. Clennin to Harding, June 15, 1920, Box 516, Folder 4128–2, No. 236869; Harding to Clennin, June 23, 1920 (carbon), Box 516, Folder 4128–2, No. 236868; Clennin to Christian, August 17, 1920 (telegram), Box 516, Folder 4128–2, No. 236866; Christian to Clennin, August 17, 1920 (telegram), No. 236867; Albert Karter to Jack Hughes, c/o Al Jolson, (n.d.), Box 574, Folder 5364–1, No. 261443.

86. Edward V. Rickenbacker, *Rickenbacker* (Englewood Cliffs, N.J.: Prentice-Hall, 1967), p. 171.

87. *Cleveland News*, October 13, 1920; *Cleveland Sunday News-Leader*, October 17, 1920. The Rickenbacker articles in the series appeared on October 7, 10, 20, 24, 27 and 31, 1920.

88. Clark to Harding, August 6, 1920, Hays Papers.

CHAPTER TWENTY-ONE

1. See chap. 7.

2. See chap. 14.

3. *Republican Campaign Text-Book, op. cit.*, p. 57.

4. Dean to Daugherty, June 15, 1920 (unclassified), No. 184131; Daugherty to Christian, July 17, 1920 (unclassified), No. 184130. Both in Harding Papers.

5. Hinkle to Harding, July 29, 1920, Box 572, Folder 4358–1, No. 260579; Harding to Hinkle, July 31, 1920 (carbon), Box 572, Folder 4358–1, No. 260580. Both in Harding Papers.

6. Hinshaw to Harding, August 26, 1920 (telegram), Box 519, Folder 4133–3, No. 237938; Harding to Hinshaw, September 3, 1920 (carbon), Box 519, Folder 4133–3, No. 237939. Both in Harding Papers.

7. Carré to Harding, October 9, 1920 (telegram), Box 621, Folder 4528–1, No. 284600; Harding to Carré, October 11, 1920 (telegram carbon), Box 621, Folder 4528–1, No. 284601. Both in Harding Papers.

8. *New York Times*, October 26, 1920; Harding to Curtis, October 20, 1920 (carbon), Harding Papers, Box 534, Folder 4201–1, No. 241050.

9. Wheeler to Harding, September 30, 1920, Harding Papers, Box 621, Folder 4528–1, No. 284606.

10. Wheeler to Harding, September 23, 1920, Box 621, Folder 4528–1; H. H. Russell, *et. al* to Harding, September 21, 1920 (telegram), Box 637, Folder 4599–1, No. 292563; Harding to Russell *et. al* September 22, 1920 (carbon), Box

637, Folder 4599–1, No. 292562; Carré to Harding, October 6, 1920, Box 621, Folder 4521, No. 284601; all in Harding Papers. *Sun and New York Herald*, September 28, 1920.

11. Wheeler to Harding, September 17, 1920, Harding Papers, Box 621, Folder 4528–1, No. 284598.

12. Canton to Harding, September 23, 1920 (telegram), Box 621, Folder 4528–1, No. 284596; Harding reply to this written at the bottom, in pencil; Wheeler to Harding, September 24, 1920 (telegram), Box 621, Folder 4521–1, No. 284697. Both in Harding Papers.

13. Secretary to Mrs. Bisbee, October 29, 1900 (carbon), Harding Papers, Box 550, Folder 4290–1, No. 250322.

14. *Cincinnati Enquirer*, October 12, 1920; *American Issue* (national monthly of the Anti-Saloon League of America) October 8, 1920, p. 3.

15. Clarence True Wilson, "The Political Campaign of 1920," *Voice* (August, 1920), pp. 2, 4.

16. Edge to Harding, July 12, 1920, Box 559, Folder 4320–1, No. 254926; Richards to Edge, July 9, 1920, Box 559, Folder 4320–1, No. 254928; Edge to Harding, July 14, 1920, Box 559, Folder 4320–1, No. 254931. All in Harding Papers.

17. Harding to Busey (editor of Springfield, Ohio *Daily Sun*), September 18, 1920 (carbon), Box 589, Folder 4416–1, No. 268159; secretary to Mrs. Willard Curren, Springfield, Ohio, September 16, 1920 (carbon), Box 591, Folder 4421–2, No. 269220; secretary to Harold G. Meyers, Barnesville, Ohio, October 2, Box 600, Folder 4452–2, No. 274142. All in Harding Papers.

18. Mrs. Upton to Harding, June 14, 1920, Harding Papers, Box 608, Folder 4478–1, No. 278421; Harding to Mrs. Upton, June 15, 1920 (carbon), Harding Papers, Box 608, Folder 4478–1, No. 278432; Mrs. Upton to Hays, May 12, June 16, 28, 1920, Hays Papers.

19. Mrs. Upton to Harding, June 23, 1920, Box 608, Folder 4478–1, No. 278426; Mrs. Upton to Harding, June 27, 1920, Box 608, Folder 4471–1, No. 278423. Both in Harding Papers.

20. *Chicago Tribune*, June 23, 1920; *New York Times*, June 23, 1920.

21. *New York Times*, July 2, 1920; Mrs. Upton to Harding, July 2, 1920, Harding Papers, Box 608, Folder 4478–1, No. 278429; Harding to Mrs. Upton, July 6, 1920 (carbon), Harding Papers, Box 608, Folder 4478–1, No. 278431.

22. *New York Times*, July 9, 13, 1920; Mrs. Upton to Harding, July 9, 1920, Harding Papers, Box 608, Folder 4478–1, No. 278434; Mrs. Upton to Hays, July 13, Hays Papers.

23. *New York Times*, July 15, 1920; Mrs. Upton to Harding, June 27, 1920, Harding Papers, Box 608, Folder 4478–1, No. 278423; July 15, 1920, Harding Papers, Box 608, Folder 4478–1, No. 278443.

24. *Hartford Times* to Harding, July 13, 1920 (telegram), Harding Papers, Box 508, Folder 4050–1, No. 234571; Harding to *Hartford Times*, July 13, 1920 (telegram carbon), Harding Papers, Box 508, Folder 4050–1, No. 234572; Mrs. Upton to Harding, July 23, 1920, Harding Papers, Box 525, Folder 4148–1, No. 246480; *New York Times*, July 17, 1920.

25. *Republican Campaign Text-Book*, p. 52; Mrs. Upton to Harding, July 23, 1920, Harding Papers, Box 525, Folder 4148–1, No. 746480.

26. Mrs. Hay to Harding, June 22, 1920, Box 572, Folder 4357–1, No. 260467; Harding to Mrs. Hay, July 7, 1920 (carbon), Box 572, File 4357–1, No. 260466;

Hays to Christian, July 3, 1920, Box 653, Folder 4692–3, No. 299463. All in Harding Papers.

27. Memorandum of a Resolution of the Republican Executive Committee Meeting in Columbus, Ohio, July 21, 1920, Hays Papers; Winfield Jones to Harding, July 29, 1920 (telegram), Harding Papers, Box 635, Folder 4586–1, No. 241722; Harding to Jones, July 30, 1920 (telegram carbon), Harding Papers, Box 635, Folder 4586–1, No. 291723; Jones to Harding, August 3, 1920, Harding Papers, Box 635, Folder 4586–1, No. 291724; Jones to Harding, August 10, 1920, Harding Papers, Box 635, Folder 4586–1, No. 291728; *New York Times*, June 26, July 22, 24, August 9, 1920; *Star*, August 6, 1920.

28. *New York Times*, August 6, 1920; *Cincinnati Enquirer*, August 17, 1920; Mrs. Upton to Harding, August 17, 1920 (telegram), Harding Papers, Box 622, Folder 4532–1, No. 284984; Mrs. Catt to Hays, August 17, 1920, Hays Papers.

29. The voluminous correspondence with Harding on the Tennessee suffrage ratification is in Harding Papers, Box 622, Folder 4532–1, No. 284979–285048. Reference to the Tennessee vote on ratification is in C. E. Linn to Harding, August 18, 1920, Harding Papers, Box 622, Folder 4530–1, No. 214846. See also Adler to Harding, August 4, 1920, Harding Papers, Box 621, Folder 4527–1, No. 284517; Harding to Adler, August 24, 1920 (carbon), Harding Papers, Box 621, Folder 4527–1, No. 284515; clipping from *Chattanooga Times*, August 4, 1920, Harding Papers, Box 621, Folder 4524–1, No. 284518.

30. Mrs. Upton to Harding, August 18, 1920 (telegram), Box 672, Folder 4532–1, No. 284983; Alice Paul to Harding, August 18, 1920 (telegram), Box 637, Folder 4597–1, No. 292332. Both in Harding Papers.

31. Lasker to Hays, September 4, 1920, Hays Papers.

32. Mrs. Upton to Harding, September 13, 1920, Harding Papers, Box 525, Folder 4148–1, No. 240476; Dexter Perkins, *Charles Evans Hughes and American Democratic Statesmanship* (Boston: Little Brown, 1956), p. 61.

33. Lasker to Hays, September 4, 1920, Hays Papers.

34. Mrs. Upton to Hays, September 30, 1920 (telegram), Hays Papers.

35. Lasker to Hays, September 20, 1920, Hays Papers.

36. Mrs. Upton to Harding, September 20, 1920, Box 525, Folder 4148–1, No. 240468; Harding to Mrs. Upton, September 23, 1920, Box 525, Folder 4148–1, No. 240470. Both in Harding Papers.

37. *Star*, October 1, 1920.

38. *Speeches of Harding*, pp. 233–43; Harding's office to Captain Victor Heintz, September 28, 1920, Harding Papers, Box 518, Folder 4133–2, No. 237816.

39. Kenyon to Harding, July 12, 1920, Harding Papers, Box 533, Folder 4187–1, No. 243547.

40. Welton to Harding, January 26, 1919, Temporary Box 3, Folder W, Part 1, No. 320621; Harding to Welton, February 6, 1919, Temporary Box 3, Folder W, Part 1, No. 320620. Both in Harding Papers.

41. *Wallace's Farmer* (January 2, 1920), p. 7; (January 16, 1920), p. 158; (March 5, 1920), p. 763; Russell Lord, *The Wallaces of Iowa* (Boston: Houghton Mifflin, 1947), pp. 191–215.

42. *Wallace's Farmer* (February 13, 1920), p. 519.

43. Orville Merton Kile, *The Farm Bureau Through Three Decades* (Baltimore: Waverly Press, 1948), pp. 47–91; Theodore Saloutos and John D. Hicks,

Twentieth Century Populism (Lincoln, Nebr.: University of Nebraska Press, 1951), pp. 255–85.

44. *Wallace's Farmer* (June 18, 1920), p. 1602; *Republican Campaign Text-Book*, p. 76–78; Howard to G. M. Wilber, Marysville, Ohio, July 12, 1920, Harding Papers, Box 607, Folder 4475–1, No. 277848.

45. *Republican Campaign Text-Book*, pp. 47–49.

46. *New York Times*, July 13, 1920. See *Congressional Record*, 65 Congress, 1 Session, July 19, 1917, p. 5269.

47. *New York Times*, July 27, 1920.

48. All of the above may be found in the Harding Papers. Memorandum Dictated by Henry C. Wallace to Kathryn Lawler for George B. Christian, Box 638, Folder 4591–1, No. 291749; Wallace to Hays, July 27, 1920 (typed copy), Box 703, Folder 703–12, No. 168505; Wallace to Heintz, July 30, 1920, Box 533, Folder 4197–1, No. 243795; Wallace to Christian, August 20, 1920, Box 533, Folder 4197–1, No. 243800; Wallace to Harding, September 3, 1920, Box 525, Folder 4150–1, No. 240602.

49. Wallace to Harding, August 1, 1920, Harding Papers, Box 533, Folder 4197–1, No. 243788; Wallace to Harding, August 2, 1920, Harding Papers, Box 533, Folder 4197–1, No. 243789; Work to Hays, August 18, 1920 (telegram), Hays Papers. Gregory was editor of the *Prairie Farmer*.

50. Wallace to Harding, August 18, 1920, Harding Papers, Box 525, Folder 4150–1, No. 240610.

51. *Speeches of Harding*, pp. 129–41.

52. Wallace to Christian, August 20, 1920, Harding Papers, Box 533, Folder 4197–1, No. 243800; Wallace to Harding, September 2, 1920, Box 525, Folder 4150–1, No. 240599; Wallace to Harding, September 10, 1920, Box 533, Folder 4197–1, No. 243784. All in Harding Papers.

53. Work to Harding, October 3, 1920, Harding Papers, Box 525, Folder 4152–4, No. 240843.

54. *Wallace's Farmer* (October 1, 1920), p. 2286; *Prairie Farmer*, October 1, 1920.

55. *New York Times*, October 3, 1920.

56. Harding to Wallace, November 1, 1920 (carbon), Box 533, Folder 4197–1, No. 243803.

57. All of the above may be found in the Harding Papers. Highly to Harding, September 11, 1920, Box 528, Folder 4160–2, No. 241737; Harding to Highly, September 23, 1920 (carbon), Box 528, Folder 4160–2, No. 241736; "Mrs. V. B. W." to Harding, September 18, 1920, Box 606, Folder 4473–1, No. 277475; Harding to "Mrs. V. B. W." (carbon), September 23, 1920, Box 606, Folder 4473–1, No. 277476; Korsgren to Harding, October 2, 1920, Box 519, Folder 4136–1, No. 231277; Lawler to Korsgren, October 19, 1920 (carbon), Box 519, Folder 4136–1, No. 231276.

58. Gossett to Harding, July 19, 1920, Box 499, Folder 3987–1, No. 230706; Christian to Gossett, July 26, 1920, Box 499, Folder 3987–1, No. 230707. Both in Harding Papers.

59. Charles F. Cole, Batesville, Arkansas, to Christian, September 13, 1920, Box 499, Folder 3987–1, No. 230678; Christian to Cole, September 17, 1920 (carbon), Box 499, Folder 3987–1, No. 230679; Christian to C. E. Hubbell of Cleveland, Ohio, October 27, 1920 (carbon), Box 596, Folder 4440–1, No. 271987. All in Harding Papers.

60. All of the above may be found in the Harding Papers. Wishar to Harding, July 31, 1920, Box 505, Folder 4010–2, No. 233274; Wishar to Christian, September 18, 1920, Box 505, Folder 4010–2, No. 233276; Melish to Harding, July 30, 1920, Box 600, Folder 4452–1, No. 274063; Huriga to Harding, July 12, 1920, Box 519, Folder 4133–3, No. 237899; Sutton to Harding, September 28, 1920, Box 610, Folder 4484–1, No. 279237; Messler to Harding, August 4, 1920, Box 577, Folder 4376–1, No. 262917; Dean to Christian, September 14, 1920, Box 592, Folder 4424–1, No. 269621; Hische to Harding, July 13, 1920, Box 519, Folder 4135–3, No. 237949; Noble to Christian, September 30, 1920, Box 609, Folder 4482–1, No. 279143; Burchard to Harding (n.d.), Box 566, Folder 4240–2, No. 257795.

61. Schwenk to Christian, October 11, 1920, Harding Papers, Box 603, Folder 4464–1, No. 276005.

62. All of the above may be found in the Harding Papers. Malcolm Jennings to George B. Hische, July 21, 1920 (carbon), Box 519, Folder 4133–3, No. 237951; Victor Heintz to Elisha Hansen, July 21, 1920, Box 518, Folder 4133–2, No. 237846; Hansen to Heintz, July 23, 1920, Box 518, Folder 4133–2, No. 237849; Jennings to Wisher, September 20, 1920 (carbon), Box 505, Folder 4010–1, No. 233279; Corwin to Howard Mannington, October 28, 1920 (telegram), Box 606, Folder 4472–1, No. 277334; Jennings to Timberlake, October 28, 1920 (telegram carbon), Box 606, Folder 4472–1, No. 277335.

63. All of the above may be found in the Harding Papers. Secretary of Marion Lodge, No. 70 F. & A. M. to Gerald L. Burchard, New York City, August 31, 1920 (form-letter copy), Box 566, Folder 4340–2, No. 257796; secretary to Allen H. Wright, San Diego, California, August 31, 1920 (form letter copy), Box 505, Folder 4010–2, No. 233339; Fred W. Schwenck to W. H. MacDonald, editor, *Masonic Home Journal*, Louisville, Ky., October 11, 1920, Box 603, Folder 4464–1, No. 276007; Andres to Harding, October 29, 1920, Box 606, Folder 4473–1, No. 277499.

64. Heintz to Christian, September 3, 1920, Harding Papers, Box 518, Folder 4133–2, No. 237898.

65. See "Eye Witness," *Chicago Tribune*, August 19, 1920; see also chap. i.

66. Torbet to Mannington, July 15, 1920, Harding Papers, Box 524, Folder 4147–2, No. 240353; Mannington to Torbet, July 16, 1920, Harding Papers, Box 524, Folder 4147–2, No. 240354; see *Register, Ohio Society Sons of the American Revolution, 1917–1921* (published by the Ohio Society, Columbus, Ohio, 1922), p. 97 (a copy of this book is on file with the Ohio Historical Society Museum Library, Columbus, Ohio); Curry to Harding, July 19, 1920, Harding Papers, Box 591, Folder 4421–2, No. 209235.

67. Galvin to Christian, July 30, 1920, Harding Papers, Box 593, Folder 4431–1, No. 270567.

68. Unlabeled typed memorandum (n.d.), Harding Papers, Box 583, Folder 4396–1, No. 265513.

69. Davis to Harding, October 16, 1920, Harding Papers, Box 613, Folder 4497–1, No. 280658. Confirmation of the appearance of the Harding message on Mooseheart was given to the author by Director General Paul P. Schmitz of the Loyal Order of Moose in the following letter dated September 10, 1965: "In referring to our library, we find that the original of the quotation mentioned in your letter of August 31 appeared on page one, issue No. 35, Volume 3—the October 30, 1920 issue of Mooseheart Weekly, with the following heading: A Statement of Senator Warren G. Harding."

70. All of the above may be found in the Harding Papers. Lentz to Harding, June 14, 1920, Box 598, Folder 4447–1, No. 273114; Lentz to Harding, June 21, 1920, Folder 4137–2, No. 238425; Lentz to Harding, June 24, 1920, Folder 4447–1, No. 273115; Harding to Lentz, June 29, 1920 (carbon), Box 520, Folder 4137–2, No. 238424; "Doc Waddell," News Letter, mimeographed (n.d.), Box 606, Folder 4473–1, No. 277490.

71. The Harding–B. A. Johnson "Hoo Hoo" correspondence is in Harding Papers, Box 519, Folder 4135–1, No. 238092–238100.

72. Donavin to Christian, August 27, 1920, Box 592, Folder 4425–1, No. 269784; Christian to Donavin, August 31, 1920 (carbon), Box 592, Folder 4425–1, No. 269785; Donavin to Christian, September 2, 1920, Box 592, Folder 4425–1, No. 269786. All in Harding Papers.

73. All of the above may be found in the Harding Papers. Leaflet of the Patriotic Knights of American Liberty, Box 543, Folder 4266–1, No. 247562; Bulletin of the Sons and Daughters of Washington, July 1920, Box 570, Folder 4351–1, No. 259584; Tract No. 1 of the Knights of Luther, Box 604, Folder 4465–1, No. 276285; Harding to Miles, August 9, 1920, Box 638, Folder 4594–1, No. 292033 (includes copy of *The Guardian of Liberty* magazine for June 1920); Clark to Harding, June 29, 1920, Box 516, Folder 4128–2, No. 236857.

74. Secretary to Mrs. Roesinger, October 25, 1920, (carbon), Harding Papers, Box 530, Folder 4170–1, No. 212585; *New York Times*, September 3, 1920.

75. Maschke to Harding, July 10, 1920, Box 607 Folder 4476–1, No. 278181; Maschke to Harding, July 15, 1920, Box 599, Folder 4449–2, No. 273590; Landman to Daugherty, June 29, 1920, Box 520, Folder 4137–1, No. 238296. All in Harding Papers.

76. Marion office to Landman, July 3, 1920 (carbon), Harding Papers, Box 526, Folder 4137–1, No. 238297; Harding to Wolsey, August 6, 1920 (carbon), Box 601, Folder 4476–1, No. 278178; Wolsey to Christian, September 9, 1920, Folder 4476–1, No. 279180; Harding to L. N. Frank, July 15, 1920 (carbon), Box 593, Folder 4430–1, No. 270349; David to Harding, July 13, 1920, Box 632, Folder 4569, No. 289445; Harding to David, July 20, 1920 (carbon), Box 632, Folder 4569, No. 289446; David to Christian, August 3, 1920, Box 591, Folder 4421–2, No. 269439; all in Harding Papers. *New York Times*, July 19, October 17, 1920.

77. All of the above can be found in the Harding Papers. Harding to Nathan D. Shapiro, July 2, 1920 (carbon), Box 580, Folder 4386–1, No. 264220; Harding to Hiram Davis, July 2, 1920 (carbon), July 2, 1920, Box 568, Folder 4345, No. 258733; secretary to a Mrs. Levy, July 19, 1920 (carbon), Box 586, Folder 4908, No. 266914; secretary to S. G. McClure, September 14, 1920 (carbon), Box 599, Folder 4450–1, No. 273725.

78. Wise to Harding, July 16, 1920, Harding Papers, Box 607, Folder 4476–1, No. 278124; Christian to Wise, July 21, 1920 (carbon), Harding Papers, Box 607, Folder 4476–1, No. 278125; Wise to Christian, July 23, Harding Papers, Box 607, Folder 4476–1, No. 278126; O. H. Karstendick to Harding, September 25, 1920, Harding Papers, Box 597, Folder 4443–1, No. 272242; galley proof of *American Israelite* editorial, Harding Papers, Box 597, Folder 4443–1, No. 272489; *American Israelite*, October 7, 1920, p. 4; Heintz to Christian, October 26, 1920 (telegram), Harding Papers, Box 518, Folder 4133–2, No. 237813; Christian to Heintz, October 26, 1920, Harding Papers, Box 518, Folder 4133–2, No. 237812.

79. Joseph David to Christian, August 3, 1920, Box 591, Folder 4421–2, No. 269439; Hartman to Harding, October 16, 1920 (telegram), Box 572, Folder

4356, No. 266385; Harding to Hartman, October 25, 1920 (carbon), Box 572, Folder 4356, No. 266386. All in Harding Papers.

80. *Jewish Independent*, October 29, 1920; *Cleveland Plain Dealer*, October 28, 1920.

CHAPTER TWENTY-TWO

1. Arthur S. Link, *American Epoch: A History of the United States Since the 1890's* (New York: Knopf, 1955), pp. 240–41.

2. John Hope Franklin, *From Slavery to Freedom: A History of American Negroes* (New York: Knopf, 1952), pp. 438–39, 478–81.

3. *Ibid.*, pp. 470–75.

4. Ralph M. Tyler to Harding, June 17, 1920, Box 606, Folder 4472–1, No. 277462; clipping from *Cleveland Advocate* (containing Republican convention report by Tyler), June 19, 1920, Box 606, Folder 4472–1, No. 277463. Both in Harding Papers.

5. Forte to Maschke, July 13, 1920, Box 599, Folder 4449–2, No. 273591; Maschke to Harding, July 15, 1920, Box 599, Folder 4449–2, No. 273590; Harding to Maschke, August 12, 1920, Box 599, Folder 4449–2, No. 273592. All in Harding Papers.

6. *Republican Campaign Text-Book*, pp. 43, 50; *Speeches of Harding*, pp. 27, 34.

7. Johnson to Robinson, August 31, 1920 (typed copy), Harding Papers, Box 618, Folder 4516–1, No. 282966.

8. T. W. Fleming to Harding, June 14, 1920, Box 593, Folder 4429–1, No. 270259; Maschke to Harding, June 16, 1920 (telegram), Box 599, Folder 4449–2, No. 273586; Harding to Maschke, June 16, 1920 (telegram carbon), Box 599, Folder 4449–2, No. 273587; Harding to Fleming, July 10, 1920 (carbon), Box 593, Folder 4429–1, No. 270261; all in Harding Papers. *New York Times*, September 11, 1920.

9. Form letter to Negro organizations, dated August 18, 1920, Harding Papers, Box 519, Folder 4135–1, No. 238111; Marion office to Johnson, August 27, 1920, Box 519, Folder 4135–1, No. 238113.

10. Pamphlets issued by Republican National Committee: "The Colored American and the Campaign Issues," Box 526, Folder 4150–3, No. 240777; "Even Justice and a Square Deal for All," Box 526, Folder 4150–3, No. 240728; John R. Lynch, "Why the Negro Is a Republican," Box 526, Folder 4150–2, No. 240774. All in Harding Papers.

11. Johnson to Daugherty, August 9, 1920, Harding Papers, Box 618, Folder 4516–1, No. 282967.

12. Robinson to Johnson, August 28, 1920, Box 618, Folder 4516–1, No. 282965; Johnson to Robinson, August 31, 1920, (typed copy), Box 618, Folder 4516–1, No. 282966. Both in Harding Papers.

13. Daugherty to Mannington, August 23, 1920, Harding Papers (unclassified), No. 183973.

14. Burton to Harding, August 11, 1920, Box 589, Folder 4416–4, No. 268129; Harding to Burton, August 13, 1920, Box 589, Folder 4416–4, No. 268132; Tyler to Christian (n.d.), Box 606, Folder 4472–1, No. 277464. All in Harding Papers.

15. Mannington to Johnson, September 2, 1920 (carbon), Box 590, Folder 4421–1, No. 209093; Mannington to Crissinger, September 8, 1920, Box 590, Folder 4421–1, No. 269091. Both in Harding Papers.

16. *New York Times*, September 11, 1920.

17. *Speeches of Harding*, pp. 144–46; *Star*, September 10, 1920; final quotation is from "Even Justice and a Square Deal For All," (pamphlet), Harding Papers, Box 526, Folder 4150–3, No. 240728.

18. *New York Times*, September 11, 1920; *Union* (Cincinnati), September 18, 1920.

19. Clippings in the Harding Papers from the *Daily Oklahoman*, October 10, 1920, and the *Tulsa World*, October 10, 1920, Box 610, Folder 4484–1, Nos. 279233 and 279234. Clippings repeat questions asked in the *Daily Oklahoman* "yesterday morning."

20. All of the above can be found in the Harding Papers. Trotter to Harding, October 20, 1920 (telegram), Box 531, Folder 4171–2, No. 242931; Christian to Trotter, October 20, 1920 (telegram carbon), Box 531, Folder 4171–2, No. 242930; Harris to Harding, October 11, 1920 (telegram), Box 635, Folder 4584–1, No. 291038; Christian to Harris, October 11, 1920 (telegram carbon), Box 635, Folder 4584–1, No. 291039.

21. New to Christian, October 11, 1920 (telegram), Box 522, Folder 4141–1, No. 239161.

22. Montgomery to Harding, October 25, 1920, Box 550, Folder 4292–1, No. 250727. See also Henry A. Wallace of New York, to Harding, October 11, 1920, Box 583, Folder 4396–1, No. 265472; J. E. Boos, Albany, N.Y. to Harding, October 19, 1920, Box 565, Folder 4337–2, No. 257138. All in Harding Papers.

23. *Union* (Cincinnati), September 11, 25, October 23, 1920.

24. Johnson to Christian, August 28, 1920, Box 574, Folder 4363–1, No. 261327; Johnson to Harding, August 28, 1920, Box 574, Folder 4363–1, No. 261330; Johnson to Christian, September 16, 1920, Box 574, Folder 4363–1, No. 261322; Malcolm Jennings to Johnson, September 12, 1920, Box 574, Folder 4363–1, No. 261323. All in Harding Papers.

25. The articles in the *Nation* by James Weldon Johnson were "Self-Determining Haiti I. The American Occupation" (August 28, 1920), pp. 236–38; "Self-Determining Haiti II. What the United States Has Accomplished" (September 4, 1920), pp. 265–67; "Self-Determining Haiti III. Government Of By and For the National City Bank" (September 11, 1920), pp. 295–97; "Self-Determining Haiti IV. The Haitian People" (September 25, 1920), pp. 345–47.

26. *Speeches of Harding*, p. 184.

27. *New York Times*, September 19, 22, October 3, 6, 10, 14, 15, 16, 17, 19, 29, 1920.

28. All of the above can be found in the Harding Papers. Johnson to Harding, September 21, 1920, Box 574, Folder 4363–1, No. 261310; Johnson to Harding, September 22, 1920, Box 574, Folder 4363–1, No. 261316; Walter F. White to Harding, October 6, 1920, Box 583, Folder 4363–1, No. 265687; Ovington to Harding, October 14, 1920 (telegram), Box 577, Folder 4377–1, No. 263118; Hill to Christian, October 30, 1920, Box 635, Folder 4585–1, No. 291144.

29. Percentages derived from election statistics for 1916 and 1920 from *World Almanac*, 1921, pp. 682–83.

30. Copy of a form letter by Governor Charles H. Brough dated Columbus, September 16, 1920 in Harding Papers, Box 594, Folder 4434–2, No. 271129.

THE RISE OF WARREN GAMALIEL HARDING

31. *New York Times,* October 22, 1920.

32. *Ibid.*

33. *Cleveland Advocate,* April 10, September 25, October 23, 1920.

34. Copies of this campaign leaflet are in the Harding Papers, Box 606, Folder 4472–1, No. 277122; Box 610, Folder 4484–1, No. 279168; Box 610, Folder 4484–1, No. 279178.

35. Mrs. Taylor to Harding, October 23, 1920, Box 606, Folder 4471–1, No. 277120; Limmy to Harding, October 26, 1920, Box 585, Folder 4404–1, No. 266335; J. D. Pierson, Norman, Oklahoma to Harding, November 1, 1920, Box 610, Folder 4481–1, No. 279168; W. G. Peters, Salisario, Oklahoma, November 1, 1920, Box 610, Folder 4481–1, No. 279178. All in Harding Papers.

36. McClure to Christian, October 13, 1920, Box 599, Folder 4450–1, No. 273780; Christian to McClure, October 22, 1920, Box 599, Folder 4450–1, No. 273781. Both in Harding Papers.

37. *Public Ledger* (Philadelphia), October 19, 1920.

38. Sutherland to Hays, August 20, 1920, Hays Papers; Hays to Sutherland, August 27, 1920, (carbon), Hays Papers; Hays to Sutherland, (carbon), September 9, 1920, Hays Papers.

39. John C. Harding to W. G. Harding, October 16, 1920, Box 518, Folder 4133–1, No. 237719; W. G. Harding to John C. Harding, October 20, 1920 (carbon), Box 518, Folder 4133–1, No. 237718. Both in Harding Papers.

40. Graham to Christian, October 28, 1920, Box 534, Folder 4205–1, No. 244165, 244166; John H. Wilkins, Tulsa, Oklahoma to Harding, November 1, 1920, Box 610, Folder 4485–1, No. 279351, 279352. Both in Harding Papers.

41. Mrs. S. B. Williams to Harding, October 27, 1920, Harding Papers, Box 607, Folder 4475–2, No. 277972.

42. George Clark quoted in *New York Times,* October 17, 1920 and in Philadelphia *Public Ledger,* October 19, 1920.

43. Paper strip and picture of Dr. George T. Harding enclosed in letter from Franklin C. Platt, Waterloo, Iowa, to Harding, October 25, 1920, Harding Papers, Box 533, Folder 4192–1, No. 243631.

44. All of the above can be found in the Harding Papers. Cox to Harding, October 18, 1920, Box 590, Folder 4420–1, No. 268959; Abee to Harding, October 31, 1920 (telegram), Box 584, Folder 4402–1, No. 266065; Williams to Harding, October 28, 1920, Box 607, Folder 4475–1, No. 277929; Ringer to Harding, October 22, 1920, Box 617, Folder 4515–1; No. 282938; Cowan to Mannington, October 28, 1920, Box 606, Folder 4472–1, No. 277335; Curren to Harding, October 27, 1920, Box 691, Folder 4471–2, No. 269617.

45. *Cleveland Plain Dealer,* August 24, 1920; *Jewish Independent* (Cleveland), August 27, 1920; *New York Times,* October 31, 1920; W. E. Chancellor, *Warren Gamaliel Harding: A Review of Facts Collected from Anthropological, Historical and Political Researches,* The Sentinal Press (n.p., n.d.), pp. 23–27, 67.

46. Poster, "To the Men and Women of America, AN OPEN LETTER" in Ohio Historical Society.

47. *Dayton Daily News,* October 30, 1920.

48. *New York Times,* October 31, 1920.

49. Poster, "The Truth Will Out" in Ohio Historical Society.

50. Poster, "The Harding Stock" issued by the Ohio Republican State Executive Committee, on display (framed) in the home of Warren Marshman, Blooming Grove, Ohio.

51. *New York Times*, November 2, 1920.

52. Election statistics from *World Almanac, 1921* (New York: Press Publishing Company, a subsidiary of the *New York World*, 1921), pp. 682–83.

53. Davis to Harding, November 1, 1920, Harding Papers, Box 388, Folder 2847–1, No. 184325.

54. *Cincinnati Times-Star*, October 31, 1920.

55. *Chattanooga Times*, November 1, 1920; Paul J. Kresi, Chattanooga vice-chairman of Tennessee Republican campaign committee, to Christian, October 29, 1920 (telegram), Harding Papers, Box 622, Folder 4530–1, No. 284811; Kresi to Christian, October 31, 1920 (telegram), Harding Papers, Box 622, Folder 4530–1.

56. Samuel Hopkins Adams to Negley Cochran, Toledo, Ohio, April 12, 1939, Cochran Papers, Toledo Public Library.

CHAPTER TWENTY-THREE

1. Hadley to Harding, June 26, 1920, Box 506, Folder 4019–1, No. 233590; Harding to Hadley, July 7, 1920 (carbon), Box 506, Folder 4019–1, No. 233595. Both in Harding Papers.

2. Root's part in framing the Republican international affairs plank is described in Jessup, *Root*, p. 410.

3. *Republican Campaign Text-Book*, pp. 117–19.

4. See chap. xiv.

5. Harding to Jennings, September 12, 1919, Jennings Papers.

6. *New York Times*, July 3, 1920.

7. *Republican Campaign Text-Book*, pp. 38–39; *Speeches of Harding*, pp. 21–25.

8. *New York Times*, July 23, 1920.

9. Harding to Johnson, July 27, 1920 (carbon), Harding Papers, Box 502, Folder 3997–1, No. 232043.

10. Robins to Hays, August 11, 1920, Harding Papers, Box 652, Folder 4692–2, No. 294277.

11. Johnson to Harding, August 9, 1920, Harding Papers, Box 502, Folder 3997–1, No. 232042.

12. Harding to Hoover, September 21, 1920 (carbon), Box 573, Folder 4360–1, No. 260912; Hoover to Harding, September 27, 1920, Box 573, Folder 4360–2, No. 266915. Both in Harding Papers.

13. Harding to Hoover, October 4, 1920 (carbon), Box 573, Folder 4360–1, No. 266918; Harding to Hoover, August 7, 1920 (carbon), Box 502, Folder 3995–2, No. 231921. Both in Harding Papers.

14. Harding to Jennings, February 4, 1920, Jennings Papers.

15. *Cleveland Plain Dealer*, October 28, 1920.

16. Hoover to Harding, August 2, 1920 (telegram), Harding Papers, Box 502, Folder 3995–2, No. 232025.

17. Schurman to Harding, August 22, 1920, Harding Papers, Box 580, Folder 4315–2, No. 264112; see also Schurman Papers in Cornell University Library.

18. Lamont to Harding, August 3, 1920, Harding Papers, Box 575, Folder 4367, No. 261731.

19. Butler to Hilles, July 27, 1920, Hilles Papers; Hilles to Butler, August 26, 1920, Hilles Papers. Butler attached to his letter a six-page essay entitled "The Republican Party in California."

20. Taft to Carson Meredith, August 2, 1920 (carbon); Taft to W. S. Rainsford, August 19, 1920 (carbon); Taft to Charles A. Stone, August 6, 1920. All in Taft Papers, Library of Congress, Letter Book, Yale 98, 1920–21.

21. All of the above can be found in Harding Papers. Hilles to Harding, August 13, 1920, Box 572, Folder 4359–1, No. 260728; Lodge to Harding, September 15, 1920 (typed copy), Box 700, Folder 700–1, No. 151757; Lodge to Harding, September 17, 1920 (typed copy), Box 700, Folder 700–1, No. 151761; Lodge to Harding, September 20, 1920 (typed copy), Box 700, Folder 700–1, No. 151764; Harding to Lodge, September 3, 1920 (typed copy), Box 700, Folder 700–1, No. 151765.

22. Schurman to Harding, August 22, 1920, Harding Papers, Box 580, Folder 4385–2, No. 264112.

23. *New York Times*, July 29, 1920.

24. Gillette to Harding, August 4, 1920, Box 543, Folder 4266–1, No. 247574; Harding to Gillette, August 8, 1920, Box 543, Folder 4266–1, No. 247579. Both in Harding Papers.

25. *Chicago Tribune*, August 24, 1920; Lasker to Bone, August 18, 1920, Hays Papers, Welliver to Bone, August 25, 1920, Hays Papers.

26. Lasker to Bone, August 18, 1920 (carbon), Harding Papers, Box 520, Folder 4137–1, No. 238359; Lasker to Christian, August 20, 1920, Box 520, Folder 4137–1, No. 238383; Lasker to Christian, August 24, 1920, Box 520, Folder 4137–1, No. 238357; all in Harding Papers. *Ladies' Home Journal* (October, 1920), p. 103.

27. *Chicago Daily Tribune*, August 27, 1920.

28. *Speeches of Harding*, pp. 85–97.

29. Harding to Moore, September 3, 1920 (carbon), Harding Papers, Box 616, Folder 4510–1, No. 282431.

30. Harding to Lodge, September 1, 1920 (typed copy), Box 700, Folder 700–1, No. 151743; Harding to Lodge, September 7, 1920 (typed copy), Box 700, Folder 700–1, No. 151751. Both in Harding Papers.

31. Hays to Hoover, Taft, and Wood, August 28, 1920, (three letters, Hays Papers); *Star*, August 30, 1920.

32. *Star*, August 30, September 7, 18, 1920; *Chicago Daily Tribune*, September 6, 1920; Cravath to Hays, September 2, 1920, Hays Papers; Hammond to Harding, August 31, 1920, Harding Papers, Box 544, Folder 4268–1, No. 247669.

33. Lodge to New, September 28, 1920, New Papers, Indiana State Library, Indianapolis, Indiana.

34. *Chicago Daily Tribune*, September 1, 1920; *New York Times*, September 22, 1920.

35. *Star*, September 15, 1920.

36. Robins to Harding, August 28, 1920 (telegram), quoted in *Star*, August 30, 1920.

37. Brandegee to Harding, August 28, 1920 (telegram), quoted in *Star*, August 30, 1920; Harding to L. A. Coolidge, September 3, 1920 (carbon), Harding Papers, Box 503, Folder 4265–1, No. 247357.

38. Harding to Hammond, September 6, 1920 (carbon), Box 544, Folder 4268–1, No. 247667; Brandegee to Harding, September 18, 1920, Box 507, Folder

4033–1, No. 234054; Harding to Brandegee, September 23, 1920 (carbon), Box 507, Folder 4033–1, No. 234057. All in Harding Papers.

39. All of the above can be found in the Harding Papers. Knox to Harding, September 16, 1920 (telegram), Box 615, Folder 4505–1, No. 281909; Harding to Knox, September 16, 1920 (telegram carbon), Box 615, Folder 4505–1, No. 281970; Knox to Harding, September 18, 1920 (telegram), Box 615, Folder 4505–1, No. 281971; Harding to Knox, September 25, 1920 (carbon), Box 615, Folder 4505, No. 281972; Knox to Harding, September 30, 1920, Box 699, Folder 699–7.

40. Spalding to Harding, September 29, 1920, Harding Papers, Box 595, Folder 4435–1, No. 271217; *New York Times*, September 7, 8, 29, October 19, 28, 1920.

41. Karger to Harding, August 29, 1920, Harding Papers, Box 636, Folder 4587–1, No. 291349.

42. Hale to Harding, September 20, 1920, Harding Papers, Box 539, Folder 4245–1, No. 246035.

43. Lodge to Harding, September 9, 1920 (typed copy), Box 700, Folder 700–1, No. 151753; Lodge to Harding, September 15, 1920 (typed copy), Box 700, Folder 700–1, No. 151757; Lodge to Harding, September 17, 1920 (typed copy), Box 700, Folder 700–1, No. 151761; Harding to Lodge, September 20, 1920 (typed copy), Box 700, Folder 700–1, No. 151764. All in Harding Papers.

44. Johnson to Harding, August 31, 1920, Box 502, Folder 3997–1, No. 232054; Harding to Johnson, September 6, 1920 (carbon), Box 502, Folder 3997–1, No. 232042; Johnson to Harding, September 10, 1920, Box 502, Folder 3997–1, No. 232051; Harding to Johnson, September 23, 1920, Box 502, Folder 3997–1, No. 232051. All in Harding Papers.

45. *Star*, October 7, 1920.

46. *Ibid.*

47. *New York Times*, October 11, 12, 1920.

48. *New York Times*, October 15, 16, 17, 18, 19, 20, 21, 22, 1920.

49. Harding to Herrick, September 11, 1920 (carbon), Box 595, Folder 4437–1, No. 271507; Harding to Treadway, September 11, 1920 (carbon), Box 546, Folder 4275–1, No. 248732. Both in Harding Papers.

50. Harding's office to Brown, October 6, 1920 (carbon), Harding Papers, Box 588, Folder 4414–2, No. 267920.

51. *New York Times*, September 16, 1920.

52. *Star*, October 1, 1920.

53. Shaw to Harding (n.d.), Harding Papers, Box 580, Folder 4386–1, No. 264238.

54. Hibben to Harding, October 2, 1920 (typed copy), Harding Papers, Box 698, Folder 698–5, No. 151041.

55. All of the above can be found in the Harding Papers. Harding to Levinson, September 20, 1920 (carbon), Box 520, Folder 4137–2, No. 238458; Harding to Street, September 22, 1920 (carbon), Box 508, Folder 4049–1, No. 234523, Harding to Hadley, September 21, 1920 (carbon), Box 506, Folder 4019–1, No. 233586. See also A. B. Fall to Harding, September 20, 1920 (typed copy), Box 696, Folder 696–1, No. 149780; Hoover to Harding, September 27, 1920, Box 573, Folder 4366–2, No. 266915; Harding to Hoover, October 4, 1920 (carbon), Box 573, Folder 4366–2, No. 266918.

56. Schurman to Harding, September 11, 1920 (carbon), Schurman Papers; Schurman to Harding, September 16, 1920, Harding Papers, Box 580, Folder

4385–2, No. 264108; Harding to Schurman, September 21, 1920 (carbon), Harding Papers, Box 580, Folder 4385–2, No. 264110; *Republican Campaign Text-Book,* p. 483.

57. Harding to Schurman, September 15, 1920, Schurman Papers; Schurman to Harding, September 29, 1920 (carbon), Schurman Papers; Harding to Schurman, October 10, 1920, Schurman Papers. A rough draft and unfinished copy of the October 10 letter is in Harding Papers, Box 580, Folder 4385–2, No. 264087. *New York Times,* September 11, 1920.

58. Schurman to Harding, September 29, 1920 (carbon), Schurman Papers; Harding to Schurman, October 5, 1920, Schurman Papers; *Who Was Who in America,* I, p. 273.

59. Schurman to Harding, October 10, 1920, Harding Papers, Box 580, Folder 4385–2, No. 264087. There is a rough draft of this letter in the Schurman Papers.

60. *New York Times,* October 8, 9, 1920; *Cincinnati Enquirer,* October 5, 6, 7, 1920; *Chicago Daily Tribune,* October 11, 1920.

61. Cravath to Hays, October 8, 1920, Hays Papers; Stimson to Hays, October 8, 1920, Hays Papers.

62. Gillette to Harding, September 27, 1920, Harding Papers, Box 543, Folder 4266–1, No. 247582.

63. Hoover to Harding, October 11, 1920 (typed copy), Harding Papers, Box 698, Folder 698–1, No. 247582.

64. Butler to Hilles, October 8, 25, 1920, Hilles Papers.

65. Hays to Cravath, October 11, 1920, Hays Papers; Harding to Hays, October 12, 1920 (carbon), Harding Papers, Box 652, Folder 4692–1, No. 299158; Harding to Stoddard, October 12, 1920 (carbon), Harding Papers, Box 652, Folder 4692–1, No. 299161; Harding to Stimson (carbon), Harding Papers, Box 652, Folder 4692–1, No. 299160; Harding to Cravath (carbon), Harding Papers, Box 652, Folder 4692–1, No. 299159.

66. *New York Times,* October 15, 1920; Root to Cravath, October 9, 1920 (carbon), Hughes Papers, Library of Congress, Box 4A, General Correspondence —1917–1921, Folder 1920.

67. Hays to Child, October 11, 1920, Hays Papers; "Johnson Rebukes the 31 Signers," *New York Times,* October 23, 1920.

68. Hays to Cravath, October 11, 1920, Hays Papers; Hays to Child, October 14, 1920 (telegram carbon), Hays Papers; Lindsay to Hays, October 14, 1920 (office memorandum), Hays Papers.

69. *New York Times,* October 16, 1920.

70. Kriebel to Harding, October 13, 1920, Box 615, Folder 4505–1, No. 281980; Harding to Kriebel, October 16, 1920 (carbon), Box 615, Folder 4505–1, No. 281979. Both in Harding Papers.

71. Harding to Brisbane, August 30, 1920 (carbon), Harding Papers, Box 566, Folder 4339–1, No. 257464.

72. Brisbane to Harding, August 11, 1920, Harding Papers, Box 566, Folder 4339–1, No. 257462.

73. Harding to Brisbane, August 30, 1920 (carbon), Harding Papers, Box 566, Folder 4339–1, No. 257464.

74. Draft of Brisbane article, Harding Papers, Box 616, Folder 4507–1, No. 282172.

75. Brisbane clipping in Harding Papers, Box 566, Folder 4339–1, No. 257465.

76. Brisbane to Harding, October 5, 1920, Box 562, Folder 4339–1, No. 257458; Brisbane to Harding, October 30 (typed copy), Box 693, Folder 693–7, No. 148560. Both in Harding Papers.

77. Brisbane to Harding, October 30, 1920 (typed copy), Harding Papers, Box 693, Folder 693–7, No. 148560; *New York Times*, October 31, 1920, Section 2.

78. Davis to Hays, October 15, 1920, Hays Papers; Davis to Christian, October 15, 1920, Harding Papers, Box 613, Folder 4497–1, No. 280654.

79. Samuel Colcord, *The Great Deception Bringing Into the League the Real Meaning and Mandate of the Harding Vote as to Peace* (New York: Boni and Liveright, 1921), p. 63.

CHAPTER TWENTY-FOUR

1. See chap. xx.

2. *Republican Campaign Text-Book.*

3. See chap. xvii.

4. *New York Times*, July 16, 1920.

5. Schortemeier, *New York Times*, pp. 105, 135, 220, 148, 192, 202, 227.

6. See chap. xvii.

7. Harding to Jennings, November 19, 1919, Jennings Papers.

8. Nicholson to Hays, November 29 and December 26, 1919, Hays Papers; Hays to Harding, January 7, 1920 (carbon), Hays Papers; Harding to Hays, January 15, 1920, Hays Papers.

9. *Electric Railway Journal*, January 17, 1920, as reprinted in *Electric Railway Journal, Vol. 55, January to June, 1920* (New York: McGraw-Hill, 1920), pp. 155–57.

10. *New York Times*, July 16, 1920, quoting *Old Colony Magazine*.

11. *Speeches of Harding*, p. 26.

12. *Ibid.*, p. 25.

13. *Forbes*, August 21, 1920, p. 364.

14. *Speeches of Harding*, pp. 25–33.

15. *New York Times*, July 7, 1920.

16. *Speeches of Harding*, p. 119.

17. *U.S. Statutes at Large*, Vol. 41, Part I, pp. 456–99.

18. Hays to Christian, August 13, 1920, Harding Papers, Box 653, Folder 4692–3, No. 299317; Mannington to Halley, July 15, 1920 (carbon), Harding Papers, Box 594, Folder 4434–1, No. 271065; Halley to Mannington, July 19, 1920, Harding Papers, Box 594, Folder 4434–1, No. 271066; see chap. xvii.

19. *Speeches of Harding*, pp. 84, 121, 125, 163–65.

20. Christian to Harry L. Fidler, October 9, 1920 (carbon), Harding Papers, Box 517, Folder 4131–1, No. 237328 (includes pamphlet "What Is the Esch-Cummins Act?"); pamphlet, "Putting the Railroads to Work," Harding Papers, Box 526, Folder 4150–3, No. 240770.

21. *New York Times*, September 29, 1920.

22. *Republican Campaign Text-Book*, pp. 91–92.

23. *Republican Campaign Text-Book*, pp. 379–97; W. F. Wakeman to Harding (telegram), August 11, 1920, Box 583, Folder 4396–1, No. 265396.

24. *American Economist* (July 2, 1920), p. 4.

25. Heisey to Christian, June 18, 1920, Harding Papers, Box 595, Folder 4436–1, No. 271414.

26. Wakeman to Harding, June 24, 1920, Box 583, Folder 4396–1, No. 265335; Harding to Wakeman, June 29, 1920 (carbon), Box 583, Folder 4396–1, No. 265338. Both in Harding Papers.

27. Wakeman to Harding, August 10, 1920 (telegram), Box 583, Folder 4396–1, No. 265394; Christian to Wakeman, August 10, 1920 (telegram carbon), Box 583, Folder 4396–1, No. 265395. Both in Harding Papers.

28. Wakeman to Harding, August 11, 1920 (telegram), Harding Papers, Box 583, Folder 4396–1, No. 265396.

29. Wakeman to Harding, August 17, 1920, Harding Papers, Box 583, Folder 4396–1, No. 265401.

30. Lindsay to Wakeman, August 12, 1920 (copy), Harding Papers, Box 583, Folder 4396–1, No. 265403; see *Republican Campaign Text-Book*, p. 389.

31. *Republican Campaign Text-Book*, pp. 487–89.

32. Wakeman to Harding, August 17, 1920, Harding Papers, Box 583, Folder 4396–1, No. 265401.

33. Wakeman to Harding, August 17, 1920, Box 583, Folder 4396–1, No. 265401; Wakeman to Harding, September 25, 1920, Box 583, Folder 4396–1, Nos. 265323–265325. Both in Harding Papers.

34. *New York Times*, August 13, 14, 15, 1920.

35. *Speeches of Harding*, pp. 121–22.

36. *Ibid.*, p. 140.

37. *Ibid.*, p. 171.

38. Hollander to Mannington, September 21, 1920, Box 573, Folder 4360–1, No. 260826–260829. This includes Hollander's "Memorandum for Senator Harding's address at Baltimore, September 27, 1920." Compare this with *Speeches of Harding*, pp. 218–24.

39. *Speeches of Harding*, pp. 218–24.

40. *New York Times*, October 7, 1920.

41. *Ibid.*, October 12, 1920.

42. *Ibid.*, October 21, 29, 30, 31, 1920.

43. *Ibid.*, October 27, 1920.

44. Maxwell C. Raddock, *Portrait of an American Leader: William L. Hutcheson* (New York: American Institute of Social Science, 1955), pp. 130–35.

45. Lentz to Harding, June 24, 1920, Harding Papers, Box 598, Folder 4447–1, No. 273115; Davis to Harding, July 26, 1920, Harding Papers, Box 516, Folder 4129–1, No. 237002; September 4, 1920, Harding Papers, Box 613, Folder 4497–1, No. 280650; Davis to Christian, October 15, 1920, Harding Papers, Box 613, Folder 4497–1, No. 280654; *New York Times*, September 7, 1920; David Brodie, *Steelworkers in America, The Nonunion Era* (Cambridge: Harvard University Press, 1960), pp. 250–57, 276.

46. *New York Times*, August 4, 1920; Welliver to Bone, August 3, 1920, Harding Papers, Box 657, Folder 4691–1, No. 299098; Welliver to Snure of the Chicago office, Harding Papers, Box 524, Folder 4146–3, No. 240025.

47. *Star*, September 13, 1920. All other quotations are from the Harding Papers: Humphries to Christian, August 4, 1920, Box 519, Folder 4133–4, Nos.

238020–238024; John W. Weaver to Harding, August 18, 1920, Box 517, Folder 4131–1, No. 237346; Mannington to Weaver, August 21, 1920 (carbon), Box 517, Folder 4131–1, No. 237343; Mannington to Fidler, August 21, 1920 (carbon), Box 517, Folder 4131–1, No. 237335; Fidler to Mannington, August 23, 1920, Box 517, Folder 4131–1, No. 237334; Mannington to J. E. Hullinger, August 20, 1920, Box 517, Folder 4131–1, No. 237345.

48. *New York Times*, October 31, 1920, Section II.

49. "Waddell" to Harding, June 20, 1920, Box 606, Folder 4473–1, Nos. 277480, 277490, 277495; Harding to Daugherty, July 8, 1920, unclassified, No. 184146. Both in Harding Papers.

50. Daugherty to Harding, July 24, 1920; Harding Papers, unclassified, No. 184151.

51. Daugherty to Harding, August 4, 1920, Harding Papers, unclassified, No. 184108.

52. Daugherty to Harding, August 4, 1920, unclassified, No. 184110; Harding to Daugherty, August 9, 1920, unclassified, No. 184109; Chapin to Daugherty, August 2, 1920, unclassified, No. 184111; clippings from *Railway Employee*, unclassified, No. 184114. All in Harding Papers.

53. Mannington to Clark, August 18, 1920 (carbon), Harding Papers, Box 589, Folder 4418–1, No. 268561; *Ohio Statistics*, 1921, p. 264.

54. *American Federationist* (official monthly magazine of the American Federation of Labor) (March, 1920), p. 233; *Cleveland Federationist*, September 9, 1920, p. 2, September 30, 1920, p. 2.

55. *American Federationist* (August, 1920), p. 737, 739–43.

56. *American Federationist*, September, 1920, pp. 810–12, 816–22.

57. *American Federationist*, October, 1920, pp. 914, 997–99, 1000–1010; *New York Times*, October 26, November 1, 1920.

58. *Columbus Labor News*, September 30, October 7, 14, 21, 1920.

59. Edge to Harding, June 25, 1920, Harding Papers, Box 559, Folder 4320–1, No. 254913.

60. *Wall Street Journal*, June 16, 1920; *Moody's Investment Service*, September 23, 1920; *Forbes*, July 24, 1920; *Forbes*, August 21, 1920; *Manufacturers News*, July 17, 1920; Harding Papers, Box 525, Folder 4150–2, No. 240646; *Bache Review*, June 19, 1920, Harding Papers, Box 601, Folder 4456–1, No. 274717.

61. *Speeches of Harding*, pp. 20–21.

62. Harriman to Harding, July 23, 1920, Box 546, Folder 4277–1, no number; Harding to Harriman, July 30, 1920 (carbon), no number. Both in Harding Papers.

63. All of the above can be found in the Harding Papers. Kahn to Harding, June 17, 1920 (telegram), Box 574, Folder 4364–1, Nos. 261414–261416; Harding to Kahn, June 24, 1920 (carbon), Box 574, Folder 4364–1, No. 261412; Harding to Kahn, August 10, 1920 (carbon), Box 574, Folder 4364–1, No. 261416; Kahn to Harding, August 16, 1920, Box 574, Folder 4366–1, No. 261685; Harding to Kahn, August 30, 1920 (carbon), Box 574, Folder 4366–1, No. 261688. See Otto H. Kahn, *Our Economic and Other Problems* (New York: Doran, 1920); Otto H. Kahn, *Two Years of Faulty Taxation and the Results* (privately printed, 1920).

64. Dawes to Harding, August 30, 1920, Harding Papers, Box 516, Folder 4129–1, No. 237014; Harding to Dawes, September 3, 1920 (carbon), Box 516, Folder 4129–1, No. 237016; see Dawes, "The Next President of the United States

and the High Cost of Living," *Saturday Evening Post*, October 2, 1920; Harding to Hoover, October 4, 1920 (carbon), Harding Papers, Box 523, Folder 4360–1, No. 266918; Harding to Hoover, September 21, 1920, Harding Papers, Box 523, Folder 4360–1, No. 266922.

65. Harding to Andreas E. Burkhardt, September 23, 1920 (telegram), Harding Papers, Box 514, Folder 4127–4, No. 236716.

66. Harding to J. A. Hall (telegram, n.d.), Harding Papers, Box 518, Folder 4133–1, No. 237660.

67. Harding to S. S. Gregory, editor of *American Bar Journal*, August 3, 1920 (telegram), Harding Papers, Box 518, Folder 4132–2, No. 237638.

68. *Speeches of Harding*, p. 23.

69. *Ibid.*, p. 46.

70. *Republican Campaign Text-Book*, p. 82.

71. *Speeches of Harding*, p. 73.

72. *Ibid.*, pp. 149–50.

73. *New York Times*, July 19, 1920.

74. *Speeches of Harding*, p. 34.

75. Moore to Harding, August 3, 1920, Harding Papers, Box 616, Folder 4510–1, No. 282476.

76. *Republican Campaign Text-Book*, pp. 134–35, 225–78, 315–30, 419–28.

77. Party pamphlets in Harding Papers, Box 526, Folder 4150–3, Nos. 240732, 240739.

78. *Speeches of Harding*, pp. 33, 150–51.

79. *American Federationist*, August, 1920, p. 821.

80. *New York Times*, January 3, 1920.

81. *New York Times*, July 20, 21, August 15, 20, 22, 23, 24, 26, 27, 28, 29, September 4, 8, 10, 12, 23, 24, 26, 1920.

82. *New York Times*, July 7, 10, 15, 21, August 21, September 15, 21, October 19, 27, 28, 29, 30, 31, November 1, 2, 1920.

CHAPTER TWENTY-FIVE

1. Wesley M. Bagby, *The Road to Normalcy, The Presidential Campaign and Election of 1920*. (Baltimore: Johns Hopkins University Press, 1962), p. 159.

2. T. Harry Williams, Richard N. Current, Frank Freidel, *A History of the United States Since 1865* (New York: Knopf, 1964), II, 389–408.

3. *Star*, May 16, 1887.

Primary Sources

MANUSCRIPT COLLECTIONS

George W. Aldrich, Rochester (New York) Public Library
Walter F. Brown, Ohio Historical Society, Columbus, Ohio
Theodore E. Burton, Western Reserve Historical Society, Cleveland, Ohio
Negley Cochran, Toledo (Ohio) Public Library
Harry M. Daugherty, Ohio Historical Society, Columbus, Ohio
Hope Donithen, Ohio Historical Society, Columbus, Ohio
Newton H. Fairbanks, Ohio Historical Society, Columbus, Ohio
Joseph B. Foraker, Historical and Philosophical Society of Ohio, Cincinnati, Ohio, and Library of Congress, Washington, D.C.
Charles R. Forbes, Princeton University Library, Princeton, New Jersey
Joseph S. Frelinghuysen, Rutgers University Library, New Brunswick, New Jersey
Arthur L. Garford, Ohio Historical Society, Columbus, Ohio
Charles E. Hard, Ohio Historical Society, Columbus, Ohio
Warren G. Harding, Ohio Historical Society, Columbus, Ohio; Library of Congress, Washington, D.C.; and New York Public Library, New York, New York
Warren G. Harding campaign book of 1914, in possession of Don L. Tobin, Columbus, Ohio
Will H. Hays, Indiana State Library, Indianapolis, Indiana
Myron T. Herrick, Western Reserve Historical Society, Cleveland, Ohio
Charles D. Hilles, Yale University Library, New Haven, Connecticut
Charles Evans Hughes, Library of Congress, Washington, D.C.
Malcolm Jennings, Ohio Historical Society, Columbus, Ohio
Mary E. Lee, Ohio Historical Society, Columbus, Ohio
Harry S. New, Indiana State Library, Indianapolis, Indiana
E. Mont Reily, New York Public Library, New York, New York
Jacob G. Schurman, Cornell University Library, Ithaca, New York
Frank E. Scobey, Ohio Historical Society, Columbus, Ohio.
J. R. Sheffield, Yale University Library, New Haven, Connecticut
William Howard Taft, Library of Congress, Washington, D.C.

MISCELLANEOUS MANUSCRIPTS AND INTERVIEWS

Oral History Research Project, Baker Library, Columbia University (New York). Reminiscences of Albert D. Lasker, Stanley Washburn, and James T. Williams, Jr.

Ray Baker Harris Collection of manuscript copies and interviews, Ohio Historical
    Society, Columbus, Ohio
Interviews by author:
Nan Britton, Evanston, Illinois
William E. Chancellor, Wooster, Ohio
Mrs. W. H. Denman, Marion, Ohio
Lehr Fess, Toledo, Ohio
Dr. George T. Harding, III, Worthington, Ohio
George B. Harris, Cleveland, Ohio (See George B. Harris typewritten manuscript
    entitled "The Ohio Republican State Convention of 1912 and Its Effect on
    United States History.")
Ray Baker Harris, Washington, D.C.
Ralph T. Lewis, Marion, Ohio
Paul Michel, Marion, Ohio
Charlton Myers, Marion, Ohio
E. V. Rickenbacker, New York, New York
Dr. Carl W. Sawyer, Marion, Ohio
James T. Williams, Jr., New York, New York

OFFICIAL RECORDS

Congressional Record, 64 Congress, 1 Session; 66 Congress, 2 Session. Election
Statistics: Edgar Eugene Robinson. *The Presidential Vote, 1896–1932.* Stanford,
California: Stanford University Press, 1934. Secretary of State of Ohio. *Annual
Report to the Governor of Ohio . . . 1871 to present. World Almanac,* 1913, 1917,
1921. Kenyon Committee. *Subcommittee of the Committee on Privileges and
Elections, 66 Congress, 2 Session, Hearings Pursuant to Senatorial Resolution No.
357 . . . to Investigate the Campaign Expenses of Various Presidential Candidates
in All Political Parties.* Washington, D.C.: Government Printing Office, 1920.
Laws: *U.S. Statutes-at-Large. Ohio Session Laws,* 1803 to date. Hearings on Treaty
of Versailles and League of Nations. *Hearings before the Committee on Foreign
Relations of the United States on the Treaty of Peace with Germany Signed at
Versailles on June 28, 1919,* 66 Congress, 1 Session, Senate Document No. 106.
Washington, D.C.: Government Printing Office, 1919. Republican National Con-
vention of 1920: *Official Report of the Proceedings of the 17th Republican National
Convention in Chicago in 1920.* New York, 1920. *Republican Campaign Text-Book,
1920.* Issued by the Republican National Committee. Shipping Board Investiga-
tions. *Hearings before Senate Committee on Commerce.* 65 Congress, 2 Session,
Resolution 170. Washington, D.C.: Government Printing Office, 1918.

OHIO NEWSPAPERS

Akron Beacon Journal
Bellefontaine *Logan County Gazette*
Bellefontaine *Logan County Index*
Bellefontaine *Republican*

Bellefontaine Weekly Examiner
Bucyrus *Crawford County Forum*
Bucyrus Evening Telegraph
Canton Evening Repository
Canton News Democrat
Carrollton Republican Standard
Cincinnati Commercial Tribune
Cincinnati Enquirer
Cincinnati Post
Cincinnati Times-Star
Cincinnati *The Union*
Cleveland Advocate
Cleveland Federationist
Cleveland Gazette
Cleveland Jewish Independent
Cleveland Leader
Cleveland News
Cleveland Plain Dealer
Cleveland Sunday News-Leader
Columbus *Catholic Columbian*
Columbus Citizen
Columbus Evening Dispatch
Columbus Labor News
Columbus *Ohio Republican*
Columbus *Ohio State Journal*
Columbus Sunday Dispatch
Conneaut Evening News
Coshocton Daily Age
Dayton Daily News
Dayton Journal
East Liverpool Crisis
Elyria Republican
Greenfield Republican
Iberia Spectator
Kenton Graphic News
Lancaster Daily Gazette
Lebanon *Warren County Record*
Logan *Hocking Republican*
Mansfield Semi-Weekly News
Marietta Daily Leader
Marysville Tribune
Mendon Herald
Mt. Gilead *Morrow County Sentinel*
Mt. Gilead Union Register

Norwalk Daily Reflector
Pomeroy Leader
Pomeroy *Tribune Telegraph*
Ravenna Republican
Ripley Bee
Sandusky Daily Register
Sandusky Evening Star
Springfield Morning Sun
Springfield Press-Republic
Steubenville Herald-Star
Tiffin *Seneca Advertiser*
Toledo Blade
Toledo News-Bee
Toledo Record
Toledo Times
Urbana Citizen and Gazette
Urbana Daily News
Van Wert Republican
Van Wert Times
Xenia Gazette
Xenia *Greene County Press*
Youngstown Vindicator
Zanesville Courier

NEWSPAPERS OUTSIDE OHIO

Boston *Christian Science Monitor*
Boston Evening Transcript
Boston Globe
Boston Herald
Boston Post
Carthage (Mo.) *Evening Press*
Chattanooga Times
Chicago Daily Tribune
Chicago Herald
Hartford (Conn.) *Courant*
Indianapolis Star
New York American
New York Journal
New York *Sun*
New York *Sun and New York Herald*
New York Times
New York Tribune
(New York) *Wall Street Journal*

New York World
Oklahoma City *Daily Oklahoman*
Philadelphia *Catholic Standard and Times*
Philadelphia *North American*
Philadelphia *Public Ledger*
Pittsburgh Gazette-Times
San Antonio Express
Tulsa World
Washington (D.C.) *Evening Star*
Washington (D.C.) *Herald*
The National Republican, Washington, D.C.
Washington (D.C.) *Post*
Wheeling (W.Va.) *Register*

HARDING SPEECHES

"Commerce and Nationalism: Pioneers of All National Development and Preserver of National Strength Is Commerce," as reported in *Prosperity: The Republican National Magazine*, April, 1916, pp. 25–27.

Address at the Republican national convention of 1916. Address on "The Problems of Business," before the Providence Chamber of Commerce, February 25, 1920. Lecture: "Alexander Hamilton," Redpath Lyceum Bureau. All in Harding Memorial Association, Pamphlet Series. Marion, Ohio, n.d.

Speeches of Senator Warren G. Harding of Ohio . . . from His Acceptance of the Nomination to October 1, 1920. Issued by the Republican National Committee.

"The Plight of the American Electric Railways." Address to the American Association of Electric Railways, reported in *Electric Railway Journal*, January 17, 1920, pp. 155–57.

"The Railways and Prosperity." Address at the annual dinner of the Railway Business Association, December 10, 1914. Pamphlet Collection of the Ohio Historical Society.

The text of other speeches can be found in the *Congressional Record*; the *New York Times*; Dale E. Cottrill, *The Counciliator: A Biography of Warren G. Harding*. Philadelphia: Dorrance & Company, 1969; and in Frederick E. Schortemeier (ed.), *Rededicating America: Life and Recent Speeches of Warren G. Harding*. Indianapolis: Bobbs-Merrill, 1920.

POSTERS

Howard Chandler Christy, 1920 campaign lithograph portrait of Harding. Ohio Historical Society.

"The Harding Stock." Poster issued in 1920 by the Ohio Republican State Executive Committee. In home of Warren Marchman, Blooming Grove, Ohio.

"The Truth Will Out." Poster issued in 1920 by the Ohio Democratic Executive Committee. In Ohio Historical Society.

"To the Men and Women of America. AN OPEN LETTER." Poster bearing name of William Estabrook Chancellor. In Ohio Historical Society.

MAGAZINES

American Issue (Westerville, Ohio)
American Economist (New York)
American Federationist (Washington, D.C.)
Argonaut (San Francisco)
Bache Review (New York)
Collier's (New York)
Country Gentleman (Philadelphia)
Forbes (New York)
Guardian of Liberty (New York)
Harper's Weekly (New York)
Harvey's Weekly (New York)
Jim Jam Jems (Bismarck, N.D.)
Ladies' Home Journal (Philadelphia)
Leslie's Weekly (New York)
Literary Digest (New York)
Manufacturers' News (Chicago)
Manufacturers' Record (Baltimore)
McClure's (New York)
Moody's Investment Service, Letters (New York)
Munsey's (New York)
Nation (New York)
North American Review (Boston)
Outlook (New York)
Prairie Farmer (Chicago)
Review of Reviews (New York)
Saturday Evening Post (Philadelphia)
Voice of the Board of Temperance and Public Morals of the Methodist Episcopal Church, Washington, D.C.
Wallace's Farmer (Des Moines)
World's Work (New York)

CONTEMPORARY BOOKS AND MAGAZINE ARTICLES

Baker, Abby Gunn. "The New President as Marion Knows Him," *Christian Herald*, November 20, 1920, pp. 1185–86, 1204.
Blythe, Samuel G. "The Fire and the Fire Alarm: The Fight in Ohio Considered." *Saturday Evening Post*, July 25, 1914, pp. 6–7.
Britton, Nan. *Mes Amours avec le President Harding*. Paris: Edition du Tambourin, n.d.
————. *The President's Daughter*. New York: Elizabeth Ann Guild, 1927.
Chancellor, W. E. *Warren Gamaliel Harding: A Review of Facts Collected from Anthropological, Historical, and Political Researches*. The Sentinel Press, n.p., n.d.

Chapple, Joe Mitchell. *Warren G. Harding, The Man*. Boston: Chapple Publishing Company, 1920.

Colcord, Samuel. *The Great Deception Bringing into the League the Real Meaning and Mandate of the Harding Vote as to Peace*. New York: Boni C. Liveright, 1921.

Cuneo, S. A. *From Printer to President*. Philadelphia: Dorrance, 1922.

Edmonds, George L. "My Boy Warren." *McClure's*, March, 1921, pp. 22–23, 49–50.

Foraker, Joseph Benson. *Notes of a Busy Life*. 2 vols. Cincinnati: Stewart D. Kidd Co., 1916.

Harding, George T. "Warren Was a Good Son." *Collier's*, March 6, 1926, pp. 16, 41.

Harding, Warren G. "Joseph Benson Foraker." *Ohio Magazine*, October, 1907.

Hendrick, Frank, ed. *Republicans of 1920*. Albany, N.Y.: Albany Evening Journal Publishing Company, 1920.

Johnson, James Weldon. "Self Determining Haiti." *Nation*, August 28, September 4, 11, 25, 1920.

Kahn, Otto H. *Our Economic and Other Problems*. New York: Doran, 1920.

———. *Two Years of Faulty Taxation and the Results*. Privately printed, 1920.

Martin, Dorothy V. "An Impression of Harding in 1916." *Ohio State Archaeological and Historical Society Quarterly*, 62 (1953), 179.

Philbrick, C. D. *What a Country Boy Did with 200 Pounds of Type*. Columbus, Ohio: McClelland and Son, 1920.

Sherman, John. *Recollections of Forty Years*. New York: Erber Co., 1895.

Secondary Material

BOOKS AND ARTICLES

Adams, Samuel Hopkins. *Incredible Era*. Boston: Longmans, Green, 1939.

Alderfer, H. K. "The Personality and Politics of Warren G. Harding." Ph.D. thesis, School of Citizenship and Public Affairs, Syracuse University.

Allen, Frederick L. *Only Yesterday*. New York: Harper, 1931.

Asher, C. *He Was "Just Folks."* Chicago: Laird E. Lee, 1923.

Bagby, Wesley M. *The Road to Normalcy: The Presidential Campaign and Election of 1920*. Baltimore: Johns Hopkins Press, 1962.

———. "The 'Smoke-Filled Room' and the Nomination of Warren G. Harding." *Mississippi Valley Historical Review* 41, No. 4 (1955), 657–74.

Bailey, Thomas A. *Wilson and the Peacemakers* [combining *Woodrow Wilson and the Lost Peace* and *Woodrow Wilson and the Great Betrayal*]. New York: Macmillan, 1947.

Blum, John M. *Wilson and the Politics of Morality*. Boston: Little, Brown, 1956.

Bremner, Robert H. "The Civic Revival in Ohio: The Fight against Privilege in Cleveland and Toledo." Ph.D. dissertation, Ohio State University, 1943.

———. "George K. Nash." Ohio Historical Society, *The Governors of Ohio*. Columbus: Ohio Historical Society, 1954.

Britt, George. *Forty Years—Forty Millions* [Munsey]. New York: Farrar & Rinehart, 1935.

Brodie, David. *Steelworkers in America: The Nonunion Era.* Cambridge, Mass.: Harvard University Press, 1960.

Butler, Nicholas Murray. *Across the Busy Years.* New York: Scribner's, 1959.

Carlson, Oliver. *Brisbane: A Candid Biography.* New York: Stackpole, 1937.

Carmadine, William H. *The Pullman Strike.* Chicago: Kerr, 1894.

Clapper, Olive. *One Lucky Woman.* New York: Doubleday Page, 1961.

————. *Washington Tapestry.* New York: McGraw-Hill, 1946.

Clapper, Raymond. *Watching the World.* New York: McGraw-Hill, 1944.

Cox, James M. *Journey through My Years.* New York: Simon & Schuster, 1946.

Crandall, Andrew Wallace. *The Early History of the Republican Party, 1854–1856.* Boston: Badger, 1930.

Crissey, Forest. *Theodore E. Burton.* Cleveland: World Publishing Co., 1956.

Croly, Herbert D. *Marcus Alonzo Hanna.* New York: Macmillan, 1912.

Curti, Merle E. *Growth of American Thought.* New York: Harper, 1943.

Daugherty, Harry M., and Thomas Dixon. *Inside Story of the Harding Tragedy.* New York: Churchill Co., 1932.

Davenport, Walter. *Power and Glory: The Life of Boies Penrose.* New York: Putnam, 1931.

David, Henry. *The History of the Haymarket Affair.* New York: Farrar and Rinehart, 1936.

Downes, Randolph C. "The Newspaper World of Warren G. Harding." *Ohioana Quarterly* III, No. 4 (1960), 122–25.

————. "A Newspaper's Childhood: The Marion Daily Star, from Hume to Harding." *Northwest Ohio Quarterly* XXXVI, No. 3 (1964), 134–45.

————. ed. "President Making: The Influence of Newton H. Fairbanks and Harry M. Daugherty on the Nomination of Warren G. Harding for the Presidency." *Northwest Ohio Quarterly* XXXI, No. 4 (1959), 170–78.

————. "Wanted: A Scholarly Appraisal of Warren G. Harding." *Ohioana Quarterly* II, No. 1 (1959), 18–20.

————. "Warren Gamaliel Harding, Man of Marion." *Beautiful Ohio* II, No. 3, 59–61.

Duckett, Kenneth W. "The Harding Papers: How Some Were Burned." *American Heritage,* February, 1965, pp. 24–31, 102–9.

Fleming, Denna F. *The United States and the League of Nations, 1918–1920.* New York and London: Putnam, 1934.

Foraker, Julia B. *I Would Live It Again.* New York and London: Harper, 1932.

Franklin, John Hope. *From Slavery to Freedom: A History of American Negroes.* New York: Knopf, 1952.

Garraty, John A. *Henry Cabot Lodge.* New York: Knopf, 1943.

Giglio, James N. "The Political Career of Harry M. Daugherty." Ph.D. dissertation, Ohio State University, 1968.

Gompers, Samuel. *Seventy Years of Life and Labor.* 2 vols. New York: Dutton, 1925.

Gunther, John. *Taken at the Flood: The Story of Albert D. Lasker.* New York: Harper, 1960.

Hagedorn, Hermann. *Leonard Wood: A Biography.* 2 vols. New York and London: Harper, 1931.

Hard, Charles E. "The Man Who Did Not Want to Become President." *Northwest Ohio Quarterly* XXXI, No. 3 (1959), 120–25.

Harris, Ray Baker. "Background and Youth of the Seventh Ohio President." *Ohio State Archaeological and Historical Society Quarterly* LII, 260–75.

———. *Warren G. Harding: An Account of His Nomination for the Presidency by the Republican Convention of 1920.* Washington, D.C.: privately printed, 1957.

The History of Marion County. Leggett, Conway & Co., 1883.

Hofstadter, Richard. *The Age of Reform from Bryan to F. D. R.* New York: Vintage, 1955.

Hoover, Herbert. *The Ordeal of Woodrow Wilson.* New York: McGraw-Hill, 1958.

Hurley, Edward N. *The Bridge to France.* Philadelphia: Lippincott, 1927.

Hutchinson, William T. *Lowden of Illinois: The Life of Frank O. Lowden.* 2 vols. Chicago: University of Chicago Press, 1957.

Ickes, Harold L. *The Autobiography of a Curmudgeon.* New York: Reynal & Hitchcock, 1943.

Jacoby, J. Wilbur. *History of Marion County, Ohio.* Chicago, 1907.

Jessup, Philip C. *Elihu Root.* New York: Dodd, Mead, 1937.

Johnson, Claudius O. *Borah of Idaho.* New York and Toronto: Longmans, Green, 1936.

Johnson, Willis Fletcher. *The Life of Warren G. Harding.* Philadelphia: John C. Winston Co., 1923.

———. *George Harvey, Passionate Patriot.* Boston and New York: Houghton Mifflin, 1929.

Kohlsaat, H. H. *From McKinley to Harding.* New York and London: Scribner's, 1923.

Leech, Margaret. *In the Days of McKinley.* New York: Harper, 1959.

Link, Arthur S. *American Epoch: A History of the United States Since the 1890's.* New York: Knopf, 1955.

———. *Wilson: The New Freedom.* Princeton, N.J.: Princeton University Press, 1956.

———. *Wilson and the Progressive Era.* New York: Harper, 1954.

———. *Wilson: The Struggle of Neutrality.* Princeton, N.J.: Princeton University Press, 1960.

Lloyd, John A. "Some Harding Anecdotes." *Northwest Ohio Quarterly* XXXII, No. 1 (1959–60), 25–29.

Livermore, Seward. *Woodrow Wilson and the War Congress, 1916–1918.* Seattle: University of Washington Press, 1968.

Lodge, Henry Cabot. *The Senate and the League of Nations.* New York: Scribner's, 1925.

Longworth, Alice Roosevelt. *Crowded Hours.* New York: Scribner's, 1933.

Lord, Russell. *The Wallaces of Iowa.* Boston: Houghton Mifflin, 1947.

Mayer, George H. *The Republican Party, 1854–1964.* New York: Oxford, 1964.

Mercer, James K. *Representative Men of Ohio, 1904–1908.* Columbus, Ohio: Heer, 1908.

Moos, Malcolm. *The Republicans.* New York: Random House, 1956.

Mott, T. Bentley. *Myron T. Herrick, Friend of France: An Autobiographical Biography.* Garden City, N.Y.: Doubleday, Doran, 1929.

Mowry, George E. *The California Progressives.* Berkeley: University of California Press, 1951.

———. *The Era of Theodore Roosevelt, 1900–1912.* New York: Harper, 1958.

———. *Theodore Roosevelt and the Progressive Movement.* Madison: University of Wisconsin Press, 1946.

Murdock, Eugene C. "Buckeye Liberal: A Biography of Tom L. Johnson." Ph.D. dissertation, Columbia University.

Murray, Robert K. *The Harding Era: Warren G. Harding and His Administration.* Minneapolis: University of Minnesota Press, 1969.

———. *Red Scare: A Study in Natural Hysteria, 1919–1920.* Minneapolis: University of Minnesota Press, 1955.

Nevins, Allan. *Grover Cleveland: A Study in Courage.* New York: Dodd, Mead, 1934.

Ohio Historical Society. *The Governors of Ohio.* Columbus: Ohio Historical Society, 1954.

Ohio Society, Sons of the American Revolution. *Register . . . 1917–1921.* Columbus: Ohio Society, Sons of the American Revolution, 1922.

Olcott, Charles S. *Life of McKinley.* Boston and New York: Houghton Mifflin, 1936.

Orth, S. P. "Municipal Situation in Ohio." *Forum,* XXXIII (1902), 435–37.

Overacker, Louise. *Presidential Primaries.* New York: Macmillan, 1926.

Paxson, F. L. *American Democracy and the World War.* 3 vols. Boston and New York: Houghton Mifflin, 1939–43.

———. *Normalcy, 1919–1923.* Berkeley: University of California Press, 1948.

Perkins, Dexter. *Charles Evans Hughes and American Democratic Statesmanship.* Boston: Little, Brown, 1956.

Pringle, Henry F. *Theodore Roosevelt.* New York: Harcourt, Brace, 1931.

———. *Life and Times of William Howard Taft.* New York: Farrar & Rinehart, 1939.

Pusey, Merle J. *Charles Evans Hughes.* New York: Macmillan, 1951.

Raddock, Maxwell C. *Portrait of an American Leader: William T. Hutcheson.* New York: American Institute of Social Science, 1955.

Roseboom, Eugene H. *A History of Presidential Elections.* New York: Macmillan, 1957.

———, and Francis P. Weisenburger. *A History of Ohio.* Columbus: Ohio Archaeological and Historical Society, 1953.

Russell, Francis. "The Harding Papers . . . and Some Were Saved." *American Heritage,* February, 1965, pp. 24–31, 102–10.

———. *The Shadow of Blooming Grove: Warren G. Harding in His Time.* New York, Toronto: McGraw-Hill, 1968.

Saloutos, Theodore, and John D. Hicks. *Twentieth Century Populism.* Lincoln: University of Nebraska Press, 1951.

Sinclair, Andrew. *The Available Man: The Life behind the Masks of Warren Gamaliel Harding.* New York: Macmillan, 1965.

Steuart, Justin. *Wayne Wheeler, Dry Boss: An Uncensored Biography of Wayne B. Wheeler.* New York: Revel, 1928.

Sullivan, Mark. *Our Times: The United States, 1900–1925.* New York: Scribner's, 1935.

Taft, Philip. *Organized Labor in American History.* New York, Evanston, Ill., and London: Harper & Row, 1964.

Walters, Everett. *Joseph Benson Foraker: An Uncompromising Republican.* Columbus: Ohio History Press, 1948.

Ware, Norman Joseph. *Labor in Modern Industrial Society.* Boston and New York: Heath, 1935.

Warner, Hoyt Landon. *Progressivism in Ohio, 1897–1917.* Columbus: Ohio State University Press, 1964.

Warwick, Jack. "Growing up with Harding." *Northwest Ohio Quarterly* XXVIII, No. 1 (1955–56), 10–25; XXX, No. 3 (1958), 116–36; XXXI, No. 2 (1959). 72–93.

———. *Growing up with Harding.* Ed. The Harding Memorial Association. Marion, Ohio, ca. 1965.

Watson, James E. *As I Knew Them.* Indianapolis: Bobbs-Merrill, 1936.

White, William Allen. *Autobiography of William Allen White.* New York: Macmillan, 1946.

———. *Masks in a Pageant.* New York: Macmillan, 1939.

GENEALOGY

Brainerd, Lawrence. "President Warren Gamaliel Harding." *New England Historical and Genealogical Register,* October, 1923, pp. 243–49.

Harding, Veryl E. *Four Centuries of the Harding Family.* Beaver City, Nebr.: privately printed, 1958.

Harding, Wilbur J. *The Hardings: A Genealogical Register of the Descendants of John Harding.* Kenwood Park, Iowa: [privately printed?], 1907.

———. *The Hardings in America.* Keystone, Iowa: The Harding Printing Co., 1925.

Miller, Clara Gardiner. "Ancestry of President Harding in Relation to the Hardings of Wyoming Valley and Clifford, Pa." *Proceedings and Collections of the Wyoming Historical and Genealogical Society.* Wilkes-Barre, Penna., 1930.

Eckley, H. J., and W. T. Perry. *History of Carroll and Harrison Counties, Ohio.* Chicago: Lewis Publishing Co., 1921.

The "Old Northwest" Genealogical Quarterly X, No. 1 (1907).

Index

Abbott, Lawrence F., 438
Abbott, Lyman, 593
Abdul Hamid, 59, 60
Acceptance speech, 434, 435, 436, 439, 457–58, 460, 497, 498, 501, 538–39, 566
Accuser, The, 212, 213
Adamson Act, 249, 269, 620, 629
Advertising, 18, 453–54, 463, 489–92, 575
Advisory committee. *See* Ohio Republican Advisory Committee
African Methodist Episcopal Church of Marion, 544
"Age of hate," 38
Aguinaldo, Emilio, 71–72, 229
Ahlwardt, Herman, 94
Aldrich, George W., 421
Aldrich, Nelson B., 165
Alexander II, 57
Alexander III, 58
Allen, Henry J., 424, 438, 444
Altgeld, J. P., 87–88
Amalgamated Association of Iron, Steel, and Tin Workers, 617
American Defense Society, 325
American Farm Bureau Federation, 515
American Federation of Labor, 599–600, 608, 617, 620
American Federation of Teachers, 531
American Federationist, 621
American Israelite, 532–33
American missionaries, 58–60
American Monthly, 481
American Protective Tariff League, 610–14

American Railway Union, 81, 92, 93
American Seeding Machine Co., 202
Anarchists, 82, 84–89, 359
Anderson, Larz, 192
Andres, W. S. (Doc Waddell), 526, 577–78
Annexation. *See* Harding: xenophobia
Anti-Catholics, 195, 211, 212, 242, 523–24, 529, 534, 639
Anti-Saloon League, 43, 118, 145–46, 149, 208, 280, 286, 290, 430, 496, 497, 499–500
"Appeal of the Thirty-One Eminent Americans," 589–95
Arbitration (industrial), 91, 92
Archbold letters, 166–67
Archer, F. B., 126
Archer, Rudolph W., 284–85, 295
Armenia, 58–59, 343
Armor Plant Bill, 240
Armstrong, Robert B., 354, 380, 432
Army Bill (Roosevelt division), 261–64
Arnold, Benedict, 176, 431–32
Article 10 (League of Nations covenant), 336, 576, 580, 581, 586, 592, 593

Backlash, 535, 549–61
Baker, Purley A., 150, 207
Barry, Edwin D., 148
Baseball game (Campaign of 1920), 471–74
Battelle, Mrs. Annie Norton, 358
Bayard, Thomas F., 37
Bell, A. R., 38
Bellamy, Edward, 49–50

Military, the, 58, 362–63, 395–97
Miller, E. J. (the "Miller letter"), 398–99, 600–601, 607, 621, 629
Milliken, Carl E., 583
Mills, Ogden L., 369, 455–57, 611–12, 627
Monroe Doctrine, 63, 332
Montague, R. W., 439, 586
Montgomery, R. B., 547–48
Moore, Alexander P., 431, 438, 443, 460, 627
Morgan, Blinkey, 51–52
Morgan, J. P., 169, 176, 622
Moses, George, 584
Most, Johann, 86
Mt. Gilead, Ohio, 21
Mt. Vernon, Ohio, 21
Mouser, Grant E., 108–9, 159, 161
Munsey, Frank A., 437

Nash, George K., 108–11, 112–13, 114, 120–21, 124–33
Nation, The, 549
National Association of Manufacturers, 11, 222–23, 239
National Association for the Advancement of Colored People, 476, 536, 541, 549, 550, 561, 636
National Citizens Committee of Non Americans, 533
National Council of Traveling Salesmen, 484
National Education Association, 531
National Magazine, 488
National Negro Baptist Association, 542
National Security League, 274
National Woman Suffrage Association, 505
National Woman's party, 504
Negroes, 51, 364, 386–87, 401, 402, 430, 454, 476, 508, 636; ambivalence of Harding on, 536–37, 546, 550, 561; and campaign of 1920, 535–61; delivering of votes of, in 1914, 203, 204; and "lily-white" politics, 371–72; and lynching problem,

51–52, 457, 536–37, 548, 550, 561; rights of, 54, 535–53
New, Harry S., 432, 435, 461, 542, 623
"New Internationalism," 564, 575, 635
New York Giants baseball club, 472
New York, Pennsylvania and Ohio railroad, 11
Nicholson, Meredith, 429
Nihilists, 58
Nitti, Francisco, 480
Non-Partisan League, 521
Normalcy, 360, 375, 410–11, 452, 454, 457–58, 490, 599, 604, 621
North American Review, 438

O'Conner, Terrance, 618
Ohio Central College, 8
Ohio Central Railroad, 7
Ohio Constitution: amendments of 1912, 192–93
Ohio League of Republican Clubs, 147–48
"Ohio man," the, 98, 101, 119–20, 206, 384, 392, 395, 415, 426, 447–48
Ohio, "Mother of Presidents," 185, 215, 232, 301, 305–6, 352, 377, 383, 391, 461, 495, 639
Ohio Progressive Republican League, 178
Ohio Republican Advisory Committee, 283–87, 293, 294, 295, 299–300, 306–11, 313–14, 633, 639
Ohio Republican party: fight for control of, in 1918, 277, 314; obligation of Harding to, 306–7. *See also* Harding: and party system
Ohio Republican primary campaign of 1920, 377–404
Ohio Society of New York, 358
Ohio State Journal, 175
Ohio v. Beacom, 128, 648
Ohio v. Jones, 128, 648
Ohio Woman Suffrage Association, 208
Oklahoma, 57, 546–48
Opper, Frederick Burr, 492–93
Order of the Eastern Star, 512, 526
Overman act, 266, 271–72, 274

DATE DUE

FEB 18 '76			
GAYLORD			PRINTED IN U.S.A.